MW00805478

WEST POINT
TWO CENTURIES AND BEYOND

WEST POINT
TWO CENTURIES AND BEYOND

Sylvanus Thayer
Class of 1808

John P. Abizaid
Class of 1973

Robert E. Lee
Class of 1829

Eric K. Shinseki
Class of 1965

Ulysses S. Grant
Class of 1843

H. Norman Schwarzkopf
Class of 1956

John J. Pershing
Class of 1886

Creighton W. Abrams
Class of 1936

Douglas MacArthur
Class of 1903

William C. Westmoreland
Class of 1936

Henry H. Arnold
Class of 1907

Benjamin O. Davis Jr.
Class of 1936

George S. Patton
Class of 1909

Leslie R. Groves
Class of 1918

Omar N. Bradley
Class of 1915

Matthew B. Ridgway
Class of 1917

Dwight D. Eisenhower
Class of 1915

The frontispiece design, with slight modification, appeared on the program cover for the bicentennial conference hosted by the USMA Department of History in March 2002 at West Point, New York.

The multi-colored emblem on the lower right is the official U.S. Military Academy crest, adopted shortly before the 1902 centennial celebration. Beside it, in black and gold, is the official emblem of the bicentennial celebration in 2002. Partially visible in the lower-left corner is the crest of the Department of History; its motto, "Sapientia per Historiam" ("Wisdom through History"), inspired the scholarship that fills this volume.

The graduates whose images appear on the frontispiece represent West Pointers' two centuries of distinguished service as war fighters, leaders of character, military professionals, and servants of the nation. First in line is Sylvanus Thayer (USMA 1808), the "Father of the Military Academy." Last is General John Abizaid (USMA 1973), the current commander of the U.S. Central Command, representing the contributions of graduates still serving in uniform. The oval formed by the graduates' images remains symbolically open at the top, as each year newly commissioned officers from the Corps of Cadets join the Long Gray Line.

WEST POINT
TWO CENTURIES AND BEYOND

edited by Lance Betros

McWHINEY FOUNDATION PRESS
McMurry University
Abilene, Texas

Library of Congress Cataloging-in-Publication Data

West Point : two centuries and beyond / edited by Lance Betros.--1st ed.
    p. cm.
    Includes bibliographical references.
    ISBN 1-893114-47-3 (cloth)
    1. United States Military Academy--History--Congresses.
2. United States Military Academy--Influence--Congresses. 3. United
States Military Academy--Alumni and alumnae--Biography--Con-
gresses. 4. United States. Army--Congresses. I. Betros, Lance, 1955-
    U410.L1W4763 2004
    355'.0071'173--dc22

                        2004015263

McWhiney Foundation Press
McMurry Station, Box 637
Abilene, TX 79697-0637
(325) 793-4682
www.mcwhiney.org

Printed in the United States of America

1-893114-47-3
10 9 8 7 6 5 4 3 2 1

Book Designed by Rosenbohm Graphic Design
Cover and Frontispiece Designed by Frank Martini

Dedicated to

Brigadier General Thomas Everett Griess
1921-2004

Professor and Head
Department of History
United States Military Academy
1969-1981

General Griess's vision, leadership, and character
formed the bedrock upon which the
Department of History
was founded
in 1969.

Contents

ACKNOWLEDGMENTS

Publication of *West Point: Two Centuries and Beyond* realizes the vision of Col. Robert A. Doughty, Professor and Head of the Department of History at the United States Military Academy. Eager to make the Academy's bicentennial in 2002 an opportunity for serious study, he initiated planning for a scholarly conference that would examine West Point's rich history of two centuries. The conference took place at the Academy during the period 7-9 March 2002, with over 60 scholars, civilian and military, presenting papers; 24 of those papers comprise the chapters in this anthology. Since the conference and anthology would have been impossible without Colonel Doughty's foresight, it is appropriate that he be acknowledged first of all.

There were of course many others within the Department of History who contributed to this project in ways big and small. Maj. Chris Prigge served as the principal planner for the bicentennial conference, and he received able assistance from the operations officer, Maj. Kevin Clark, and the financial officer, Maj. Kevin Murphy. Many other members of the faculty and staff worked hard to host the conference and publish the anthology. They are too numerous to name individually, with a few exceptions. Col. Matthew Moten and Prof. Samuel Watson provided substantial assistance in the early phases of editing the conference papers for publication. Mr. Frank Martini, the Department's talented cartographer, designed and constructed many of the graphical displays for the conference; his design for the primary conference poster, with slight modification, graces the dust jacket and frontispiece of this book. Ms. Melissa Mills, one of the Department's veteran administrative assistants, supported all aspects of the conference with boundless energy and enthusiasm; her support was a significant, albeit largely unheralded, reason for the success of the conference.

The authors of the papers appearing in the anthology deserve great credit for their scholarly work and for their cooperation throughout the editorial process. They comprise a talented and multidisciplinary group: distinguished members of the historical profession, faculty members from other disciplines at West Point, and independent scholars. Significantly, four chapters were penned by officers in the Tactical Officer Education Program, a one-year course of study at West Point leading to a master's degree for captains preparing to become company tactical officers. Their chapters are revised versions of the research papers they submitted for the course, *The American Military Experience and the United States Military Academy*, taught by senior faculty members of the Department of History. The quality of these papers is a powerful reminder of the intellectual and professional benefits derived from serious historical study and reflection.

The Dean of the Academic Board, Brig. Gen. Daniel Kaufman, arranged the funding for this project. From the outset, he and his able staff recognized the scholarly importance of the project and never wavered in their commitment to finding the money to complete it, despite many competing demands.

Mr. A. Ross Wollen, USMA Class of 1965 and a longstanding friend of the Department of History, helped bring the publication effort to completion through a substantial monetary grant. His support of this and other Department projects reflects his belief in the power of history to enhance our understanding of the Military Academy.

Col. (Retired) Lloyd J. Matthews, the textual editor, deserves special thanks. His attention to detail and mastery of the English language are evident on every page. His interest in producing a high-quality volume went beyond normal professional considerations. As a graduate of West Point, a former Professor of English in the Department of English, and the former Associate Dean at West Point, he was uniquely qualified to provide technical, as well as substantive, advice on all aspects of the volume. His counsel was sage and always appropriate.

Last but not least, I thank my wife, Laurel, and our daughters, Holly, Heather, and Rosemary, for their emotional support and understanding as I labored to complete this project. Though not historians, they helped me in more ways than they will ever know.

Lance Betros
West Point, New York

List of Illustrations

Photographs

Figures

List of Tables

INTRODUCTION

Lance Betros

The United States Military Academy at West Point celebrated its bicentennial on 16 March 2002. The yearlong commemoration had many highlights, such as a bridge-building competition, the unveiling of a U.S. postage stamp, and a prominent exhibit at the Smithsonian's Museum of American History. President George W. Bush issued a proclamation honoring the Academy, and the print and broadcast media produced many special programs that underscored the institution's long history of service to the nation in war and peace. While these and other such recognitions were fitting tributes to West Point, they were also uniformly uncritical. They illuminated the shiny surface of things rather than offering the probing analysis that might have deepened our understanding of the institution and its role in American society.

The Department of History at West Point made great efforts to fill this scholarly void. First, it appointed the noted historian of Thomas Jefferson and the Military Academy, Dr. Theodore Crackel, to serve as a visiting professor during the 2001-2002 Academic Year. During his time on the faculty, he published *West Point: A Bicentennial History*, now the most authoritative general history of the institution.[1] Additionally, the Department conducted two scholarly conferences—one on the founding of West Point, another on its subsequent history. The scholarship of the former conference was published under the title *Thomas Jefferson's Military Academy: Founding West Point*.[2] The present volume is devoted to the scholarship of the latter conference.

The Military Academy has a long, rich history that parallels the broad historical themes of the nation. At the center of issues relating to the American military establishment, it also reflects developments in the larger society. In the chapters that follow, several interpretive themes emerge bearing witness to the nexus between the Military Academy and the society it serves.

(1) *West Point's influence on the military profession goes well beyond its role as a provider of commissioned officers.* More than any other commissioning source, West Point inspires its officers to be military professionals. This is different than simply providing a first-rate education and military training opportunities, although the Academy does both. More important, the Academy immerses cadets in a values-laden environment populated with officer mentors devoted to cadet development. Over the course of four years these conditions exert a powerful influence on cadets, who gradually develop habits of thought and action consistent with a military career. Cadets learn to appreciate in historical terms their roles as war-fighter, leader of character, servant of society, and member of a time-honored profession. These insights heighten the professional self-awareness of USMA graduates, but they also leaven the professionalism of the officer corps in general.

(2) *The Military Academy is by nature a conservative institution that favors continuity over change.* Steeped in military tradition and proud of its long legacy of service, West Point stands like granite against the tide of shifting social currents. In this light, continuity is a virtue; it allows the Academy to nurture and perpetuate the noble values that have brought Americans success in war. While the record of West Point seems to justify the institution's conservatism, critics view the emphasis on continuity as an obstacle to salutary change. They view the Academic Board, the dominant policy-making body for most of the Academy's existence, as the main culprit; consequently, they applaud the diminution of the Academic Board's influence relative to the superintendent's over the past 25 years. Only time will tell if the new balance of power will keep the Academy at the forefront of innovation or overwhelm it with constant change.

(3) *Once change is unavoidable, Academy leaders normally make the best of it.* Because of the conservative nature of the institution, change comes most quickly at West Point when external forces

impose it. Spirited debate usually precedes a decision requiring significant change and, on occasion, follows it. In the vast majority of cases, however, Academy leaders quickly accept the new policies and implement them effectively once they are made. This is especially true with regard to sensitive social issues such as racial and gender integration; in both cases, the Academy (and the armed forces in general) overcame its initial resistance and became a model of equal opportunity and meritocracy for the rest of society. The Academy's adaptability in managing change should not be surprising. As the nation's foremost leader-development institution, the school is committed to the ideals of loyalty, service, and responsibility. Moreover, Academy leaders subscribe fully to the professional military ethic, which emphasizes subordination to the will of civilian leaders.

(4) *Despite West Point's distinguished history, Americans remain uneasy about a school devoted exclusively to producing military professionals.* The hierarchy, regimentation, and organization for violent action that characterize military service make it an object of suspicion and hostility in a liberal democracy. Americans typically embrace their military during times of crisis, but support wanes quickly once the life of the nation returns to normal. This ambivalence has translated into repeated attempts to dilute the military trappings of the West Point experience and, in the extreme, to abolish the institution altogether.

(5) *On the whole, the West Point academic program has effectively prepared cadets for the challenges of a military career.* The academic program has come under continual criticism ever since Sylvanus Thayer established it in the early 19th century. The critics have pointed to several major shortcomings: a one-size-fits-all core curriculum that stifles intellectual curiosity and in-depth study; heavy emphasis on mathematics, science, and engineering at the expense of the humanities; a heavy academic load that leaves little time for reflection; weak academic credentials among the teaching faculty; and a pedagogical style that elevates form over substance. While the validity of these criticisms is debatable, Academy leaders have addressed all of them to varying degrees. Despite these issues, however, the academic program has done well in preparing cadets to anticipate

and respond to the changing nature of war, something critics tend to overlook when they focus narrowly on curricular issues. West Point's fundamental mission is to prepare cadets for successful careers as Army officers, and the record of 200 years suggests that the Academy has usually been closer to "right" than "wrong" when it comes to structuring the curriculum. Here is a case, perhaps, in which the institution's conservatism works in its favor.

No single volume can provide a definitive history of an institution as significant and complex as the U.S. Military Academy, and this volume makes no pretense of doing so. Rather, its purpose is to survey the highlights of that history, with particular emphasis on the salient trends and personalities of West Point's second century. The chapters offer glimpses of the environment and internal workings of the Academy, but overall they underscore West Point's influence on the American military establishment and the institution's connection to American society.

The scholarship contained in these chapters, organized into five sections, is new and insightful. Part I considers West Point's role in developing the nascent professionalism of the officer corps in the 19th century. Part II examines the influence of West Point on the careers of prominent graduates, suggesting the extent to which West Point succeeded in creating 20th-century military professionals. Part III surveys some of the institutional challenges the Academy has faced through its history and the efforts to overcome them. Part IV addresses women and minorities, whose integration into the Corps of Cadets represents one of the most dramatic changes in the history of the Academy. The anthology closes with Part V, the longest section, which updates the histories of a representative sampling of academic departments. Individually, these chapters build on the departmental histories that appeared in the published record of West Point's 100th anniversary; collectively, they provide an excellent overview of the dramatic curricular changes at the Academy during the past 50 years.[3] In every case, they help explain why West Point today ranks as one of the nation's most prestigious undergraduate institutions.

The graduates of a century ago would view the modern Academy with awe. Impressive new buildings and modern facilities serve a Corps of Cadets more than doubled in size. Instead of leading cloistered lives, cadets now travel broadly and gain virtual access to people, places, and information around the world through digital technology. An expanded curriculum, with dozens of majors and hundreds of elective courses, provides more educational opportunities than ever before. The Long Gray Line, once exclusively male and white, now includes men and women of virtually every racial and ethnic group.

Despite these and other significant changes, however, the most fundamental aspects of West Point have endured. Cadets still face the demands of a heavy academic load, a rigorous program of physical fitness, and the weighty responsibilities of leadership within the Corps. Devoted faculty mentors, consisting primarily of Army officers, nurture the cadets' intellectual and professional development. Above all, the values of Duty, Honor, Country still inspire the cadets, as confirmed once again by the gallantry in battle of West Point's most recent graduates.

As the chapters in this book attest, continuity—not change—is what most characterizes West Point and the Corps of Cadets. By perpetuating the noble values of the profession of arms, West Point continues to accomplish its vital mission of producing leaders of character for the nation. In this regard, the Corps of today still treads "where they of the Corps have trod."

THE CORPS
H. S. Shipman, former USMA Chaplain

> The Corps! Bareheaded salute it,
>   With eyes up, thanking our God
> That we of the Corps are treading
>   Where they of the Corps have trod.
> They are here in ghostly assemblage,
>   The men of the Corps long dead,
> And our hearts are standing attention,
>   While we wait for their passing tread.

We sons of today, we salute you,
　　You, sons of an earlier day.
We follow, close order, behind you,
　　Where you have pointed the way;
The long gray line of us stretches
　　Through the years of a century told,
And the last man feels to his marrow
　　The grip of your far-off hold.

Grip hands with us now though we see not,
　　Grip hands with us, strengthen our hearts,
As the long line stiffens and straightens
　　With the thrill that your presence imparts.
Grip hands, though it be from the shadows,
　　While we swear, as you did of yore,
Or living, or dying to honor
　　The Corps, and the Corps, and the Corps.

---

[1] Theodore J. Crackel, *West Point: A Bicentennial History* (Lawrence: University Press of Kansas, 2002).

[2] Robert McDonald, ed., *Thomas Jefferson's Military Academy: Founding West Point* (Charlottesville: University of Virginia Press, 2004).

[3] United States Military Academy, *The Centennial of the United States Military Academy at West Point, New York, 1802-1902*, vol. 1 (Washington, DC: Government Printing Office, 1904), 223-438.

PART I:

WEST POINT AND OFFICER PROFESSIONALISM

Introduction

The nature of war changed dramatically during the 19th century. Large standing armies, supported by the growing populations, wealth, and governments of industrialized nations, replaced the smaller conscript armies of an earlier era. Technological advances—steam engine, telegraph and telephone, Bessemer process, powerful new explosives, and rifled, breech-loading weapons, to name a few—greatly increased the scope and lethality of war. These changes created the need for a new breed of military professional who could manage the processes and systems of war in addition to leading soldiers in combat. Toward that end, the major powers of the world took measures to create professionally trained officer corps committed to mastering military art and science.

In the United States, West Point was the most important influence on officer professionalism in the first half of the 19th century. One reason was simply the preponderance of USMA graduates in the Army—on the eve of the American Civil War they comprised about three-quarters of the officer corps. Moreover, they were a homogenous and well-educated elite acculturated to the profession of arms by a regimented lifestyle and a common academic curriculum. West Point cadets, young and inexperienced, were the beneficiaries of the nation's only institutionalized program devoted to the study of military art and science. Their successes and failures as officers reflected the strengths and weaknesses of that program.

In the opening chapter, William Skelton examines West Point's influence on officer professionalism in the early 19th century. Although critical of the Academy's heavy emphasis on mathematics, science, and engineering, he acknowledges the excellence of the technical education. More important, he notes the effect of social indoctrination as a shaping influence at West Point. Impressionable young cadets were isolated in a Spartan environment where the principal role models were successful Army officers. The experience imparted to cadets the concepts of duty, self-sacrifice, and service to the nation—essential elements of the professional military ethic.

While the origins of military professionalism lay in the antebellum period, the decades after the Civil War brought the greatest professional growth. American military leaders, with wartime experiences behind them, could no longer ignore the increasingly complex nature of war. Only then did they create and begin to sustain the institutional trappings of professional life—service organizations, scholarly journals, and graduate education—that characterize modern professions.

Theodore Crackel affirms the importance of post-Civil War reforms in promoting military professionalism. Newly established service schools and journals, among other improvements, provided opportunities for serious professional study that benefited the nation's military. By 1901, for example, there was an Army War College, and by 1903 an Army General Staff.

Taken together, Skelton's and Crackel's chapters portray an American military establishment of growing sophistication and maturity. In particular, the officer corps increasingly exhibited the three defining qualities of a profession described by Samuel Huntington in his landmark study, *The Soldier and the State*.[1] The first quality, "expertise," is the theoretical knowledge of the occupation that laymen do not possess. The second is "responsibility," the felt obligation to use professional expertise for the benefit of society. "Corporateness," the collective identity of professionals that sets them apart from other occupational groups, is the third quality. As Skelton points out, the experiences of U.S. officers in the early 19th century imparted responsibility and corporateness; Crackel's chapter explains their growing level of expertise. By any measure, officer professionalism was very high by the end of the 19th century and, fortunately for the nation, has only improved since then.

—Editor

---

[1] Samuel Huntington, *The Soldier and the State* (Cambridge, MA: Harvard University Press, 1957), 8-10.

⊰ CHAPTER 1 ⊱

WEST POINT AND OFFICER
PROFESSIONALISM, 1817–1877

William B. Skelton

On the evening of 10 December 1847, Maj. Gen. Winfield Scott hosted a dinner party for a group of high-ranking Army officers and other dignitaries in occupied Mexico City, captured after a bitter struggle three months earlier. He began his post-dinner address by instructing the three West Point graduates who were present to hide their faces and pretend that they were under the table. He then expounded at length on the contributions of West Pointers to the overwhelming success of American arms in the struggle against Mexico. In Scott's opinion, "but for the science of the Military Academy 'this army, multiplied by four, could not have entered the capital of Mexico.'"[1]

Scott repeated his encomium to the Military Academy on other occasions, and it has become part of West Point lore. Despite the dose of hyperbole, it reflects a major change in both the military school and its relationship to the profession of arms during the decades following the War of 1812. The baseline for this transformation is the early West Point of Jonathan Williams and Alden Partridge. From its official founding in 1802 to the year 1817, the U.S. Military Academy was very much what its name suggests—an academy rather than a formal institution of higher learning. Scattered across the landscape of the early republic, academies were small and informal institutions existing in a hazy educational borderland between secondary schools and four-year colleges. Usually short-lived, they offered a hodgepodge of course work to scholars who ranged widely in age and preparation, who began their studies individually and remained for varying lengths of time, and who left after completing the standards required for admission to a four-year college or obtaining the basic credentials needed for launching a professional career—or simply when their funding ran out.[2]

Except for its military connection and its curricular emphasis on mathematics and engineering, the little school on the Hudson fit very much into this academy tradition. Cadets, ranging in age from their early teens to their thirties, arrived at irregular times throughout the year and remained for varying periods, some for a few months and others for five years or longer. In the absence of an academic calendar, course work was rudimentary and fluctuating in content, and the school was recurrently racked by bitter personal dissension. Moreover, West Point's impact on the early Army was marginal. Prior to the War of 1812, the Academy produced only 89 graduates, many of whom chose not to continue long in the Army. As late as 1817, the West Point contingent made up only 15 percent of the commissioned officer corps, and the great majority of graduates concentrated in the Corps of Engineers and artillery.[3]

As every West Pointer knows, the transformation of the Military Academy began in 1817, when President James Monroe appointed Sylvanus Thayer to replace Alden Partridge as superintendent. An Academy graduate himself (Class of 1808) as well as a Dartmouth graduate and a career officer of engineers, Thayer had visited France in the aftermath of the Napoleonic wars and studied the curriculum of the École Polytechnique, the prestigious school for French military and civil engineers. With the support of Secretary of War John C. Calhoun, Thayer set out to convert the Military Academy into an American version of the French institution.

In 1818, the War Department approved a comprehensive set of regulations for the Academy, largely compiled by Thayer. These firmly established the authority of the superintendent as commander of the Academy, directly responsible to the secretary of war. New cadets were to report for their entrance examination at the same time each year and begin their studies as a unified class in the fall. None was to receive a commission until he had completed the full academic course, now fixed for the first time at four years. The regulations established a uniform curriculum, centering on mathematics and engineering, and prescribed a system of general examinations to determine cadets' progress. An aloof, rather ascetic bachelor, Thayer exerted tight control over all aspects of cadet life, readily dismissing cadets who failed to meet his strict academic and disciplinary standards.[4] Controversial though they were, the Thayer reforms converted West Point from a loose-knit country academy into a formal four-year technical college. They also established the basic tone that the military school would retain into the late 20th century.

Thayer's reforms in the internal administration and curriculum of West Point constituted only part of the changing relationship between the Military Academy and the Army at large. Of only slightly lesser significance was the systemization of the cadet selection process. Before 1815, cadet appointments followed no clear standards. The secretary of war and chief engineer controlled the selections and tended to favor northeasterners and members of families with strong martial connections. Seventy-three percent of the pre-War of 1812 graduates had been residents of the New England states or New York, and a full quarter had been appointed from the lone state of Vermont.[5] This geographical bias probably arose less from intentional favoritism than from the very obscurity of the Military Academy in its formative years: northeasterners were simply in a better position to know of the tiny school's existence and seek admission. The effect, however, was that West Point was a regional rather than a truly national institution.

Beginning about 1815, the War Department made an effort to broaden the Academy's geographical base. As Secretary of War in James Monroe's cabinet, John C. Calhoun relied increasingly on Congressional recommendations in selecting cadets. His successors carried the trend further, distributing the cadetships among the states based on Congressional representation. By the 1830s, the executive branch had transferred control of most cadet appointments to Congress, a policy confirmed by an 1843 act that set the school's enrollment at the total number of Congressmen and territorial delegates, plus one slot for the District of Columbia and ten "at large" positions that were generally reserved for sons of military officers.[6]

The Congressional appointment system, which has persisted in basic form to the present day, significantly shaped both West Point and the military profession. First, it gave Congress a direct stake in the survival of the Academy and thus helped deflect popular criticism of the military school as a bastion of aristocratic privilege in the "Age of the Common Man." Second, it ensured that West Point would be a truly national institution and that the West Point contingent in the officer corps would form a geographical "portrait of Congress," with no region or section predominating.[7] (While northerners composed a majority of the officer corps throughout the antebellum era, the South was somewhat overrepresented in comparison to its part of the free white population. But this situation resulted mainly from the three-fifths clause of the Constitution, which allowed the slave states to count a portion of their slaves for purposes of representation in the House of Representatives. The South's proportional advantage in the House, of course, translated into a proportional advantage in securing West Point appointments.)

Finally, the Congressional appointment policy tended to defuse political partisanship in the Army by weakening and dividing the political identities of the officer corps. Assuming that Congressmen selected mainly families of political supporters as sources for their cadet appointments, the partisan allegiances that these men brought to the Army—dampened of course by four years of professional training—resembled the party composition of Congress and presumably of the nation as a whole. By ensuring that the officer corps would not be dominated by a particular party or faction, Congressional control of cadet appointments encouraged the separation of the military profession from the mainstream of civilian politics, a key development in the stabilization of civil-military relations in America.

Another point about the impact of the reformed Military Academy on the Army after the War of 1812: It was during this period that West

Point became by far the most important gateway to the military profession. Earlier, the West Point contingent had been a small minority of the officer corps. Under Thayer, however, West Point graduating classes increased, then stabilized at between 35 and 45, totals generally well above the available vacancies in the Army's junior grades. Moreover, the rising prestige of West Point led Army administrators to favor the commissioning of graduates over alternative modes of officer recruitment—namely, the direct appointment of citizens and the promotion of enlisted men. In any case, the proportion of graduates in the officer corps rose dramatically: from 15 percent in 1817, to 64 percent in 1830, and to 76 percent in 1860 (exclusive of paymasters and medical officers).[8] This West Point predominance clashed with the democratic values of the Jacksonian era—the emphasis on equality of opportunity for all white male citizens—and it produced charges of favoritism and calls for reform. Nevertheless, it resulted in a high degree of uniformity in the training and socialization of American officers. By the mid-19th century, the officer corps of the little United States Army was surely one of the world's most homogeneous and professionally educated military elites.

Internally, West Point shaped future officers in two ways: formally, through the academic curriculum, and informally, through the general influence of the Academy as a force for professional socialization. The basic curriculum established under Thayer remained virtually the same into the 1850s and reflected the strong technical emphasis of the Ecole Polytechnique and other French military schools.[9] Indeed, Thayer saw West Point as primarily a school of engineering and showed little interest in cultivating either liberal arts or strictly military courses. The academic program of the first two years centered on mathematics and the French language. Mathematics was considered an essential foundation for the more advanced technical courses, while a knowledge of French—in Thayer's opinion, the "sole repository of military science"—was deemed necessary for future officers to read the literature of their profession.[10] Third and fourth year cadets continued their technical studies by taking natural philosophy, chemistry, geology, and mineralogy. The central feature of the final year was a course entitled "Military and Civil Engineering and the Science of War," taught after 1832 by Dennis Hart Mahan, one of the most famous and influential members of the West Point faculty. Despite Mahan's reputation as a military thinker, the main thrust of his course was civil engineering and fortification, with only a few days at the end spent on military organization and strategy.[11]

Other than French, cadets had only limited exposure to the liberal arts, mainly in the form of an omnibus course during the final year, taught by the chaplain, that supposedly embraced history, geography, ethics, grammar, rhetoric, and national and international law. In addition, they studied the technical aspects of artillery and ordnance and received training in infantry, artillery, and, after 1853, cavalry tactics at the summer encampments and at daily drill sessions during the academic year. Overall, however, cadets devoted well over twice as much classroom time to mathematics, science, and engineering as to liberal arts and strictly military subjects combined.

This technical orientation did not go unchallenged. As early as 1819, Inspector General John E. Wool recommended more attention to history, geography, and languages, especially in the training of infantry officers. In his opinion, the great victories of history "were not achieved by the 'rule and compass' or the 'measurement of angles.' They were the product of enlarged minds, highly cultivated and improved by a constant survey of human events." Criticism of this kind continued through the antebellum period and in the 1850s led to a brief experiment with a five-year course of instruction, which allowed greater emphasis on liberal arts and military topics.[12] West Point authorities remained committed to the technical curriculum, however, and they countered their critics by stressing the need of both the Army and the nation at large for trained engineers. They also developed the argument that mathematics and engineering honed the reasoning powers of cadets, resulting in tough-minded, mentally disciplined officers capable of cutting through ambiguity and making coldly logical decisions under pressure. Thus West Point benefited all of its graduates, regardless of their future branch of service.[13]

Whatever the validity of the concept of "mental discipline," the engineering curriculum did provide excellent technical training for the small minority of cadets who entered the "scientific" branches of the Army: the Engineers, Topographical Engineers, and Ordnance. It also prepared many others for successful careers as civil engineers when they left the service. In terms of content, however, the formal course work at West Point probably proved of little direct value to the great majority of line officers, who were destined for service on the Indian and international frontiers and combat in the Mexican and Civil wars.

Far more important than the curriculum in shaping future officers was a second, nonacademic function of the Military Academy—its role as a powerful institution of professional socialization. As shaped under Thayer, its tone was rigidly authoritarian, quintessentially military. On arriving in June, cadets entered a spartan, structured world, almost totally isolated from civilian influences. During the first summer, they lived in tents on the Plain, the West Point drill field, where they were subjected to a regimen of strenuous drill and exaggerated discipline, administered by the upperclassmen. The regimentation continued in the fall, when they moved into permanent quarters and began their academic studies. To facilitate control and give upperclassmen experience in command, the cadets were organized as a battalion of infantry under the overall supervision of the commandant of cadets, the officer charged with their discipline and tactical training. Each day followed a fixed pattern, punctuated by roll calls, parades, and inspections. Regimentation even extended into the classroom: cadets were seated on the basis of their academic standing and recited according to a rigidly prescribed system.[14]

If regimentation was the central feature of the "Thayer system," another ingredient was competitive pressure. Early in his tenure, Thayer introduced the merit roll, by which cadets were continually evaluated on their academic course work, tactical proficiency, and general conduct. Their cumulative standing determined both their class rank and branch of service upon graduation. Perhaps an even greater source of pressure was the fear of failure. The technical curriculum was demanding, especially for cadets who lacked a strong academic background or an aptitude for mathematics. Approximately a quarter of the cadets entering between 1833 and 1854 were discharged for failing one or more of their courses, and many others resigned because of academic pressure.[15]

The West Point environment did not convert cadets into military automatons, but it did exert a potent influence. Aside from a furlough after their second year and occasional social contacts with visitors, cadets spent four years of impressionable adolescence in a closed, authoritarian institution where the principal role models were professional soldiers. Although they complained about the excessive discipline and competitive stress—and constantly tried to beat the system—most cadets absorbed the prevailing values and were drawn into a distinctly military culture. Of special importance was the romantic mystique that came to surround the Academy—a blend of breathtaking scenery, heroic traditions, and the pomp and ceremony of military life. This aura grew especially strong after the Mexican War assured West Point a place in the nation's mythology of martial glory. A first-year cadet described the wild, rugged beauty of the Academy's setting: "In some places you can read at the distance of a quarter of a mile the names of 'Palo Alto,' 'Buena Vista' and 'Monterey,' where they have been carved in the solid rock. Here too the ruins of Fort Putnam look down upon us, with its Revolutionary memories, reminding us of the gallant men who fought and perished—as we may fight and perish—in their country's cause."[16]

West Pointers made much of the leveling and nationalizing effects of the Academy. Supposedly the broad recruitment base of the school and the intensive program of military indoctrination blurred sectional and social class lines and produced an egalitarian community among West Point classmates—a "band of brothers." Indeed some graduates saw the school as a powerful force for national unity, offsetting the divisive impulse of sectionalism. Writing in 1822, Capt. James Dalliba (Class of 1811) expressed this idea perfectly:

> If there is a means stronger than any other of cementing the union of the States, and of perpetuating our government, it is the national Military Academy at West Point. To this institution, young gentlemen are sent from all sections of the Union. They come together with all their sectional prejudices, habits, and knowledge. . . . Their former habits, manners, and prejudices

soon become extinct. They form a new character, a national character, which is no where else formed in the country. . . . They separate and are scattered to every part of the country; but their feelings are not separated, and their interests are not divided, and generally never will be. . . . From this source an uniformity of political principles and opinions and national and personal attachments will be formed and disseminated, which will bind together our States, and perpetuate our union, when without this cord they might separate.[17]

One should be skeptical, of course, of descriptions of West Point as the seedbed of a nationally-minded brotherhood of arms. After all, the majority of southern-born graduates resigned in 1861 to fight for the Confederacy. Nevertheless, the West Point experience did lay the foundation for a development profoundly significant for the future of the American military profession—the emergence of a service ethic within the officer corps. This term connotes a sense of public duty and professional responsibility and a commitment to nonpartisan service and accountability to the national government. The sources of this spirit are not entirely clear. In part it stemmed from the Congressional appointment policy, which nationalized and partially depoliticized the cadet body. In part it was the message contained in the West Point textbooks on ethics and law. But the most important source was probably the consistent efforts of Thayer and other West Point leaders, in large part through setting an example of professional objectivity, to discourage partisan conduct among the cadets and instill in them the idea that they were first and foremost servants of a broad national community. Thayer adamantly resisted political intervention into the Academy and personally clashed with President Andrew Jackson over Old Hickory's toleration of cadets' political actions. In 1833, he resigned in protest as superintendent when Jackson readmitted dismissed cadets who had appealed through political channels, thereby becoming a martyr for the Academy's professional integrity.[18]

So what was the total effect of the Academy experience in shaping the officer corps? First and most fundamentally, it familiarized cadets with military discipline, administrative procedure, and small-unit tactics. Thus it assured the Army of a uniform and dependable "product" in the junior officers' grades—a basic level of professional competence that had been lacking in the military force of the early republic. Surely Winfield Scott referred principally to this feature when he praised the Academy's contribution to victory in the Mexican War.

Second, West Point provided a cohesive element that had been missing in the officer corps of the early national period. Four years in the Spartan atmosphere of West Point developed in cadets a distinctive military ethos, causing them to internalize hierarchical values, identify with the Army and its heroic traditions, and, in many cases at least, make a strong commitment to military service. Moreover, the personal friendships and institutional loyalties forged at the Academy continued long after graduation, providing a network of shared habits, memories, and experiences that united officers of diverse backgrounds and branches. One effect of these bonds was a significant decline in quarreling and dissension among junior and mid-level officers. Indeed, the habit of dueling, pervasive prior to the War of 1812, virtually disappeared within the Army's West Point contingent. While other conditions contributed, the West Point bond was certainly a factor in the dramatic lengthening of officers' careers during the antebellum era, from an average of ten years for those in service in 1797 to 23 years for those on the 1860 Army list.[19] Long-term career commitments, of course, formed an essential social foundation for the professional consolidation of the officer corps.

Third and most important, West Point helped shape the relationship between the Army and the civilian world. On one hand, the special circumstances of the Academy—its isolation, romantic mystique, and intense program of indoctrination—produced an elitist mindset within the officer corps, a sense of separateness from and moral superiority to the mainstream of civilian society. Compared to the rowdy individualism, partisanship, and materialism that allegedly characterized the civilian world, the Military Academy—and by extension the Regular Army as a whole—appeared an island of order, integrity, and devotion to duty. Reinforcing this attitude was the widespread criticism of the Academy during the Age of the Common

Man as a bastion of aristocratic privilege, which caused West Pointers to close ranks in defense of their institution. The result was the formation of a collective self-image within the officer corps, exaggerated but nonetheless powerful and remarkably persistent: that of a devoted band of brothers, faithfully cultivating professional expertise and performing dangerous, unpleasant, yet essential duties for an ungrateful and somewhat decadent public.[20] (Interestingly, a by-product of this elitism was a near universal contempt for citizen-soldiers—militia and short-term volunteers—that ironically clashed with the officer corps' self-proclaimed central mission: to serve as a leadership cadre for a wartime mobilization of those same citizen-soldiers.)

On the other hand, the officer corps' elitism remained within limits, confined mainly to officers' personal letters and diaries. Despite their grumbling about self-serving politicians and greedy civilians, West Point-trained officers accepted the primacy of civilian control and the ethic of nonpartisan service to the national government. During the antebellum era, this spirit was clearly revealed in the Army's professional competence and political neutrality while handling a series of difficult civil-military and constabulary crises, extending from the South Carolina nullification controversy, Indian removals, and Canadian border disturbances of the 1830s to the Kansas violence, filibustering troubles, and "Mormon War" of the 1850s.[21] Under orders to serve in the nasty guerrilla war against the Seminoles in Florida, Lt. William Wall (Class of 1832) summed up succinctly the officer corps' emerging service ethic: "I feel that I cannot bear so much glory as is about to be obtained from this Florida concern. However as Uncle Sam wills it I shall try to bear up."[22] Moreover, the officer corps' professional detachment was manifested under even more trying conditions during the civil-military tensions of the Civil War and especially in navigating the political minefields of postwar Reconstruction.

So what were the shortcomings of the Military Academy as a nursery for the American profession of arms? Mainly these stemmed from the narrowly focused engineering curriculum and the rigid, authoritarian character of the West Point mode of instruction. Certainly, the Academy instilled in most of its graduates a basic respect for professional study and the idea that military ability is acquired, not inborn. Whether or not they read professional books, they knew that they should be reading them. This was especially true of a group of officer-graduates who served tours of duty at West Point as assistant professors in the academic departments and instructors of tactics. During the 1840s and 1850s, Chief Engineer Joseph G. Totten and other Academy authorities attempted to organize a program of postgraduate professional studies for these officers. For assistant professors in the Department of Engineering, this program consisted of a two-year course in military engineering under Dennis Hart Mahan's overall supervision, which required extensive reading in military history and strategic theory. After the Mexican War, Mahan expanded this circle of military scholars by forming the Napoleon Club, open to any officer at West Point. Participants researched and presented papers on Napoleonic campaigns that were critiqued by Mahan and the other members. Officers who served on the West Point junior faculty accounted for much of the Army's professional publication during the antebellum period.[23]

Overall, however, the West Point approach to military science was narrow, technical, and derivative, as Matthew Moten has argued in his recent study of the Delafield commission to Europe in 1854-1855. With a few exceptions, most notably Mahan himself, Academy-trained military thinkers focused mainly on traditional fortification, tactics, and the particulars of military weaponry and equipment rather than on strategy or broad military policy. Moreover, they tended to accept uncritically European models rather than seeking flexible solutions to military problems within the context of American conditions.[24]

Obviously, the Academy should not be faulted for failing to prepare its graduates for fighting the Civil War. Who before 1861 could have reasonably predicted a division of the Union followed by a brutal four-year internal struggle involving mass volunteer armies numbering in the hundreds of thousands? Even if West Point officials had had such foresight, the Academy's commitment to national service and the avoidance of political and sectional controversy would have prevented them from acting upon it. But the Academy also failed to provide its graduates with a broad intellectual foundation in history and military theory that might have helped them to grow in their profession, and it neglected to address the practical duties that would occupy the careers of most line officers: frontier police work and Indian campaigning.

Finally, among its highest graduates, those who entered the Corps of Engineers, West Point's narrowly technical focus and enshrinement of 18th and early 19th-century French models encouraged a rigid commitment to an orthodox system of seacoast defense based on large masonry fortifications, designed in the years following the War of 1812. Throughout the antebellum period, the Engineers lobbied tenaciously and successfully to preserve and expand this program as the centerpiece of national defense policy—despite the development of rifled artillery, steam-powered naval vessels, ship armor, and railroads that by mid-century were making such a system obsolescent.[25]

Only a brief look is warranted at the role of the military profession in the sectional crisis, which constitutes a vast topic in its own right. Admittedly, the depiction of West Point as a catalyst for military professionalism would be more convincing if a quarter of the Army's commissioned officers, including two-thirds of those from the seceding states, had not resigned to join the Confederacy. History does not always follow the course that one would prefer. Nevertheless, both West Point and the officer corps as a whole remained remarkably immune from the sectional controversy until the election of 1860 and the actual secession of the southern states imposed an unavoidable crisis of conscience.[26] When push finally came to shove in the winter and spring of 1861, the majority of southern-born graduates discovered that older loyalties to section, state, and especially family and community outweighed their emerging professional ties. No doubt, many southern officers sincerely believed that the secession of their home states and the formation of the Confederate government had effectively voided their Constitutional oath and that they were justified in shifting their allegiance to a new and equally legitimate national authority. In any case, most seem to have made the decision reluctantly, after considerable wrestling with their consciences, and, with a few exceptions, they performed their duties faithfully up to the time of their departure.[27]

The Civil War split the officer corps, but it did not destroy the military profession. As the firing subsided at Fort Sumter, Regular

Army officers scrambled to obtain high commissions in the vast volunteer army raised in the North. Forty-four percent of the generals in the Union army were veterans of the prewar establishment, and 37 percent were graduates of West Point, including the great majority of army, corps, and division commanders. On the southern side, the Academy's influence was likewise extensive.[28] The traditions, procedures, and personal loyalties forged at West Point and honed in the regular service pervaded the high commands of both armies and shaped in myriad ways the conduct of the war: strategy, tactics, logistics, staff work, and civil-military relations.

Recently, Mark Grandstaff has made a persuasive case that the postwar period marked a partial and temporary break in the Army's professionalization. The reductions of the Army in 1866 and 1869, which involved the blending of volunteers and regular officers, left the West Point contingent at barely a quarter of the total officer corps, and only one fifth of the commanders had experience in the antebellum service. Inevitably, the retention of a majority of volunteers, rankers, and citizen appointees diluted the Army's cohesion and institutional memories.[29] Moreover, the unprecedented problems of reconstructing the South and the Constitutional crisis resulting in the impeachment of Andrew Johnson partially eroded the barrier separating the military profession from the political mainstream. As the sectional crisis passed, however, and as West Point reestablished its position as the principal gateway to the officer corps, prewar patterns of thought and conduct reemerged. During the late 1870s and 1880s, when William T. Sherman, John M. Schofield, Emory Upton, and a rising generation of West Point-trained military reformers renewed the professionalization process, they built on a firm foundation laid in Sylvanus Thayer's Military Academy and the small Regular Army of the antebellum era.[30]

---

[1] Ethan Allen Hitchcock, *Fifty Years in Camp and Field: The Diary of Major-General Ethan Allen Hitchcock, U.S.A.*, ed. William A. Croffut (New York: G.P. Putnam's Sons, 1909), 310. An officer reported hearing Scott twice make similar remarks before large crowds. Capt. Benjamin Alvord to Marcus C. M. Hammond, 24 February 1848, James H. Hammond Papers, Library of Congress.

[2] Christopher McKee, *A Gentlemanly and Honorable Profession: The Creation of the U.S. Naval Officer Corps, 1794-1815* (Annapolis, MD: Naval Institute Press, 1991), 92-94; Joseph F. Kett, *Rites of Passage: Adolescence in America, 1790 to the Present* (New York: Basic Books, 1977), 18-20.

[3] Calculated from the Army register of 1817, *U.S. Army Registers*, 2 vols. (Washington, DC, 1815-1839), 1: 107-117; Francis B. Heitman, comp., *Historical Register and Dictionary of the United States Army, from Its Organization, September 29, 1789, to March 2, 1903*, 2 vols. (Washington, DC: Government Printing Office, 1903), 1: passim. On the early history of the Military Academy, see Stephen E. Ambrose, *Duty, Honor, Country: A History of West Point* (Baltimore: Johns Hopkins University Press, 1966), 24-61; George S. Pappas, *To the Point: The United States Military Academy, 1802-1902* (Westport, CT: Praeger, 1993), 26-96.

[4] Ambrose, *Duty, Honor, Country*, 62-86; Pappas, *To the Point*, 99-117; Peter M. Molloy, "Technical Education and the Young Republic: West Point as America's Ecole Polytechnique, 1802-1833" (Ph.D. diss., Brown University, 1975), 384-464.

[5] Calculated from George W. Cullum, comp., *Biographical Register of the Officers and Graduates of the U.S. Military Academy at West Point, NY, from Its Establishment, in 1802, to 1890; with the Early History of the United States Military Academy*, 3 vols. (Boston: Houghton, Mifflin, 1891), 1: 51-110.

[6] William B. Skelton, *An American Profession of Arms: The Army Officer Corps, 1784-1861* (Lawrence: University Press of Kansas, 1992), 137-39.

[7] West Point Board of Visitors to John H. Eaton, June 1830, U.S. Congress, *American State Papers*. Class V: *Military Affairs*, 7 vols. (Washington, DC: Gales and Seaton, 1832-1861), 4: 608.

[8] Calculated from Army register for 1830, ibid., 4: 251-61; Army register for 1860, 36th Cong., 2d sess., House Exec. Doc. no. 54; Heitman, *Historical Register*, 1: passim.

[9] On the West Point curriculum, see Ambrose, *Duty, Honor, Country*, 87-105, 131-37; James L. Morrison, Jr., *"The Best School in the World": West Point, the Pre-Civil War Years, 1833-1866* (Kent, OH: Kent State University Press, 1986), 87-101; James L. Morrison, Jr., "Educating the Civil War Generals: West Point, 1833-1861," *Military Affairs* 18 (October 1974): 108-111; Samuel J. Watson, "Professionalism, Social Attitudes, and Civil-Military Accountability in the United States Army Officer Corps, 1815-1846" (Ph.D. diss., Rice University, 1996), 262-85.

[10] Sylvanus Thayer to George Graham, 28 August 1817, file T-122(10), National Archives, Records of the Office of the Secretary of War (Record Group 107), Letters Received by the Secretary of War, Registered Series, 1801-1870.

[11] Thomas E. Griess, "Dennis Hart Mahan: West Point Professor and Advocate of Military Professionalism, 1830-1871" (Ph.D. diss., Duke University, 1968), 209-48 and passim; Morrison, "Educating the Civil War Generals," 109; Russell F. Weigley, *Towards an American Army: Military Thought from Washington to Marshall* (New York: Columbia University Press, 1962), 38-53.

[12] Col. John E. Wool to John C. Calhoun, undated inspection report, approved by Maj. Gen. Jacob Brown, 12 December 1819, John E. Wool Papers, New York State Library, Albany. For the five-year program, see Morrison, *"Best School in the World,"* 114-25.

[13] Col. Joseph G. Totten to William Wilkins, 30 November 1844, 28th Cong., 2d sess., Sen. Exec. Doc. no. 1, 199-200; Totten to Jefferson Davis, 3 August 1860, 36th Cong., 2d sess., Sen. Misc. Doc. no. 3, 233; Morrison, *"Best School in the World,"* 43-44.

[14] On West Point as a mechanism for professional socialization, see Watson, "Professionalism," 725-54; Skelton, *American Profession of Arms*, 172-80.

[15] Morrison, *"Best School in the World,"* 101.

[16] Cadet Thomas Rowland to his mother, 9 August 1859, Thomas Rowland, "Letters of a Virginia Cadet at West Point, 1859-1861," *South Atlantic Quarterly* 14 (July and October 1915): 214-15.

[17] James Dalliba, *Improvements in the Military Establishment of the United States* (Troy, NY, 1822), 9.

[18] James W. Kershner, "Sylvanus Thayer: A Biography" (Ph.D. diss., West Virginia University, 1976), 231-48; Ambrose, *Duty, Honor, Country,* 106-11; Hitchcock, *Fifty Years,* 64-68.

[19] Calculated from Army list of 1797, Thomas H. S. Hamersly, comp., *Complete Army Register of the United States for One Hundred Years (1779-1879)* (Washington, DC: T. H. S. Hamersly, 1880), 47-49; Heitman, *Historical Register,* 1:passim.

[20] Skelton, *American Profession of Arms,* 210-12, 283-87, 297-300, and passim.

[21] Ibid., 299-304, 312-17, 332-38, 351-53; Samuel J. Watson, "United States Army Officers Fight the 'Patriot War': Responses to Filibustering on the Canadian Border, 1837-1839," *Journal of the Early Republic* 18 (Fall 1998):485-519; Watson, "Professionalism," 1041-1344 and passim; Robert W. Coakley, *The Role of Federal Military Forces in Domestic Disturbances,1789-1878* (Washington, DC: Center of Military History, 1988), 92-226.

[22] Lt. William Wall to Lt. Robert Anderson. 19 August 1836, Robert Anderson Papers, Library of Congress.

[23] Griess, "Mahan," 162-64, 236-37; Ambrose, *Duty, Honor, Country,* 138-39; Col. Joseph G. Totten to Major Richard Delafield, 29 August 1842, National Archives, Records of the Office of the Chief of Engineers (Record Group 77), Letters and Reports of Col. Joseph G. Totten, 1803-1864.

[24] Matthew Moten, *The Delafield Commission and the American Military Profession* (College Station: Texas A&M University Press, 2000), 26-38, 54-72, 205-11, and passim.

[25] Samuel J. Watson, "Knowledge, Interest, and the Limits of Military Professionalism: The Discourse on American Coastal Defence, 1815-1860," *War in History* 5 (July 1998):280-307.

[26] Skelton, *American Profession of Arms,* 348-53; Edward M. Coffman, *The Old Army: A Portrait of the American Army in Peacetime, 1784-1898* (New York: Oxford University Press, 1986), 92-96. The principal historian of the antebellum Military Academy found little overt sectional antagonism prior to the mid-1850s. Morrison, *"Best School in the World,"* 128-31.

[27] Skelton, *American Profession of Arms,* 353-58.

[28] Compiled from Ezra J. Warner, *Generals in Blue: Lives of the Union Commanders* (Baton Rouge: Louisiana University Press, 1964), xx; and lists in James Spencer, *Civil War Generals: Categorical Listings and a Biographical Directory* (New York: Greenwood Press, 1986).

[29] Mark R. Grandstaff, "Preserving the 'Habits and Usages of War': William Tecumseh Sherman, Professional Reform, and the U.S. Army Officer Corps, 1865-1881, Revisited," *Journal of Military History* 62 (July 1998): 521-35.

[30] Ibid., 535-45; Coffman, *Old Army,* 269-84; Kenneth J. Hagan and William R. Roberts, eds., *Against All Enemies: Interpretations of American Military History from Colonial Times to the Present* (New York: Greenwood Press, 1986), 183-234; Stephen E. Ambrose, *Upton and the Army* (Baton Rouge: Louisiana State University Press, 1964); James L. Abrahamson, *America Arms for a New Century: The Making of a Great Military Power* (New York: Free Press, 1981); Peter Karsten, "Armed Progressives: The Military Reorganizes for the American Century," Peter Karsten, ed., *The Military in America from the Colonial Era to the Present* (New York: Free Press, 1980), 246-60.

CHAPTER 2

WEST POINT'S CONTRIBUTION TO THE ARMY AND TO PROFESSIONALISM, 1877 TO 1917

Theodore J. Crackel

Introduction

For much of the last half century scholars have engaged in a debate about the cause of 19th century reform and professionalization in the United States Army. It was Samuel Huntington who launched the debate in 1957 with his book *The Soldier and the State*.[1] Huntington argued that whatever professionalization occurred prior to the Civil War resulted from a tradition of military interest resident chiefly in the South. Still, he argued, "Southern support was insufficient to enable military professionalism to prevail" in the ante-bellum years. Rather, he said, "Southern interest sparked the emergence of military professionalism as a concept and paved the way for the institutional reforms of the post-Civil War era."[2]

Marcus Cunliffe disagreed. "There is plenty of evidence to show," he wrote, "that by the 1840s the American regular army had developed professional styles which had little in common with the folklore of amateur soldiering."[3] Although his *Soldiers and Civilians: The Martial Spirit in America, 1775-1865* examined only the pre-Civil War years, he laid the groundwork for future scholars who would argue that in the ante-bellum period there was a remarkable emergence of professionalism.

Russell Weigley saw more merit in Huntington's view. In *The American Way of War* (1973), he argued the case for the post-Civil War emergence of professionalism. "In the United States," he wrote, "the twenty years of neglect of the armed services following the Civil War produced the somewhat surprising result of a cultivation of professional military study and discussion among the officers."[4]

The two sides of the debate have continued to voice their views to this day. William Skelton, beginning in the mid-1970s, argued persuasively for an earlier reform impulse—one that stressed formal and continuing military training, bureaucratic efficiency, and a full career of service.[5] But, in 1986, Edward Coffman made the case once more for the later emergence of professionalism. In the antebellum years, he argued, life in the Army's small garrisons simply did not encourage the development of military professionalism. "Prior to the Civil War," he wrote, "circumstances thwarted its evolution." Rather, he argued, it was during the last three decades of the century that professionalism finally emerged within the army.[6]

Most recently, in 1998, Mark Grandstaff argued that there were significant impulses of Army professionalization both before and after the Civil War.[7] There were, Grandstaff said, two eras of professionalization, each with a distinct origin that reflected the different makeup of the officer corps before and after the Civil War. Only time will tell whether or not the members of the two warring camps can be reconciled. I must say, however, that I find Grandstaff's position persuasive—the more so because the argument I will make about West Point's contribution to the professionalization of the Army in the late 19th and early 20th centuries will draw on events and activities that have roots in the antebellum years.

Before I go further in that direction, however, it is necessary to examine what are considered by many the more important components of reform contributing to this era of professionalization. Among those is the rise of professional military associations and their journals, which together constituted a secondary but significant element of that reform movement. Included among them are the Military Service Institution of the United States (established 1878) and its *Journal*; the United States Cavalry Association (1885), which published the *Cavalry Journal*; the Association of Military Surgeons (1891) and its *The Military Surgeon*; and the Infantry Association (1893), which published the *Infantry Journal*. In addition, in 1892, the Artillery School at Fort Monroe began to publish *The Journal of the United States Artillery*. These organizations and periodicals quickly became an important medium for the exchange of professional ideas across a widely scattered army. Also important in the dissemination of professional ideas and information was the *Army and Navy Journal*, which began publication in 1863. Although a weekly newspaper and not a professional journal in the sense the others were, it carried articles, correspondence, news, and social notes of particular interest to officers, and it was the most widely read. Moreover, its editor, William Church, made the *Army and Navy Journal* a proponent of many of the era's Army reforms.[8]

The primary impetus of professionalization, however, was the emergence of the service schools, and much of the credit for these must be given to Gen. William Tecumseh Sherman (USMA 1840). It was during his long reign as Commanding General of the Army (1869-1883) that many of them were launched. As early as 1872, Sherman was saying that "the Army should be a school."[9] "The Army, as a school," said Mark Grandstaff, "would be the initial premise for his conceptualization of a professional officer corps."[10] Of course, Secretary of War John Calhoun had established the Artillery School at Fort Monroe in 1824 which, though closed in 1860, was revived in 1868 by Ulysses S. Grant (USMA 1843) in his last year as Commanding General. But Sherman went further. In 1866 he was instrumental in the creation of an Engineering School at Willet's Point, New York.[11] Then, of even more enduring import, in 1881 he established a School of Application for Infantry and Cavalry at Fort Leavenworth, Kansas.

Sherman's ideas on military education shaped the Leavenworth school's early years. Let us consider that school in some depth, for it is here that most scholars have discovered the mother lode of early Army professionalization. "Sherman envisaged Leavenworth as a model post," wrote Timothy Nenninger, "where students carried out their duties as though at a well regulated garrison in time of war."[12]

Although Sherman stressed the value of practical work, he also acknowledged the place of theoretical study: "In war, as in science, art, and literature, for the higher branches we must look to books—the recorded knowledge of the past."[13] The Leavenworth course was to be two years in length, and at any given time each cavalry and infantry regiment would have one lieutenant assigned as a student. These students would serve with the units then stationed at the post, rotating billets a couple of times a year. In that way they would learn by doing as well as by studying, and would be exposed in the process to all three of the combat arms—infantry, cavalry, and artillery.[14]

In the beginning, the students were divided into two classes. The most advanced were placed in the first class, whose curriculum stressed practical work in such military subjects as organization, tactics, and drill. The second class (those less prepared) would also study these subjects, but would first review the basic studies they should have mastered before commissioning—reading, writing, and arithmetic, plus grammar, geography, history, algebra, geometry, and trigonometry.[15]

The school at Leavenworth began classes in January 1882, but it got off to a rocky start. There were no current textbooks, no approved curriculum, and no adequate classrooms or quarters. Moreover, many students lacked "either the ability or the industry necessary to master studies with which a school boy should be familiar."[16] It was not until the assignment of Alexander McCook (USMA 1852) and his regiment in 1887 that the school was able to shed the moniker of "The Kindergarten." Under McCook, the remedial or second class was eliminated, and a new and approved curriculum was installed. McCook insisted that only officers who had aptitude and motivation be sent to him. Those without a diploma from either the Military Academy at West Point or some civilian college would have to pass an entrance examination. McCook's reforms brought quick and dramatic improvements.[17]

Also central to the school's new success were two instructors: Arthur Wagner (USMA 1875) and Eben Swift (USMA 1876). It was their work during the late 1880s and 1890s that laid the foundation for Leavenworth's development until World War I. Its methods, its courses, and its doctrine all reflect their work. In looking beyond the mere functioning of officers as tacticians and administrators, Wagner and Swift began the process that would eventually break down the Army's garrison mentality. Increasingly they came to acknowledge more abstract and theoretical concerns, thus imbuing the curriculum with increasing sophistication. During the time that this enlightened pair were at Leavenworth, the school became a font of new and original thinking in the Army.[18]

Their object was for the Army as a whole ultimately to adopt a uniform set of doctrines and techniques, but it would have been a slow process had it been left only to the initiative of those who attended the school at Leavenworth. Although the graduates of Leavenworth were imbued with a strong sense of professionalism and immersed in the doctrines and techniques that Wagner, Swift, and later John Morrison (USMA 1881) fostered, there were simply too few graduates in the years before World War I to have reshaped the Army alone. Leavenworth's Infantry and Cavalry School was closed in 1898 at the beginning of the Spanish-American War. It was reopened in 1902 as the General Service and Staff College, which, after 1904, included two separate schools: the School of the Line (with a one-year curriculum) and the Army Staff College (offering a second year for the best students from the School of the Line). In the years between 1904 and 1916 the Army graduates from the School of the Line numbered just 529, and less than half of these continued on for a second year at the Staff College.[19] During World War I these Leavenworth graduates played an important role on the corps, field army, and headquarters staffs of the American Expeditionary Force, but few trickled down below the level of divisions. In fact, only five of 26 divisions were commanded by Leavenworth graduates, and though the chiefs of staff of most of the divisions were Leavenworth-trained, few other members of division staffs, and virtually none of those at brigade or below, held that distinction.[20] Thus, if one wanted an educational institution within the Army that provided a source of professional education and training for the officers at large, he would have to look elsewhere.

"The Army should be a school that can at will infuse into the masses of our volunteers and militia a spirit that shall [leaven] the whole people into a regular army," said Sherman in late 1872.[21]

After a trip to Europe, he had decided that reform of the American Army must be driven by the circumstances in which it operated. No European model would suffice. Rather, he concluded, the Army must reform itself on an American model. Because the Army was so very small, he wrote in his *Memoirs* just a few years later, "I hold that it should be the best possible . . . and that in time of peace we should preserve the 'habits and usages of war,' so that, when war does come, we may not again be compelled to suffer the disgrace, confusion, and disorder of 1861."[22] The whole of the regular establishment, he believed, should be a school. The formal schools he had established—including the Infantry and Cavalry School at Fort Leavenworth—were elements of that vision, but it fell to his successor as the Army's Commanding General, John Schofield (USMA 1853), to move the Army another step closer to the school house writ large that Sherman had envisioned.

The Officers' Lyceum and the Garrison Schools

Schofield's solution was a little understood and oft maligned component of the Army's education system—the officers' lyceum, a "school" that could reach every company grade line officer in the Army. Schofield's choice of the name lyceum reflected his belief that officer education should continue all through life. In the Lyceum Movement in America before the Civil War, continuing adult education was the centerpiece. Professional lecturers eventually came to make the circuit from one lyceum to another, but in the early days members of the lyceums took turns at the lectern. Schofield's lyceums provided every line officer of the Army the opportunity to address professional subjects, questions, and problems. Widely ignored by military historians, these schools were the only ones at this time that reached out to all the lieutenants and captains of the Army. Moreover, for most of these officers it was their one organized opportunity to develop themselves as professional officers. Schofield hoped that his new institutions, like the lyceums of early American communities, would become centers of intellectual life at Army posts across the nation.[23]

In 1890, Congress provided for a system of examination to determine the fitness for promotion of all officers of the Army below the grade of major. A year later, when Schofield published rules to guide these examinations, he also ordered into being a new component of the Army education system—the officers' lyceum:

> On November 1, 1891, or as soon thereafter as practicable, there shall be established at every post in the Army, garrisoned by troops of the line, an officers' lyceum. From the work connected therewith no officer of the line shall be excused excepting under such circumstances as would exempt him from any other duty at the post. The commanding officer of the post shall be president of the lyceum, and in that capacity act as director of instruction, subject to the supervision of the department commander.[24]

Post commanders were directed to prepare a "carefully considered scheme of theoretical instruction" selected from the subjects covered on the examinations for promotion. The annual lyceum season was to be no less than six months (not necessarily consecutive), to be determined by local conditions. The number and periodicity of meetings was not specified, but commanders were advised that instruction was intended to be carried on from year to year, and it was therefore to build on earlier work whenever practicable. Field officers were not required to participate as members of the lyceum, but might be used as instructors. In addition to the foregoing directions, each officer regardless of rank was required, every year, to select a professional subject to investigate and to write a report thereon. These reports would be read to a meeting of the lyceum after which a full discussion was encouraged. No minutes of these discussions were to be kept, and after the papers were read they were considered the private property of the author. A schedule showing the subject assigned each officer and the dates on which the papers were to be read was to be forwarded to the department commander.[25]

The first reports from the field were generally favorable. Brig. Gen. John Brookes of the Department of the Platte reported that "the lyceum seems to have been well inaugurated."[26] Brig. Gen. Thomas

Ruger (USMA 1854), commanding both the Department of Columbia and the Department of California, said that the lyceums "have had a good effect, and as improvements in methods will come with experience in their management, the final results of their operation must be very beneficial."[27] Maj. Gen. Nelson Miles of the Department of the Missouri noted that 135 essays on professional topics were read by his officers during the first year. "These essays and the reports of the discussions thereon," he reported, "contain much valuable and interesting information concerning military matters. The work already done clearly demonstrates that these lyceums will be of much value in stimulating professional zeal and ambition."[28]

Brig. Gen. Wesley Merritt (USMA 1868), Department of the Dakota, reported that his assistant inspector general, Capt. Charles Miner, had attended a number of the lyceums and discussed their operation with the junior officers involved, reporting back that "in the opinion of all an immense amount of good had resulted and was likely to result from the system." The principal value, Merritt concluded, was "giving officers an incentive to study, and objects on which to make research." The discussions of the papers, Miner noted, "have been interesting, and in every case have been the means of valuable instruction."[29] Miner's observations are particularly interesting because he was one of the older officers—about 50 years old—and a senior captain who would soon be promoted to major. Many of his contemporaries opposed the new lyceums. "Too many of the older officers," wrote George Van Horn Moseley (USMA 1899), "had no interest in new ideas of training, for it disturbed the rest and ease of their status quo."[30] Not so Miner.[31]

Maj. Gen. Alexander McCook, who had helped set the school at Leavenworth on the right course, now commanded the Department of Arizona. In his report to Schofield he judged that the officers' lyceum "has proved a great success" in his department, and that "much good" had resulted from it. The work done on the essays "by a large majority of the officers is most commendable," he noted. He had read the essays with interest, he reported, and had commented in writing on each of them. "This good work," he said, "should be persevered in."[32]

Maj. Gen. Oliver Howard (USMA 1854) of the Department of the East also believed that the lyceums would contribute to professional proficiency, but he suggested that at "the smaller garrisons, where but two or three officers can attend, the recitative feature becomes somewhat tiresome." He recommended doing away with the recitations in such situations—but wished to retain the research papers.[33] What reservations there were among the senior officers concerning the lyceums were minor indeed.

By late 1893, after two years' operation, Schofield reported, "In the permanent establishment, education was never so general or so high as at the present time. Not only are the established schools at West Point, Willet's Point, Fort Monroe, Fort Leavenworth, and Fort Riley, as efficient as ever, but the Military Service Institution and the general system of lyceums established throughout the Army are adding largely to the voluntary individual work of nearly all officers of the Army."[34]

The department commanders agreed. Howard now reported that "the work accomplished in post lyceums in this department . . . exhibit on the whole a commendable zeal in professional study and enterprise. Many of the papers read would, if published, prove of much interest and profit to the service . . . [and] would add a stimulus to officers in this work."[35]

McCook reported in some detail the efforts of the Department of the Colorado:

> The following are the subjects taken up and the posts at which they were entered upon: Military law (abridged), Forts Bayard, Grant, and Huachuca. Military law (unabridged), Forts Apache, Bayard, and Marcy. General Orders No. 100, Adjutant General's Office, series 1863, Forts Stanton. The Articles of the Geneva Convention, Fort Apache. Field engineering, etc, Forts Marcy, Bayard, and Whipple Barracks. Drill regulations, Forts Apache, Bayard, Bowie, Grant, Huachuca, Stanton, and Wingate, San Diego Barracks, and Whipple Barracks. Minor tactics (Shaw), Forts Apache, Wingate, and San Diego Barracks. Infantry fire (Batchelor), Forts Marcy and Stanton, and San Diego Barracks. Army regulations, San Diego Barracks and Fort Stanton.

He noted, however, the lack of uniformity occasioned by relying on the post commanders to determine the curriculum. He suggested that a "uniform course of study . . . should be prescribed for all posts, so that each and every subject required by the War Department to be studied should have its regular turn." Otherwise, he argued, "judging from past experience, the entire course may never be covered, whilst there will be a repetition of certain subjects, such as each post commander at the time may see fit to adopt, [resulting in] as many different courses and as many varieties in the amount gone over in each as there may be different commanders."[36]

In 1893, Col. Zenas Bliss (USMA 1854), who commanded the 24th Infantry at Fort Bayard, New Mexico—a part of McCook's Department of the Colorado—said he believed the lyceum "to be a good institution, and that the line officers especially will derive great benefit from it."[37] The next year, Brig. Gen. Elwell Otis, the new commander of the Department of the Columbia, added his positive assessment of the officers' lyceums. It had "produced beneficial results and has been of a character which should continue to occupy the attention of officers. Such labors, if properly conducted, keep fresh in their minds a knowledge of their accustomed duties, broadens their perception of military science, and furnishes healthy intellectual occupation. The training derived from the preparation of essays on professional subjects must greatly assist the mental development of our officers in the desired direction."[38]

Over time, however, a growing number of senior commanders came to favor exempting the older and more senior officers from the various requirements associated with the officers' lyceums. "Many are not in favor of requiring field officers to lecture," wrote General Howard in 1894, "as this places them on a par with junior officers and opens the way to criticism, which, they allege, is not in the interest of discipline."[39] Colonel Bliss of the 24th Infantry had made a similar argument the year before: "For the older officers, field officers, I think the writing of essays should be optional. Those who like to write and have anything to impart will be glad to [present] essays. To those who neither like to write nor have anything valuable to impart, it is disagreeable and productive of no good. Their habits are pretty well formed, and it is hard and perhaps unwise to attempt to change them."[40] In 1895, Schofield exempted both field officers and captains over 50 years of age from any required participation as members of the lyceum, except as might be needed to use them as instructors.[41]

Nelson Miles replaced Schofield in late 1895. Given Miles's record as a department commander, it was no surprise that he supported the officers' lyceums when he became the Army's commanding general. He almost immediately made provision to publish (with the permission of authors) those lyceum essays that were considered especially valuable by the department commanders.[42] In his first annual report he pronounced the officers' lyceums a sound enterprise, noting "good results from systematic readings from advanced text-books, from recitation, from essay readings, and from discussions at post lyceums during the year." "The professional papers prepared," he added, "covered a wider range of subjects than heretofore and have given evidence of reading, intelligent thought, and industry. The system furnishes an incentive for study and research, and it assists in keeping officers abreast of the development of military science and of the ever-increasing demands of their profession."[43]

No system, of course, can be perfect. The lyceums were only as effective as the participants would allow, and not every officer was a willing participant. "One officer, I remember," wrote George Van Horn Moseley, "bragged that during all his service he always read the same paper, only changing the name each year. First, it appeared as 'The Pistol Versus the Saber,' then under the title 'The Relative Merits of the Saber and Pistol,' and later 'What Arms for the Cavalry,' and so it survived from year to year."[44]

In 1896, General Miles made adjustments in the system that restored any of the rigor that might have been lost and attempted to deal with opposition of some of the officers. He increased the number of lyceum meetings each year but shortened the lyceum season. Now the lyceums met for only four months instead of six, but lyceum participants were required to gather at least twice a week during that term. Moreover, all officers of the line were once again required to attend, although field officers and captains over 50 could be excused from preparing essays. Miles pointed out, however, that he considered their experience to be particularly valuable in the meetings, and he urged them to "use their best efforts to make the Lyceum exercises valuable, not only to themselves, but also to those of less experience." Discussions were to begin with the junior officers who desired to participate, the more senior officers going last. Miles was very specific on one point: "All discussions and essays are to be free from personalities and in terms of the strictest courtesy towards both superiors and inferiors"; indeed, Colonel Robert's Rules of Order were to govern.[45]

Interestingly, the essays they prepared were no longer considered to be the officer's property; instead they were now counted "official documents" and were to be forwarded to the department headquarters "for examination and criticism, and finally for file." (Essays could, however, be published by their authors if authorized by resolution of three-fourths of the members of their lyceum.) Miles also required department commanders and their inspectors to attend lyceum sessions as a part of their regular inspections. Finally, he ordered each post commander to "endeavor to obtain a select library of standard professional works for the use of the members of the Lyceum at the post." These lyceum libraries would be funded by a one dollar per annum charge to each member of the lyceum.[46]

The lyceums continued under the Miles regime until 1898 when their activities were dramatically curtailed and in many cases wholly abandoned as a result of the Spanish-American War. At war's end, however, the lyceums picked up where they had left off. Change, however, was afoot. In the War Department Annual Report of 1901, Secretary of War Elihu Root made a strong argument in support of theoretical instruction, but after Root's departure in 1904 those who favored "practical" instruction gained the upper hand. Root's words were now stood on their head and made to support the new mode. "Though [Root's argument] is contained in a report advocating theoretical instruction, it affords direct evidence that this talented, clear-seeing, great Secretary of War had not lost sight of the value of 'practical qualities in a soldier.'" After all, Root had said, "It is a common observation, and a true one, that practical qualities in a soldier are more important than a knowledge of theory." Favored now was "the ambitious, industrious, zealous and courageous professional soldier who is conspicuous for possessing 'practical qualities.'"[47]

In 1905, the lyceums were replaced by "garrison schools for officers" which emphasized more practical work. General Order No. 124 of 1905 specified a progressive system of military education that began with the Military Academy and the garrison schools for officers, and moved through the competitive special service schools (such as those at Fort Monroe, Fort Riley, and Fort Leavenworth), the Staff College, and finally to the War College.

The new garrison schools met for an hour each day from early November to late March. All company grade officers were required to attend, except captains with ten or more years of commissioned service, and prior graduates of any of the special service schools.[48] The course of instruction for the garrison school was divided into three parts, one to be taught in each of three successive years. During the first year, the officers studied administration, manual of guard duty, field service regulations, drill regulations, and small arms regulations. The next year, the course work consisted of tactics, military law, and international law. In the last year, the officers received field engineering, military hygiene, military topography, and a program of branch specific training. At the end of each topic or course an examination was given, and those passing the examination were awarded certificates of proficiency.[49] In 1910, a branch-specific "preliminary" course was added for lieutenants during their first year of commissioned service.[50]

Despite this more "practical" orientation, some of the theoretical aspects of the earlier lyceum were retained. Officers who had completed the three-year garrison school curriculum were then subject to undertake "postgraduate work." The postgraduate officers might be given map problems to solve or essays to write, and, as in the days of the officers' lyceum, their presentations would be followed by discussion and critique. The map problems were to be scaled to division-size units and below, and emphasized marches, deployments, and the attack and defense of positions. The essays were to focus on "special studies of subjects bearing on and important to the military service." Those essays and solutions of map problems that possessed marked excellence were forwarded to the Chief of Staff for possible publication.[51]

"In the garrison schools," reported Chief of Staff Leonard Wood in 1911, "every effort should be made to make the instruction as practical as possible. The scope of the postgraduate work is particularly fixed by commanding officers. The importance of this work cannot be overestimated, but its success depends wholly upon the practical and thorough nature of the work. The subjects most worthy of attention in this course are tactics, supply in the field, and military history."[52] The garrison school, and its postgraduate program, persisted in this form until 1917, when the program was closed as the United States prepared to enter the Great War in Europe. New branch schools and a new program of officer education after the war meant that the garrison schools would not be reopened.

Contribution of the Officers' Lyceums and the Garrison Schools

In examining the impact of the U.S. Army's educational reforms of the late 19th and early 20th centuries, one is immediately drawn to an analysis of the work of Leavenworth (and to a lesser degree War College) graduates. "Because of their training Leavenworth graduates were among the best qualified officers to plan, organize, train, and staff a large expeditionary force," wrote Timothy Nenninger. "Pershing recognized this," Nenninger continued, "and placed Leavenworth men in important positions because the schools had taught them the proper functioning of a general staff, operational planning, teaching tactics, and simply coping with large numbers of troops."[53]

The officers' lyceum experience had been too recent to have significant impact on the experience of officers in the Spanish-American War, but that was not the case in World War I. The same predictable want of Leavenworth graduates that had prompted Schofield to create the officers' lyceums in the first place soon began to plague the American Expeditionary Force (AEF) in France. A hastily established AEF Staff College at Langres produced only 537 graduates, a number of whom did not finish until after the war was over. An AEF School of the Line was also established, but it did little better. The fact is that most of the regular officers had only their lyceum and garrison school instruction to rely upon, and it was these officers who formed the backbone of the AEF's officer corps.[54]

Gen. John Pershing (USMA 1886) was concerned about the shortage of officers trained at Leavenworth, and feared for the worst. "But Pershing's own misgivings," wrote Russell Weigley, "proved greater than necessary, and the deeper misgivings of the French and British certainly were excessive." There were failures on the part of both commanders and staffs, but overall the AEF did surprisingly well. Moreover, the quality of the staff work of subordinate commands— typically made up almost wholly of those with no Leavenworth schooling—often rivaled that of the higher headquarters.[55]

As so often happens, the early American operations in World War I did not go according to plan, but the AEF learned to fight by fighting. The staff officers at AEF General Headquarters who planned operations were usually Leavenworth men, but that was not so true at Army level, and, as we have noted, much less so of the staffs at division, brigade, and regiment. Most of these men had only their officers' lyceum and garrison school experience to call upon. In the end it proved an adequate, if sometimes imperfect, foundation.

The West Point Connection

Now, let us take up the matter of how West Point figures in this equation. It is, I suggest, in the officers' lyceums and in the postgraduate element of the garrison school that one finds a connection to West Point. It seems clear that Schofield, when he created the lyceums, envisioned a program much like those he had known at West Point as an instructor and later as the superintendent—the Napoleon Club of Dennis Hart Mahan (USMA 1824) and the West Point branch of the Military Service Institution which sprang from the former.

In the early or mid 1840s, Mahan founded and presided over the Napoleon Club, an organization dedicated to the study of the campaigns and battles of its namesake. It soon became the center of the officers' intellectual recreation at West Point. Professor Mahan, as president, assigned other members study topics—usually related to one of Napoleon's campaigns. They would then research the subject thoroughly and prepare a presentation on the topic for the other members. These presentations would be followed by a discussion in which any member might join. With very authoritative references in both French and English at the Academy's library, officers were allowed six weeks for diligent research and preparation.[56]

Although cadets were not allowed to become members of the club, they were often very aware of it. Cadet William Harris wrote in 1858:

> In History we have been studying the French Revolution and Napoleon's campaigns, and these have come hard to me as I have never read much about them, but I have "maxed" it so far on them. We have a large room in the Academic Building, on the wall of which are painted very large maps of Napoleon's campaigns. It is called the "Napoleon room" and cadets are taken in there to study his marches and battles. The officers are very particular about the study of all military campaigns and they are generally well "posted" on them, so that the study is interesting.[57]

The room Harris refers to had been assigned to the Napoleon Club by Robert E. Lee (USMA 1829) while he was superintendent.

After Mahan's death in 1871, the Napoleon Club was reorganized as the Thayer Club. Mahan had kept the focus on Napoleon and sometimes Frederick the Great. The name change was, in part, a recognition of a broader range of topics that would be covered under new leadership. Emory Upon (USMA 1861), who had returned to West Point in 1870 as Commandant of Cadets, was a member of the Thayer Club, and in 1874 delivered a paper on Prussian tactics.[58]

In 1879, with the creation of the Military Service Institution of the United States at Governor's Island, the Thayer Club became the West Point branch of that organization. Schofield, then the superintendent at West Point, gave the inaugural address for the parent club and urged the members to study and prepare themselves for whatever came next. "War is a grave and serious business. . . . Our business is to prepare ourselves to the extent of our ability to make it effective for the security of our country whenever the public necessity may call it into operation."[59]

A dozen years later, now the commanding general of the Army, Schofield faced the need to better educate the whole of the officer corps. When he sculpted the new officer lyceums, he must have recalled the papers, discussion, and learning that went on at West Point in the Napoleon Club and at the meetings of the Military Service Institution.

What was once the center of intellectual life at the Military Academy at West Point, when adapted for a larger purpose, became the one center of military professionalism that served all of the line officers of the Army. For some, the staff school, and perhaps the War College later, elevated them further, but for most it was the officers' lyceum or the postgraduate programs of the garrison schools that provided them an opportunity to explore and discover—in an intellectual way—the profession of arms.

---

[1] Samuel Huntington, *The Soldier and the State: The Theory and Politics of Civil-Military Relations* (Cambridge, MA: Harvard University Press, 1957).

[2] Huntington, *The Soldier and the State*, 211-14.

[3] Marcus Cunliffe, *Soldiers and Civilians: The Martial Spirit in America, 1775-1865* (Boston: Little Brown and Co., 1968), 149.

[4] Russell F. Weigley, *The American Way of War: A History of United States Military Strategy and Policy* (New York: Macmillan Publishing Co., 1973), 171.

[5] See Chapter 1 by William Skelton in the present anthology. Three of Professor Skelton's other works are of particular interest in this context: "Professionalism in the U.S. Army Officer Corps During the Age of Jackson," *Armed Forces and Society*, 1 (Summer 1975): 4; *An American Profession of Arms: The Army Officer Corps, 1784-1861* (Lawrence: University Press of Kansas, 1992); and "Samuel P. Huntington and the Roots of the American Military Tradition," *Journal of Military History* 60 (April 1996): 325-38.

[6] Edward M. Coffman, *The Old Army: A Portrait of the American Army in Peacetime, 1784-1898* (New York: Oxford University Press, 1986), 100-01, 269-86.

[7] Mark R. Grandstaff, "Preserving the 'Habits and Usages of War': William Tecumseh Sherman, Professional Reform, and the U.S. Army Officer Corps, 1856-1881, Revisited," *The Journal of Military History* 62 (July 1998):524-25.

[8] Donald Nevius Bigelow, *William Conant Church and the Army and Navy Journal* (New York: Columbia University Press, 1952, reprinted AMS Press, 1968), 204-07.

[9] "General Sherman on the Army," *Army and Navy Journal*, 28 December 1872, 308-09.

[10] Grandstaff, "Sherman," 538.

[11] Russell F. Weigley, *History of the United States Army* (New York: Macmillan, 1967), 273.

[12] Timothy K. Nenninger, *The Leavenworth Schools and the Old Army: Education, Professionalism, and the Officer Corps of the United States Army, 1881-1918* (Westport, CT: Greenwood Press, 1978), 22-23.

[13] William T. Sherman, "Address to the School of Application," School of Application, Fort Leavenworth, KS, 1882.

[14] Nenninger, *Leavenworth*, 22. By 1908 units almost uniformly sent captains and not lieutenants to the school. *Commandants, Staff, Faculty, and Graduates of the Command and General Staff School, Fort Leavenworth, Kansas, 1881-1939* (Fort Leavenworth, KS: The Command and General Staff School Press, 1939), 20. [Cited hereafter as *Commanders, Staff, Faculty and Graduates.*]

[15] Nenninger, *Leavenworth*, 24.

[16] Todd R. Brereton, *Educating the Army: Arthur L. Wagner and Reform, 1875-1905* (Lincoln: University of Nebraska Press, 2000), 14-15; Arthur L. Wagner, "The Military Necessities of the United States, and the Best Provisions for Meeting Them," JMSI 5 (September 1884):262. [Hereafter cited as Wagner, "Military Necessities."]

[17] Brereton, *Educating the Army*, 16-18.

[18] Nenninger, *Leavenworth*, 35-36.

[19] *Commandants, Staff, Faculty, and Graduates*, 18-27. There were a total of 545 graduates from the School of the Line between 1804 and 1816, but 16 of them were from other services or other nations.

[20] Jonathan M. House, "The Fort and the New School, 1881-1916," in *A Brief History of Fort Leavenworth*, ed. John W. Partin (Fort Leavenworth, KS: U.S. Army Combined Arms Center, 1983), 25. (Available on-line at www-cgsc.army.mil/carl/resources/ftlvn/briefhist/briefhist.asp)

[21] "General Sherman Interview," *Army and Navy Journal*, 28 December 1872, 308-09.

[22] Sherman, *Memoirs*, 2:406.

[23] On the Lyceum Movement in America, see Carl Bode, *The American Lyceum* (New York: Oxford University Press, 1956).

[24] Headquarters of the Army General Orders [HQAGO] No. 80, 1891.

[25] HQAGO No. 80, 1891.

[26] War Department Annual Report [WDAR], 1892, 1:125.

[27] WDAR, 1892, 1:105.

[28] WDAR, 1892, 1:102.

[29] WDAR, 1892, 1:119.

[30] George Van Horn Moseley, "One Soldier's Journey," manuscript autobiography, 55, George Van Horn Papers, Library of Congress.

[31] Minor was near 50 or older in 1892 and one of the Army's most senior captains. His birth date is not known, but he entered the service as a private of Ohio Troops in April 1861 and was made a captain the next year. He was surely 18 or older upon entering the service, and that would make his birth year 1843 or earlier. Just two years after his 1892 investigation of the officers' lyceums, Minor was promoted to major. He was promoted to lieutenant colonel in 1898, and to colonel the next year.

[32] WDAR, 1892, 1:129.

[33] WDAR, 1892, 1:94.

[34] WDAR, 1893, 1:63.

[35] WDAR, 1893, 1:114.

[36] WDAR, 1893, 1:137-138.

[37] WDAR, 1893, 1:137.

[38] WDAR, 1894, 1:159.

[39] WDAR, 1894, 1:106.

[40] WDAR, 1893, 1:137.

[41] HQAGO No. 23, 1895.

[42] HQAGO No. 58, 1895.

[43] WDAR 1896, 1:83.

[44] Moseley, "One Soldier's Journal," 55.

[45] HQAGO No. 51, 1897.

[46] Ibid.

[47] J. Franklin Bell, Chief of Staff, Memorandum for the Secretary of War, subject: Selection of officers for detail at the Army War College, 18 August 1908, War Department Circular No. 69, 22 August 1908.

[48] War Department General Order [WDGO] No. 124, 1905.

[49] WDGO No. 124, 1905.

[50] WDGO No. 70, 1910.

[51] WDGO No. 124, 1905.

[52] WDAR, 1911, 155.

[53] Nenninger, *Leavenworth*, 134.

[54] I have drawn this data from Nenninger's *Leavenworth* (pp. 136-38), but the analysis of it is my own.

[55] Weigley, *History of the United States Army*, 387-88.

[56] Theodore J. Crackel, *West Point: A Bicentennial History* (Lawrence: University Press of Kansas, 2002), 118; Dabney Herndon Maury, Recollections of a Virginian in the Mexican, Indian, and Civil Wars (New York: Scribner's Sons, 1894), 50.

[57] William H. Harris [USMA, June 1861] to father, 4 April 1858, William H. Harris Papers, New York Public Library.

[58] Stephen E. Ambrose, *Upton and the Army* (Baton Rouge: Louisiana State University Press, 1964, 1992), 83.

[59] Schofield, "Inaugural Address," *Journal of the Military Service Institution* 1 (1879): 16-18.

PART II:

DISTINGUISHED WEST POINTERS

Introduction

As part of West Point's centennial in 1902, the Academy heralded the many achievements of its graduates. The published record of the celebration devoted over 250 pages to recounting the success of West Pointers during the conflicts of the preceding century; another 100 pages described their contributions to the political, social, economic, and technological life of the nation. A separate chapter, unabashedly titled "The Genius of West Point," explained the secret of the success—the gradual application of "principle, personnel, and environment" over the course of the four-year Academy experience. The noble values of the profession of arms, modeled by committed faculty members, in a location offering regimentation and isolation from the distractions of the world, produced officers capable of responding to the challenges of war and peace.

The record of West Pointers in the 20th century was no less impressive than that of the 19th. Academy graduates assumed most of the top positions in every war and major campaign. During peacetime they contributed at the highest levels, both in uniform and as civilians. Measured by these accomplishments, the "genius" of West Point showed no signs of abating.

All of the authors in this section would agree that West Point was a significant influence in the lives of their subjects. They differ, however, on the extent of that influence. On the one hand, Carlo D'Este views West Point as a life-shaping experience for the young George Patton, who needed help overcoming physical and temperamental obstacles to professional success. On the other hand, Lewis Sorley focuses on pre-cadet character traits and professional experiences after West Point to interpret the greatness of Creighton Abrams. Dik Daso's study of Henry "Hap" Arnold, and Robert Norris's study of Leslie Groves, fall somewhere in between in assessing West Point's influence on these two distinguished graduates.

The authors' narratives are particularly revealing about cadet life at West Point in the early 20th century. Less than half the size of the modern Academy, the West Point of Patton, Arnold, Groves, and Abrams was a more intimate place than today. Cadets knew virtually all of their classmates on a personal level, and the deeds and misdeeds of each were common knowledge. They shared each other's hardships and joys, successes and failures, loves and losses. The friendships forged by these common experiences were intense and enduring; they provided a source of strength and comfort during the years of crisis that lay ahead. Such human ties still obtain, of course, though probably not to the degree as when the Corps was smaller.[1]

Whether or not "genius" is the best description of the Academy's four-year developmental program is debatable. What is certain, however, is that West Point has achieved resounding success in producing leaders of character for the nation. President Theodore Roosevelt—who knew something about leadership and public service—told the 1902 centennial gathering, "No other educational institution in the land has contributed so many names as West Point to the honor roll of the nation's greatest citizens."[2] His words were as true in 2002 as they were a century before.

—Editor

---

[1] The size of the Corps of Cadets has fluctuated. From the founding of the Academy through the 19th century, the authorized strength of the Corps increased gradually to just under 400. Major increases in authorized strength occurred in the 20th century: to 491 in 1900; to 748 in 1914; to 1332 in 1916; to 1960 in 1936; to 2496 in 1942; and to 4417 in 1964. Congress reduced the size of the Corps by ten percent—to about 4000—in 1993, but subsequently authorized an increase by the same amount starting in 2003. Theodore J. Crackel, *West Point: A Bicentennial History*, (Lawrence: University Press of Kansas, 2002), 170, 199, 220-21, 232, 273.

[2] United States Military Academy, *The Centennial of the United States Military Academy at West Point, New York, 1802-1902*, vol. 1 (Washington, DC: Government Printing Office, 1904), 9-10.

❧ CHAPTER 3 ❧

GENERAL GEORGE S. PATTON, JR., AT WEST POINT, 1904–1909

Carlo D'Este

From the time of his youth in Southern California when he decided he would one day become a great general, it seemed unlikely that George S. Patton, Jr., would ever achieve his dream. Patton suffered from lifelong, undiagnosed dyslexia, a malady that is far more than a learning disorder. Dyslexia is a complex disorder that, in addition to creating difficulties with reading and writing, includes an inability to concentrate, sharp mood swings, hyperactivity, obsessiveness, impulsiveness, compulsiveness, and feelings of inferiority and stupidity.[1] Patton was 11 years old before he even learned to read and write, and during his six years of formal schooling he did poorly in most academic subjects. His intense desire to attend West Point and attain an Army commission seemed little more than a farfetched, childish dream.

Instead, his father sent him to the Virginia Military Institute in 1903 where he was a model cadet. By dint of intense study and dedication, Patton succeeded in obtaining a Senatorial appointment to West Point in 1904, after beating out his competition to finish first. That Patton even survived West Point to receive a commission in the cavalry was one of the crowning achievements of his life and the subject of this article.

Established in 1802, West Point during that first century of its existence had become a national institution that supplied the U.S. Army with the majority of its professional officers. In the early days of the 20th century, not only was the Military Academy considerably smaller than today's imposing facility, but also the Corps of Cadets was only a fraction of the size of today's Corps. (The Class of 1905, for example, graduated 114 cadets compared with the Class of 2002, which graduated 966.) In June 1904, when George Smith Patton exchanged VMI gray for that of a West Point plebe (or Fourth Classman, the equivalent of a freshman), the Academy was little changed from the remote outpost created at the turn of the 18th century as a military school for engineers.

By the post-Civil War years, hazing had become an integral part of plebe life and a West Point tradition. Its excesses included strenuous and often harmful physical exercise, and petty harassments such as liberal doses of hot sauce in a plebe's food. There to greet each incoming freshman class were the upperclassmen, many of them yearlings newly liberated from their own year of hell as plebes. The arrival of a new class marked the start of what is still inelegantly dubbed "Beast Barracks," a rite of passage designed to indoctrinate civilians in the West Point way and to identify and weed out those unable or unwilling to function as future officers.

Nevertheless, the harassment accorded plebes by upperclassmen during Beast Barracks (known as "plebe camp" in Patton's time) had a far lesser impact on Patton than on his new classmates. He was in superb physical condition, and the abuse, shouting, and hazing differed only semantically from that of his previous year of ordeal at VMI.

Patton relished the pomp and ceremonial aspects of military life and thought West Point was less oppressive than VMI. During the summer of 1904, two generals were buried at the Academy, spawning in him romantic visions of great warriors and death: "I certainly think it is worth going in the army just to get a military funeral. I would like to get killed in a great victory and then have my body born between the ranks of my defeated enemy escorted by my own regiment and have my spirit come down and revel in hearing what people thought of me." [2]

His first days at West Point also precipitated what would become a lifetime penchant for saying the wrong things in public. He wrote of "catching a good deal of *hell* lately because in an unguarded moment I said that we braced harder at VMI than here." Ever since, "All the corps [Third Class corporals] have been trying to show me my error and they have succeeded."[3] Like all cadets then and now, Patton complained endlessly of the grind of cadet life, of the poor food (meat so tough "the more you chewed it the bigger it got"), too little sleep, and West Point's quaint customs. "If General Sherman's definition of war [as hell] be right," he wrote home in one of the first of many letters to his father, "west point *is* war."[4]

From his first days as a cadet, Patton was a loner, deemed arrogant and remote, with few friends and a great many detractors. Whether it was a vendetta or mere hazing, while on guard duty Patton was attacked by three cadets during plebe camp. When one attempted to seize his rifle, Patton threatened to bayonet the first person to approach him. Fortunately, the catch on his bayonet slipped and it retracted into its sheath or he might have killed the attacker. Henceforth he was left alone.[5]

Early on, Patton confided in a letter to his father, "I belong to a different class, a class perhaps almost extinct or one which may never have existed yet [is] as far removed from these lazy, patriotic, or peace soldiers as heaven is from hell. I know that my ambition is selfish and cold yet it is not a selfishnes for instead of sparing me, it makes me exert myself. . . . I may be a dreamer but I have a firm conviction I am not and in any case I will do my best to attain what I consider—wrongly perhaps—my destiny."[6]

Patton was not at first particularly tolerant of the West Point system, believing that VMI was tougher and had better discipline. "Our whole class will have more demerits than any preceding class," he said, "for since the upper class-men are not allowed to speak to us or correct us, they naturally bone us [with demerits] and they are quite right. Indeed I think that the system which they have adopted here . . . toward plebes will ruin the academy in a very few years."[7]

His constant complaining notwithstanding, Patton soon realized that West Point was indeed special: "The absolute honor of this place is amazing. . . . There is nothing but truth here and even the worst of the rabble to whom the name 'plebean' is *most* fitly applied soon learn this and conform to it."[8]

The intense training was physically exhausting and the hazing often infuriating, but what bothered Patton the most during the summer of 1904 was his uncertain academic prospects. "We begin studying on the first of september. I shall be rather glad when we do this and I at last find out just what my chances of being able to stick are," he wrote to his father with considerable trepidation.[9]

Plebe year academics were especially difficult for Cadet Patton, who lamented that English was pure memorization and "pretty hard for me because it is simply grammar and I know nothing of it. . . . I don't believe that there is any possibility of my being found at least this year for there are some absolute fools in the present third class who got through. You should see this place at night it is absolutely soundless yet there are five hundred men in it and every one of them studying like hell."[10]

Patton was torn between an ability to see future greatness for himself and the promptings of his dyslexia, which served unceasingly to implant the notion that he was both ordinary and stupid. On at least one occasion that summer, he was unable to read an order posted on the bulletin board. Thus, his plebe year was an uneven struggle to overcome an affliction of which he had no conception. "I have always thought that I was a military genius or at least that I was or would be a great general," he wrote his father soon after classes started. "Well . . . at present I see little in which to base such a belief. I am neither quicker nor brighter in any respect than other men nor do they look upon me as a leader as it is said Napolions class mates looked upon him. In fact the only difference between me and other people is that I have ideals with out strength of character enough to live up to them and they have not even got them."[11]

Another aspect of Patton's struggle centered on his deliberate, sustained efforts to project a personality not his own. He began to affect personality traits intended to deceive others into believing he was someone entirely different—in short, to reinvent himself in the guise of a rugged macho male. When Patton entered VMI in 1903 he had already begun to display unmistakable signs of a significant personality change from his happy-go-lucky youth in California. As a teenager he had perceived that a military leader must present an image of invincibility and toughness, traits then utterly alien to him. Determined to prepare himself for generalship, Patton began acting in a manner that bore scant resemblance to his true persona. He concocted his own personal conception of how a leader and a general ought to look and behave, and he spent the remainder of his life honing that image by becoming profane, ruthless, and aristocratic. His famous scowl became so much a part of his persona it was as if he had been born with it permanently engraved on his face. Nevertheless, despite his attempts to portray himself as a tough guy, the ultramacho image that Patton cultivated so successfully in later years was not yet fully present in the youthful West Point cadet. Inside he remained a tenderhearted young man, always anxious to please his father and requiring constant parental approval and encouragement.

His bravado was actually part of the defensive wall he erected to compensate for the impairments associated with his dyslexia. Patton's classmates, however, perceived his single-mindedness as naked ambition. There was nothing wrong with aspiring to become the first general from his class, but it was boastful and tactless to let this become common knowledge. Patton also bragged that he would letter at West Point in football, a feat he was unable to accomplish. His belief that he was different from other cadets, that he possessed a unique sense of commitment they lacked, that he was special where they were simply ordinary, was bound to breed resentment—and it did.

When the upperclassmen learned he had been at VMI, the hazing intensified. Other military institutions were regarded as "tin schools," but none more so than VMI. During the summer of 1904 Patton was frequently and often forcefully reminded that he was now at West Point. His classmates soon scornfully dubbed him, "Georgie," a nickname he loathed.

Although Patton struggled with academic subjects, he had no such problems on the parade ground, where he was far more comfortable and nearly flawless. "I have been perfect so far in drill regulations," he proudly wrote to his father.[12] When it came to confidence in his soldiering, Patton was unequivocal, declaring that "God willing

. . . and given the chance I will carve my name on some thing bigger than a section room bench."

Yet, with his continued struggle in the classroom, Patton openly spoke of his uncertainty as to surviving academically. One of the daily dilemmas faced by dyslexics is that others believe they are merely stupid. There are few torments worse than being publicly identified as "slow." The harder he tried, the worse he seemed to do. What he could not understand, of course, was that his problem had nothing to do with his intelligence or study habits, but rather was a learning disorder that included several personality impairments. One of his most anguished letters read: "I am a characterless, lazy, stupid, yet ambitious dreamer; who will degenerate into a third rate second lieutenant and never command anything more than a platoon."[13]

Patton tried out for the football team but was cut and played intramural football for his cadet company, vowing he would try harder than ever the following year to make the varsity team. He never did. In the autumn of 1904, as the time neared when his academic progress would be formally evaluated, he wrote, "The best thing—the only thing now left for me to do is by doubly hard work [to] live down the effects of a poor start."[14] Although he managed to pass his first series of examinations, his mood swung from elation to pessimism. In December 1904, fearful of taking a forthcoming written recitation he was convinced he could not pass, Patton deliberately faked illness (an act that in later years would have been a violation of the Honor Code—for which the penalty was dismissal).

Athletics became a valuable outlet from the ordeal of the classroom. During the Christmas holidays in 1904 he decided to make the best of the winter and take up ice skating, but his early attempts brought frequent contact between his posterior and the ice, leaving him assured that his future as an outdoor sportsman lay elsewhere.

Other than in playacting as a child, Patton had never fenced before entering West Point. Although fencing with a saber was a formal part of the curriculum, he also began to practice with a broadsword in the anonymity of the gym where he could give free expression to his perception that being a great swordsman was an essential trait of a great general. Patton practiced incessantly over time and improved his skill with the sword to the point that he began to refer to himself as "Master of the Sword," a prophetic gesture that would eventually be fulfilled as a young officer.

Patton also joined the track team where he described himself as "turning into a gray hound." But he became the victim of the first of what would become a lifetime of accidents that might have killed unluckier or less well-conditioned men. "I almost brought my fiery life to a sudden and tragic conclusion," he wrote after tripping over a hurdle at full speed, falling on his head, and badly skinning his knees. Not only was Patton accident prone, but his impatience with the everyday problems of life sometimes led to acts of outright folly, such as the time he deliberately cut his gum with a pocket knife in a fruitless attempt to "let the beast of a [wisdom] tooth through."[15]

His enthusiasm waxed and waned, and his moods reflected the uncertainty felt by all dyslexics. "I amount to very little more than when I was a baby. . . . I am fare in every thing and good in nothing. . . . I some times fear that I am one of these darned dreamers with a willing spirit but a weak flesh of a man who is always going to succeed but who never does."[16] To Patton, perception was everything, and his low self-esteem left him convinced he had little to offer anyone. Other than his father, there was no one to tell him he was dead wrong. After receiving one of his son's plaintive letters, Mr. Patton offered these blunt but wise and compassionate words: "You must school yourself to meet defeat and failure without bitterness—and to take your comfort in having striven worthily and done your best."[17]

To that end, Patton approached his year-end exams determined to do his best. It was not enough; he failed mathematics and was "found" (i.e., failed) and ordered to repeat his plebe year. Free of recriminations from his understanding parents, Patton looked forward to his second year at West Point with an ambivalent hope that he might eventually graduate: "It is scarcely possible that I may ever again be so happy and so sad at the same time."[18]

While home in California during the summer of 1905, Patton began recording in a small black notebook a hodgepodge of thoughts, poetry, principles of war, diagrams, and admonitions affirming that his terrible first year at West Point had matured him. One of his first entries was "Do your damdest always." To his death, Patton never fully understood that during his first year at West Point he had indeed "done his damdest" and had fallen victim not to stupidity or laziness but to a cruel disorder that we today call dyslexia. In the notebook, Patton also outlined the principles that would guide him:

- Genius is an immense capacity for taking pains.
- Always do more than is required of you.
- What then of death? is not the taps of death but first call to the reveille of eternal life.
- We live in deeds not years.
- You can be what you *will* to be.[19]

Patton returned to West Point in 1905 to begin his military career all over again. Although still technically a plebe, but exempt from the hazing and harassment of plebe life, Patton in his second year at West Point existed in a sort of limbo where he was looked upon as neither plebe nor Third Classman. He continued to study hard and for the first time saw his efforts rewarded. Patton began to anticipate the delights of advancement to the Third Class and set his sights on promotion to corporal, not just any corporal, but first corporal, the most prestigious office in his class: "I think I shall die when I get it."[20]

During his five years at West Point, Patton courted his future wife, Beatrice Ayer, the daughter of a self-made Yankee millionaire from Boston. With her beauty, brains, musical talent, and family wealth, the sophisticated debutante Beatrice Ayer was the very antithesis of George S. Patton. She attracted a number of suitors, but from the time of their first meeting in California in 1892, when she was only six years old, Beatrice Ayer only had eyes for Patton. Their courtship was largely conducted by letter (his were mostly vain and "I"-oriented), interspersed by occasional visits by Beatrice to West Point, and by Patton to Massachusetts. She proved the perfect foil for the emotional downside of Patton's dyslexia. Her letters bolstered his morale and made him begin to feel good about himself.

Patton continued throughout the 1905-1906 school year to fill his notebook with ideas and quotations, ranging from Clausewitz to observations on cavalry. Some reflected his isolation: "Let people talk and be damed," and "I think that there must be a Destiny. . . . Look well whether the game is worth the candle. . . . I hope and pray that *what ever* it cost I shall gane my desire."[21] On his 21st birthday, doubtless toughened by his long bout with dyslexia, he repeated one of his earlier stated principles of life: "Man lives by deeds not years."[22] Patton's second year at West Point ended on a high note when he not only routinely passed his exams with grades in the top third of his class but also was selected second corporal.[23]

Predictably, as a cadreman in the plebe summer camp of 1906, Patton was overzealous and managed to irritate virtually everyone from his classmates to the tactical officers, and, of course, the hapless plebes who ran afoul of him. Nevertheless, he soon learned that harassing plebes did not "afford me much amusement as I had hoped."

He was excited by the opportunity to be in command but seemed to have no concept of when enough was enough: "I believe that I reported more men than any other Officer of the Day this summer," he told Beatrice, who admonished him not to become over-exuberant. Patton's first taste of authority ended in shock and disappointment when he was demoted from second to sixth corporal in late August. Although angry and hurt, Patton displayed no inclination to change his basic precept of demanding very high standards of those under his charge. "It is true that they don't like me but when I get out in front of them the foolishness stops," he proclaimed. In March 1907, Patton regained his second corporal stripes and jovially wrote to his father, "I take the opportunity of telling you I am in matters vegetable, animal, and mineral, the very living model of a modern Second Corporal."[24]

Academically, Patton remained a mediocre student, standing near the bottom of his class in French and in the middle in drawing and mathematics, and was a borderline student in Spanish as well. Nevertheless, he successfully passed his exams and was promoted to sergeant major in the Second Class (i.e., junior class).

Although he disdained academics, Patton had no qualms about the value of history. He proclaimed that becoming a great soldier entailed learning from history. To his death he never lost his passion for reading and learning from the past: "To attain this end I think it is necessary for a man to begin to read military history in its earliest and hence crudest form and to follow it down in natural sequence permitting his mind to grow with his subject until he can grasp with out effort the most abstruce question of the science of war. . . ."[25]

Following the words of Napoleon, he wrote that "to command an army well a general must think of nothing else."[26] Throughout his West Point days Patton continued to dream of glory and triumph in his chosen profession. He also reminded himself that by perseverance, study, "and eternal desire any man can be great." His words of advice to himself bore the stamp of maturity far beyond his years, and later became the essence of his military philosophy. An entry in his notebook in November 1907 served as a vivid exhortation of the inner fire that burned within: "George Patton you have seen what the enthusiasm of men can mean. . . . You have done your damdest and failed now you must do your damdest and win. Remember that is what you live for. Oh you must! You have got to do some thing! Never stop until you have gained the top or a grave."[27] Patton never conceived of any other career for himself. Again and again he wrote passionately of his desire to become a successful soldier: "I am fool enough to think that I am one of those who may teach the world its value."

Nevertheless, even as he used his black notebook to devise the tenets by which he would later govern his military career, his dyslexia continued to ambush his self-esteem in what became a daily struggle for recognition, an aim that continued to haunt his dreams. Shortly before the February 1908 cadet promotion list was announced, Patton wrote to his father about a disturbing dream: "I was the adjutant and I was having a fine time then next night I dreamed I was found and everybody was pointing their fingers at me and calling me stupid. I was so scared that I woke up. . . . the only thing I am good at is military. I can't to save my life care about studies and if I did care about them I have not got the head for them. I can not sit down and study because I like to as some of these fools do."[28]

In the summer of 1908, eight of his classmates, now First Classmen, were expelled after being caught hazing. Although he saw no harm in what they had done, Patton now seemed disinclined to haze, preferring instead to enforce discipline. When the Commandant of Cadets, Lt. Col. Robert L. Howze, demoted most of the First Class cadet officers during a shakeup in the summer of 1908, Patton was unaffected.

Patton's fifth and final year at West Point was his most successful. At the Annual Field Day in June 1908, he established a new school record in the 220-yard hurdles. He also won the 120-yard hurdles and rounded out the most triumphant day of his athletic career at West Point as the runner-up in the 220-yard dash.[29] His feats won him notice in the *Howitzer* along with the 15 other wearers of the coveted letter "A."[30] Patton also fired "Expert" with the rifle and continued to excel in swordsmanship. The *Howitzer* text accompanying the photograph of those First Classmen who had won letters included this remark: "It is said that Georgie Patton has compiled for future generals, a rule for winning any battle under any combination of circumstances."[31]

In a manner of speaking, Patton had indeed compiled such a "rule." Many years after his death, his son donated part of his father's vast collection of books to the Friends of the West Point Library. Unearthed on the final page of a textbook called *Elements of Strategy* was Patton's exhausted farewell to academics at West Point: "End of last lesson in Engineering. Last lesson as Cadet, Thank God." Then, inscribed on the back cover in Patton's hand, was his prescription for those who aspired to be battle-winning generals: [32]

Qualities of a Great General
1. Tactically aggressive (loves a fight)
2. Strength of character
3. Steadiness of purpose
4. Acceptance of responsibility
5. Energy
6. Good health and strength

/signed/ George Patton
Cadet
U.S.M.A.
April 29, 1909

Patton's early writings substantiate the proposition that his West Point years were far more than an essential period of preparation for his Army commission. When the time came, Patton would put into practice his tenets for how men should be led and battles fought. These tenets were fostered at the Military Academy, finally coming to fruition in December 1944 during the Battle of the Bulge.

Although Patton's early writings reflect undeniable brilliance, he had yet to demonstrate to his contemporaries that his fiery intensity was anything more than the ravings of a temperamental opportunist. To the end of his cadet days, he remained a dogmatic and unpopular cadet, a young man on the make with a reputation as a "quilloid"—a cadet who was overly zealous in writing demerit reports on other cadets.[33] In the years following his graduation from West Point, this perception of Patton would not change.

Beatrice Ayer attended the West Point-Yale football game in the autumn of 1908, pronouncing it "great fun watching him prance up and down the field at inspection, chest bulging and chevrons shining, serenely. . . . He seemed by far the most military person on the post that day; our only anxiety was that he might break in two at the waistline."[34]

If Patton's belief in discipline was seen by others as excessive, it failed to deter his ambition, for when he was promoted to regimental adjutant in 1908, he exulted that he had at last begun to live up to the high standards he had set for himself. As cadet adjutant, Patton was always center stage in front of the Corps of Cadets. Impeccably dressed and a master of military posture, Patton was now the focus of their attention. The adjutant read the orders of the day each morning and led the Corps wherever they marched. It was what he had long coveted and he made the most of it.

He also began to display the enigmatic traits that would later characterize the public perception of him as a general. One day on the rifle range, as Patton toiled in the pits, raising, lowering, and marking targets during rifle practice, he inexplicably stood up during the firing. He faced the firing line, unflinching as bullets angrily splattered all around him, and later declared he had done it to test his courage under fire.[35] More to the point was the miracle that he was not wounded or killed while giving in to the urge to satisfy his curiosity and prove his courage.

Patton's stubborn independence was demonstrated one day at the noon meal when he led the Corps of Cadets into the mess hall. As they awaited his "Take Seats" command, an unpopular tactical officer entered. Cadet custom was to stand silently at attention until the officer got the message and left the hall. Patton, however, believed that any officer, whatever his alleged misdeeds, was deserving of proper respect for his rank. On this occasion, when the Corps began to give the officer the silent treatment, Patton became so disgusted that he marched them out of the mess hall.[36]

Historian and Patton biographer Martin Blumenson here assesses Patton's often stormy relations with his classmates: "They accepted him generally with affection and admiration for his sincerity, candor, and fairness. They smiled in condescension over his naive earnestness and enthusiasm. They believed that he tried too hard, had too much spirit, and they were uncomfortable with his obsessive concern with future glory, which he could not resist confessing from time to time. He had no close friends."[37] Sadly, despite his lengthy sojourn at West Point, by the time Patton graduated in 1909, he could claim none of his classmates as intimates.

Reflecting on his years at the Academy, Patton recalled his first day as a plebe. "How scared I was that day how earnest in my desire to succeed. I failed a little and did not succeed in much . . . but I did my best as I found it."[38] After five grueling years, George S. Patton's ordeal at West Point ended on 11 June 1909 when he was commissioned a second lieutenant of cavalry. Of the 103 graduates in the Class of 1909, Patton's final class standing was number 46.[39] If that seemed average, it was not, for had it not been for his dyslexia he undoubtedly would have graduated near the top of his class.

With his dream of a commission as a cavalry officer fulfilled, Patton left West Point for an uncertain future in the Lilliputian Regular Army of the time. Patton had good reason to be proud, for not only had he overcome what he thought was his natural stupidity, but he had achieved the all-important first step in the long road toward fulfilling his driving ambition and perceived destiny of becoming the celebrated warrior whose statue today guards the entrance to the West Point library.

To his death Patton loved West Point and treasured what it had taught him. The words of the Academy motto, "Duty, Honor, Country," were no mere symbols but the literal embodiment of his deepest convictions as nurtured at this institution. Indeed, so abiding was Patton's desire to return to West Point that he tried without success on several occasions between the two world wars to be appointed commandant.

It was always Patton's desire to be buried at West Point. When he died an unsoldierly death in December 1945, shortly after being paralyzed from the neck down in a traffic accident in war-torn Germany, his wife fully intended to fulfill his wishes until dissuaded by Patton's lifelong friend, Geoffrey Keyes (USMA 1913), then the commanding general of the U.S. Seventh Army. Keyes pointed out that it was customary (at that time) for soldiers who died in Europe to be buried there in a military cemetery. Beatrice Patton agreed, and George Smith Patton, Jr., was buried in the American military cemetery outside Hamm, Luxembourg, beside the soldiers of the Third Army he had led so well. Ultimately, his place of burial did not matter, for his spirit lives on at West Point.

---

[1] This article is adapted from the author's *Patton: A Genius For War* (New York: Harper-Collins, 1995). Note to the reader: Patton's dyslexia led him to frequently omit punctuation and misspell words. In order not to clutter the text his exact words are reproduced, and the use of *sic* has been omitted. Further information about dyslexia can be found in a landmark book by a leading expert in dyslexia: Harold N. Levinson, *Smart But Feeling Dumb* (New York: Warner Books, 1984).

[2] GSP to his father, George S. Patton II, 15 August 1904. Unless otherwise cited, all correspondence and diary entries written at West Point are in Box 6, Patton Papers, Manuscript Division, Library of Congress, and in "Excerpts from Cadet Letters of GSP to Father," Patton Papers, USMA. See also chaps. 6-8 of *Patton: A Genius For War*.

[3] Ibid., 3 July 1904.

[4] Robert H. Patton, *The Pattons: The Personal History of an American Family* (New York: Crown, 1994), 128.

[5] GSP to GSP II, 15 August 1904.

[6] Ibid., 3 July 1904.

[7] Ibid., 31 July 1904.

[8] Ibid., 21 August 1904.

[9] Ibid.,17 July 1904.

[10] Ibid., 4 September 1904.

[11] D'Este, *Patton: A Genius For War*, 77.

[12] GSP to GSP II, 18 September 1904.

[13] Ibid., dated 1904 and written sometime in November or December.

[14] Ibid., 4 September 1904.

[15] Ibid., 14 and 21 May 1905.

[16] Ibid., 12 November 1904.

[17] George S. Patton II to GSP, 10 June 1905.

[18] GSP to Beatrice Ayer, 10 July 1905.

[19] The opening date of Patton's small black notebook is August 1905. There were actually two notebooks, a small one begun in 1905 ("1905 Notebook") and a second cadet notebook begun in 1906 ("Cadet Notebook"). Patton's principles were: (1) Cut line of communication; (2) Cause enemy to form front to flank; (3) Operate on internal lines; (4) Separate bodies of enemy and fight in detail; and (5) Direct attack. This observation also appeared in his notes: "A Saxon can die without a murmer. A French man can die laughing. But only a Norseman can laugh as he kills."

[20] D'Este, *Patton: A Genius For War*, 90.

[21] Entries in "1905 Notebook," late August 1906.

[22] GSP to GSP II, 11 November 1906.

[23] Patton was topped for first corporal by Cadet Edwin St. John Greble, Jr., one of the outstanding members of the Class of 1909, and a cadet against whom he competed throughout his tenure at West Point.

[24] GSP to GSP II, 17 March 1907.

[25] First written in 1903 and later copied into the "1905 Notebook."

[26] "1905 Notebook" entries recorded sometime in early 1909.

[27] Entry in "1905 Notebook," 27 November 1907.

[28] GSP to GSP II, 5 February 1908.

[29] Martin Blumenson, *The Patton Papers*, vol. 1 (Boston: Houghton Mifflin, 1974), 147.

[30] 1909 USMA *Howitzer*.

[31] Ibid.

[32] Col. Roger H. Nye, USA, Ret., "The Patton Library Comes to West Point," in Friends of the West Point Library *Newsletter*, 1988; and lecture, "The Professional Reading of General George S. Patton, Jr.," April 1988. Lt. Col. G.J. Fieberger, a USMA Professor of Engineering, wrote *Elements of Strategy*, the standard cadet text of Patton's period.

[33] Thomas J. Fleming, *West Point* (New York: Morrow, 1969), 288. Patton had in fact written his own rules for "quilling" in his notebook, called "Essentials of Quill." Designed for himself as rules he attempted to follow, they later became tenets by which Patton enforced his own standard of discipline: 1. Start the day you enter. 2. Do every thing possible to attract attention. 3. Brace hard and at all times. The less you are spoken to the more you should brace. 4. Always be very neat and when you get any new clothes let every one know it. 5. Do with all the snap and power you possess whatever you do. 6. When ordered to do a thing carry out the spirit. 7. Brace through publication of orders and when "at ease" and never stop quilling.

[34] Beatrice Ayer Patton, quoted in the unpublished memoir of her daughter, Ruth Ellen [Patton] Totten.

[35] Martin Blumenson, *Patton: The Man Behind the Legend, 1885-1945* (New York: Morrow, 1985), 55.

[36] Ibid., 58.

[37] Blumenson, *The Patton Papers*, vol. 1, 176.

[38] D'Este, *Patton: A Genius For War*, 107.

[39] Patton's final class standings in his last academic report were: Civil and Military Engineering - 37; Law - 80; Ordnance and Science of Gunnery - 62; Drill Regulations - 5; Practical Military Engineering - 10; Conduct, First Class - 16. He accumulated 42 demerits for the year 1908/09. *(Official Register of the Officers and Cadets of the USMA,* June 1909, USMA Special Collections, and Blumenson, *The Patton Papers*, vol. 1, 175.)

⫷ CHAPTER 4 ⫸

HENRY H. ARNOLD AT WEST POINT, 1903–1907

Dik Alan Daso

When the Class of 1907 entered the United States Military Academy on 15 June 1903, man had not yet flown aloft in a powered aircraft. On 17 December of that year, however, the Wright brothers accomplished what many believed impossible—they flew. Not long afterward, the concept of using the airplane as a military tool was officially sanctioned in the Army. The first aviation unit was created in 1907, the year Henry Harley "Hap" Arnold graduated from West Point. Perhaps it was destiny that a member of this class thus became so intimately linked to aviation.

Examining Arnold's cadet career provides the means to understand more clearly how this adventurous young native Philadelphian during the Second World War came to command the greatest air armada in military history. Not a gifted student, Arnold found that the Military Academy worked under a strict set of rules and practices. During his years there, he found ways to work around that system by knowledge of its function and familiarity with its strengths and weaknesses.

Inevitably, Arnold's methods and his behavior came into conflict with the good order and discipline that were considered essential to military efficiency—in the ground Army anyway. When he graduated, however, the fledgling aviation branch required unique officers that were dynamic and somewhat possessed of a devil-may-care attitude. Arnold, although he did not clearly understand it at the time, exemplified those dynamic qualities of fearlessness and rebelliousness that turned out to be essential to a career as a military pilot in those early days of flight. After a brief stint as an infantryman, Arnold launched on what became a career that ended with five stars and command of 2.4 million airmen of the Army Air Forces.

When Henry Harley Arnold entered the Military Academy in 1903, it was an isolated fortress nestled against rock-bound highlands overlooking a sharp bend in the Hudson River. Narrow, difficult dirt roads were the only way to reach the place. The countryside remained sparsely populated, and there were no routes leading directly north. Only one unimproved road headed west out of the Academy grounds. The West Shore Railroad was the principal means of transportation both in and out.

For the most part, except for special occasions such as graduation, the only people at the Military Academy were cadets, faculty, and the faculty's families. A local tram, described as a "funny little train," was the most comfortable way to get from the closest mainline train station to the hotel near the post. It was the chosen method of transport by out-of-town visitors, particularly lady friends. The ride up the hill, the final leg of the journey to the grounds, was provided by an early version of a taxi, a hack.[1]

Cadet training was as rugged and difficult as the terrain. To gain admission into the Corps of Cadets, young men first had to pass a series of examinations. Entrance exams were difficult, and only a fraction of those taking them passed. Passing the exams was no guarantee that a young man—women were not permitted to attend any of the service academies until 1976—would enter with the new class that numbered 134 at the end of Arnold's first year.

Harley Arnold was one of those who passed the competitive exams, which he had taken with five other young men from Philadelphia, his hometown.[2] Unfortunately, he was not immediately accepted into the Class of 1907 because another candidate from Arnold's district had scored higher on the May entrance exams and was first in line. Although Beast Barracks, as the plebe indoctrination training during the first summer was called, began at precisely 11:45 a.m. on 15 June

Major Henry H. Arnold at his 20th class reunion at West Point, 1927. His 1905 photo is inset at the lower left of the image. (Courtesy of Robert Arnold, Sonoma, CA)

1903 without Arnold, one month later, on 18 July, Arnold was notified that the candidate who had aced him out of the first slot had, inexplicably, married the day before training began. That man was immediately disqualified and sent home and Arnold was to take his place.[3]

At the age of 17 years, one month, and two days, barely meeting the minimum age requirement, Arnold entered West Point on Monday morning, 27 July, as a member of the Class of 1907. He, along with several others, was to arrive before 8:00 a.m. for the entry physical examination.[4] This was more than luck: it almost strikes as an act of fate. If Arnold had been first in line to attend West Point, he would have reported on 15 June 1903. And Army regulations were explicit that "no candidate shall be admitted who is under seventeen." Arnold did not turn 17 until the 25th of June; on 15 June, he was still 16 and would have been turned away. But in July, along with four other classmates with similar birth dates, he met the entry requirement for age.[5]

The challenge before him was formidable. Many cadets had prior experience at civilian colleges, and virtually everyone was older than Arnold. More than one-third of the class was over 20 years old. The experiences these older cadets gained in the years between high school and West Point endowed them with greater maturity and the ability to handle more deftly the plebe or Fourth Class (freshman), year. Arnold, almost before he realized it, had gone from high school senior to plebe in less than one month without such a benefit.

Nearly one-third of those who entered West Point did not graduate. Arnold fell into the successful two-thirds, a feat he accomplished with seemingly shallow effort and, accordingly, minimal formal distinction. Nonetheless, he was destined to become an important part of the ever-extending Long Gray Line.[6]

Entering late did not come without penalty. The majority of the cadets already had moved out of the permanent barracks area and established the summer encampment, where basic field procedures were taught. The tents were erected past the cavalry plain near the tactical training ranges, less than a mile from the barracks. The 28 stragglers who belatedly began training in July received special, almost individual, training attention. They were dubbed, according to tradition, "Juliets," a term originating in the combination of *July* and *-ette*.[7] The allusion to one of Shakespeare's feminine characters served to heighten the derogatory effect of the nickname.

Beast Barracks was unlike anything these young men had ever experienced before. It was sardonically defined in the 1906 version of the cadet yearbook *The Howitzer* as "Cadet barracks during the period when beasts use it for a summer resort." Gen. Carl "Tooey" Spaatz, Class of 1914, first chief of staff of the independent Air Force and a Pennsylvanian himself, described summer camp as "primarily not a hazing but a disciplinary period, a different kind of discipline than what you're used to when you're pretty much on your own around a small country town."[8]

Different is perhaps a mild understatement to describe the plebe experience. Incoming candidates were first labeled beasts (from the French *bêtes*, meaning "animals" or "stupid"), then plebes (from the Latin *plebs*, meaning "mob" or "common herd") or Juliets, if applicable. For those first three weeks they were beasts; they did not qualify as plebes until they moved from the barracks out to the tent city.

From the moment the Juliets were ushered to the cadet area, the endless barking of commands and corrections began—plebes called it ragging and bracing. "Get your chin in. . . . Shoulders back and down. . . . Tack a 'sir' on to that statement, mister. . . . Drag in that chin!" The act of "dragging" in one's chin was immortalized in many cadet annuals in cartoon form. One of Arnold's classmates was particularly impressed that Arnold could, on demand, produce up to seven wrinkles under his chin.[9]

On the second day, the Juliets were ordered to sing a running song as they double-timed to the cadet store, sporting crisp, maroon-colored flags that represented their class. At the store, the fledglings were issued bedding, uniforms, a mattress, and a dipper for water. Then it was on to the barracks. Rooms were Spartan. There was a plain iron bunk for each man and two alcoves in which to hang uniforms in a specified order. All other worldly belongings went in a footlocker. "Everything was prescribed," as Arnold's classmate Hayden Wagner recalled. "The top drawer of your clothes press [closet organizer] was the only place you got to take any liberties whatsoever to arrange personal things. Most of them [cadets] had photographs of girls up there." One of Arnold's personal items was a photograph of his father and mother.[10]

Latrine facilities for the cadets were as Spartan as the barracks. Each cadet had a washbasin and washstand, but the water had to be carried from the quadrangle—the area in the center of the barracks—back to the rooms. Renovations in 1906 eventually remedied the situation, but that did not mitigate the problem for the plebe's of the Class of 1907. Toilet facilities, or "sinks," were inconveniently located on the second floor of a separate building on the quad. They were divided by class rank: the First Class sink, the Second Class sink, and so on. Toilets lined one wall and tubs another, as straight and tidy as a cadet parade formation. After a quick latrine break, it was double-time back to the rooms, where the ragging increased in intensity again until the next scheduled duty.[11]

Next came a trip to the Ordnance Department for rifles, bayonets, and entrenching tools, a holdover practice from the successful siege campaigns of the Civil War. Then back to the rooms again to stow their newly acquired gear. Drill formations began next. A beast was not a soldier until he could march in lockstep with a company of other soldiers while carrying a highly polished, bolt-action Springfield .30 caliber rifle. Incredibly, by dinner on Arnold's very first day, the Juliets were keeping in step and looked like a sharp, gray-clad company of soldiers sans rifles; marching with rifles came a few days later.[12]

Day two established the model for the rest of Beast Barracks and was much more challenging than the partial first day. The newest members of the Corps of Cadets were rousted from bed for the breakfast formation by the unnerving blast of the reveille cannon at 5:30 a.m. Immediately following the meal, the Juliets met the notorious 1st Lt. Herman Koehler, instructor of military gymnastics and physical culture. His job was to get the Juliets on an even physical par with those who had entered on 15 June.[13] For many, the workout was a brutal assault on their bodies, and one suspects that Koehler relished the misery he inflicted on them. After the first half-hour of nonstop calisthenics and running in place, several plebes fainted, vomited, or took a knee to catch their breath. Arnold handled the physical exercise with relative ease; his high school track and football experience had left him in excellent physical condition.[14]

After a quick but necessary morning shower, the cadets conducted rifle drill. During drill periods, as one cadet wrote, "the sun was hotter, the guns heavier, the drills longer and the rests rarer than in any vocation in any other country on the planet."[15] Short break periods, from the plebes' point of view anyway, were hardly worthy of the name. Plebes rushed back to their rooms to polish their brass buckles and buttons, clean rifles, or memorize upperclass cadet names and ranks. Then drill, drill, and more drill.

Meanwhile, most of the upperclassmen conducted artillery and cavalry training. Many rode horses, and some worked on engineering projects. The First Classmen trained hard all morning, but played polo, tennis, or went swimming in the afternoon. For them summer camp was fun, even relaxing. There were even upperclass hops, sometimes three evenings a week during the summer. Sometimes local girls—faculty daughters or from nearby towns—made the journey. Hops were a privilege reserved exclusively for upperclassmen, who attended whether or not there were dance cards to fill. The plebes just drilled.[16]

Finally, at the end of the day, stomachs filled with "sammy" (molasses) and "slum" (mysterious stew meat), the new cadets found physical and mental relief. As Ben Castle, Arnold's class athletic representative, recalled, "When tattoo [the bedtime bugle call] came at nine o'clock—that was the earliest we could go to bed—we just dropped into bed and went to sleep, a dreamless sleep. You were so damned tired, physically tired. Then, the next morning, up at quarter to six, breakfast at six, and the routine would be repeated. . . . It was amazing how quick they whipped us into shape."[17]

By the end of the third week, now indoctrinated into West Point's strict military regimen, the Juliets joined the rest of the cadets at summer encampment as plebes. Understandably, the new additions felt second-rate compared with those plebes who had been subjected to the entire eight weeks of beast barracks. The scornful but still vigilant eyes of the upperclassmen in charge of plebe training did little to diminish this self-inflicted guilt. But the initial disparity vanished as the first official dress parade brought all the cadets together for the first time. It was the beginning of a four-year experience that transformed the individuals who entered the Academy in 1903 into a united class that graduated four years later.

The first parade formation was not, however, an opportunity to relax. Upperclass cadets, now surrounding the newly tailored, stiffly starched, parade-dressed plebes on all sides, took the liberty of making verbal corrections even while the formation passed directly in front of the West Point superintendent, Brig. Gen. Albert Mills. The constant din of corrections rumbled like distant thunder over the visitor stands, causing the uninitiated to wonder what the commotion was all about. None of the plebes enjoyed the harassment, but all of them took solace in knowing that their West Point forbears had endured the same treatment. They were taking their place in the Long Gray Line beside such distinguished luminaries as Ulysses S. Grant, Robert E. Lee, and Philip H. Sheridan.[18]

The Corps of Cadets returned from summer encampment to the barracks on 31 August 1903. A large stack of textbooks awaited them, having been delivered to their rooms while they were yet in the field. The next day classes began. "There wasn't any fooling around. You had a lesson assigned the day before and you started in the first day to recite and be marked." In addition to textbooks, cadets were issued the "Black Book," a manual on guard duty and drill. Failure to follow precisely the book's rules resulted in demerits and punishments.[19]

Cadet daily life during the academic year conformed to a rigid routine. In addition to studies and sports, cadets served periodic guard duty in 24-hour shifts. Sunday chapel attendance was mandatory, as were all meals. All activities were preceded by a formation in the barracks courtyard and then a march to the appointed destination. Weekends afforded the only opportunity for cadets to entertain visitors. On Saturdays and Sundays, even plebes had limited privileges of visitation.

The rigors of cadet life kept everyone so busy that time passed quickly, even for the plebes. There was so much to be accomplished that "weeks were stretched quite out of shape and could scarcely be made to fit into the little thirty-day month."[20] Academic studies took up the majority of free time. During their first year all plebes studied mathematics, French, and English. In fact, there were no electives in the entire cadet academic curriculum. Each cadet received his diploma as a prerequisite for commissioning. Mathematics was generally considered the most important subject, as far as studying went, and deficiency usually resulted in dismissal without appeal.

Arnold's grades in mathematics were just good enough to prevent any academic reviews, despite the fact that he memorized more than 30 pages of logarithmic tables. His French teacher, 2d Lt. Frank P. Lahm, remembered only that the boyish Arnold was average—nothing outstanding. Perhaps his less-than-stellar performance in French, 98th out of 136, was the reason for Lahm's lackluster assessment.[21] Arnold finished even lower in English, 103d out of 136, but no one was expelled for low marks in English. Remarkably, 50 years of handwritten letters to his wife contain only a handful of misspellings, along with continual apologies for sloppy writing or breaches in style. Many of Arnold's letters were eloquent, demonstrating a gifted economy of language. In the English classroom, however, it appears that he did not put in much effort.[22]

Despite marginal academic achievement, Arnold's grades for military conduct were consistently high. Conduct grades were inversely related to the number of demerits accumulated during the academic year. For his first three years, Arnold was near the top of his class in that area, having received relatively few demerits. It was these marks that actually saved him from a lower final class standing than his mediocre academic scores alone would have reflected.

Football season brought welcome relief to the bleakness of cadet life. It helped build esprit de corps, and victories over regional powerhouses like Navy often earned the Corps of Cadets special privileges such as postponed inspections or a canceled parade. Football in those days was a particularly brutal endeavor. There was no forward passing allowed until 1906, so every play was a running play of some kind. Helmets were little more than leather caps, if worn at all. Players were tough and resilient. Cadets placed tremendous emphasis

Cadet Arnold (second from right of the five seated cadets) did not excel at academics. He finished 66 of 111 in the Class of 1907, elevated only by solid military performance scores. (Courtesy of Robert Arnold, Sonoma, CA)

upon football. As testimony to that fact, 23 pages in the 1907 *Howitzer* were devoted exclusively to the football squad and the games. The three lower classes, in contrast, were allotted only a skimpy five pages each.[23] Army football was more than just a game: it was a reason to wear the gray proudly and on one future day to recount the year's greatest struggle over arch rival Navy.

During the cadets' limited free time, particularly during evening hours, there were other diversions available. Plebes were encouraged, likely by the ever present Lieutenant Koehler, to visit the gymnasium. Participation in fencing, swimming, or tumbling activities helped maintain their hard-earned summer physical condition. They had to take personal responsibility for their fitness level during winters, especially after parades ceased in November at the first snow, beginning again only after the spring thaw. Upperclassmen could sign for a horse and ride the cavalry plain until dark. During the winter months, the cavalry plain was sometimes flooded to create a huge ice-skating area. Those who remained at West Point during the holidays were treated to a variety of entertainments in an effort to raise fading cadet spirits. Lectures by guest speakers and other entertainment—like cadet dramatic productions—were arranged, particularly on the weekends.[24]

One event, viewed as an uncommonly memorable privilege by the Corps of Cadets, occurred on 4 September 1903, at 6:19 p.m. The corps adjutant issued an order permitting all cadets to smoke pipes and cigars in their rooms during the evening academic period, as well as after studies and drill during the weekend. Cigarettes, commonly referred to as skags, were hand-rolled in those days with Bull Durham tobacco. That night it appeared to some that the barracks were oozing smoke from every possible crack and crevice—everybody was smoking. This event was so noteworthy that it was immortalized in the *Howitzer* that year: on one page appeared a poem, on another a drawing of a cadet lighting up his skag.[25]

These invincible cadets in the Class of 1907 had just completed the most grueling two months of their lives. "You have the confidence that you can do any damn thing," recalled Tooey Spaatz.[26] Tobacco was an integral part of military culture then; today it is different. Cavalrymen particularly enjoyed it, chewing a big wad of leaf tobacco—"brown"—and seldom keeping the subsequent dark spittle from dribbling out the corners of their mouths. The chewing of tobacco was expected of a true cavalry officer, at least in the minds of many still impressionable young cadets, including Harley Arnold.[27]

With the graduation for the Class of 1904 approaching, and having weathered both physical and mental stress unlike any before in their lives, the plebes received a needed break from the rigors of the preceding year. The entire Corps of Cadets traveled by train to the St. Louis World's Fair, staying for ten days. It was an enjoyable and exciting time for all—especially the plebes, who were released from "bracing" during the trip. For many of them, this was the first time they had ever seen a city.[28] Before leaving the fair, the cadets marched in a dress parade in honor of the Liberty Bell, which was on display there.

Unfortunately, their timing was bad: torrential rains soaked them, and their woolen uniforms took on the odor of wet sheep.

Now back at West Point after the delightful ten-day junket, plebes' chins were dragged back in (for a few days, anyway) during exams. "Thirteen days of ninety-two hours each, and then oblivion," was the exaggerated perspective of the final exam period as expressed by a member of the Class of 1905.[29] The most significant event yet to occur was "recognition," marking the Fourth Class's acceptance as an integral part of the Corps of Cadets. No more squared corners, no more drawn-in chins. Recognition was a monumental step back into a more human, less pressure-packed world.

Recognition took place after "hell week," immediately preceding graduation. Third Classmen, sophomores in civilian parlance but called yearlings at West Point, were responsible for administering most of the detailed training to the plebes. Hell week was the last occasion for the yearlings to correct the plebes' posture and military bearing. After the graduation ceremony, the plebes' elevation to yearlings was official. For one day, there were no plebes at West Point. The graduating First Classmen were commissioned as second lieutenants in the Army, while everyone else moved up one class in rank. The transition from plebe to yearling was both instantaneous and miraculous. "What a glorious day it was," the class scribe trumpeted in the *Howitzer*; it marked a "complete metamorphosis of the class."[30]

The next day the new yearlings moved lock, stock, and barrel to summer encampment, where the new beasts arrived the following day. Some of Arnold's classmates stayed in the area to "greet" the new arrivals, and the rest of the class hiked out to yearling camp at nearby Camp Forse, north of the cadet area.

The routine for yearlings was far more relaxed than for plebes. Artillery drill and riding skills were practiced each morning, while afternoons were reserved for strolls with friends up Flirtation Walk or for deadbeating under a shade tree. There was a noticeable, and welcome, lack of mental pressure as yearlings. But summer encampment was not a total breeze. Cadets began the process of learning about leadership at the basic level, while refining followership skills

Cadet Arnold loved the idea of serving with the Cavalry Branch. He wrote that the horse cavalry was the "last romantic thing left on earth." His impertinence prevented his being rated a "Special Qualification" that was requisite to such an assignment after graduation. Here he is on a summer ride to the Gettysburg battlefield circa 1906. (Courtesy of Robert Arnold, Sonoma, CA)

at an elevated level. For Arnold, the most pleasurable hours of year-ling camp were likely those he spent riding. The yearlings rode at least once every day regardless of weather. Arnold loved to ride—it was like being in the cavalry, the branch of service he wanted to enter upon graduation.[31]

Arnold may have excelled in summer camp, but his performance in the classroom remained mediocre. Of all the courses he took, his highest ranking was in Third Class mathematics—49th out of 119. Although Arnold had entered the Academy with an undeserved reputation as a highly capable student (probably based upon his achieving admission at such a young age), by the time he was in his final semester, yearbook scribes noted that "he has overcome any hankering for work that he may have once had and now doesn't do any more than anyone else."[32]

Although Arnold never won a varsity letter, he was a tough competitor. He ran track during all four years at West Point, and he consistently placed in the top three in the 16-pound shot-put event during his junior and senior years—his best distance being almost 36 feet. He played polo every summer and was a skilled equestrian, good enough to earn a spot on the graduation-ceremony drill team that year.[33]

In March 1905, the Corps of Cadets marched in the presidential inaugural parade for Theodore Roosevelt. It was customary for the Corps to participate in the quadrennial inaugurals, so every cadet had the opportunity of doing so once during his four-year stay at West Point. Before departing for Washington, cadets were reminded of their obligation to behave. There would be no unbuttoning of their tunics, no unauthorized visits to schools for women, and no language stronger than "Oh, Spludge."[34] The 1905 train trip to the national capital was long and slow; damp drizzle ensured the streets would be a mud bath the next morning—if they had not frozen first. After the oath was administered at noon on 5 March, the parade began. Officers, whose colorful sashes formed a stark contrast to the cadet's gray uniforms, were scattered along the parade route. One of Arnold's classmates noted sarcastically: "Of course the President couldn't have safely been inaugurated without us . . . and the moral responsibility we felt was exceeded only by our appearance."[35]

By his Second Class (junior) year, Arnold was entrenched in the cadet routine. He ran both indoor and outdoor track and played football. Athletic programs in any college environment frequently inhibited academic excellence, particularly for football players. Time devoted to practice was extreme, usually lasting until the evening meal. Following the three-hour field workout and dinner, the mental effort necessary for study in light of physical fatigue created much more of a challenge than for those who spent most of their after-school time memorizing—or "specking"—their assignments. For the football squad, the entire academic semester served only one purpose: to support preparations to beat Navy in the annual late-fall grudge match.

During his Second Class year, Arnold played on the scrub team against the first string that was learning a new strategem called the forward pass.[36] The task of the scrubs—pretending to be the upcoming rival team—was vital but thankless. Arnold described a day at practice in a letter home to his mother in 1905, undated except for the indication "263 days till June"—still customary for cadets to this day.

> My Dear Mother,
>
> I went out for foot-ball last week and today I played on the scrub against the varsity. I tell you the life of a man on the scrub is no cinch. He is used for a dummy. If the varsity wants to try a new play they use the scrub to see if it is a success . . . the scrub gets battered and bumped and cussed out and everything else coming just because they are not as good as the varsity. I don't want you to think I am knocking or have the blues for I am not knocking and haven't the blues but I just feel like writing for the top of my head is full of bumps the size of hens eggs.[37]

By his First Class year he had moved up the football roster from junior scrub team to second-string halfback on the varsity squad. He never started a game, but he played against Tufts, Trinity, and Williams Colleges as injuries took their toll on the first stringers. While at West Point, Arnold saw two victories and one tie against Navy; unfortunately Army suffered a 10-0 defeat against the midshipmen in Arnold's senior year.[38]

Although he participated in many officially sanctioned cadet activities, Arnold demonstrated leadership and ingenuity in a less conventional, yet highly effective way. This brash, foul-mouthed Pennsylvanian found his calling at the head of a small group of 29 cadets from E and F Companies (he was in F Company) known as the Black Hand. These young men were tough and enjoyed spirited, rough games like tackle football. Their trademark was a bandanna worn around the head or neck. They did not go to hops and did not "drag girls" very often because they were too busy with other spirited pursuits. Arnold was a prime mover in the Hand until he graduated. The Hand was not a secret organization—members' pictures were in the yearbook, adorning a huge outline of an outstretched, dark-colored hand. Their outrageous activities were how they earned their reputation as bold pranksters.[39]

The Hand's adventures included rolling cannonballs down rickety, cavernous stairwells in the dark of night, hiding the reveille cannon, and—the most famous—a fireworks display honoring the Class of 1907 from atop the barracks. All of their operations were carefully planned and well executed.[40] Accomplishing these pranks required a certain amount of guile and, more important, mutual trust among Hand members. These young men risked severe punishment if they were ever caught, not only in the form of demerits, but also periods of confinement and disciplinary tours marching around the cadet area.

They knew the West Point system inside and out. They knew the guard and officer-of-the-day schedules and developed a form of covert communications and night disguises to conceal their antics. After three years of this type of activity, the members had forged a close comradeship. They learned how to circumvent the system and accomplish their missions. They were the rabble-rousers of the Academy—the originators of what are today called "spirit missions." Arnold, their leader, was expert at these secret missions. There was the Army way, and there was the way of the Hand. There is no doubt that the 20-year-old Arnold, though he understood both methods, favored the Army way.[41] But it was in the Hand that he found his niche at West Point.

Arnold saw the cavalry as his sole purpose in attending West Point: "It was what we lived for—our whole future. The Horse Cavalry!" Arnold once wrote that "it was the last romantic thing left on earth."[42] The cavalry had a culture all its own, and to be a cavalryman meant one must act the part. It was a culture of hard-playing, hard-working officers who exhibited panache and a devil-may-care attitude. Cavalrymen nurtured a separate culture within the Army that valued a sense of adventure and the deafening sound of the charge. Moreover, they loved the look of the wide yellow stripe on their trousers and the indefinable attraction that most women could

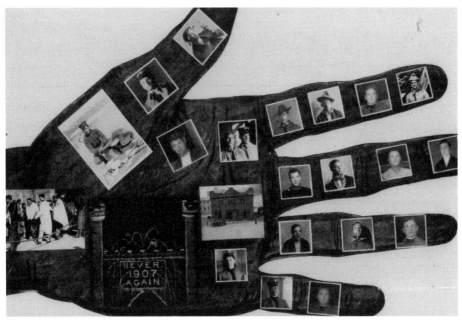

"Pewt" Arnold (center bottom) found his niche as the leader of the Black Hand, a group of cadets known for midnight pranks and rowdy behavior. (Courtesy of Robert Arnold, Sonoma, CA)

not resist—not that Arnold cared much about that.[43] It was a culture that transferred, largely intact, to the cavalry's successor—the Army Air Service—as the embodiment of speed, maneuverability, and danger in a three-dimensional battlefield. The horse differed from the airplane as it was a two-dimensional weapon. In spirit, however, the cavalryman and the pilot remained as one.

But Arnold's infatuation with traditional cavalry was so great that he was not immediately receptive to the potential application of military aviation. Even the novelty of a hot-air balloon launch he observed on 11 February 1906 did not impress him much, though he did write home to tell his parents about it. He described matter-of-factly the launch of the 25-foot-diameter balloon crewed by a single man. Having been filled with "illuminating gas" the sphere climbed upward, floated due north, and just kept on going. Arnold never fully appreciated why the event was scheduled as it was—temperatures were near zero and fresh snow had covered the area two days earlier.

Nor did he comprehend why the event attracted such a large crowd, particularly in light of the freezing temperatures.[44] Such an event was, for most, only a novelty.

In fact, the launch was arranged by a delegation of the newly formed Aero Club of America. Courtland Bishop, Augustus Post, and A. Leo Stevens traveled from New York City to West Point, where they called upon Lieutenant Lahm—an accomplished balloonist himself, later one of the Army's first two aircraft pilots, and Arnold's former French instructor—to assist with the balloon flight.[45] The nearly silent balloons were a far cry from the deadly thunder of a cavalry charge. Possibly, as he watched the balloon drift from sight, the possibilities for its use in combat were in the back of his mind. In his military training or history classes, he would have heard of observation ballooning during the American Civil War. But ballooning could not compete with the lure of equestrian pursuits and the romance that the cavalry branch represented.

Arnold, virile and handsome, exhibited as little interest in the fairer sex as he did in ballooning. His experience with women at West Point is not an account worthy of a Harlequin love story. Courting at the Military Academy in the early 1900s might best be described as traditional and extremely formal; as with everything else at West Point, there were very strict rules governing behavior for both the cadets and their female guests. Young ladies and their chaperones—be it mother, sister, or family friend—usually arrived by train and proceeded to the quaint little hotel located at the base of the hill just off the campus. They found themselves "all jammed in together [having] a great time," while the hotel's housemother ensured that protocol was strictly enforced.[46] A statue of Gen. George Washington upon his horse stood in front of the building, his arm outstretched as if delivering a benediction. Cadet lore held that Washington instead was admonishing, "Keep away from the hotel, boys."[47]

Washington's presence notwithstanding, cadets would present their calling card at the hotel door and announce who it was they were to meet. The card made its way up the long staircase to the anxious, primping visitors. The girls would peer out over the railing and flirt with their cadet, who remained in the house foyer until the bugle call announcing the parade formation. After Saturday classes and the noon meal were over, cadets were free to stroll on Flirtation Walk—a winding path overlooking the Hudson River that afforded some privacy—arm-in-arm with their dates. The walk could not have been totally pleasant for the young ladies, sporting slipper-like shoes and long dresses while negotiating hilly, unpaved terrain. Saturday and Sunday afternoons were the only time that cadets enjoyed any measure of privacy with their dates. Flirtation Walk was filled with cadets, all of whom knew each other. There were frequent stops and conversations about cadet happenings and life in general, but in reality cadets and their girlfriends were never truly alone.[48]

Following the evening meal on Saturday, cadets dressed for the evening hop while the women changed into their own hop attire. The dances highlighted everyone's weekend entertainment except for the plebes, who were not yet permitted to attend hops. The upperclassmen escorted the plebes' ladies to the dance if they wanted to go. The hop ended promptly at the playing of "Army Blue," the last dance at midnight. Escorts and guests headed back to the hotel on a bus, and then the cadets ran for the barracks. On Sundays, after mandatory chapel service and a dress parade, cadets met their dates for a few more hours of visitation. Late in the afternoon they escorted the ladies to the tram for the short trip to the main rail station and the journey home. Guests were gone by 4:00 p.m.[49]

That was how it worked for most cadets, but not Arnold. He was painfully reserved around women. Having been reared in an extremely restrictive environment, he never had time and was never instructed as to the ways of the world, particularly those involving the fair sex. This inexperience resulted in undue shyness, even insecurity; Arnold was so bashful that he did not attend a hop voluntarily until his First Class year. Whatever the reason, women did not much enter the picture until after he left West Point.

Arnold's involvement with the Black Hand, particularly the leadership role he played during his First Class year, dropped him from 21st to 52d out of 111 cadets in conduct. His attitude had become cocky in the extreme, even to the point of making an impertinent remark to the senior cavalry instructor after being ordered to spit out a large chunk of "brown" he had crammed into his mouth. "Sir," Arnold quipped, "I thought all good cavalrymen chewed tobacco." Such flippancy was indicative of his immaturity and his inability to hold his sharp tongue at critical moments. Punishment was swift and severe: he would "march the area" until graduation. When he was not marching the area, he was confined to quarters.[50] In the short term, the punishment hurt by taking away what little free time he had; in the long term the consequences were far greater because they probably affected his branch selection adversely.

Graduation day on 14 June 1907 was as much a relief as a triumph. As he had been in 1903 when he left his home in Ardmore, Pennsylvania, for West Point, Arnold was once again free of strict rules and seemingly ridiculous punishments. Leaving West Point brought no teary good-byes; in fact the departure embodied the essence of the unofficial class motto, "1907 . . . Never Again!"[51] This motto, actually a cheer, had been adopted by the class on the final day of summer encampment in 1906 and was dutifully repeated upon the completion of any number of significant "last time" events during their First Class year. Arnold went home on furlough anxiously awaiting news of which cavalry unit he would join. Commissioning paperwork and notification of first assignments were expected in the mail by the end of June. While not standing high enough in his class to enter the prestigious Corps of Engineers, his ranking should have easily qualified him for cavalry duty. In those days graduation order was arguably treated with much more import than today.[52]

When Arnold's orders finally came, his mother's eyes registered impending disaster. Sympathetically, she could only watch as Arnold read, then re-read, the papers she had just handed him—"Henry H. Arnold, 2nd Lieutenant of Infantry."[53] He could not believe his eyes. He was shocked, perplexed, and then angry. Arnold had invested four years of his life at West Point with only one purpose in mind—to become a cavalry officer. Now that dream was gone. Hundreds of hours perfecting "equitation" at that "Godforsaken school" now appeared wasted.

The Class of 1907, whose class motto was, "Never Again!" (Courtesy of Robert Arnold, Sonoma, CA)

Arnold knew there was little chance of changing his assignment. Each of the major branches—infantry, cavalry, artillery, and engineers—was a close-knit community of officers that resisted transfers in or out. Moreover, because the cavalry was so popular, Arnold could gain entrance only if a current cavalry officer transferred out. "Nobody would do it," recalled Tommy Milling (USMA 1909), whose first assignment was in the cavalry.[54]

Arnold's father, Dr. Herbert Arnold, despite his son's growing independence, took it upon himself to resurface the issue of his son's assignment to the cavalry. In January 1908, he wrote a friendly letter to the Superintendent, Col. Hugh Scott, in which he described his son's exceptional equestrian skills. A year later, he sent another message to the West Point surgeon and head of the Department of Hygiene, Lt. Col. Charles Gandy, to question the circumstances surrounding Arnold's assignment to the infantry.[55] Gandy, as had Scott, explained that Secretary of War William Howard Taft had listened to complaints about assignments from several cadets in the Class of 1907, not just Arnold's. Although Taft expressed interest, it was simply a polite bureaucratic dodge and nothing came of the initiative.

Locked away in the West Point archives was the real reason for the rebuke. In a 14 October 1907 internal response to a staff request for Arnold's transfer to the cavalry, Maj. Gen. Fred Ainsworth, the Army's Adjutant General (commissioned in the Medical Corps), wrote, "Henry H. Arnold is not S.Q. and regretfully, transfer is not possible."[56] Ainsworth's letter thus revealed the existence of a "Special Qualification" status for cavalry that was unknown to all but the Military Academy's highest authorities. There is no evidence that Arnold, his father, his Congressional representatives, or even Lieutenant Colonel Gandy, a Department Head, were ever made aware of such a thing as "S.Q." status.[57] Arnold did not hold S.Q. status and was therefore ineligible for the cavalry, apparently permanently.[58]

How this rating was awarded remains a mystery. It seems clear that Arnold's impertinence during his cadet years—perhaps best represented by his childish remark concerning chewing tobacco made to the Chief Cavalry Officer only days prior to graduation—cost him S.Q. status. Special Qualification selection required a certain amount of off-the-record evaluation by Academy faculty. None had more influence in selecting cavalry officers than the Chief Cavalry Officer himself. Regardless of the reasons, for Lt. Harley Arnold, it was a fateful assignment with the infantry that eventually lifted his military career skyward.

In retrospect, none who knew Arnold at West Point would have picked him to rise to five-star rank in the Army. He never fit the traditional cadet mold. Academically, he was fortunate to have graduated at all. In the end, however, the boldness and cocky self-assurance that ironically cost him the opportunity ever to fulfill his dreams as a cavalry officer were precisely the traits essential to his survival in the skies, first as an infantryman and later as a Signal Corps officer. This observation was particularly applicable during the dangerous days of early military aviation. Arnold's cadet career serves as an instructive caveat to those who might otherwise be quick to judge officer potential on the basis of a cadet's performance at West Point. The Military Academy, by design, has trained and graduated a body of officers representing a broad spectrum of leadership qualities, styles, and techniques. It was the right personality and character fitted to the right circumstances that eventually saw General of the Army Hap Arnold command the greatest air armada in history.

---

[1] The author wishes to acknowledge the assistance in editing and stylizing this chapter received from members of the USMA faculty. In particular, Col. Lance Betros went above and beyond the call during this process, and his efforts directly contributed to making this a more readable chapter. I owe additional thanks to Col. Lloyd J. Matthews (USA, Ret.), whose keen eye and pointy red pen helped tighten phrases and smooth other breaches in writing style. This piece is adapted from parts of my biographical treatment, *Hap Arnold and the Evolution of American Airpower* (Smithsonian Press, 2000). Much of the background for the descriptive narrative comes from Columbia University Oral History Interviews, The Reminiscences of Gen. H.H. Arnold's Friends and Family. Dr. Donald Shaughnessy conducted all interviews from 1959 to 1960 (hereafter, CUOHI). The following interviews were particularly useful: Col. Benjamin Castle, July 1959, 1-39; Gen. Carl Spaatz, January 1959, 4, 18, 20; Col. Hayden Wagner, 1 August 1959, 1-35; and Mrs. H.H. Arnold, 6 May 1959. Specifically for this paragraph, Mrs. Arnold, CUOHI, 7; and Wagner, CUOHI, 3.

[2] Henry Harley Arnold did not become "Hap" until his mother's death in 1931. Harley gave way to the nickname Pewt during his Third Class year. Pewt had its origins in a newspaper serial of the time (also a best-selling book in 1902), "The Real Diary of a Real Boy," by Henry A. Shute. This real-life diary, written by the main character "Plupy" Shute, chronicled the youthful adventures of a group of boys growing up in a small New England town in the 1860s. Among the sidekick characters was Pewter "Pewt" Purinton, a hayseed cigar-smoking, girl-hating mischief-maker who frequently had to chop wood or had "the time licked out of him" to atone for his devilish behavior. The popularity of both the serial and the 1903 book made it an obvious source for secret names. Other cadets also purloined tags from the popular series. "Beany," the third major sidekick character, was adopted by Cadet George R. Harrison (USMA 1907), a bawdy, song-writing member of the Hand. The stories were usually about some form of mischief—smoking behind the barn, shooting peas in school, exploding "snapcrackers" in each other's faces, or rough-housing instead of doing chores. So the nicknames were appropriately reserved for members of West Point's most mischievous organization.

[3] "List of Cadet Candidates Authorized to Report for Examination at West Point on the 27th day of July, 1903, Before 8 O'clock A.M." In War Department Letters and Telegrams Sent Relating to the United States Military Academy, 1867-1904, M2048, USMA Archives, West Point, NY; also H. H. Arnold Folder, USMA Archives, West Point, NY.

[4] Ibid.; and Wagner, CUOHI, 2.

[5] *Official Register of the Officers and Graduates of the United States Military Academy, West Point, New York*, June 1904. (Hereafter, *Official Register*), 34.

[6] *Official Register*, June 1904, 18-21; also Papers of H.H. Arnold, Library of Congress, West Point Records, Box 262A (hereafter, HHA).

[7] A number of cadet candidates entered West Point in the latter part of July each year to round out the class. These gentlemen faced an intense training period before they were allowed to join the on-time plebes. Mrs. H. H. Arnold, 6 May 1959, CUOHI, 17; and Wagner, CUOHI, 2-3.

[8] *The Howitzer*, 1906 (New York: The Hoskins Press, 1906), 261; Gen. Carl Spaatz, 26 January 1959, CUOHI, 4.

[9] *The Howitzer*, 1907, 306. Picture trying to pull your chin into your neck so that the bottom of the chin touches the Adam's apple. That was the act of dragging in your chin. The more wrinkles produced, the more impressive the effort.

[10] *The Howitzer Advertiser, 1907* (New York: The Hoskins Press, 1907), 53. An appendix to the 1907 yearbook features a photograph of the proper alignment of the cadet closet and clothes press; also Wagner, CUOHI, 9.

[11] Wagner, CUOHI, 7-9; Col. Benjamin Castle, 24 July 1959, CUOHI, 1.

[12] Castle, CUOHI, 2-3.

[13] *Official Register*, 1904, 5. First Lieutenant Koehler was promoted to captain the following year. He eventually authored an exercise manual for the entire U.S. Army while a colonel. Upperclassmen still refer to the entering freshmen as "beasts" during their summer indoctrination, then plebes for the rest of the first year. An Air Force Academy freshman is commonly called a "dooly" which is defined as "that insignificant whose rank is measured in negative units; one who's potential for learning is unlimited; one who will graduate in some time approaching infinity." *Contrails, 1977-78.*

[14] Castle, CUOHI, 4.

[15] *The Howitzer*, 1904, 113.

[16] Wagner, CUOHI, 5-6. The average cadet height at that time was near 5' 6". Many of these dance cards are displayed in the West Point visitor center.

[17] Castle, CUOHI, 1-4; Castle was also a *Howitzer* staff member in 1906-1907, which was undoubtedly helpful in his ability to recall many of these early events with such clarity. Tragically, Castle's son Freddie was killed during WW II. His heroic actions earned him the Congressional Medal of Honor.

[18] *Official Register*, 1904, 5; Castle, CUOHI, 5.

[19] *The Howitzer*, 1905, 119; and Wagner, CUOHI, 9.

[20] *The Howitzer*, 1907, 113.

[21] Brig. Gen. Frank P. Lahm, CUOHI, 1.

[22] Lahm, CUOHI, 1; for academic standings see Arnold references in *Biographical Register of the Officers and Graduates of the USMA at West Point New York*, Supp. Vol. V, 1900-1910; also see *The Official Register of the Officers and Cadets of the USMA, 1904*; and *The Howitzer*, 1907; for early Signal Corps aviation history, see Rebecca Robbins Raines, *Getting the Message Through: A Branch History of the U.S. Army Signal Corps* (Washington: Center for Military History, U.S. Army, 1996), Part IV.

[23] To read the accounts in *The Howitzer*, 1900-1907, of Army football during these years is a story in its own right. The prose describing the Army-Navy contest in each yearbook contains spectacular drama and description. Games were played in 30-minute halves rather than the familiar four quarters of today, and the rules were more like those of English rugby than modern-day football. Touchdowns were worth only five points, and field goals were worth four. This explains many of the odd scores that decided the winners at the turn of the century. A hard-fought, often low-scoring victory was appreciated in ways modern football fans might not understand.

[24] Castle, CUOHI, 11-17.

[25] *The Howitzer*, 1904, 214-215; and *The Howitzer*, 1906, 264.

[26] Spaatz, CUOHI, 20.

[27] *The Howitzer*, 1907, 306. Smokes were hand-rolled in those days. Photographic evidence shows Arnold with cigarettes in hand as late as 1925.

[28] Wagner, CUOHI, 24.

[29] *The Howitzer*, 1906, 98.

[30] *The Howitzer*, 1904, 115.

[31] *The Howitzer*, 1904, 116.

[32] *The Howitzer*, 1907, 42; and *Official Register*, 1907, 13.

[33] Castle, CUOHI, 36-37. The cadet record for the shot put was 37' 11¾" set in 1899; see *The Howitzer*, 1907, 185.

[34] *The Howitzer*, 1905, 121.

[35] *The Howitzer*, 1905, 121.

[36] *The Howitzer*, 1907, 159-164.

[37] Henry H. Arnold to Mrs. Herbert A. Arnold, 263 Days Until June 1905, Robert Arnold Collection, Sonoma, CA (hereafter, RAC).

[38] *The Howitzer*, 1907, 146-164; also West Point Records, Box 262A, HHA.

[39] Wagner, CUOHI, 19; see *The Howitzer*, 1907, 42, 214. Arnold's photo is nearest the center and next to the drawing of his most famous prank, a fireworks display saluting the Class of 1907.

[40] *The Howitzer*, 1907, 214.

[41] For accounts of the Hand's activities, see Thomas Coffey's, *HAP*, 20-22; first hand accounts can be found in Wagner, CUOHI, and Castle, CUOHI; also, photos of The Hand are present in H.H. Arnold's West Point Scrapbook, RAC.

[42] Henry H. Arnold, *Global Mission* (pre-publication proof, actually titled *Global Missions* in its original cover) located in RAC, 3; similarly, many pilot-qualified members of the cadet wing at the Air Force Academy have attended with the sole purpose of becoming a pilot. The education process was a necessary hurdle to overcome, but was not the singular reason for attending the "Blue Zoo." This attitude reflects that of H. H. Arnold during his West Point days.

[43] Milling, CUOHI; 58. Lucian K. Truscott, Jr., *The Twilight of the U.S. Cavalry: Life in the Old Army, 1917-1942* (Lawrence: University Press of Kansas, 1989), highlights the glories of cavalry life. Pewt was not Arnold's only West Point name. His First Class yearbook photo and description noted that he was also called Benny, a shortened version of the obvious "Benedict Arnold." It is likely that he enhanced this nickname by illegally frequenting the only local pub, a known cadet hangout that was close enough to visit by foot and return without too much difficulty. The name of the pub was Benny Havens, immortal in the history of West Point. It was a ribald place, where cadets could smoke freely and drink a few tankards of beer, if they chose. Arnold likely joined in the drinking and the smoking, as did other impressionable, "pretend" cavalry officers.

[44] H.H. Arnold to Mrs. Herbert Arnold (mother), "108 days till June," RAC. This letter is in reference to the 11 February 1906 launch of the *L'Alouette*, a small one-man reconnaissance balloon. Another account of the event may be found in the 10 February 1906 *Army/Navy Journal*, 673.

[45] Charles DeForest Chandler and Frank P. Lahm, *How Our Army Grew Wings: Airmen and Aircraft Before 1914* (New York: The Ronald Press, 1943), 54-55; U.S. Military Academy, *Register of Graduates and Former Cadets* (2002), 4-87.

[46] Mrs. H.H. Arnold, CUOHI, 5-6; Grove to author, 9 December 1997, West Point, NY.

[47] Wagner, CUOHI, 12; also see *The Howitzer*, 1907 for the words and music to Army Blue.

[48] Promiscuity held far greater consequences for young ladies in those days than in modern times. Young officers rarely sought to marry a woman having such a reputation, for such was often detrimental to one's career in the old Army.

[49] Mrs. H.H. Arnold, CUOHI, 5-10; and Castle, CUOHI, 11-12.

[50] Castle, CUOHI, 36-37.

[51] *The Howitzer*, 1907. Not an uncommon feeling for many Academy graduates even in contemporary times. As a member of the USAF Academy Class of 1981, I ended up going back as a history instructor in 1992, much to my own astonishment.

[52] *The Howitzer*, 1907, 11-32.

[53] Arnold, *Global Mission* (draft), 3½.

[54] Brig. Gen. Thomas DeWitt Milling, CUOHI, 7; in the early 1980s, pilot assignments had similar consequences for young airmen. Once assigned to fighter or bomber duty, it was nearly impossible to change from one to the other later in one's career.

[55] Herbert A. Arnold to Col. H. L. Scott, 17 Jan 1908; and Lt. Col. Charles M. Gandy to H. A. Arnold, 8 February 1909, West Point, NY, in MGC, roll #1 (ref: West Point Archives); also see *The Howitzer*, 1907, 11, 32, for both Colonel Scott's and Lieutenant Colonel Gandy's faculty positions.

[56] Maj. Gen. F.C. Ainsworth to unknown, 14 October 1907, MG, roll #1, Ref: National Archives, RG 94, W-3, 201 Files. This letter was supported by further staff follow-up on 25 November 1907 when Lieutenant Colonel Bell passed a message to Colonel Scott verifying that Arnold was not "S.Q." For background on that "efficient administrator," see Russell F. Weigley, *History of the United States Army* (New York: Macmillan Publishing Co., Inc., 1967), 323-39.

[57] Lt. Col. Charles M. Gandy to H.A. Arnold, 8 February 1909, West Point, NY, in MGC, roll #1 (ref: West Point Archives).

[58] A similar process existed even in the 1980s to determine pilot qualifications for fighter, attack, or reconnaissance qualification (known as "FAR qual"). Flying training academic scores, actual flight performance, and a third undefined quality were examined in detail before FAR qual was awarded to a pilot trainee. The final decision usually rested with those instructors with "fighter time" in operational units. This "undefined" quality equated to the 1907 S.Q. for cavalrymen.

CHAPTER 5

LESLIE R. GROVES, WEST POINT, AND THE ATOMIC BOMB

Robert S. Norris

How did West Point shape Leslie Richard Groves and how did the Academy contribute to the skills he used to oversee one of the nation's most ambitious enterprises, the building of the atomic bomb during World War II?[1] The Manhattan Project was, among other things, a gigantic engineering, construction, and industrial effort, run by the Army under great secrecy, accomplished rapidly through unorthodox means to deal with uncertain technologies. Overemphasis of the roles played by a few individual scientists has distorted our understanding and appreciation of these features. A closer look at Groves the administrator and builder will supplement—and partially correct—common misperceptions of the project and provide us with a fuller understanding of how the atomic bomb was built.

The Manhattan Project did not just happen. It was put together and run in a certain way: Groves's way. His is a classic case of an individual making a difference. Being in the right place at the right time is the secret of winning a place in history, but rarely does a person arrive there by accident. Groves ran the Manhattan Project in precise and resolute ways, recruiting some of the giants of American industry and science to design, build, and run his atomic factories and laboratories. Without Groves's organizational and managerial skills, and construction know-how, the project might have failed; in any case it would have taken longer to accomplish. Individuals do make a difference, and in this instance Groves was indispensable to the project's success.

Many factors contributed to the development of Groves's personality and character, ranging from family influences and growing up on military posts at the beginning of the 20th century, to service in the interwar army with the Corps of Engineers. West Point was one of the most significant of those factors leaving an indelible mark upon him. It transformed an ambitious and aggressive but disorganized and carefree boy into a remarkably self-disciplined man imbued with assiduous work habits and a sound technical education. In addition, the Cadet Honor Code provided him with a moral compass that he followed throughout his life.

Dick Groves (he was known by Dick after his middle name Richard) entered the Academy on 15 June 1916 as a member of the Class of 1920. He later recalled that "entering West Point fulfilled my greatest ambition" and went on to give his reasons for wanting to attend the Military Academy:

> I had been brought up in the army, and in the main had lived on army posts all my life. I was deeply impressed with the character and outstanding devotion of the officers I knew. I had also found the enlisted men to be good solid Americans and in general far superior to men of equal education in civil life. I was imbued with the idea that the West Point graduates were normally the best officers and on the whole enjoyed higher respect from the enlisted men.[2]

Like many cadets of his day, he had completed several years of university level education prior to entering. Groves had spent one year at the University of Washington and two years at MIT. The decision to go to West Point was his, and it was something he wanted intensely. His father, an Army chaplain for 20 years, did not encourage his son to follow him, and in fact preferred he choose another career. His mother, before her death in 1913, tried in discreet ways to influence her son against an Army career. It was to no avail.

Groves attended West Point for less than two and a half years, graduating with the Class of November 1918. The standard four-year course was cut short by the expected need for officers for World War I, though as it turned out he graduated only ten days prior to the armistice.

What was West Point like? In those early years of the 20th century West Point was a smaller, more tradition-bound institution, resistant to, even fearful of, change. As one scholar has described it:

> At West Point, graduates had all taken the same classes, undergone the same hazing, marched in the same formations. This common experience gave them a sense of community, of fraternity, that they could not bear to see destroyed. A change in the continuity at the Academy would have the effect of disturbing their bond. To tamper with West Point would be to tamper with the cement that held the army officer corps together.[3]

West Point influenced family priorities and practices. Sons of graduates were usually encouraged to attend the Military Academy. Classes were small enough that a cadet would probably know most of his classmates, and even many in the classes just ahead or just behind.[4] Graduates would often marry young women whose fathers were graduates themselves. (Thus Groves married the daughter of a member of the Class of 1877.) The Regular Army officer corps was inbred and in many ways isolated from the society at large.

Like every new cadet, Groves wanted to realize the promise of West Point. In a contemporary account a former instructor describes what a cadet feels when he arrives.

> To the candidate [his arrival at West Point] conjures a vision of all that he hopes to be. The honor of being a cadet, the privilege of wearing the uniform, the immense possibilities of physical and mental achievement, the soul-satisfying fear of an ambition about to be realized, the glamour of military life, and, it must be admitted, a secret feeling of righteous superiority over his boy friends at home—all these thoughts crowd his imagination so that for once he sees frozen the vague ideal that he always has had of himself.[5]

No sooner did one class graduate in early June than a new plebe class—formally, Fourth Class—arrived, trudging up the hill from the train station on the west bank of the Hudson River.[6] Groves was one of the 322 cadets of what would have become the Class of 1920 who entered that summer of 1916, the largest class up to that time. Two days before Groves's arrival, President Woodrow Wilson had delivered a half-hour address to the graduates of the Class of 1916 and awarded them their diplomas.

From all Groves had heard he knew that his first three weeks as a cadet in "Beast Barracks," the indoctrination into West Point ways, would be the most demanding experience of his young life. And indeed it was, with early reveille and long hours of physical training and military drill. This rite of passage also included considerable hazing by upperclassmen on the Beast detail.[7] The severe treatment of plebes had its purpose. As a contemporary of Groves said,

> The standards of West Point are entirely unlike those of any other institution. To preserve those standards unchanged it is considered necessary that a young man entering the Academy be subjected to the severest discipline, that even his personality be more or less suppressed in order to give the spirit of West Point time to get hold of him, to allow him to adapt himself to the ideals of the Corps, and to keep those ideals from being, through him, perverted.[8]

After two months in summer camp at the northwest corner of the Plain, Groves moved into cadet barracks to begin the first academic term. Like every plebe, he was issued a copy of *Bugle Notes*, a pocket-sized handbook known as the Plebe bible and containing useful information about the rites and rituals, schedules and procedures of West Point. It stated, "The purpose of the Academy is to shape a man and a soldier—an honorable, loyal, courageous, self-reliant, disciplined, intelligent gentleman and officer." There was also a section titled "English as She Is Spoke at the U.S.M.A."[9] The plebe was required to learn a new vocabulary that helped describe his new life. In the first year he was frequently "braced" (ordered to assume a severe position of attention); "skinned" (reported as being in violation of regulations); and "quilled" (reported as having committed one of the offenses listed in the "Black Book"). But if he "hived" (understood) his study assignment or "specked" (memorized without understanding) his assignment, he might "max" (achieve a maximum grade on) the lesson.

The cadets lived in either South Barracks or North Barracks. Each room was identical, 14 feet by 22 feet, with the same furniture for its two cadets: two iron cots, two plain wooden tables, two wooden chairs, two steel clothes lockers, and two washbowls. Bathing or toilet call required a trip to the "sinks" (lavatories) in the basement. Rugs on the floor and pictures on the wall were prohibited. The mirror was flanked by notice of the hours of instruction and the schedule of the cadet. Failing to have it correctly posted was an offense. There were also hooks on the wall to hang clothing, in the proper order: the first hook for the raincoat, the second for the overcoat, the third for the dress coat, and so on. Shoes were aligned toes-out alongside the bed, in order of size from biggest to smallest. During the day mattresses were folded, with bedding folded and piled on top, ready for any inspection that might occur.

Activities were prescribed for almost every minute of the day. The cadet was up at 6:00 a.m. with breakfast at 6:30. Normally there were two classes from 8:00 a.m. to 12:35 p.m. Dinner lasted 40 minutes and was followed by another class until 3:45 p.m. Then it was drill, athletics, and parade, with supper at 6:25 p.m. Call to quarters followed, with a study period from 7:30 to 9:30, taps at 10:00 p.m., and lights-out.[10]

A cadet was issued an extensive wardrobe of uniforms of different types and combinations, depending upon the season, weather, and function.[11] Cadets knew the proper uniform for each occasion by looking out of their barracks room window to see which uniform flag flew in the courtyard. A cadet was not allowed to have money; before admission he had to deposit sufficient funds with the treasurer to cover the cost of his uniforms, about $160 when Groves was a plebe. His pay was $600 per year, but that too was deposited, and all costs he incurred were drawn against it. The cost of meals—$29.19 per month in 1918—books, laundry, blankets, sheets, pillowcases, mattresses, candy, tobacco, uniform replacements, and furloughs kept the cadet constantly on the verge of debt, or in it.

During meals there were ordered procedures that had no variation. A bugle or drum call summoned the cadets to formation for marching to Grant Hall, the cadet mess. Cadets marched everywhere, at all times. If even two cadets were going from the chapel to the library, they kept in step. Once inside the mess hall the cadets arranged themselves at tables according to seniority, standing at attention behind their chairs. After the order "Take seats," the meal began. A First Classman (senior), known as the table commandant, was in charge of each table, and he sat at its head. Second Classmen (juniors) and Third Classmen (sophomores) came next, positioning themselves down the table until at the foot sat three or four lowly plebes, who performed the menial duties of serving their superiors. One plebe, known as the water corporal, poured the water and milk; another, the meat corporal, carved the "bone"; and a third, the coffee corporal, poured the coffee. The gunner supervised the supply of food brought from the kitchen by civilian waiters. If plebes were in short supply, they might have to double up on their duties. Busy with their chores, the plebes ate in spasms when they had a free minute. Meals were not leisurely affairs. Including announcements from the officials about various matters, the meal was over in half an hour. At its conclusion the cadets were called to attention and dismissed, to make their way back to their rooms.

During plebe year many drop out for one reason or another. In Groves's class seven were gone in the first three weeks, not making it past Beast Barracks; others departed as a result of academics, and a few were lost to the Honor Code, the strict rules that demand the reporting of dishonorable behavior. The Cadet Honor Code—"A cadet does not lie, cheat, or steal, or tolerate those who do"—stands as the keystone in fulfilling West Point's mission.[12] The code is about trust. If officers in the Regular Army could not trust one another, especially in war, then the prospects for battlefield success would be undermined.[13] West Point graduates believed in the values taught there and used them as the central principles of conduct throughout their lives. Groves was a prime example: he lived by the code and expected others to do so as well.

Some of the more dramatic differences between then and now are to be found in the course of instruction. The curriculum of Groves's day, as well as the nature and purpose of a West Point education, was still deeply rooted in 19th-century traditions, though some reforms were occurring.[14] A uniform course of study for all helped forge a unified and homogeneous officer corps. Mental discipline and character-building were the essential ways to prepare young men to be Army officers.[15] Thus the curriculum at the time offered no choices. No matter what his previous schooling, every cadet took every subject, every cadet had to recite every day and was graded on his answers, and every cadet had to be proficient in every subject to advance. There were no exceptions.

Cadet Groves's first-year courses included mathematics, English, history, practical military engineering (surveying), and drill regulations (infantry and artillery).[16] The technical curriculum was heavily weighted in the first two years toward mathematics, consuming about 45 percent of the course work. Groves had already taken several math courses at the University of Washington and MIT, so he did well in math and surveying, placing fifth and second, respectively. Overall at the end of plebe year, he ranked 23d and was one of the 26 distinguished cadets of the Fourth Class entitled to wear stars on his collar.[17]

The cadets were marched by sections to class in the East Academic or West Academic (now Pershing Barracks) Building. After the cadets were in the classroom, the section marcher closed the door, faced the instructor, saluted, and reported either that all were present or that those noted were absent. In Groves's day there were probably a dozen or so cadets per section. After the order "Take seats," the instructor asked if there were any questions about the day's assignment. Answering them took about half the period. Then the instructor would say, "Take boards," and each cadet would stand and face a blackboard, write his name in chalk in the corner, and listen for instructions. If it were a math class, for example, the boards were marked odd and even. Cadets at the odd blackboards would work on two or three problems over the next 30 or 40 minutes, while their neighbors at the even boards would work on two or three different ones. Whereas the honor system was operative every minute of the day, the odd-even system helped prevent an inadvertent observation that might arise due to peripheral vision.

With the order "Cease work," the cadet stopped where he was. The instructor would then give the pointer to a cadet, who would have to explain how he solved his assigned problem. After the class was dismissed, the instructor assessed each of the boards and recorded a grade. At the end of the week all the marks were compiled into the weekly report ("tenth sheets" reflecting the numerical grading system that discriminated to the first decimal place) and posted on Saturday on bulletin boards in the sally ports of the barracks, where all could see every cadet's progress or lack thereof. Once a month the cadets were "resectioned" according to merit, with the most capable moving up to higher sections and those less so moving down. Each month the grades were mailed to the parents to keep them informed. This was a highly competitive environment where tenths of a point The instructors gave grades using a scheme laid down by Sylvanus Thayer, superintendent from 1817 to 1833. Perfect was scored 3.0; passing was 2.0. Thus there were only 11 possible passing grades between 2 and 3—2.0, 2.1, 2.2, 2.3, and so on—and the grade competition was fought out there ("fighting for tenths"). Anything below 2.0 of course was a failure. The system was slightly skewed, with instructors of the top sections more likely to continue to give higher grades to those cadets, often for identical work, than did instructors in the middle or bottom sections.[18]

From the daily recitations to weekly compilations, to the monthly, semester, year, and finally entire four years, an aggregate grade, to the second decimal point, was calculated. This score—along with demerits—determined the General Order of Merit, or class rank, and would follow the cadet to the end of his days (and even beyond), determining what branch he would enter and thus where he would be assigned, when he would be promoted, even which set of quarters he would be assigned.[19] It was a system that fostered competition, and Groves thrived on it, for he truly enjoyed competing; he liked nothing better than excelling at whatever he undertook. His copies of the annual Official Register are full of his penciled computations, carried to five significant figures, of his standing relative to that of his classmates—keeping track of progress toward his goal of being Number One, a goal that he likely would have attained if his class had not graduated early.[20] Even so, he finished fourth out of 226 in the Class of November 1918. The Thayer system developed Groves's will to win and made it a lasting part of his makeup.

Early in the 20th century a new emphasis came to be placed on the physical conditioning of cadets.[21] In 1905 President Theodore Roosevelt ordered all cadets to attend gymnasium daily. By 1910 they used the new gymnasium for boxing, fencing, bowling, and squash. The following year an indoor swimming pool was installed. Physical exercise also came in the courses that exposed the cadet to the other branches of the Army besides engineering: field artillery, infantry, and the cavalry. Equestrian exercises were practiced in the huge riding hall.

Exercise also came in daily drills and parade. In order to drill in formation and appear visually as a coherent whole, the Corps was "sized." This involved lining up the cadets by height and assigning them to companies based on how tall they were. The number of companies depended upon the size of the class; always beginning with A it might run to I, as it did for Groves's class. The tallest cadets were in Companies A and I, the next tallest in Companies B and H, next C and G, and so on. Thus when the Corps was formed in a line of companies on the parade ground, it appeared as though everyone was the same height. Cadets in A and I Companies were known as Flankers. Cadets assigned to the center companies were known as Runts. While the purpose of sizing was for the Corps to appear of uniform size when drilling, the cadets used it as a means of social differentiation, leading to some real animosity and contempt among them. Flankers held themselves superior to the lowly Runts, who were considered officious, aggressive, and overly military—a combination that was commonly termed a "runt complex." During his plebe year, Groves was in H Company and at five feet ten and one-half inches (tall in his day), a Flanker. This was a source of great satisfaction to him, leading him to make shorter classmates the butts of his derisive comments.

There was also an extensive athletic program, with intramural and some intercollegiate competition. Groves favored the contact sports, football and wrestling. In his plebe year he played on the junior varsity football squad, and in his yearling year he played on the varsity, whose only loss in eight games was to Notre Dame. The schedule did not include arch rival Navy, the contest being canceled for the duration of the war. Groves did not play in two-thirds of the games and thus did not earn an A letter.[22] The star of that team was Elmer "Ollie" Oliphant, a year ahead of Groves, an All-American fullback and co-captain. On 10 November 1917, Army played the Carlisle Indian School and beat them 28–0. Groves was the second-string center behind his roommate, Arthur Pulsifer, and played in the game.[23] In the winter months there was intramural wrestling. In his plebe year during the indoor meet he came in second in the light heavyweight class.

Groves kept somewhat apart from his classmates. While his room-mates and hall mates were spending their free time in the evenings gossiping, playing cards, or horsing around, Groves studied or wrote letters home, while lecturing the other cadets about not wasting their opportunity to excel. Although some considered him a bit of a grind, he was respected for his ambition and his dedication; it was clear to several of his classmates, even then, that he was destined for higher leadership.

The commandant of cadets, assisted by the tactical officer for each company, is responsible for the military instruction and discipline of the Corps. In Groves's time the commandant was Lt. Col. Guy V. Henry. The officers in the tactics department prescribed the order of the barracks, the mess hall, and just about every other detail of cadet life. For breaches of regulations cadets were skinned, or reported, as we noted earlier. With so many rules there were ample opportunities for infractions, ranging from being late for class to inattention to instruction to missing a button on one's uniform. The cadet had to submit a written explanation of his delinquency and, depending on the severity of the offense, might receive punishment in lieu of or in addition to demerits. It might be a "punishment tour," one hour of walking an assigned pattern on Wednesday or Saturday afternoon in the central courtyard known as the Area. It might mean confinement to one's room, loss of furlough, deprivation of privileges, reprimand, or, in the most serious cases, suspension or dismissal. Conduct was factored into overall class standing and when relative class standing could hinge on tenths of a point, demerits could make the difference in where one eventually ranked.

Groves never had any serious disciplinary problems.[24] As a plebe he ranked in the middle in conduct; like most of his classmates he was awarded the bulk of his demerits during the first six months.[25] At that time there were seven classes of offenses. A Class 1 offense was the most severe; playing at cards or games of chance, for example, could result in 11 to 20 demerits. Least severe were Classes 5, 6, and 7, which resulted in the fewest demerits (three, two, and one, respectively). Almost all of Groves's demerits were 7s and 6s, with an occasional 5. His worst day came on 14 October 1917, when, under the watchful eye of tactical officer Captain Kelly, Groves was awarded six demerits for three separate offenses at inspection: a dirty rifle, a soiled collar, and a tarnished breastplate—awards that were considered to be "character building." In his case, they most certainly were. For, though he walked the area on account of them, he decided that doing so was a waste of his time; after that he walked no more.

Although Groves's academic performance at the University of Washington and MIT had been mediocre to average, at West Point he was an excellent student. Considering his entire two and a half years, Groves ranked fourth in his class. He graduated and was commissioned a second lieutenant on 1 November 1918.[26]

The developments of the European war, under way since 1914, had been slow to influence the conservative Academy.[27] Occasionally the war intruded in the form of distinguished visitors. Gen. Joseph Joffre, hero of the Marne, visited West Point in May 1917. The following May, a group of French combat veterans, the Blue Devils, visited. The West Point Band played "The Marseillaise" and 900 cadets marched as one in their honor.[28]

The initial response at West Point to the Great War in Europe was that no change was needed at all in the tradition-bound crucible forging America's officer class. Until 1917, the Academy refused to acknowledge the changes brought about by the war, adhering to the curriculum that had been established prior to the American Civil War. In military instruction, the well-established great captains—Alexander, Caesar, and Napoleon, as well as the Civil War leaders—were studied intensively, while such modern developments as the Gatling gun and trench warfare were largely ignored.

But when the United States formally entered the war on 6 April 1917, the War Department, badly in need of officers, accelerated the graduation dates of West Point cadets. Eventually the six wartime classes that entered between 1913 and 1918 would all graduate in the 38-month period between April 1917 and June 1920, leaving the Military Academy practically empty.[29] This rush to produce West Point officers through accelerated graduation was controversial within the Army's high command. Granted, large numbers of officers were needed to lead the huge numbers of men going off to war. A partial solution to that problem was to give commissions to thousands of civilians, so-called emergency officers.[30] In 1916 there were 5,175 officers in the Army. The following year there were 34,224; in 1918, 130,485.[31] When the war was over, many of these wartime officers became Regulars. The long-term impact of this infusion, known as the "Hump," profoundly affected the interwar army, freezing officer promotions throughout two decades and causing Groves and his classmates to remain first lieutenants for 16 years.

On the morning of 2 October 1918, a rumor began spreading through the Corps that the Classes of 1920 and 1921 would graduate on 1 November of that year. At dinner that evening an announcement confirming the rumor was made in the main mess hall. It was a moment of high drama. Immediately after the order had been read, the acting commandant held up his hand for silence and said, "Now let's see what sort of discipline you have . . . . I want everyone to keep absolutely silent for five minutes."[32] After what seemed to be an excruciatingly long period the cadets were told to make as much noise as they wanted; what followed was pure pandemonium. A hectic four weeks followed, "a nightmare of lectures and drill . . . busy morning, noon, and night . . . a mad attempt to give us a year's work in three months."[33]

Because of his high class standing Groves could choose his branch. He opted for the prestigious Corps of Engineers, the almost automatic choice of the smartest cadets decade after decade. West Point was, after all, founded as an engineering school, and traditionally the top-ranking graduates chose engineering as their vocation. Indeed, leadership of the Academy was confined to the Corps of Engineers until 1866, when Congress passed a law allowing those from other branches of the Army to serve as superintendents. Nevertheless, of the 30 who served from 1802 to 1918, 20 were from the Corps of Engineers.

There was a large number of engineer spaces available, so Groves had lots of company. Twenty-nine out of the top 30 cadets in his class, and 44 out of the top 50, chose the Corps of Engineers. Twenty-five percent of the entire class—62 cadets—chose the Corps. The choices for most of the remaining second lieutenants were infantry (50), field artillery (32), coast artillery (29), and cavalry (22). One other option was available, air service, and Eugene Luther Vidal (a famous football star, later known for being Gore Vidal's father) and a few of his classmates took it.

The hurriedly arranged graduation ceremony took place on the parade ground in the presence of about 3,000 people. In a short address Assistant Secretary of War Benedict Crowell told the 511 new second lieutenants (the Classes of November 1918 and 1919 graduated at the same time) that it was the government's intention to have them in France within four months. Ten days later the Armistice was signed, proving once again that it is not always easy to predict when wars might end.

The imprint of Groves's experience at West Point on his personality, character, professionalism, and leadership runs deep, and though we will treat this subject more expansively toward the end of the chapter let us pause briefly to note those traits that appear to reflect most directly the correspondence between his Academy training and his approach to officership.

The Academy regimen imbued Groves with extraordinary self-discipline—the will to harness his energies, impulses, inclinations, thoughts, and acts, and focus them laser-like upon the accomplishment of a larger purpose. The math-science orientation of the Academy curriculum produced in Groves an analytic mind, one marked by remorseless objectivity, logic, and organization. It was a mind able to apply scrupulous attention to the particularities of a problem when such was required, but which never lost sight of the overarching principles leading to answers to the great and complex questions. The Academy's continued emphasis upon the causal connection between leadership and mission accomplishment remained with Groves for life. He was a master artist in adapting his accustomed leadership and managerial style to the various exigencies of the moment, always with a tenacious regard for getting the job done. Most important of all, of course, was the Cadet Honor Code, which infused Groves with the grand imperative that an officer's word is his bond, an imperative informing every act in his subsequent professional life.

Over the next 20 years, from 1919 to 1939, Groves served in the interwar Army in several capacities with the Corps of Engineers. An understanding of this experience and his indoctrination into the special culture of the Corps are essential to appreciating the skills and abilities Groves put to use in building the bomb. The interwar Army was an interesting institution, minuscule by contemporary standards, but miraculously able to provide much of the military leadership for World War II. Its average strength was about 135,000, some 12,000 of whom were commissioned officers. The number of officers in the Corps of Engineers during the period was only around 600, about five percent of the Army's officers.

It was a very small group in which everyone knew one another, and it was easy to spot who had ability and intelligence and who did not. The Corps of Engineers has traditionally seen itself as the elite branch of the Army, the best and the brightest with their own motto, "Essayons" (Let us try), and special buttons on their uniform. In many ways the Corps was a caste apart, semi-independent from the main Army and not really integrated into it at all. The other branches felt that distance as well. Engineers, with a few exceptions, normally were not chosen for the highest levels of command in the Army. Nevertheless the Corps fostered a tradition of excellence and was proud of its accomplishments of exploring, surveying, developing, and improving the expanding nation from colonial days to the present.

In 1918, the Chief of Engineers was concerned that the war-accelerated graduations at West Point had produced officers who were inadequately prepared to perform engineering duties, so he established a special course at the Army Engineer School designed to round out their education. Thus, Groves's first assignment was to that course. From there he went on to serve in a variety of duties from Hawaii to Delaware and from Vermont to Nicaragua—always closely observed and guided by outstanding senior officers. He learned a great deal from them; he did well in every assignment and gradually gained a reputation of being a man who could get things done.

He spent four years in Washington, DC, in the Chief of Engineers' office in the early 1930s, and then attended the Command and General Staff School (as it was known at the time) at Fort Leavenworth, Kansas. Clearly on the fast track, he attended the Army War College at Fort McNair in Washington, and then served on the General Staff just as World War II began in Europe. In late July 1940, as the Army mobilized for war, he was assigned as special assistant to the Quartermaster General where responsibility for military construction lay. The story of how the Corps of Engineers took control of construction over the next year and a half is too complicated to recount here, but it was a classic bureaucratic battle over turf with Groves in the middle of it. Eventually Groves ended up as Deputy Chief of Construction and in that capacity was responsible for all domestic Army construction during the period leading up to Pearl Harbor and for nine months afterwards, overseeing the construction of dozens of Army camps, depots, air bases, munitions plants, airplane plants, and hospitals, as well as building the Pentagon. His daily challenges were monumental and unrelenting. In July 1942, the construction peak was reached, with a million men at work and a monthly expenditure of $720 million, the cost equivalent of 15 Pentagons or about $14 billion in today's dollars. It was here that he became widely known as someone who could get things done, and in a hurry. He knew how wartime Washington functioned with its emergency boards and committees that allocated resources and manpower to priority projects. And as he worked with the large construction and industrial firms he came to know their executives and engineers. He would soon be calling upon them to help him build the bomb.

Groves was a classic example of the right person being in the right place at the right time. His prior experience and record made him the most logical choice to head the Manhattan Project. From the day when he first took charge and for every day that followed he put his skills to work to build the bomb in the fastest time possible. The element of speed was overriding in all of his actions. From the outset he dedicated his efforts to winning the war. His assignment to the project had denied him the opportunity to go overseas and serve as a combat engineer; yet his actions make it clear that, after a few moments of disappointment, he decided that building the bomb would be his life's achievement. Knowing that it might end the war was the main source of Groves's extraordinary determination and energy.

His mission order, dated 17 September 1942, was all-inclusive: "Colonel Groves' duty will be to take complete charge of the entire project . . . [and] draw up plans for the organization, construction, operation, and security of the project, and after approval, take the necessary steps to put it into effect." At the beginning Groves was engineer and builder, charged with constructing the plants and factories that would make the atomic fuels—highly enriched uranium and plutonium. As the project accelerated, he came to oversee a vast security, intelligence, and counterintelligence operation with domestic and foreign branches. Through his power to make final decisions, he was ultimately in charge of all scientific research and weapon design, including keeping close watch on the laboratory at Los Alamos. He was involved in many key high-level domestic policy issues and in several international ones as well. By 1945, in addition to all else, he effectively became the operational commander of the bomber unit he established to drop the bomb, and was intimately involved in the planning, targeting, and timing of its missions. One is struck, in discovering all of his many activities, by just how much power Groves accrued. As a West Point classmate and friend later observed, "Groves was given as much power in that position as any officer ever has had."[34] A remarkable statement.

Groves's education at West Point and elsewhere clearly did not qualify him to solve personally the scientific challenges of the Manhattan Project. Nor did it need to. Yet, the Academy's technical curriculum gave him the foundation necessary to build upon. Groves was always a quick study. He did his homework, asked questions, and had a rudimentary knowledge of the physics and chemistry of the atom; he did not need to be a world-class scientist since he had scores of them working for him. Eight on the project had already won a Nobel Prize, and more than a dozen others would do so after the war. Issues requiring scientific analysis were thoroughly reviewed by his advisers; still, in the end it was Groves's choice about which path to take. And these were not easy decisions; the proposed solutions were not always clear-cut and often more than one alternative seemed promising, each backed by sound scientific advice.

In the face of the baffling, enigmatic nature of the scores of such problems, arriving at the right solution in two or three cases could have been mere luck or chance. But to do so repeatedly over a period of three full years, as Groves did, bespeaks an engineer-administrator with uncanny judgment and the keenest of scientific-technological instincts.

Equally important to the project's success was Groves's broad, integrative perspective. The clashing worldviews of the theoretical physicist and the practical engineer were ever present in their different approaches to the bomb. This point was brought home to him a few weeks after getting the job. In October 1942 Groves visited the University of Chicago to assess the status of the project and to meet some of the scientists. He asked them the practical question of how much fissionable material—either highly enriched uranium or plutonium—would be needed for a bomb. Expecting a reply within a narrow range of uncertainty, he was horrified when they told him that they could estimate only within a factor of ten. In other words if it was determined that 100 pounds of plutonium might be needed, the correct amount could be anywhere from ten pounds to 1,000 pounds, not a good basis upon which to start building production facilities. In the months that followed Groves was relentless in demanding an answer to the crucial question of how much material was needed for a bomb. Eventually an answer was found and producing that amount became the determining factor of when there was a bomb ready for use.

Groves possessed to an unusual degree four of the essential qualities of leadership, be it on the battlefield or off: the ability to choose able subordinates and let them work without interference; the self-confidence to take decisive action when needed; the will to win; and personal integrity. Groves's dozens of personnel choices speak for themselves. He had an extraordinary ability to size people up almost instantly and to know whether they could perform the job he was assigning them or not. As for decisions, he made most of the important ones, risking hundreds of millions of dollars in the process and not getting too many of them wrong. When there was a misstep he was usually able to reverse himself quickly. Since so many of the steps in the theory-to-hardware production cycle were first-time engineering ventures—literally steps into the unknown—and since in those early years even the theory itself was uncertain and untested, the fear of failure hung over the project from the beginning. Not until 16 July1945, when the first atomic explosion occurred in the New Mexico desert, were the doubts dispelled. Though the weight of his responsibilities must have borne heavily upon him, he never let it show. Exhibiting any doubt would have eroded the morale of everyone. He knew that leaders must project a confident exterior to maintain enthusiasm and focus.

These first two qualities of the man—shrewd insight into his fellowman and robust self-confidence—were probably a part of his birthright; as he matured, service with the Corps of Engineers developed and strengthened them. The last two—the will to win and integrity—are more directly attributable to his time at West Point, when constant exposure to the highly competitive atmosphere of the Thayer system imbued him with a fiercely competitive spirit and an indomitable will to win. After that, he would allow nothing to deter him from accomplishing his mission, however distasteful to him it might be and no matter who stood in the way. And the Cadet Honor Code provided the rock upon which his personal integrity was founded. As Sir James Chadwick said of him: "[H]e was a man of his word. He could be trusted. When he said he would do something, it would be done."[35]

Throughout his life he kept close ties to West Point. A former officer under whom he served (Francis B. Wilby), a close friend (Maxwell D. Taylor), and his executive officer (James B. Lampert) became Superintendents. His son and grandson were graduates and Groves served as President of the Association of Graduates for four terms. As he said late in life, "To be a graduate of West Pont is an honor that comes to few and one that is never forgotten by any former cadet."[36]

---

[1] This chapter is derived in part from Robert S. Norris, *Racing for the Bomb: General Leslie R. Groves, the Manhattan Project's Indispensable Man* (South Royalton, VT: Steerforth Press, 2002). I would like to thank James L. Abrahamson for his comments on an earlier version.

[2] Leslie R. Groves, *For My Grandchildren,* Entry 7530N, Papers of LRG, Record Group 200, NARA, 103.

[3] Stephen E. Ambrose, *Duty, Honor, Country: A History of West Point* (Baltimore: The Johns Hopkins Press, 1966), 207.

[4] For the classes from 1910 to 1919, the average number of graduates was 140; from 1920 to 1929 it was 225; from 1930 to 1939 it was 456. For the classes from 1990 to 1999 the average number of graduates was 970.

[5] Robert Charlwood Richardson, Jr., *West Point: An Intimate Picture of the National Military Academy and the Life of the Cadet* (New York: G.P. Putnam's Sons, 1917), 103. Captain Richardson (Class of 1904) was an assistant professor of English in Groves's plebe year. His book is an account of what it must have been like when Groves was there. See also Jeffrey Simpson, *Officers and Gentlemen: Historic West Point in Photographs* (Tarrytown, NY: Sleepy Hollow Press, 1982).

[6] *Plebe* is short for the Latin word *plebeian,* referring to a member of the lower or ordinary class—or, in the West Point dictionary, "less than nothing." *The Howitzer: The Yearbook of the Class of 1919,* 361.

[7] Theoretically it ended with his class. *The Howitzer: The Yearbook of the Class of 1920* says that they "were the last plebe class to go thru the mill under the old regime of intensified hazing." 14.

[8] Brig. Gen. William W. Ford, "Plebe Life 1918," *Assembly,* June 1982, 37.

[9] The Young Men's Christian Association beginning in 1908 published *Bugle Notes* annually. In 1924 it was edited and distributed by the upperclassmen. The plebe was refunded his money if he knew the contents.

[10] *Regulations for the United States Military Academy,* 1 April 1918, para. 109; *Bugle Notes* 10 (1918–1919), 96–97.

[11] *Regulations for the United States Military Academy,* 1 April 1918, paragraphs 178–195; *Annual Report of the Superintendent, United States Military Academy, 1918,* 39; Frederick P. Todd, *Cadet Gray: A Pictorial History of Life at West Point as Seen Through Its Uniforms* (New York: Sterling Publications, 1955).

[12] The Honor Code goes back to the beginnings of the Academy, deriving its basic precepts from the code of honor of the Army's officer corps. The first part of the current Code ("A cadet does not lie, cheat, or steal") was not formalized until 1947, and the second part ("or tolerate those who do") until 1970. See Department of the Army, Cadet Honor Committee, *Honor System and SOP*, 1 April 1999. The wording changed slightly in 2001. It now reads, "A cadet will not lie, cheat, steal, or tolerate those who do."

[13] Never better expressed than by Secretary of War, Newton D. Baker (1920): "Men may be inexact or even untruthful, in ordinary matters, and suffer as a consequence only the disesteem of their associates, or even the inconveniences of unfavorable litigation, but the inexact or untruthful soldier trifles with the lives of his fellowmen, and honor of his government: and it is, therefore, no matter of idle pride but rather of stern disciplinary necessity that makes West Point require of her students a character of trustworthiness which knows no evasions."

[14] Roger H. Nye, "The United States Military Academy in an Era of Educational Reform," (Ph.D. diss., Columbia University, 1968).

[15] A compilation of data of the academic standings of all West Point graduates who held the rank of major general or higher in the Civil War, World War I, and World War II (a total of 618), shows a correlation between academic proficiency and later career success. Of the 275 cadets who later became major generals or higher in World War II, 119 graduated in the top third of their class (43 percent), 98 in the middle third (36 percent), and 58 in the bottom third (21 percent). The percentages are comparable for the Civil War and World War I. Col. Charles P. Nicholas, "Six Hundred and Eighteen Major Generals," *Assembly*, January 1952, 10–11.

[16] The courses he took in his plebe year and the textbooks he used are described in *Official Register of the Officers and Cadets, United States Military Academy for 1916* (West Point, NY: USMA, 1916), 75–79.

[17] *Official Register of the Officers and Cadets, United States Military Academy for 1917* (West Point, NY: USMA, 1917), 34, 52–53. A distinguished cadet is one who exceeds 92 percent of the possible total. The Hon. John C. Calhoun, Secretary of War, instituted the practice of reporting distinguished cadets on 10 February 1818.

[18] Through special tests at the end of the term called Written General Reviews, the system provided a way for cadets in the middle or lower sections to improve their ranking. A cadet who did well on WGRs could add points and thereby move upward.

[19] There are many exceptions to the rule. Ulysses S. Grant (Class of 1843) graduated 21st in a class of 39. Four generals who recently served as Chairman of the Joint Chiefs of Staff (John W. Vessey, Colin L. Powell, John M.D. Shalikashvili, and Henry H. Shelton) did not attend West Point, having been commissioned through OCS or ROTC.

[20] In a letter to Chaplain Groves, his brother Owen reported Dick claiming "that if they stay there the full four years, he will emerge at the top of his class. If they are cut short he expects to be third or fourth." Letter, Owen Groves to Chaplain Groves, June 1917, author's collection.

[21] Nye, "The United States Military Academy," 115–124.

[22] To receive credit for playing a game the cadet must be in at least one full period of the game. *Bugle Notes* 10 (1918–1919), 67.

[23] "Carlisle Easy for Army," *New York Times*, 11 November 1917. The eight games are described in some detail in *The Howitzer: The Yearbook of the Class of 1919*, 262–69.

[24] *Register of Demerits*, Class of November 1918, Part 1 (A–L), USMA Archives; *Abstract of Delinquencies*, 11 vols., 1 June 1916–30 November 1918, USMA Archives; *Regulations of the United States Military Academy*, April 1916.

25 Demerits were not recorded for one month after admission. For the remainder of the period to 31 May, one-third of the number of demerits received each month was deducted. *Regulations for the United States Military Academy,* 1 April 1916, 81.

26 For well over a century since its founding, graduates of West Point received a commission in the Army. In 1933, all graduates also began receiving a Bachelor of Science degree, retroactively conferred to those who had graduated after the Academy had been accredited by the American Association of American Universities in 1925.

27 The authorized strength of the Corps of Cadets for 1915 was 706. For 1916 this nearly doubled, to 1,332, though it took some time before that level was actually reached.

28 *New York Times,* 12 May 1917; *New York Times,* 7 May 1918: "'Blue Devils' of France Pay a Visit to West Point," *News of the Highlands,* 11 May 1918.

29 The Class of 1920 (Groves's class) graduated on 1 November 1918, 19 months early, 10 days before the armistice, after having spent 28 months at West Point. The class was originally called the Class of 1920. Later when there was another class that actually graduated in 1920, it became the first Class of 1920. Finally it became the Class of November 1918.

30 When World War I broke out there were 4,900 officers of the Regular Army who had at least one year of commissioned service. When the U.S. entered the war over 193,000 emergency officers were commissioned. Thomas J. Fleming, *West Point: The Men and Times of the Military Academy* (New York: William Morrow & Company, Inc., 1969), 303.

31 *Historical Statistics of the United States, Colonial Times to 1970,* Bicentennial Edition (Washington, DC: U.S. Department of Commerce, 1975), pt. 2, 1141.

32 As quoted in Brig. Gen. William W. Ford, "Plebe Life 1918," *Assembly,* June 1982, 38

33 *The Howitzer: The Yearbook of the Class of 1920,* 16.

34 Wesley G. Jones, "A Conversation with an Engineer Legend: Retired Major General Claude Henry Chorpening— Class of November 1918," *Assembly,* September 1992, 20.

35 Edward Teller with Allen Brown, *The Legacy of Hiroshima,* (Garden City, NY: Doubleday & Company, Inc., 1962), 33.

36 Handwritten note by LRG on letter, Jacob Bacal to LRG, 15 January 1968, Box 3, Entry 7530M, Papers of LRG, RG 200, NARA.

⊰ CHAPTER 6 ⊱

PRINCIPLED LEADERSHIP: CREIGHTON WILLIAMS ABRAMS, CLASS OF 1936

Lewis Sorley

Creighton Abrams brought with him to West Point fine personal values, the capacity for hard work, tolerance for austerity, and enormous energy. He found life at the Military Academy perfectly compatible with these attributes, and departed four years later admirably prepared to lead soldiers and advance in the profession of arms.

Abrams came from a modest background, his father a railroad mechanic and his mother the daughter of an estate caretaker. The family motto, said one of his sisters, was "We're going to be the best regular people we can be."[1] Her brother, she recalled, "always did his job. Nobody ever had to tell him." In fact, "it really used to kind of grate on me because he never had to be asked to do anything. He always did it. If he was in the Chicken Club, then he took care of the chickens." Then they graduated to the Pig Club, and "while we were in the Pig Club, he fed his pig and my pig and took care of it."[2]

Abrams attended West Point somewhat by chance. Raised in the small, semi-rural town of Agawam in western Massachusetts, he worked hard as a youth, throwing himself into his studies, plus everything from football to dramatics outside the classroom and a succession of part-time jobs. His academic and athletic achievements earned him a scholarship to Brown University, but the stipend was only for tuition. His parents were unable to cover the costs of room, board, and books, so Abrams had to pass up the offer. Then he heard a talk by the principal of a nearby high school. The man was a West Point graduate, and he spoke of what an opportunity the Military Academy offered young men. "Abrams liked what he heard," later wrote Keyes Beech, and that speech "changed his life."[3] Abrams was able to obtain an appointment and, in the summer of 1932, entered West Point.

When Abrams left home to become a cadet, it was his first trip outside his native state. Given his modest upbringing, his fairly limited experience, and the fact that America was then in the depths of the Great Depression, he did not find the austerity of West Point difficult to accommodate. He had routinely worked hard as a youth, while in his family there had been few amenities, perhaps the only "frivolous" thing (as his parents would view it) a dog named Pal who became Abrams's constant companion.

Despite the ease with which he adapted, however, Abrams was not enthusiastic about some aspects of the West Point of his day. In later life Abrams would claim a more checkered cadet career than the record supports, often for humorous effect. At West Point, he told one reporter, "there were so many rules it was not uncommon for me to be found violating one."[4] And, many years after the fact, he still felt strongly enough about cadet days to tell Will Lang of *Life* magazine that "the Military Academy was hard to take. People there were hard to take. They were frequently rude and issuing orders continually. We plebes had to pick up things, and then set them right down, put on our coat, and then take it off, and I was punished if upperclassmen found paper in my wastebasket. Now, a wastebasket is a simple functional thing, and that's where paper belongs. How silly can one get?"[5]

In particular Abrams deplored the harsh treatment given the plebes: "It was a pretty brutal experience. The hazing was degrading, and certainly not character-building," he remembered.[6] Many years later, when he was Army Chief of Staff, Abrams had an opportunity to influence such matters by appointing a new Superintendent of the Military Academy. He selected Maj. Gen. Sidney Berry and called him in for a talk. "Build on what a man is—don't tear him down," began

Berry's notes of a meeting that lasted for two and a half hours. Abrams told Berry that he was concerned with West Point's isolation, that it did not resemble the real Army, and that its graduates were accordingly unprepared to deal with the professional environment in which they had to operate after graduation and commissioning. Berry should strive to build a bridge that one could travel without too much risk from the Military Academy to the Army in the field.[7] It seems clear that Abrams would approve the current system of training all four classes in lieu of the "plebe system" of earlier days, as well as the contemporary emphasis on the dignity of the individual and on mentoring and teaching as opposed to harassment and humiliation.

Despite his misgivings, Abrams was an enthusiastic and fully committed cadet. He lettered in football as a First Classman after four years of struggling to earn that distinction, and was appointed a cadet lieutenant in the days when only about a quarter of the First Class became cadet officers. He was famous throughout Central Area as a daredevil rider of the laundry carts, an exercise that involved maneuvering a skate-wheeled cart with canvas sides down the metal stairs from the second floor of barracks, out the entryway (where an accomplice would give a swift sideways kick to line up the cart with the slightly offset door), then across the barracks stoop and down more steps, these made of stone, onto the concrete apron, whooping gleefully all the way. That drill never failed to draw a crowd.[8]

Upon graduation Abrams chose cavalry as his branch—*The Howitzer*, the cadet yearbook, observing that "the horses will have to work hard to keep up with him"—then married his sweetheart Julia Harvey, newly graduated from Vassar College. Together they joined the famous 7th Cavalry at Fort Bliss, Texas, beginning 38 years of shared service which culminated with Abrams's appointment as Army Chief of Staff.

The values the Military Academy seeks to instill in its graduates were evident in Abrams's conduct from the outset of his commissioned service. Those of greatest interest in connection with his West Point background might well be exceptional compassion for the soldiers he led (not universally regarded as an attribute common to West Pointers) and absolute personal integrity (at the heart of West Point's teachings).

Leading a platoon of horse cavalry, his first command, Abrams demonstrated an already sure grasp of how to deal with soldiers. The 7th Cavalry in those days was understrength in troops but full up with horses. To ensure that all the horses got adequate exercise, they would often ride out with each man mounted on one horse and trailing two others on leads. On one occasion Pvt. Daniel Sanford, new to the outfit, decided to go around the left side of a sand dune with the horse he was riding, while those he had on lead chose the opposite side. There was a brief tug of war, inevitably lost by Sanford, who was pulled out of his saddle and dragged across the sand dune, which was covered with mesquite and cactus.

When the troops had gotten back to the stable and looked after the horses, Abrams lined his soldiers up, then said to them: "You men can take Private Sanford here as an example. They pulled him right off his horse but, by God, he didn't let loose of his lead horses!" This had a tremendous effect on Sanford, who later remembered: "There I stood, with my ass full of mesquite and cactus stickers—but proud as hell!"[9]

Before long war came, the horses went away, and Abrams and many other young cavalrymen became leaders of the emerging armored force. In July 1942 Abrams took command of a tank battalion. He was 27 years old, six years out of West Point, and a captain. By September he was a lieutenant colonel in the 4th Armored Division, where he would serve throughout the coming conflict.

The motto of the 37th Tank Battalion, the outfit Abrams would lead across Europe during World War II, was "Courage Conquers." Abrams trained his unit hard, insisting on what sometimes seemed to others impossible standards of performance. Responding to complaints that his requirements for reaction time and first-round hits in tank gunnery were too stringent, Abrams organized a pick-up crew from members of his staff, gave them a little drill, then went down range in his own tank "Thunderbolt" and met the standards. That ended complaints on that matter. Then, as other tanks from the battalion negotiated the gunnery course, Abrams or one of his staff officers would ride along on the back deck. Some company commanders then complained that this made their men nervous. Abrams's reaction was direct. "If that makes them nervous," he asked, "what are they going to do when the Germans start shooting at them?" There were no further complaints on that score, either.[10]

Abrams's battalion accomplished a great deal while he was in command. In recommending him for a battlefield promotion to colonel, his division commander stated that "the brilliant combat record of Lt. Col. Creighton Abrams constitutes one of the sagas of this war . . . . His command was first to cross the Moselle River, he led the advance which resulted in the relief of Bastogne, and his was the first element in Third Army to reach the Rhine."[11] Abrams got the promotion, complementing two Distinguished Service Crosses and two Silver Stars he had won in the drive across Europe.

Abrams gave the credit to others, writing to his wife Julie late in the war, "I have travelled in gallant company." Later Abrams lauded what he called the division's "fantastic record of human endeavor. I feel for one," he added, "that this all was possible because . . . the Fourth Armored Division took unto itself the banner of our American heritage and never relinquished it. This heritage is faith, sacrifice, determination, and consciousness of destiny."[12]

Abrams's essential modesty remained intact despite his success and increasing reputation within the profession. "He was no change from a captain to a colonel," said his reconnaissance sergeant, who had watched him all the way.[13] Many years later, to his great delight, Abrams received this introduction at a 4th Armored Division reunion: "Ladies and gentlemen, the Chief of Staff of the United States Army, Colonel Abe!" Abrams himself liked to remind people that "there is no limit to what you can accomplish if you don't care who gets the credit."[14] His wife Julie said he got that from Gen. George C. Marshall, the Army's sterling Chief of Staff during World War II.

Despite driving his unit hard in both training and combat, and leading it into harm's way time and time again, Abrams was regarded by his troops with respect, admiration, even affection. He demonstrated extraordinary courage, leadership, and professional competence, but many also remembered the compassion he had shown for the soldiers under his command, and how he shared every danger and every hardship with them. Wrote one of his soldiers many years later, "Abe had a tremendous effect on me. His strength of character and the kindness he was wont to show to civilians soldiers such as myself is a memory I cherish." Recalled another, "I have fond memories of the kind of man Abrams was. He never made things more difficult and unhappy than they were, as did some of the officers of far less rank." And yet another, writing to Abrams during his final illness many years later, "I still respect you as a soldier and love you as a fine human being. I teach children to grow up to be like General Abe."[15] In later years people would remember that Abrams had a number of "sayings," observations that appealed to him and that he would use over and over. One of his favorites was "soldiering is an affair of the heart." The outlook that observation reflected was understood and appreciated by his soldiers.

Fairness was also a hallmark. Reporter Jimmy Cannon once asked Abrams to name the key to the success of his outfit, to which Abrams responded: "Firepower and ability to move it around, and the fact that there is no first weapon in this outfit. The tanks, the infantry, the artillery, the engineers, they're all first. When it's that way you have a good outfit."[16] Abrams was echoing the wisdom of Maj. Gen. Adna R. Chaffee, Jr., widely recognized as "the father of the armored force," who insisted that that force must be "a balanced team of combat arms and services of equal importance and equal prestige."[17] The beauty of the concept is that if all are equal in importance and prestige, if there is no first team, then no one is on a second team. All are equal partners, all valued for their essential contributions to what together they accomplish as a team. Abrams ran the 37th Tank Battalion that way, and to good effect.

Their insightful comments indicate that Abrams's soldiers saw, and appreciated, a side of him not perceived by many. The more typical view was of Abrams as a gruff, hard-charging, "cigar-chomping" combat leader who constantly reminded his men that "the shortest way home is east" and demanded that they "attack, attack, attack!"[18] That aspect was real, and important, as acknowledged by Third Army commander Gen. George S. Patton. "I'm supposed to be the best tank commander in the Army," Patton observed, "but I have one peer—Abe Abrams. He's the world champion."[19] That was not, however, the whole man, and Abrams's soldiers knew it.

Reporters who encountered Abrams during the war also perceived that they had come across someone special, especially in terms of his personal modesty and love of the soldier. "He was out of West Point," wrote Jimmy Cannon, "but he understood this was a civilian army and he knew what the drafted soldiers endured." Cannon observed that Abrams was "cherished by his people because he respected them for what they did and they reciprocated. In two wars," he added, "Abe was the most impressive officer of any grade I met. He never seemed to use the force of his rank as a weapon of command. That was the style of his greatness beyond his immense ability as a military man."[20]

As he rose in rank and responsibility, Abrams often used self-deprecating humor to connect with those he sought to influence. He joked about his humble existence as a third-string member of the West Point football team and sometimes even claimed to have been elected to the Jewish All-American team. "The only Methodist so honored," he would add with a straight face.

Soon after rising to general officer rank, Abrams was assigned very challenging duties as the Chief of Staff's representative at places where domestic civil rights disturbances required the deployment of Army elements. He handled those crises with coolness and understated confidence, leading to command of the 3rd Armored Division and then V Corps in Germany, followed by return home to become Army Vice Chief of Staff under Gen. Harold K. Johnson. "The Army has long needed such a happy combination," wrote noted military affairs commentator S.L.A. Marshall of the Johnson-Abrams team.[21]

The two men shared deep misgivings about how the war in Vietnam was being conducted, even as they worked tirelessly to expand and train an Army that was being asked to send more and more troops to the conflict. Of one mind professionally and ethically, the two struggled with some of the most difficult tasks imaginable in the atmosphere of pervasive mistrust and antagonism in civil-military relationships that characterized the Pentagon of the day. Abrams told Lt. Gen. Arthur S. "Ace" Collins, Jr., newly assigned to the Army Staff, that "working in this building . . . you'll have reason to quit every day. You just don't see any point in going on, or how you're going to get things done. But we know the soldier and we know the conditions of the battlefield, so no matter what they [the politicians] do, or how tough they make it, our job is to hang in there, day in and day out, so that when that soldier has to fight, he can be as well equipped and as well prepared as we can make him. And *that's why we hang on!*"[22]

Abrams both articulated and exemplified what he viewed as the essential qualities of a professional military officer. Describing the decision-making process in the Pentagon to a group of junior officers, Abrams pointed out the enormous impact of many of the decisions that were made. This, he stressed, rendered it essential that the people working on these problems be professionally qualified and honest, men of sound judgment to be sure, but above all honest and straightforward. "We have it," said Abrams, "but we don't have it one hundred percent." That wasn't good enough. The Army had to be the conservator of values, especially in turbulent times. "Regardless of standards that are set in any other walk of life in our country," he stressed, "regardless of standards in any business or anything else, this must be preserved in the military. It must be enhanced in the military. While we're guarding the country, we must accept being the guardian of the finest ethics. The country needs it and we must do it."

After visiting an Officer Candidate School, Abrams wrote this out in longhand: "What we want in our officer corps: character, integrity, respect for and devotion to the fundamental precepts of our government and our evolving way of life, intelligence, professional competence in a highly technical age, and a fundamental belief and confidence in human beings."[23]

In May 1967 Abrams was sent to Vietnam as deputy commander of all U.S. forces there. Later, when it was announced that he was moving up to the top job, Gen. Harold K. Johnson was interviewed by *Time* magazine for a cover story about Abrams. "I said he was the finest individual in uniform in any of the services at that time," Johnson recalled. "I said that included me, that included the Chairman of the

Joint Chiefs of Staff, that included the chiefs of the other services as well." The reporter from *Time*, taken aback, said he could not print that. Johnson's reply was direct: "As far as I'm concerned you can, and you can quote me." The quotation was not used, but Johnson meant what he said: "I always found him to be very, very straightforward with me, a very compassionate and human man, thoroughly knowledgeable, and I think professional in every sense of the word. Just a unique being."[24]

Abrams had been told that within a few weeks of his arrival in Vietnam, he would succeed to the top post as Commander, U.S. Military Assistance Command, Vietnam. Instead, that move was delayed for over a year. In the meantime there occurred events of great import, especially the enemy's 1968 Tet Offensive, the watershed event of the war from the American standpoint. Domestic support for continued American involvement nose-dived, the long years of building up U.S. forces gave way to their progressive withdrawal, and Abrams presided over a massive effort to train and equip the South Vietnamese to maintain their own security once the Americans had all gone home. Thus, when General Abrams took command of MACV in June 1968, he charted a radically different course, stressing in particular the necessity of conducting "One War" of military operations, pacification, and improvement of South Vietnam's armed forces.[25]

As he had done at every stop along the way, Abrams also staked out his ethical stance early in the assignment. The first order he issued upon assuming command was that there would be no bombing or rocketing or heavy artillery used against an inhabited area without his personal permission. He emphasized this to the Vietnamese as well, telling senior Vietnamese military and civilian officials that "we cannot apply the full firepower capabilities of our military force throughout the countryside at will, for to do so would further endanger the lives and property and the governmental relationships with the very people we are all fighting to protect: your own citizens of Vietnam."[26]

In another action with a strong ethical component, Abrams early on made clear his antipathy to "body count," the primary measure of merit under his predecessor. "It is important that the command move away from the over-emphasized and often irrelevant 'body count' preoccupation toward measures of progress more oriented to attainment of U.S. objectives," he stressed to his subordinate commanders. In fact, maintained Abrams, in a total repudiation of the approach of his predecessor, "I don't think it makes any difference how many losses he [the enemy] takes. I don't think *that* makes any *difference*."[27]

Nor was Abrams ambivalent about reversing another inherited outlook. "The mission," he thundered, "is not to seek out and destroy the enemy. The mission is to provide protection for the people of Vietnam."[28] Reinforcing that, he linked the two concepts: "The body count does not have much to do with the outcome of this war. Some of the things I do think important are that we preempt or defeat the enemy's major military operations and eliminate or render ineffective the major portion of his guerrillas and his infrastructure—the political, administrative, and paramilitary structure on which his whole movement depends." And, he added, "it is far more significant that we neutralize one thousand of these guerrillas and infrastructure than kill 10,000 North Vietnamese soldiers."[29]

Abrams's stance on media relations also reflected his emphasis on integrity. "Effective now," he told commanders throughout MACV in an early message, "the overall public affairs policy of this command will be to let results speak for themselves. We will not deal in propaganda exercises in any way, but will play all of our activities at a low key." It was a total repudiation of the policy he had inherited. "Achievements, not hopes, will be stressed," he added.[30] A few days later he followed with a message prescribing how bad news was to be handled. "If [an] investigation results in 'bad news,' no attempt will be made to dodge the issue. If an error has been made, it will be admitted . . . as soon as possible."[31] Responding to his senior Marine subordinate, who complained that Armed Forces Radio was carrying too much coverage of dissent, protests, and violence in the United States, Abrams reported having looked into the matter and concluded that the broadcasts were "presenting a balanced set of facts." And, he added, "It is our job to persevere in the atmosphere of the facts."[32]

This outlook was recognized and appreciated by many reporting on the war. Abrams gave no press conferences, but in a series of backgrounders, informal suppers with journalists, and occasional one-on-one interviews he managed to keep the press informed. George McArthur of the *Los Angeles Times* noted that Abrams clearly viewed much of the press and television coverage of the war as one-dimensional and negative. "Yet on the whole," he concluded, "the gruff-spoken general has retained the respect of most Saigon newsmen, hawk and dove alike." Indeed, observed McArthur, "Abrams' wry humor, candor, and earthy intellect have combined to produce a paradox—a popular leader in an unpopular war."[33]

As American units were progressively withdrawn from Vietnam, Abrams went to tell them goodbye and to thank them for their service. On those occasions he invariably revealed much about his own character and the values he most admired in others. When the 1st Infantry Division was headed home after four and a half years in combat, Abrams told its soldiers that "in a changing world, changing times, and changing attitudes . . . the 1st Infantry Division, more than any other division in our Army, represents a constancy of those essential virtues of mankind—humility, courage, devotion, and sacrifice." And, he added, "I choose to feel that this is part of the cement, and the rock, and the steel that holds our great country together." Then he closed by quoting back to them their own inspirational division motto: "No Mission Too Difficult, No Sacrifice Too Great—Duty First."[34]

Lt. Col. Andy Coffey worked as a staff writer for Abrams in Vietnam during the period 1969-1970. He prepared, among other things, responses to letters from the next of kin of deceased or missing soldiers. "The mail he received was often heart-rending," said Coffey, and the carefully researched replies were "nearly as moving as the incoming mail." Coffey worked hard to ensure that each letter was perfectly composed and typed, but he was bothered to note that often, when they came back out with Abrams's signature, there were smudges and strange brown splotches on the paper. He held those letters up and examined them in the light. Eventually he concluded that the marks were Abrams's tear stains. "I am grateful for leaders like General Abrams who show it is acceptable for a leader to cry over his men," Coffey said later. "I am grateful for leaders like General Abrams who show us that every soldier's death diminishes every other soldier's life."[35]

Senior officers completing their tours often had visits from Abrams, or with him in Saigon. When Sidney Berry was en route home after serving as assistant division commander of the 101st Airborne Division, Abrams invited him to his quarters. Berry remembered the occasion vividly, and later spoke of it in a eulogy for General Abrams delivered in the Chapel of the Most Holy Trinity at West Point. Abrams, he said, "described two qualities he considered essential in senior leaders of the United States Army: first, sensitivity to other people, human understanding, compassion, a concern for the human beings entrusted into one's care, and second, the love, gentleness, constructiveness, and fulfillment of good family life to counterbalance the harshness, toughness, and destructiveness of war and combat." Concluded Berry, "General Abe was a sensitive man."[36]

Abrams's compassion for soldiers remained strongly in evidence during this most difficult assignment, including compassion for even his most senior subordinates. Maj. Gen. John T. Carley was assigned to MACV as the J3, Deputy Chief of Staff for Operations, in June 1971. Within a short time, he said in a message to a friend, "Things had piled up on me. Lots of pressure. Thirty-five fourteen hour days in a row had left me worn out. I just felt that I could not go on. Took yesterday off, thought it all out and concluded that it was best for me to call it quits . . . . I put in my papers."

Learning of this abrupt request for retirement, Abrams invited Carley to his quarters for dinner, just the two of them. "During the course of the evening," Carley told his friend, "I talked myself out of quitting and went home carrying my papers under my arm. I emphasize that I talked myself out of my own decision and General Abrams only helped by his understanding and wisdom. It was a fascinating evening with a wonderful man."[37]

Carley returned to duty, while others were astounded by Abrams's understanding and compassion. Said another very senior officer serving in Vietnam at the time, "My reaction is 'Jesus, make him a colonel.'"[38] But Carley served well, finishing out his year in Vietnam, and upon departure received the Distinguished Service Medal from Abrams. On his last evening in Vietnam, Abrams again had him to dinner.

Enclosing a copy of that earlier despairing message to his friend, Carley later wrote to thank Abrams for the sendoff. "There will be medals and tributes in recognition of your major contributions here," said Carley, "but none for the small acts of great leadership known only to those concerned. However, I know about this particular one and will always be grateful to you for providing wise council and a shoulder to lean on when it was badly needed. I hope that you never had cause to regret salvaging me. I never did."[39]

Abrams served five long and difficult years in Vietnam, becoming eventually MACV's institutional memory. He bore it all with stoicism, even with what might be termed, for all his volatility of temperament and monumental moodiness, a certain serenity. But he, too, felt the need for reassurance and refuge. He found them in conversion to Catholicism, undertaken during his service in Vietnam. Years before, speaking at a prayer breakfast, Abrams had remarked how "each of us, by our prayers and by our faith in God, is seeking not only an inner peace, but also the courage to face what lies ahead and to do what must be done."[40] Now, explained his wife Julie, "he just felt that he had to have some extra help."[41]

Soon after Abrams had been baptized in the Catholic faith, the visiting Francis Cardinal Cooke confirmed him. Moved by what he had witnessed during the visit, Cooke wrote to tell Abrams that being with him in his command "gave me the balanced picture of a great human being and a great gentleman—a man of peace striving to come successfully to the end of a difficult and awful war and anxious to guarantee a just peace for his own people and for those others to whom he had been sent to help and support. I never have the chance to be with you but that I come away grateful to God for the dedication and for the courage which you have."[42]

"Some of the days are kind of long, but the years go by very quickly," Abrams observed near the end of his service in Vietnam.

Much had been accomplished. By the time of the enemy's 20-division conventional invasion of South Vietnam in what came to be known as the 1972 Easter Offensive, the pacification program had succeeded remarkably, genuine land reform had given over 400,000 farmers title to 2.5 million acres of land, some four million citizens had been organized into a People's Self-Defense Force armed with 600,000 weapons, and South Vietnam's armed forces had achieved the capacity—with important help from U.S. airpower—to successfully defend against North Vietnam's massive assault. On his last night in command, reflecting on all he had seen during the previous five years, Abrams stated his settled conviction to officers assembled in the mess: "The longer I serve, the more I become convinced that the single most important attribute of the professional officer is integrity."[43]

In the summer of that year Abrams returned from Vietnam to head an Army that was widely viewed, both by the nation and from within its own ranks, as dispirited and desperately in need of reform. His appointment as Chief of Staff was the first step in getting on with the job of rebuilding. "Unvarying honesty touched everything he did,"[44] Secretary of Defense Melvin Laird said of Abrams. His reputation for integrity and competence, and the universal respect and admiration for him that ran through the Army's ranks, were in themselves important parts of dealing with the manifold problems of the day. He set out to achieve two key tasks, restoring combat readiness and taking care of the soldier, the touchstones of his entire career.

"I consider the basic task of the Army to be readiness," Abrams told Army officers assigned to the senior service schools. Readiness as he defined it involved training, equipment, and people, but even more important it involved a state of mind including "devotion to duty and service, and a dedication to being competent, professional soldiers" with a positive approach to tasks, mental flexibility, receptivity to change both inside and outside the Army, and action instead of lip service.[45] In his public talks Abrams emphasized the critical need for readiness, detailing how in past conflicts "we have paid, and paid, and paid again in blood and sacrifice for our unpreparedness. I don't want war," he maintained, "but I am appalled at the human cost that we've paid because we wouldn't prepare to fight."[46]

Along with readiness was constant emphasis on the importance of the soldier. "People are not *in* the Army," Abrams reminded leaders at every level, "people *are* the Army." Often he would add, "and by people I do not mean personnel. I do not mean end strength. I do not mean MOSs. I do not mean files. I do not mean any such categories that deal with people as a commodity. I mean people as individual human beings who make up the squads and the companies and the divisions, and upon whom our security ultimately depends."[47] The key to solving all the many problems at hand, thought Abrams, was people—their commitment, leadership, competence, and integrity. "Nobody can take your integrity away from you," he told young officers. "[If you're going to lose it,] you've got to give it up yourself."[48] Cabling commanders worldwide, he delivered a straightforward message: "I cannot emphasize too strongly the critical necessity for candor. Tell it like it is."[49]

The post-Vietnam Army was having trouble with race relations, an especially sad thing since for many years the Army had led the way in providing opportunities for all soldiers to advance on merit without respect to race or other such characteristics. Abrams knew that principled leadership meant treating everyone fairly and with dignity. Speaking at an Army-wide conference on racial relations held at Fort Monroe, Virginia, in 1974, he laid it on the line. "The most important thing we have in the Army is people," he stressed. "It is the spirit, the faith, the attitudes of people that make a winning Army." The Army, in his unswerving view, could achieve its objectives only if its soldiers have confidence in one another, have faith in each other, and recognize their dependence on one another. Unless there is equal opportunity for all in the Army, these necessary outlooks cannot be achieved.[50]

The Army had not yet reached that objective. "We all like to think that we have two lives," said Abrams,

> our official military life and our private life . . . . But I know that any leader in the military who believes that is wrong. He only has one life, and that's his military life. He can't have a dual personality, on the post an advocate for equal opportunity and when off the post—in so-called private

life—a member of a club or society that is not in keeping with equal opportunity. Is there anyone left who thinks his soldiers don't know all that—and realize what a damned fraud he is? If you're a leader, you can't do it. If you can't live with that, you're just in the wrong outfit. You should seek employment elsewhere.[51]

In the last year of his life Abrams attended the annual Armor Ball held in Washington. After dinner he was invited to say a few words. Dancing had already begun, so Abrams just stood at the side of the floor while people gathered around him. He spoke quietly, in a very husky voice, about service, about the privilege of service. For many who heard him, the experience was unforgettable. Later that night, tired and slumped down in the rear seat of the sedan on the way back to Fort Myer, Abrams asked his wife Julie how she thought the talk had gone. "All I can tell you," she responded, "is what I heard afterward in the ladies room. Two young women were talking, and one said to the other: 'I've been urging my husband to get out of the Army, but after hearing that I hope he will stay in.'"[52]

When General Abrams passed away while serving as Chief of Staff, the only Chief ever to die in office, there were many tributes. At Carlisle Barracks, Pennsylvania, home of the Army War College, a modest memorial was erected. Just a chunk of rock, really, it was placed so that every student would see it as he or she departed the school each day. On it were these few words of Abrams's own: "There must be, within our Army, a sense of purpose and a dedication to that purpose. There must be a willingness to march a little farther, to carry a heavier load, to step out into the dark and the unknown for the safety and well-being of others."

The way of the soldier was made for Creighton Abrams. He found in it the ideal manifestation of his strength of character, depth of commitment, ability to lead and move men, grasp of complex organizations and fast-paced events, physical bravery, intellectual integrity, endurance, spirituality, and need for a sense of purpose. Abrams was something quite rare in the profession of arms, a soldier of tactical brilliance, personal bravery, and inspiring leadership who was also compassionate, modest, and wise. He had qualities, difficult to define but easy to apprehend, that have variously been described as presence, command authority, and aura.

He was, withal, in many ways a man of contradictions. He was not a good student at West Point, but he was intelligent and able, full of common sense. He was not well turned out, but he was impressive. He did not make much small talk, but he was an outstanding communicator. He did not curry favor, but he was respected and moved along by senior people. He did not care about public opinion, but he was effective in shaping it in ways supportive of what he was trying to do. He did not pander to the press, but in leveling with them he gained a level of trust and support that eluded many senior officers. He had embedded qualities acquired in the environment of the family and community in which he grew up, and only honed and given wider scope by the professional environment in which he performed so ably. What Abrams had cannot be taught, although others may seek to learn from and emulate it.

Clearly Creighton Abrams's attributes of selflessness, personal modesty, physical and moral courage, love of the soldier, and commitment to service were wholly congruent with West Point's ideals of Duty, Honor, Country. It seems likely, however, that he brought most of those values with him when he entered as a cadet rather than learning them during his years at the Military Academy. The West Point experience may, indeed must have, reinforced those attributes and outlooks on Abrams's part, but no more than that. "He was a dependable boy," recalled his high school teacher Miss Marjorie Ward when Abrams became Army Chief of Staff. Harmon Smith, the football coach when Abrams captained an undefeated, untied, and unscored upon team as a senior at Agawam High School, agreed: "The same qualities he has shown in the last few years, when he was in the public eye, were qualities we teachers could see in him then."[53]

At the front of West Point's New South Post is a plaque designating the entryway as Abrams Gate. Such memorials are established so that others may be inspired to manifest in their own lives the same values of principled leadership, to understand—as Abrams did—the privilege of service, and to commit themselves wholeheartedly to its dictates. As Abrams once said to a group of cadets nearing graduation, "What the country needs and expects from you as leaders . . . has to come from the heart."[54]

Clearly, too, West Point found a place in Abrams's heart. Not long before the Normandy invasion, as a young lieutenant colonel carrying a lot of responsibility, he wrote a poignant love letter to his young bride. "For me," he told her, "I can hear the last strains of the 'Star Spangled Banner' across the plains at West Point, I can hear the majestic beat of 'The Corps' at chapel, I can hear the noble words of the Cadet Prayer, and with all this I can see in Grant Hall the girl who stole my heart, my most beautiful girl, my sweetheart, my wife forever and ever."

---

[1] Dr. Jeanne Abrams Daly, Interview, Fort Leavenworth, KS, 22 February 1988, recalling what her aunt had once told her.

[2] Elizabeth James, Oral History Interview, General Creighton Abrams Story, U.S. Army Military History Institute, Carlisle Barracks, PA. Hereafter MHI.

[3] *Chicago Daily News*, 10 July 1968.

[4] Keyes Beech, *New Orleans Times-Picayune*, 21 July 1968.

[5] "Colonel Abe," *Life*, 23 April 1945.

[6] Ibid.

[7] Interview, Lt. Gen. Sidney B. Berry, 3 May 1989.

[8] Maj. Gen. Delk Oden, "Abrams Story" Interview, MHI.

[9] Correspondence File, Creighton W. Abrams Papers, MHI.

[10] Col. William A. Dwight, Interview, 23 May 1989.

[11] Maj. Gen. Hugh Gaffey, as quoted by Will Lang in filing of 3 October 1961 for *Time* cover story on Abrams as Commanding General, 3rd Armored Division. Copy in Abrams family papers.

[12] 4th Armored Division Association, "Eighteenth Annual Convention Booklet," 23. No publication data.

[13] Sgt. Marvin Mattingly, Interview, 6 August 1987.

[14] As recalled by Gen. Walter T. Kerwin, Jr., "General Abrams and Professionalism," U.S. Army War College Lecture, 15 August 1983.

[15] Quotations are from letters in Correspondence File, Abrams Papers, MHI.

[16] *New York Post*, 23 November 1955.

[17] As inscribed on the Armored Forces Monument, Washington, D.C.

[18] Col. James H. Leach, "Tank Leaders Lead," Typescript. Leach commanded B Company, 37th Tank Battalion, throughout World War II.

[19] Official Army Obituary Notice, "Creighton W. Abrams," 4 September 1974.

[20] "General Abe," *World Journal Tribune*, 26 April 1967.

[21] *Los Angeles Times*, 12 July 1964.

[22] Lt. Gen. Arthur S. Collins, Jr., Oral History, MHI.

[23] Memorandum, Abrams for DCSPER, Subject: Basic Objectives in Acquiring Officers, 3 March 1965, Abrams Papers, MHI.

[24] Gen. Harold K. Johnson, Oral History, MHI.

[25] For a comprehensive account of the changes Abrams made in the conduct of the war, and the results, see the author's *A Better War: The Unexamined Victories and Final Tragedy of America's Last Years in Vietnam* (New York: Harcourt Brace, 1999).

[26] Discussion with students of the first class of the National Defense College, Vietnam, 9 August 1968, in Marshall Papers, Indochina Archive, University of California, Berkeley.

[27] Commanders Weekly Intelligence Estimate Update, Headquarters, MACV, 27 September 1969.

[28] Col. Donald S. Marshall, Interview, 12 October 1988.

[29] As quoted by Beverly Deepe, *Christian Science Monitor*, 23 October 1968.

[30] Message, Abrams to Multiple Addressees, MAC 7236, 020158Z JUN 1968, Office, Chief of Military History, U.S. Army, files. Hereafter CMH.

[31] Abrams, Message to Multiple Addressees, MAC 7429, 060620Z JUN 1968, CMH files.

[32] Message, Abrams to Cushman, MAC 04619, 061734Z APR 1968, CMH files.

[33] George McArthur, *Los Angeles Times*, 26 February 1970.

[34] Audio-Archives, MHI.

[35] *Army*, November 1990, 24.

[36] Lt. Gen. [then Maj. Gen.] Sidney B. Berry, Superintendent, United States Military Academy, Eulogy for General Abrams. Chapel of the Most Holy Trinity, West Point, NY, 6 September 1974.

[37] Message, MAC 08982, MG Carley, MACJ3, Saigon to MG Orwin C. Talbott, CG USAIS, Fort Benning, 180642Z SEP 1971. Copy in Abrams Family Papers.

[38] Interview, 16 January 1989.

[39] Letter, Carley to Abrams, 26 June 1972, Abrams Family Papers.

[40] As recounted by Col. Thomas T. Jones in a letter to Abrams, 16 June 1974. "In looking over some of the speeches I had the privilege of helping you write about 8 years ago," wrote Jones, "I found the following sentence you had added to your prayer breakfast speech in Helena, Montana," and he quoted the line.

[41] Julie Abrams, Interview, 8 December 1987.

[42] Letter, Francis Cardinal Cooke to Abrams, 14 January 1972, Abrams Family Papers.

[43] Recollections of Maj. Gen. Stan L. McClellan on 4 September 1974, Enclosure to Letter to Mrs. Abrams, 8 October 1974, Abrams Family Papers.

[44] Melvin R. Laird, "Unforgettable Creighton Abrams," *Reader's Digest*, July 1976, 72-76.

[45] Remarks, Briefing for Senior Service College Army Personnel, 14 October 1972, Abrams Papers, MHI.

[46] Remarks, TRADOC-FORSCOM Chaplains Conference, Kansas City, 11 September 1973.

[47] For one example of many, Abrams's remarks to the Massachusetts Bay Chapter of the Association of the United States Army, Middletown, MA, 6 April 1974, as subsequently published in *Command Comment No. 109* (Washington: Office of the Chief of Information, Department of the Army, 17 May 1974).

[48] As quoted in *U.S. News & World Report*, 6 August 1973.

49 Message, Abrams to Multiple Addressees, WDC 09073, 121949Z JUN 1973.

50 Remarks, Department of the Army Race Relations/Equal Opportunity Conference, Fort Monroe, VA, 16 January 1974.

51 Ibid.

52 Interview, Julia Abrams [Mrs. Creighton W. Abrams], 23 June 1988.

53 Quoted by David Wilkes, *Union*, 21 June 1972. Newspaper not further identified. Clipping file, Caraganis Collection, Chilton Library, Norwich University, Northfield, VT.

54 Remarks to the Class of 1965, U.S. Military Academy, West Point, NY, 18 January 1965, Abrams Speech File, MHI.

PART III:

Challenges and Changes

Introduction

At the time of this writing, the armed forces of the United States are heavily engaged in combat operations. Virtually the entire Army, which has borne the greatest burden in Afghanistan and Iraq, is in one stage of deployment or another. Americans so far have been enthusiastic in expressing their appreciation and support for the men and women in uniform. The fighting forces have vindicated those sentiments with extraordinary courage, sacrifice, and determination on the battlefield.

Regardless of the current situation, Americans traditionally have been ambivalent toward their military. On the one hand, Americans love winners, and for most of the nation's history the military has been a winner. On the other hand, they resent the burden of maintaining professional military forces, especially in peacetime. Moreover, they recoil from the regimentation, discipline, and autocracy of the military culture, which many consider out of step with the individualism of American society. Finally, they fear the potential threat of the military to civil liberties; it does not matter that the American military has an unblemished record of subordination to civilian authorities.

The views of Americans about West Point reflect their ambivalence toward the military. Since its founding in 1802, the Academy has been the target of critics who would change its mission, scope, focus, and organization; some would eliminate the institution altogether. The attacks started early, with particular vehemence during the presidency of Andrew Jackson. They have continued on and off ever since, most recently during the Army drawdown of the early 1990s. The chapters in this section provide a chronological sampling of some of the most contentious issues.

The conditions that generated attacks on the Academy were often external to West Point. As Robert Wetteman points out in his chapter, for example, West Point was an obvious target for Jacksonians who sought to root out special privilege in American society; to them, the Academy was a bastion of military elitism that favored the sons of the rich and powerful and threatened American liberties. At the other end of the chronological spectrum, Gerardo Meneses examines the challenges West Point faced following the first Gulf War. With the size of the armed forces decreasing, Congress seized the opportunity to impose a variety of reforms to reduce costs and streamline operations at the service academies. Viewing the measures as arbitrary and detrimental, Academy and Army leaders fought hard to temper them.

In some cases, conditions internal to the Academy caused problems. Donald Connelly, for example, examines the difficulties of eradicating indiscipline and abusive practices within the Corps of Cadets during the 1870s and 1880s. Frank Walton describes how the negative publicity of a hazing scandal shortly before the centennial undermined Academy interests in Congress. Finally, Brian Linn examines the consequences of the Academy's reluctance to upgrade the academic credentials of the teaching faculty in the early Cold War years.

Given the nature of the American political system, it is unlikely that attacks on West Point will ever cease. The Academy is more than just a first-rate academic institution; it is one of the most visible icons of the American military establishment. As such, it feels the push and pull of the competing political and personal agendas that vie in the arena of national policy-making. If the past is any indication of the future, however, West Point will emerge from each challenge stronger than before.

—Editor

⊰ CHAPTER 7 ⊱

WEST POINT, THE JACKSONIANS, AND THE ARMY'S CONTROVERSIAL ROLE IN NATIONAL IMPROVEMENTS

Robert P. Wettemann, Jr.

In November 1837, disgruntled former West Point cadet Ver Planck Van Antwerp took venom-dipped pen in hand and informed President Martin Van Buren that the "power and patronage thrown into the hands of officers of the Army" had cost fellow Indiana Democrats 2,000 votes in recent elections.[1] Much of the discord between the Jacksonians and the military stemmed from the 1824 General Survey Act, which took U.S. Army officers away from their regiments and, for the first time, authorized their employment on surveys for "such roads and canals as [the president] may deem of *national importance, in a commercial or military point of view.*"[2] Rife with promise, this act was not without fault. By allowing the president to define "national importance," the General Survey Act soon placed U.S. Military Academy graduates in a perilous crossfire between forces of privilege and emerging advocates of equality.[3]

By 1828, a more liberal definition of "national importance," coupled with the decision to employ Army officers on internal improvements projects, opened a new door of opportunity for critics of West Point and the officers it produced. Officers were no longer regarded as purely military men, commanding companies of soldiers in the field, but were cast as agents of private enterprise, directing companies bent on returning profits to their shareholders. With this in mind, the Jacksonian attacks on the Academy must be considered in light of social, political, and economic issues as well as the military motives, specifically the creation of an aristocratic officer corps and what role it would perform. Recognizing the crucial role played by West Point graduates in national development under the Survey Act, Jacksonian Democrats portrayed former cadets not only as recipients of this new-found privilege, but also as being responsible for its extension to select segments of American society that benefited from a burgeoning list of internal improvements projects directed, at least in part, by the U.S. Army. West Point, Democratic critics argued, had become little more than a school in behalf of special interests. As self-regarded representatives of the people, the Democrats saw it as their duty to restore equality to the United States.

The immediate political goals of the Jacksonians were met by the limitation of officer employment on private projects imposed by the 1838 repeal of the General Survey Act and the extension of Academy graduates' service commitment from one to four years. This prohibition had other, ultimately more beneficial consequences as well. Limiting the work of U.S. Military Academy graduates to more clearly defined martial duties also contributed to a growing sense of military accountability to civilian leadership that developed while the U.S. Army struggled to find a peacetime role.

Accepting President James Monroe's offer for him to serve as Secretary of War, John C. Calhoun wrote that "I was actuated by a strong desire to contribute as much as possible to the publick prosperity, by giving our military establishment the strongest utility and perfection."[4] Having witnessed firsthand the desolation of a destroyed national capitol in the wake of the War of 1812, Calhoun took action to ensure that such indignities would not be repeated. Central to these efforts was recognition of a need for a peacetime military establishment and the reorganization of the Military Academy into the nation's premier engineering school. By supporting a scientifically trained officer corps, Calhoun (and his successors) would have at their disposal a skilled cadre of engineers that could assist in the development of roads and canals to promote economic development and provide for a more effective national defense.[5] While President Madison had vetoed Calhoun's Bonus Bill in 1816, the South Carolinian still harbored designs of a national system of internal improvements as an adjunct to a standing Army, and in his new position as Secretary of War planned to use a reduced standing force to achieve these ends. On 30 April 1824, Calhoun's hopes were fulfilled (at least in part) when the General Survey Act was passed, permitting the employment of U.S. Army officers on internal improvements surveys.[6] With the 1821 military reduction in force providing an "expansible" skeleton Army with a disproportionate number of officers, the handful of supernumerary officers each regiment retained could be put to good use for the benefit of the entire nation.[7]

Embracing nationalistic ideals but conscious of the political dangers potentially associated with using Army officers in nonmartial roles, Calhoun cautioned that troops (and by implication their officers) should be employed only on projects "of a military character," lest their actions "give rise to unpleasant [political] reflections."[8] His final departmental report, issued six months after the Survey Act's passage, echoed these views. The secretary opined that the work of officers on internal improvements must not only benefit "the whole Union" but should "bind all of the parts [of the republic] together . . . thereby facilitating commerce and intercourse among the States, enabling the Government . . . to extend protection to the whole."[9]

Less than one year after the passage of the Survey Act, John Quincy Adams became president, defeating Andrew Jackson through the contentious "Corrupt Bargain" of 1824, in which Henry Clay threw his support behind Adams in return for appointment as secretary of state. A pragmatic politician might have recognized a lack of political consensus and used his skills to broaden a base of support. The uncompromising Adams did not, however, and proceeded to wreck his presidency on the horns of the American System, the combination of protective tariff, internal improvements, and national bank devised by Henry Clay to promote national growth in the wake of the War of 1812. In utilizing the General Survey Act to promote seemingly unfettered national development, Adams's actions would have profound repercussions on West Point, the Army officer corps, and the U.S. military establishment.[10]

Although recognizing that "great powers" were "liable to great abuses," Adams did not limit federal projects undertaken by the government.[11] Observing that the "roads and aqueducts of Rome have been the admiration of all," Adams, a nationalist of stature equal to that of now-Secretary of State Henry Clay, decided that comparable monuments would benefit the American republic. Though there was "some diversity" of opinion regarding federal power over roads and canals, Adams hoped the "practical public blessing" of internal improvements would work for "the common satisfaction of all," and he prosecuted the General Survey Act to the utmost.[12] Ignoring words of caution, including those offered by his own vice president, John C. Calhoun, Adams saw virtually every project as nationally important and employed Army officers in unprecedented numbers, actions that caused discord when the Survey Act appropriation bills reached Congress.[13]

From the outset, many who would ultimately fall in behind the Democratic banner challenged the measure as an unfair extension of government favor. Virginia Congressman William Rives claimed that the "radically vicious" Survey Act led to a "*disproportionate increase of prerogative and patronage*," where none had existed before. He argued that Army officers spread privilege by their mere presence, as they represented "the vast fiscal power and resources of this Government." When they appeared, "we embrace the mere phantoms of hope" that a survey would lead to an internal improvement, hopes that connected loosely defined "national" surveys with (as Rives saw it) the transparent efforts of the Adams administration to bribe the electorate. For evidence, Rives cited a series of obscure surveys in New England, calling for the "prompt application of prophylactics" to stop such practices.[14]

Likewise, William Smith of South Carolina saw "ample field for governmental patronage," accusing the administration of embracing the opportunity to use the General Survey Act to deploy military engineers with the express goal of "buy[ing] the people with their own money." Nor was West Point safe from Smith's vitriol. If internal improvements were halted, he alleged, the "sons of members of Congress, and the sons of their friends and favorites" could no longer be educated at the expense of the government, given commissions, "high pay," and "additional pay as engineers . . . for amusing themselves through the country."[15]

Senator Thomas Hart Benton criticized Adams's loose definition of "national" improvements, as the routes originally designated by Calhoun had "rapidly degenerated from national to sectional, from sectional to local, and from local to mere neighborhood improvements." He offered the most recent list of routes prepared by the Corps of Engineers that included "places hardly heard of before outside of the state or section in which they were found." These included sites like Saugatuck, Amounisuck, Pasumic, Winnispiseogee, and nearly a dozen others of equal obscurity. While the General Survey Act had been designed with an eye towards national defense and promoting domestic prosperity, these new surveys, in Benton's view, represented little more than a "condemnation of the act under which they were selected."[16]

To a certain degree, these critics were correct. By the end of Adams's first term, officers employed under the Survey Act were supervising 45 different building projects and 20 "incipient surveys . . . promotive of the public interest," designed to "assist the labors, increase the comforts, and enhance the enjoyments of individuals throughout the United States.[17] But, as Benton correctly pointed out, many of these projects stretched a national definition to the extreme. It was this latitudinarian definition of "national," coupled with the continued employment of trained military engineers, that subjected the U.S. Army, and West Point, to increased Democratic scrutiny.

Seeking "reform . . . [and] the correction of those abuses that have brought the patronage of the Federal Government into conflict with the freedom of elections," opponents of the Adams administration had already begun rallying around Andrew Jackson. Shortly after the election of 1824, proponents of equality looked to the hero of New Orleans, hoping that he could deliver the nation from the forces of privilege and promote equity in government.[18] Not only would Jackson's election mark the dawn of a new era of American democracy, but it would lead to a dramatic shift in policy regarding national development, internal improvements, and the Military Academy.

By virtue of his victory over the British at New Orleans, many regarded Andrew Jackson as the ultimate example of the democratic citizen-soldier, regardless of the fact that he had served as one of the two principal generals in the Regular Army for seven years. In his first State of the Union address, he argued that not only did West Point-trained officers promote the "moral and intellectual character" of the regular Army, they provided an important adjunct to the common defense, as "their knowledge of the military art will be advantageously employed in the militia service," where it would be beneficial to all Americans[19]

Jackson's early views on internal improvements followed a commendatory vein. During his tenure as U.S. Senator, Jackson favored internal improvements to promote national military and economic strength.[20] This came with a certain caveat, one commonly embraced by early critics of the General Survey Act, for he considered such works a task for the states, where the people had the greatest input. Once in the White House, Jackson attacked the "flagicious *logg-rolling legislation*" embraced by his predecessor with a series of presidential vetoes.[21] A close examination of Jackson's vetoes reveals the consistent position that "all internal improvements funded by the national government" should be "opened to the enjoyment of all our fellow citizens." He rejected any union of the financial or corporate concerns of the federal government with those of the "States or individuals" as "inconsistent with [the nation's] institutions" and highly "impolitic."[22] This union of federal and private interests represented one of Andrew Jackson's greatest fears. If the federal government financed intrastate improvements like the Maysville Road—a measure that Jackson vetoed—or detailed officers to conduct surveys for state or private projects, these actions not only ran contrary to the notion that the "majority is to govern," but represented the extension of federal privilege to either an isolated locality or incorporated company. From Jackson's perspective, continued extension of patronage like the proposed federal financing of a state road wholly within Kentucky linking the communities of Maysville and Lexington would lead to "prejudice to the public interest or an alienation of the affectations to the general discredit" of government, a consequence dangerous to the liberties of the people.[23] In his view, federal aid should be limited to "those great leading and navigable streams from the ocean, *passing through two or more states*," and "obstruction[s] . . . which when removed will give an uninterrupted passage to those other states." If this definition was exceeded, he wrote to Martin Van Buren in 1830, "then every creek, or small river, emptying into a navigable stream . . . may claim to be survayed and improved at the national expence."[24]

Since 1824, the liberal attitudes of the Adams administration and the realization that West Point graduates held a monopoly over both military appointments and technical engineering skills had also changed Jackson's opinion on what he once called "the best school in the world." [25] Professing that "the bulwark of our national defense is the national militia," Jackson, like so many of his political allies, soon came to question the form and utility of the Military Academy, which had seemingly strayed from the Jeffersonian vision.[26] Not only did the automatic promotion of graduating cadets to brevet second lieutenant foster an apparent military aristocracy, but Jacksonian critics claimed a West Point education now led to a personal benefit from the public purse. This argument seemed more credible considering that cadets were required to serve only one year in uniform after graduating, and many served even less than that.

Moreover, Academy graduates' technical skills allowed them to extend privileges to those who employed military engineers on private and local improvement projects, as evidenced by a steady increase in the number officers detached to serve with one of the engineering branches during the Adams administration. In 1824, there were 18 line officers detached to engineering duty (3.3 percent of the officer corps), of whom 17 (3.1 percent) were engaged in topographical (surveying) projects. By 1829, the number detached to engineering duty had increased to 44 (8.1 percent), with 36 officers (6.6 percent of a total officer corps of 540 men) serving on topographical duty.[27] When considered in the light of the repeated calls for manpower for the direction of fortification construction by the Corps of Engineers, diverting line officers to civilian transportation projects clearly represented an extension of federal privilege by methods new to the republic.[28] Thus, while Old Hickory led a crusade against internal improvements, his political compatriots, increasingly aware of the absence of military officers from their regiments while they were employed on state, local, and private works, focused their enmity on the Military Academy, with Jackson himself joining in on a few occasions.

Considerable attention has been given to the Jacksonians' assault on West Point as an attempt to limit the growth of an American military aristocracy.[29] While this interpretation accurately depicts their intent, few scholars have examined those attacks in the context of the struggle over federal assistance for internal improvements. When examined more closely, another relationship between these phenomena is apparent. Not only were Academy graduates receiving the favors of the government, but, as noted above, in providing their expertise to internal improvement projects, they, at least in the eyes of the Jacksonians, extended federal patronage as well. To a president who believed that government must "shower its favors alike on the high and low, the rich and the poor," any extension of privilege, regardless of how small or seemingly insignificant, must be curtailed.[30]

This stance was echoed by like-minded members of Congress, who hoped to arrest the extension of federal favors before it threatened the equality on which American democracy was based. James Blair of South Carolina labeled the Military Academy as a "hot-bed of a military aristocracy perverted from its original and legitimate object, and change[d], by 'piecemeal' into what it is at present," an institution whose "patronage, favors, and benefit . . . were principally bestowed upon those least in need of them."[31] David Crockett of Tennessee resolved that the Academy should be abolished altogether, as it granted "exclusive privileges to its cadets," and was "a downright invasion of the rights of the citizens and a violation of the civil compact called 'the constitution.'" Cadets were after all "generally the sons of the rich and influential," while "the sons of the poor, for want of active friends, are often neglected."[32]

The attack on the military establishment did not cease with the tabling of Crockett's bold proffer. Starling Tucker of South Carolina focused his enmity against the Army, the Military Academy, and internal improvements, drawing all three together in a single, scathing drive for military reform. Citing a current War Department report on cadet applications and appointments between 1802 and 1829, he chastised what he viewed as the pernicious practice of educating officers at public expense, considering that the nation's greatest military hero, President Jackson, had no formal military training whatsoever.[33] Department records showed that 2,053 young men had been offered admission to West Point since its establishment in 1802. Of these, 1,655 actually entered the Academy, 591 graduated, and in 1830 only 361 remained in the Army. Citing current trends (though lacking a solid understanding of statistics), Tucker believed that "more than one half of the cadets who had been admitted" to the Academy, had, as "soon as they acquired sufficient education to answer their purposes," left the military to engage "in such profession as would best promote their private interest." The practice of providing engineering expertise for internal improvement projects led Tucker to pronounce West Point "the main prop for this deceptive name called the American System." Nor was Tucker enamored of the Army's Corps of Engineers, which served,

> to blind [the people] . . . and . . . get them to embrace this deceptive American system, with the vain and delusive idea that they are not only to have the public money distributed among them, but that all their watercourses are to be made navigable, their paths and highways made smooth and firm; that all their produce is to be sent to market, and every other facility afforded them that vain hope can imagine; and all this they call national.[34]

As president, Andrew Jackson sought equity in his military policy, confining survey projects to those of national significance, as outlined in his letter to Van Buren in 1830. Jackson wanted internal improvements to benefit all Americans, and to curtail the "pernicious consequence of a scramble for the favors of government" that had taken place under Adams.[35] Thus, military engineers continued conducting surveys for roads, canals, and railroads throughout Jackson's presidency, albeit on a limited basis. However, the engineers came under increased scrutiny as they continued to gain advantages from the exclusive opportunities made possible by a West Point education. With the Army barely absorbing each class of West Point graduates, the Academy became a lightning rod for Democratic criticism. Not only did the Jacksonians believe that the Academy was generating an aristocratic officer corps, but this "prop" for Clay's American System appeared to assist only those best able to secure political patronage for private gain. Surely, Democrats reasoned, permitting well-connected Academy graduates to undertake lucrative employment developing roads and canals for state governments and private companies while retaining the military rank and emoluments otherwise granted to officers of the line (the regiments of infantry, artillery, and dragoons), did not represent the most equitable promotion of the public prosperity.

With former West Point Superintendent Alden Partridge now labeling the Academy as the "idol and pet" of the political elite, Democrats in Congress launched another wave of attacks against privilege, West Point, the military establishment, and the practice of employing officers on internal improvements.[36] Conscious of a growing number of supernumerary officers (many of whom were employed by state and private companies in addition to their military duties), Charles Wickliffe of Kentucky complained that the "principle object" of Mr. Jefferson's institution was apparently lost. In his view, West Point was no longer a school to educate future officers in the military arts, it had become a free national academy, training civil engineers who went on to enjoy the pecuniary benefits of private employment. Harboring no objections to a national university, Wickliffe would have wanted one to be established openly, not disguised as something it was not. A far worse practice was the extension of federal privilege to the 250 young men annually selected to be cadets at the Military Academy who would "receive their education at public expense," and be paid $16 per month, only to have "three out of four of them return to their homes and pursue some [other] profession" upon graduation.[37] Although Wickliffe's statistics were, at best, an overstatement, he and other Jacksonians argued tellingly that the prevailing system did not represent the best allocation of "national" resources.[38]

Nor was the administration silent in the wake of these new allegations. In November 1831, Secretary of War Lewis Cass ordered that officers "absent from their military duties . . . and engaged in any employment" not under direction of the War Department return to their regiments.[39] Possibly issued at President Jackson's request, the order was a reaction to an earlier report from Cass's predecessor showing 140 officers detached from their regiments for staff or other duties, with 57 absent on furlough. Thirty of the detached officers were with the engineers: eight with the Corps supervising fortification construction and 22 on topographical duty.[40]

Cass's order represented part of a two-pronged attempt to apply the equalitarian principles of the Jacksonian Democrats to the operations of the Army engineers. First, ordering all officers on detached duty back to their regiments struck a blow in behalf of reducing the large number of supernumerary officers (the brevet second lieutenants) maintained on the Army register since Calhoun's 1821 reduction in force. By forcing officers back to their regiments, the duties being carried out by supernumerary officers (whom the Jacksonians considered superfluous) would be carried out by regimental officers. This practice would eliminate the need for the extra officers produced by West Point, thereby promoting economy, frugality, and small government, since the size of this "privileged" institution could be reduced. Second, the principles outlined in the Maysville Veto were applied to War Department engineers. By limiting the extension of military assistance to truly national projects, the work of military engineers would be strictly curtailed. In the future, the secretary of war could limit their operations to three classes of *national* projects: surveys "directed by resolutions of Congress," incomplete surveys, and finally those surveys "requisite to ascertain the military peculiarities of our frontier and for position of fortifications."[41]

Two years later, the War Department issued an additional call to end the exclusive opportunities enjoyed by West Point graduates and return them to nationally beneficial martial duties as favored by President Jackson. In May 1833, Cass limited Academy graduates' opportunities for staff duty. To prevent young officers from leaving the Army prior to the end of their one-year commitment to pursue employment on civilian projects, Cass tried to confine their services to their regiments. His order specified that no officer would be "allowed to fill any Staff appointment . . . until he has served at least three years with his regiment," with specific reference to engineer and topographical officers.[42]

Midway through his second term, Andrew Jackson seemed to be winning the war against perceived privilege on many fronts.[43] While it appeared that the Maysville Veto and Jackson's rejection of subsequent internal improvement measures would cause the favors of government to fall equally upon all Americans, Democrats believed that the Army continued to receive and extend federal privilege. Despite Congressional outcries, West Point remained the primary source for new Army officers, although a number of civilians were posted to the new mounted regiments. Moreover, the Corps of Engineers and the Bureau of Topographical Engineers, not to mention officers of the line detached for staff duty, continued to aid states and private companies on engineering projects, and others resigned after only a brief period in uniform to seek their fortunes.[44]

Democrats therefore continued their attacks on the Academy. Observing in 1834 that "West Point as it was" was not the same as "West Point as it is," New Hampshire Democratic Congressman Franklin Pierce advocated ending what he saw as a blatant abuse of privilege by reorganizing the institution. He proposed transforming the Academy into a school for practice and application for Army officers, "not an institution for educating, gratuitously, young gentlemen, who . . . resign their commissions and return to the pursuits of civil life." Under Pierce's plan, West Point would still educate future officers, but only in the skills necessary to command militia in the field. As we have seen, following Thayer's revitalization of the institution, the Academy began to graduate officers with engineering skills who, in many cases, applied their expertise on internal improvement projects that neither contributed directly to the defense of the United States nor were associated with military service. Having observed this development, Pierce believed that the Academy had "outlived . . .

its original design," and he would refuse to "appropriate the first dollar" for its upkeep.[45]

While Congressional Democrats targeted the Academy, Jackson's focus remained on the officer corps. In June 1836 Secretary Cass repeated his order for officers on detached duty to return to their regiments, specifically naming 37 junior officers, 25 of whom were on engineering or topographical duty.[46] When this order was ignored, the president took more concerted action to force Army officers to perform his vision of military duty. General Order No. 69, issued on 13 October 1836, contained a forcefully worded message straight from Jackson's pen. The recently initiated Second Seminole War demanded officers of the line for active service in the field, and the old general now pronounced that an officer's duty was commanding men in battle, not taking jobs that separated them from their troops. To these ends, Jackson ordered the line officers "not on duty with their companies" to "immediately . . . join their regiments." Not only did he list officers absent on engineering duty, but he specified that in the future, no more than two officers from an artillery company and one from an infantry company would be simultaneously detailed for detached duty.[47]

These orders did not solve the problem completely; despite his best efforts, Old Hickory was ultimately unable to halt the privileges extended by the Survey Act. When sworn in as president, Martin Van Buren offered very few words regarding the status of the Army, its military engineers, and the internal improvements debate. Instead, the drafter of Jackson's Maysville Veto announced his guiding principle to be simply the "strict adherence to the letter and spirit of the Constitution as it was designed by those who framed it."[48]

However, on 5 July 1838, President Van Buren signed the "Act to Increase the Present Military Establishment of the United States, and for Other Purposes," and two days later supplemental legislation put an end to military efforts conceived to promote public prosperity. The act expanded the rank and file of the U.S. Army, adding 16 privates to each artillery company and 38 men to each company of infantry, making these units more combat-effective. At the same time, Van Buren increased the size and pay of the Corps of Engineers, reorganized the Topographic Corps, placing it on an equal footing with the Engineers and fulfilling a call for more engineer officers heard since 1825. As popularly perceived, these two legislative initiatives represented a triumph of Jacksonian egalitarianism and democracy over the forces of privilege, patronage, and military elitism, for they ultimately struck a death blow at the links between West Point, engineering, and private enterprise that Democrats opposed.[49]

Increasing the size of the companies was intended to help force officers detached from their regiments to return to field duty, as these men were now needed to command additional troops. Raising the pay for engineer officers worked to keep talented officers in the Army, a task made easier by the 1837 economic crisis that halted many internal improvements projects. But that was not the most significant change regarding privileges heretofore extended to West Point graduates, for the new law now required officers to serve for a longer term after graduation from the Military Academy. Beginning in 1838, any Academy graduate would serve in the Army for four years after commissioning, an amount of time equal to that which they spent at West Point.

By the stroke of a president's pen, cadets were no longer educated at public expense and then given opportunities, as Lt. George Cullum phrased it, to "doff their chapeau" to pursue civilian employment. Now, officers educated at West Point would reimburse the nation through service to it, another factor contributing to a growing sense of accountability ascribed to officers by other scholars of the period.[50] At the same time, the loopholes in the Survey Act permitting the employment of officers by state and private companies were closed. By prohibiting officers from working on civilian internal improvement projects, and preventing them from aiding corporations while still in uniform, the Jacksonians dissolved any union between the national government and private companies, an arrangement that Jackson had decried since the Maysville Veto.[51]

Traditional histories of the U.S. Military Academy contend that attacks on West Point during the Jackson administration were simply an attack on privilege by the forces of equality. Jacksonians extolled the virtues of the common man exercising the citizen-soldier tradition, and their rhetoric chastised the aristocratic tendencies of the Academy, its graduates' near monopoly over appointments and promotions, and the anti-egalitarian nature of military service. However, to view the attacks on West Point strictly in these terms overlooks the role played by Academy graduates in the development of the American economy, particularly the actions of Army officers under the terms of the General Survey Act. A closer examination of President John Quincy Adams's definition of "national" internal improvements and the myriad opportunities for employment made available to scientifically trained Army officers gives new significance to this struggle between privilege and equality. Not only was West Point considered the source of a privileged officer corps, but, under the General Survey Act, it became an instrument to promote Clay's American System, with Army officers extending federal patronage to those best able to secure the favors of the national government.

Thus, the attacks on privilege that began with Jackson's Maysville Veto and ended with the 1838 repeal of the Survey Act must be viewed in conjunction with Congressional attacks on West Point, repeated orders for officers to return to their regiments, the prohibition of Army officers from working for private companies, and the statute requiring West Point-trained officers to serve four years in the Army. These actions were designed not only to limit the extension of federal privilege, but, in doing so, were central to defining the peacetime role of the U.S. military establishment and contributing to a growing sense of military accountability to civilian leadership. In the future, the U.S. Military Academy, and the officers it produced, would be charged with serving and securing *all* Americans, not just promoting prosperity for a privileged few.

---

[1] Ver Planck Van Antwerp to Van Buren, 20 November 1837, roll 25, Lucy Fisher West, ed., *Papers of Martin Van Buren*, 55 rolls (Alexandria, VA: Chadwick-Healey, 1987). Originally from Albany, New York, Ver Plank was "well reported" in the "U.S. Military Academy Cadet Application Papers, 1805-1866," M2037, roll 1, Records of the Adjutant General's Office, RG 94, National Archives and Records Administration (hereafter referred to as NARA). A J. P. Van Antwerp of New York is listed in the roster of cadets accepted to West Point in 1823 that appeared in "History of the Military Academy," 1 March 1837, *Ameri-*

can State Papers: Military Affairs, 7 vols. (Washington, DC: Gales and Seaton, 1832-61), 7: 33 (hereafter referred to as ASP:MA). Thomas H.S.Hamersly, *Complete Regular Army Register, 1779-1879* (Washington, DC: T.H.S. Hamersly, 1880), 236, notes that a cadet of the same name was accepted to West Point from New York in 1823, but did not graduate. Van Antwerp was accepted into the Academy the same year as Abraham Van Buren (the future president's son), which might explain the connection between the two New Yorkers. Marcus Cunliffe, *Soldiers and Civilians: The Martial Spirit in America, 1775-1865* (New York: Little, Brown and Co., 1968), 275, characterizes Van Antwerp as a "Western Democrat" based largely upon his condemnation of the language used by engineer Capt. Cornelius A. Ogden and his Indiana patrons in describing the Jacksonians: "The terms 'Mobocracy,' 'vulgar rabble,' 'ignorant herd,' etc. etc. are as common among these gentlemen as household words; and I venture to assert that three of them can not be got together, at any time and place, and the subject introduced, without there escaping from at least two of them, as applied to the name of Mr. Jefferson, the epithet 'd——d demagogue,' 'mobocrat,' or something equally complimentary; while those of 'd——d old fool,' 'scoundrel,' etc. etc. will just as certainly be appended to that of General Jackson." Van Antwerp closed his letter to the president by proposing that the Military Academy be forced to "stand upon its own footing and merits, without aid or praise from who it is the pride of the Democratic party to honor." As far as he was concerned, "the institution not only is not a favorite, but in my opinion, it does not deserve to be one with the people."

[2] "An Act to Procure the Necessary Surveys, Plans and Estimates upon the Subject of Roads and Canals," *Statutes at Large* (1824), 4: 22-23. Emphasis added.

[3] Framing "Jacksonian Democracy" in the context of the struggle between privilege and equality is not new. Other historians have relied upon similar themes to explain the political, economic, and social developments of the period, but in doing so have generally neglected any part played by the U.S. Army and its officer corps. See Arthur Schlesinger, Jr., *The Age of Jackson* (New York: Little, Brown and Co., 1945); Bray Hammond, *Banks and Politics in America: From the Revolution to the Civil War* (Princeton, NJ: Princeton University Press, 1957); Richard Hofstadter, *The American Political Tradition and the Men Who Made It* (New York: Alfred A. Knopf, 1948); Marvin Meyers, *The Jacksonian Persuasion: Politics and Belief* (Stanford, CA.: Stanford University Press, 1957); John Ashworth, *'Agrarians' and 'Aristocrats': Party Political Ideology in the United States, 1837-1846* (Cambridge: Cambridge University Press, 1987); Lawrence F. Kohl, *The Politics of Individualism: Parties and American Character in the Jacksonian Era* (New York: Oxford University Press, 1989); Harry L. Watson, *Liberty and Power: The Politics of Jacksonian America* (New York: Hill and Wang, 1990), 8, 9, 135. The use of the Market Revolution to present Jacksonian Democracy as an egalitarian challenge to the forces of privilege culminated in 1991 with Charles Sellers's publication of *The Market Revolution: Jacksonian America, 1815-1846* (New York: Oxford University Press, 1991). The transportation revolution was central to Sellers's synthesis, which connects the economic changes of the Jacksonian Era with the concurrent political transformations of the era. Sellers argues that the national discourse in the decades following the War of 1812 centered around how politicians tried to answer three principal questions. First, how democratic—how responsive to popular majorities—would government be? Second, would government power become extensive and concentrated at the federal level or limited and diffuse among the states? And, finally, to what extent and in what ways would both the federal and state governments promote economic growth? Central to answering these questions was the role played by John Calhoun and the military establishment. Sellers briefly explains that by modeling West Point on the French École

Polytechnique, Calhoun provided the nation with a source of military engineers to explore and map the frontier, survey rivers and harbors, and "provide free engineering services for transportation improvements by the states or state-chartered corporations" (83-84).

[4] John C. Calhoun to General Gen. Jacob Brown, 17 December 1817, *The Papers of John C. Calhoun*, 23 vols., ed. Robert L. Meriwether (Columbia, SC: University of South Carolina Press, 1959-96),1: 22-23 (hereafter referred to as *Calhoun Papers*). During the course of the War of 1812, Calhoun, a former War Hawk Congressman, had seen firsthand the devastation an enemy could bring to a city, having returned to a national capital left in ruin by the British in 1814. In the post-war period, he aligned himself with members of the 14th Congress who promoted a national bank, protective tariff, and system of internal improvements to enhance economic development in the United States. In future years, Henry Clay would refer to this as the "American System." See Sellers, *Market Revolution*, 70-103. The orthography of Calhoun, Andrew Jackson, and other public figures of the period was often colorful by modern standards. In quotations from these figures, their original spelling is preserved intact without further notice.

[5] Calhoun first expressed his hopes for a national system of roads and canals in his "Speech on Internal Improvements," 4 February 1817, ibid., 1: 403.

[6] "An Act to Procure the Necessary Surveys, Plans and Estimates upon the Subject of Roads and Canals," *Statutes at Large* (1824), 4: 22-23. This act was passed in conjunction with others conceived for improving harbors, and providing for stock purchases in the Chesapeake and Delaware Canal Company. See also "An Act to authorize the building of light-houses, light-vessels, and beacons, therein mentioned, and for other purposes," a bill of lesser scope, ibid., 3: 780-81; and "An Act authorizing the subscription of stock in the Chesapeake and Delaware Canal Company," ibid., 4: 124.

[7] See Roger J. Spiller, "Calhoun's Expansible Army: The History of a Military Idea," *South Atlantic Quarterly* 79 (Spring 1980): 189-203. Although the reduction of 1821 did not truly create an expansible Army as Calhoun had originally envisioned, the retention of supernumerary officers in each of the Army's regiments made the General Survey Act a possibility. With only a captain and the first and second lieutenants necessary for the command of a company of 42 men (with actual company strength frequently much lower), the potential certainly existed for supernumerary officers (usually junior officers recently graduated from West Point and holding a brevet rank) beyond the aforementioned three called for by regulation to be employed elsewhere.

[8] Calhoun to Jacob Brown, 22 September 1819, Meriwether, ed., *Calhoun Papers*, 4: 342.

[9] By the end of his tenure, four clearly national projects were under the supervision of U.S. Army engineer officers: the survey of the Chesapeake and Ohio Canal; connecting the Ohio River with Lake Erie via canal; a canal uniting the bays of the North Atlantic states; and a national road from Washington to New Orleans. "Condition of the Military Establishment and the Fortifications," ASP:MA, 2: 699.

[10] Mary W.M. Hargreaves, *The Presidency of John Quincy Adams* (Lawrence: University Press of Kansas, 1985), 20. Throughout his presidency, Adams struggled to achieve moral perfection and exercise conscientious civic leadership, efforts frequently undertaken at the expense of practical politics. See Paul C. Nagel, *John Quincy Adams: A Public Life, a Private Life* (New York: Alfred A. Knopf, 1997), the first biography to utilize Adams's manuscript diary. See also Marie B. Hecht, *John Quincy Adams: A Personal History of an Independent Man* (Newtown, CT.: American Political Biography Press, 1972).

[11] Charles Francis Adams, ed., *Memoirs of John Quincy Adams*, 12 vols. (Philadelphia: J.B. Lippincott, 1874-77), 6: 451-52.

[12] Ibid., 2: 298-99.

[13] In correspondence with Gen. Joseph G. Swift, Calhoun observed that the actions of the administration appeared to be those conducted "by a few ambitious men with a view to their own interest." As a result, he looked to the next four years with "deepest discontent." Calhoun to General Joseph G. Swift, 10 March 1825, *Calhoun Papers*, 10: 9-10.

[14] *Register of Debates*, 19th Cong., 2nd Sess., 3: 1275. Emphasis in the original.

[15] Ibid., 20th Cong., 1st Sess., 4: 634-43.

[16] Benton also listed Piscataqua, Titonic Falls, Lake Memphramagog, Conneaut Creek, Holmes' Hole, Lovejoy's Narrows, Steele's Ledge, Cowhegan, Androscoggin, Cobbiesconte, and Ponceaupechaux, alias Soapy Joe. See Thomas Hart Benton, *Thirty Years' View; or, A History of the Workings of the American Government for Thirty Years, from 1820 to 1850* (New York: D. Appleton and Co., 1854), 26.

[17] John Quincy Adams, "Fourth Annual Message," 2 December 1828, *A Compilation of the Messages and Papers of the Presidents, 1789-1902*, 10 vols., ed. James D. Richardson (Washington, DC: Government Printing Office, 1904), 2: 416-17.

[18] Andrew Jackson, First Inaugural Address, 4 March 1829, ibid., 2: 438. Emphasis in the original.

[19] Jackson, First Annual Message, 8 December 1829, *Messages and Papers of the Presidents*, 2: 456.

[20] Jackson to President James Monroe, 26 July 1822, *The Papers of Andrew Jackson*, 5 vols., eds. Harold D. Moser et al. (Knoxville: University of Tennessee, 1980-present), 5: 207-08.

[21] Jackson to John Overton, 31 December 1829, *The Correspondence of Andrew Jackson*, 6 vols., ed. John Spencer Bassett (Washington, DC: Carnegie Institution of Washington, 1926-35), 4: 109. Emphasis in the original. Jackson is once reported to have said that "it is a damned poor mind indeed that can't think of at least two ways of spelling any word." Consequently, the colorful spellings he frequently utilized in personal correspondence have been preserved. See note 4 above.

[22] For a detailed discussion of Jackson's vetoes, see Carlton Jackson, "The Internal Improvements Vetoes of Andrew Jackson," *Tennessee Historical Quarterly* 25 (Fall 1996): 261-80, although the present chapter challenges Jackson's assessment as to the "inconsistency" of Jackson's relationship to internal improvements. Quoted passages are found in Jackson, Second Annual Message, 6 December 1830, *Messages and Papers of the Presidents*, 2: 508-10. For other comparable messages, see Jackson, Veto Message, 27 May 1830, ibid., 2: 483-85.

[23] Second Annual Message, 6 December 1830, ibid., 2: 510.

[24] Jackson to Martin Van Buren, 18 October 1830, *Correspondence of Andrew Jackson*, 4: 185-86. Emphasis in the original.

[25] Jackson to Andrew Jackson Donelson, 5 March 1823, ibid., 3: 190-91.

[26] Andrew Jackson, "Inaugural Address," 4 March 1829, Richardson, ed., *Messages and Papers of the Presidents*, 2: 438.

[27] Beginning with the ten lieutenants detailed to the brigades of Maj. John J. Abert and Capt. William Gibbs McNeill in May 1824, the vigorous prosecution of the General Survey Act by the Adams administration resulted in not only a greater number of

internal improvements surveys, but also in an increase of the number of line officers detached from their regiments and ordered to temporary staff duty with the Corps of Engineers and the Topographical Engineers. As authorized by law, only ten officers (six majors and four captains) were authorized to serve with the Topographical Engineers, a "bureau" administratively subordinate to the Corps of Engineers. In light of the ever-increasing operations called for by the Board of Internal Improvements, it became necessary to detach young officers educated at West Point from the line regiments and order them to serve as assistant engineers, a practice made possible by the 1821 Army reduction, which retained more officers in each company than absolutely necessary. While only seventeen17 junior officers were ordered to topographical duty in 1824, by 1829 their ranks had swelled to over twice that size, with 36 officers serving in 1829 (see Table 7-1 below). When considered in conjunction with those officers ordered to supervise the building of fortifications, this represented a considerable federal effort. Although the officers detailed to staff functions were, in most cases, often supernumerary officers (those maintained beyond the number designated by law), the Jacksonians' principal fear stemmed from their role in extending privilege to state and private companies. The young officers serving on surveying details soon found themselves engaged on fewer and fewer national projects, with these important endeavors gradually replaced by projects of regional and local concerns.

Year	1824	1825	1826	1827	1828	1829
Officer Corps (authorized)	540	540	540	540	540	540
Topographical Duty (Surveying)	17	25	30	29	35	36
Percent of Officer Corps	3.1	4.6	5.5	5.3	6.5	6.6
Engineering Duty (Fortification Construction/Supervision)	1	2	2	1	1	8
Percent of Officer Corps	0.2	0.4	0.4	0.2	0.2	1.5
Total Officers on Detached Duty	18	27	32	30	36	44
Percentage of Officer Corps	3.3	5.0	5.9	5.5	6.6	8.1

Table 7-1. Line Officers Detached to Engineering Duty, 1824-1829.

[28] Although an independent Topographical Corps bureau had been established previously in 1832, manpower for this organization in the face of state and private companies seeking assistance left the Corps unable to function effectively. In April 1836, Col. John J. Abert offered Secretary of War Lewis Cass a litany of reasons as to why the bureau could not fulfill a request for a simple road survey proposed by Whig Representative William Ashley of Missouri. The bureau, Abert wrote, was composed of only 10 officers, to which was attached "a few" civilian engineers, and from "25-30 officers of the Artillery and Infantry." Thus, the "emergencies of the service from the disturbances in Florida" necessitated that the "great body of assistants" return to their regiments, leaving the bureau with inadequate means to make any additional surveys. Abert to Cass, 27 April 1836, Letters Sent, Topographical Bureau, M66, roll 2, RG 77, NARA.

[29] See Leonard D. White, *The Jacksonians: A Study in Administrative History, 1829-1861* (New York: Macmillan Co., 1954), 208-12. White views the Jacksonian attack as an expression of the "great currents of opinion that prevailed" during the period, caused by "old distrust of a standing army and a democratic resentment at what was alleged to be an aristocratical institution." Cunliffe, *Soldiers and Civilians*, 106-11, considers the employment of Academy graduates on internal improvements in only constitutional terms, as cited by the 1840 West Point Board of Visitors report. Stephen E. Ambrose, "The Jacksonians and the Academy," in *Duty, Honor Country: A History of West Point* (Baltimore: Johns Hopkins Press, 1966), 106-24, recognizes the important contribution made by West Point trained engineers, but his analysis stops there, as he fails to link Jacksonian views on privilege and equality, internal improvements, and the Military Academy. William Skelton, *An American Profession of Arms:The Army Officer Corps, 1784-1861* (Lawrence: University Press of Kansas, 1992), 134, 138, 142-43, reviews the criticism of the Academy and the question of civilian appointments both to the Academy and to the Army, but only as they relate to the growth of military professionalism. Sellers's *Market Revolution* has shaped much of the discourse on Jacksonian America, but aside from addressing Secretary Calhoun's efforts to revitalize the Military Academy and take advantage of its graduates to develop a network of internal improvements, relatively little is offered on the form and function of "privilege" in the Jacksonian-era military establishment.

[30] Jackson, Veto Message, 10 July 1832, *Messages and Papers of the Presidents*, 3: 590.

[31] *Register of Debates*, 21st Cong., 1st Sess., 6: 551-54.

[32] Ibid., 21st Cong., 1st Sess., 6: 583-84. During the winter of 1818, Crockett successfully ran for the colonelcy of the Franklin County, Tennessee, militia. He answered to the title of "Colonel" for the remainder of his life. See William C. Davis, *Three Roads to the Alamo: The Lives and Fortunes of David Crockett, James Bowie and William Barret Travis* (New York: Harper Collins, 1998), 67-69.

[33] See "Applications and Appointments as Cadets at the Military Academy at West Point from its Establishment to 1829, and the Annual and General Expenses of the Same During that time," ASP:MA, 4: 307-364.

[34] Ibid., 21st Cong., 1st Sess., 6: 808-10.

[35] Jackson, Sixth Annual Message, 1 December 1834, *Messages and Papers of the Presidents*, 3: 122.

[36] Americanus [Alden Partridge], *The Military Academy at West Point Unmasked or Corruption and Military Despotism Exposed* (Washington, DC: J. Elliott, 1830), 1, Thayer Papers, USMA.

[37] *Register of Debates*, 21st Cong., 2nd Sess., 7: 522-527.

[38] Wickliffe certainly overstated his case. Recognizing that 260 cadets were allowed to be enrolled in the Military Academy in any given year, he was, however, misinformed in implying that three out of every four left the army for civilian employment shortly after their appointments. In 1831, 40 graduates were expected to graduate from the institution and be commissioned. Considering that in that same year, 18 officers resigned their commissions, even if all 18 who resigned were junior officers, Wickliffe was exaggerating. Even if Wickliffe was speaking of *all* Academy graduates, the statistics cited previously by Starling Tucker indicated only a 60 percent attrition rate, not 75 as cited by Wickliffe.

[39] Order No. 63, 15 November 1831, Orderly Book, Entry 128, vol. 2, RG 77, NARA.

[40] "Statement of the Number and Rank of Officers of the Army on Duty in the Line, Staff, or Detached Service, and Those Absent on Furlough," 8 February 1831, ASP:MA, 4:

683-86. The detached officers were all on orders from the War Department or its subordinate bureaus and regiments, mostly detailed to ordnance and recruiting duty, but a number of those on furlough were employed by state and private transportation companies in addition to their military duties.

[41] Abert to Cass, 3 February 1832, Letters Sent, Topographical Bureau, M 66, roll 1, RG 77, NARA.

[42] Order No. 48, 18 May 1833, General Orders and Circulars, M 1094, roll 3, RG 94, NARA.

[43] By halting Calhoun's efforts to nullify the Tariffs of 1828 and 1832, Jackson had prevented the minority from exerting its will over the majority. Similarly, his "Killing" of the Second Bank of the United States through the removal of deposits to his "Pet Banks" had ended the bank's monopoly over foreign and domestic exchange, ensuring that the favors of government would be more equitable.

[44] Between the beginning of the Jacksonian attacks on the Academy in 1830 and the repeal of the Survey Act in 1838, more than 300 officers resigned from the Army, as follows:

Years	Number of Resignations	Percent
1830	15	4.6
1831	18	5.6
1832	23	7.1
1833	37	11.5
1834	14	4.3
1835	33	10.2
1836	111	34.7
1837	44	13.6
1838	27	8.4
Total	322	100.0

Table 7-2. Officer Resignations, 1830-1838.

After 1838, a number of factors came together to dramatically reduce the numbers of officers resigning from the military annually (only 65 resignations took place between 1839 and 1844: 22 in 1839, 13 in 1840, 10 in 1841 and 1842, 4 in 1843 and 6 in 1844). Although military service in the Second Seminole War continued to be onerous duty, the onset of the Panic of 1837 and the repeal of the General Survey Act limited most other opportunities for civil employment, forcing most officers to remain in uniform, and thereby ending the "resignation crisis." Of those who did resign, most did so early in their career before coming to accept emerging notions of military professionalism as indicated in the table below. These early departures provided yet more grist for the mills of the Democratic critics of the Military Academy.

Years as Commissioned Officer	Number of Resignations	Percent
One or less	81	21.4
Two to Five	121	32.0
Six to Ten	77	20.4
Eleven to Fifteen	44	11.6
Sixteen to Twenty	27	7.1
Twenty-one to Twenty-five	21	5.6
Twenty-six or more	7	1.9

Table 7-3. Officer Resignations by Time Served, 1830-1844.

[45] *Register of Debates*, 24th Cong., 1st Sess., 12: 4574-76.

[46] General Order No. 43, 28 June 1836, General Orders and Circulars, M1094, roll 4, RG 94, NARA. The following officers were ordered to return to their regiments from engineer duty: Lt. James Allen, First Dragoons; Lt. Louis A.D. Walbach, First Artillery; Lts. Harrison Loughborough and William McKee, Third Artillery; Lts. Alfred Brush, Franklin E. Hunt, and Raphael C. Smead, Fourth Artillery; Lts. Thomas B. Stockton and Jonathan K. Greenough, First Infantry; Lt. Thomas Stockton, Fifth Infantry; Capt. Henry Smith, and Lts. Albemarle Cady and Jonathan Freeman, Sixth Infantry; Lt. George W. Cass, Seventh Infantry. The following officers were ordered to return to their regiments from topographical duty: Lts. Edwin Rose and Edward White, Third Artillery; Lts. Joseph E. Johnston and John N. Macomb, Fourth Artillery; Lt. James Cooper, Third Infantry; Lts. Alexander Center and John M. Berrien, Fifth Infantry; Lt. Thomas Drayton, Sixth Infantry; Lts. Roger S. Dix, Seneca Simmons, and James G. Reed, Seventh Infantry. The following officers were ordered to return to their respective regiments from Indian duty: Lt. Isaac P. Simonton, First Dragoons; Lts. Joseph W. Harris and George G. Meade, Third Artillery; Lts. Francis L. Jones and Edward Deas, Fourth Artillery; Lt. Julius J. Kingsbury, Second Infantry; Lt. Jefferson Van Horne, Third Infantry; Capt. John B.F. Russell, Fifth Infantry; Capt. Jacob Brown, Sixth Infantry. Bvt. Maj. Thomas C. Legate of the First Dragoons, Lt. Alexander D. Mackay of the First Artillery, and Lt. Robert H.K. Whitely of the Second Artillery were also ordered to return from detached duty at the federal lead mine, the U.S. coast survey, and from the Ordnance Corps, respectively.

[47] General Order No. 69, 15 October 1836, General Orders and Circulars, M1094, roll 4, RG 94, NARA.

[48] Martin Van Buren, Inaugural Address, 4 March 1837, *Messages and Papers of the Presidents*, 3: 319.

[49] "An Act to Increase the Present Military Establishment of the United States, and for Other Purposes," 5 July 1838, and "An Act Supplemental to the Act to Increase the Military Establishment of the United States, and for Other Purposes," 7 July 1838, in Callan, *Military Laws of the United States*, 329-39, 340-41. Specifically, the act authorized increasing the Corps of Engineers by adding one lieutenant colonel, two majors, six captains, six first lieutenants, and six second lieutenants, to be paid the same as officers of the dragoon regiments. The act also organized the Corps of Topographical

Engineers on an equal footing, establishing a corps composed of one colonel, one lieutenant colonel, four majors, ten captains, ten first lieutenants, and ten second lieutenants, to be compensated identically to the Corps of Engineers.

[50] This action extended a cadet's overall service commitment from five to eight years. See "An Act to Increase the Military Establishment," 5 July 1838, Callan, *Military Laws of the United States*, 337. On military accountability to the civilian realm, see Samuel J. Watson, "Professionalism, Social Attitudes, and Civil-Military Accountability in the United States Army Officer Corps, 1815-1846," (Ph.D. diss., Rice University, 1996), 888-912, 1497-1527.

[51] See "An act to Increase the Military Establishment," 5 July 1838, Callan, *Military Laws of the United States*, 338.

CHAPTER 8

THE ROCKY ROAD TO REFORM: JOHN M. SCHOFIELD AT WEST POINT, 1876–1881

Donald B. Connelly

Between 1800 and 1900 the United States Army experienced dramatic swings in its size and the scope of its missions, yet the institutions and structure of the Army changed remarkably little. The road to military reform was pitted with numerous obstacles. The American military establishment largely reflected American constitutional principles of separation and division of powers amid the rough and tumble of partisan politics and factional infighting. During and after the Civil War, military policy was routinely contested in constitutional disputes between the Congress and the President and arguments over the role of the states and the federal government. The Army was the object of partisan political battles between Republicans and Democrats and regional quarrels between northerners and southerners, easterners and westerners. The Army itself was riven by disputes over the powers of the Secretary of War and the General-in-Chief, institutional struggles between the general staff and the commanding generals, and clashes within the officer corps over who would gain and who would lose by various "reforms."

At West Point, these conflicts were replicated in clashes between the Secretary, the Commanding General, and the Adjutant General;

between the superintendent, the Academic Board, and the Board of Visitors; and, perhaps most surprisingly, between the Academy leadership and the Corps of Cadets. In the late 1870s, a resurgent William T. Sherman hoped to remove military policy from politics and unify and reform the Army under the control of the Commanding General. Sherman enlisted his wartime subordinate, Maj. Gen. John M. Schofield, in this effort. As the Commander of the Department of West Point, Schofield became a pointman in Sherman's quest for reform of the Army and of West Point. The story of Schofield's hopes and frustrations, his successes and failures reveals much about the state of the Army, the Academy, and the nation in the latter half of the 19th century.

With the election of Gen. Ulysses S. Grant to the Presidency, Gen. William T. Sherman was exhilarated at the prospect that he would be able to unite the various elements of the Army under the command of the Commanding General of the Army. Sherman's hopes were quickly dashed as Grant's political friends and enemies made it clear they would not accept expanding the power and authority of the Commanding General at the expense of the Secretary. Sherman's situation went from bad to worse as Secretary William Belknap overwhelmed the Commanding General politically. Rather than fight the bureaucratic battle for influence over military policy, Sherman, like Lt. Gen. Winfield Scott before him, withdrew from Washington, DC. In Sherman's absence, Belknap ran the War Department unmolested until his resignation and impeachment for corruption in the spring of 1876. Sherman returned to the capital in March 1876. The following month, Grant agreed to issue an order placing the Adjutant General and Inspector General under Sherman's command. To consolidate his grip on the various components of the Army, Sherman brought General Schofield from his post in San Francisco to wrest control of the Military Academy from the Secretary of War and the Adjutant General. He also assigned his new Superintendent to the task of revising Army regulations to bring the entire General Staff under Sherman's authority.[1]

John Schofield, as commander of the Army of the Ohio, had been one of Sherman's most dependable subordinates in the Atlanta and

Carolinas campaigns of the Civil War. The 45-year-old major general was bald and somewhat pudgy, but Schofield impressed people with his keen intelligence and calm demeanor. While Sherman was the fiery advocate, Schofield was a pragmatic judge. Sherman recognized this and used Schofield's judicial temperament to build consensus within a divided Army. Schofield was also respected for his political skills in surviving the cutthroat political infighting as commander of the Department of the Missouri during the war, as commander of the First Military District during Reconstruction, and as Secretary of War. Of Schofield's ability to maintain his political balance, Gen. John Pope reputedly said Schofield "could stand steadier on the bulge of a barrel than any man who ever wore shoulder straps."[2]

In March 1876, Sherman wrote to Schofield of his plan to enhance the status of the Military Academy by appointing Schofield as superintendent. Citing Adm. David Porter's revitalization of the Naval Academy, Sherman sought to elevate the stature of the Academy and place it under his authority.[3] Comfortably ensconced as commander of the Military Division of the Pacific, Schofield was very reluctant to give up his division command for a colonel's command.[4] While Sherman claimed that Schofield would elevate the status of West Point, Schofield feared that the new command would degrade the officer assigned as superintendent. Both Sherman and Grant rejected this argument, but Sherman promised Schofield a position worthy of his rank.[5] Schofield finally acceded to Sherman's appeals and in June 1876 departed California.

The assignment to West Point was a bit of a homecoming for the Schofield family. Though Schofield grew up in Illinois, he was born in the town of Gerry, Chautauqua County, New York, on 29 September 1831 and still had relatives in the area. He graduated seventh in his class from the Academy in 1853, and from 1856 to 1860 Lieutenant Schofield served as an assistant professor of natural philosophy under the renowned Prof. William H.C. Bartlett. Bartlett, USMA Class of 1826, was one of America's foremost astronomers. In 1857, Schofield married Bartlett's daughter Harriet, and their first two children were born at West Point.[6]

Schofield assumed command at West Point in September 1876. Beyond placing the Academy under his personal command, Sherman seems to have given Schofield few specific instructions about reforms at West Point. But Schofield had his own ideas, and within weeks of assuming command, the new superintendent, who had himself squeaked through the Academy with 196 demerits, secured President Grant's approval to revise the demerit system. The new rules provided for a reduction of previous demerits based on later good conduct.[7] Despite Schofield's special competence in mathematics and science, his chief academic objective was to improve the instruction of English composition. The careers of Grant, Sherman, and Schofield himself illustrated the importance of writing with facility and clarity, and Schofield lamented that too few graduates possessed the necessary proficiency.[8]

On the military side of training, Schofield attempted to update the practical aspects of the instruction. He brought in several experienced frontier officers to improve cavalry instruction and stress marksmanship. He combined the Fourth and Third Classes (freshmen and sophomores) for purposes of conducting battalion-level drill. Perhaps recalling his embarrassing reduction from cadet lieutenant to cadet private after his court-martial while a cadet, Schofield instituted a system in which all Second and First Classmen (juniors and seniors) would be promoted to cadet noncommissioned officer and officer status, instead of having many continue as privates. He introduced swimming instruction and boat handling at the expense of close-order drill. The boats were not racing shells, which had become a craze in the elite civilian colleges; they were the barges and watercraft that the Army would employ to transport supplies and equipment. For the young military faculty, Schofield created a "post-graduate course" to keep them abreast of professional developments and encouraged their participation in the newly formed Military Services Institution of the United States, based in New York City.[9]

Schofield's reforms were modest, in part because his goals were modest, but more importantly because the powers of the superintendent were severely constrained. For a soldier, even an astute political soldier like Schofield, the fragmented governance of the Military Academy was a nightmare. Until 1866, the Military Academy had been under the supervision of the Chief of Engineers, when authority was transferred to the War Department and the position of superintendent opened to officers of the line. Nominally under the Secretary of War, the Adjutant General generally supervised routine matters. Additionally, Congress regulated the Academy through a Board of Visitors made up of prominent politicians and educators who annually visited the Academy and made an official report. Finally, there was the Academic Board composed of the senior faculty, who had control of academic policy and made decisions on dismissing cadets for academic failure.

Schofield achieved a major institutional victory when on 2 March 1877, the day before Grant left office, the War Department created the Department of West Point, with Schofield reporting directly to Sherman.[10] Despite Schofield's new status as a department commander and his generally good relations with President Rutherford Hayes and Secretary of War George McCrary, the superintendent still had to deal with numerous political interventions. The most common were the appeals from prominent citizens or their Congressmen when their sons or constituents either failed to pass the entrance exams or were about to be dismissed for academic or disciplinary failure. Schofield resented this political pressure, but was himself relatively soft-hearted and often sympathetic to such appeals. There were, however, limits to the superintendent's authority. The Academic Board was the statutory authority for academic qualifications and the superintendent had only one vote ("first among equals"). Dominated by the senior professors who were relatively impervious to outside pressure, the Board was the chief bulwark against reducing academic standards.[11]

The Academic Board's power to resist outside political influence also enabled it to frustrate academic reform measures. In the post-Civil War era, the Military Academy was no longer the premier engineering school of the nation, but the senior professors in the mathematics, engineering, and natural sciences departments were unwilling to change the strong technical orientation of the school.

Schofield's academic goal to improve the English composition skills of the cadets had also been a long-standing issue with the Board of Visitors. Yet, it took Schofield most of his first year to persuade the Board to enhance the English instruction for Fourth Class cadets, and then only at the expense of Spanish instruction which had been placed in the curriculum as a result of the Mexican War and the five-year curriculum expansion instituted in 1854.[12]

The Board also attempted to extend its authority to the military side of the curriculum. Schofield fought a continuing battle with the Board over who had the authority to dismiss cadets "deficient in discipline." Schofield appealed to Sherman and the Secretary of War, urging that the Superintendent and his Commandant of Cadets should have primary authority in this arena. Writing to the Secretary in 1880, Sherman emphatically supported his superintendent, insisting that "the prescribed academic course was not meant to embrace 'Discipline,' which is the province of the Superintendent, who has the power at all times to remit or pardon the breaches of discipline which go to make up the Conduct Roll." The Secretary agreed, but the Board continued its protracted struggle for power with Schofield's successors.[13]

Frustrated by the Academic Board's obstruction and encroachment on his sphere of responsibility, Schofield frequently challenged the Board and sought to reduce its power and independence. He worked with Sherman to increase his control, for example in limiting the tenure of the military officers assigned as assistant instructors. However, Schofield overreached when he struck directly at the permanent professors themselves by suggesting that they should also have limited tenure by periodically returning to Regular Army duty. Doubtless Schofield's father-in-law, Professor Bartlett, was not pleased with this impertinent idea. Despite Schofield's admiration and affection for him, Bartlett in some ways epitomized the superintendent's difficulty with reforming the Academy. Bartlett had served as the Professor of Natural and Experimental Philosophy for 37 years (1834-1871). Along with his colleagues, Dennis Hart Mahan (Professor of Military and Civil Engineering, 1830-1871) and Albert E. Church (Professor of Mathematics, 1837-1878), Bartlett dominated curriculum design and resisted any attempts to alter its heavy orientation on mathematics and science. His successor, Peter S. Michie (1871 to 1901), would become the next champion of West Point traditions.[14]

The longevity of the senior professors meant they could wear down or wait out the superintendent. But the superintendent and the Academic Board were not always at odds. They shared the desire to improve the educational standards for admission to the Academy. Just as the intervening decades had seen universities surpass the Academy as the foremost engineering school of the nation, dramatic changes had taken place in secondary education. The Board of Visitors routinely commented on the relatively low admission standards when compared to the major universities. Unfortunately, the new standards of academic preparation could be met by only a very small portion of the nation's youth, and the efforts to raise admission standards were met with howls of elitism and charges of "military aristocracy" by members of Congress. Politicians were loath to have the sons of their constituents rejected, and no amount of explanation that poorly prepared cadets would merely flunk out later on helped. Indeed, there was increased pressure on both Schofield and the Board to recycle those dismissed for academic failure.[15]

Echoing the politicians, Quartermaster General Montgomery Meigs (USMA 1836) complained that the number who failed the admission test proved the Academy's standards were too high. Schofield replied that though the Academic Board favored the raising of admission standards, since the subjects were fixed by statute, the admission standards were "as low as statute will justify or the conditions of good education permit." He went on to argue that from the time new standards were adopted in 1866, the number of cadets passing the new admissions tests had improved the overall graduation rate. "Therefore," Schofield concluded, "the effect of raising the standard seems to have been the rejection of incompetents instead of their dismissal at some future time." The effort to improve admission standards prompted Schofield to later suggest that new cadets with high admission examination scores might join the Third Class after their participation in the Fourth Class summer encampment. The majority of the Board concluded, probably correctly, that those successfully passing such tests would be few and would create a precedent to reduce the regular curriculum. Schofield, in his annual report, proposed the even more radical idea of expanding the Academy by creating a program of two to three years for the training of officers for state militias.[16]

This last proposal afforded a glimpse into Schofield's concept of the importance of West Point, and the Army, to the nation. "The Military Academy at West Point," he wrote to Representative James Garfield, "is the one institution of the country which is, above all others, eminently national in its character and influence." He explained that the population, except in times of war, was generally preoccupied by their local, sectional, and party interests, but "a nation, however free, requires the services of a certain number of men whose ambition is different from, if not higher than, that for personal wealth or station." To educate such a body of young men was "the primary object of the national school." The military training was merely incidental to this national education, wherein states and sections are "almost forgotten" and party strife "scarcely heard." Noting the failure of many militia organizations during the recent Great Strike of 1877, Schofield went on to recommend the training of militia officers at the national institution. Thus, "the true mission of the Military Academy" was not only to provide officers for the national army, but to furnish states with a body of scientifically trained young men—young men inculcated with the principles of public service and "a high sense of duty to the state and the nation."[17]

While the "Gilded Age" comprising the post-Civil War boom time would create the basis for a genuinely national economy, it was not until the "Progressive Era" of social and political reform during the early years of the 20th century that many national institutions were formed. The Army was one of the very few truly national institutions of the 19th century. And though Schofield's extravagant argument for the expansion of West Point was institutionally self-serving, in some measure it captured the spirit—the thoughts and concerns—of the larger society as well. Even in the greatest of commercial republics, it is not surprising that some people longed for ideals and aspirations beyond those of the marketplace. Many veterans and non-veterans yearned for the sense of great national purpose of the Civil War. Not everyone agreed with Schofield's benign view of the West Point education as a way to reduce party or sectional friction. For those who saw the world in terms of sectionalism, localism, or class conflict, the "nationalization" of the militia was simply another ploy of the vested interests. Schofield's legislative recommendations were accorded little interest or support from Congress.[18]

As if wrestling with Congress, the War Department, and the Academic Board were not enough, Schofield also had to battle the cadets. Hazing plebes had long been a part of the West Point experience, but by the 1870s it far exceeded in severity the kind of hazing practiced by Schofield and his classmates when they were cadets. In particular, the Third Class had become more abusive, and the period of abuse extended beyond the summer encampment into the academic year. Each new class seemed resolved to impose on the new cadets all that they had endured and more. While a certain amount of freshman hazing had become traditional in private universities, it was especially problematic at a public institution like the Academy. Many parents and politicians complained loudly about abuses, yet others protested punishments for the abusers. Hazing was also the dark side of the inculcation of military discipline and authority. To learn the art of military command, the Academy gave cadets a certain amount of authority over their juniors to teach them the rules and regulations of the institution and the military service. Too often, the young men abused their authority, sometimes in embarrassingly juvenile ways.[19]

Shortly after taking command, Schofield issued an order against hazing, making the repudiation of such behavior a matter of honor:

> For the comparatively intelligent and strong to take unfair advantage of the inexperienced to harass and annoy them is an act unworthy of a civilized man, and much more unbecoming an officer and gentleman. On the other hand, to secure justice and protection to the defenseless is the office of the gentle and brave. The honor of the Corps of Cadets, as well as that of the officers of the Academy, requires that the unkind treatment of new cadets shall be wholly eradicated.

There had always been a certain code of silence about hazing among the cadets, but Schofield's order rejected that tradition and made the reporting of such incidents obligatory.[20]

Over the first few years, Schofield attempted to balance punishment with mercy in controlling the problem, but by the summer of 1879 he faced open rebellion. In July, the Third Class cadets descended on the new cadets with curses, demands for physical stunts, and even physical violence. The superintendent asked the War Department for authority to summarily dismiss the culprits. While the War Department pondered the matter, Schofield, mistakenly thinking the problem solved, went on vacation to New London, Connecticut. Within days, his trusty assistant, William Wherry, telegraphed him that the Academy was in a state of near mutiny. The Third Class cadets were attempting to impose the code of silence about the hazing and retaliated against two of their classmates who had testified about the earlier episodes. The problem had gone beyond youthful horseplay; as Schofield wrote the Secretary, the main source of the trouble was the attempt by "a combination of the members of the third class to screen their comrades from punishment by refusing to testify against them."[21]

Schofield insisted on severe action: "The discipline of the Academy requires prompt dismissal of every cadet who has been guilty of hazing or of shielding the principals." He wrote Sherman that he hoped the President would sustain his efforts to enforce compliance, but that "unfortunately the cadets rely upon the President's well known kindness to save them from extreme penalties." Of course, Schofield was often just as kind-hearted, though in some instances Schofield may have reduced punishments so as to spare the President the political repercussions. Within days the Secretary authorized the dismissal of six cadets. This had the desired effect and recalcitrant cadets began cooperating. To ensure that cadets did not get the wrong message from the episode, Schofield resisted all efforts to speedily reconsider the cases of the dismissed cadets for the next academic year. In postponing their reinstatement, Schofield believed he could break the hazing cycle by holding the fate of these former cadets hostage to the good behavior of their fellows.[22]

Schofield took other actions. He strengthened rules that required regular officers to supervise the training activities of the cadets and for at least one to sleep in the cadet bivouac. He strengthened the authority of the Commandant of Cadets, making it clear that refusal to answer his questions constituted "disobedience of orders" punishable by dismissal. On 11 August 1879, Schofield gave a formal address to the Corps of Cadets on hazing and military discipline. He characterized hazing as a "venerable vice," one like slavery that was now condemned throughout the civilized world. "The practice of hazing," the superintendent declared, "is both injurious and humiliating to its victims and degrading to those who engage in it." The old grad ominously warned, "You can never be a 'brother officer' to him whom you once degraded."[23]

Schofield also dissociated the poisonous activity of hazing from military discipline in a democratic republic. He observed that "the very foundation of civil society is mutual respect for individual rights," and that military honor demands not only obedience to orders, but detection and punishment of those who abuse their authority. He went on to utter words on the subject of leadership that have since become indelible in the minds of all Academy graduates:

> The discipline which makes the soldiers of a free country reliable in battle is not to be gained by harsh or tyrannical treatment. On the contrary, such treatment is far more likely to destroy than to make an army. It is possible to impart instruction and to give commands in such manner and in such tone of voice as to inspire in the soldier no feeling but an intense desire to obey, while the opposite manner and tone of voice cannot fail to excite strong resentment and a desire to disobey. The one mode or the other of dealing with subordinates springs from a corresponding spirit in the breast of the commander. He who feels the respect which is due to others cannot fail to inspire in them regard for himself, while he who feels, and hence manifests, disrespect toward others, especially his inferiors, cannot fail to inspire hatred against himself.[24]

This section of the address became known as Schofield's Definition of Discipline. After Schofield's death, a superintendent directed that it be inscribed on a bronze tablet and placed at a barracks sallyport for the edification of the cadets. Eventually, the upperclassmen came to require the new plebes to memorize Schofield's words as "plebe poop," the menu of miscellanea that plebes were required to learn by rote as part of their initiation ritual. That his speech denouncing hazing should itself become instrumental in the more benign form of hazing based on enforced memorization, is an irony that even Schofield would have relished. But he probably would have observed that memorizing his sage words was superior to vulgar insults and physical assaults, or the memorization of nonsense ditties like "How's the Cow." As a final irony, most contemporary graduates know little about Schofield the Civil War general and Army General-in-Chief, but they still associate his name with enlightened discipline and recite his famous definition of the term.[25]

Schofield succeeded in diminishing, but never eradicating, hazing at the Academy. Perhaps part of his difficulty was the lingering rumors of Schofield's own court-martial as a cadet. As one cadet later wrote, "We used to hear that John M. Schofield was turned back a class for deviling plebes."[26] This characterization both exaggerated and romanticized Schofield's transgression. In 1852, Schofield as a cadet had been court-martialed for neglect of duty. As a math tutor of prospective cadets, he permitted other upperclassmen to enter the classroom. While Schofield was busy coaching several weaker candidates, the older cadets asked the other candidates vulgar questions and had them draw obscene figures on the blackboard. The court-martial convicted Schofield and sentenced him to dismissal, but the court majority remitted the sentence for Schofield's previous good conduct. Years later, as Secretary of War for the last year of the Johnson administration, Schofield learned that the two officers who voted to dismiss him from the Academy and abort his military career were George Thomas and Fitz-John Porter.[27]

Schofield also had to contend with other forms of youthful exuberance and disorder. On New Year's Eve of 1879, underclassmen locked cadet officers in their rooms, set off illegal fire works, and blew horns to ring in the new year. Later, cadets fondly remembered "Old Scofe" storming into barracks square, calling the Corps to formation, and then confining them to barracks on New Year's Day.[28] While the cadets thought of the incident merely as a manifestation of "high spirits," Schofield had a darker interpretation. He believed that the recent announcement of clemency for one of the culprits of the July hazing rebellion had encouraged further "reckless deviltry and love of mischief." The Commandant of Cadets, he confided to Sherman, "is nearly broken down by the weight of responsibility to which he does not feel equal." The strains on the Academy leadership and a perceived lack of support by civilian authorities would have disastrous consequences a few months later, when the Whittaker case threatened to tear the institution apart.[29]

On 6 April 1880, Cadet Johnson Chestnut Whittaker, the only African-American cadet then enrolled, was discovered bloody and unconscious on the floor with his hands and feet tied to his bed. According to Whittaker's later testimony, three masked assailants had set upon him in the night. Such an attack went well beyond routine hazing and the fights that periodically erupted among the young cadets. From the beginning, the Commandant of Cadets, Lt. Col. Henry M. Lazelle, doubted Whittaker's story. The Academy doctor who examined Whittaker that morning believed the cadet had been feigning unconsciousness. They suspected that Whittaker, who was close to failing—a second time—Professor Michie's Natural and Experimental Philosophy course, had staged the incident in order to avoid academic dismissal.[30]

Superintendent Schofield initiated an immediate investigation, convening at Whittaker's request a court of inquiry. The newspapers, especially those in New York, covered the story extensively. The resultant publicity generated a political outcry, prompting President Hayes to send a legal representative to ensure the young African-American cadet got a fair hearing. The court of inquiry concluded that Whittaker faked the incident, and a subsequent court-martial found Whittaker guilty, but recommended clemency. Superintendent Schofield, to his lasting shame, joined the posse against Whittaker by aggressively taking sides during the trial. The Army Judge Advocate

General wrote a highly critical report of the trial and Schofield's part in it. In the end, the Arthur administration set aside the court-martial, but ordered Whittaker's dismissal for failing his June 1880 Natural and Experimental Philosophy exams, which had been taken during the investigation.[31]

In the Whittaker case, Schofield was painstaking, but never evenhanded. While declaring his interest in getting to the truth, he had clearly made up his mind. His private journal indicates that he accepted Lazelle's assessment that Whittaker's wounds were self-inflicted. Schofield seethed as the lawyer sent by President Hayes attempted to turn the investigation away from Whittaker's actions toward the actions of others at the Academy. Even as the inquiry was getting underway, Schofield told the press that he was sure that no other cadets were involved and suggested Whittaker had made some false statements. In later comments, Schofield declared that since all cadets were honor-bound to expose any complicity in the attack, this proved the Corps of Cadets was innocent.[32]

Schofield's statements during the investigations embarrassed the Academy, and his subsequent Annual Report, which excused the social ostracism of African-American cadets and blamed their troubles on their own lack of qualifications, became an enduring disgrace. Even newspapers that suspected Whittaker may have faked the attack denounced his treatment at West Point. Schofield's prejudicial conduct in this case is surprising, but not inexplicable. Schofield shared what he termed the "universal prejudice" against African-Americans. But as commander in Reconstruction Virginia, Schofield had never let his racial antipathy so openly influence the administration of justice. In too hastily accepting Lazelle's theory of the event, he became committed to proving Whittaker's guilt. Later, he blamed the political turmoil on those who were traditionally hostile to the Academy and would seek any pretext to discredit it. Schofield, who had quietly aspired to the Democratic presidential nomination in 1880, saw his admittedly slender hopes vanish in the controversy.[33]

Yet Schofield actions went beyond simple racism: they repre-sented a capitulation to the attitudes and prejudices of the Corps of Cadets. Schofield's argument that the military could not impose social equality, and that it should not attempt to enforce rules of social interaction "different from those which prevail among the people of the United States," contained a double message. In his career, Schofield had enforced many policies with which he disagreed. Now he argued that the opinions of the cadets and the public justified his opposition to administration policy. Moreover, his assertion that the Corps of Cadets would never lie, although Whittaker apparently would, was clearly something he did not truly believe. In his efforts to stamp out hazing, he had seen too many contrary examples. Indeed, Schofield shared the frustration and growing pessimism over hazing that he attributed to the Commandant, Lieutenant Colonel Lazelle. Both the Superintendent and Commandant preferred to believe in Whittaker's guilt, not just because of their hostility to blacks, but also to avoid another destructive clash between the Academy leadership and the largely racist Corps of Cadets.[34]

The cadets probably did not realize they had won such a victory over the Academy leadership. The Whittaker case seems to have had little direct impact on their lives, and no one seems to have given Johnson Whittaker a thought as they much later collected their memories of their Academy years. Of Schofield, they seemed to have had a genuine affection. Looking back on their cadet days, they wrote:

> Schofield, a fine man, perfectly fair to the boys. . . .
> Schofield was a real man, with a fine sense of justice. . . .
> He was all discipline, all justice, all good will, all wisdom. And he had such a way with him that, for all his dignity and aloofness, it would not have been difficult to think that he would have been well content to leave the high place over at the Adjutant's Office and leave his noble quarters, and come running across the Plain to be a cadet again. When I come to think of it I am sorry that General Schofield left West Point without some worthy tribute to him.[35]

Schofield left without a "worthy tribute" because President Hayes replaced him with Maj. Gen. Oliver O. Howard. Schofield contended that he was the innocent "over-kind" victim of partisan politics, but he had clearly lost the confidence of the President. Moreover, while his behavior conformed to the racial attitudes of most white Americans, he seriously misjudged the political reaction, especially in an election year.[36]

Schofield's willingness to sacrifice Whittaker and his own reputation for judicious conduct to protect the Cadets and the Academy are all the more striking, given his previous pattern of conduct which was marked by caution and prudence. In Civil War Missouri and Reconstruction, Schofield had learned that only a commander who possessed the trust and confidence of the political leadership, and not just the President, could survive, much less thrive. Professional competence alone was not enough for a senior general. Civil authorities would grant soldiers authority only if they could be trusted, and they would be trusted only if they displayed some appreciation of the political implications of military policies. Of course, not even the most politic general can always please all sides.[37]

Schofield's relief was especially ironic because Sherman had brought him east to help with military reform and tap his skill in handling thorny, politically-charged issues. For example, in 1879 Sherman appointed Schofield president of a board to reexamine the court-martial and cashiering of Maj. Gen. Fitz-John Porter for dereliction of duty during the Second Battle of Bull Run. Porter, a vocal supporter of Gen. George McClellan, had been bitterly denounced by Gen. John Pope and his radical Republican supporters in Congress for purposely sabotaging Pope. Though Schofield knew that Porter had been one of the officers who nearly ended his career, Schofield and the other board members, Gen. Alfred Terry and Col. George Getty, scrupulously reexamined the evidence and called former Confederates to testify about the battle. The Board unanimously recommended that Porter's conviction be reversed and his rank restored. This conclusion caused a political ruckus. The Speaker of the House and future President James Garfield, who had been a member of the original court-martial, considered the decision a personal insult. Republicans continued to oppose Porter's restoration and it was not until 1886 when Democrat President Grover Cleveland finally signed a bill reinstating Porter. Unlike the Whittaker case, in investigating the charges against Porter, Schofield was meticulous and fair-minded. In rendering his decision, he ran political risks and alienated friends.[38]

Schofield's successor as superintendent, Oliver Howard, was one of the foremost supporters of African-American rights in the Army. Yet, he had little opportunity to change the racial climate, as no black cadets were appointed during his brief tenure. Hazing continued, and the Department of West Point did not survive Howard's term of office. Howard described the assignment as "the hardest office" he ever had to fill. Five more African-Americans were appointed in the 19th century and two graduated—John Alexander in 1887 and Charles Young in 1889. No more would graduate until 1936. Thus, racial integration of the Military Academy, one of the Academy's most significant reform efforts during the first century of its existence, ended in failure. This does not excuse Schofield, but it reminds us of the difficulty of meaningful reform against entrenched social and institutional opposition, especially when these mirrored conditions throughout the rest of the nation.[39]

Reform at West Point failed through lack of consensus and lack of interest. Moreover, while the failure of integration was a genuine tragedy, most of Schofield's reform proposals were either minor or potentially harmful. The creation of the Department of West Point in order to bring the Academy under Sherman's control was a short-sighted expedient. The political dimension of West Point could not be ignored or evaded. Sherman had little inclination to replace the Secretary of War as the buffer between the Superintendent and importuning Congressmen and their constituents. Since most of the governing rules of the Academy were enshrined in statute, any reform needed to pass through Congress where enemies of the Academy would have had opportunities to attach unwise, and possibly damaging, changes in the name of reform.

Even more short-sighted were Schofield's efforts to diminish the autonomy of the Academic Board. True, the Board was a genuine obstacle to many academic reforms, and even minor changes prompted fierce bureaucratic fights. Yet the Board was also the bulwark that maintained academic standards against political pressure in the 19th century. Its very autonomy gave the Superintendent, the Secretary, and even the President cover against irate Congressmen and their constituents. The engineering curriculum was becoming outdated, but was in many ways secondary to the school's real purpose. West Point had always been more about building leaders than producing trained engineers. Hazing notwithstanding, the curriculum continued to insist upon intellectual application and academic responsibility.

Reform efforts at the Academy served as a microcosm of the larger problems of reforming the Army. While Schofield was embroiled in the fractious and futile efforts to reorganize and reform the Military Academy, he was also engaged in an equally frustrating struggle in assisting Sherman in the general reform of the Army, a quest that demonstrated even more vividly the perils and pitfalls of reform efforts. Schofield's dual position as department commander and superintendent intensified his resentment of the entrenched fiefdoms of the bureau system. Even before Schofield officially assumed his duties at West Point, Sherman assigned him the task of revising Army regulations so as to place the staff departments under the Commanding General's supervision.[40] Schofield's time at West Point marked the beginning of his intensive study of military command and administration. The necessity of an integrated general staff system became the abiding concern of his professional life. In 1876, Schofield came up with the shrewd solution of defusing political opposition by forthrightly acknowledging the Secretary of War's authority over the entire Army, including the Commanding General. He argued that administration and command could not be readily separated and that the Secretary and Commanding General should share the General Staff departments. Sherman rather reluctantly accepted these constraints as the price of power over the staff, but the staff departments vociferously opposed any efforts to curtail their autonomy. Schofield's efforts to forge a historic breakthrough in the command and control of the Army were soon overwhelmed by a larger political assault on the Army, an attack that placed the existence of the Army in jeopardy.[41]

Earlier, as Democrat "redeemers" took over more southern states, and northern voters recoiled from the turmoil in the South, the Democrats gained power in the Congress. In the 1874 elections, the Democrats gained control of the House of Representatives. The Army's role in protecting Republican governments and guarding the polls in the South had united the Democratic Party in intense antipathy to the regulars. The electoral crisis of 1876 (the year Schofield reported to West Point as Superintendent) generated a new rallying cry for the Democrats, while the Army's role in helping suppress the Great Railroad Strike of 1877 further inflamed many northern Democrats against the Army. With control of the House of Representatives, the Democrats in the House conducted a two-pronged attack against the Army—to obstruct its appropriations as a means of extracting concessions and to propose draconian cuts as "reform" measures.

In 1877, the Democrat-controlled House Appropriations Committee refused to approve the Army appropriations bill unless the Army was restricted from guarding polls and intervening in labor disputes. The resulting impasse produced the suspension of Army pay from July to November along with the irony of unpaid professional soldiers using force against railroad workers striking for higher pay. The next year, the Democrats renewed their demands; the Republican Senate finally capitulated and Congress passed the Posse Comitatus Act of 18 June 1878, which restricted the use of the Army as a posse to enforce civil law.[42] The southerners who had encouraged the use of the Army as a posse comitatus to enforce the fugitive slave laws now congratulated themselves for protecting the nation from military tyranny.[43] The President could still employ the Army in some domestic roles, such as protecting federal property and assisting the militia in suppressing insurrection, but the act meant that the use of the Army required presidential approval. No longer could local commanders use their troops to aid U.S. marshals at their own discretion.

Although it was not the Democrats' intent, the Posse Comitatus Act was a symbolic turning point for the Regular Army. First, the act spurred the development of the National Guard. Unable to readily call out the regulars, local officials were forced to create another more reliable force than the old largely unorganized militia system.

The Guard not only displaced the Army as the primary force to handle domestic unrest, but it embodied the ideal of the "volunteer soldier, " who, in many American minds, constituted the real source of American military strength. The growth of the Guard would severely hamper the Regular Army's efforts to create an "expansible army" or an "army reserve."[44] Second, the Posse Comitatus Act declared that soldiers who pledged to "defend the Constitution against all enemies, foreign and domestic," should focus their attention on foreign enemies.[45]

Meanwhile, in the House Military Affairs Committee, the Democrats crafted a legislative reform and retrenchment program that cunningly combined genuine reforms with draconian reductions of the Army.[46] These Democratic initiatives eventually led to the creation of a joint Congressional Committee, chaired by Senator Ambrose Burnside (R-RI).[47] Unfortunately, the Joint Committee's proposed bill, known as the Burnside bill, became a true piece of committee "sausage," mingling goods with bads. The bill included such genuine reforms as the creation of four-battalion regiments and a retirement system. In a victory for the authority of commanders over the staff, it required that all staff department orders to staff officers in the field be issued through the Headquarters of the Army. The Republicans also fended off Democratic efforts to radically reduce the Army's enlisted strength, but were forced to accept a dramatic proposal to reduce the number of regiments and the size of the officer corps.[48]

Schofield at West Point welcomed the Committee's efforts and provided lengthy responses to its questions and requests for information.[49] Though troubled by the proposed officer cuts and some of the details, he concluded that the bill "merits the cordial support of the Army."[50] Schofield was especially heartened by the provision strengthening the Commanding General's control over the staff. The sections on the War Department and the Headquarters of the Army closely followed the language of Schofield's proposed regulations, especially the part directing that the Commanding General "shall, under the direction and during the pleasure of the President, have command of the entire Army, command and staff"; that the chiefs of the bureaus shall act under the immediate supervision of the Secretary of War in "all matters of accountability and administration not connected with military operations"; and that they would also act as "Chiefs of Staff to the Commanding General" and report directly to him on matters "appertaining to the command of the Army."[51]

Because the Burnside bill would markedly reduce the staff and curtail its autonomy, the staff chiefs were the leading opponents of the legislation. But staff officers were not the only critics within the Army. While Schofield and Sherman were generally supportive, other senior officers like Philip Sheridan and John Pope were more critical. Many officers, as well as the editor of the *Army and Navy Journal*, attacked the bill especially for its reduction of over 300 officers. Amid the criticism, Sherman let it be known he would take no active measures to support or defeat the Burnside bill. However, he went on to say that he considered the legislation, on the whole, as the best the Army could expect and that if it were defeated, the next bill would be even worse.[52] The three years of legislative battles over the Army had deepened Sherman's natural pessimism. Both Sherman and Schofield saw the Burnside bill as an opportunity to advance their case on the control of the staff departments and thus worth the price of the other more disagreeable provisions. But even Schofield acknowledged that the suffering it would impose on officers forced out or denied promotion gave their staff opponents an important advantage in defeating the overall bill.[53]

For Congressmen who lacked specific convictions about the reorganization plan, this lack of military consensus became an excuse for rejecting the bill. Beyond a lack of consensus, there was simply no pressing need for a radical and contentious reorganization of the Army. Congress had proven to be just as divided as the Army, but, more important, it was largely uninterested. There were no external pressures on Congress to take up the complex and controversial issues of Army reform. In fact, Civil Service reform was a more salient issue than Army reform. The tariff policy was more important than military policy. Most Congressmen and most Americans had bigger, more important concerns related to the rapid geographic, demographic, economic, and technological expansion the nation was undergoing. There were no serious military threats; just as the nation could enjoy the strategic luxury of maintaining a tiny Army, so it could afford the inefficiency of an antiquated military system.[54]

In retrospect, the failure of the Burnside bill and the institutional obstacles to Army reform in the late 1870s were a blessing for the Army. Every proposed reorganization included reductions of either the enlisted or officer strength of the Army and would have inflicted severe damage. The demands of Indian warfare were diminishing, but not extinguished. The battalion structure meant little to an Army still scattered in numerous one- and two-company posts. Austerity programs required the ever greater diversion of the present-for-duty strength to tend troop vegetable gardens or maintain post facilities. Meanwhile, the greater lethality of weapons and complexity of tactics demanded that more time be devoted to training, not less. The marksmanship of individual soldiers was replacing reliance on the brute force of massed formations. Meanwhile, the already under-strength Army was spread ever more thinly.[55]

A severe reduction in the officer corps would also have had devastating consequences, especially on morale. The reductions would have further reduced the dismal promotion prospects. Fewer officers would have diminished the chances for officers to escape dreary garrison duty and find more attractive temporary assignments as staff officers, military instructors at colleges, or foreign observers. The cuts would have hindered the Army's ongoing nation-building missions and would have made it more difficult to assume new ones. A large reduction in the officer corps would have materially hampered the creation of Army professional schools, for which Congress provided few additional resources. It would have been far more difficult to form the new military professional organizations and journals, which were vital to the tiny, underfunded Army during these years of rapid technological change.[56]

Finally, Schofield's ambition to end the conflict between the Secretary of War and the Commanding General would probably have failed as well. First of all, Sherman was not emotionally committed to being the loyal subordinate of the Secretary of War. Later, as Commanding General, Schofield fully subordinated himself to the Secretary in the hope of insinuating himself between the Secretary and the staff, yet this did not stop the Secretary or the staff from going around him. Schofield's insight concerning the interrelatedness of administration and command was correct but not widely accepted, while the concept of the civilian administrator and military commander sharing the same staff was inherently unstable.

Through the 1870s, Sherman and Schofield attempted to wrest West Point and the Army from their institutional adversaries. As commander at West Point, Schofield learned that, given the adversarial nature of American institutions, some reforms come with too high a price, while the hope of separating the Army from politics was illusory. Schofield saw that professional development could be achieved only by subordination to, not independence from, political leaders. His embarrassing relief as superintendent served paradoxically to reinforce his belief that civilian control required accommodation to politics, not separation. Both the Army and West Point represented distinct military values, but they could never be isolated from the nation's values and institutions.

As Commanding General from 1888 to 1895, Schofield came to understand that in the absence of crisis or consensus, only incremental reform was possible, and that the Commanding General needed the active support of the Secretary of War. Rather than contending with the Secretary of War, he subordinated himself to the Secretary and became his closest advisor. In retirement, Schofield advanced his reform agenda by testifying before Congress and serving as President of the Academy's Board of Visitors. Schofield mastered the art of bureaucratic in-fighting. His political education, both in the Civil War and at West Point as Superintendent, taught him to value the hidden hand of influence over the peremptory habit of command. He learned that not all reforms are improvements, and a system that impedes progress can also thwart ill-advised measures masquerading as reform. Schofield's experience illustrates that the nature, speed, and direction of military reform and professionalization were dictated primarily by the need to conform to the nation's deliberately fragmented and contentious constitutional system—an intentionally rocky road to reform.[57]

---

[1] The 19th-century General Staff was far different from a modern general staff. The Adjutant General, Quartermaster General, Commissary General, Judge Advocate General, etc. were the chiefs of separate staff departments and bureaus. They were not a coordinating staff and sought to act independently from other departments and the line Army. In theory, the Commanding General commanded the Army, while the Secretary of War administered the Army. But the delineation between administration and command is as difficult as between political and military questions. While the Commanding Generals believed the "General Staff" should operate under their supervision, the staff chiefs preferred to report directly to the Secretary. Dependent on the staff, the Secretaries of War generally sided with the bureaus. Without control of the staff, the Secretary feared he would be a glorified clerk, dependent on the Commanding General for all information. See Leonard D. White, *The Republican Era: A Study in Administrative History, 1869-1901* (New York: MacMillan, 1958), 134-153; James E. Hewes, Jr., *From Root to McNamara: Army Organization and Administration, 1900-1963* (Washington, DC: Center of Military History, 1975), 3-6; Lloyd M. Short, *The Development of National Administrative Organization in the United States* (Baltimore, MD: Johns Hopkins University Press, 1923), 119-39, 236-68. For an excellent summary of the institutional politics of Army reform, see "Patching the Army: the Limits of Provincial Virtue," in Stephen Skowronek, *Building a New American State: The Expansion of National Administrative Capacities, 1877-1920* (New York: Cambridge University Press, 1982), 85-120. For an excellent account of the origins of the Commanding General position, see William B. Skelton, "The Commanding General and the Problem of Command in the United States Army, 1821-1841," *Military Affairs* 34/4 (December 1970): 117-22.

[2] David S. Stanley, *Personal Memoirs of Major-General D.S. Stanley, U.S.A.* (Cambridge, MA: Harvard University Press, 1917), 214.

[3] John F. Marszalek, *Sherman: A Soldier's Passion for Order* (New York: The Free Press, 1993), 385-88. Sherman to Schofield, 28 March 1876 telegram, Box 42, Schofield Papers, Library of Congress (LC). Sherman's plans for West Point were rather vague. Most basically, he seems to have believed that since the Naval Academy had an admiral in charge, USMA should have a general in command. Adm. David Porter (Superintendent USNA, 1865-1869) added instruction on new technological developments, but his main influence seems to have been in the introduction of athletics and social programs to the school. USNA was not founded until 1850 (Naval School, 1845) and had fewer traditions than West Point. Sherman did not have an explicit "reform agenda"; instead, he sought to place men of intelligence in important positions under his command, and then encourage and promote their efforts.

[4] At that time, Col. Thomas Ruger, Infantry, one of Schofield's wartime division commanders, was the Superintendent.

[5] Sherman to Schofield, 28 March, 30 March, 8 April, 4 May, 25 May, 1 June 1876; Schofield to Sherman, 29 March, 30 March, 7 April, 10 May 1876, Box 42, Schofield Papers, LC; Marszalek, *Sherman*, 385-88; Walter Scott Dillard, "The United States Military Academy, 1865-1900: The Uncertain Years" (Ph.D. diss., University of Washington, 1972), 176-78. Schofield departed California in June, but did not assume command at West Point until September. Sherman detailed Schofield to revise the Army Regulations in a renewed effort to gain control over the general staff.

[6] Harriet Bartlett Schofield died in 1889 and is buried at West Point with her first child, John Rathbone Schofield.

[7] Schofield to President Grant, 18 September 1876, Cullum Files 1585, USMA.

[8] Schofield to President Grant, 18 September 1876, Cullum Files 1585, USMA; Schofield to Secretary of War, 29 (or 30) June 1877, Schofield Letters, vol. I, Special Collections Archives, USMA; Schofield to Sherman, 25 October 1877, Schofield Letters, vol. I, Special Collections Archives, USMA; *Annual Report of the Secretary of War*, 1877, vol. 1, Serial # 1794, 153.

[9] Schofield to Sherman, 25 October 1877, Schofield Letters, vol. I, Special Collections Archives, USMA; *Annual Report of the Secretary of War*, 1877, vol. 1, Serial # 1794, 150-51; Dillard, "The United States Military Academy, 1865-1900," 283-84.

[10] Schofield to Secretary James D. Cameron, 27, 28 November, 1 December 1876, 5 January 1877; Schofield to Sherman, 12, 19 December 1876, Schofield Letters, vol. I, Special Collections Archives, USMA; Schofield, "Private Military Journal, 1876-1880," 94, Box 1, Schofield Papers, LC; Dillard, "The United States Military Academy, 1865-1900," vi-ix, 177-79. Above the regimental level, the line of the Army was organized into geographical military departments and the departments into military divisions. Though within the Division of the Atlantic, commanded by Gen. Winfield S. Hancock, Schofield's Department of West Point reported directly to Sherman.

[11] Dillard, "The United States Military Academy, 1865-1900," 253-54.

[12] Schofield to Secretary of War, 29 (or 30) June 1877, Schofield Letters, vol. I, Special Collections Archives, USMA; Schofield to Vincent, 22 June 1877, Box 42, Schofield Papers, LC; Dillard, "The United States Military Academy, 1865-1900," 162-63, 267-69. The Five Year program was finally abandoned in 1861. Interestingly, Congress suggested introducing German language instruction since so many Union volunteers spoke German. The Academic Board rejected the idea. James L. Morrison, Jr., *"The Best School": West Point, 1833-1866* (Kent, OH: Kent State University Press, 1986), 143-35.

[13] Dillard, "The United States Military Academy, 1865-1900," 163-68, 175; Theodore J. Crackel, *West Point: A Bicentennial History* (Lawrence: University of Kansas, 2002), 149-53.

[14] Schofield to Sherman, 14 April 1877, Schofield Letters, vol. I, Special Collections Archives, USMA; *Annual Report of the Secretary of War*, 1877, vol. 1, Serial # 1794, 152-154; Schofield to Sherman, 27 November 1877, Box 89, Schofield Papers, LC; Morrison, *"The Best School,"* 59-60. Bartlett retired at the age of 67 only because he was enticed by the professional and financial prospects of becoming the Actuary for the Mutual Company of New York. He died in 1893 at Yonkers, NY. USMA Alumni Association, *Annual Reunion of June 9th 1893*, 105-12.

[15] *Annual Report of the Secretary of War*, 1879, vol. 1, Serial # 1903, 173-175; Dillard, "The United States Military Academy, 1865-1900," 253-60. The Congressional attack on Academy standards was part of a general Democratic assault on the Army. Efforts to reduce the size and pay of the Army were extended to USMA instructors. The *Army and Navy Journal* argued that standards were not too high. Between 1832 and 1876: 4599 appointments, 3302 admitted (72%), 763 rejected by the Academic Board (17%), 145 rejected by the Medical Board (3%), 389 did not report or declined appointment (8%). *Army and Navy Journal*, 27 January 1877, 392-93.

[16] Schofield to Secretary of War George W. McCrary, 30 August 1877, Cullum Files 906, Special Collections Archives, USMA; Schofield, "Suggestions for the consideration of the Academic Board," 9 October 1879, with Replies, Box 89, Schofield Papers, LC; *Annual Report of the Secretary of War*, 1879, vol. 1, Serial # 1903, 175.

[17] Schofield to Garfield, 26 January 1878, Box 89, Schofield Papers, LC.

[18] Schofield, *Forty-Six Years*, 438; Russell F. Weigley, "The Military Thought of John M. Schofield," *Military Affairs* XXIII/2 (Summer 1959): 77-78; John P. Mallon, "Roosevelt, Brooks Adams, and Lea: The Warrior Critique of the Business Civilization," *American Quarterly* VIII/3 (Fall 1956): 216-30.

[19] Dillard, "The United States Military Academy, 1865-1900," 89-97, 290-301; Crackel, *West Point*, 143-44.

[20] *Army and Navy Journal*, 26 July 1879, 939.

[21] Schofield to Mrs. John Wendenhall, 20 July 1879; Wherry to Schofield, 21 July 1879, Schofield Letters, vol. II, Special Collections Archives, USMA; Dillard, "The United States Military Academy, 1865-1900," 295.

[22] Schofield to Adjutant General, 21 July 1879; Schofield to Sherman, 23 July 1879; Schofield to President Hayes, 15 August 1879, Schofield to Editor, New York Times, 17 August 1879; Schofield to Sherman, 18 August 1879; Schofield to Adjutant General, 2 October 1879, Schofield Letters, vol. II, Special Collections Archives, USMA. For examples of Presidential pressure, see President Hayes to Schofield, 17 December 1879, Cullum Files, USMA Archives and Schofield to Hayes, 19 December 1879, Schofield Letters, vol. II, Special Collections Archives, USMA.

[23] Schofield Memorandum for the Commandant, 30 July 1879; Schofield to Commandant, 19 August 1879, Schofield Letters, vol. II, Special Collections Archives, USMA; "An Address Delivered By Major General J.M. Schofield to the West Point Cadets," Monday, 11 August 1879, West Point, NY, Box 91, Schofield Papers, LC. Schofield was so proud of this speech that he had it printed and sent copies to Gen. Sherman and President Hayes.

[24] "An Address Delivered By Major General J.M. Schofield to the West point Cadets," Monday, 11 August 1879, West Point, NY, Box 91, Schofield Papers, LC.

[25] Adjutant to Edward Holden, 11 August 1908, Adjutant Letter Book, vol. 20, USMA Archives. While most West Pointers associate Schofield's name with the "Definition of Discipline," most Americans associate it with only Schofield Barracks on Oahu and the 1941 attack on Pearl Harbor. Such are the vagaries of fame.

[26] Williston Fish, *Memories of West Point, 1877-1881*, 3 vols., USMA Archives, 490. Stephen Ambrose calls Schofield "a notorious hazer" who loved to steal plebes' clothing. While practical jokes and minor hazing were not beyond Schofield's capacity, none of the primary sources link Schofield by name to such activity. Stephen E. Ambrose, *Duty, Honor Country: A History of West Point* (Baltimore, MD: Johns Hopkins Press, 1966), 158; Hartz to his sister, 14 June 1851, Hartz Papers, LC. In his memoirs, Schofield admitted to a "misunderstanding" when, as corporal of the guard, he attempted to sneak up on a young sentinel. Schofield, *Forty-Six Years*, 4. Schofield's Academy obituary also related an incident in which Schofield, as a new cadet, crossed bayonets with a corporal of the guard for not challenging promptly. USMA, *Annual Reunion*, 11 June 1906, 128.

[27] Schofield, *Forty-Six Years*, 10-13, 241-42; Captain B.R Alden to Adjutant, USMA, 26 June 1852, and John M. Schofield to B.R. Alden, 30 June 1852, RG 94 Engineer Dept., Letters Received Relative to USMA 1819-1866, Reel 27, USMA Archives; Captain Henry Brewerton to BG Joseph G. Totten, 8 July 1852, Superintendent's Letterbook No. 2, 2 July 1849 - 5 February 1853, USMA Archives; HQ Army, Special Orders No. 141, 9 September 1852, and Special Orders No. 216, 13 December 1852, Orders volume 11, 1852, USMA Special Collection. The letters signed by Fitz-John Porter that I have

show no hyphen between Fitz and John. However, his official name as reflected in the annual *Register of Graduates and Former Cadets of the United States Military Academy, West Point, New York* does contain the hyphen, so it will be spelled accordingly in the present chapter.

28 Williston Fish, *Memories of West Point, 1877-1881*, USMA Archives, 490, 853.

29 Schofield to Sherman, 4 January 1880, Schofield Letters, vol. II, Special Collections Archives, USMA; John F. Marszalek, *Assault at West Point: the Court Martial of Johnson Whittaker* (New York: Collier Books, 1972), 13-14.

30 Whittaker had failed the course in 1879, and Schofield had permitted him to repeat a year rather than be dismissed. For a detailed account of the case see Marszalek, *Assault at West Point.*

31 Marszalek, *Assault at West Point*, 239-249. On 24 July 1995, Whittaker was posthumously commissioned as second lieutenant in the Army by special act of President Bill Clinton. *2002 Register of Graduates and Former Cadets of the United States Military Academy*, 4-64.

32 Schofield, "Private Military Journal, 1876-1880," 104-28, Box 1, Schofield Papers, LC; Marszalek, *Assault at West Point*, 63-64. John Bigelow, who had visited Schofield two days after the attack, later wrote that Schofield was already quite confident that Whittaker was the real culprit. John Bigelow to Edward Holden, 24 October 1906, John Bigelow, Sr. File, USMA Archives.

33 "Annual Report, Department of West Point, 1880," (5 October 1880) Box 93, Schofield Papers, LC. Schofield had written much of the section on "The Freedman at West Point and in the Army" in May 1880. See Schofield's handwritten draft, "Notes on the Colored Cadet," May 1880, Box 89, Schofield Papers, LC; Schofield, *Forty-Six Years*, 445-47; J.D. Broadhead to Schofield, 1 March 1880, Box 37, Schofield Papers, LC; John Bigelow to Edward Holden, 24 October 1906, John Bigelow, Sr. File, USMA Archives.

34 Schofield once chastised the Commandant for not investigating statements of cadets that the Commandant believed to be untrue. To Schofield, the acceptance of "false denials" by cadets tended to "teach the habit of falsehood." Schofield to Commandant of Cadets, 14 September 1878, Schofield Letters, vol. III, Special Collections Archives, USMA.

35 Williston Fish, *Memories of West Point, 1877-1881*, USMA Archives, 490-93, 820, 853.

36 Schofield, *Forty-Six Years*, 445-47.

37 Schofield, ironically, recognized the central importance of such political confidence as opposed to simple seniority in the selection of the Army's senior officers. Writing to Elihu Root in 1902 about the creation of a Chief of Staff, he advised, "Let the President have full freedom of choice, from among those legally eligible, of the officer who he is willing to entrust with military power and then give that officer ample authority, and hold him responsible." Schofield also told Root that he preferred the title General-in-Chief to Chief of Staff. Schofield also saw this officer as departing shortly after the rest of the Cabinet at each election. Schofield to Elihu Root, 29 March 1902, Schofield Papers, Box 38, LC.

38 For in-depth accounts of the Fitz-John Porter case see, Otto Eisenschiml, *The Celebrated Case of Fitz John Porter* (New York: Bobbs-Merrill, 1950), and Henry Gabler, "The Fitz John Porter Case: Politics and Military Justice" (Ph.D. diss., City University of New York, 1979). Schofield's decision strained his friendship with Jacob D. Cox, Schofield's most trusted wartime subordinate. Cox, a friend of fellow Ohioan Garfield and Ambrose Burnside, whom Porter had disparaged, inundated Schofield with long impassioned letters about the Porter case.

[39] John A. Carpenter, *Sword and Olive Branch: Oliver Otis Howard* (Pittsburgh, PA: University of Pittsburgh Press, 1964), 273; Coffman, *The Old Army*, 228-29; Dillard, "The United States Military Academy, 1865-1900," 213-25, 301-16, 351-55.

[40] For a lengthy discussion of Schofield's "regulations," see Richard A. Andrews, "Years of Frustration: William T. Sherman, the Army, and Reform, 1869-1883" (Ph.D. diss., Northwestern University, 1968), 156-69. The proposed regulations were reprinted in *Senate Reports, No. 555*, 45th Congress, 3d Session, Serial #1837. Large portions of these proposed regulations were incorporated in the unsuccessful "Burnside Bill" for Army reorganization. Army regulations had become a political football between the executive and legislative branches. The Army Regulations of 1861, with a few additions in 1863, remained the governing instructions for the Army. Congress, in 1866, had redirected that the Secretary of War report on necessary changes as a result of the experiences of the war. Congress ignored the work of Sherman's board and in 1870 required that any revision of Army Regulations be approved by Congress. By 1875 Congress had revoked that requirement and authorized the President to publish new regulations, hence Schofield's project.

[41] Schofield's aborted proposals marked a small milestone in the evolution of Sherman's thinking about the command of the Army. Prior to assuming the task, Schofield made his thoughts on the matter clear to General Sherman. Schofield reiterated his view that the Secretary of War, at the discretion of the President, "exercises 'supervision,' 'control' or 'direction' over all branches of the military service, while the General-in-Chief, subject to such supervision, control, and direction, exercises command over all parts of the Army." Schofield admitted that to achieve the ideal of unity in administration and command would require combining the positions of Secretary and Commanding General, but rejected that as "politically impossible" and ultimately bad for the Army because of "the lack of sympathetic connection with the party at any time in power." Schofield's proposed regulations forthrightly recognized the Secretary's control over the entire Army, though it still reflected the enduring problem of distinguishing between administration and command and having the staff serve two masters. This ambiguity did not assuage everyone's concerns, but in appointing Schofield and endorsing his work, Sherman, at least grudgingly, accepted the view that the Commanding General's authority was not independent of the Secretary of War. Schofield to Sherman, 8 May 1876, Reel 23, WTS Papers, LC.

[42] The act reads: "From and after the passage of this act it shall not be lawful to employ any part of the Army of the United States, as a posse comitatus, or otherwise, for the purpose of executing the laws, except in such cases and under such circumstances as such employment of said force may be expressly authorized by the Constitution or by act of Congress; and no money appropriated by this act shall be used to pay any of the expenses incurred in the employment of any troops in violation of this section. And any person willfully violating the provisions of this section shall be deemed guilty of a misdemeanor and on conviction thereof shall be punished by fine not exceeding ten thousand dollars or imprisonment not exceeding two years or by both such fine and imprisonment." Posse Comitatus Act. Pub. L. 97-86, 1 December 1981; 95 Stat. 1114; 10 U.S.C. (sections) 371-78.

[43] For the role of the Army in enforcing fugitive slaves laws, see Robert W. Coakley, *The Role of Federal Military Forces in Domestic Disorders, 1789-1878* (Washington, DC: GPO, 1988), 128-37.

[44] See Jerry Cooper, *The Rise of the National Guard: The Evolution of the American Militia, 1865-1920* (Lincoln: University of Nebraska Press, 1997).

45 By limiting the Army's role in enforcing the power of the federal government, the government was forced to develop its own civilian law enforcement agencies. This process was slow in the 19th century, but accelerated in the 20th. Today's federal government has multiple law enforcement agencies, many with extensive paramilitary elements. Yet, ironically, the gap between military and law enforcement seems to be narrowing to the extent that some people call for the use of the military assistance in domestic law enforcement while others see overseas military operations as law enforcement operations. For a discussion of the modern implications of the Act, see Matthew Carlton Hammond, "The Posse Comitatus Act: A Principle in Need of Renewal," *Washington University Law Quarterly* 75/2 (Summer 1997): 953-84; Gregory D. Grove, *The U.S. Military and Civil Infrastructure Protection: Restrictions and Discretion under the Posse Comitatus Act* (Stanford, CA: Stanford University Center for International Security and Cooperation, October 1999).

46 The new chairman of the Military Affairs Committee, Henry B. Banning (D-OH), led the Democratic charge against the Army. In Banning, the Democrats had the perfect leader for their agenda. Banning had enlisted in the Union Army in April 1861, rose to command an Ohio regiment in the Atlanta Campaign, and was breveted as a major general of volunteers in 1865. Elected to Congress in 1872 as a liberal Republican, he joined the Democrats in 1874. As chairman, Banning advocated both military economy and reform, though he was most wedded to reductions in Army strength and pay. He lost his bid for renomination in 1070 and was defeated in the general election in 1880. Banning was a member of the West Point Board of Visitors in 1877, but declined to attend. This disappointed many Academy officers, who were eager to show him the "palatial quarters" he railed against in Congress. *Army and Navy Journal*, 9 June 1877, 704.

47 For an in-depth examination of the Burnside bill, see Richard A. Andrews, "Years of Frustration: William T. Sherman, the Army, and Reform, 1869-1883" (Ph.D. diss. Northwestern University, 1968); and Donna Marie Eleanor Thomas, "Army Reform in America: The Crucial Years, 1876-1881" (Ph.D. diss., University of Florida, 1980). For an internal Army perspective on professionalism and reform, see William R. Roberts, "Loyalty and Expertise: The Transformation of the Nineteenth-century American General Staff and the Creation of the Modern Military Establishment" (Ph.D. diss., Johns Hopkins University, 1980).

48 The Burnside bill included many of the mischievous reforms proposed by Banning. The authorized Army enlisted strength would remain at 25,000, but the bill called for significant officer reductions. It included consolidations and major reductions in the staff corps and required the rotation of line officers to staff positions. It reduced the number of regiments: Infantry decreased by 7 to 18; cavalry decreased by 2 to 8; artillery retained 5 regiments, with internal officer reductions. It authorized the four-battalion infantry regiment with two battalions remaining unmanned. It provided for mandatory retirement at age 62 and 65 for general officers. It also reduced through attrition the number of general officers from eleven to six (2 major generals and 4 brigadier generals). Senate Reports, No. 555, Serial 1837, "Burnside Report on the Proposed Reorganization of the Army" (12 December 1878), 1-4, 1-78. The complete text of the Burnside bill was also published in the *Army and Navy Journal*, 21 December 1878, 325-41.

49 Schofield to Sherman, 20 December 1878, Schofield Letters, vol. III, Special Collections Archives, USMA. Schofield had initially been reluctant to tell Sherman of his true feelings about the bill, because "this plan appears to be closer to mine than yours." Sherman's plan was more orthodox than Schofield's. Sherman did not propose lineal

promotion, though he advocated that general officer positions of the staff be selected from the Army at large rather than from the staff branch—clearly an attempt to break up the insularity of the staff branches. Sherman did not propose a formal battalion structure although his plan could accommodate one. He offered few changes in the staff structure. He appealed especially for additional regimental first lieutenants to meet the need for staff and other special duty details. He urged the authorization of general officers based on one brigadier for every three regiments and one major general for every three "brigades." Combat brigades and divisions were not peacetime formations in the 19th century. Sherman's letter to the committee also referred to Emory Upton's manuscript titled "The Military Policy of the United States." Though he expected that it would be in press soon, he told them that it would not be accessible before their report had to be submitted in December 1878. Alas, Upton's work would not see publication for 26 years. Senate Reports, No. 555, Serial 1837, "Burnside Report on the Proposed Reorganization of the Army" (12 December 1878), 78-89.

[50] Schofield to Sherman, 20 December 1878, Schofield Letters, vol. III, Special Collections Archives, USMA. Schofield wrote two letters to Sherman that day. The first reflected his initial qualms about submitting his views, and the second contained a longer analysis, which he may have assumed Sherman would publish to garner further support. Sherman passed the latter on to William Conant Church, who published it in his *Army and Navy Journal*, 28 December 1878, 359; *Army and Navy Journal*, 25 January 1879, 438. Sherman also passed on Philip Sheridan's and John Pope's letters on the bill, who were less supportive. *Army and Navy Journal*, 18 January 1879, 409-10.

[51] Senate Reports, No. 555, Serial 1837, "Burnside Report on the Proposed Reorganization of the Army" (12 December 1878), 7-8, 354-55.

[52] *Army and Navy Journal*, 11 January 1879, 398; 18 January 1879, 409-10. Despite the close connections between Sherman and editor William Conant Church, the *Army and Navy Journal* dismissed the idea that the Army must accept the Burnside bill or face something worse. The *Journal* believed that since previous efforts to harm the Army had been defeated, the friends of the military need not accept bad measures in the fear of even worse measures to follow. *Army and Navy Journal*, 25 January 1879, 436.

[53] Schofield to Sherman, 21 January 1879, Schofield Letters, vol. III, Special Collection, USMA Archives, 253-55.

[54] A "distinguished Senator, interested in the Army," told the *Army and Navy Journal* that the future of the bill depended entirely on its manager in the Senate. According to this old hand, it takes a "very old stager" to know how to combat all of the opponents of a bill. He feared that Burnside, in a desire to accommodate, had given way too often and it was then too late in the session to recover the lost momentum. The anonymous Senator marveled at the way the opponents of the bill had managed their fight. They were able to divert attention from their own self-interests by dwelling on the supposedly "unconstitutional" efforts to give power to General Sherman at the expense of the President and the Secretary of War. Even though he knew this was false, he knew the charge resonated especially with southern members of Congress. *Army and Navy Journal*, 25 January 1879, 438. A week earlier the Washington correspondent of the *Army and Navy Journal* also noted the effectiveness of the opponent's argument when he predicted that any bill that seemingly gave authority to Sherman at the expense of the Secretary would fail. The correspondent also noted increasing opposition to enshrining West Point in statute as a military department. *Army and Navy Journal*, 18 January 1879, 417; *Army and Navy Journal*, 11 January, 8, 15, 22 February, 1, 8 March 1879; Thomas, "Army Reform in America," 254; *Congressional*

Record, 45th Congress, 3d Session, 660, 847-52, 897-926, 963-76, 1034-51, 1132-45, 1707-14, 1755-67, 1809-25.

[55] This condition prompted most officers to prefer long-term enlistments rather than having to regularly train large numbers of recruits. This conflicted with efforts of those like Secretary of War Redfield Proctor to create shorter enlistments in order to attract a younger, more ambitious enlisted soldier.

[56] Artillery School, 1868; Signal School, 1868; School for Application of Cavalry and Infantry, 1881; Engineer School for Application, 1885; School for Cavalry and Light Artillery, 1893; Army Medical School, 1893. *Journal of the Military Service Institution*, 1880; *Cavalry Journal*, 1885; *Journal of the Artillery Corps*, 1889; *Infantry Association Journal*, 1904.

[57] Schofield also served as the chairman of the architectural committee for major expansion and renovation of the school. In selecting the distinctive Gothic architecture so closely associated with the Academy, he probably had a greater lasting impact on the Academy than when he served as Superintendent. Schofield to Elihu Root, 16 April 1901; Mills to Schofield, 3 January 1903; Mills to Schofield, 26 June 1903, Box 38, Schofield Papers, LC. Crackel, *West Point*, 170-74.

⇥ CHAPTER 9 ⇤

THE WEST POINT CENTENNIAL: A TIME FOR HEALING

Frank J. Walton

And be it further enacted, that the said corps,
when so organized shall be stationed at West Point,
in the state of New York, and shall constitute a
military academy.

**—From Congressional Act
establishing U.S. Military
Academy, 16 March 1802**[1]

The U.S. Military Academy was ready for a celebration as the 100th anniversary of its founding approached in 1902. There was much to be proud of. Academy graduates had served the nation with distinction in war and peace, and the institution had developed a worldwide reputation for excellence. With so much to celebrate, Academy leaders planned a centennial observance to occur in conjunction with the June commencement exercises. They chose June rather than March, the actual birth month, to avoid disrupting the academic schedule with the multi-day event. The celebration took place from 9 to 12 June, with each of the four days having a separate theme—alumni day, field day, centennial day, and graduation day, respectively.

Despite its impressive legacy and reason to celebrate, however, West Point faced a growing chorus of criticism in the late 19th and early 20th centuries. The public was aroused by an ugly incident of hazing in 1900 that brought intense media scrutiny and shed an unfavorable light on the cadets and Academy leaders. "Old grads" were dismayed by the deteriorating infrastructure that was stretched to the limit with the expansion of the Corps of Cadets. Educators disparaged the Academy for its low admission standards and for failing to adopt curricular and pedagogical reforms that other prestigious schools had implemented. To these and other observers the Academy was floundering, and Congress had not seen fit to rescue the institution with adequate funds and concern.[2]

If these problems were not bad enough, the Academy continued to suffer from the lingering wounds of the American Civil War. Many northerners had still not forgiven the school for providing the Confederacy so many officers whose martial skills prolonged the four-year agony. In this regard, West Pointers themselves were deeply divided. A large number of graduates who had served loyally in the Union Army were still alive, and they resisted reconciliation with those who had abetted the rebellion.

Academy leaders planned the bicentennial with these challenges in mind. To be sure, they would celebrate the positive contributions of West Point and its graduates to the nation. But they also would use the occasion to improve the Academy's relations with the public and to forge the political consensus necessary to redress institutional problems. Moreover, they would attempt once and for all to exorcise the demon of the Civil War as it affected relations within the Long Gray Line.

If Academy leaders needed a reminder about the power of America's free press, an unfortunate hazing incident provided it. In December 1900 former cadet Oscar L. Booz died of tuberculosis. Booz had entered the Academy in June 1898 with the Class of 1902 and resigned the following October because of declining health; during his five months at the Academy he endured a variety of hazing rituals. Booz's father believed that the hazing had aggravated the medical condition that led to Oscar's death, which occurred over two years after he left

West Point. He took his accusation to the press, which sensational-
ized the story. According to the press accounts, the younger Booz had
been severely beaten in a fistfight, endured punitive and exhaustive
physical exertions, and been forced to consume large doses of hot
sauce.[3] A military board of inquiry substantiated the hazing, but did
not find it to be the proximate cause of death; Congressional hearings came to the same conclusion.[4] Regardless, the harmful effects
of hazing, wrote one reporter, "has aroused a demand" for reform
at the Academy. Other journalists chimed in with headlines such as
"Victim of Hazing at West Point Dies in Agony" and "West Point Bitterly Scorned at the Funeral of Dead Cadet."[5]

Superintendent Albert L. Mills resented the "wonderful hysteria"
caused by the press. He accused "Yellow Journals" of exploiting the
Booz story "regardless of facts and truth" in order to sell their newspapers.[6] Although some reporters had noted Mills's efforts to curtail
hazing following Booz's death, others ranted with such speculations
as "Mills to Lose the West Point Billet" and "Mills May Have To Go."[7]
The latter headline prompted Mills to write a letter to the editor of
the *Washington Times*, in which he referred to statements in the
article as "untrue and . . . without foundation in fact" and requested
that they be corrected.[8]

The Booz incident was a public relations fiasco for the Academy.
The *New York Sun* used the opportunity to compare West Point unfa-
vorably with the Naval Academy: "There is no hazing at Annapolis,
that is to say, none of the brutal hazing which has brought scandal
upon West Point."[9] Given this opening, other journalists resurfaced
the old debate about the wisdom of having a military academy at all.
One such editorialist argued for the school's abolition:

> We do not need it [the Academy] in our business; a mili-
> tary course included in our leading universities would fully
> answer all purposes, and minimize all the disadvantages
> from which West Point now suffers; and we should no lon-
> ger labor under the scandal of supporting at the national
> expense in this twentieth century of civilization and
> enlightenment, a school where boys are deliberately taught
> how to kill their fellow creatures.[10]

The Booz incident not only garnered news media attention, but also generated passionate debate in Congress. Some Congressmen believed that the media's exposure of the scandal and the consequent public outcry would be enough to spur the Academy to police itself; others preferred legislation to end the practice of hazing.[11] Senator William J. Sewell, a New Jersey Republican, noted that the "country was astonished at what developed. The press of the country from one end to the other cried out against that condition of affairs."[12] Like many Americans, Sewall was deeply influenced by the media and supported the Congressional efforts to outlaw hazing. Sewell's colleague, William V. Allen of Nebraska, went further: "If hazing cannot be suppressed, abolish the academy."[13] Mills tried to assure Congress of his commitment to reform, but to no avail. In the end, Congress decided that the Academy could not be trusted to eliminate hazing on its own, so it outlawed the practice through legislation passed on 2 March 1901.[14]

With the anti-hazing law behind it, Congress finally could address other Academy business that had been put on hold. Most significant was the Military Academy appropriations bill. The issue of funding was particularly sensitive because of the dilapidated condition of the buildings and infrastructure at West Point, a situation worsened by the expansion of the Corps of Cadets from 381 to 481 in 1900.[15] The Army battled with Congress annually over the appropriation of funds for the buildings and facilities at West Point, which were in desperate need of repair and expansion. With scanty funding from Congress through the years, the Academy was limited to sporadic makeshift construction to meet its immediate needs. Hence the buildings at West Point lacked a coherent architectural plan, last seen in any form in the 1840s under Superintendent Richard Delafield.[16] Prof. Charles W. Larned accurately assessed the physical plant in a December 1901 report:

> The existing plant is a series of additions progressively bettering older conditions, but each, when made, inadequate for more than immediate wants. As a consequence many of the public buildings are now not only entirely inadequate, but in some cases incongruous and inconvenient.[17]

Larned included with his report a summary of the Board of Visitors' reports from 1882 to 1901, which consistently noted the inadequacy of the Academy's buildings. He concluded, "It can be truthfully said there is a pressing necessity for a complete tearing down and a new building up."[18] This may have been true, but in 1901 Congress was unconvinced of the need for major new construction and provided no funds for this purpose.

Despite Congress's inaction on money for new construction, Mills was successful in gaining supplemental funds for the centennial. In his 1900 annual report he had anticipated needing extra money "to meet in part the expenses attendant upon a fitting commemoration of the one hundredth anniversary of the opening of the military academy."[19] The War Department brought the matter to Congress, which looked favorably on the request. In 1901 Congress voted to provide funds "for partly meeting the expenses incident to the exercises in commemoration of the one hundredth anniversary of the opening of the United States Military Academy, to be expended under the direction of the Superintendent, ten thousand dollars."[20] Mills's advance planning paid off, figuratively and literally, as he secured both the political and financial support for an event that potentially could lead to greater patronage in the future.

Perhaps nothing better illustrated the need for new construction at West Point than the dearth of housing for the many guests who would attend the centennial. With a paucity of hotel accommodations at West Point and in the local area, event planners had to improvise. They directed the cadets to vacate the barracks and encamp, thus freeing space for 200 graduates. Press reports of the lodging plan were uncharacteristically positive. The *New York Sun* noted approvingly:

> The graduates were quartered in their old rooms in cadet barracks, the corps having been sent into camp. Over the alcoves where they had slept as boys the Adjutant, Capt. Rivers, with thoughtful care had posted their names on placards just as they had been posted forty, fifty, sixty years ago. . . . [E]very detail had been thought out by the Superintendent, Adjutant, and Quartermaster.[21]

In the end there were accommodations for everyone. West Point's most distinguished centennial guest, President Theodore Roosevelt, stayed in the Superintendent's quarters, and lesser dignitaries lodged at officers' quarters scattered about post.[22] Still others were billeted in sleeping cars provided by the West Shore Railroad, as the official guest list grew ever larger in the weeks preceding the centennial. The guests could not possibly have missed the significance of the improvised lodging, which reflected the inadequacy of the Academy's buildings and facilities.

Many of those attending the celebration returned to Washington more eager than before to help, and it was not long before Congress appropriated the necessary funds. The press noted the connection:

> The centennial celebration at West Point this week gives additional interest to the announcement that the practical reconstruction of the United States Military Academy has been decided upon by Congress. It is now simply a question between the national Senate and the House of Representatives whether the appropriation shall be five million or six million dollars.[23]

In fact, the 1902 Congress appropriated a hefty $5.5 million for new construction at West Point. The architectural firm of Cram, Goodhue, and Ferguson won the design competition with a Gothic architectural plan that would complement existing buildings and enhance the natural beauty of the location. The buildings constructed during this time were a new riding hall, academic building, administration building, gymnasium, barracks, and chapel. At the south end of the post were the new artillery and cavalry barracks. These projects were completed by 1914 and virtually all of them remain prominent features of the West Point landscape today.[24]

Despite the several problems the Academy confronted at the start of the 20th century, most Americans held West Point in high esteem. Even the press, in the absence of sensational news stories, found good things to say. One newspaper report, for example, noted the significance of the approaching USMA centennial in comparison to Yale's bicentennial and Princeton's sesquicentennial: "Now that West

Point comes before the public with an anniversary," the reporter opined, "there should be rejoicing that will make the others seem in a way insignificant."[25]

Superintendent Mills agreed. Accordingly, he worked hard to make the West Point centennial a memorable celebration as well as a public relations success. He recruited President Roosevelt to be the keynote speaker, recognizing the positive press coverage that would result. In correspondence with Roosevelt's secretary prior to the centennial, Mills asked the President to recognize the contributions of West Point in words that "can be placed in bronze letters" on a plaque.[26] Roosevelt obliged the Superintendent, although it is not clear whether the plaque was ever cast.[27] Roosevelt noted that during the previous 100 years "no other educational institution in the land has contributed as many names as West Point has contributed to the honor roll of the nation's greatest citizens."[28] Roosevelt's remarks, covered widely in the press, delivered to Congress and the public precisely the message Mills had hoped for. Americans around the country read such headlines as "GREATEST SCHOOL—President Gives First Place To West Point."[29]

If West Point were to continue producing great leaders and citizens, it would have to admit only the best cadet candidates. As the centennial celebration approached, Academy leaders therefore asked Congress to raise the school's admission requirements, which had changed little over the years. This was not a new request, but one that Academy leaders had made repeatedly—and Congress had rejected repeatedly—throughout the 19th century. Congress purposely had established low entry standards out of respect for the democratic sentiments of a nation that prized equal opportunity for all of its citizens, regardless of social, economic, or academic background. The lenient requirements of the 19th century allowed young men from all socio-economic and educational backgrounds to have equal access to the Academy.[30] Another reason for favoring the status quo was the Congressmen's fear that tightening entry standards would undermine their political patronage. They understood that it would be better to let the son of an important constituent gain entry as a cadet and then fail, than to deny the young man access from the start because of poor academic preparation. In the former case, the failure could be blamed on Academy leaders; in the latter, on Congressionally approved entry requirements.

With these ideological and political considerations in mind, Congress had established loose entry requirements in 1812. Cadet candidates needed to show proficiency only in basic mathematics, writing, and reading skills; in 1866 Congress added English grammar, geography, and U.S. history. Provided a reasonably astute applicant had secured a Congressional nomination, the likelihood of being disqualified for inadequate academic preparation was slim. The consequence, of course, was that many cadets struggled to keep up, and the Academy spent much time providing remedial instruction. As academic standards generally rose in higher education during the latter half of the 19th century, West Point began to lag noticeably behind other colleges and universities in the quality of its entering classes.[31]

Mills testified before Congress on this subject during committee hearings on the Military Academy appropriation bill in 1900. "The entrance examination to a public high school," he noted, "demands substantially the same requirements as does the Military Academy. . . . This fact is a heavy handicap to the academy in the work that it does and the work that it should do."[32] With so much academic ground to make up once they were admitted, many cadets flunked out. "The records of the past years," Mills added, "show that about one-third of the applicants fail to enter and about one half of those who enter fail to graduate, the majority of failures in the first year."[33] If the entrance requirements were stricter, cadets would be better prepared to complete the academic program; consequently, more of them would graduate, and the Academy would be able to commission as many officers as Congress authorized.[34] The lawmakers were unmoved by these arguments and voted against changing the current system.

The mood in Congress was different the following year. Early in 1901, with no prompting from Mills, the Senate Military Affairs Committee resurfaced the proposal to raise entry requirements. In joint conference, senators and representatives wrote into the bill a provision authorizing the Secretary of War—and by extension the

Academic Board—to set admissions standards. Congress passed the measure with surprising speed, and the bill was signed into law on 2 March 1901—the same day as the bill outlawing hazing.[35] The bill's easy passage no doubt was influenced by the spirited debate on hazing. Lawmakers could see a beneficial connection between raising admission standards and eliminating the adolescent hazing rituals that had led to the Booz scandal.

Academy leaders acted quickly to make the changes. Beginning with the class entering in 1902, cadet candidates had to be "well versed" in a variety of new subjects, as well as those tested previously. The new subjects included spelling, English composition, English literature, algebra through quadratic equations, geometry, descriptive and physical geography, world history, and "the general principles of physiology and hygiene."[36] These changes went into effect just as planning for the centennial celebration was in its final phase, and they could be touted to the press and within academic circles as evidence that the Academy was changing for the better.

Despite the momentum for improved entry standards, educators criticized the academic program for failing to keep pace with developments in higher education. In particular, they noted the lack of educational choice for cadets and the continued use of a regimented teaching methodology dating back to Sylvanus Thayer. Other colleges and universities had established curriculums with discipline-specific majors and elective courses that gave students ample choice in structuring an educational program. Moreover, their pedagogical techniques were changing. At schools like Harvard, Yale, and the Massachusetts Institute of Technology, students used a hands-on approach to learning rather than the strict recitation system at West Point. Moreover, the Academy curriculum remained largely unchanged and, from the viewpoint of the reformers, the institution's stubbornness reflected the stereotypical conservatism of the military. The composition of the Academic Board, with its long-term, tenured military faculty members, lent credence this view.

Members of the Academic Board were not oblivious to the changes going on around them. On the contrary, they studied the new techniques and considered their utility at West Point. In 1872, for example, Peter Michie (Professor of Natural and Experimental Philosophy) and Henry Kendrick (Professor of Chemistry) visited several prominent schools to compare their curriculums and methodologies with West Point's. However, they returned convinced that "so far as the Military Academy is concerned, the character, scope, and method of its instruction *considering the end in view*, is much superior to that of any institution either technical, special, or general."[37] Their principal concern, of course, was the professional needs of the cadets as opposed to the general educational needs of civilian students. They viewed mathematics, science, and engineering—and the rigid pedagogy that went with them—as the building blocks of the mental discipline necessary to deal with the uncertainties and frictions of war. They concluded, "We may safely challenge any institution either in this country or in Europe to display results of study as favorable as those exhibited in the careers of our graduate cadets."[38]

This is not to say that West Point was immutable. The Academic Board continued to compare the USMA curriculum and pedagogy with those of other schools and came to realize that some changes were prudent. In 1883, it sent Samuel Tillman (Professor of Chemistry) and George Andrews (Professor of Modern Languages) on a fact-finding trip to Harvard, Yale, Dartmouth, and the Massachusetts Institute of Technology. They concluded that the USMA curriculum was fundamentally sound although "susceptible of improvement."[39] The momentum for change was slow but steady; in this case it resulted in an expansion of the humanities curriculum that would continue through the 20th century.

Superintendent Mills, young and energetic, was impatient with the slow pace of curricular reform. As a combat veteran of the Spanish-American War—he had lost an eye in the Battle of San Juan Hill and won the Medal of Honor—he was sympathetic to the view that the curriculum should be more applicable to the professional needs of graduates. He doubted the utility of so much mathematics, science, and engineering; furthermore, he voiced heresy by suggesting that cadets need not take exactly the same courses.[40] Not surprisingly, he endorsed the unambiguous recommendation of the Board of Visitors:

> The Academy is a training school for soldiers. In place of mathematics and the applications of mathematics, which now dominate the course, a body of subjects should now come to a hearing that have direct bearing upon the human life and needs of the soldier—general history, military history, English, oral study of modern languages, military ethics, military hygiene, etc.[41]

To underscore his commitment to reform, Mills dispatched Tillman and Wright Edgerton (Professor of Mathematics) on a fact-finding mission to other academic institutions. The purpose was to gather information "with a view of better equipping ourselves for considering desirable changes in the Military Academy's curriculum, a work now in progress."[42] The timing of their trip—February 1902—was no coincidence. Mills had planned the review to conclude just prior to the centennial, when West Point would be the focus of national attention. Perhaps he believed that Tillman and Edgerton, with all eyes upon them, would be reluctant to appear as opponents of reform.

As it turned out, the main outcome of the trip dealt more with admission standards than curricular reform. Tillman and Edgerton noted that cadets spent almost twice as much time on mastering basic mathematics as their civilian peers in other schools. The finding highlighted the need for higher entry standards and, as noted earlier, Congress responded with the appropriate legislation.

Despite the near-term focus on admission standards, the Tillman-Edgerton trip helped ignite a public debate about curricular issues at West Point. Letters from the presidents of six prestigious academic institutions—Harvard, Yale, Columbia, Brown, the University of Chicago, and the University of the City of New York—appeared in the 14 June 1902 edition of the *Army and Navy Journal*. Their comments reflected the lively interest of civilian educators in the West Point curriculum.[43] Most of the letters avoided direct criticism of West Point, no doubt out of a courteous regard for the centennial celebration, and a few were quite positive. On the other hand, Harvard President Charles Eliot remarked sharply on West Point's "perpetuation of its own methods, uninfluenced by the great changes in educational methods which have been gradually evolved during the past eighty years."[44] Collectively, these educators gave public voice to the curricular and pedagogical issues being debated in academia between proponents of the old ways and those of the new. Dr. William R. Harper, President of the University of Chicago and an admirer of West Point, acknowledged the sensitivity of the curriculum debate in his centennial address:

> I appreciate the fact that the question I am raising touches vitally the most sacred articles in the creed of the modern educator. I understand that it is today a piece of pedagogical heterodoxy to look with any favor upon an educational policy which is not based upon the idea that the student must be allowed to follow his own sweet will in selecting his courses of study, his hours of study, and his methods of work. At the same time I venture to ask whether in the application of this modern educational policy we have not gone too far . . . . But this is not the time for pedagogical discussion.[45]

The public debate reflected Mills's shrewdness in harnessing the energy of the centennial to advance the agenda of curriculum reform. Because of the nature of the institution, the changes resulting from the discourse would be slow. But even slow change was progress. Over the course of several decades, subsequent superintendents—Douglas MacArthur, Maxwell Taylor, and Garrison Davidson, among others—would champion curricular reform. These efforts would reach fruition in the second half of the 20th century (see Chapter 16 of the present volume).

Of all the purposes served by the centennial celebration, none was as conspicuous as reconciliation between graduates who had fought against each other in the Civil War. Many of those who remained loyal to the Union never forgave the West Pointers who did not. Foremost among the hardliners were Peter Michie, George Cullum, and Charles Larned, who resisted all efforts at reconciliation during their tenures as senior members of the West Point faculty. Until his death in 1901, Michie harbored animosity toward the

Confederates, to whom he ascribed dishonorable motives for their choice to fight for the South.[46] Cullum quashed all efforts to extend the olive branch during his tenure as superintendent (1864-1866) and long afterward. He felt strongly enough to bequeath $250,000 from his estate—a sizable sum in those days—to build a memorial hall on the southwest corner of the Plain. The building, known today as Cullum Hall, honored the "distinguished deceased officers and graduates of the Military Academy," pointedly omitting those from the Confederacy.[47] Larned, as well as Michie, Cullum, and others, worked tirelessly to erect Battle Monument in tribute to the officers and men of the Regular Army of the United States who gave their lives in the Civil War. On a breathtaking site overlooking the northern reach of the Hudson River, this monument dwarfs all others at West Point in size and majesty, and it conspicuously ignores the sacrifices of those who fought for the South.

In contrast to the ongoing rift among Academy graduates, Americans in general had begun to put the sectional dispute behind them. The disputed presidential election of 1876 signaled a desire to close the sectional divide; the Republicans eventually won the presidency, but only after agreeing to withdraw federal troops from their occupation duty in the South. Although Republicans continued to "wave the bloody shirt" to partisan advantage, the political life of the nation was slowly getting back to normal. The two-party system was thriving in most parts of the country, and former Confederates were being elected to Congress. The greatest catalyst for reconciliation was the Spanish-American War, which provided common purpose in creating a truly national army to defeat a foreign foe.[48] The U.S. victory culminated a long process of sectional healing that coincided with America's entry on the world stage as a major power. For West Pointers, however, it was only the beginning of the reconciliation process.

The Association of Graduates, founded in 1869, was an early attempt to bring healing within the West Point community. Created to "cherish the memories of the Military Academy at West Point, and to promote the social intercourse and fraternal fellowship of its graduates," the Association held scant initial appeal for Confederates.[49] The sting of defeat and knowledge of the bitterness directed at them by so many of their northern compatriots kept them away. By the turn of the century, only a handful routinely attended the annual meetings, and not until 1902 did the Association officially recognize their wartime achievements.[50]

Of the few Confederates who joined the Association of Graduates, Joseph Wheeler was by far the most influential. A cavalry officer who rose to the rank of major general in the Confederate army, he championed the cause of sectional reconciliation in a variety of capacities following the war. As a congressman from Alabama elected in 1882, he fought passionately against the politics of sectionalism. In a rousing speech to the House of Representatives he intoned:

> Were our people of the North and South to use the same effort in promoting harmony as is often used in kindling strife, would not the sweet influences thus aroused . . . close our ears to the clamors of sectional strife and direct us safely in our search for . . . a newly regenerated Union, happier and grander than before, more prosperous and more united, more Christian and more enlightened?[51]

Later, as a member of the House Military Affairs Committee, Wheeler was West Point's most devoted and powerful advocate in Congress. He continuously fought for more funding (or against reductions in funding) for the Academy, helped improve the credentials of the faculty, and was instrumental in securing money for a new academic building. His commitment to the welfare of his alma mater won him the respect of Academy leaders, who helped engineer his appointment as President of the Board of Visitors in 1895. Wheeler's rehabilitation was complete when he volunteered to serve as an officer during the Spanish-American War. Appointed a major general of U.S. Volunteers on 5 May 1898, he won national recognition as the first Confederate to be recommissioned in the U.S. Army.[52]

Mills was a keen supporter of reuniting the West Point alumni. This was partly because of his relative youth—as an 1879 graduate, he was the first superintendent after the Civil War who had neither been in the Army nor lived at West Point during the conflict.[53] With few personal memories of the upheavals that led to the rift among graduates, he was less reluctant than older graduates to put those troubles behind him. Within one month of his appointment as superintendent in 1898, he invited Wheeler to the Academy. Mills treated Wheeler to a mounted escort and other official honors, marking the first time the Academy had accorded a former Confederate such recognition.[54] Mills's magnanimity led to other expressions of solidarity and good will toward graduates who had served the South, and it set the stage for the dramatic events of the centennial celebration.

West Point graduates, distinguished visitors, and members of the press filed into Cullum Hall on 9 June 1902—Alumni Day—for the opening ceremonies of the centennial. Event organizers had carefully planned the seating, with Union and Confederate veterans side by side. The aging Confederate Lt. Gen. James Longstreet, for example, took his place next to Union veteran Col. John McCalmont; the two men had graduated together in 1842. The large hall was abuzz with the excited reminiscences of old friends and wartime foes. Reporters noted that some of the men "almost gave way to their emotions at the sight of the old enemies of forty years ago renewing their friendships of their days at Alma Mater before the war."[55]

The program for Alumni Day included speeches by distinguished West Pointers on the history of the Academy and the service of its graduates during its first century. Lt. Gen. John Schofield, Class of 1853, addressed the founding of the Academy and its growth as an institution under Sylvanus Thayer. Brig. Gen. Thomas J. Wood, Class of 1845, spoke next on the service of West Pointers in the war with Mexico. The audience listened politely, but all of them knew the most sensitive topic was still to come.

Maj. Gen. Thomas Ruger, Class of 1854, addressed the service of West Pointers who served the Union in the Civil War. He praised the "instant return to the military service" of virtually every living graduate from the Union states; these officers were the "very life of the armies as disciplined and fighting organizations."[56] He praised the valor of Union soldiers, regular and volunteer, and emphasized the success of Union armies in achieving the original purpose of the war—"the principle of the supremacy of the nation."[57] Ruger's intent was not to boast, however, and he ended his address with conciliatory words for the Confederates in the audience:

> No one who faced such graduates in battle doubts the sincerity of their intent. . . . Hypocrites do not combine for fighting. When the end came there was found in their hearts an echo to the words, 'Let us have peace.'" It is gratifying to meet many such graduates on this occasion . . . and to further renew the tie of good-fellowship, and especially to meet them at this place, where, as in the days of our youth, honesty and duty are still watchwords; where a man is estimated according to his qualities, and where favor can not be purchased.[58]

Ruger's carefully crafted words hit the mark. While he avoided praising the Confederate cause, he stated unequivocally his belief in the sincerity of those who embraced it. That was a key point in the struggle to reconcile the Long Gray Line.

Brig. Gen. Edward P. Alexander, Class of 1857 and a former Confederate, followed Ruger to the podium. As expected, he eulogized the wartime heroes of the South and paid special tribute to the soldiers who bore the heaviest burdens of the war. His most significant remarks, however, addressed the sensitive issue of the southern cause. With the hindsight of a generation, Alexander asked rhetorically,

> Whose vision is so dull that he does not recognize the blessing it is to himself and to his children to live in an undivided country? Who would to-day relegate his own State to the position it would hold in the world were it declared a sovereign, as are the States of Central and South America?

Answering his own question, Alexander declared, "It was best for the South that the cause was 'Lost!'"[59] These ringing words, unequivocal in meaning, were the focus of press reports of the event. One headline read, "Addresses Recounting What They Have Accomplished—Glowing Tribute to the Heroism of the South—Would not Now Accept State Sovereignty as a Gift, General Alexander Says."[60] Other speakers followed Ruger and Alexander, but the most important words in reconciling graduates on both sides of the sectional divide already had been uttered.

The four-day centennial celebration was impressive in many respects. One needs only to review the substantial two-volume history of the centennial, published in 1904, to appreciate the magnitude of the event and the thoroughness of the planning effort. Academy leaders succeeded in celebrating the positive contributions of West Point and its graduates to the nation. At the same time, they improved the Academy's public image and, with some difficulty, obtained significant Congressional support to redress institutional problems. Most significant, they encouraged a genuine rapprochement between graduates who had fought on opposite sides during the Civil War. Each of these accomplishments was significant in itself; collectively they brought tangible benefits to the Academy and reflected well on the vision of Mills and his associates. The Academy would enter its second century with new buildings, better facilities, improved academic standards, high public approval, and peace within the Long Gray Line. The centennial had much to do with those accomplishments, as noted in a *Public Opinion* article shortly after the event:

> West Point's centennial celebration served to give the institution a much-needed advertisement. We doubt if half the people who read the accounts of last week's ceremonies ever realized before the many reasons why the nation has cause to be proud of its military academy.[61]

Clearly there were many reasons to celebrate the centennial, and Academy officials made the most of them.

---

[1] Military Peace Establishment Act, 16 March 1802, Annals of Congress, 1st Sess., Seventh Congress, Appendix, 1306ff.

[2] Mary Elizabeth Sergent, *An Unremaining Glory—A Class Album for the Class of June, 1861 (Custer's Class)* (Middletown, NY: Prior King Press, Inc., 1997), 11.

[3] Multiple newspaper clippings from 4 December 1900, Booz Scrapbook, Vol. I, 25-41, Special Collections, USMA Library, West Point, NY.

[4] Roger Hurless Nye, "The United States Military Academy In An Era of Educational Reform, 1900-1925" (Ph.D. diss., Columbia University, 1968), 151.

[5] "Victim of Hazing at West Point Dies in Agony," *New York Journal*, 4 December 1900, Booz Scrapbook, Vol. I, 27; "West Point Bitterly Scorned at the Funeral of Dead Cadet," *Philadelphia Enquirer*, Booz Scrapbook, Vol. I, 57, Special Collections, USMA Library.

[6] Albert Mills to Maj. Julius A. Penn, 21 December 1900, Superintendent's Letter Book, Volume 11, No. 637, 460-61, USMA Archives.

[7] "Mills to Lose the West Point Billet," *New York Journal*, 4 December 1900, Booz Scrapbook, Vol. I, 147; Mills to editor of *Washington Times*, 21 December 1900, Superintendent's Letter Book, Vol. 11, No. 639, 460, USMA Archives.

[8] Mills to editor of *Washington Times*, 21 December 1900, Superintendent's Letter Book, Vol. 11, No. 639, 460, USMA Archives.

[9] *New York Sun*, 12 December 1900, Booz Scrapbook, Vol. I, 125, Special Collections, USMA Library.

[10] Julian Hawthorne, "The Trial of West Point," *The* (Philadelphia) *Rebel*, March 1901, Booz Scrapbook, Vol. II, 105-06, Special Collections, USMA Library.

[11] The 56th Congress engaged in lengthy and animated debate on the topic of hazing at West Point. Congressman Butler defended hazing as "absolutely essential if administered in moderation." He argued that the adverse public reaction to the Booz incident would sufficiently motivate Academy leaders to correct the worst abuses. United States Senate, Hearings, *Military Academy Appropriations Bill*, 19 February 1901, 56th Congress, 2nd Sess., 2626.

[12] Ibid., 2625.

[13] "West Point Hazing is Denounced at Academy and in the Senate," *New York World*, 17 January 1901, Booz Scrapbook, Vol. II, 228, Special Collections, USMA Library. In contrast to Senator Allen's opinion, some Congressmen defended hazing. Senator Edward O. Wolcott, a Colorado Republican, thought the practice was necessary to avoid "making milksops and prigs out of our soldiers." *Army and Navy Journal*, 23 February 1901, 617.

[14] *Military Academy Appropriations Act of 1901, Statutes at Large*, Vol. 31 (1901), 911; Theodore J. Crackel, *West Point: A Bicentennial History* (Lawrence: University Press of Kansas, 2002), 145.

[15] Nye, 73.

[16] Crackel, 111-15.

[17] Charles W. Larned, *Reorganization of the Plant of the USMA* (U.S. Military Academy, West Point, NY: 1901), USMA Archives. The Report of Buildings, 1882-1902, includes Larned's report, other documents, and copies of the Congressional minutes where Mills and Larned are present and questioned regarding the large appropriation for the major building project.

[18] USMA, Board of Visitors, *Annual Report of the Board of Visitors to the United States Military Academy for the Year 1901* (Washington, DC: Government Printing Office, 1901), 7-8, 14, 23.

[19] *Annual Report of the Superintendent of the United States Military Academy, 1900*, 15, USMA Archives.

[20] *The Statutes at Large of the United States of America*, from December 1899 to March 1901 (Washington, DC: Government Printing Office, 1901), 919.

[21] *New York Sun*, 22 June 1902, Jubilee Scrapbook 1902, Vol. 1, Special Collections, USMA Library.

[22] Ibid.

[23] Unidentified newspaper clipping, Boston, MA, Jubilee Scrapbook 1902, Vol. I, 59, Special Collections, USMA Library.

[24] Crackel, 169-74.

[25] Unidentified newspaper clipping, 13 June 1902, Trenton, NJ, Jubilee Scrapbook 1902, Vol. I, 50, Special Collections, USMA Library.

[26] Albert Mills to George B. Cortelyou, 24 May 1902, Superintendent's Letter Book, Vol. 12, Letter No. 413, 446, USMA Archives.

[27] A search of the Academy grounds and official records produced no evidence of Roosevelt's words in bronze at the Military Academy.

[28] USMA, *The Centennial of the United States Military Academy at West Point, New York, 1802-1902*, Vol. 1 (Washington, DC: Government Printing Office, 1904), 20.

[29] Unidentified newspaper clipping, Jubilee Scrapbook, Vol. I, Special Collections, USMA Library.

[30] The obvious exception was race. Only three African-Americans graduated from West Point in the 19th century, and none would do so in the 20th century until 1936. In this regard, the Corps of Cadets reflected the same racist attitudes as the larger society.

[31] Walter Scott Dillard, "The United Sates Military Academy, 1865-1900: The Uncertain Years" (Ph.D. diss., University of Washington, 1972), 226-45.

[32] H.R. 11538, Military Academy Appropriations Bill, 1901, 56th Cong., 2nd sess., *Congressional Record*, 5.

[33] Ibid, 15.

[34] Ibid.

[35] Nye, 81. The Antihazing Bill was an amendment to the Military Academy Appropriations Act of 1902; see n. 14, supra.

[36] USMA, *The Centennial of the United States Military Academy at West Point, New York: 1802-1902*, Vol. 1 (Washington, DC: Government Printing Office, 1904), 228.

[37] Crackel, 160. Italics added.

[38] Ibid.

[39] Ibid.

[40] Ibid., 180-81.

[41] *Board of Visitors Report, 1901*, 29, USMA Archives.

[42] Albert Mills to Presidents of Yale, MIT, and Cambridge, Superintendent's Letter Book, Vol. 12, No. 130-32, 354, USMA Archives.

[43] *Army and Navy Journal*, 14 June 1902, 1023-24.

[44] Ibid., 1023.

[45] USMA, *The Centennial of the United States Military Academy at West Point, New York, 1802-1902*, Vol. I (Washington, DC: Government Printing Office, 1904), 114-15.

[46] Dillard, xiii.

[47] Ibid.; Crackel, 158.

[48] Paul H. Buck, *The Road To Reunion, 1865-1900* (Boston, MA: Little, Brown and Company, 1937), 306.

[49] USMA, *The Centennial of the United States Military Academy at West Point, New York, 1802-1902*, Vol. 1 (Washington, DC: Government Printing Office, 1904), 27.

[50] Dillard, 323.

[51] Quoted in John P. Dyer, *"Fightin' Joe" Wheeler* (Baton Rouge, LA: Louisiana State University Press, 1941), 271.

[52] Dillard, 324-26.

[53] Ibid., 327.

[54] Ibid.

[55] *New York Sun*, 10 June 1902, Jubilee Scrapbook, Vol. I, Special Collections, USMA Library.

[56] USMA, *The Centennial of the United States Military Academy at West Point, New York, 1802-1902*, Vol. I (Washington, DC: Government Printing Office, 1904), 72.

[57] Ibid., 74.

[58] Ibid., 76.

[59] Ibid., 78-79.

[60] *Ledger*, 10 June 1902, Jubilee Scrapbook, Vol. I, Special Collections, USMA Library.

[61] *Public Opinion*, 19 June 1902, Jubilee Scrapbook, Vol. I, Special Collections, USMA Library.

⇥ CHAPTER 10 ⇤

CHALLENGE AND CHANGE: WEST POINT AND THE COLD WAR

Brian McAllister Linn

In the two decades prior to the Vietnam War seemed like a different world from today's institution.[1] It was all male and virtually all white and the faculty were overwhelmingly West Pointers. The curriculum was rigorously prescribed: cadets not only took the same curriculum, they often took the same tests. There were other differences from today as well, not least that the Academy in the 1950s was very much in the public eye. Its graduates were nationally known and played significant roles in the national government—including the presidency. National journals such as *The Saturday Evening Post, Holiday, Colliers*—even *National Geographic*—all ran highly laudatory stories. The Academy's football team was a national powerhouse and some of its players were household names. The Academy experience, or its fictional equivalent, provided the plots for "Red" Reeder's Clint Lane series and for television's *West Point Story*, which featured future stars such as Clint Eastwood, Leonard Nimoy, and Barbara Eden. Hollywood's elite—Tyrone Power, Doris Day, Jimmy Cagney, and Francis the Talking Mule—starred in movies which extolled the Corps of Cadets' abilities, be it on the football field or the dance floor.[2] West Point appeared, both to its graduates and to many Americans, as a bastion of honor, patriotism, and duty, its cadets impervious to the dangerous influences of individualism, materialism, and adolescent rebellion.

Yet despite its apparent solidity, the Academy in the two decades after the end of World War II was an institution in flux, seeking to retain its traditions while moving towards a troubled future. To prepare a new generation of officers for the challenges of the Cold War would require West Point to overcome a variety of difficulties. The legendary unity of the Corps of Cadets would be tested by unprecedented expansion: West Point's student body increased to over 2,000, forcing the creation of a second regiment. But at the same time, the reinvigoration of ROTC and the integration of hundreds of wartime and OCS officers into the large postwar Army greatly diluted the Academy graduate's presence and influence and posed a further challenge to West Point's claim to be *the* school for officers. Moreover, until 1958 the newly established Air Force took nearly a quarter of the Academy's graduating class, an expropriation made even more galling by the fact that for many Americans in the atomic era, the pilot, not the soldier, had come to symbolize the nation's military might.

West Point's reputation as a cherished American institution was also in flux. The Academy had garnered a great deal of prestige as the school that had educated over half the Army's senior commanders in World War II, including such luminaries as Dwight D. Eisenhower, Douglas MacArthur, Omar Bradley, George S. Patton, and Henry "Hap" Arnold. The contributions of the Academy's graduates inspired military writer Col. R. Ernest Dupuy to claim that "upon no other one group of men has fallen in such finality the fate of our nation through the years."[3] Correspondents praised West Point both for its character-building regimen and as a source of "soldier-statesmen."[4] A young woman "pinned" to a cadet told readers of *The Pointer* that he represented "the laughing, gallant, trained willingness of our American men to continue to devote their lives to the protection and preservation of these homes from all outside dangers" and "the beginning of unity and world peace, based on the study of war."[5] In his hugely influential 1957 work *The Soldier and the State*, Samuel Huntington contrasted the "discordancy of small-town commercialism" of neighboring Highland Falls with the "ordered serenity" and "beauty and utility" of West Point. To Huntington, the virtues taught at the Academy—loyalty, duty, restraint, dedication—were the ones that America in the 1950s most needed, leading him to conclude that "today America can learn more from West Point than West Point from America."[6]

But the Academy's reputation rested on fragile foundations. Although it had doubled in size, it was unable to fill the gaping holes in the ranks of the Army's junior officers. On average, any one of the annual incoming classes lost roughly a quarter of its strength between its freshman (Fourth Class or "plebe") year and senior (First Class or "firstie") year; and a fifth of its graduates would resign their commissions soon after they fulfilled their obligatory term of service. Both statistics may well have been indicative of the rigors of a West Point education and the marketability of its graduates, but both meant fewer Pointers in the Army.

More disturbing was evidence of a relative decline in the Academy's reputation. Critics, and even some supporters, pondered its continuing role in Cold War America. Within and without the Army there were complaints about "ring knockers" and the "WPPA" (West Point Protective Association), an alleged secret society of graduates dedicated to "protect its membership from hard jobs, insure their promotions, guarantee them prestige, and give each member some advantage over nonmember contemporaries in the service."[7] Norman Ford's 1961 novel *The Black, the Gray, and the Gold* portrayed a school in which cadets were victimized by a hypocritical, self-serving school administration. A year later, academic specialist David Boroff characterized the Academy as "a second-class college for first-class students."[8] Even veteran-turned-correspondent Charlton Ogburn, who admired the Military Academy, questioned whether in 1960 West Point was not "an institution with the single purpose of ensuring the safety of the United States by inculcating in those who must face its enemies a set of values directly antithetical to those that prevail in American life."[9] During the Vietnam War, William C. Westmoreland and other graduates were pilloried by leftists and by right-wingers; by the early 1970s this had escalated to accusations that the Academy was the incubator of the military-industrial complex and the source of the Vietnam debacle.[10] How did the darling of the American public and an institution that Huntington saw as the teacher of the nation suffer such relative decline? In part, but only in part, the answer may be found in the choices West Point made, and some it did not make, during the 1950s.

The Cold War era at West Point may be said to have begun as early as September 1945 with the three-year tenure of Superintendent Maxwell D. Taylor. Encouraged by comments from the Academy heroes who had directed the Army in World War II, Taylor instituted the first of what would become almost biannual self-studies. After consulting alumni and educators, Taylor made three relatively narrow, but highly significant changes: he modified the curriculum, adding more social sciences and humanities classes as well as a course on military leadership; he adopted a new criterion to evaluate each cadet's military aptitude; and he began a public relations effort to improve the Academy's academic reputation.

The first of these reforms came from a concern expressed by General Eisenhower and others that cadets needed far more training in how to lead the citizen-soldiers that made up the nation's wartime armies. Taylor eliminated anachronistic requirements such as fencing and horsemanship and tried to balance West Point's heavily engineering-oriented curriculum with more emphasis on languages, international relations, economics, and what might now be termed applied psychology. He introduced the Gallagher-Landrum Military Aptitude Test to evaluate not only each cadet's academic skills, but also his leadership, his athletic ability, and his relations with his peers. In an effort to end the Academy's self-imposed isolation from other academic institutions, Taylor encouraged intercollegiate athletic competition and established an annual symposium on national issues at which West Point hosted hundreds of students from other schools. A 1951 *Newsweek* feature noted approvingly that cadets were learning not only international relations and atomic theory, but also about such practical issues as how to deal with a pregnant girl who accused a member of their company of fatherhood.[11]

Taylor's reforms were perceived by some as an attack on West Point's cherished Thayer System, the all-inclusive approach to cadet education that comprised "the modes of discipline and character-building, the pedagogical techniques that were utilized, and the academic curriculum that was prescribed." Established by Superintendent Sylvanus Thayer (1817-1833), the system sought to create a "total environment" wherein a cadet's mental, spiritual, physical, and moral character could be forged.[12] Structure and uniformity were imposed in almost obsessive detail: all cadets marched together, all played and prayed together, all solved the same class problems, and all took the same examinations. The life of each cadet was rigorously supervised: he was required to comply with a host of regulations and could be awarded "quill" (demerits) for any infraction. Thayer had designed his system to accommodate a student body of some 100 cadets, but by 1950 the Corps numbered over 2,000. It was becoming harder and harder for West Point to provide a "total environment" for each cadet and to prevent competing loyalties and interests from subverting the single-minded dedication to the Academy that the Thayer System demanded.

The Thayer System's pedagogical methods were based on the belief that all learning could be broken into small, discrete units. Students met in small classes—perhaps a dozen students—using a pedagogy that emphasized "recitations": instructors would assign problems and selected cadets would solve them at the blackboard. Better suited for teaching engineering and mathematics than the liberal arts, the system required cadets to absorb an enormous amount of information, to summarize it rapidly, and to present it clearly and succinctly under the critical supervision of faculty and fellows. But it also discouraged intuitive thinking, intellectual speculation, indepth research, and the study of complex problems that could not be solved rapidly.

In his own day, Thayer had educated the small but elite student body with the help of an equally small but elite faculty, and in the process made West Point the best engineering school in the nation. The Academy's post-World War II expansion revealed an embarrassing, but very significant fact: the Army had a plethora of officers with sufficient experience and character to train the cadets, but very few with the necessary academic credentials to educate them in the increasing military complexities of the atomic age. West Point drew its junior teaching faculty from senior lieutenants and captains, many of them Academy graduates. Often combat veterans of World War II and Korea, they usually had considerable leadership and teaching skills and a sincere desire to help the cadets. But many lacked specialized postgraduate degrees, and all were kept so busy with teaching the curriculum and with administrative, athletic, and disciplinary duties, that they had little time for their own academic pursuits. Lacking tenure and very aware of the importance of a good evaluation for their subsequent careers, they fulfilled their three- or four-year teaching tour and then rotated back to the "real Army."

The lack of academic specialization among the junior faculty would not have been so serious had there been a senior faculty of great intellectual breadth, distinguished scholarship, and impressive teaching ability. But, with some conspicuous exceptions, this does not appear to have been the case. Most senior faculty had graduated from West Point several years—if not decades—earlier; few had the doctoral degrees that were becoming a virtual requirement for collegiate teaching in the 1950s; and even fewer were professionally active in their disciplines. Many of the senior faculty faced a problem relatively common in academia: their field of specialization had undergone such radical changes in theory and practice that much of their own education had been rendered obsolete. Indeed, some of the disciplines that were most needed in the post-World War II Army had barely existed when the senior faculty were cadets.

The problem of intellectual obsolescence was greater for West Point's faculty than for their contemporary civilian academics because the former had started out with less education and had, for the most part, remained isolated from their academic disciplines for several years. Unlike civilian institutions, the Academy had not provided its senior faculty the opportunity to take sabbaticals so that they might re-learn their disciplines. Nor, at least in comparison with civilian schools, did the Academy reward faculty who excelled in their chosen field. Although the nation's postwar universities increasingly defined themselves as research institutions and hired professors with doctoral degrees and demonstrable research abilities, the Academy's mission placed cadet, not faculty, development first. To outsiders, this growing gap between the academic qualifications of West Point's faculty and those of the civilian universities with which it chose to compare itself was disturbing. Unless it was rectified, the Academy faced the prospect of becoming an increasingly mediocre institution no matter how high the quality of the cadets it attracted. More seriously, West Point might lose its academic accreditation.[13]

Given the composition of its senior faculty, nearly all of whom were West Point graduates, it is perhaps not surprising that many of them resisted efforts to reform their cherished Academy. But their opposition was more than simple dog-in-the-manger obstructionism. Most of them took for granted both that the Thayer System was appropriate for the training of military officers and that they were well qualified to employ it in teaching the current generation of cadets. Some felt that there already had been sufficient curricular reform when West Point in 1946 added courses in military history and international relations. Also, they contended that the Academy's heavy concentration on mathematics, engineering, and the sciences—however limited in application to command and staff duties in the post-atomic Army—was essential to teach mental discipline, rapid decision-making, and efficient time management. Many firmly believed Taylor's innovations threatened the very virtues that had made West Point successful for almost a century and a half, most particularly the emphasis on the cadet's character development.

They recognized that many of the reforms, particularly Taylor's call to broaden the curriculum, would require a far more diverse and specialized faculty than West Point or the Army at large could provide.[14] Moreover, electives struck at the heart of the Academy's egalitarian tradition that every cadet faced the same opportunities and challenges. A common curriculum was also indicated, given that most of West Point's faculty rotated after only a few years and lacked both the qualifications and the time to teach more specialized courses. With more than a little justification, the permanent faculty questioned whether the Superintendent's reforms would achieve a better balance of professional education and character-building, and wondered whether they might not turn the Academy into just another college. Considering that many of the problems that the top contemporary public institutions faced from their own students in the 1960s were due to the decision made in the 1950s to emphasize faculty research over contact with students, the West Point faculty's hesitations were certainly understandable.

Those who opposed Taylor looked to the Academic Board, which controlled the curriculum. Composed of the department heads, it could serve as a valuable and essential check to West Point's falling victim to whatever educational or doctrinal trend was popular in the Department of the Army. However, the Board was also, in the words of one 1957 study, "better designed to insure stability than progress."[15] It had considerable powers because, unlike the Superintendent, who was limited to a four-year term, its members had years (in some cases decades) of experience in the Academy's antiquated bureaucratic methods and could, if they chose, impose change with glacial speed.[16]

Taylor sought to circumvent the faculty, and especially the Academic Board, in a variety of ways. He solicited outside support for his reforms from authorities such as Eisenhower. He encouraged some of the more innovative, better educated faculty such as George A. Lincoln and Herman Beukema in their emphasis on teaching international relations and current military issues.[17] He tried to moderate the Academy's internally focused faculty selection process and to hire a few respected civilian scholars—a move that was resisted by both the Academic Board and the cadets themselves. Finally, he bypassed the Board altogether by working with his close friend, Commandant Gerald J. Higgins and the Department of Tactics. Indeed, in 1947 Taylor pointedly ignored the Board when he hired Dr. Douglas Spencer, a civilian, for the newly created Department of Military Psychology and Leadership under Higgins' supervision. Taylor's troubles with conservative faculty and the Board, as well as the methods he adopted to work around them, would be repeated by subsequent reformers.[18]

Taylor's zeal was not shared by his immediate successors—Bryant E. Moore (1949-1951), Frederick A. Irving (1951-1954), and Blackshear Bryan (1954-1956)—all of whom tended to place more emphasis on the development of moral character. Successive internal self-studies presupposed there was nothing fundamentally wrong with the Academy and deliberately avoided comparing its curriculum and academic reputation with those of civilian institutions. Accordingly, they concluded that West Point was more than doing its job, that the Thayer System was the best method for teaching cadets, and that there was no need for electives in the curriculum.[19]

The Academy's opinion was shared by many, but some insiders questioned both its methods and its mission. In 1952 the Board of Visitors—many of whose members rarely accompanied the group during its annual visit and even more rarely made constructive suggestions—complained that "the error of over specialization is quite apparent in the present format of the curriculum," and urged less attention to mathematics and science and more to history, English, and the social sciences.[20] The Board also criticized the requirement that a quarter of the Academy's temporary faculty be reservists, on the grounds that the desperate shortage of qualified academics among civilian universities would ensure that only inferior scholars would volunteer for military duty. The Board's solution—to draw West Point's temporary faculty from the Regular Army—begged the question of whether the Regulars could provide the required scholars, particularly in the fields in which the Board believed West Point most deficient. The following year, after observing that the Academy hierarchy had ignored virtually all its recommendations, the Board repeated its demand for more "diversification." Escalating its attack, it challenged the long-hallowed assumption that every cadet must receive identical instruction, noting that the "greater number of roles the Army is called upon to perform" rendered obsolete the traditional rationale for a "uniform education."[21] The Board also drew attention to a number of other problems, including a rise in cadet resignations, the dilapidated condition of some cadet barracks, and, most tellingly, the fact that "in classrooms, lecture halls, and laboratory space West Point is not to be compared with most of our state universities."[22]

In addition to this internal criticism, West Point also came in for some pointed, albeit comparatively rare, censure from outsiders. In a 1947 *Look* article, Maxine Davis, the wife of a career naval officer and the mother of an Annapolis midshipman, blasted both academies for their "smug, time-marking mentality" and charged that their graduates were "incapable of self-criticism" and poorly prepared for the challenges of the postwar world.[23] In 1956 Congressman John F. Kennedy attacked the service academies' selection process. Although his main target was Congressional appointments, he noted that many cadets were poorly motivated and intellectually deficient, factors he believed contributed to an attrition rate twice that of Harvard and to the resignation of many graduates as soon as they fulfilled their military commitment.[24] In their generally sympathetic 1957 work *Soldiers and Scholars*, sociologists John W. Masland and Laurence I. Radway concluded that both West Point and Annapolis suffered from a number of problems, including an obsolescent and overly technical curriculum, an emphasis on training rather than education, a propensity towards stereotyped thinking and "school solutions," a faculty composed of "amateurs and drillmasters," and a "study and recite" pedagogy.[25]

In at least one way, West Point was very much like a civilian academic institution—in its aspirations for a national champion football team. After a decade of mediocrity which had seen Army football tumble from its once lofty reputation, Coach Red Blaik had revitalized the program, winning 57 games between 1944 and 1950, recruiting All-Americans such as Doc Blanchard and Glen Davis, and winning national championships.[26] Such success had come at some cost to the Academy's reputation, not least in that it aroused a great deal of external animosity and revived wartime criticism of West Point as a haven for draft dodgers. Within the Academy, Blaik's influence was huge, and not altogether beneficial. Superintendent Taylor recalled him as "a magnificent coach, but a man who felt that winning football games was a primary responsibility of the Military Academy."[27] Some West Pointers, including Commandant Paul D. Harkins (1947-1951), believed that the acclaim accorded the football program was inappropriate for a military academy and that Blaik was subverting discipline. Blaik had succeeded in changing the height and weight qualifications for cadets; he encouraged the creation of an off-campus "cram school" which prepared students, athletes prominent among them, for the West Point entrance examinations; and he sequestered his players in a number of ways, including a separate mess hall training table. The players were also segregated from the other cadets in their priorities: George Barney Poole, a stellar college receiver, was "drafted" onto West Point's team during the war, then left the Academy to resume his football career at the University of Mississippi.[28] The prestige, power, and independence of the team grew to such an extent that one correspondent was only half joking when he commented that in 1949 the American public believed the Corps of Cadets was "divided into two parts, half of which spends all its time parading, and the other half playing football."[29]

The Academy's pedagogical methods and the pressures of balancing football with classwork both contributed to academic dishonesty. In order to follow Thayer's stricture that each cadet receive exactly the same education at the same time, cadets from one regiment would attend class and recite the day's problems. In the afternoon (or sometimes the next day), cadets from the other regiment would take the same class and recite the same problems. This extended even into testing, so that half the cadets might take a test on one day, and the other half the same test the next. The two regiments' separation from each other and, more important, the Honor Code—which stated that a cadet would not lie, cheat, or steal, or tolerate those who did—were believed more than sufficient to avoid misconduct. But at the football training table, in the locker room, and at the special tutorial sessions for athletes, cadets from both regiments mixed freely, creating a tempting opportunity to exchange information on class problems. By 1951 these unhealthy arrangements came to produce "rings" of complicit cadet athletes who shared test questions and answers.[30]

Cheating was not only an academic issue, it also highlighted the potential confusion in the Academy's efforts to inculcate "character." Orders, regulations, and restrictions were everywhere at West Point, and cadets were expected to follow each of them to almost ludicrous extremes. None was stronger than the Honor Code, which was perceived by the cadets themselves as the cornerstone of their integrity and had overwhelming support among the student body. But unlike the Academy's regulations, the Code was a moral and ethical guide that the Corps enforced on itself. No less an authority than Eisenhower cautioned Superintendent Taylor in 1946 that faculty must understand that "the honor system is something that is in the hands of the Cadets themselves, . . . and that under no circumstances should it ever be used at the expense of the Cadets in the detection of violations of regulations."[31] Perhaps in response, Taylor issued a pamphlet, *West Point Honor System: Its Objectives and Procedures*, emphatically stating that "the authorities are careful not to use the Honor System to prevent the violation of regulations" and that the "Honor System is not a means of disciplining the Corps of Cadets."[32] However, it is evident that some of the faculty, particularly tactical officers, did use the Honor Code as a means of enforcing discipline, and some abused it in ways that forced cadets to incriminate themselves and their classmates in violations of what, at least in the cadets' minds, often were petty regulations. This, in turn, may have contributed to the rationalization among some cadets that evading regulations was acceptable, and from there to an elastic interpretation of the Honor Code itself.[33]

In April 1951 a cadet told Commandant Harkins that he had been invited to join a ring which shared information about recitations and exams. Shortly afterwards, another cadet reported a similar invitation. With perhaps insufficient thought to the ethical and legal issues involved, Harkins asked, or ordered, the pair to inform on their comrades. Armed with their testimony, and with evidence of a test in which a suspiciously high number of cadets had entered the identical wrong answer, he appointed a board under Lt. Col. Arthur "Ace" Collins, Jr. In a series of hearings, the Collins Board ultimately identified 39 Second Classmen (Class of 1952) and 54 Third Classmen (Class of 1953) as cheaters. Blaik, in an action he may later have regretted, urged members of the football squad to cooperate, with the result that 37 players, including Blaik's son, voluntarily gave evidence that they had either cheated or knew people who had. The Collins Board penalized only the Second and Third classes, exempting the entire Fourth and First classes from punishment and thus in all probability allowing the leaders of the cheating rings to be commissioned. The Department of the Army behaved even more questionably, defining the review board's duties so narrowly as to insure guilty verdicts, sequestering the cadets, and then, at the order of President Truman, separating 90 cadets from the service.[34]

The repercussions of the football scandal are difficult to determine. One writer termed it the greatest blow West Point had suffered since classmates had divided over the Civil War.[35] In the past decade alone it has been the subject of two books and a *Sports Illustrated* article. Over time, the consensus seems to be that the scandal was primarily the result of Blaik's and the football team's separation from the Military Academy and the Corps of Cadets. To West Point's credit, and in contrast to more than a few universities, both then and now, the conflict between integrity and football excellence resulted in a victory for integrity. It is clear that many cadets violated the Code, though many of these violators were not cheaters themselves but had merely tolerated cheating. It is also true that many of those who were punished (and perhaps several more plebes and firsties) deserved expulsion. Yet it is also true that the Military Academy was due some censure for allowing football to become such a threat to the Academy's integrity, for allowing the conditions that one board termed "a perpetual inducement" to cheating, and for mishandling the affair so that punishment fell unequally and, in more than a few cases, unjustly.[36] Finally, the scandal revealed, if in a somewhat negative way, that the vast majority of cadets, including several who were expelled, took the Honor Code very seriously and viewed it as an essential part of the West Point education.

In its immediate consequences, the "honor incident" seems to have done little but reinforce the Academy's already noticeable tendency to see itself as unique and misunderstood. The faculty continued the rotation system of recitations and examinations, and some tactical officers continued to abuse the Honor Code as a means to enforce discipline. The football team recovered quickly and was again a national powerhouse by 1953, enthusiastically supported by a superintendent and commandant who were both former gridiron stars.[37] The significant problems revealed by the scandal—the flawed self-policing methods, the inherent difficulty in ensuring the Thayer System's precepts of an equal education to a large student body, and the administration's use of questionable procedures—were apparently overlooked. Indeed, in its annual report the Board of Visitors ignored the entire affair except to express its horror at a "manifestation of a wholly undesirable type of liberalism": two cadets had exercised their constitutional right against self-incrimination.[38] It is difficult to disagree with West Point's own 1989 self-study, which concluded that by fixing blame on the football team, the Academy avoided a more thorough examination of other problems.[39]

The football scandal ushered in a decade that would prove one of the most frustrating in the entire history of the U.S. Army. The early defeats of the Korean War had tarnished the Army's reputation, as did highly colored accounts of prisoners of war collaborating with the Communists. Nuclear weapons appeared to make the Army's hard-won World War II experience, indeed, its entire history, largely irrelevant. To the dismay of his former subordinates, Eisenhower's New Look stressed the primacy of nuclear weapons and air power, and throughout the 1950s the Air Force received the lion's share of the budget as the Army shrank. With considerable spirit, if less than considerable historical accuracy, West Point's former superintendent and by this time Army Chief of Staff Taylor declared in 1955, "An army without atomic weapons on the battlefield of the future will be more helpless than the French knights at Crécy before the English cannon."[40]

But the Army's efforts to create an atomic field army capable of fighting on the nuclear battlefield had mixed success, prompting such dubious experiments as the Pentomic division and the "Davy Crockett" tactical nuclear weapon. In movies, television, novels, and cartoons the service was often portrayed as a haven for goldbricking Beetle Baileys and conniving Sergeant Bilkos. If the Army's World War I soldier-hero was Alvin York, and for World War II Audie Murphy, then perhaps its Cold War personification was the reluctant draftee Elvis Presley. Despite unstinting efforts at public relations, the Army remained convinced that it was unappreciated and misunderstood by the American public. Responding to the incessant demands from superiors to "tell the Army's story," one exasperated major wrote in 1954: "I do not know what the Army's mission is or how it plans to fulfill its mission. . . . At a time when new weapons and new machines herald a revolution in warfare, we soldiers do not know where the Army is going and how it is going to get there."[41]

Such complaints revealed an undercurrent of doubt and demoralization in the 1950s officer corps. In 1953 the Secretary of the Army had warned: "It is a disturbing fact that the Army is finding it increasingly difficult to attract and hold career soldiers."[42] Among West Pointers who graduated between 1954 and 1960, an average of 19 percent had resigned by 1964, including 27 percent of the Class of 1954.[43] In a 1958 *Look* article, J. R. Moskin followed the careers of two 1952 USMA classmates, Lt. Robert Burke, commander of an isolated NIKE battery, and salesman Warren Hayford. Burke, who had lived in nine homes in five years, customarily worked 97-hour weeks in a job characterized by routine, paperwork, and petty detail—one picture showed Burke accompanying his colonel on latrine inspection.

The lieutenant collected an annual salary of $5,724 and hoped that in 15 years he might make $9,000 as a colonel. Hayford was already earning more than that, and his occupation promised even greater financial rewards. He owned a beautiful home in a fine neighborhood, far better than the Burke family's miserable Army quarters. Asked why he had resigned, Hayford responded he had been among the most enthusiastic of cadets, but the Army he joined proved to be a stultifying, hidebound bureaucracy, unwilling to recognize merit, and indifferent to the sacrifices its members made. Other ex-officers echoed Hayford, both in praising the financial and emotional joys of civilian life and in criticizing the Army's lack of opportunities. *Look* noted that the Class of 1952 had already lost two of its top five cadets and that Hayford had ranked in the top 20, whereas Burke had been 514th out of 527. Valid or not, the message was clear: West Point's best and brightest were getting out of the Army, leaving only those who couldn't find another occupation.[44]

Much of the retention problem may have been the result of the selection process itself. In the immediate postwar era, Army service was not overly popular: from 1947 to 1951 only 73 percent of the Academy's slots were filled.[45] Throughout the 1950s roughly one out of every four cadets admitted did not graduate, and the Academy

usually met only 80 percent of its Army-imposed quota of junior officers, indications that in some ways West Point's own elitism worked
against the Army's need for officers.[46] Until 1958, the Academy's
admissions requirements focused narrowly on academic and physical skills; only later was there an effort to evaluate the "whole man."[47]
Perhaps as a result, throughout much of the 1950s West Point may
have admitted a high proportion of cadets who were temperamen-
tally unsuited to an Army career. Even those graduates who wanted
to stay in the Army could be frustrated when its assignment system,
based on class standings, assigned them to branches that were professionally and personally unsatisfactory.[48]

The limited information now available on cadet life provides
some clues for why many of West Point's 1950s graduates were so
lukewarm in their commitment to their service. The collected letters of Harper Brown Keeler (Class of 1957) show a gifted individual
who was a credit to his school and his nation. But until his senior
year—when he found he could join the Air Force—they are remarkable for their revelation of the Academy's lack of emphasis on, and
the cadets' lack of interest in, military subjects. Keeler found his
course work hard but not intellectually challenging: his strongest
criticism was reserved for a mathematics teacher who graded below
the accepted "C" or 2.4; his highest praise was for a physics instructor "who does not try to confuse you with theory but . . . just tells
you the proper application of formulas."[49] To outsiders the most
interesting aspect about the student magazine *The Pointer* is the
absence of military focus. In the 1954 editions, for example, there
is almost no discussion of events in Korea, or of the Cold War, or
of which branch or specialty cadets might opt for. Army subjects
intrude only with such mundane and unmilitary issues as housing,
uniforms, mess facilities, and athletics.[50]

In retrospect, it appears that West Point's greatest chance for
reform in the 1950s was during the tenure of its most controversial
superintendent, Maj. Gen. Garrison H. "Gar" Davidson (1956-1960).
A star athlete as a cadet, Davidson had been one of the Academy's
most successful football coaches, Patton's chief engineer in North
Africa and Sicily, and a tenacious and charismatic combat com-

mander. During his tenure as commandant of the Command and General Staff College he began changing its curriculum to emphasize the Army's new responsibilities in the atomic age.[51] His experience both with CGSC and his own children, who had attended excellent universities, opened him to new methods of education. He was also in close contact with many of the Army's most brilliant officers, some of whom, such as James M. Gavin, were convinced that West Point was weeding out many cadets possessed of the very traits the Army most needed to meet the challenges of the Cold War. Finally, on a personal level, Davidson was convinced that both the cheating scandal and the administration's conduct were indicative of a deep-rooted moral and ethical malaise within the Academy.[52]

Davidson moved rapidly to change what he viewed as the Academy's outmoded curriculum. In 1957, with support from the Department of the Army, he initiated a new summer course that required cadets to visit military installations and learn about new developments in weapons and doctrine, particularly atomic warfare.[53] He began a revision of the Honor Code that would eventually make any question that required a cadet to incriminate himself or others an "improper" one. He liberalized the regulations about alcohol and eliminated the tradition of organizing cadet companies by height, thereby making company intramural athletic competition far more equal, and perhaps mitigating somewhat the cadet prejudices about the personality impairments associated with so-called "runt" and "flanker" complexes. Davidson emphasized leadership by example and greatly increased the responsibilities of the First Classmen, insisting they be mentors and discouraging their tendency to blow post for the weekend. His message was clear: command brought with it obligations; it required a highly moral, ethical, and principled person to be a U.S. Army officer.

One of Davidson's first, and most public, actions was to curb the power of Blaik and the football program. He and Red Blaik had disliked each other from the time they had both been assistant football coaches in the 1920s. Blaik believed the Superintendent's views on athletics were not only anachronistic, but also a direct threat to the football program and to himself. For his part, Davidson was convinced Blaik had entered the Academy to avoid service in World War I and he considered the coach's methods incompatible with the school's athletic and academic priorities. Most important, Davidson believed Blaik shared responsibility for the 1951 cheating debacle. The two men clashed immediately when Davidson restricted the football recruiting program, and again in 1958 when Davidson vetoed the team's appearance in the Cotton Bowl. Timing his actions to exact the most publicity, and inflict the most damage, Blaik abruptly resigned in 1959. At some cost, Davidson had accomplished one part of his mandate for change.[54]

Far more controversial, at least in the long run, were Davidson's efforts to reform the curriculum. To justify his changes, he could cite a Secretary of the Army report that declared that West Point would offer new courses "as required by developments in nuclear and missile warfare and by the pentomic Army."[55] Through a series of "Plain Talk" articles in the alumni magazine *Assembly*, he sought support from graduates. That the Department of Tactics was under former teammate and close friend Commandant John Throckmorton and included two stellar officers—Cols. Richard G. Stilwell and Julian J. Ewell—must have greatly increased Davidson's confidence.[56] To prepare the Academy for reform, Davidson began a series of studies, surveying the entire Class of 1957 and polling active duty graduates. These demonstrated both that the current Academy curriculum was unbalanced and that it was not comparable to those of other undergraduate schools, including West Point's chosen "peer competitors."[57] The data from these studies were used by two boards, one under Stilwell, which focused on military leadership, and the other under Ewell, which mapped out the Army's needs for officers in the decade 1968 to 1978. The boards' reports, delivered in early 1958, confirmed much of what Davidson had suspected. The Ewell Board in particular presented "a manifesto for sweeping reforms." Among these were the inclusion of more humanities and social sciences, and, most radical of all, the recommendation that cadets be allowed to take electives and to specialize in specific disciplines.

Davidson was convinced that West Point needed to be more like a top-tier university, and that meant a faculty that combined teaching and scholarship. In 1957 he declared that all statutory professors would be expected to complete their doctoral degrees, and, moreover, they would take sabbaticals every seven years with the specific injunction of improving their professional credentials.[58] Since fewer than 10 percent of the Academy's instructors had earned a doctorate, and the percentage of those professionally active in their disciplines was even smaller, Davidson's reforms inevitably brought him into conflict with the Academic Board. Headed by a dean who had taught at West Point for 27 years, its members averaged eight years as permanent professors and all had at least a decade as faculty members.[59] The Academic Board's own study, conducted by Col. John R. Jannarone, Head of Physics and Chemistry, concluded that the Army's future officers would require mathematics and engineering, advocated only token increases to the social sciences, and recommended electives only for truly exceptional students.[60]

In fairness to the Academic Board, it might well have argued that the needs of the "Atomic Army" and the Soviet threat more than justified West Point's traditional emphasis on mathematics, science, and character-building. The fact that graduating West Point cadets consistently scored higher in standardized tests in mathematics, humanities, and social sciences then did their civilian counterparts seemed to demonstrate both the Academy's academic rigor and the diversity of its curriculum. The Board may also have recognized that electives would revolutionize both the curriculum and the composition of West Point's faculty. As long as West Point cadets all took the same curriculum it was possible to insure uniformity not only of cadet education, but of faculty quality. But should electives be introduced, it would be necessary to have a far more specialist and diverse teaching faculty that would have to devote at least a part of its time to continuing its own research.

This raised the problem, common in civilian universities, of a faculty divided between scholars and teachers, not to mention the potential for officers to accord a higher priority to the completion of their degrees or their research than to their responsibilities to cadets. Moreover, as the Board of Visitors had noted earlier, it was extremely doubtful that West Point could attract faculty with scholarly credentials equivalent to those of the top civilian universities it compared itself to. The implications of Davidson's reforms for both the Academy and the Army were thus far-reaching indeed, and Army Chief of Staff Lyman Lemnitzer was unwilling to deal with them. He tacitly supported the Academic Board when he refused either to change the curriculum or to reappoint Davidson.

Davidson soon appeared to be vindicated in his belief that if West Point did not reform it would lose both academic and popular prestige. A 1962 *Harper's Magazine* article by David Boroff, an authority on undergraduate education, may have marked a significant turning point in the Academy's reputation. Boroff was impressed with the cadets' high entrance standards—the equal of any elite university, by their "awesome" academic load, and by their courtesy, discipline, and strong work ethic. But he was depressed by the "deadening uniformity" of cadets' responses to his questions, their rigid adherence to the "party line," and, perhaps most alarming, their complete lack of enthusiasm for learning.[61]

To Boroff, the major problem was that "academically, West Point is a second-class college for first-class students. The limitations of the program can be summed up in this fashion: The faculty isn't good enough."[62] Even by the standards of second-tier civilian institutions, the academic credentials of West Point's 358 faculty were weak—93 possessed only their baccalaureate, a little more than two-thirds (251) held a master's, and only 14 held doctoral degrees.[63] As in Taylor's time, with a few conspicuous exceptions, they neither published nor made any other scholarly contribution to their respective disciplines. Boroff claimed that the pedagogical principles underlying the Thayer System had been discredited throughout academe, as had the view that knowledge could be broken down into easily digestible segments, consumed, and then regurgitated at recitation. He insinuated that the primary reason the Academy retained its by-the-numbers lesson plans was that they protected the under-educated faculty.

Although much of Boroff's article seems, in retrospect, too critical, he did raise an interesting question: did the Army and the West Point authorities miss a real opportunity to "grow" officers in the same way that universities "grow" accomplished scholars and teachers? In stressing that the faculty's primary mission was to teach the Army leaders of the future, the faculty's own potential contribution as future leaders—the faculty being far more likely than the average cadet to remain in the Army—appears to have been effectively overlooked. The insistence that the cadets came first prompted complaints such as that of Donald V. Bennett, a faculty member in the 1950s (and later a four-star general), who recalled that 95 percent of his time was spent with those 5 percent of cadets who were doing poorly.[64] Had Taylor and his successors shown more flexibility and foresight, they might have relieved a few selected faculty of some of their administrative, athletic, and social duties, and encouraged them to pursue their postgraduate education. This might have not only provided a core of officers better able to deal with the intellectual and professional challenges of the 1960s, it could have solved West Point's shortage of qualified faculty and a looming problem with academic accreditation.[65] This need not have required a substantial shift in the faculty's teaching commitments. Prior to the Civil War, Academy faculty duty served as a postgraduate school for the best officers in the Army. Today, some of West Point's permanent faculty are internationally recognized as scholars, and many of the rotating faculty have earned their doctorates.[66] West Point's decision to make its priorities the graduation of a few more marginal second lieutenants—Bennett's 5 percent—may not have justified the long-term cost of under-educating dozens of the Army's brightest captains and majors.[67]

Boroff's article may have also been indicative of an increasingly critical view of the Military Academy among the American public and press. In the early 1950s virtually all media treatments were favorable; the Academy was hailed as a bastion of conservative values and manly virtues. Two 1952 articles—"The Making of a West Pointer" in the *National Geographic* and "Plebe at the Point" in *Colliers*—are typical in their laudatory coverage of West Point's ability to turn young boys into men.[68] A 1954 article in *McCalls* even assured parents they could profit by following West Point's example in disciplining and motivating their own children.[69] Writers of juvenile fiction also praised the Academy. In Russell G. Emery's *Warren of*

West Point, the hero arrives a shy and insecure boy, but "with the help and understanding of his instructors, his friends, and the methods by which this great military school develops the best in its students" he becomes a star basketball player.[70] In "Red" Reeder's Clint Lane series, the hero overcomes a number of adversities—mostly in the classroom—on his way to glory on the gridiron and baseball diamond. In a perhaps unintentional omission, Clint Lane does almost nothing at West Point that would seem, at least to an outsider, to prepare him for the profession of arms.[71] To Hollywood, the Academy was a hard-but-kindly boys school whose faculty and students were always ready to march, sing, dance, and play football. Thus in the 1950 musical *West Point Story* starring Jimmy Cagney, Virginia Mayo, Gordon MacRae, and Doris Day, all problems are resolved when the Corps breaks into the "Military Polka" at the hop.[72] In contrast, there were very few movies, television shows, or juvenile books about West Point in the 1960s, nor were there nearly as many laudatory articles in the popular press.

Like virtually every other institution Americans had revered in the 1950s, the U.S. Military Academy in the 1960s was subject to a barrage of criticism. As Rick Atkinson's *The Long Gray Line* so movingly illustrates, the 1960s would see a further erosion of the school's popularity as well as far more internal troubles.[73] As many of the nation's best students sought to avoid service during the Vietnam War, West Point was forced to lower its entrance standards, admitting more and more marginal students. Another cheating scandal in 1966 resulted in the expulsion of 42 cadets. Some faculty members' abuse of the Honor Code in order to reverse what they regarded as a decline in discipline prompted resistance from cadets who covered up for their comrades and even intimidated Honor Committee members.[74] When correspondent Ward Just visited in 1969, he found a school uncertain of its purpose and its place. Many of the best (and worst) cadets were leaving—attrition was over 20 percent—and there were the same complaints about the Thayer System, the time-consuming but often superficial course work, and the quality of the teaching. But according to Just, what was far more disturbing was the casual comment of one cadet, selected by the Academy as a representative, who told him "there isn't a single member of the junior class who is going to stick with this Army after the five-year commitment."[75]

Nowadays, of course, it is all too easy to assume that West Point's high reputation, military and academic, is the natural outgrowth of a century's uninterrupted progress. In an entry in a work on military education, for example, one ex-faculty member concluded that in the 1950s the Academy "evolved with the times and prudently adjusted its program" and thus "maintained its front rank among American undergraduate institutions."[76] A more accurate appraisal would be that excessive prudence slowed evolution and contributed to a decline in the Academy's place among the nation's undergraduate institutions. Some of this decline was due to factors entirely outside of West Point's control, for example, the dramatic growth and improvement of civilian academic institutions, the increasing emphasis on academic research, and the availability of higher education to more and more Americans. So too, OCS, ROTC, and the comparatively high manpower levels of the Cold War Army weakened the Academy's influence. In retrospect, it is difficult to imagine how the Academy's leaders of the 1946 to 1965 period could have prepared for the trauma of Vietnam. Nevertheless, some of this decline was due to West Point's own conservatism. Although reformers such as Taylor and Davidson could point to improvements in the curriculum, the 20-year battle to allow electives is indicative of the slow pace of change at that time. So too is the faculty's sustained resistance to higher academic standards. In an era in which the Army faced a myriad of new challenges both at home and abroad, the Academy often seems to have found too much inspiration in the customs and traditions of the past.

Fortunately, both the Army and West Point recognized the seriousness of the situation and took strong, and effective, measures to restore the Academy's proud status. Many of the academic developments that were initiated in the immediate postwar period would be instrumental in this revitalization. In 1961 for the first time First Classmen were offered the opportunity to select two electives. Today, cadets can pursue any one of 24 optional majors, selecting ten electives among over 600 courses. Between 1952 and 2002, the proportion of mathematics, sciences, and engineering courses in the core curriculum declined from 69 percent to 45 percent, so that today there is an essential parity between the technical and the social/ humanities components. That former bastion of conservatism, the West Point faculty, have played an essential role in this revitalization. Whereas in 1962 only 4 percent of Academy's faculty had doctoral degrees and 71 percent had master's, now the figures are 40 percent and 57 percent, respectively.[77] Thus if the pace of change was overly slow at the Academy in the 20 years immediately following World War II, it accelerated greatly thereafter. The result has been a Military Academy far better prepared to face the challenge of the next century.

---

[1] I would like to thank John W. Shy (USMA 1952), Thomas W. Collier (USMA 1952), Robert A. Doughty (USMA 1965), Paul H. Herbert (USMA 1972), Conrad C. Crane (USMA 1974), Lance A. Betros (USMA 1977), and Jeffrey W. French (USMA 1991) for their often critical but always helpful comments on earlier drafts. Many thanks also to Susan Lintelmann and the staff at Special Collections and Archives, USMA Library. All mistakes are my own.

[2] The West Point experience did not always engender loyalty to the U.S. Army. Students of popular culture will note that Tyrone Power flew for Great Britain in *A Yank in the RAF*, Barbara Eden took up with a USAF pilot in *I Dream of Genie*, Clint Eastwood and Francis the Talking Mule swabbed together in *Francis Joins the Navy*, and Leonard Nimoy later had a distinguished career with the United Federation of Planets.

[3] R. Ernest Dupuy, "This is West Point," *Combat Forces Journal* 2 (May 1952): 25.

[4] "West Point Producing Soldier Statesmen," *Newsweek*, 26 March 1951, 88-89.

[5] Judy Parkinson, "West Point," *The Pointer*, 16 March 1955, 6. The term "pinned" refers to the cadet custom of giving an A-shaped (for Army) brooch to his "steady" girlfriend.

[6] Samuel P. Huntington, *The Soldier and the State: The Theory and Politics of Civil-Military Relations* (New York: Vintage Books, 1957), 465-66.

[7] C. V. Clifton, "A Pointer Looks at the WPPA," *Combat Forces Journal* 2 (May 1952): 32. Maxine Davis, "What's Wrong with West Point and Annapolis," *Look*, 13 May 1947, 32-36.

[8] David Boroff, "West Point: Ancient Incubator for a New Breed," *Harper's Magazine*, December 1962, 59. Norman R. Ford, *The Black, the Gray, and the Gold* (Garden City, NY: Doubleday and Co., 1961).

[9] Charlton Ogburn, "The United States Army," *Holiday*, September 1960, 98.

[10] K. Bruce Galloway and Robert B. Johnson II, *West Point: America's Power Fraternity* (New York: Simon and Schuster, 1973); Ward Just, *Military Men* (New York: Alfred A. Knopf, 1970), 15-52; Richard C. U'Ren, *Ivory Fortress: A Psychiatrist Looks at West Point* (Indianapolis: Bobbs-Merrill Co., 1974). A balanced appraisal of these rather biased West Point critiques appears in Joseph J. Ellis and Robert Moore, *School for Soldiers: West Point and the Profession of Arms* (New York: Oxford University Press, 1974), 14-22.

[11] "West Point Producing Soldier Statesmen," 88-89. On Taylor's tenure as Superinten-
dent, see *Annual Report of the Superintendent, 1947* (West Point, NY: U.S. Military
Academy, 1947), 23; *Annual Report of the Superintendent, 1948* (West Point, NY: U.S.
Military Academy, 1948); Stephen E. Ambrose, *Duty, Honor, Country: A History of West
Point* (Baltimore, MD: Johns Hopkins University Press, 1966), 298-99; Harold H. Mar-
tin, "Is West Point Doing its Job?" *Saturday Evening Post*, 7 June 1952, 32-33, 155-58;
Steven E. Smith, "Maxwell Taylor and the Establishment of the Department of Military
Psychology and Leadership," 15 November 1996, Tactical Officer Educational Program
[TOEP], Special Collections, U.S. Military Academy Archives [USMAA], West Point, N.Y.

[12] James P. Lovell, *Neither Athens Nor Sparta? The American Service Academies in Transition* (Bloomington: Indiana University Press, 1979), 18. For a detailed study of the
Academy's curriculum and pedagogical methods in the 1950s, see John W. Masland
and Laurence I. Radway, *Soldiers and Scholars: Military Education and National Policy*
(Princeton, NJ: Princeton University Press, 1957), 197-231. On Thayer, see Ambrose,
Duty, Honor, Country, 62-105. For a laudatory in-house treatment of the Military Academy, see R. Ernest Dupuy, *Men of West Point* (New York: William Sloane, 1951).

[13] Ellis and Moore, *School for Soldiers*, 219-22. The problem of an inbred faculty that
was neither as well educated as peer civilian institutions nor professionally active had
been true in both service academies since the Civil War; see Lovell, *Neither Athens Nor
Sparta*, 24-27.

[14] This was a legitimate concern. In 1962, for example, among the U.S. Army's officer
corps, some 7.4 percent had master's degrees and .43 percent had doctoral degrees.
Moreover, educational levels were skewed by branch, so that in the Regular Army 44
percent of engineer officers had master's degrees, but only 9 percent in armor and
field artillery and 6 percent in infantry did; see "Civilian Education Level as of mid-
month November 1962, Army Department Commissioned Officers," File 63/6, Box 63,
George A. Lincoln Papers, Special Collections, USMAA.

[15] Masland and Radway, *Soldiers and Scholars*, 248. Conflict between instructors and
senior faculty is a primary theme of Ford's *The Black, the Gray, and the Gold*.

[16] I am indebted to Col. Robert Doughty for pointing out the importance of the Academic Board and suggesting a comparison with CGSC.

[17] John Shy noted that both Lincoln and Beukema were in the social sciences-liberal arts
faculty. That these two were considered the "academics" and not the faculty in West
Point's traditional strengths of engineering or mathematics is perhaps further indication that Taylor's concerns were justified.

[18] *Annual Report of the Superintendent, 1947*, 23; Tom Hayden, "Improving the Image of
the Tactical Officer," 1989, TOEP. Spencer's appointment was even more controversial
after copies of his confidential reports were found in the possession of tactical officers; see Smith, "Maxwell Taylor," 14.

[19] Ellis and Moore, *School for Soldiers*, 49-51; Lovell, *Neither Athens Nor Sparta?* 93-94.

[20] "Report of the Board of Visitors to the U.S.M.A.," 24 April 1952, 4-5, USMAA. The Board
of Visitors' lack of commitment can be indicated by its four-day inspection in 1951. Of
the four Senators, five Congressmen, and six presidential nominees, only nine attended the initial meeting on 23 April and none remained for the final day; see "Report
of the Board of Visitors to the U.S.M.A.," 28 April 1951, USMAA. In 1953 only seven
members participated and two of these left after one day; see "Report of the Board of
Visitors to the U.S.M.A.," 24 April 1952, USMAA.

[21] "Report of the Board of Visitors to the U.S.M.A.," 30 April 1953, 4, USMAA.

[22] Ibid., 6.

[23] Davis, "What's Wrong," 32-36.

[24] John F. Kennedy, "Take the Academies Out of Politics," *Saturday Evening Post*, 2 June 1956, 36-37, 46-50.

[25] Masland and Radway, *Soldiers and Scholars*, 232-49; *Annual Report of the Superintendent, 1959* (West Point, NY: U.S. Military Academy, 1959), 31-47.

[26] Frank Deford, "Code Breakers," *Sports Illustrated*, 13 November 2000, 86. Conrad C. Crane noted that the Military Academy was the unanimous pick as national champion in 1944 and 1945, but that in 1946 the Helms Foundation proclaimed Army champions and the AP poll awarded that honor to Notre Dame.

[27] Maxwell D. Taylor Oral History, 1972, 3:12, Senior Officer Oral History Program, U.S. Army Military History Institute, Carlisle, PA. [hereafter MHI].

[28] Poole was the most famous wartime Black Knight, but not the only one. Thomas E. "Shorty" McWilliams, who played for Mississippi State University, switched to the Academy team, then returned to college, where he played against Barney Poole. According to John Shy, the "cram school" taught Army appointees as well as athletes.

[29] Kahn, "West Point," 53.

[30] In the words of one board, the guilty cadets "were led into this situation by men in classes ahead of them, most of whom are now graduates and beyond anything but very complicated punitive action. In other words, the cadets with whom we are now dealing inherited the system of cheating, they did not voluntarily establish it, and many ahead of them have gone free." Report of Board to Secretary of Army, 25 July 1951, West Point Honor System Review File, Box 23, J. Lawton Collins Papers, Dwight D. Eisenhower Library, Abilene, KS.

[31] Dwight D. Eisenhower to Maxwell D. Taylor, 2 January 1946, cited in Louis Galambos, ed., *The Chief of Staff*, vol. 7, *The Papers of Dwight David Eisenhower* (Baltimore, MD: Johns Hopkins University Press, 1978), 709.

[32] Maxwell D. Taylor, *West Point Honor System: Its Objectives and Procedures* (West Point, NY: USMA, 1950), copy in West Point Honor System Review File, Collins Papers.

[33] For an overview of the Honor Code and the "improper question," see Craig Whiteside, "Honor vs. Regulations: An Important Victory for the Honor System and West Point," 22 November 1999, TOEP. For contrasting views on the relations between tactical officers and cadets; see Martin, "Is West Point," 157; Ellis and Moore, *School for Soldiers*, 190.

[34] It is worth noting that the review board upheld the Superintendent's decision to expel the cadets by a 2-1 vote. The board based its decision largely on the grounds that the Corps of Cadets "expects the drastic penalty which the Code imposes upon those who violate it" and that to do otherwise "would seriously risk destruction of the Honor Code"; see Report of Board to Secretary of Army. One of the accusations leveled at the time, and subsequently, was that the accused cadets were denied both the procedures provided by the UCMJ and the right to a court-martial. The Academy's own rules stated, "Cadets who are found guilty of violations of the Honor Code are either allowed to resign or required to stand trial by court-martial"; see Taylor, *West Point Honor System*, 7. In the Department of the Army's and Truman's defense, their actions may have been prompted by concern for the cadets' own best interests. Had individual cadets been tried by court-martial and found guilty, their professional careers would have been permanently damaged. Several former cadets did reenter the armed forces via ROTC.

[35] Martin, "Is West Point," 158; "Honor Issue at West Point," *U.S. News*, 17 August 1951, 14-16; "Dishonor Under the Honor System," *Life*, 13 August 1951, 37; "Grave Days at West Point," *New York Times Magazine*, 12 August 1951, 8-9.

[36] Report of Board to Secretary of Army. For recent treatments of the Honor Incident, see Deford, "Code Breakers," 82-98; Phil Bardos, *Cold Warriors: The Story of the Achievements and Leadership of the Men of the West Point Class of 1950* (privately printed, 2000); James A. Blackwell, *On Brave Old Army Team: The Cheating Scandal That Rocked the Nation: West Point,1951* (Novato, CA: Presidio Press, 1996); Bill McWilliams, *Return to Glory: The Untold Story of Honor, Dishonor, and Triumph at the United States Military Academy, 1950-1953* (Lynchburg, VA: Warwick House Pub., 2000). For the Military Academy's own study; see Anthony Hartle et al., "Honor Violations at West Point, 1951: A Case Study," 1989, Special Collections, USMAA. The scandal is also covered in Ambrose, *Duty, Honor, Country*, 318-20; Ellis and Moore, *School for Soldiers*, 184-90; Thomas J. Fleming, *West Point: The Men and Times of the United States Military Academy* (New York: William Morrow and Co., 1969), 333-38; Dave Hagg, "The Last Word: The Resignation of Red Blaik as Army Football Coach, 1958," 1989, TOEP.

[37] "The New Commandant," *The Pointer*, 15 October 1954, 11.

[38] "Report of the Board of Visitors to the U.S.M.A.," 24 April 1952, 4, USMAA. Interestingly, this censure of the cadets appeared on the same page as the Board's condemnation of West Point's curriculum.

[39] Hartle, "Honor Violations," 36-37.

[40] Maxwell D. Taylor, "The Role and Capability of the Army World-Wide," Address before Quantico Conference on Defense Leaders, 16 July 1955, Maxwell D. Taylor File, Box 13, Bio Files, Record Group 407, Records of the Adjutant General, National Archives II, College Park, MD.

[41] John H. Cushman, "What Is the Army's Story?" *Army Combat Forces Journal* 5 (October 1954): 49. On the 1950s Army, see Andrew J. Bacevich, *The Pentomic Era: The U.S. Army Between Korea and Vietnam* (Washington, DC: National Defense University Press, 1986); Don Alan Carter, "From G.I. to Atomic Soldier: The Development of U.S. Tactical Doctrine, 1945-1956" (Ph.D. diss.: The Ohio State University, 1987).

[42] *Semiannual Report of the Secretary of the Army, January 1, 1953, to June 30, 1953* (Washington, DC: GPO, 1953), 101.

[43] "Report of Board of Visitors to the U.S.M.A.," 11 April 1964, 4. The loss of officers, particularly company-grade, was of much concern to the Army leadership; see Maxwell D. Taylor, "Remarks on meeting Army Staff as C/S," 7 July 1955, Item 2, Fldr A, Box 5, Maxwell D. Taylor Papers, National Defense University Library, Fort McNair, D.C.

[44] J. Robert Moskin, "Our Military Manpower Scandal," *Look*, 18 March 1958, 27-33. John Shy commented that *Look* failed to address the major reasons for the "manpower scandal," i.e., the Eisenhower Administration's decision to cut conventional forces, slash the Army's budget, and build up the Reserves. Tom Collier believes that had Moskin examined an airborne unit or the forces in Germany he would have come to very different conclusions about morale and career satisfaction. Col. Robert Lawrence Burke retired in 1977.

[45] *Annual Report of the Superintendent, 1952* (West Point, NY: U.S. Military Academy, 1952), 6.

[46] *Annual Report of the Superintendent, 1957* (West Point, NY: U.S. Military Academy, 1957), 18.

[47] *Annual Report of the Superintendent, 1958* (West Point, NY: U.S. Military Academy, 1958), 3.

[48] In what may be some indication of how many officers were forced into career tracks, under the quota system the Class of 1956 had 158 cadets assigned to the Infantry and 91 to the Artillery, whereas the Class of 1958, which in contrast was allowed to select branches, had 155 choose the Artillery and only 129 the Infantry; see *Annual Report of the Superintendent, 1956* (West Point, NY: U.S. Military Academy, 1955), 2; *Annual Report of the Superintendent, 1958*, 19.

[49] "Hop" to Family, 1 November 1954, Harper Brown Keeler Letters, #2127, Special Collections, USMAA.

[50] See, for example, *The Pointer* 32 (1953-54), Special Collections, USMAA.

[51] Garrison H. Davidson, "After-Action Report," 9 July 1956, N-13423.02, Combined Arms Research Library, Ft. Leavenworth, KS.

[52] The section on the Davidson years is based on Lovell, *Neither Athens nor Sparta*, 91-124; Garrison H. Davidson, "Grandpa Gar," (1974), MHI; Ellis and Moore, *School for Soldiers*, 51-54; Fleming, *West Point*, 353-54; Conrad C. Crane, "Garrison H. Davidson," in *Professional Military Education in the United States*, ed. William E. Simons (Westport, CT: Greenwood Press, 2000), 116-118; Philip A. Scibelli, "Vision Not Shared: Garrison Davidson and Resistance to Curricular Change and the U.S.M.A., 1956-1960," 6 November 1990, TOEP; Michael C. Dorohovich, "Lieutenant General Garrison Davidson: Success at Long-Term Reform," 5 December 1991, TOEP.

[53] *Semiannual Report of the Secretary of the Army, January 1, 1957, to June 30, 1957* (Washington, DC: GPO, 1957), 127. West Point cadets had gone on summer tours of military installations prior to Davidson's tenure, but these often were social junkets; see "Hop" to Dear Ma, 11 May 1955, Keeler Letters.

[54] Davidson, "Grandpa Gar," 170-74. For a balanced treatment of the Blaik-Davidson conflict, see Hagg, "The Last Word."

[55] *Semiannual Report of the Secretary of the Army, January 1, 1958, to June 30, 1958* (Washington, DC: GPO, 1958), 155.

[56] Wally Clark, "The Association of Graduates of the U.S.M.A, 1946-1959: More than Just a Fraternal Fellowship," 30 November 1994, TOEP.

[57] USMA, *Institutional self-examination* (November 1958), USMAA. Ellis and Moore, *School for Soldiers*, 52. The self-study showed that West Point's curriculum was unbalanced. Each cadet took 1748 course hours (62.5%) of engineering and mathematics, including 425 hours of mathematics, 295 of mechanics, and 271 hours of military engineering. He also took a total of 1,048 hours (37.5%) of courses in the social sciences and humanities, including 214 hours of foreign languages, 180 of English, and 178 of combined history, government, and geography. It might be argued that, unbalanced curriculum or not, cadets spent more classroom time in liberal arts and social studies classes than did students at comparable civilian universities. On the other hand, it would be a mistake either to confuse time in the classroom with quality of education, or to ignore that the cadets' extensive extracurricular requirements substantially reduced their potential study time.

[58] *Annual Report of the Superintendent, 1960*, 29. Interestingly enough, Davidson declared he was "unalterably opposed" to any regulation that would require professors to have a Ph.D., insisting that each individual had to be considered on individual merit and the Academy's needs; see Garrison H. Davidson to DCS for Military Operations, 25 April 1960, File 63D/2, Box 63D, Lincoln Papers.

[59] USMA, *Institutional Self-Examination* (November 1958), USMAA.

[60] Ellis and Moore, *School for Soldiers*, 53-55; Fleming, *West Point*, 353-55.

[61] Boroff, "West Point," 56. John Shy notes that Boroff may have not understood that cadet culture often requires a pretense of apathy towards academic and military subjects. Both my own limited classroom experience with cadets and the anecdotal evidence of several colleagues who have taught at the Academy would emphatically contradict Boroff's assertion that cadets lack enthusiasm for learning.

[62] Ibid., 59.

[63] According to USMA data, during the academic year 1962-63, among a total of 341 faculty, 4 percent had doctoral degrees and 71 percent had masters or professional degrees; see Appendix J, *Annual Report of the Superintendent, 1 July 1969 through 30 June 1970*. As with all academic institutions, Academy data requires some interpretation. In 1963, for example, Dean William W. Bessell suggested counting 30 of the junior faculty as "graduate students," thus raising the percentage of faculty with postgraduate degrees from 76 to 82; see William W. Bessell, Memo to Superintendent, 15 March 1963, File 63D/2, Box 63D, Lincoln Papers. On an attached note, Lincoln wrote, "The Dean is overreaching—dangerously!"

[64] Donald V. Bennett Oral History, 1:4:2-3, Senior Officer Oral History Program, MHI.

[65] In 1967, after a long meeting with a member of the accrediting board, Lincoln commented that he shared the board member's doubts about West Point's faculty. He concluded that the Academy would eventually be forced to adopt a majors program, but "our faculty is too thin to support such a program before a skeptical board of visiting civilians." Memorandum for Dean, Sub: Quality of Faculty and Teaching, 1 March 1967, File 63/12, Box 63, Lincoln Papers.

[66] For example, in the last decade among the instructional faculty in the History Department alone, H.R. McMaster, Peter Mansoor, Michael Doubler, Ty Smith, William Odom, Daniel Bolger, and David M. Toczek have all published highly regarded scholarly works. In the Political Science Department, Col. Don M. Snider's work on military professionalism has received wide recognition. An important benefit has been the increased prestige of Army officers and the Army itself among civilian academics. At my own school (Texas A&M University), even faculty who are generally critical of the military acknowledge the Army officers in our graduate program have been among the best of our students.

[67] A similar point was made by Army Chief of Staff J. Lawton Collins, who not only urged that the faculty be given the opportunity to "broaden" itself, but noted that many of the most valuable officers in World War II as well as the top officers in the postwar Army had been instructors at the service schools; see J. Lawton Collins, Remarks to Army School Commandants, 13 November 1952, Service School Speeches File (6), Box 43, J. Lawton Collins Papers, Dwight D. Eisenhower Library, Abilene, KS.

[68] Sey Chassler, "Plebe at the Point," *Colliers*, 5 January 1952, 15-16; Howell Walker, "The Making of a West Pointer," *National Geographic* 101 (May 1952): 597-626; see also E.J. Kahn, "West Point," *Holiday*, September 1949, 50-55, 91-94; Martin, "Is West Point."

[69] F.J. Stare, "Parents Can Learn From West Point," *McCalls*, October 1954, 110.

[70] Russell G. Emery, *Warren of West Point* (Philadelphia: Macrae Smith Company, 1950), frontispiece. For a study of earlier works, see Aloysius A. Martin, "A Case Study of the Customs and Traditions of West Point in the American Novel," (M.A. thesis: Columbia University, 1950).

[71] Red [Russell Potter] Reeder's Clint Lane series consists of: *West Point Plebe; West Point Yearling; West Point Second Classman; West Point First Classman; 2nd Lieutenant Clint Lane: West Point to Berlin;* and *Clint Lane in Korea*.

[72] Ralph McKnight, review of *The West Point Story*, available from www.dorisday.net.

[73] Rick Atkinson, *The Long Gray Line: The American Journey of West Point's Class of 1966* (Boston: Houghton Mifflin Co., 1989).

[74] Ellis and Moore, *School for Soldiers*, 184-90.

[75] Just, *Military Men*, 32. Several alumni have noted that the cadet's comment was factually inaccurate and questioned whether it reflected the views of the majority of the Corps. There is some corroborative evidence: a 1971 survey of cadets indicated 46 percent intended to leave the Army before 20 years and 40 percent stated they would not have attended West Point had they the chance to choose again; see U'Ren, *Ivory Fortress*, 141.

[76] Herbert Y. Schandler, "U.S. Military Academy," in *Professional Military Education*, 330.

[77] For comparative data, see Chapter 16 of the present volume, and Appendix J, *Annual Report of the Superintendent, 1 July 1969 and 30 June 1970*. Figures on the academic qualifications of USMA faculty were supplied via e-mail from the Office of the Dean, USMA [Debra Scully], 6 October 2003.

⊰ CHAPTER 11 ⊱

WEST POINT AND THE POST-COLD WAR DRAWDOWN

Gerardo V. Meneses

In the early 1990s, after the end of the Cold War and the stunning military success in the Persian Gulf War, the United States once again underwent a seemingly traditional post-conflict demobilization. The Department of Defense began shedding as many as 100,000 uniformed personnel per year. By the end of the decade, active forces had gone from a prewar peak of 2.2 million to less than 1.5 million troops.[1]

Unlike other postwar reductions, in which the service academies went unscathed, this reduction included them as well. The 1992 National Defense Authorization Act directed each of the service academies to drop its enrollment by 10%, from 4,400 students to 4,000 for the class years beginning after 1994.[2] While the nation rushed to grasp the so-called "peace-dividend," critics saw an opportunity to resurrect a debate almost as old as West Point itself, the idea of abolishing the service academies altogether.[3] This time, opponents focused on a particular allegation, that academy graduates were scarcely better, but much more expensive to produce, than their counterparts from the Reserve Officer Training Corps (ROTC) and Officer Candidate Schools (OCS).[4] The academies were once again being asked to justify their existence. West Point, with the highest price tag per graduate among the academies, faced the most serious challenge.[5]

Still, in the forum that mattered most, the U.S. Congress, the Military Academy did not have to justify its existence so much as to refute vociferous accusations of inefficiency. While Congress debated reducing enrollment at service academies and several related issues, it never considered shutting them down. West Point survived this latest storm of criticism because it responded with cogent arguments that it produced lieutenants at prices comparable to ROTC programs at selective universities. West Point demonstrated that its graduates, contrary to common criticisms, consistently exceeded Army averages for retention, promotion, and command. Most important, Army and Academy leaders clearly demonstrated that West Point was an integral part of the Army's officer accessions system, uniquely organized to produce leaders of uncommon character, integrity, and ability.

Through much of its history, critics have questioned the Military Academy's place in a democratic society. President Andrew Jackson built a political movement around advocacy of the common man, including the heroic citizen-soldier. The very existence of the Academy was loathsome to the more radical Jacksonians, who believed it was a waste and an inappropriate use of money to maintain an institution for the development of an elite professional officer corps.[6] West Point's harshest Jacksonian critic was the famous frontiersman and Tennessee Congressman, Davy Crockett, who asserted that the institution was "better calculated to make dandies than soldiers."[7] He found it unfair and anti-democratic that only select young men should receive higher education at the expense of the country as whole. Crockett thought he had enough support for his views to introduce a resolution that the Military Academy "should be abolished and the appropriations annually made for its support discontinued." Although the legislation was ultimately defeated, Crockett's views reflected a traditional American suspicion of a large standing army and distaste for aristocracy.[8]

With the overwhelmingly laudable performance of West Pointers in the Mexican War, criticism of the Academy subsided, only to reach another crescendo during the Civil War. Within a week of Fort Sumter's fall, almost all southern cadets and several officers of the Academy staff and faculty had resigned. Similar situations occurred throughout units in the Army.[9] As hundreds of West Pointers left for service with the Confederacy, the Academy's critics began to question the loyalty and competence of its graduates. This time, the criticism had more sting because it came from the civilian leaders of the Army. Secretary of War Simon Cameron was disgusted that so many graduates failed to remain "faithful to the flag." He specifically faulted the Academy disciplinary system because it "failed to distinguish between immorality and simple violations of regulations."[10]

Cameron's criticisms of West Point spurred Congressional debates on the competence of the Academy's graduates. Some charged that early Union defeats were a direct result of the officers' flawed West Point educations. As Maj. Gen. George B. McClellan's Army of the Potomac loitered near Washington and then failed in the Peninsula Campaign of 1862, Radical Republicans latched onto his passive generalship as the prime exemplar of the Academy's failings. As Crockett had done 30 years earlier, Congressional opponents attempted to abolish West Point by proposing legislation to kill its appropriation.[11] Friends of the Military Academy eventually defeated this act. With the improving fortunes of Union forces under West Point generals Grant, Sherman, Sheridan, and others, the controversy passed.[12]

West Point's harshest critics have not always been in Congress. Authors putatively promoting the best interests of the military community, and even Academy alumni, have sided with those seeking to abolish West Point. Alden Partridge, a graduate and former superintendent, was one of those who echoed Crockett's attacks in the early 19th century. Although Partridge's ignominious dismissal as superintendent tainted the objectivity of his criticisms, he nonetheless found people at the highest levels of government willing to listen.[13] He criticized the Academy for breeding a military aristocracy, challenged its constitutionality, and recommended its replacement with a commissioning source that selected officers from the enlisted ranks.[14]

In the late 20th century, Academy critics began to echo Partridge. Periodicals as varied as *The Officer, Retired Officer Magazine,* and *Time* argued for replacing West Point with other commissioning sources. While the arguments and solutions varied, they all posit the allegation that the Academy is a wasteful, inefficient source of average-quality commissioned officers that should be replaced with more cost-effective alternatives.[15]

In this latest round of attacks, Benjamin Schemmer, a 1954 USMA graduate, echoed Partridge in questioning West Point's usefulness. His commentary in *Armed Forces Journal*, aptly titled "Is It Time to Abolish West Point?" opens with the question "How many *Journal* readers would pay $225,000 to send a son or daughter to undergraduate school?" Then, assuming the answer is few or none, he follows with: "Why should the taxpayer?"[16] Schemmer quotes unreferenced data suggesting that a West Point education costs 16 to 23 times more than OCS lieutenants and six to nine times more than ROTC lieutenants.[17] He then points to a drop in the retention of West Point graduates in the Army, attributing that trend to changes in the West Point curriculum that made it more like a typical college. Schemmer also quotes statistics indicating that relatively fewer West Point graduates were achieving general officer rank than in earlier times. While graduates made up 13 percent of the officer corps at the time, they comprised "only" 40 percent of the two- and three-star generals and only 19 percent of brigadier generals.[18] The implication was that USMA graduates, if truly superior, should have outperformed their peers to a far greater degree. Schemmer's argument was that since West Point officers were no longer far better than ROTC or OCS graduates in terms of quality, the nation should stop spending taxpayer dollars on expensive Academy graduates and let other sources of commission make up the shortfall.

As the drawdown continued into the early 1990s, other service academy critics joined the debate. In *The Officer*, Maj. Gen. Robert Upp, USA Ret., urged closing all service academies. His argument again attacked West Point's price tag per graduate, but added a new dimension. Reminiscent of Jacksonian attacks, he linked the active Army's "second class" treatment of the National Guard and Army Reserve with elitism supposedly bred at the Military Academy. He implied that Academy graduates are less connected to the society they defend than their ROTC counterparts.[19] Upp proposed eliminating the service academies as undergraduate institutions and "using ROTC as a primary source of commissions, [so that] officers would bond better with public opinion, and elitism would be diminished," all while realizing significant budgetary savings.[20] Later, Scott Shuger of the *Washington Monthly* began a similar polemic with cost-effectiveness arguments and then went on to attack the cultural isolation of the academies and their graduates. To him, "abolishing the service academies and picking up the slack via other commissioning sources would make the U.S. military less isolated, more well-grounded, more cohesive, and more meritocratic."[21]

All these attacks shared a common thread, the cost of the West Point experience.[22] Many of them relied upon a single, but authoritative source, a 1991 General Accounting Office (GAO) investigative report entitled "Department of Defense Service Academies, Improved Cost and Performance Monitoring Needed." The report addressed four areas of academy operations: financial reporting, academic programs, performance and retention of graduates, and the effectiveness of external oversight. The primary and most often cited finding of the investigation was that "the academies are the most expensive commissioning source." The GAO figured 1989 costs per graduate at West Point, Annapolis, and Colorado Springs at $228,500, $153,200, and $225,500, respectively.[23] The report found the academies lacking in each area investigated except the progression and retention of their graduates. However, it largely attributed the higher retention and progression rates to "academy graduates receiving regular, rather than reserve, commissions and a higher allocation of combat-related occupations," as well as favoritism from senior academy graduates.[24] With the official imprimatur of the GAO, calls for reform and abolition of West Point picked up renewed vigor. Worse, critics often falsely attributed abolitionist sentiments to Congressmen charged with oversight of the academies.[25]

Members of Congress *did* criticize the service academies for their inefficiencies. However, unlike Davy Crockett, no contemporary member called for closing the academies. The two senators most often associated with the idea of closing down the service academies were John Glenn of Ohio and Sam Nunn of Georgia. While they often criticized the academies, no evidence exists that they specifically wanted to shut them down. Arnold Punaro, the Senate Armed Services Committee (SASC) staff director, specifically noted that they "have pressed the academies hard to become more efficient in recent years, but never once did they suggest closing them."[26] They were, however, responsible for the investigation that produced the critical July 1991 GAO report discussed above.

As SASC chairman, Senator Nunn oversaw all military authorizations, including legislation affecting the service academies. Nunn pressed the service academies to become more efficient and to produce graduates of a quality commensurate with the significant appropriations they received. Lt. Gen. Howard D. Graves, then superintendent of USMA, felt that Senator Nunn had some biases against the military academies, specifically West Point and the Army. Graves attributed this animosity to Nunn's earlier work as chairman of the Personnel Subcommittee: "There were some changes that they wanted to have made, and they were resisted by the Army and the Academy, and there was resentment from that."[27] For his part, Nunn denied any ill will toward the Academy. As Lieutenant General Graves noted after a Congressional visit to West Point, Senator Nunn conceded to him, "I've never really been opposed to the military academies, I'm just concerned about how expensive you are."[28]

Similarly, Senator Glenn, chairman of the SASC Subcommittee on Manpower and Personnel, exercised oversight of the post-Cold War military personnel drawdown. His subcommittee was keenly interested in the pace and nature of personnel reductions, and thus the accession of new officers. As one of the requestors of the GAO study, he too was critical of service academy operations, but not to the extent that he wanted to close them. Senator Glenn categorically disavowed abolition in opening remarks to the subcommittee when the GAO presented the preliminary results of its investigation:

> These institutions [the service academies] have always had a key role in producing career officers for our military services, and I believe we need these institutions and the officers they produce. My interest is in the effectiveness and efficiency of these institutions in accomplishing their

> mission and not, as someone suggested, to close them down or reduce their output or reduce their role as the bedrock source of our military officers. I would add that I am probably as big a booster as there is on Capitol Hill of our service academies. In fact, one of the reasons for having this hearing is to find out how we can increase the number of people that go through the academies and stay in the service. . . . Let me say again, I do not have a hidden agenda, as has been suggested, to close down the military service academies. . . .[29]

Senator Glenn expressed these views at the same hearing in which Mr. Robert F. Hale of the Congressional Budget Office and Mr. Paul L. Jones of the GAO presented findings that the academies were the most expensive commissioning sources. However, Glenn was adamant that he was not out to close the academies, but did want to extend Congressional oversight to academy operations to ensure that they produced quality graduates as efficiently as possible. He was interested in keeping the academy graduates in the services longer, not in dismantling the academies.

These views were similar to those held by members of the House Armed Services Committee (HASC). Less than a year later, as the House debated how officer accessions would be curtailed in consonance with the ongoing drawdown, the chairman of the Military Personnel and Compensation subcommittee championed the efficacy of the service academies. Representative Beverly B. Byron stated in her opening remarks that "there is no question in my mind that the academies are part—and an integrated part—of our national defense. It is vitally important that we keep the academies."[30] Her views were prevalent in the House. Representative Ike Skelton of Missouri expressed his support: "The service academies have more than paid for themselves in leadership and on the battlefield. There's no bar chart, or pie chart, or graph that will show that; we need these schools as an anchor for each service, to set the standard for all officers."[31] Political scientist John Lovell accurately summed up the Congressional sentiment against closing the academies, arguing that the academies are symbols of the American military profession because they represent professional values. Therefore, in Lovell's view a Congressional attempt to abolish the academies would call into question the legitimacy of the entire armed forces.[32]

If no members of Congress were really looking to shut down the academies, what then did West Point have to fear? The most worrisome problem was the negative perception that West Point was a wasteful, inefficient institution that produced mediocre leaders for the Army. This perception threatened to damage West Point's reputation in the eyes of the American public with attendant adverse effects on recruiting and political support. In response, Superintendent Graves spearheaded a dual effort in Congress and contemporary military periodicals to refute the GAO's assertions and to articulate a position justifying the Academy's existence and its reputation as a premier leader development institution. He argued not only that West Point's costs were comparable to ROTC programs at selective institutions such as "Duke, Princeton, Stanford, Notre Dame, Cornell, and Johns Hopkins," but more importantly that the Military Academy was a unique and essential part of the Army's commissioned officer accessions system that provided unique and competent leaders to the Army.[33]

Graves began by rebutting West Point's most often alleged fault—its high cost per graduate. As noted earlier, the 1991 GAO study found that in fiscal year 1989 West Point's cost per graduate was $228,500, contrasting that to the relatively inexpensive average cost per ROTC graduate of $53,000 to $58,000 or OCS graduate of $15,000 to $20,000.[34] Graves and GAO calculated West Point's cost per graduate by dividing the Academy's annual operating expenditures by the number of cadets graduating that year. This method produces a comprehensive and robust figure. However, GAO calculated average ROTC costs by dividing Department of Defense (DOD) costs for annual ROTC scholarships (i.e., tuition charges) by the number of ROTC graduates. Graves argued that this comparison ignored the aggregate or "societal cost" to produce an ROTC lieutenant.[35] This "societal cost" provided a fairer basis for comparison with USMA, not the artificially low tuition cost.

Looking at just the tuition costs to the DoD, the GAO overlooked the fact that the taxpayer was in many ways subsidizing all institutions of higher learning, public or private. The majority of college costs "are paid from earnings on endowments, from tax subsidies from state and local government, federal grants, and philanthropic gifts."[36] In many instances the federal government spent more in grants and other aid to private institutions than it did in supporting the entire budget of West Point or the other service academies. Three examples of federal financial support in 1985 include the California and Massachusetts Institutes of Technology, which received $909,701,000 and $493,671,000, respectively, as well as Johns Hopkins University, which received $437,557,000; in 1985 West Point's budget was $231,751,000.[37] These figures represent substantial amounts of taxpayer funds appropriated to support various programs at private institutions of higher learning. When all these federal monies and the other government costs of a four-year college education were considered, the difference between ROTC and West Point graduates was not so apparent.

In response to the GAO study, West Point's Office of Institutional Research (OIR) conducted research also showing that commissioning costs were much more comparable. Using the most up-to-date cost figures available after the release of the GAO report, the OIR compared the costs to graduate West Point's Class of 1992 to a similar cohort of ROTC cadets. The Class of 1992 cost an average of $254,754 per graduate.[38] OIR reached the figure by taking the total cost to run the Academy, multiplying it by the percentage of the Corps of Cadets that the Class of 1992 made up during each of the four years, and then summing the four figures. It then divided this sum ($244,564,162) by the total number of graduates for the Class of 1992 (960) to get the total cost per graduate.[39]

To ascertain the total costs of the ROTC graduates, the OIR estimated the average cost of a four-year civilian college education using data from *Snyder's Digest of Educational Statistics* and the Army's fiscal year 1992 ROTC expenditures. The OIR research team calculated the average college's four-year expenditures divided by the number of bachelor degrees it awarded during the four-year period. This figure, which included tuition costs normally paid by the student, or in this case the government-paid ROTC tuition, turned out to be $98,170.[40] To this the researchers added the additional indirect support that dependent students typically (83.4 percent of them) receive from parents over four years of college; this accounts for an additional $19,401 per student.[41] The total costs of a college education in the United States thus averaged approximately $117,571 per graduate. This figure however, did not take into account the Department of the Army's ROTC expenditures, which included such items as cadet and instructor pay, travel allowances, training, maintenance, and other overhead costs. This amount (after scholarship costs) totaled $287,274,000 in fiscal year 1992.[42] Dividing that figure by the number of ROTC graduates yielded an average cost of an additional $69,006 per graduate. Adding that cost to the $117,571 typical four-year college expenditures produced a 1992 ROTC average cost per graduate of $186,577.[43]

While this estimate of the average *real* costs of an ROTC commissioned lieutenant was still 35 percent less than the $254,754 per graduate price tag for West Point's Class of 1992, it was not four or more times less as the 1991 GAO investigation indicated. Additionally, this figure represented an average institutional cost of education for the nation as a whole, not the cost at institutions of academic excellence to which West Point is typically compared. As Graves argued, based on its selectivity and the entrance qualifications of its student body, it would be more appropriate to compare the costs of West Point with some of its Ivy League counterparts. The superintendent further noted, "If you are going to compare programs you've got to compare us to Stanford, Harvard, MIT, Caltech; and if you look at the overall costs of these programs, you find that we are comparable."[44] Graves also made this argument in a speech reprinted in *Assembly* magazine in which he quoted a figure from a 1991 issue of *U.S. News & World Report* indicating that the average cost of a four-year education at the nation's top-ten-ranked universities was $234,400.[45] That figure is actually higher than the cost per graduate of a West Point education so often quoted from the 1991 GAO report. Even if it is compared to the $254,754 cost per graduate of the Class of 1992, the Academy took the position that the difference was minor given the uniquely qualified graduate that it produced.

The second half of Graves's argument was that USMA is a unique and essential institution, the crux being that West Point plays a key role in the accessions system and that its graduates could not be replicated elsewhere. In testimony before Congress as well as in columns and speeches, Graves explained how officers were procured to meet the Army's needs, and how West Point fit into that accession system. "Our Officer Corps," he explained, "is sustained by all sources of commission, and the nation needs the Reserve Officer Training Corps, Officer Candidate Schools, and the Military Academy as complementary and essential programs for attracting and developing the Army's leaders."[46] The superintendent made no invidious comparisons between West Point and other sources of commission, but rather emphasized that all sources were necessary to meet the needs of the Army. West Point had a Congressionally mandated mission to prepare highly qualified officers for the Army and the nation, and it was successfully fulfilling that mission.

Graves received important support from the highest levels of the Army in making that case. At a 1994 HASC hearing, Army Deputy Chief of Staff for Personnel, Lt. Gen. Thomas P. Carney, testified as to West Point's success in meeting its historical mission requirements to the nation. "USMA has a distinct place in the Army structure for pre-commissioning education of officers," he said. "It is focused on meeting Regular Army officer needs in peace and war."[47] Welcome assistance also came from Army Chief of Staff Gen. Gordon R. Sullivan, one of the Academy's staunchest advocates. Graves noted that "as an ROTC graduate of Norwich University, [General Sullivan] had a unique ability to articulate the role and contributions of the Military Academy . . . as the standard bearer for the Army Ethic," without being suspected of favoritism.[48] Indeed, General Sullivan's support was public and enthusiastic. He opened his 1992 USMA commencement address by placing the importance of West Point in historical context:

> At the end of his term as our country's first president,
> George Washington declared that America needed a Military

Academy, convinced that it would be vital to America's future. The contributions of this institution in building our great country can be seen everywhere, and are reflected in the lives of its graduates. Since 1802, in peace and in war, West Point has held a treasured place in America. It has a role in America today, and it will continue to symbolize what is good about us as soldiers and Americans for years to come. America needs West Point. America needs young officer-leaders such as yourselves.[49]

Sullivan's approach with various audiences, as Graves recalled it, was: "Look, I'm not a graduate of that institution. I've looked at it, . . . and I support it wholeheartedly. This is what the *Army* needs. I speak for the Army."[50] The heartfelt and reasoned advocacy of an Army Chief of Staff who was not a USMA graduate, as well as support from other Army leaders, was immensely helpful to the Academy leadership.

Graves's most convincing argument was that West Point produced a quality of leader not attainable elsewhere. "The most important outcome of an Academy education is that these highly talented young people are imbued with strong traditions of character, leadership, and service to the Nation."[51] Peter Drucker, one of the nation's foremost experts on organizational dynamics, found that the Military Academy is ideally designed to produce graduates who have a profound moral and ethical foundation. Since its inception, West Point's core competence has been to produce leaders worthy of the nation's trust.[52] West Point is uniquely organized to accomplish this mission. External educational assessments note that the emphasis on such values as integrity and respect for others "permeates a cadet's four-year experience at West Point, from the signing of the Cadet Honor Code and taking of 50 hours of substantive instruction on honor and ethics to serving on cadet honor education teams and on honor boards."[53] In an editorial rebutting the GAO and Congressional criticisms of the service academies, Brig. Gen. John D. Lawlor, USA Ret., further championed the character-building nature of the West Point experience. He saw it as critical that "the cadet is immersed 24 hours a day in a system designed to teach values that are intended to last a lifetime. The cadet is taught not to lie, cheat, or steal, nor tolerate those who do. . . . This immersion in character-building cannot be replicated in the ordinary civilian institution."[54]

Drawing on such data and analysis as the foregoing, Graves's argument carried the day. In time, West Point began to attract support from outside the Army community. In a 1997 review of professional military education, a Center for Strategic and International Studies (CSIS) panel headed by former Secretary of Defense and later Vice President Richard Cheney found that "rather than making comparisons of dollars and cents and promotion rates," the "far more compelling argument [is] that each of the academies supplies its service with a unique product."[55] The CSIS panel based this conclusion on three distinct areas in which West Point excels. These strengths included the extremely high academic qualifications of its entrants, the cultural diversity of its Corps of Cadets, and the preponderance of technical degrees awarded to its graduates.[56] Because of its highly selective admissions process, West Point draws most of its candidates from the most gifted college-bound seniors. The average SAT score for West Point's Class of 1993 (taken in 1988) was 1213 of a possible 1600 points—several points higher than the average at other highly rated schools.[57] Moreover, these scores far outstripped those of the average ROTC student of the same time period. SAT scores of the USMA class entering in 1987 averaged 1210, while students in ROTC programs across the country averaged 1030.[58] The CSIS panel argued that by starting with a more gifted student body, West Point was well positioned to produce superior graduates.

The CSIS panel report employed a similar argument in behalf of the Academy's recruitment of women and minorities. During the period from 1989 to1992, West Point recruited and enrolled seven to nine percent African-American students, four to six percent Hispanic students, two to three percent Asian/Pacific Islanders/Native American students, and ten to fifteen percent women.[59] These percentages stemmed from Academy goals to graduate cohorts of junior officers whose demographic composition approximated that of the Army as a whole. Beginning with a highly selective group of women and minorities, then educating and training them well, West Point produced a core of junior officers uniquely well equipped to lead the Army's demographically diverse soldiers.

The third unique West Point strength that the CSIS panel identified was the high percentage of technical degrees its graduates earn before departing to serve the technologically driven modern Army. West Point has traditionally had a curriculum based on math, sciences, and engineering. While options for majors have broadened considerably through the years, these areas still represent a significant part of the curriculum. The panel report suggested that graduates from these disciplines have transferable skills that they will be able to use on behalf of the Army.[60] For example, so far as operations research and systems analysis are concerned, West Point graduates made up 53 percent and 34 percent, respectively, of the Army officers in these fields.[61] In 1991, while West Point produced only 25 percent of the Army's basic branch lieutenants, that 25 percent met 81 percent of the Army's need for officers with degrees in the physical and applied sciences.[62] Whether in direct use of their skills in technical branches or in secondary functional areas, Academy graduates supplied the Army with technological capabilities that it could not get elsewhere. However, even if, as the CSIS panel suggests, the "unique attributes" of graduates were the most compelling argument in favor of the Military Academy, its graduates also excelled in the military's more traditional measures of success.

In a continuing effort to dampen animosity between products of the various commissioning sources, West Point officials have tried to couch the institution's defense in terms that avoided inter-source comparisons. Graduate performance, however, was one of the issues brought up in the 1991 GAO study that inevitably resurfaced in any discussion of cost versus value. West Point could remain quiet only at its own risk. In the words of West Point's Director of Policy, Planning, and Analysis, "We have to promote the fact that our graduates do well in comparison with their officer cohorts in a way that is not divisive, (because ROTC and OCS remain critical components of our officer accessions), but taken together, it's not true that all three groups perform equally."[63]

West Point's graduates have historically exceeded the Army averages for retention, promotion, and command. In his 1992 Congressional testimony, Graves pointed out with regard to the West Point Class of 1972—a class that suffered particularly from retention problems associated with the Vietnam War—as that class approached 20 years of service it still had 35 percent of its members in uniform, compared to only 21 percent for the other commissioning sources.[64] A more comprehensive longitudinal study completed in 1989 showed that, on average, USMA graduate cohorts always exceeded the retention rates of comparable ROTC cohorts. When measured at the sixth year of service (one year after the active duty service obligation expired), West Point graduates contributed 13-14 percent more years of service; when measured at the 30th year of service they contributed 26 percent more years of service.[65]

Graves also presented data indicating that West Point graduates performed more successfully in terms of promotion: over the "past three years, selection to major for West Point officers was 80 percent. The Army average was 64 percent. Selection to lieutenant colonel was 76 percent; the Army average 59 percent. Colonel 46 percent versus the Army average 38 percent."[66] Graves did not address the issue of selection to general officer, but as noted earlier in Schemmer's article critical of West Point, a 35 percent selection rate to brigadier general seemed quite an accomplishment when Academy graduates made up only 13 percent of the original officer accession pool. Lieutenant General Graves did address the allegation that West Pointers were the unwarranted recipients of favoritism. He specifically noted that the Department of the Army selection boards that produced the promotion results recapitulated above contained a majority of ROTC and OCS officers.[67] In sum, the statistics presented before Congress and elsewhere showed that West Point graduates consistently exceeded the average Army promotion rates.

Additional measures of graduate achievement presented in Congressional hearings, as well as to West Point's Board of Visitors during the early 1990s, supported the argument that West Point produced uncommonly talented leaders. In 1991, the average Graduate Record Examination (GRE) scores for First Class cadets were as follows: verbal 506; quantitative 645; and analytical 609. The national averages for seniors were 481, 556, and 526, respectively.[68] A parallel achievement was evident in the number of postgraduate scholarships that Academy graduates earned. Through 1991, graduates of USMA earned a total of 109 Rhodes, Marshall, and Hertz scholarships, putting it ahead of MIT and fifth behind Harvard, Yale, Princeton, and Stanford.[69] That is a significant accomplishment considering the high priority that physical, military, and other developmental requirements enjoy alongside academics at the Academy. Finally, in a letter to West Point's dean, Brig. Gen. Gerald Galloway, the dean of the University of Pennsylvania strongly praised those graduates who conducted postgraduate work at his institution. These officers "have all performed superbly in virtually every respect; not only have they met or exceeded Penn's academic standards, but they have—through their extraordinary energy, commitment, and, most important, *self-discipline*—set a marvelously high standard for our other graduate students to emulate."[70]

In sum, the Academy did withstand the wave of criticism that followed the 1991 GAO report, as it had withstood periodic attacks over nearly two centuries of its existence. In the context of the post-Cold War drawdown, critics had accused the Academy of elitism on one hand, and inefficiency on the other. Numerous critics, in and out of the Army, had looked at the GAO report and begun to advocate West Point's closure. They argued that it was questionable to keep West Point and the other service academies operating when ROTC and OCS commissioning programs produced lieutenants of the same quality at a fraction of the cost. They compelled West Point's champions to defend the institution by bringing the truth before Congress and the public. Members of Congress with oversight responsibility sought only to make West Point more efficient. Key members of the Senate Armed Services Committee went to great lengths to ensure that West Point and the other service academies spent the taxpayers' money wisely. Though they were often critical of some academy practices and the apparently high relative cost of producing graduates, they stopped well short of the calls for the Academy's closure heard in the Jacksonian and Civil War era.

West Point withstood criticisms of inefficiency and elitism because its leadership demonstrated the Academy's unique value to the nation. The superintendent and other Army leaders made it clear that even at a slightly higher cost, West Point plays an indispensable role in producing Army leaders. West Point showed that while its cost per graduate exceeded that of the average ROTC program, the difference was not nearly as striking a the GAO report made it appear. West Point's leaders demonstrated that a student body comprising a diverse but highly talented selection of America's youth, immersed in an unparalleled academic and leader development experience, will produce graduates exceptionally well prepared to face the challenges of a career in the Army. Furthermore, the Academy showed that it could accomplish this feat at a cost comparable to other prestigious undergraduate institutions. As the Board of Visitors concluded in 1987 and continued to echo through the 1990s, the U.S. Military Academy produced leaders of character for the Army "at a bargain for the taxpayer."[71]

In the cycles of American history, political attitudes toward the U.S. Military Academy have experienced wide swings, but support and admiration for the Academy among the public at large has rarely wavered. West Point and Army leaders in the 1990s demonstrated that not only must the Academy maintain the standards of a high-caliber institution at a reasonable cost to the national treasury, but that it must continually be prepared to demonstrate that capacity to the American people and their elected representatives. The efforts of Lt. Gen. Howard Graves and the Army's leadership provide a useful model for their successors to follow in carrying out that duty to the country.

---

[1] Katherine M. Peters, "The Drawdown Drags On," *Government Executive*, March 1996, 20.

[2] U.S. Public Law 102-190, 5 December 1991, Sec. 511, "Limitation on the Number of Cadets and Midshipmen Authorized to Attend the Service Academies."

[3] Critical articles include Benjamin F. Schemmer, "Is It Time to Abolish West Point?" *Armed Forces Journal International*, September 1985; Scott Shuger, "The Case Against the Military Academies," *Washington Monthly*, October, 1994; Thomas Philpott, "The Service Academies: Are They Still Worth the Cost?" *The Retired Officer*, October 1995; Robert D. Upp, "Are the Service Academies Obsolete?" *The Officer*, May 1992; and Mark Thompson "Academies Out of Line," *Time*, 18 April 1994.

[4] Schemmer, 80.

[5] General Accounting Office, "Department of Defense Service Academies, Improved Cost and Performance Monitoring Needed," July 1991, 3.

[6] Stephen E. Ambrose, *Duty, Honor, Country, A History of West Point* (Baltimore, MD: Johns Hopkins University Press), 1999, 107-108.

[7] *Erie Gazette*, 11 March 1830.

[8] House of Representatives, 21st Congress, 1st Session, 25 February 1830.

[9] Sidney Forman, *West Point, A History of the United States Military Academy* (New York: Columbia University Press, 1950), 121.

[10] Theodore J. Crackel, *West Point: A Bicentennial History* (Lawrence: University of Kansas Press, 2002), 134.

[11] Crackel, 134.

[12] Ibid., 134-35.

[13] Mark Rice, "Defending the Ramparts: USMA's Struggle for Survival in the Age of Jackson" (Master's thesis, U.S. Military Academy [Tactical Officer Education Program], 1995), 3.

[14] Stephen R. Grove, "Memo For the Superintendent: Historical Criticisms of West Point," 15 March 1990.

[15] Philpott, Upp, and Thompson, cited in n. 3 above.

[16] Schemmer, 80.

[17] Ibid.

[18] Ibid.

[19] Upp, 37.

[20] Ibid.

[21] Shuger, 2.

[22] Political scientist John Lovell, USMA 1955, argues that "proposals to abolish the academies completely have less plausibility now than they did, say, in the 19th century or even as recently as the end of WWII." He points to the amount of money that Congress has appropriated for the military academies. He estimates that in the 1960s and 1970s the nation invested millions of taxpayer dollars in new buildings and modern facilities at each of the academies. Considering the construction projects undertaken in the 1980s and 1990s at West Point alone, the figure is appreciably greater. To Lovell, "despite the per-student cost that the maintenance and operation of such facilities entails, the sunk cost of the initial investment represents a persuasive argument on behalf of 'seeing the investment through.'" Still, the arguments against the taxpayer's investment continued to appear in periodicals. John P. Lovell, *Neither Athens nor Sparta?* (Bloomington: Indiana University Press, 1979), 276.

[23] GAO "Department of Defense Service Academies, Improved Cost and Performance Monitoring Needed," July 1991, 3.

[24] Ibid., 4.

[25] Philpott, 31-32 and Upp, 35.

[26] Philpott, 36.

[27] Stephen R. Grove, "Oral History Interview with LTG Graves," second session conducted on 5 June 1996, 23.

[28] Ibid., 34.

[29] Department of Defense Authorization for Appropriations for Fiscal Year 1991, U.S. Senate, Subcommittee on Manpower and Personnel, Committee on Armed Services,

"Officer Procurement Programs of the Military Services and the Management of Operations at the Military Service Academies," 4 April 1990, 214.

[30] House of Representatives Armed Services Committee Hearings 102-46, "Officer Production in a Drawdown Environment," 31 March 1994, Sec. 511.

[31] Richard B. Cheney, *Professional Military Education: An Asset for Peace and Progress* (Washington DC: CSIS, 1997), 28.

[32] Lovell, 277.

[33] Howard D. Graves, Letter to "Graduates and Friends," *Assembly*, May 1995, 1.

[34] General Accounting Office "Department of Defense Service Academies, Improved Cost and Performance Monitoring Needed," July 1991, 3.

[35] Howard D. Graves, "Why America Needs West Point," Speech reprinted in *Assembly*, November 1992, 9.

[36] Ibid.

[37] Ronald P. Elrod, "The Cost of Educating a West Point Cadet" (Master's thesis, U.S. Military Academy [Tactical Officer Education Program], 1994), 16-17.

[38] "Cost Per Graduate," Attachment D to Memorandum For [USMA] Chief of Staff & Superintendent, Subject: Congressional Inquiry on Cost Per Graduate, 4.

[39] Ibid.

[40] Robert F. Priest, Office of Institutional Research, "Cost Per Commissioned ROTC Lieutenant," 1993, Attachment E to Memorandum For [USMA] Chief of Staff, Subject: Congressional Inquiry on Cost Per Graduate, 18 November 1993, 1.

[41] Ibid.

[42] Ibid., 2.

[43] Ibid., 1.

[44] Mark Feeney quoted Lieutenant General Graves in reference to West Point ranking among the most selective institutions of higher learning in "Changing with the Times, The Military Academy Links the Army's Tradition-filled Past to its Nontraditional Future," *Boston Globe*, 19 March 1995, 75.

[45] Graves, "Why America Needs West Point," 9.

[46] Graves, "Letter to Graduates and Friends," 1.

[47] House of Representatives Armed Services Committee Hearings 102-46, "Officer Production in a Drawdown Environment," 31 March 1994, 343-44.

[48] Stephen R. Grove, "Years of Continuity and Progress," USMA, 1996, 27.

[49] Gordon R. Sullivan, "Address to the 1992 USMA Graduating Class: Leading Tomorrow's Army," West Point, NY, 30 May 1992, 1.

[50] Stephen R. Grove, "Oral History Interview with LTG Graves," second session conducted on 5 June 1996, 25.

[51] Ibid., 384.

[52] Peter Drucker, as quoted by Lieutenant General Graves in *Assembly*, May 1995, 1.

[53] Richard B. Cheney, CSIS Panel Report, 30.

[54] John D. Lawlor, "Do We Need West Point?" Editorial in *Officer Review*, May 1992, 7.

[55] Richard B. Cheney, 27.

[56] Ibid., 27-28.

[57] Ibid., 27. The CSIS report states that USMA SAT scores were higher than those for students at the University of California at Berkeley and Vanderbilt University, but it does not specify the actual scores.

[58] "West Point: Efficient & Effective," Office of the Superintendent, USMA. This is a single page document available through OIR, but there is no date or other publication reference.

[59] Richard B. Cheney, 27.

[60] Ibid.

[61] Ibid., 28.

[62] Lieutenant General Howard D. Graves's testimony before the House of Representatives Armed Services Committee Hearings 102-46, "Officer Production in a Drawdown Environment," 31 March 1994, 348.

[63] Patrick Toffler, West Point's Director of Policy, Planning, and Analysis, as quoted in Richard Cheney's CSIS Panel Report, 27.

[64] Graves, testimony before the House of Representatives Armed Services Committee Hearings 102-46, "Officer Production in a Drawdown Environment," 31 March 1994, 384.

[65] Larry Donnithorne, "Price/Cost/Worth of West Point," Attachment A to Memorandum For [USMA] Chief of Staff, Subject: Congressional Inquiry on Cost Per Graduate, 18 November 1993, 1.

[66] Graves, testimony before the House of Representatives Armed Services Committee Hearings 102-46, "Officer Production in a Drawdown Environment," 31 March 1994, 384.

[67] Ibid.

[68] Prepared by USMA OIR (GRE Scores of Class of 1991), 23 September 1991.

[69] USMA OIR Scholarship Statistics, 1991.

[70] Letter from Richard R. Beamed, University of Pennsylvania Dean, Enclosure 8 to the 1991 Board of Visitors Report.

[71] USMA, Board of Visitor Reports, 1987-1994, and 1996.

PART IV:

WOMEN AND MINORITIES

Introduction

The most dramatic change in the history of the U.S. Military Academy was the demographic shift in the Corps of Cadets during the second half of the 20th century. Starting in the mid-1960s, West Point undertook a concerted effort to recruit minority applicants, particularly African-Americans. Within a short time the novelty of color in the Corps had worn off as the number and success of minority cadets rose steadily. By 1980 West Point had its first black First Captain; seven years later an Asian-American held the honor for the first time.

African-Americans received appointments to West Point as early as 1870, but their numbers were few and their experiences difficult. Their white classmates, reflecting the prevailing racial attitudes of the day, treated them at best with indifference and at worst with scornful hostility. Not surprising, most black cadets never made it to graduation. Henry O. Flipper became the first African-American to run the gauntlet successfully; he was commissioned in the cavalry in 1877.

Flipper had a short and troubled career as a junior officer. Isolated socially by his peers, and lacking the mentorship of more senior officers, Flipper was especially vulnerable to the consequences of professional inexperience. Trouble came in the form of a court-martial when his commander discovered he had mishandled government funds. In proceedings tainted by racial prejudice, Flipper was convicted and dismissed from the Army.

In 1999 President Bill Clinton pardoned Flipper. It was the first posthumous pardon ever granted by a U.S. president, and it followed the exhaustive efforts of a team of advocates working on Flipper's behalf. The team included several West Point graduates; Thomas Carhart, USMA Class of 1966, was one of them. His chapter focuses on the proceedings of the court-martial, but he devotes several pages to the remarkable efforts to restore Flipper's reputation. The story provides a fitting closure to the Flipper saga, as West Pointers of the modern era gripped hands with one of an earlier day.

African-Americans are but one of many racial and ethnic groups at West Point. Beginning in the early 19th century, young men from several countries were offered admission into the Academy. The appointments were intended primarily to foster good relations with countries of strategic importance to the United States; one such country was China. As Charles Krumwiede points out, the Chinese comprised one of the most prominent foreign contingents, at least until the Communist takeover of China in 1949. Despite the obsta cles of language and culture, the Chinese excelled at West Point. Their record of success helped institutionalize the Academy's foreign cadet program, which continues strong today.

Even more dramatic than recent racial and ethnic trends at West Point was the admission of women into the Corps in 1976. Congress directed the change in late 1975; although the proposal to admit women had been gaining momentum for years, the decision hit the Academy like a thunderclap. With less than a year to prepare, Academy leaders scrambled to modify the barracks, academic buildings, training facilities, and the corpus of regulations, policies, and operating procedures to accommodate the new arrivals. More challenging, however, were the attitudinal changes necessary to ensure fair and equal treatment of the women. This was a tall order given the negative reactions with which virtually every member of the West Point community—faculty and cadets alike—greeted the decision.

Lance Janda's chapter analyzes the early experiences of female cadets. Although he pulls no punches in describing the indignities visited upon them, he praises the efforts of Academy leaders to overcome the obstacles to full integration. Within a few years the initial shock of a coeducational Academy had worn off, and the performance of women at West Point and in the Army had vindicated the decision to admit them. An indicator of how far they had come was the appointment of the first female First Captain in 1989.

Historical accounts of West Point often overlook the dedicated enlisted soldiers—many of them African-American—whose service was essential to supporting and training the cadets. Tanya Kabel-Ballard helps to redress the historical record with an examination of the "Buffalo Soldiers" of the all-black 9th and 10th Cavalry Detachments, assigned to West Point from 1907 to 1947. Her chapter offers an intriguing look into the life of West Point away from the glare of the statues and monuments of the cadet area. Although not perfect, the West Point community offered a far higher level of equality and respect than Buffalo Soldiers—or African-Americans in general—could find elsewhere in American society. Perhaps this is why aging Buffalo Soldiers, in an annual ritual, keep coming back to West Point to muster on the grassy field that still bears their name.

—Editor

CHAPTER 12

THE TRIAL, TRIBULATION, AND PARDON OF LIEUTENANT HENRY O. FLIPPER, USMA 1877

Thomas M. Carhart III

Henry O. Flipper graduated from West Point in 1877; in 1878, Flipper's memoir of his days at West Point, *The Colored Cadet at West Point*, was published in New York by Homer Lee & Company. Thus, by the age of 21, Flipper had earned a degree from West Point, was finishing his West Point memoir, and had orders to head for the frontier, where he would command United States cavalry troops and play a role in the taming of the West.

The 10th Cavalry Regiment, commanded by Col. B.H. Grierson, was one of the four all-black regiments (9th and 10th Cavalry, 24th and 25th Infantry) in the Army. Flipper's first posting was with A Troop (a military unit of a hundred-odd soldiers, called a "company" in the infantry, a "troop" in the cavalry) at Fort Sill, Indian Territory (later, commencing in 1907, Oklahoma).

Flipper took up his duties in January 1878, and as the only African-American officer in the entire Army, his social circumstances were no doubt strained. But he denied that he would be more alone in his regiment than he had been at West Point, as had been predicted in the *New York Herald*:

> From the moment I reached Sill, I haven't experienced anything but happiness. I am not isolated. I am not ostracized

by a single officer. I do not "feel it more keenly," because what the Herald said is not true. The Herald, like other papers, forgets that the army is officered by men who are presumably officers and gentle-men. Those who are will treat me as become gentlemen, as they do, and those who are not I will thank if they will "ostracize" me, for if they don't, I will certainly "ostracize" them.[1]

Happy words these, and surely more optimistic and upbeat than circumstances warranted. Flipper, however, was soon to be rudely awakened to the fact that the officers of the Army were not yet willing to accept an African-American, no matter how intelligent, competent, and well-educated at the "right" school, as their full equal.

For several years after his arrival, Flipper's unit moved around to different forts in Texas and Indian Territory while fighting Indians and/or outlaws. In the spring of 1880, A Troop arrived at Fort Davis, Texas, where it had been transferred with two other troops of the 10th Cavalry in order to fight Victorio's hostile Mescalero Apaches. Fort Davis was less than 60 miles from the Rio Grande, and after a brief stop at the fort, A Troop took up the chase of Victorio and his men, along with several troops of the 8th Cavalry (white) and a company of Texas Rangers.[2]

Fierce fighting resulted in the deaths of 19 Indians and three troopers. Flipper was designated to read the Episcopal service over the dead troopers, who were buried where they fell, after which a volley was fired and the buglers played taps. At the end of November 1880, Flipper and A Troop returned to Fort Davis.[3] It is clear that in this early experience, Flipper, under arms, risked his life for his country.

In early December 1880, Flipper was made Acting Post Assistant Quartermaster and Acting Post Commissary of Subsistence. These and other such staff duties were usually filled for short periods by designated junior officers. Flipper put a most positive light on what he clearly saw as an opportunity to excel rather than a burden to bear: "I had charge of the entire military reservation, houses, water and fuel supply, transportation, feed, clothing and equipment for the troops, and the food supply."[4] Such administrative jobs are more tedious than complex. The junior officers filling them are generally supported by sergeants below them who are familiar with the routine and senior officers above them who watch to make sure that young officers avoid blunders. Flipper, unhappily, was to commit some youthful blunders, but without the kindly oversight of a concerned superior officer who might have guided him painlessly back to solid ground.

Because of the particular nature of his position as the only African-American commissioned officer in the Army, he held himself, and was held by others, to a higher-than-normal standard of conduct. That standard was of almost superhuman proportions, and the nature of his social environment discouraged senior officers or even his peers from offering him advice or assistance. Such isolation also prevented Flipper from sharing the confidence of, or seeking counsel or support from, his fellow officers. Thus, truly alone and rather unprepared to deal with the snares inherent in administrative or financial matters, to say nothing of the cloaked cupidity of his fellow man, Flipper seemed destined, sooner or later, to trip himself up and take a hard fall.

Flipper's social life during his troop's peregrinations in Texas was certainly strained. His troop commander, Capt. Nicholas Nolan, was a widower over 50 years of age with two small children. As soon as A Troop was established in quarters at Fort Sill in 1878, Nolan went to San Antonio, where he wooed and wed Annie Dwyer. He brought his bride back to Fort Sill, and her sister Mollie came along. Nolan insisted that Flipper dine with them, and he did. Mollie and he became what he called "fast friends" and soon enough they were going on long horseback rides together.[5]

This is an instance of what can only be termed at best as incredible naiveté on the part of Flipper, stationed as he was in the formerly Confederate state of Texas that had only recently rejoined the Union, and living and working in the all-white community of officers. He believed the Army to be led by officers and gentlemen who would not ostracize him, and if they were so intolerant as to be unable to accept him on that basis, he preferred them to keep their distance.

He tried to live according to those rules, fully acting out the role of a West Point graduate and commissioned officer while trying to ignore officers prejudiced against him. But they were legion, and surely he was not ignorant of their feelings.

For instance, while A Troop was at Fort Elliott, Texas, the wife of one of the other officers wrote to Eastern newspapers criticizing Nolan and his wife for receiving and entertaining Flipper in their quarters. In response, Captain Nolan wrote a letter of reply that was published in the *Army and Navy Journal.* This publication made a practice of reprinting official orders, excerpts from court-martial proceedings, and other military news items during the late 19th century, thus capturing the flavor of the social and military life of the officer corps. In his letter, Nolan admitted his bias in favor of Flipper because, as a much-persecuted Irishman himself, he felt a shared bond of persecution with African-Americans.[6]

Flipper resumed his rides with Mollie Dwyer at Fort Davis in December 1880, but a new lieutenant arrived, Charles Nordstrom, who promised to unsettle the waters again. In a few words from his frontier memoir, a rigidly correct Flipper only hints at what must have been his broken dreams and the galling hell of Nordstrom's proximity. Even if his relationship with Mollie Dwyer was truly nothing more than a platonic friendship, he had precious few of those to spare:

> We got Charles E. Nordstrom as 1st Lieutenant. He also came from the Civil War Army, was a Swede from Maine, had no education and was a brute. He hated me and gradually won Miss Dwyer from her horse back rides with me and took her riding in a buggy he had. Lieut. Nordstrom and I occupied the same set of double quarters. There was a common entrance and a common hall, but other-wise our quarters were separate. He married Miss Dwyer after I was dismissed.[7]

Sadly, this story makes Flipper's efforts to defy tradition seem all the more foolish.

In the spring of 1881, Fort Davis changed dramatically. Until that time, the fort had been commanded by Maj. N.B. McLaughlen of the 10th Cavalry. During the months of March and April, all the cavalry units except A Troop were dispatched to other posts, and the headquarters of the 1st Infantry arrived, commanded by Col. Rufus Shafter, who also took over command of Fort Davis. Shafter's regimental adjutant, 1st Lt. Louis Wilhelmi, relieved the post adjutant, and his regimental quartermaster, 2nd Lt. Louis Strother, relieved Flipper as the Post Quartermaster. Shafter told Flipper that he would also be relieved as Acting Post Commissary of Subsistence as soon as possible so that he might devote his time fully to his role as a cavalry officer, but that he would retain the position for an indeterminate period while personnel were shifted around. He ended up retaining the job until 11 August when he was replaced by Lt. Frank Edmunds.[8]

Despite the fractionalized nature of the frontier officers' corps, with its dispersal among numerous small, widely separated forts and outposts, theirs was in many respects still a small world inhabited by many familiar faces owing to the West Point connection. Consider, for example, Lieutenant Wilhelmi. Several years older than Flipper, Wilhelmi had started his military career as a cadet at West Point in 1872, only to fall ill during his first year and start again in 1873, this time with Flipper's class. But the sickness returned, and he left West Point for good at the end of 1873. He recovered and was commissioned a second lieutenant in 1875, then was appointed regimental adjutant, a post for which he was promoted to first lieutenant in 1880. Thus, when he arrived at Fort Davis, although he outranked Flipper, the latter had the cachet of a West Point degree, and thus a far superior military education as well as vastly superior potential political power (in theory) within the Army.[9] That potential, however, was of course neutralized by Flipper's ethnicity.

In fact, there were at least five other West Point graduates at Fort Davis who either were Flipper's classmates or had graduated within a few years of him. Ordinarily, on a lonely frontier post West Pointers would have been the fastest of friends, and they have historically maintained a sort of "insiders' club" that, coupled with their traditional dominance of the higher ranks in the Army, has long caused considerable bad feeling and resentment among officers who did not graduate from West Point. Though he did not graduate, his time at West Point would have qualified Wilhelmi for inclusion in this closed circle. But for Flipper, a freed slave and an African-American, this social world remained almost as closed to him in the Army as it had been at West Point.

The old "silence" from West Point days was effectively back again—the institutional message, broadcast in the past to Flipper and all other African-American cadets by the entire Corps of Cadets: We do not want you here, and despite the national governmental authorities that have appointed you a cadet, we refuse to recognize your presence and will do everything we can to force you to leave. And now some of his fellow officers on a remote Western post were sending him the same message. Thus, the Army's racist mentality to which Flipper had first been exposed at West Point was still alive after he left that institution. At first, such slights must have been very hurtful indeed. But after four years of it at West Point, followed by five years in the frontier Army, it seems Flipper had come to expect such treatment.

Flipper, of course, was very popular among the African-American enlisted soldiers who filled the ranks of the 10th Cavalry. But the barrier of rank created an impenetrable wall between them socially: even had the disparity of education and experience not been enough to keep them apart, the rules of the Army precluded social fraternization between officers and the enlisted ranks.

In his small quarters, he kept a violin, a typewriter (he had, after all, already written a book that was being commercially published and from which he was awaiting royalties), a "student's lamp," three photo albums, and 79 books, providing ways to fill his frequent solitary moments.[10] But he also gravitated to the town that had sprung up outside Fort Davis, which lay about 165 miles southeast of El Paso, befriending many of the European-American, African-American, and Mexican civilians who lived there. His best friend was probably W. S. Chamberlain, a watchmaker, whom he apparently visited every day, with whom he often went on rides and other social outings, and in whose company he often took his meals. He was also close to Joseph Sender, a merchant whose store, Sender & Seidenborn, was the largest in town.[11]

At his court-martial, about which we shall have more to say later, both Sender and Chamberlain had only the highest praise for Flipper, a man they described as being of the highest personal honor and integrity. Moreover, when the chips were down and Flipper needed financial help, they were able within a few days to come up with more than $2,000 in personal loans to him from the civilian community at Fort Davis.

Though his service as quartermaster had ended in March, Flipper continued to serve as the Post Commissary, with an office and a storehouse. Most of the details of buying and selling food for the soldiers and families at Fort Davis were taken care of by Commissary Sergeant Carl Ross, who recorded sales, prepared letters and receipts for Flipper's signature, and generally kept the books in order.[12] Flipper's duties were primarily those of passing on instructions, taking responsibility for all funds received, and the efficient management of the commissary service.

All foodstuffs were purchased from the commissary by the soldiers at the post or by their families. Officers were allowed credit, usually paying their accrued debt by check periodically, but soldiers were supposed to present cash at each transaction. Each week, the total amount of money on hand, in checks and specie—American and Mexican bills and coins—was tallied and approved by the post commander, Colonel Shafter. Each Saturday, Sergeant Ross prepared appropriate forms for Flipper's signature, which Shafter in turn signed on Sunday morning. A copy of the Statement of Funds was sent to the Chief Commissary of Subsistence of the Department of Texas in San Antonio, and another to the Commissary General in the War Department, Washington, DC, while a third copy stayed in the post commissary office records. The funds themselves were to be sent to San Antonio as soon as practicable after the end of each month.

For March through May 1881, Colonel Shafter described Flipper's performance of his duties as follows: "I found Mr. Flipper, as far as I could observe, always prompt in attending to his duties—performed them intelligently and to my entire satisfaction."[13] But then in May, Flipper began to notice apparent shortfalls in cash and checks collected. Until that time, Flipper's performance of his professional duties, even given the racist walls that surrounded him, had never even remotely been called into question. Moreover, his record as an Indian- and outlaw-fighting cavalry officer had been superb. His regimental commander, Col. B.H. Grierson, was later to write a very positive appraisal of him for consideration during Flipper's court-martial:

> [His] veracity and integrity have never been questioned, and his character and standing as an officer and a gentleman have certainly been beyond reproach. He came under my immediate command in 1880, during the campaign against Victorio's band of hostile Indians, and from personal observation, I can testify to his efficiency and gallantry in the field. General Davidson, Captain Nolan, and others under whom he has served have spoken of him in the highest terms, and he has repeatedly been selected for special and important duties, and discharged them faithfully and in a highly satisfactory manner. . . . In any event: in view of his manly and successful struggle; his past excellent record; his heretofore faithful and meritorious services to the government; . . . considering too the very severe punishment he has already undergone . . . I, as his colonel, . . . believing in his great promise for future usefulness; knowing that his restoration to duty would give great satisfaction to the regiment, . . . most heartily and earnestly commend him to the leniency of the court and reviewing authorities.[14]

As we begin to consider the actions for which Lieutenant Flipper would find himself ultimately driven from the Army in disgrace, it is important that we recognize the particularity of his position in certain ways. As the only black officer in the Army, he saw the social conditions of others in a way that white officers did not. His sensitivity to the plight of, and resultant charity toward, those who filled more menial roles at Fort Davis than he did were to become an important underlying factor in his own personal commissary debt problems.

Flipper was especially sensitive to the plights occasioned by the accident of birth of other people of color who had not been so fortunate as himself. An obvious place where he could make their lives incrementally less difficult was in their purchase of foodstuffs from the commissary. Since he was an officer, he could buy on credit, while enlisted personnel had to pay cash. Though his pay as a second lieutenant was only $125 per month, Flipper made it a custom to allow enlisted men, laundresses, and others in unfavored circumstances to buy from the commissary stores, drawing on his own credit for payment but keeping little or no systematic record of such transactions. He eventually came to allow others to spend on credit in his commissary an amount that, when combined with his own modest requirements, came close to consuming all his pay.[15] At his court-martial, his counsel, Capt. Merritt Barber, pointed this out:

> Look at the condition of his personal accounts, as illustrated by his monthly purchases from the commissary, steadily running up from $72.08 in December to $262.20 in July. Open hearted and not realizing upon what shoals and quicksands he was drifting, generous to a fault, every one who came to him got what they asked, so that during the eight and one half months he was commissary his personal account was $1121.71, at least half of which he thinks is still outstanding, and there is scarcely a scrap of paper or a memorandum of any kind to show how much is owing to him or who owes it.[16]

By the end of May 1881, he was short some $800. Though in his reports to his post commander he began to reflect the amount of money he actually had on hand rather than the amount he *should* have had, he continued to declare the larger amounts, which he should have had, on reports to San Antonio and Washington, DC. At his trial his attorney explained:

> It was simply a matter with himself and all there was of it, Lieut. Flipper, 10th Cavalry, did not pay his commissary bills to Lieut. Flipper, A.C.S. [Acting Commissary of Subsistence]. . . . He knew there was considerable lacking, and he knew

there was considerable due from him to make it up, and as
the funds and weekly statements were not to be transmitted
for some time, he made the statements to correspond with
the actual cash on hand and held himself responsible to pay
his commissary bills when it became necessary to transmit
the funds. That some person had begun at this time to visit
his trunk and carry off money would seem probable.[17]

The reference to "some person" visiting "his trunk" and carrying
off money broaches another central issue: the way Flipper maintained security of the commissary funds of which he was custodian.
In his statement to the court, Flipper said:

The funds for which I was responsible I kept in my own
quarters in my trunk, the trunk I procured at West Point and
have used ever since I entered the service. My reasons for
keeping them there were that as far as I was responsible for
their safety I felt more secure to have them in my own personal custody.[18]

One wonders why Flipper didn't seek to keep the funds in one of
the two quartermaster safes. The only mention he made at trial of
why he kept the funds in his trunk appears above. But in 1898, he
attempted to have Congress intervene in his behalf, and submitted a
statement in which he commented on why he kept the funds in his
quarters:

When I was relieved from duty as Quartermaster I had no
secure place to keep the commissary funds, and so reported
to Colonel Shafter. He expressly told me at that time to keep
them in my quarters, that they would no doubt be safe
there for a few days until he relieved me and I turned them
over to my successor. Colonel Shafter denied all knowledge
of this interview.[19]

Colonel Shafter's words and deeds figured in the case in other
regards. Once allegations began to surface, he ordered Flipper's quarters searched and had him arrested on the flimsy pretext of having

seen his saddled horse on the street in town carrying saddlebags,[20] the implication being that the saddlebags showed he intended to flee. But Flipper's horse *always* carried both saddle and saddlebags, and Flipper was often in town during the day or evening.

But regardless of whether Flipper was ordered to keep the funds in his quarters or simply decided to do so on his own, it was a highly imprudent act, given that there were official safes that he might have used instead. And no matter how secure the trunk itself and its lock may have been, there was at least one other person who had access to the keys and thus to the contents of the trunk: Flipper's servant, Lucy Smith.

Lucy claimed to sleep in a room at one Mrs. Olsup's house in town,[21] but there was evidence that she was Flipper's mistress as well as his servant. Apparently the morality of the time discouraged mentioning this relationship at trial (she is called "Lucy Flipper" or "Mrs. Flipper" in the trial transcript at least four times, and each time the slip was hurriedly corrected), but she kept her clothing and personal possessions in Flipper's trunk in his post quarters, which implies more than just the convenience to her he claimed:

> My servant having no place to keep her clothing safely had asked me if she could put some of it in that trunk and I granted her permission; keeping the keys myself, and only handing them to her when she desired to get something out or put something in, and then but for a short time; cautioning her to be very careful of my goods and papers and to never leave anything unlocked or insecure.[22]

On other grounds also, Lucy's connection to him was clearly more than the normal master-servant relationship one might have expected. In defending his client against the charges of embezzlement, his attorney Capt. Merritt Barber took it upon himself in his summation to refute certain rumors:

> The next was the theory that my client had been touched by the tender passion and his heart melting under the gentle influences of a first love had lavished the gold of government on the object of his passion in gorgeous presents of

jewelry and attire. But alas for that theory, upon investigation we find he has been guilty of presenting his servant girl
an old gold ring which he didn't want and was of no use to
her.[23]

But however old and unwanted by either, what other plausible circumstances could induce a young black bachelor officer, isolated
and adrift in a white world, to give a gold ring to his black female
servant?

In early May, Flipper got a message from San Antonio telling
him not to send funds in until June,[24] and during this period Flipper simply stopped his weekly accounting of funds. Weekly reports
were prepared during this period by Commissary Sergeant Ross and
signed by Flipper, but were *not* signed by the commanding officer,
Colonel Shafter, or his designee in his absence.[25] Shafter did not
inspect them again until 8 July. When Flipper prepared his records
for the colonel on 7 July, he found that he was now some $1440
short. So he wrote a check that was to be drawn on his account at
the San Antonio National Bank, for $1,440.43,[26] even though he had
no account in that bank. He showed this check to the colonel on 8
July, and with that additional amount, the other figures tallied for the
preceding fiscal period at $3,791.77.

After the 8 July inspection, Colonel Shafter told him to submit the
$3,791.77 to San Antonio. Flipper agreed to do so, and ordered Ser-
geant Ross to make out the invoices and receipts of the funds, which
he did. Flipper took them with him, then returned on 10 August
and ordered Ross to make out a letter of transmittal for these funds,
which he also did. Flipper signed these papers on 11 August, which
was the day that, in conformity with Shafter's earlier commitment,
Flipper was to be relieved as Acting Commissary and replaced in that
role by Lieutenant Edmunds.

He had expected to collect a large amount from soldiers in A
Troop who owed him money from their credit purchases in his name
when the troops returned to Fort Davis on 10 July, but for reasons
that remain unclear he was unable to make any such collections. He
then contacted the Homer Lee publishing company in New York and

asked them to send his royalty check to the San Antonio National Bank. He was expecting to receive some $2,500,[27] an amount sufficient, once deposited, to cover his earlier check for $1440.43. But the weeks dragged by with no word from New York. Without having forwarded the necessary funds, he signed three consecutive weekly reports, on 9, 13, and 24 July, all falsely indicating that the $3,791.77 was in transit to San Antonio. Flipper explained his motives to the court:

> As to my motives in the matter alleged in the first specification of the second charge [having written the check for $1440] I can only say that some time before I had been cautioned that the commanding officer would improve any opportunity to get me into trouble, and although I did not give much credit to it at the time, it occurred to me very prominently when I found myself in difficulty; and as he had long been known to me by reputation and observation as a severe, stern man, having committed my first mistake I indulged what proved to be false hope that I would be able to work out my responsibility alone and avoid giving him any knowledge of my embarrassment.[28]

When the royalty check finally arrived on 17 August, it was too small and too late—only $74.00—and by then Flipper had been arrested.[29] Maj. Michael Small, the Chief Commissary in San Antonio, had begun pressing for the money. After several messages to Flipper that drew no response, he informed Shafter, first by mail, then by telegram, that he had received nothing.

Initially, Shafter suspected nothing more than the normal "slows" of all matters administrative. Then, as time passed, he said, he began to suspect wrongdoing. He had confronted Flipper as early as 10 August, who assured him the checks and currency were in the mail. But more telegrams came in from San Antonio, and now having come to believe that Flipper had not sent the money to San Antonio, Shafter had Flipper's quarters searched by Lieutenants Wilhelmi and Edmunds. He told them to arrest Flipper if they found "anything suspicious."[30] They found nothing suspicious, but they also did not find the commissary money they thought Flipper had retained. They put a guard on Flipper, then reported to Shafter, who told them to go back and make a more thorough search.[31]

Thereupon Shafter interrogated Lucy Smith, Flipper's servant. She played dumb, but almost by accident Shafter discovered that she had two envelopes concealed in her dress. He forced her to produce them, and one contained some $2,800 in checks (including the $1440.43 check Flipper had written on the San Antonio bank), the other a mass of invoices and receipts.[32]

It seems improbable Lucy was trying to steal the checks since she would not have been able to negotiate them; rather, it looks like she was trying to cover for Flipper, as he had certified both in signed reports and orally to the colonel that the checks were already in the mail to San Antonio. Now, things looked bad for Flipper. Colonel Shafter had him placed in the guardhouse and told Flipper he believed that he had stolen the difference between the $2,800 in checks recovered and the total liability of $3,700.[33]

Two days later, he learned that Flipper did not have an account at the San Antonio National bank, which made the check he had written for $1440.43 (included among the $2,800 in checks Shafter had found on Lucy's person) worthless. Shafter went to the guardhouse and informed Flipper of this, that his total liability had now risen from $900 to some $2,300 or $2,400. Their conversation, according to Shafter, went as follows:

> He said "Yes, Colonel, I had to deceive you in some way and took that way to do it." I then said "You need not criminate yourself, I don't want you to do so unless you choose to, but I would like to know where that money has gone to if you are willing to tell me." He said "Colonel, I don't know where it has gone to." I said "It is very strange that you should be short $2400 and not know where it is." He said "Yes, that is so, but I can't account for it unless some of them have stolen it from me." I said "who do you mean by 'some of them'?" He said "I don't know." I said "Do you think that woman at your house has it or any of it?" He said "No, sir, I do not." He said then that if he could see three or four of

his friends in town he thought he could make his deficiency good. I said "Do you think you can make the whole $2400 good?" He said "Yes, I think I can."[34]

Flipper was held in a small (6'6" x 4'6") cell in the guardhouse for four days. The only other inmates were enlisted black soldiers from the 10th Cavalry, who were held in a large adjoining room in which they were free to move around and interact. Flipper's cell was separated from the enlisted section by a wall, and communication was further barred by the social barrier that separated officers from the enlisted ranks. But the enlisted men were fully aware of Flipper's presence and the public shame that went with his being held in the guardhouse. Such treatment would have been unheard of for white officers. Normally, an officer in similar circumstances would have simply been restricted to his quarters, unguarded, while the charges against him were investigated. But for the only black officer in the Army, such treatment was not surprising.[35]

However, when Shafter sent news of the affair and Flipper's arrest and confinement up the chain of command to Headquarters, Department of Texas, in San Antonio, the immediate response from his commander, Gen. Christopher Augur, was to release Flipper from the guardhouse. But the telegram was delayed for four days. After that, Flipper was released to return to his quarters, where an armed guard was posted.

Some of Flipper's friends from town had visited him in jail, including Chamberlain and Sender. By the fourth day, they were able to come up with a total of $2,300, which they gave to Flipper, who in turn gave it to Colonel Shafter. This amount, combined with the $1,400 in sound checks found on Lucy, cleared up Flipper's liability to the government, and his restriction to quarters was accordingly lifted. Shafter contributed $100 to the $2,300 himself. It should be noted, however, that his expressed sympathy is somewhat suspect since he insisted on retaining Flipper's watch (already in his possession, as were all of Flipper's personal possessions, collected and catalogued on Shafter's order at the time of Flipper's arrest) as collateral for what the colonel would later refer to as his "loan" to Flipper.[36] But the game was not yet over: on 29 August, Flipper was served with the formal charges filed against him by Shafter. He would have to face a court-martial.

Flipper asked for a month's delay in order to allow him time to secure the services of a civilian lawyer from New York. This delay was granted, and Flipper negotiated with a lawyer in New York who ultimately declined to act as his attorney in the case. When the court-martial convened, Flipper was defended by Capt. Merritt Barber.

The court-martial took place at Fort Davis in November and December 1881, before a board of ten officers, a Judge Advocate, Capt. John W. Clous (a military prosecutor with enlarged powers), and Captain Barber. There were two charges: the first was that he had embezzled $3,791.77; the second, that he had engaged in conduct unbecoming an officer as set forth in five specifications. These were: (1) writing a fraudulent check for $1440.43; (2), (3), and (4) signing three false reports in July 1881, each of which indicated that the $3,791 was in transit to San Antonio; and (5) telling Colonel Shafter on 10 August that he had sent the funds to San Antonio, when in fact he had not.

The trial was complex, and there are many apparent conflicts in the record that will probably never be resolved. For instance, while Lucy may have looked like Flipper's selfless protector by concealing the envelope filled with checks on her person, her motives become suspect when, as Shafter explained it, she tried to claim money that had come from Flipper's trunk. Here is the exchange between Captain Barber and Colonel Shafter:

> *Barber:* You have said in your testimony that you thought what was in Lucy's pocket book was commissary money. What was there, if anything, that led you to think so?
> *Shafter:* The amount of money which was something in the neighborhood of $100.00, I think I stated something over $80.00, there were three twenty dollar bills and a twenty dollar gold piece. I thought it was a good deal of money for a servant girl to have in her pocket book and from the

fact that Lieutenant Flipper had presented to me week after week a solitary means of identifying either the bills or the gold and cannot do so, but there was no gold, that I knew of or as I am aware of found by the officers who made the search, and this twenty dollar gold piece was found in a little pocket book that she claimed was her money and was given back to her.[37]

Also, many witnesses at the trial commented on the number of civilians, mostly Mexicans, who seemed to be in and around Flipper's quarters when he was not there, and about the large amounts of checks and currency that seemed to be almost carelessly strewn around his rooms.[38] There was considerable suspicion expressed that some of these individuals, perhaps in collusion with Lucy, were thieves. But Flipper, who had learned Spanish at West Point and enjoyed using it with those who did not shun him because of his color, trusted his new friends even in financial affairs:

I had no reason to question the honesty of any of the persons about my house as I had never missed anything that attracted my attention, and when the officers searched that trunk and failed to find the funds which I had put there three days before I was perfectly astounded, and could hardly believe the evidence of my own senses. As to where that money went and who took it, I am totally ignorant.[39]

Most of Flipper's own commissary bill of $1,121.57 was for credit he had extended to enlisted men and civilian workers not normally allowed credit, and which was doubtless covered by the check for $1,440.43 he had written and kept in his trunk while awaiting royalties from New York.[40] This check may also have covered amounts that had been pilfered from his quarters, but Flipper's records of debts from his loans and extensions of credit to others were too scanty to determine this point. When the $1,121.57 is coupled with the $1,400 in checks that were found on Lucy, a gap of $900 remains that he should have had and that he did not realize was missing at the time of his arrest. Flipper said he believed that this amount was in his trunk and was stolen from him by unknown persons. But whether it was stolen by Lucy, the Mexicans, or other officers such as Lieutenant Wilhelmi, whom he did not trust, is largely irrelevant. When the time came, Flipper was unable to produce the money of which he was custodian.

Given the time and place of the court-martial, it has to be said that Captain Barber's defense was quite thorough. To a layman, some of the points he made may seem to be mostly "form over substance," but in the law, form can be all-important. In answering the first charge, that of embezzlement, Barber reviewed the events of the preceding year, showing that Flipper had never evidenced any intention to convert the money entrusted to him, any newly-acquired wealth, or any secrecy or other suspect behavior. Barber showed that after his arrest, Flipper evinced a strong determination to make good, through his own resources, the amount lost, thus indicating a lack of desire to acquire such ill-gotten gains. Barber then showed that Flipper was expecting the amount of $2,500 to arrive by check from his publishers in New York, and argued that Colonel Shafter's handling of the case was either procedurally inept or reflective of active hostility against Flipper.

But given that some money was missing, Barber argued that the bookkeeping practices and record maintenance procedures of the commissary service were fatally flawed even before Flipper arrived at Fort Davis, and that the missing funds were less his fault than that of the system itself. Then he took up the definition of embezzlement, showing that if the funds were in fact stolen, Flipper was not even aware that that had happened until after he was arrested. The disappearance of the money, Barber argued, was not caused by Flipper nor done with his knowledge, so that the element of intent was missing. Flipper, in this construction of events, simply could not have kept the money and used it for his own purposes.[41]

Barber next addressed the second charge, that of "conduct unbecoming an officer and a gentleman." The first specification was that he lied to his commanding officer, telling him that the checks were in the mail to higher headquarters when he knew they were not—we shall return to this specification shortly. The second, third, and fourth were that he had submitted false reports to his commanding officer, when in fact he had kept the money and used it for his own purposes. Barber quickly disposed of these three specifications:

> In each one of the second, third, and fourth [specifications], certain weekly statements of public funds are specified with the averment [allegation] that they are false, pointing to an averment in the papers which is characterized as being so, and winding up with an averment in the alternative that Lieutenant Flipper had applied the funds represented by that entry to his own use and benefit, thus charging embezzlement in those three specifications as well as conduct unbecoming. All the testimony in this case is directed to the inaccuracy of one single entry of the funds in transit to the Chief Commissary of Subsistence, Department of Texas, and as there is nothing said of the other entries it must be presumed they are all true. It is necessary that every part of a specification should be covered in testimony and found by the court, and all that is not covered must be found for the accused, and in regard to the last averment of applying to his own use and benefit we feel as confident that you will not find Lieutenant Flipper guilty of embezzlement under this charge as under the first.

The fifth specification under this charge was that Flipper had presented a fraudulent check with the intent to deceive his commanding officer, Colonel Shafter. Barber took this specification on first:

> It must have been known to the officer drawing the charges that the check had never been out of Mr. Flipper's hands, had never been uttered, published, or presented, had never been negotiated or used in any manner except as an exhibit. If a man draws a check on a bank in which he has no funds and puts the check in his pocket, the *check* is not fraudulent, or if he shows it to his neighbor to impress him with the idea of his responsibility, the *check* is not fraudulent, or if he shows it and purchases goods on the credit of having it in his possession, the *check* is not fraudulent, but if he

buys goods and gives the check in payment and makes no provision to meet it, when presented for payment, it is then fraudulent. The element which makes it fraudulent is uttering it, negotiating it, putting it in circulation. As nothing of the kind was done in this case, the averment that the check was fraudulent gives an entirely false coloring to the transaction and is a misuse of the term.[42]

Barber showed that, on the only date the check was shown to Shafter, it was for an amount, $1440.43, that was much greater than any difference could have been on that date between the amount Flipper had on hand and the amount for which he was responsible. Therefore, the check was neither fraudulent nor meant to deceive Shafter.[43]

Returning to the first specification, Barber conceded that his client had not been truthful with Shafter, but he also showed that Flipper had been warned that Shafter would destroy him if he could, and that Flipper was desperate to stay out of trouble. Ever conscious of the fact that he was the only black officer in uniform and aware of the added attention that drew to his every act, Flipper made every effort possible to be seen as the sort of ideal officer who would meet the theoretical standards he had learned at West Point. Among other things, that included being a man of high principles who would withstand any temptation to lower his standards for personal gain. But in negotiating the financial shoals of the Army's logistical support system, he desperately needed the guidance of a mentor, an older and wiser man, who could help him along his path. Unfortunately, his race seems to have rendered such an arrangement a practical impossibility, and he had to tell Shafter small lies to buy time in the hope that he could somehow acquire the money necessary, even if it was out of his own pocket, to make his promises good.

Barber then discussed recent courts-martial of white officers, one a Paymaster Reese who had been charged with 15 specifications of "embezzlement" and seven of "conduct unbecoming an officer and a gentleman." After being found guilty of lowered charges by court-martial, he suffered only a reprimand in general orders and was restored to duty. Barber's closing argument emphasized the double standard by which Flipper was being measured and urged an honest focus on the impending damage to the image of justice in the Army. But his arguments were to no avail, and the judgment handed down in January 1882 seems to have been predictable from the start: on Charge 1(embezzlement), not guilty; on Charge 2 (conduct unbecoming an officer and a gentleman), guilty of all five specifications. The sentence prescribed that Flipper "be dismissed from the service of the United States."[44]

An automatic review then occurred through the military chain of command all the way up to the President (the 106th Article of War at the time said that, in time of peace, no sentence of a court-martial directing the dismissal of an officer shall be executed before it has formally been confirmed by the President of the United States).

The first review, by General Augur, recommended that Flipper be found guilty of both charges. General Augur was not a lawyer, but he was clearly a stern man. The next reviewing officer was indeed a lawyer, the man responsible for advising the Secretary of War on issues of law. That was the Judge Advocate General of the Army, David Swaim. His report to the Secretary was the last comment before the President would review the case. His review was lengthy, but its conclusion bears repeating:

> It is believed that there is no case on record in which an officer was treated with such personal harshness and indignity upon the causes and grounds set forth as was Lieut. Flipper by Col. Shafter and the officer who searched his person and quarters taking his watch and ornaments from him; especially as they must have known all the facts at the time and well knew that there was no real grounds for such action. . . . I would recommend that the sentence be confirmed but mitigated to a lesser degree of punishment.[45]

All that was left now was a final review by President Chester Arthur. Given the recommendation for mitigation of punishment by Judge Advocate General Swaim, the senior lawyer in the Army, it would not have been unreasonable to expect some leniency from the

White House. But on 14 June 1882, President Arthur signed a simple statement at the bottom of the cover letter forwarding the Flipper case to the White House from the War Department. It read: "The sentence in the foregoing case of Second Lieutenant Henry O. Flipper 10th Regiment of U.S. Cavalry, is hereby confirmed."[46] Accordingly, Flipper was discharged from the Army.

He decided to remain in the southwest United States working as a civil and mining engineer, not only in that area but also, given his facility in the Spanish language, in Mexico as well. However, until the day he died in 1940, he adamantly insisted on his innocence in the matters for which he had been court-martialed and driven from the Army in disgrace.

As he recovered his composure and equilibrium, Flipper began to establish a very favorable professional reputation, such that he gained many friends and admirers. Eventually, he became close to governmental leaders and, through their agency, was able to have bills introduced in both Houses of Congress that would have restored him to the officer corps in the Army.[47]

In the body of these bills, he proposed a number of new defenses to the charges made against him, most of them structural (that the attempt to force two new members on the court after it had been organized and accepted by Flipper seemed an effort to fix the composition of the court so as to guarantee conviction; that the merging of the functions of prosecuting and reviewing officer in one individual was prejudicial to Flipper; that three of the members of the court-martial were assigned to the 1st Infantry and so worked for Colonel Shafter, the man who preferred the charges; etc.). These defenses strike as mainly technical, however, and, short of a Presidential pardon, it is difficult to see how an appeals court might have used them to overturn an earlier decision.

One of his new defenses, however, seems worthier than the others, i.e., the defense he makes to specifications (2), (3), and (4) of Charge 2: they all specify that certain funds he had falsely said were in transit had actually "been retained by him or applied to his own use or benefit." But that is simply a statement of the crime of embezzlement, a crime of which he had been found "not guilty" under the first charge, and so these three specifications of the second charge must also fall.[48]

Flipper's efforts to attain legislative reversal of a court-martial verdict, however, were strongly opposed by the War Department, and all such bills died in committee, never being brought to a vote on the floor of either the House of Representatives or the Senate. But Flipper was relentless, and he was able to secure the introduction of bills as late as 1922, although all failed. His efforts to have Congress officially clear his record and so return his good name to him unfortunately occurred at the same time that Jim Crow laws were springing up in the South to oppress blacks, while indifference to or even acquiescence in the second-class citizenship of blacks swept unimpeded through the nation.

On 3 May 1940, Flipper died a quiet death in Atlanta. But his cause did not die with him. In the early 1970s, Henry Flipper's nephew, Festus Flipper, and niece, Irsle King, submitted an appeal to the U.S. Army Board for Correction of Military Records. A Georgia schoolteacher, Ray MacColl, who had become interested in the case, prepared and submitted a 52-page supporting brief.

The brief drew heavily on Judge Advocate General Swaim's lengthy letter, and pointed to a number of apparent technical errors or miscarriages of justice in the composition of the court or in its proceedings, defenses that had been employed by Flipper in his attempt to get bills passed by Congress that he hoped would have restored him to military service. But the U.S. government is frequently assailed by appeals of supposed injustices from the past, and it is very difficult for them to be heard. Fortunately for the Flipper family, they had an ally inside the Pentagon. Mr. H. Minton Francis, USMA Class of 1944 and the eighth African-American to graduate from West Point, was at the time a Deputy Assistant Secretary of Defense. In this role, he was able to help obtain serious consideration of the appeal.

The Army Board for Correction of Military Records heard the appeal, delivering its decision on 17 November 1976. Early on, the Board states the following important prefatory limitation on its action:

> That the Attorney General of the United States (40 Opinions
> Attorney General 504) has held that the language of the stat-
> ute which established the Board for Correction of Military
> or Naval Records cannot be construed as permitting the
> reopening of proceedings, findings, and judgments of courts-
> martial so as to disturb the conclusiveness of such proceed-
> ings; and that, however, such Boards might properly
> correct records as a matter in clemency or mitigation with
> reference to the sentence of such courts, including fines, for-
> feitures, reduction in grade, character of discharge, etcetera.[49]

Subsequently, the Board made a number of statements about the
harshness of the punishment meted out in 1882 and the record of
service that Flipper had established both before and after the events
surrounding his court-martial. The Board then recommended that
the Army's official records be corrected to show that Flipper was separated from the Army on a certificate of honorable discharge on 30 June
1882.[50] On 13 December 1976, the Assistant Secretary of the Army for
Manpower and Reserve Affairs formally approved the findings of the
board and directed that the Army records be so changed. But while the
nature of his discharge was thus changed, his conviction of conduct
unbecoming an officer remained on the books unchallenged.

In 1989, Mr. Francis was at a meeting of the Board of Trustees of the
West Point Association of Graduates, where he met one of the newest
trustees, Federal Judge Eugene Sullivan, USMA Class of 1964. One of
their conversation topics was a recent article about Flipper and the
correction of his military records. Mr. Francis was surprised to hear
from Judge Sullivan that, in the eyes of the law, Flipper remained a
convicted felon notwithstanding the successful action at the U.S.
Army Board for the Correction of Military Records. Moreover, in Judge
Sullivan's view, only a federal court could void the conviction. The
only other option was a pardon by the President. Mr. Francis asked
Judge Sullivan if he would assist him with further legal action to clear
Flipper's name. Though sharing the concerns of Mr. Francis, Judge
Sullivan could not practice law as a sitting judge, but he decided to
read the historical records about the Flipper conviction.

Judge Sullivan asked his secretary, Barbara Burley, an African-American, if she would volunteer to obtain the Flipper court records on microfiche from the U.S. Archives and reproduce them on paper. Burley was eager to assist in clearing the name of an American officer of great moral courage whose skin happened to be black. Once she had secured the relevant records, Judge Sullivan was surprised to find that the stack of papers was easily ten inches high. He asked his wife, Lis Sullivan, to read through the documents and mark the relevant sections of the legal proceedings, to include noting any perception on her part of bias or unfair treatment in the court-martial. A major undertaking, this was an important weeding of handwritten records that were often difficult to read.

Once this step was completed, Judge Sullivan reviewed the distilled records and concluded that there were numerous instances of injustice in the trial. These included the illegal confinement of Flipper before the trial, which was a violation of the 65th Article of War in effect at the time; command influence by Colonel Shafter; attempted jury tampering, again by Colonel Shafter; improper review of the conviction by the Prosecutor, Captain Clous; inconsistent verdicts; lack of sufficient evidence to support the verdict; prosecutorial misconduct in charging the wrong offense; and other prejudicial factors. But now Judge Sullivan had a problem: even though he could see that justice had not been done in this particular case, he could take no action to remedy the injustice. In fact, he had decided that if the case ever came to his court, he would recuse himself because of prior knowledge.

Judge Sullivan's frustration with forced inaction seemed to be resolved when he and I had lunch together one day, and I told him I was writing my Ph.D. dissertation at Princeton on African-American West Pointers in the 19th century. I am also both a graduate of West Point and a lawyer, and Judge Sullivan was delighted to find someone who might help him in working to clear Flipper's name. I obtained his stack of historical records and read them almost immediately. I agreed with Judge Sullivan's conclusions that injustices had occurred, and decided to make this issue a key part of my dissertation. But as a lawyer admitted to practice in federal courts, I also wanted to take legal action in Flipper's behalf.

My dissertation covered the factual and legal history of the Flipper case, to include the relevant official records and the specific instances of seeming injustice, both in the trial and on appeal. After completing the dissertation, I started drafting a legal brief intended for filing in federal court in an attempt to overturn Flipper's conviction. But as I worked, it became increasingly clear that I might be opposed in court by the U.S. government on many grounds—legal, political, administrative, bureaucratic, etc. This could be a long, difficult, and expensive fight, and it was just too risky and too important for me to pursue by myself. What I really needed was a large District of Columbia law firm that had the resources and the will to accomplish this most worthy goal.

Fortunately, I had a close friend who could provide an entrée to the necessary means, a man who graduated from West Point with me in 1966 and with whom I had shared student days at the University of Michigan law school, Jeffrey H. Smith. It happened that Smith was a partner in a large Washington law firm, Arnold & Porter. After I proposed the case to him, he was eager to help. I gave him my dissertation, my draft work on a legal brief, the trial transcript, and other legal papers. Then Smith and his partner Darryl Jackson spearheaded the firm's effort to explore the possible legal avenues for redress. Eventually, they decided that the best and most practical route would be a Presidential pardon. It took more than five years, but their effort was eventually successful. Bill Clinton pardoned Henry Flipper on 19 February 1999, the first posthumous pardon ever granted by a U.S. president.

The initiative resulting in a Presidential pardon for Flipper was a team effort: several necessary links in a chain of West Point graduates who worked to right a wrong done to another graduate long ago, not because he was a graduate, nor because he was an African-American, but because he was a victimized young Army officer who deserved better. That Minton Francis, Gene Sullivan, and Jeff Smith succeeded is not a mark of their personal or professional success. Rather, it was a simple act of duty they performed for the sake of duty alone.

[1] Henry O. Flipper, *The Colored Cadet at West Point* (New York: Homer Lee & Co., 1878), 247-48.

[2] Flipper, *Negro Frontiersman* (El Paso: Texas Western College Press, 1963), 14-16.

[3] Ibid., 15-17.

[4] Ibid., 18.

[5] Ibid., 2-3.

[6] *Army and Navy Journal*, 11 October 1879, 176; and Theodore D. Harris, "Henry Ossian Flipper: the First Negro Graduate of West Point" (Ph.D. diss., University of Minnesota, 1971), 139.

[7] Flipper, *Negro Frontiersman*, 19.

[8] In November 1881, Flipper was tried by General Court-Martial. The record of these proceedings, 744 pages in length, is found in the National Archives as "Court Martial Proceedings of Henry O. Flipper," File QQ2952, Record Group 153. This information is drawn from pages 300-304 of that record. Hereafter, these Court Martial records will be referred to as "CMR."

[9] CMR, 53-54.

[10] Flipper's posessions in his quarters were inventoried on 13 August 1881 after his arrest, the list appearing as Exhibit 83, CMR, 724.

[11] CMR, 477-84.

[12] The testimony of Sergeant Ross contains much detail about how the commissary was run (CMR 391-412).

[13] CMR, 54.

[14] CMR, exhibit 109, 745.

[15] CMR, 535-40.

[16] CMR, 575.

[17] CMR, 538.

[18] CMR, 503.

[19] U.S. Congress, House Committee on Military Affairs, Committee on Military Affairs, *In the Matter of the Court-Martial of Henry Ossian Flipper*, 55th Congress, 2nd Session, 1898,12.

[20] CMR, 122, 129.

[21] CMR, 444.

[22] CMR, 504.

[23] CMR, 522.

[24] CMR, 508.

[25] CMR, 655-58, 503-05, wherein Flipper stated that the weekly verification of funds did not occur from 28 May through 8 July, corroborated by the weekly statements not having been signed by Shafter or his designee. On pp. 507 and 508, the Judge Advocate called a witness to testify that the books *had* been checked on 4 June but, after a conference, the court refused to allow such testimony.

[26] CMR, 649.

[27] CMR, 306-07.

[28] CMR, 506.

[29] CMR, 193.

[30] CMR, 67-68.

[31] CMR, 68-73.

[32] CMR, 75-77.

[33] CMR, 50.

[34] CMR, 51.

[35] CMR, 25-60.

[36] CMR, 150-52.

[37] CMR, 121.

[38] CMR, 284-90.

[39] CMR, 504.

[40] CMR, 410-11.

[41] CMR, 523-53.

[42] CMR, 557.

[43] CMR, 57, 524-26, 565-68.

[44] CMR, 605.

[45] Letter to the Honorable Robert T. Lincoln, Secretary of War, from Judge Advocate General David G. Swaim, dated 3 March 1882; copied on unnumbered pages located in Record of Proceedings of Henry O. Flipper's Trial by General Court Martial, File QQ 2952, Record Group 153, National Archives.

[46] CMR, 607.

[47] E.g., 55th Congress, 2d Session, H.R. 9849, 13 April 1898; 56th Congress, 1st Session, S. 1260, 11 December 1899.

[48] CMR, 607.

[49] Proceedings, In The Case of Henry O. Flipper (Deceased), U.S. Army Board for Correction of Military Records, 17 November 1976, 6.

[50] Ibid., 7.

⇥ CHAPTER 13 ⇤

CHINESE CADETS AT WEST POINT

Charles D. Krumwiede

The graduating class of West Point cadets assembled for commencement ceremonies in Cullum Hall on 11 June 1909. As the diplomas were handed out, cadets cheered their classmates in a rousing display of affection and respect. The loudest cheers of all that day went to the Military Academy's first and—up to then—only Chinese cadets, Ting C. Chen and Ying H. Wen.[1] It had not been easy for Chen and Wen, the third and fourth foreign cadets at West Point and the first and second from the Far East. Despite their difficulty with the English language and unfamiliarity with Western culture, they completed every graduation requirement through determination and hard work. Their success paved the way for the admission of eight more Chinese men—six of whom graduated—between 1914 and 1937.[2]

The experience of Chen, Wen, and the other Chinese West Pointers signaled important developments at the Military Academy. First, it led to lasting and positive changes in the Foreign Cadet Program, which still guides the admission procedures used today. Second, it heightened the cadets' awareness of the Chinese people, culture, and military affairs. Finally, it fostered an appreciation of the importance of China to American national security. Ironically, these developments coincided with a period of U.S. nativism during which Congress passed the Chinese Exclusion Act and Americans in general exhibited irrational prejudice against Chinese-Americans. At West

Point, however, the mood was different, and cadets developed an awareness and appreciation of foreign cultures that would help them throughout their professional careers.

Foreign Cadets at West Point

The authority to admit foreigners to West Point derived from a law that was originally intended for U.S. citizens in American territories. The law empowered the Secretary of War to nominate for appointment ten territorials every year; the nominees were subject to the approval of Congress and the President. In 1884, Secretary of War Robert Todd Lincoln interpreted the law liberally and nominated a Guatemalan, Antonio Barrios, for an appointment.[3] Antonio was the son of Justo Rufino Barrios, who had been Guatemala's president and army commander until his death in 1864. Barrios and his successors had maintained friendly relations with the United States at a time when U.S. relations with other Central American nations were tenuous. Consequently, Congress viewed the nomination favorably. Congressman Henry Slocum—an influential New York democrat, a USMA graduate of the Class of 1852, and a major general in the Civil War—agreed with the Secretary of War that "it is advisable to extend this courtesy." Congress approved the nomination without further debate. In establishing such a precedent, it granted the Secretary of War the implied power of nominating foreigners, as well as territorials, to West Point.

The next time a secretary of war used his implied power to nominate a foreigner was in 1902, when Elihu Root nominated Arturo Calvo of Costa Rica.[4] At the time, American investments in Costa Rican business and agriculture were growing rapidly. The influence of the United Fruit Company, a huge American conglomerate, in the economic and political life of Costa Rica was emblematic of the magnitude of American interests in the region.[5] With U.S. economic interests in mind, Congress approved Calvo's appointment to West Point without discussion.

Taken together, the admission of Barrios and Calvo created an admissions policy for foreign cadets that was distinctly different from the policy applied to their American classmates. Countries with whom the President wished to gain favor would be offered appointments to the Academy. The diplomatic benefits of such a policy far outweighed the particular circumstances surrounding the individual foreign cadet. Accordingly, beyond the Academy's general concern for the quality of all products anointed with the West Point title, there was no compelling reason to subject foreign cadets to the same rigorous standards to which U.S. cadets adhered; moreover, the entry requirements were not in West Point's control. The foreign students were admitted solely on the recommendation of their government to the U.S. government and under the special Acts of Congress. When the editor of the *Chinese Student Monthly* inquired of the Superintendent about foreign cadet admissions testing, the West Point adjutant, 1st Lt. F.H. Farnum, replied, "Foreign cadets are admitted to the Academy without any mental or physical examinations."[6]

The admission of Barrios and Calvo reflected the American preoccupation with hemispheric affairs during the 19th century. In the latter years of the century, however, as U.S. trade expanded westward across the Pacific, Americans viewed with eager anticipation the exploitation of trade with China. In 1904, as part of America's outreach to China, the time was right to create an open door policy in reverse by admitting Chinese cadets to West Point.

The Admission of Chinese Cadets: 1905–1933

Chen's and Wen's nominations reflected China's emergence as a focal point of U.S. foreign relations. The United States' growth as a global power ran parallel to the development of its relations with China. The development of United States foreign policy in China from 1900 to 1940, in turn, correlated to the nominations of eight other Chinese cadets to West Point and the prospects of how their future service in the Chinese military and government could benefit the United States.

It was not until the mid-19th century that the United States began to take an interest in China for economic and missionary reasons. American capitalists and missionaries were some of the first Americans to live in China. In 1899, following the Spanish-American War, the United States annexed the Philippine Islands. American interest in China increased because with this acquisition the Philippines could then serve as a resupply station and base of operations for conducting trade with China.[7] Unfortunately for the new American interests, Great Britain, France, and Russia had traded with China for over 50 years and had already gained control of key coastal and economic centers.

The United States had no further territorial ambitions, but wanted to keep trade with China unrestricted. As a result, Secretary of State John Hay negotiated the "Open Door" policy with Great Britain, France, Germany, Russia, Italy, and Japan. The agreement called for equal and impartial trade with all areas of China, while declaring that all nations would respect China's "territorial and administrative integrity."[8] The Open Door agreement remained the basis of United States policy towards China until the Communist Party took control in 1949.

In gratitude for the U.S. role in negotiating the Open Door policy, the Chinese contacted Secretary of State John Hay to seek admission of Chinese cadets to West Point. The first of these requests occurred in February 1905, when Hay received a letter from the Chinese Legation in Washington. Noting the "friendly disposition" of the United States towards China, the letter requested that Chen and Wen be admitted to West Point as cadets.[9] The Chinese Imperial Government would consider these appointments to be "evidence of the friendly spirit which animates the government of the United States in its relations with [China]."[10] In contrast, it will be recalled, the administration's objective with regard to the appointments of Barrios and Calvo had been to please their influential fathers.

Hay discussed the matter of the Chen and Wen appointments with the Secretary of War, William H. Taft, who supported the action and submitted the nominations to Congress. In this instance, however, Taft added verbiage to the nomination request that would become policy for subsequent appointments of foreign cadets to West Point. First, he stipulated that "no expense shall be caused to the United States," by the appointments—the Chinese government would have to pay for sending their cadets to the Academy.[11] Second, he proposed that foreign cadets not take the oath of allegiance to the U.S.

government (required by all U.S. cadets) nor be required to serve in the U.S. Army upon graduation.[12] Taft's provisos on reimbursement, the oath of allegiance, and service obligation were all accepted by Congress, remaining central features of the Foreign Cadet Program to this day.

Congress's approval of Chen's and Wen's appointments was not without difficulty. Unlike the minimal debate over Barrios and Calvo, the Chinese nominations raised spirited objections. Congressman John Maddox, a Democrat from Georgia, argued that allowing foreign cadets to attend West Point was "bad policy" because "we ought not to teach these people our secrets and methods of warfare in the Army."[13] Congressman George Gilbert, a Democrat from Kentucky, agreed, noting the instability in China reflected by the Boxer Rebellion a few years earlier.[14]

Congressman John Hull, a Republican from Iowa and chairman of the Committee of Military Affairs, assuaged his colleagues' fears. He reminded them that the request for nomination came personally from the Secretary of State through the Secretary of War with their assurance that the Chinese cadets did not pose a threat to the Army or to West Point. He emphasized the extent of "our trade relations" and the fragile state of "friendly relations" with China regarding which "it would be in bad form and prove a wrong to the Government for the House to refuse to pass the resolution."[15] He concluded by reminding his colleagues how the admission of the Chinese cadets would advance American foreign policy objectives in the Far East. Hull's arguments helped the nominations carry the House by a vote of 123 to 38. The Senate also approved, and the result was that Chen and Wen reported to West Point on 15 June 1905 for the start of their plebe summer training.[16]

While the two were attending West Point, a revolutionary movement to overthrow the Chinese emperor was underway in China. For many Chinese, the Boxers' defeat in 1900, their inability to reverse Western encroachment on their lifestyle, and the terms of the surrender that imposed heavy fines and public trials were an utter humiliation. Chinese dissatisfaction intensified support for Sun Yat-sen, the Nationalist revolutionary leader. Sun Yat-sen frequently traveled to the United States to solicit support and funds for his Nationalist party and their goals of overthrowing the Manchu Dynasty, unifying China, and establishing a Chinese republic.[17] This movement gained widespread support in China from 1900 to 1911. The United States took notice and sought dialogue with the Nationalist leaders.

With China in the midst of revolution, future relations with the United States were uncertain. In 1911, Secretary of War Henry Stimson asked Congress to authorize the appointment of two more Chinese cadets to be designated later by the government of China. Stimson acted on his own initiative to make this request; his purpose was to use the appointments at some point in the future as a foreign policy incentive for China. As in 1905, several Congressmen objected and debated the issue on the House floor. It did not matter that Chen and Wen had done well at West Point or that since their graduation in 1909 eight other foreign cadets—one each from Costa Rica and Cuba and six from the Philippines—also had graduated.[18] As the appointments of cadets from other countries were uncontested in Congress, the objections seemed to reflect the prevailing mood of American society against Chinese immigration.[19]

Congressman Hull, as he had in 1905, reminded his colleagues that the request embodied issues beyond West Point:

> The Secretary of War and the Secretary of State are both exceedingly anxious that this resolution shall pass, for reasons which I am sure [you] will appreciate when [you] stop to think. We have adopted the rule almost always of granting to any nation requesting it, especially the South and Central American Republics. . . . It is an act of friendship to a friendly nation. It is something that has never been denied to any nation up to this time, and to deny it now to China would be virtually a statement or notice of hostility to that nation.[20]

There were no further objections and Congress ultimately passed Joint Resolution 131, "authorizing the Secretary of War to receive, for instruction at the Military Academy, two Chinese subjects to be designated hereafter by the Government of China."[21]

The Secretary of War and the Secretary of State thus used the U.S. Military Academy to help generate friendly relations with nations and to assist the implementation of foreign policy objectives. Congressional nominations and West Point admission of Chinese cadets in 1905 and 1911 created the foundation upon which USMA's Foreign Cadet Program was built. The Secretary of War assumed the power to nominate foreign cadets without regard to their physical or academic examination standards. Congressional approval of the nominations hinged on U.S. foreign policy objectives and the agreement of the foreign countries to offset their cadets' expenses.[22]

Chinese Cadets and the Corps

The ten Chinese cadets who entered West Point during the period 1905-1937 gained attention at West Point first for the novelty they presented, then eventually for the respect and reverence they earned from their classmates. They made lasting friendships with their American classmates, worked hard to meet the rigors of cadet life, and exhibited a high level of commitment and discipline. The first among them, Chen and Wen, arrived at West Point together on 15 June 1905 to begin plebe summer training, appropriately nicknamed "Beast Barracks." They were the only foreigners and the only non-white members of the 161-man Class of 1909.[23] The American cadets knew little about Chen and Wen other than that Congress had approved of their presence at the request of the Secretary of War. Because of the special treatment, rumor had it that Chen and Wen were from the upper class of Chinese society.[24]

In 1905 Beast Barracks and plebe year were extremely difficult. The Corps of Cadets was re-imposing the Fourth Class system on the plebes after the ramifications of the Booz hazing scandal of 1900 had tempered their behavior for the previous five years. Fourth Class cadet Oscar L. Booz, a member of the Class of 1902, died of tuberculosis in 1900, some two years after he resigned as a plebe. His parents charged that his death was the result of having been forced to drink hot sauce and consume other objectionable food items as part of the Corps's systematic hazing rituals. A Congressional investigation into the hazing of Booz concluded that West Point had a "complex system of unseen hazing."[25] Subsequent legislation outlawed hazing on 2 March 1901.[26] By the summer of 1905 the hazing issue had faded and the once constant scrutiny and monitoring of the Corps of Cadets by Academy leaders had dissipated.

Readjustment by the Corps back to the traditions of hazing coupled with the arrival of two Chinese cadets made Beast Barracks 1905 particularly difficult. The *New York Times* covered Chen and Wen's story, reporting that "there is a tradition that the upperclassmen had a lot of fun with Chen and Wen" during plebe year.[27] Chen and Wen's dignity and stoical sense of tolerance during the hazing introduced their classmates to cultural aspects of Chinese society and their ethnic perspective. Wen also became an upperclass target for addressing himself as "George Washington" Wen in his letters home.[28] The two Chinese cadets endured their plebe year and began to earn the respect of their peers and upperclassmen as 38 other plebes resigned from a class of only 161.

The U.S. cadets suspected that Chen was a Chinese prince and that Wen was his attendant. The suspicion grew from Chen's mannerisms and his special treatment by the Chinese Legation in Washington. For example, during graduation ceremonies on 11 June 1909, the Chinese Ambassador brought white lilies for Chen but ignored Wen, fueling the cadets' imagination of Chen's royalty.[29] If there was any truth to the story of the Chinese cadets' origins, however, it was the opposite of what the American cadets thought. Wen's father was a District Governor and his uncle was the Chinese Minister of Foreign Affairs and the Viceroy of Tibet.[30] Chen's father, by way of contrast, was "a dealer in foreign goods."[31] As Wen began to excel at West Point, the Corps of Cadets considered his success an enduring example of the "American dream" in which Wen the "commoner" eventually surpassed Chen the "aristocrat" in all areas.

Ying Wen graduated number 82 in his class of 103 members, while Ting Chen was the "immortal," the term given at the time to the cadet who finished last in his class in order of merit. Both Chinese cadets exhibited hard work, sincerity of effort, and attention to detail throughout their West Point experience. These attributes positively influenced the Corps's attitudes toward the Chinese people. Their disciplinary record was particularly impressive—Wen finished first in the Class of 1909 in conduct with 121 of 125 points, while Chen finished in the top quarter.[32] Of the two, the Corps favorite was Wen. As a *New York Times* reporter noted, "When Wen received his diploma the cheers of the cadets shook the building, and Wen was so pleased that he winked at his classmates and left the rostrum all smiles."[33]

The third Chinese cadet, Tze-lan Wang, arrived four years after Chen and Wen graduated, filling one of the two appointments Congress had authorized in 1911 under Joint Resolution 131. Wang had graduated from the Chinese Paotingfu Military Academy prior to entering West Point in June 1913 with what would come to be designated as the Class of April 1917. He was a captain in the Chinese Nationalist Army and the brother of Maj. Gen. Ting-Jerh Wang, commander in chief of the China Provincial Army garrisoned in Peking.[34] Wang's appointment reflected the efforts of the Wilson administration to establish positive relations with the new Chinese Nationalist regime, which had overthrown the Imperial government in 1911.

Wang had a difficult time at West Point. At 23 years of age, Wang was about four years older than most of his classmates. This disparity in age and maturity made it difficult for him to adapt to the severities of the West Point regimen. Additionally, in another example of the preferential status of the Chinese cadets compared to the institutional standards, his age directly violated West Point admission criteria, which stated, "No candidate shall be admitted who is over 22 years of age."[35]

In the middle of plebe year Wang took an eight-month leave from West Point. Academy leaders granted Wang a leave of absence that began in January 1914. The reason for his sudden departure was a request that he return home to support the Nationalist Party in a developing civil war against supporters of the former Chinese monarchy.[36] However, the Nationalists' own strong efforts, renewed Japanese aggression, and the beginning of World War I defused the civil war and the Nationalists remained in power. Wang returned to the United States and reentered West Point in August 1914. He began his second plebe year with the incoming Class of 1918.[37] This time he struggled academically, failing mathematics, English, and history.

He appeared before the Academic Board on 14 June 1915. The Board decided to retain him, allowing him to rejoin "his class without class standing." Why the Academic Board decided to keep Wang, who failed three classes, yet dismissed 15 other cadets who had failed only one class, is not officially known. Probably the Academic Board simply extended Wang the same exceptions and leeway within the politically established policies that characterized his entire cadet experience.[38] Wang proceeded to fail plebe math once again. Before the Academic Board convened in the spring of 1916, the USMA Adjutant recorded that "the Chinese Government ordered him home." Captain Wang resigned from the Academy on 27 March 1916 and immediately returned to China.[39] Perhaps Wang's sudden departure was a result of the Chinese Legation's frustration and embarrassment over his poor performance, his need by the Chinese army owing to the continued unrest in China, and the pending selection of more qualified Chinese cadet candidates.

In contrast to Tze-lan Wang's cadet career was the performance of Cadet Ken Wang. Ken Wang entered West Point in June 1915 with what would come to be designated the Class of June 1918 as the second of the two appointments under Joint Resolution 131. Amazingly, Ken Wang arrived without Congressional knowledge and without any scrutiny by the Office of Admissions. He was certainly well prepared for the academic rigors of West Point: he had been living in the United States for two years, spoke and understood English, and had been attending Princeton University.[40] Furthermore, he possessed the personality and temperament of the beloved Chen and Wen. At the end of his plebe year, after Captain Wang had returned to China, Cadet Ken Wang finished 13th in the Fourth Class order of merit. Amazing everyone with his intelligence and hard work, on graduation day 12 June 1918, he finished 12th in a class of 137. The *Howitzer* staff wrote that if China could produce more men like Ken Wang then the country is surely "ordained to the achievement for great things."[41]

The fourth Chinese cadet, Linson Edward Dzau, filled the position from Joint Resolution 131 vacated by Tze-lan Wang. The manner in which he joined his classmates at West Point was as remarkable as that of his predecessors. In 1915 West Point policy stated that an appointment vacancy created by a cadet resignation or expulsion was not held for the appointer, such as a state senator or congressman, to fill. This policy, however, did not deter the Chinese government. The Chinese Minister in Washington discussed a replacement for Captain Wang with the U.S. State Department. On 7 September 1916, the State Department sent a telegram to the USMA Superintendent, Col. John Biddle, with instructions that he immediately admit Linson Dzau, a Chinese student who was attending the Choate School in Wallingford, Connecticut, into West Point.[42] Dzau wanted to wait until the following summer and join the class arriving in the summer of 1917, which would have been the sensible thing to do. The Chinese Minister thought differently, however, and ordered Dzau to report to West Point immediately. In this case diplomacy superseded personal preference, and Dzau joined the incumbent plebe class (November 1918) without ever taking an entrance exam or even going through Beast Barracks. Dzau joined his classmates on 13 September 1916, three weeks into the academic year.

The special treatment accorded Dzau underscored the influence of the Secretary of War and the Secretary of State in managing U.S. relations with China. Both officials recognized the benefits of maintaining good relations with the Nationalist Chinese government, and opening West Point to Chinese cadets was a conspicuous display of good will. It therefore did not matter, at least in their view, that they violated Academy policy by waiving the entry requirements or that they acted without the approval of Congress. This would be the last time there would be such blatant flouting of policy, but it demonstrated the importance of the Foreign Cadet Program in the conduct of diplomatic relations.

The matriculation of five more Chinese cadets between 1920 and 1933 reflected Congress's growing acceptance of West Point as a tool of diplomacy. During this time frame Congress approved three Joint Resolutions concerning Chinese cadet admissions. Zeng Tze Wong and Tao Hung Chang both gained admission to West Point through the first of these acts.[43] Wong did not arrive until 11 August 1919, and thus, like Dzau, missed plebe summer training and met his class-mates at the start of the academic year. Chang did not report to West Point until the following summer, but entered with his classmates and had the full Fourth Class experience. The next Chinese cadet nominations did not occur until 1928. China was able to secure two more open nominations to West Point through another Congressional resolution. Secretary of State Bainbridge Colby nominated Chih Wang and I Chang. Wang entered West Point on 24 July 1928, while Chang entered on 11 July 1931. The last Chinese cadet to attend West Point was Posheng Yen. Congress passed the final Joint Resolution concerning Chinese cadets on 5 June 1933. Three weeks later, on 1 July 1933, Yen reported for summer training.[44] No one could have known that Yen's nomination would be the tenth and final appointment to the U.S. Military Academy from China. The decrease in prolonged debate during the passing of these final three joint resolutions signifies the broad acceptance by Congress of the need to extend West Point appointments to China and other foreign nations as a diplomatic sign of friendship and good will.

Cadet Zeng Tze Wong continued the high standards set by his predecessors. Joining Company F, he graduated 14th of 293 in the Class of 1922, earned the rank of cadet sergeant, and played on the intercollegiate soccer team. Wong's celebrity and stellar performance prompted his company to change its nickname from "Runt Company" to the "Foreign Legion."[45] The term "runt" had come about from the Academy's practice of assigning cadets to companies according to height to facilitate precision and soldierly appearance during drill and ceremonies. Company A had the tallest cadets, and Company F the shortest. With Wong now among their ranks, the cadets of the Foreign Legion were pleased to shed the opprobrious nickname.

The next Chinese graduate was Tao Hung Chang, who graduated in 1924 ranked 404th of 405 cadets. Chang entered West Point directly from China and spoke the least fluent English of any of the Chinese cadets. His own classmates remarked that his inexperience with English "handicapped him from the start," but that his determination and "a reputation for stoicism" enabled him to overcome the challenges of West Point.[46] After Chang, Chih Wang graduated in

1932. Wang graduated with the highest percentile order of merit of any Chinese cadet, 12th out of 262 cadets. Curiously, Wang's classmates noted that he exhibited "a rare mixture of indifference and militariness. He is a good soldier and a conscientious one."[47]

I Chang, who entered West Point in July 1931, had a cadet experience as difficult as Tze-lan Wang's in 1913. Chang failed plebe English, but the Academic Board allowed him to continue with his class and retake the English examination when he was ready (23 of his classmates were not as fortunate). Chang failed English two more times, as well as history in his Third Class year, despite the dedicated efforts of the faculty and classmates to pull him through. Embarrassed by Chang's poor performance, the Chinese Legation forced him to resign from the Academy and return to China.[48] Of the ten young Chinese men who entered West Point, only Tze-lan Wang and I Chang did not graduate. Although Chinese officials were chagrined at the failure of these two, the 80 percent graduation rate of Chinese cadets overall far exceeded the graduation rate of American cadets.

The last Chinese cadet to attend West Point was Posheng Yen, who graduated 137th of 324 in the Class of 1937. In a manner similar to that of other Chinese cadets over the last 30 years, his classmates described him in the following words: "Characterized principally by a congenial, unpretentious nature, he has conscientiously applied himself in academics, being rewarded with a highly commendable class standing."[49] Yen was the son of a distinguished diplomat who had served as China's ambassador to the United States. During his cadet years, his father became the Chinese Ambassador to the Soviet Union and his family lived in Moscow.

This period was a turbulent time in Yen's homeland, with the Chinese Communist Party vying with the Nationalists for control of the country. The civil war cast a shadow of uncertainty over the future of Sino-American relations since the United States would be unwilling to recognize a communist regime in China. The Nationalists were eager to secure whatever support—material or moral—the Americans could give; sending Ambassador Yen's son to West Point was a well-timed effort in this direction.[50] Unfortunately, the outbreak of war between China and Japan in 1937, coupled with the Communist victory over the Nationalists in 1949, brought an end to the Chinese presence at West Point. [51]

In generalizing about Chinese cadets at West Point, their American classmates typically used such language as "good-natured, hard-working, stoic, and helpful."[52] Regarding the Chinese cadets' future endeavors, their classmates remarked, "We expect great things"; "our interest in his future will be keen"; and "[he will] bring honor to this Alma Mater." Such tributes are remarkable given the intolerance toward immigrants—especially from the Far East—that characterized American society during this time. The most blatant manifestation of such intolerance was the Chinese Exclusion Acts. First passed in 1902 and not repealed until 1948, the act prohibited entry into the United States and its territories of "Chinese and persons of Chinese descent."[53] Congress passed this law to allay public concern over Chinese immigration to the West Coast and worries that during times of economic uncertainty and scarce jobs, the Chinese would displace American workers. Such cultural ignorance and fears joined to create racism and prejudice against the Chinese. Such attitudes certainly existed at West Point, but the presence and overall performance of the Chinese cadets did much to mitigate them. The Chinese and American cadets developed bonds of friendship and respect that heightened cultural awareness and tolerance within the Corps of Cadets.

Chinese Cadets and their Classmates After Graduation

The relationships formed between American and Chinese cadets at West Point endured long beyond graduation. The *New York Times* first reported on these strong ties in a 1911 article about the Class of 1909's Chen and Wen. [54] The article stated that "Chen and Wen were among the most popular cadets," and their friends wanted to know what part Chen and Wen were playing in the Nationalist overthrow of the Manchu dynasty. In fact, they were very involved in the overthrow. Wen was a military aide to Dr. Sun Yat-sen, the founder of the Nationalist movement. Chen received a brevet promotion to lieutenant general and commanded the Tiger Hill fortifications at Canton.[55]

The Class of 1909 kept in close contact with Chen and Wen, and American officers who traveled to China often visited them and reported back to their classmates. Classmate Forrest Harding served for three and a half years in China, eventually becoming regimental commander of the 15th Infantry, garrisoned in Tientsin. He wrote in an annual class update that he had visited Wen during the Christmas holidays and provided other current information about the two.[56] Wallace Philoon, captain of the football team, served as the U.S. Military Advisor to China, where he was very close with both classmates. The class received with great pride news that the Chinese and British governments had presented Chen the Chinese Tiger Cross and the British War Cross, respectively, for his gallantry in the Chinese Nationalist Revolution.[57]

Some of the instances of classmate loyalty and friendship were extraordinary. When the Communist government took over in 1949, Linson Dzau was stripped of all his possessions and fined $500,000 dollars for being a "pro-west capitalist." The government denied exit permits for him and his family, and he was sent to a concentration camp in Peking. He finally escaped and surfaced in Macau, China (a special administrative region under Portuguese rule), as a refugee in 1951. Some West Point classmates inquired about his whereabouts and learned of his desperate situation. They came to his aid, providing him money for an apartment and, later, for establishing Linson College, a Western Preparatory school for Chinese in Macau. Gaining prominence and respect in the Macau community, he was finally able to have his family join him there.[58] In another case, classmates of Tao Chang, USMA Class of 1924, rallied to Chang's aid when he was trying to immigrate to the United States in 1960. With the help of anonymous classmates and the Chief Delegate to the United Nations from Nationalist China, Chang was able to get visas for himself and a daughter.[59]

The assistance provided to Dzau and Chang by their West Point classmates is significant for two reasons. First, the fact that the Americans even knew of their Chinese classmates' hardships reflects the determination of all of them to stay in touch across time, space, and political upheaval. Second, the extent of the assistance underscored the powerful and enduring bonds they had developed as West Point cadets. Dzau, Chang, and the others were not just foreign cadets, but coequals in the Long Gray Line. Their performance as cadets and during service in China proved how completely they had internalized the Military Academy's bedrock values of Duty, Honor, Country.

Chinese Cadets' Fulfillment of Duty, Honor, Country

The Chinese graduates of the U.S. Military Academy were leaders of character who served their own country with distinction and honor. They were closely associated with the Nationalist government and fought heroically against the Japanese and the Chinese Communists. When the Communists came to power in 1949, many of the graduates suffered additional hardships imposed by the new regime. An example of such sacrifice is the story of the Class of 1909's favorite—Ying Wen.

Starting his career as the military aide to Nationalist founder Sun Yat-sen, Ying Wen rose to the rank of lieutenant general, serving as deputy commanding general of Chiang Kai-shek's National Gendarmarie in 1930. In 1931 he took command of the Revenue Guard, an elite 70,000-man unit that fought against the Japanese and the Chinese Communists from 1932 to 1937.[60] In 1945 Chiang Kai-shek appointed him a National Senator.[61] When the Nationalist government fled to Taiwan in 1949, Wen served as the senior military delegate to the United Nations Military Staff Committee, and he was actively involved in planning to overthrow the fledging Communist government on the mainland.[62] Wen was ardently anti-Communist, and his strong commitment to the Nationalist cause sometimes brought him into conflict with his superiors. His disillusionment with Chiang Kai-shek, the Nationalist leader, prompted Wen to travel to the United States in 1950 to garner support for an independent invasion of the mainland.[63] He made the trip against Chiang's wishes, and the resulting animosity led to Wen's retirement after 42 years of service. Shortly thereafter he moved with his family to the United States where he lived out the rest of his life. He died in 1968 and is buried in the West Point cemetery—a long way from his birthplace but yet in the hallowed grounds of his adopted Alma Mater. In a sad and poignant example of just how much this West Point graduate had offered up on the altar of Duty, Honor, Country, he lived out his last years managing a small laundromat in Northern Virginia.[64]

Soon after graduation, Ken Wang, USMA Class of June 1918, served as a member of the Chinese delegation at the Versailles peace conference. Afterwards, he commanded an artillery brigade near Shanghai. During the Nationalist movement, he initially maintained his brigade as an independent unit but later joined actively in support of the Nationalists. As the Nationalist effort gained momentum, he and his brigade were responsible for uniting the northern provinces.[65] During the war with Japan, Wang was captured at the Battle of Shanghai in 1937. When captured he had on his person valuable strategic maps that his commanders regarded as deeply compromising to the Nationalist cause. After the war, the Nationalists court-martialed him and sentenced him to be executed for treason.[66] While in prison, popular opinion had it that he was being set up as a scapegoat for the Nationalist army's failures at Shanghai. In another example of classmate loyalty, Wang was visited in prison by a West Point classmate who carried the word to the other members of the class.[67] The local commander released him a year later, but this incident tarnished his reputation and he left the Army. Despite poor health, he took up a mission to the United States to negotiate Chinese lend lease funding during World War II. He died enroute to the United States in Cairo at the age of 46.[68]

Brig. Gen. Zeng Wong, Class of 1922, served with the Nationalists and fought several battles against the Japanese. When the Communists gained power he fled to Taiwan, and in 1951 moved his family to Japan. During the Korean War he served in the U.S. Army as an advisor to the 1st Radio Broadcast and Leaflet Division of the Army's Psychological Warfare Unit, operating from Japan. His expert knowledge of China, its people, and language helped the United Nations propaganda efforts.[69]

Concerning the Chinese cadets' service following graduation, Chih Wang, writing in a letter to his class scribe, states: "All Chinese graduates from West Point are striving hard for the welfare of their country and for the fame of their Alma Mater." He adds, "Although their obstacles are numerous, they have not failed and will always attempt to live up to the motto of the Corps—Duty, Honor, Country."[70]

Conclusion

At the beginning of the 20th century, the U.S. Military Academy, just as the Army and nation it served, awakened to the political and cultural significance of China. The direct impact of ten Chinese cadets on West Point during this era had profound ramifications before, during, and after their attendance for what it meant to the Academy and to West Point graduates. Begun by Ting Chen's and Ying Wen's appointments in 1905 and culminating in Posheng Yen's graduation in 1937, the Chinese cadets became a significant element of West Point's history.

The Chinese cadets stimulated the Military Academy to develop and then to reexamine its admissions policies for foreign cadets. In analyzing the circumstances of these ten cadets' admission to West Point, one finds unprecedented entrance conduits and unique diplomatic considerations that together evolved into West Point's Foreign Cadet Program. The only aspect of the modern program that did not derive from the Chinese cadets' experiences is a law passed in 1983 making all foreign cadets subject to the same physical and academic admission standards as their American counterparts.[71] The Foreign Cadet Program during its long history has produced 288 graduates, growing to such an extent that West Point invited 131 countries to submit nominees for the Class of 2004.[72]

Allowing Chinese admissions to West Point was intended to contribute to the present and future of American foreign policy. However, equally significant in impact were the Chinese contributions to the Corps of Cadets. For West Point cadets, interacting with their Chinese classmates, saw their sensitivity and awareness of an important world culture greatly heightened in professionally useful ways.

After handing the diplomas to members of the Class of 1909, Secretary of War Jacob Dickinson pulled Ting Chen and Ying Wen aside and said to them: "I congratulate you, and trust that when you go home you will do all that is in your power to maintain friendly relations between your country and the United States."[73] Chen and Wen along with the Chinese cadets who followed them to West Point took Dickinson's words to heart and did just that.

---

[1] "West Point Cadets Graduate With Pomp: Cheers for Chinese Boy," *New York Times*, 12 June 1909, 16.

[2] Steve Grove, USMA Historian, to Maria Hsueh-yu Cheng, Taiwan, 25 November 1997, Memorandum about foreign cadet program, with enclosures, Office of Policy, Planning, and Analysis, USMA, West Point, NY.

[3] Paul W. Child, Jr., ed., *Register of Graduates and Former Cadets 1990* (West Point, NY: Association of Graduates Press, 1990), 1026.

[4] United States Military Academy, *Official Register of the Officers and Cadets of the United States Military Academy*, "Register for 1909" (West Point, NY: USMA Press and Bindery, 1906), 12.

[5] "Costa Rica: History," available from http://www.funkandwagnalls.com/encyclopedia/; Internet; accessed 13 November 2000.

[6] F. H. Farnum, Acting Adjutant of USMA, to Min Wong, editor of *Chinese Student Monthly*, 6 May 1911, Memorandum discussing admissions procedures of foreign cadets, Special Collections, Pershing Center Archives, USMA, West Point, NY.

[7] "Emergence to World Power: 1898-1902," *American Military History*, chap. 15, Office of The Chief of Military History, United States Army, available from http://www.1-14th.com/boxerhist.htm; Internet; accessed 13 September 2000.

[8] "Open Door Policy," *Funk and Wagnall's Encyclopedia*, available from http://www.funkandwagnalls.com/encyclopedia/; Internet; accessed 30 October 2000.

[9] Congress, House, *Granting Permission to Yning Hsing Wen and Ting Chia Chen, of China, To Receive Instruction at the Military Academy at West Point*, 58th Cong., 3rd sess., H.J. 222, *Congressional Record*, 39, pt. 4, daily ed. (25 February 1905): 3417.

[10] Ibid.

[11] Congress, House, *Ying Hsing Wen and Ting Chia Chen*, 58th Cong., 3rd sess., H.J. 222, *Congressional Record*, 39, pt. 4, daily ed. (27 February 1905): 3545.

[12] Congress, House, *Admission to Military Academy*, 48th Cong., 1st sess., H.R. 113, *Congressional Record*, 15, pt. 1, daily ed. (15 January 1884): 433.

[13] Congress, House, *Ying Hsing Wen and Ting Chia Chen*.

[14] The Boxer Rebellion was an insurrection inspired by native opposition to the presence of foreigners—the United States, France, Britain, and Germany—in China. Coupled with the intense efforts of the missionaries, the presence and policies of western foreigners caused anger and sporadic violence among the Chinese, who detested what they regarded as the exploitation of their country. A secret society, known as the "Boxers," rose to power. Their rebellion against foreign influence swept China into anarchy and terrorism. The United States assembled military forces already garrisoned in the Philippines to create the "China Relief Expedition" with the mission of restoring order and protecting American citizens. This military effort, working cooperatively with forces from Britain, Germany, France, and Japan moved on the stronghold of Peking and quelled the insurrection on 14 August 1900. The success of the U.S. Army against the

uprising did not change the fact that the political situation in China was still volatile as Congress debated Chinese cadet nominations in 1905.

[15] Congress, House, *Ying Hsing Wen and Ting Chia Chen.*

[16] Ibid.

[17] "Chinese Cultural Studies: Concise Political History of China," *Compton's Living Encyclopedia,* available from http://acc6.its.Brooklyn.cuny.edu/~phallsall/texts/chinhist.html; Internet; accessed 29 October 2000.

[18] Paul W. Child, Jr., ed., *Register of Graduates and Former Cadets 1990* (West Point, NY: Association of Graduates Press, 1990), 1026.

[19] Congress, House, *Chinese Students at West Point,* 62nd Cong., 1st sess., S. J. 131, *Congressional Record,* 46, pt. 1, daily ed. (21 February 1911): 3050.

[20] Ibid.

[21] Ibid., 3051.

[22] In 1912 the Nationalists overthrew the Chinese government, ending 2000 years of imperial rule. After a period of internal struggle, Chiang Kai-shek united the new Republic of China in 1928. Despite American assistance to the Chiang Kai-shek government, the Communist revolution was ultimately successful. In 1949 the Nationalists fled to Taiwan, and the Communist Party formed the People's Republic of China. China's political unrest, untapped economic resources, and strategic location in Asia had placed that nation in the forefront of U.S. foreign policy from 1900 to 1930. This timeline of Chinese political history after 1900 is relevant to developments at West Point because it reflects why China became a mainstay of USMA's Foreign Cadet Program.

[23] United States Military Academy, *Official Register of the Officers and Cadets of the United States Military Academy,* "Register for 1909," 31.

[24] "Cadets Think Chen a Chinese Prince," *New York Times,* 21 June 1909, 16.

[25] Theodore J. Crackel, *The Illustrated History of West Point* (New York, NY: Harry N. Abrams, Inc., 1991), 164.

[26] Ibid.

[27] "Cadets Think Chen a Chinese Prince."

[28] United States Military Academy, *The Howitzer,* Yearbook for the Class of 1909 (New York, NY: Charles L. Willard, 1909).

[29] "West Point Cadets Graduate With Pomp: Cheers for Chinese Boy."

[30] "Personal Biography Fact Sheet: LTG Ying Wen," *New York Times,* 15 June 1913, II-10.

[31] "New Cadet Biography Instructions: New Cadet Ting Chai Chen," Special Collections, Pershing Center Archives, USMA, West Point, NY.

[32] United States Military Academy, *Official Register of the Officers and Cadets of the United States Military Academy,* "Register for 1909," 12.

[33] Ibid.

[34] "Personal Biography Fact Sheet: LTG Ying Wen," *New York Times,* 15 June 1913, II-10.

[35] United States Military Academy, *Official Register of the Officers and Cadets of the United States Military Academy,* "Register for 1915" (West Point, NY: USMA Press and Bindery, 1906), 64.

[36] In 1912, the founder of the Nationalist movement, Sun Yat-sen, resigned; his successor, Yuan Shih-kaia, became the first president of the new republic. Throughout 1913 Yuan schemed to assassinate Nationalist leaders and resume the Chinese monarchy in which he would become emperor. These developments made another civil war appear likely. Under these conditions at home, Captain Wang returned to China.

37 Ibid., 36.

38 Clifton C. Carter, USMA Adjutant and Secretary of the Academic Board, 14 June 1915, Academic Board Results, USMA Staff Records, no. 7, Special Collections, Pershing Center Archives, USMA, West Point, NY, 170.

39 *Casualties, US Corps of Cadet*, "Casualty Book 1915-Present," Adjutant's Office, Special Collections, Pershing Center Archives, USMA, West Point, NY.

40 United States Military Academy, *The Howitzer*, Yearbook for the Class of 1919 (West Point, NY: The Howitzer Board, 1919), 129.

41 Ibid.

42 Assistant U.S. Secretary of State to Col. John Biddle, USMA Superintendent, Western Union Telegram, 7 September 1916, Special Collections, Pershing Center Archives, USMA, West Point, NY.

43 Congress, House, *Zeng Tze Wong*, 66th Cong., 1st sess., H.J. 120, *Congressional Record*, 58, pt. 3, daily ed. (14 July 1919): 2518.

44 Congress, House, *Instruction at Military Academy of Posheng Yen*, 73rd Cong., 1st sess., S. J. 48, *Congressional Record*, 77, pt. 4, daily ed. (22 May 1933): 3890.

45 United States Military Academy, *The Howitzer*, Yearbook for the Class of 1922 (New York, NY: The Schilling Press, Inc., 1922), 89

46 United States Military Academy, *The Howitzer*, Yearbook for the Class of 1924 (West Point, NY: The Howitzer Board, 1924), 129.

47 United States Military Academy, *The Howitzer*, Yearbook for the Class of 1932 (West Point, NY: The Howitzer Board, 1932), 218.

48 Adjutant's Office, The United States Military Academy, "Form 5-19-32-1000," Special Collections, Pershing Center Archives, USMA, West Point, NY. This form is an information card kept on cadets.

49 The United States Military Academy, *The Howitzer*, Yearbook for the Class of 1937 (Garden City, NY: Country Life Press, 1937), 182.

50 Posheng Yen, Last Surviving Chinese Cadet, Class of 1937. Telephone interview by author, 13 November 2000, West Point, NY.

51 Interestingly enough, despite support of and benevolent foreign policy toward Taiwan, the state of the Nationalist Chinese for 50 years, it was not until 29 June 2000 that the first Taiwanese cadet entered West Point (Class of 2004).

52 Taken from assorted Howitzer Yearbooks: 1909, 1919, 1922, 1924, 1932, 1937.

53 "Chinese Exclusion Act of 1902," available from http://www:itp.berkeley.edu/~asam121/1902.htm; Internet; accessed 31 October 2000.

54 "Army Asks About West Point Chinese," *New York Times*, 24 December 1911, 6.

55 *Class of 1909 Forty Year Reunion Book*, "Personal Updates," Special Collections, Pershing Center Archives, USMA, West Point, NY, 53. "Tiger Hill" is a famous cultural and historical area in the Canton region. Tiger Hill's history is entwined with that of the ancient city of Suzhou, both traceable back 2,500 years. The command of the Tiger Hill fortifications is considered a great honor.

56 "Class Update: The Far East," USMA Class of 1909, Special Collections, Pershing Center Archives, USMA, West Point, NY, 43.

57 *Eleven Years After*, Class of 1909 Update, Special Collections, Pershing Center Archives, USMA, West Point, NY.

58 B.A. Dickson, "Class History, USMA, November 1918," Special Collections, Pershing Center Archives, USMA, West Point, NY, 18.

59 "Tao Hung Chang," *Assembly*, Obituary of Chang, March 1978, Special Collections, Pershing Center Archives, USMA, West Point, NY.

[60] "Personal Biography Fact Sheet: LTG Ying Wen," Special Collections, Pershing Center Archives, USMA, West Point, NY.

[61] S. L. Fishbein, "Former China Army General Commands Laundromat Here," *Washington Post* (date unknown), Pershing Center Archives, USMA, West Point, NY.

[62] "Personal Biography Fact Sheet: LTG Ying Wen."

[63] Ibid.

[64] S.L. Fishbein, "Former China Army General Commands Laundromat Here," *Washington Post* (date unknown), Pershing Center Archives, USMA, West Point, NY.

[65] "Ken Wang," *Assembly*, Obituary of Wang, July 1943, Special Collections, Pershing Center Archives, USMA, West Point, NY.

[66] Ibid.

[67] Ibid.

[68] Ibid.

[69] Dick Berry, "Group Boasts Distinguished Chinese Advisor," *PSYWAR Newsletter*, June 1952, Special Collections, Pershing Center Archives, USMA, West Point, NY.

[70] Chih Wang, personal letter to his classmates, Special Collections, Pershing Center Archives, USMA, West Point, NY.

[71] Edmund Moore, "Integrating International Cadets at USMA," LD720 Historical Paper, TOEP (West Point, NY: U.S. Military Academy, 1997), 8.

[72] Steve Grove, USMA Historian, to Maria Hsueh-yu Cheng.

[73] "West Point Cadets Graduate With Pomp: Cheers for Chinese Boy," *New York Times*, 12 June 1909, 16.

⇥ CHAPTER 14 ⇤

THE LIVES OF WEST POINT'S BUFFALO SOLDIERS

Tanya Kabel-Ballard

The U.S. Military Academy at West Point has earned worldwide fame for its success in producing commissioned leaders of character. Millions of people have visited the Academy to see cadets on display, and millions more have read of the accomplishments of West Point graduates who have contributed to the nation in war and peace and in virtually every walk of life.

In contrast to the celebrity of cadets and officers, however, the enlisted soldiers of West Point have received little public or historical attention. Enlisted soldiers called West Point their home well before the establishment of the Military Academy; they were the infantrymen, artillerists, and engineers who manned Fortress West Point during the Revolution and the early years of the New Republic. Subsequent to the founding of the Military Academy in 1802, they were instrumental in training and supporting the cadets, as well as performing missions vital to the efficient operation of the installation.

If enlisted soldiers have traditionally walked in the shadow of their commissioned partners at West Point, black enlisted soldiers received even less notice. Unlike some of the early black graduates whose experiences have been well documented of late—Lt. Henry O. Flipper, Col. Charles Young, and Gen. Benjamin O. Davis, Jr.—the

Cadets conducting cavalry drill on the Plain. (Courtesy of USMA Archives)

lives of black enlisted soldiers have remained historically obscure.[1] Segregated by both race and rank, they nonetheless represented an important part of the West Point community for several decades in the early 20th century. Black soldiers comprised three separate units—cavalry, medical, and mess—all critical to the West Point mission.[2] The most prominent among the three were the "Buffalo Soldiers" of the famed 9th and 10th Cavalry Regiments, two of the Army's most distinguished units.[3]

The Buffalo Soldiers of West Point left only a faint historical footprint. While there is a fair amount of documentation relating to their conduct of cavalry training for cadets, the records reveal little about other aspects of their existence. Why did they come to West Point and how well did they perform their mission? How were they treated by white officers, soldiers, and civilians? Did they assimilate into white society or remain aloof? What were the physical and emotional boundaries of their existence? The few surviving records, including the testimony of some of the last living Buffalo Soldiers, suggest intriguing answers. Although black enlisted soldiers at West Point encountered various degrees of discrimination by virtue of their race and rank, Academy leaders went to great lengths to ensure that blacks and whites interacted routinely and cooperatively in all professional and most community venues. The result was a racial climate that, while far from perfect, was superior to virtually any other in the Army or the nation.

USMA Cavalry Detachment on the Riding Field with stables in the background. (Courtesy of USMA Archives)

The first black soldiers assigned to West Point were the 89 troopers of the 9th Cavalry Detachment—a contingent of the larger 9th Cavalry Regiment at Fort Leavenworth, Kansas—who arrived on 23 March 1907.[4] Their arrival occurred during an era when American race relations were especially difficult. Jim Crow laws imposed rigid segregation throughout the South, with the consequent restriction of social mobility, civil rights, and financial freedom for black Americans. Racial hatred led to over 1,100 lynchings between 1900 and 1915.[5] Although not as severe in the North, even there discrimination and de facto segregation effectively blocked the entry of black Americans into the mainstream of white society. This was true despite the recognition for valor that black soldiers had earned in the Spanish-American War and the steady economic and cultural advances in the black community.

Race relations, if not already bad enough, took a turn for the worse shortly before the 9th Cavalry Detachment made its way to West Point. Six months earlier, an unfortunate situation in Brownsville, Texas, located in the extreme southern tip of the state, appalled and frightened many Americans and put the issue of race relations on the front page of many newspapers. Texas was already a hotbed of racial tension when the 170 black soldiers of the 25th Infantry were ordered to Fort Brown, on the edge of Brownsville, in the summer of 1906. On 13 August 1906, shots were fired near the fort. The black soldiers, fearing a white riot, alerted their fellow soldiers and drew their weapons. Soon, one man was dead and a few others wounded, and a trial eventually took place. During the pre-trial investigation, which was overseen by President Theodore Roosevelt, none of the black soldiers reported having any knowledge of the shootings. Eye witnesses claimed seeing black gunmen armed with revolvers. However, one crucial fact was overlooked during the investigation—25th Infantry soldiers carried only rifles, not revolvers.

A separate investigation following the trial concluded that the bullets fired during the incident did not come from any of the weapons used by the men in the 25th. Although none of the soldiers was found guilty, 167 of the soldiers were recommended for dismissal without a public hearing. President Roosevelt accepted the recommendation for dismissal, and ordered that the black soldiers be dishonorably discharged, stating that some of the men were "bloody butchers" who "ought to be hung". The incident was dubbed the "Brownsville Raid," and it remained an emotional flashpoint for both black and white Americans for many years. [6]

Despite public interest in the Brownsville incident, the arrival of the Buffalo Soldiers at West Point brought little fanfare. The *New York Times* made no mention of it, despite the city's proximity to West Point and the extensive coverage the newspaper had given the racial problems in Texas. Likewise, the *Newburgh Daily News*, the most widely read local paper, ignored the story. Only The *News of the Highlands*, a small weekly hometown newspaper serving the area immediately around West Point, covered the event. Under the headline, "The Negro Cavalrymen Will Reach West Point Today," the following short announcement was made on the day of their arrival:

> Negro cavalrymen have been ordered to West Point for duty for the first time in the history of the United States Military Academy.

The sending of Negro troopers is an experiment on the part of the War Department. The present detachment on duty at West Point have been dissatisfied with the extra duties devolved upon them in the care of the horses used by the military cadets. It is alleged that while they were willing to look after their own individual mounts, they did not like the duty of caring for all the horses in the cadet battalion.

The detachment of negro cavalrymen at West Point will constitute all the Negro troops in the United States, all the others, including the greater part of the Ninth Cavalry and all of the Tenth Cavalry and Twenty-fourth and Twenty-fifth Infantry, being in the Philippines or on their way.[7]

The next week, the paper printed a short follow-up story. Despite the positive spin, however, the news was almost hidden, having been placed inside a larger article about West Point on the very last page of the paper:

The long expected colored cavalrymen arrived on Saturday at about 4 p.m. Colored troops at the academy are a decided innovation, and much curiosity was evinced by the large crowd which awaited their arrival at the depot. Much can be said in their praise, for upon the whole they are a young and bright looking lot, and thus far have been a credit to themselves and to the uniform they wear. They have been divided among the artillery and cavalry detachments, and will in a few days form the entire force of the cavalry detachment, the white troops of the organization having been assigned to other posts.[8]

Given the significance of an all-black unit coming to the Hudson Valley, it is hard to fathom why it received so little public notice and no coverage from the area's more widely circulated papers. Newspapers of all sizes in the early 20th century typically devoted extensive coverage to the local social scene, and national newspapers like The *New York Times* prided themselves on including "all the news that's fit to print." Certainly the arrival of the Buffalo Soldiers would have an impact on the political, social, and economic life of the region; just as certain, it was viewed with a mixture of apprehension and revulsion by at least some of the local inhabitants. Perhaps newspaper editors sought to avoid stirring trouble by not reporting the story. Whatever the reason, from the very beginning, it appears that the Buffalo Soldiers were kept in the shadows of the history being made at West Point.

In addition to the blatant prejudices of the times, the Buffalo Soldiers faced an immediate professional challenge at West Point. In the years prior to their arrival, the all-white cavalry detachment carried the worst reputation of all the enlisted units in the garrison. Year after year the Annual Report of the Superintendent noted the poor performance of the cavalry troopers, their low morale, and the poor condition of the horses. The 1899 report was typical in this regard: "The combination of cavalry and light artillery duties this detachment with its horses is called on to perform in connection with cadet instruction do not give the desired results."[9] As the state of the cavalry detachment continued to decline, superintendents in subsequent years were not so subtle. In 1906, the year prior to the arrival of the Buffalo Soldiers, the Superintendent reported,

> All of the Military Academy detachments are in satisfactory condition, except the cavalry detachment. In that detachment, despite untiring efforts to improve its condition, there is a great lack of the proper military spirit and deportment. There are practically no reenlistments in this detachment and the number of desertions is very large.[10]

The cavalry detachment's poor performance was due primarily to its heavy work load, greatly compounded by the fact that they received as much as 50 cents less per diem than the general service soldiers. Much of the work was considered "menial" and beneath even the lowest-ranking white enlisted man.[11] The troopers worked long hours grooming the horses and preparing them for training, conducting drill exercises for the cadets, and performing guard and other duties. In the winter, many of the troopers were tasked to harvest ice to be used for refrigeration—that is, sawing ice on the ponds and reservoirs into appropriate sizes and using their horse teams to

Ice harvest at West Point, circa 1925. This was one of many installation-support missions assigned to the Buffalo Soldiers. (Courtesy of USMA Archives)

haul the ice away. In the more temperate months, the cavalry soldiers often found their days lengthened by having to perform maintenance on roads and buildings in addition to having to care for their unit's horses and equipment. On top of all this, they often were required to care for the personal mounts of officers or their families. [12]

In recognition of the difficulty meeting these requirements, Academy leaders sought reforms. Prof. Charles W. Larned, a prominent member of the Academic Board, recommended lightening the work load by assigning each trooper only one horse instead of the usual four; unfortunately, a one-to-one ratio between man and horse was impossible given the cavalry detachment's current low strength. [13] The Superintendent, Hugh L. Scott, considered hiring civilian hostlers to take over many of the duties of the cavalry troops. Other than paying the enlisted soldiers extra money, the Superintendent believed that bringing in civilians was "the only other method that would [bring] satisfactory results." [14] When Larned's and Scott's proposals proved unworkable, the best hope for improvement came in the form of the

Buffalo Soldiers of the 9th Cavalry Detachment. Although there still were not enough men to assign them only one horse each, the black troopers proved equal to the demanding tasks before them.[15]

Within six months of their arrival, the Buffalo Soldiers had earned a sterling reputation. Both in duty performance and personal conduct, they established a standard of excellence in stark contrast to that of the white cavalry detachment they had replaced. Scott noted glowingly the "good results" of the 9th Cavalry troopers.[16] They "are better satisfied, the equipments and horses are in better condition than when the detachment was composed of white men, and no desertions have occurred among the colored men as compared with the desertions among the white men from September 1, 1906, to date of March 7, 1907."[17] A year later the Superintendent was even more emphatic: "The detachment is believed to be in better state of contentment than any period of its history."[18]

The local community was quick to notice the improved performance of the cavalry detachment once the black troopers took over. Within weeks of their arrival, The *News of the Highlands* began printing short yet highly positive accounts of the Buffalo Soldiers. On a bimonthly schedule, the newspaper published articles on such topics as increased troop strength, promotions, deaths of family members, official ceremonies, and dances and parties hosted by the detachment. When Japanese Army Gen. Tamemoto Kuroki and his entourage visited West Point in May 1907, the cavalry troop was detailed to provide official escorts. The newspaper complimented the soldiers for their fine performance: "The colored troop of cavalry, mounted, as escorts . . . presented a fine appearance in their natty uniforms."[19] A week later the paper reported the unit as being much more disciplined than the former detachment comprised of white soldiers: "There has not been a case of absence without leave since the new Cavalry detachment arrived, which is very different from the former detachment."[20] The paper also commended the black troopers for being well-mannered and sociable at their monthly dances.[21]

By virtue of their excellent performance, it did not take long for the Buffalo Soldiers to earn the respect and affection of the local community. The detachment was popular on account of its well-disciplined troops, successful athletic teams, well-attended monthly dances, and excellence in horsemanship and official duty performance. On the rare occasions when black troopers got into trouble, the overall reputation of the Buffalo Soldiers allowed the locals to keep things in perspective. In June 1907, for example, The *News of the Highlands* published a front-page defense of a Buffalo Soldier who had been arrested and subsequently defamed by a New York City newspaper. Under the headline, "West Point Colored Troops Unnecessarily Criticized," the article made clear that the transgression of one soldier could not besmirch the fine reputation of the rest of the soldiers of the cavalry detachment.

> The New York World on Monday morning contained a column of sensational matter which made it appear that the colored troops stationed at West Point were behaving badly and terrorizing the people of Newburgh, Cornwall, and Highland Falls. The story was built on a very trivial foundation. It came about by the arrest and incarceration in Newburgh of Trooper Williams, upon whose person was found an empty revolver and some cartridges. He was charged simply with intoxication and received a 10 day's jail sentence. That is all there is to the matter. White persons not infrequently do the same and are punished the same. In Highland Falls, the colored soldiers, as a rule, conduct themselves in an orderly manner, and there are no grounds for statement that fear exists for the safety of life or property. No complaints have been made to the West Point authorities of the conduct of the colored troopers.[22]

As it turned out, the trooper was the detachment gardener who lived off the military reservation and was therefore allowed to carry a gun for his own protection.[23]

The detachment's excellent reputation facilitated recruiting. By 1908, only one year after the 9th Cavalry's arrival at West Point, there was a waiting list to get into the unit. Over the years, the officers (all white) of the detachment became increasingly selective, accepting only those men with former service and excellent records.[24] Much later, with the approach of WWII, they looked for the most highly qualified men on recruiting trips to the black farming communities of the mid-Atlantic and lower New England states.[25] One such was, Joe Dunn, a former cavalry trooper, recruited back into the Army in 1946 and assigned to the cavalry detachment at West Point. Ironically, his recruitment came two years after he was released by the draft board for being too short. In his words,

> I was working with racehorses in Kentucky when I was initially drafted in 1943. When I reported in for duty, they found out I was only 4 feet 8 inches and 81 pounds . . . I didn't qualify. . . . Back then a man had to be 5 feet and 115 pounds. So, I left and went back to work.[26]

A few years later, Dunn moved back home to Pennsylvania. Somehow word got out about his experience with horses and that he had worked at some of the most well-known tracks, including Churchill Downs. "So, the recruiters came around again. This time they signed me up. I went off to initial training and then ended up [at West Point]."[27] Whether the Army granted an exception to policy concerning his height or the recruiters looked the other way is not clear; what is certain is that Dunn returned to service a year after the war ended and joined the Buffalo Soldiers stationed at West Point.[28]

The bounty of recruits was plentiful, and from the very beginning the numbers swelled as the glowing reputation of the 9th Detachment continued to spread. Soldiers who met the high standards of membership and desired an assignment to the unit typically had to wait until a currently serving member was discharged, retired, or died; the same was true for soldiers seeking an assignment to the detachment's parent unit at Fort Leavenworth.[29] With such exceptional young men filling the ranks, it is not surprising that the troopers of the 9th Cavalry Detachment were able to maintain a level of performance and morale that their predecessors could not match.

Besides the fine reputation of the 9th Detachment, another reason for the popularity of West Point for black soldiers was the policy on marriage. West Point was an anomaly as far as duty assignments for enlisted soldiers were concerned. Throughout the Army

Jack Gaines of Coatsville, PA, on "Loretta." Gaines enlisted for duty in the 10th Cavalry in September 1938. (Courtesy of USMA Archives)

it was common practice to prohibit enlisted soldiers from marrying, regardless of race. The transient life and low pay of enlisted soldiers were the principal reasons for the policy. Other than West Point, Fort Leavenworth was the only other Army post in which enlisted soldiers were permitted to marry.[30]

West Point could permit enlisted soldiers to marry because of the nature of the assignment. As noted in a Board of Visitors report,

> The status of married men on this post has no parallel in the remainder of the army. . . . The enlisted men permanently attached to this post are not subject to being ordered away; they are thus stationary troops, and to increase their reliability and efficiency at this plant they are allowed to marry and bring up families.[31]

Lured by the prospect of a normal family life, enlisted soldiers had a strong motivation to stay at West Point for as long as they could, sometimes even for their entire military careers. Moreover, it was not uncommon for the sons of West Point soldiers to follow in their fathers' footsteps. In some cases, sons enlisted in the same units in which their fathers and grandfathers served.[32] As a result, West Point developed a sizable population of enlisted dependents, including the largest population of school-age children anywhere in the Army.[33]

The peculiarity of the enlisted situation at West Point was compounded by the fact that a significant portion of the enlisted population was black. Academy leaders, sensitive to the delicacy of race relations in America in the early 20th century, had to grapple with potentially controversial issues. If they allowed white enlisted soldiers to marry, would they allow the same for blacks? How would they handle such family needs as housing, schooling, and medical treatment? If segregated neighborhoods were the norm in the American society, would West Point replicate that social arrangement? These and other issues were vexing, but for the most part Academy leaders handled them in an enlightened and efficient way.

Housing was the most immediate concern for the newly arrived Buffalo Soldiers. Fortuitously, a new set of cavalry barracks had just been built on the south end of post, just inside the gate separating the post from Highland Falls.[34] Although not originally intended to house black soldiers, the barracks were perfectly suited to the new arrivals. The accommodations were modern and spacious and were among the very few barracks considered "livable" well into the 1920s.[35] The new cavalry barracks were a source of pride for the black troopers and a source of envy for the other enlisted soldiers, many of whom lived in substandard housing that was almost a century old. In addition to providing quality housing for the single soldiers, the cavalry barracks served a social purpose by coincidence of location. They were conveniently located near the horse stables— the troopers' usual place of duty—and almost a mile away from the central post area, where white cadets, officers, and families lived and worked. The social gulf between white and black in the early 20th

Buffalo Soldier with guests, late 1920s. (Courtesy of USMA Archives)

century was conveniently reinforced by the physical separation of the two races at West Point.

Although there are no records to prove it, some of the Buffalo Soldiers may have been married and had families even before they arrived. Most of them came directly from Fort Leavenworth, the only other post in the Army where enlisted soldiers could marry. Even if there were no families initially, within a few years there were several. The earliest enlisted records from the West Point housing office date back to 1916; in that year the roster of "Names and Quarters of Married Enlisted Men Occupying Quarters at West Point" confirmed that housing was indeed provided for married Buffalo Soldiers.[36]

At first glance, it appears that West point followed the prevailing social norm of requiring segregated housing. Married Buffalo Soldiers were grouped separately in quarters 125-128. The segregation, however, was not based on race, but on unit of assignment.

Engineers, for example, lived in quarters 106-111 and artillerymen in quarters 132-135.

Unit-based housing assignment prevailed until 1936 at West Point; subsequently, the housing office assigned quarters individually based on availability. Whereas in 1916, the cavalry families lived in a segregated cavalry detachment neighborhood,[37] in 1936 a similar number of black families were spread throughout the enlisted housing area. In the latter years, none of the Buffalo Soldiers had neighbors from their own all-black unit; enlisted soldiers regardless of race or unit of assignment lived side by side, sharing duplexes.

Academy leaders handled the issue of education as unremarkably as the issue of housing. In February 1907, West Point proposed establishing the first Congressionally funded school on an Army installation. The Board of Visitors provided the justification, which centered on the large population of school-age children of married soldiers:

> Who are these children? They are the children of the soldiers who make up the enlisted personnel of the Academy. At this Academy we have, for assistance in the education of cadets, a battery of artillery, a troop of cavalry, a band, a detachment of ordnance, a company of engineers, and greatest of all a company of Army servicemen, that is, laborers and mechanics of all sort, blacksmiths, wheelwrights, carpenters, painters, masons, teamsters, janitors, etc.[38]

In preparing the proposal, the Board of Visitors did not distinguish between youngsters of different races. The decision to integrate the children of the Buffalo Soldiers into the post schools was made with little fanfare. Despite the race issues elsewhere in the country and strict segregation in the South, the local community of Highland Falls already had integrated schools.[39] In terms of providing for the children's education, the communities of Highland Falls and West Point were in unison. With the arrival of the Buffalo soldiers in March 1907 and the establishment of the first federally funded school on an Army installation in September 1907, West Point set a precedent for integrated schooling, which endured despite the national policy of "separate but equal."

Access to medical care and facilities was the same for black and white soldiers and their families. There was a distinction, however, between the commissioned and enlisted ranks, at least in the early years of the century. Officers, their families, and cadets used a hospital separate from the one used by the enlisted ranks; this was a practice common to the Army at the time. The policy changed, however, when a new hospital was built in the late 1920s.[40] At that point, all ranks and all races used the same facilities.[41]

Surviving Buffalo Soldiers and their family members have fond memories of on-post health care. Saunders Matthews served as a Buffalo Soldier from 1939 to1947. He and his family used the same hospital as everyone else on post, and he recalls the treatment being very good.[42] Loretta Burns, the daughter of Buffalo Soldier Arthur Johnson, remembered her mother's special treatment at the post hospital in the late 1930s. Mrs. Johnson was a maid for the wife of Superintendent Jay L. Benedict. When Mrs. Johnson became ill, she was admitted to the post hospital and reportedly received excellent treatment. When the post hospital could not treat her advanced thyroid condition, Mrs. Benedict personally oversaw Mrs. Johnson's transfer to a hospital in Newburgh, ensuring that she received the proper treatment.[43]

Despite the enlightened Academy policies on housing, education, and health care, Buffalo Soldiers often experienced subtle, and sometimes not so subtle, discrimination. Informal policies established boundaries designed to keep black soldiers hidden from view and separate from the social world of white officers and their families. The Buffalo Soldiers could go to the central post area—site of the cadet barracks, academic buildings, and main parade grounds—only if they had official business. Even more restricted were the officers' housing areas. The black soldiers could not simply traverse the area on a shortcut, for a leisurely stroll, or even to provide personal tours for proud family members. If black soldiers were spotted in these areas, the military police would stop and question them; unless there was a good (i.e., official) reason for their presence, they would be harassed and forced to leave.[44]

Saunders Matthews recalled a time when he wanted to visit his girlfriend, who worked as a house servant for a white officer's family in the Lee housing area. Like all the single Buffalo Soldiers, he lived in the cavalry barracks located on the opposite end of post from the officers' housing area. He was aware of the unwritten rule that forbade the black soldiers from walking through the central post area or by the officers' housing areas and officers' facilities. To abide by this rule, he would have had to take a long and circuitous route: from his barracks, down to the river by the South Dock, around the border of the cadet area over rough and uneven terrain, along the river to the North Dock, then up to the Lee housing area. On one occasion he decided to attempt a shortcut. Instead of the inconvenient river route, he took a more direct route on the west side of the central post area. He cut through a wooded area by Delafield Pond, a recreation area reserved for officers and their families. Unfortunately, the military police spotted and quickly detained him. To reinforce the message that he did not belong in a white enclave, particularly where white women and children were swimming, the military police took stern action. As Matthews recalled, "The MPs roughed me up pretty bad."[45]

Such incidents were hard to endure and from time to time black soldiers would complain. One anonymous soldier took his case to the highest authority in the Army. Here, with spelling and punctuation preserved, is his poignant letter dated 26 September 1913:

> Secretary of War, Sir,
>
> We are here in West Point and we are doing our duty the best we now how and we take interest in doing our duty . . . they will let all the white enlisted men walk on the west side walk in front of the Commanding officers quarters and they wont let the collered enlisted men walk over there. if they will let the white enlisted men walk over there and dont let the collered, they might as well let us all go . . . we all have brothers and sisters, Mothers and Fathers and when they come to visit us wanted to see the Post. it would hurt me awfull bad to let them now that I were [unequal?] with white enlisted men. and not allowed the same privilege.[46]

It is not recorded whether this trooper's complaint was ever resolved, but it is clear that racial discrimination was no stranger to West Point. Good housing, education for their children, and health care notwithstanding, black soldiers deeply resented policies suggesting they were inferior to their white brethren in arms.

In summing up, we may note that in providing for the needs of the Buffalo Soldiers, the post administration considered factors such as logistics, funding, and the relatively tolerant racial attitudes of the local community. While policy encouraged soldiers to marry and have families, the resulting numbers of dependents were never large enough to induce the administration even to explore the idea of separate facilities. There were only six married Buffalo Soldiers on post in 1936, the same number as in 1916. Although Buffalo Soldiers received equal facilities, their interaction with cadets and officers and their families—all white—was limited to official business only. Their private world remained separate and hidden, circumscribed within the boundary of racial prejudice prevalent in American society.

The official chapter on West point's Buffalo Soldiers came to an end on 1 September 1947 when the Army entered a period of force modernization.[47] Trucks, jeeps, and trailers replaced the horses, and cadets no longer received instruction in equitation; the modernization of equipment, however, did little to change old racial attitudes. With the horses gone, Academy leaders faced the issue of what to do with the 9th Cavalry Detachment. Despite their splendid history of over 40 years of superior performance, the prevailing social norms still restricted the cavalrymen from being utilized as trainers and instructors for cadets. A letter written by Col. Philip E. Gallagher, Commandant of Cadets, to Superintendent Francis B. Wilby, dated 27 May 1942, highlights the struggle the senior officers faced in balancing issues of discrimination and the most effective use of the cavalrymen:

> Please note the attached draft regarding having the Cavalry Detachment, *colored*, conduct some of the weapons training during summer. Personally, I am not much in favor of this idea . . . . I believe the general feeling is . . . that they do not like having a colored soldier giving such intimate

instruction where they get down on their stomachs to teach cadets on the range while firing or teach them how to handle the bayonet and the grenade.

It seems a shame that we are unable to get more value from the Cavalry Detachment. However, I do not feel it is their fault, but it is based on probably a sound prejudice. Under the scheme of training during the summer there is very little call for mounted detachment training. . . . This leaves the Cavalry Detachment out of the picture almost entirely . . . except probably, for cooks and mess attendants.[48]

A response "by order of the Superintendent" and signed by Post Adjutant General Col. Arthur C. Purgis arrived a week later: "It is not desired that members of the Cavalry Squadron be used for individual instruction of cadets."[49]

The men of the cavalry detachment never again would serve as instructors or trainers for the Corps of Cadets. Upon deactivation of the detachment in September 1947, the troopers were absorbed into the Cadet Mess Detachment, the only other black unit on post.[50] It would remain for President Harry S. Truman with his Executive Order 9981 in 1948 to eradicate racial segregation in the U.S. armed forces.[51]

The competence, pride, and patriotism that characterized West Point's Buffalo Soldiers are still evident today. Following the deactivation of the 9th Cavalry Detachment, many of the troopers continued to serve on active duty until retirement. Detachment alumni maintained close friendships over the years and eagerly shared their memories of life as cavalry troopers; one of the outlets for their creative energies was the dedication of the Buffalo Soldier Monument at Fort Leavenworth, Kansas, in 1992.[52]

The Buffalo Soldier "family" includes some of the officers and cadets who had the honor of serving with the troopers. John Baker, a 1942 graduate of the Military Academy, fondly recalled the equestrian training he received from the cavalrymen: "We liked and respected the men of the 10th Cavalry. They were great horsemen."[53] Lt. Col. John Nazarro, the last detachment commander before the

A very emotional day for the troopers. The horses are auctioned off as the detachment prepares for deactivation, August 1947. (Courtesy of USMA Archives)

unit was deactivated, speaks highly of his men and the successes of his unit: "They were the best soldiers; the NCOs were the best in any unit I ever served with."[54] Colonel Nazarro, now retired, is still actively involved with many of his former soldiers and sees them on special occasions. He has recently established a scholarship in honor of his son for the descendants of West Point's Buffalo Soldiers.

While their numbers diminish each year, the men continue to meet annually to reminisce, honor their fallen comrades, and share their stories with younger generations. On 31 August 2003 one group met again—the 42nd Annual Reunion of the West Point Chapter of the Buffalo Soldier Association. As they visited the installation, they marveled at the new buildings and modern facilities that have been added since their enlisted days. But the highlight of the event was the gathering on the field below the cavalry barracks—now appropriately named "Buffalo Soldier Field"—to recall their days of service to West

Ceremony marking the dedication of Buffalo Soldier Field, 19 May 1973. From left to right, William Banks, Lt. Gen. William A. Knowlton, and Maj. Frank Steele (ret.). (Courtesy of USMA Archives)

Point and the nation. They brought their children, grandchildren, and great-grandchildren to the reunion to view the old photographs and documents that preserved, much like a patchwork quilt, the record of their admirable service. Their patriotism shone bright as they paid tribute to their country during a Pledge of Allegiance Ceremony and to their fallen brothers during a wreath-laying memorial service. The official records of the Buffalo Soldiers may have left only a faint historical imprint, but their contributions loomed large in lengthening and strengthening the Long Gray Line.

---

[1] Gail Buckley, *American Patriots* (New York: Random House, 2001). Henry O. Flipper was the first black graduate of the U.S. Military Academy. He graduated in 1887, served in the 10th Cavalry, and had a successful career as a civilian surveyor. See Chap. 12 in the present volume for further details. Charles Young was the third black to graduate from USMA. He graduated in 1889 and achieved the rank of colonel. He was the last black cadet to graduate until 1936 when Jim Crow laws became less influential in

American society. In 1936 Benjamin Davis, Jr., graduated from USMA. He commanded the famous WWII Tuskegee airmen and became the first black man to achieve the rank of lieutenant general in military service. He retired from the Air Force in 1970 as a lieutenant general, but was promoted to full general in 1999 while retired.

[2] There were three all-black units that served at West Point during the 20th century. The 9th Cavalry served from 23 March 1907 to 10 February 1932 when it was reorganized as the 10th Cavalry. The 10th Cavalry served from 10 February 1932 to 1 September 1947. During these years the unit was also referred to as the USMA Cavalry Squadron and the USMA Cavalry Detachment. The second all-black unit, the Hospital Corps to the Medical Department Detachment, served at West Point from 1925 through 1941. The third unit, the Cadet Mess, was activated in 1947 as an all-black unit and absorbed part of the 10th Cavalry when the 10th Cavalry was deactivated.

[3] The name "Buffalo Soldiers" originated circa 1860 when black troops of the 10th Cavalry served in the west during the Indian Wars. The Indians saw a resemblance between their sacred animal the buffalo, the black hair of the soldiers, and their warrior spirit. Although originally applied only to the cavalry troops, it was soon applied to all black soldiers serving in the west.

[4] Leonard McWherter, *The Buffalo Soldiers at West Point : A Distinguished Record, A Forgotten Past, 1907-1947* (West Point, NY : U.S. Military Academy, 1991) , 3.

[5] Buckley, 160.

[6] Buckley, 160-62. In 1971, Augustis Hawkins, a Democratic Congressman from Los Angeles, led the fight to clear the men of their dishonorable discharges. The next year President Nixon ordered that the men be granted honorable discharges.

[7] "The Negro Cavalry Men Will Reach West Point To-Day," *News of the Highlands* (Highland Falls, NY), 23 March 1907.

[8] "West Point Edition," *News of the Highlands* (Highland Falls, NY), 30 March 1907.

[9] *Annual Report of the Superintendent*, 1899, West Point, NY, 10.

[10] *Annual Report of the Superintendent*, 1906, West Point, NY, 8.

[11] *Annual Report of the Board of Visitors to the United States Military Academy,* West Point, NY, 14 June 1907, 12

[12] *22d Anniversary Day Program* (West Point, NY: United States Printing Office, 1929).

[13] Charles W. Larned, *Enlargement of the Military Academy, West Point, August 1899* (West Point, NY: U.S. Military Academy Press and Bindery, 1908), 24.

[14] *Annual Report of the Superintendent*, 1906, West Point, NY, 8.

[15] Saunders Matthews, interview by author, 22 October 2001 .

[16] *Annual Report of the Superintendent*, 1907, West Point, NY, 11.

[17] Ibid.

[18] *Annual Report of the Superintendent,* 1908, West Point, NY, 10.

[19] "Visit at West Point of Japanese General," *News of the Highlands* (Highland Falls, NY), 18 May 1907.

[20] "Cavalry Detachment Notes," *News of the Highlands* (Highland Falls, NY), 25 May 1907.

[21] Ibid.

[22] "West Point Colored Troops Unnecessarily Criticized," *News of the Highlands* (Highland Falls, NY), 15 June 1907.

[23] Ibid.

[24] *Annual Report of the Superintendent*, 1908, 9.

[25] Saunders Matthews, interview by author, 22 October 2001.

[26] Joe Dunn, interview by author, 31 August 2003.

[27] Ibid.

[28] Ibid.

[29] George Knapp, *Buffalo Soldiers at Fort Leavenworth in the 1930s and early 1940s* (Fort Leavenworth, KS: Combat Studies Institute, 1991).

[30] *Annual Report of the Board of Visitors to the United States Military Academy,* West Point, NY, 14 June 1907, 25-27.

[31] Ibid., 25.

[32] Ibid., 27.

[33] Ibid., 25.

[34] *Annual Report of the Superintendent,* 1906, appendix H. The Cavalry Barracks, currently used as barracks for 1-1 Infantry, were located on the south end of the post approximately ¾ mile from the central post area. The barracks overlook what is now called Buffalo Soldier Field.

[35] *Annual Report of the Superintendent,* 1923, 20.

[36] "Names and Quarters of Married Enlisted Men Occupying Quarters at West Point," 1916, Archives, U.S. Military Academy.

[37] Of the six cavalry soldier families listed on the roster "Names and Quarters of Married Men Occupying Quarters at West Point," four families lived in a four-plex building in a separated area. The other two were those of the unit First Sergeant, the senior enlisted man in the unit, who lived in a separate housing area, and the unit gardener, who lived off post at the garden itself.

[38] *Annual Report of the Board of Visitors to the United States Military Academy,* West Point, NY, 14 June 1907, 26.

[39] Loretta Burns, interview by author, 18 September 2001.

[40] West Point Telephone Directory Guide Map, 1936, Archives, U.S. Military Academy

[41] Saunders Matthews, interview by author, 22 October 2001.

[42] Saunders Matthews served as a Buffalo soldier from 1939 to 1947, when the unit was deactivated. He continued to serve as a civil servant until mandatory retirement and continues to work at West Point as a bus driver. Matthews is the President of the West Point Buffalo Soldier Association.

[43] Loretta Burns, interview by author, 18 September 2001. Burns is the daughter of Buffalo Soldier Arthur Johnson, who served at West Point in the late 1910s and early 1920s. Her mother also served as a house servant for the officers' families on post including Superintendent and Mrs. Benedict in the late 1930s

[44] Saunders Matthews, interview by author, 22 October 2001.

[45] Ibid.

[46] Anonymous letter to Secretary of War, 26 September 1913, Archives, U.S. Military Academy.

[47] McWherter, 4.

[48] Col. P.B. Gallagher, Commandant of Cadets, official correspondence to the Office of the Superintendent, U.S. Military Academy, 27 May 1942. Unaccountably, Gallagher's name is shown as "P.B. Gallagher" in the signature block of the letter, but it is carried as "Philip Edward Gallagher" in the USMA *Register of Graduates and Former Cadets.*

[49] Col. Arthur C. Purgis, Adjutant General, official correspondence to the Office of the Commandant, 4 June 1942.

[50] The 1802nd Special Regiment, Archives, U.S. Military Academy, 27.

[51] John Whiteclay Chambers, ed., *The Oxford Companion to American Military History* (Oxford : Oxford University Press, 1999), 8-9.

[52] Saunders Matthews, interview by author, 22 October 2001.

[53] Col. John Baker (USA, Ret.), from a speech given at the 42nd Annual Buffalo Soldier Reunion at West Point, 31 August, 2003.

[54] Lt. Col. John Nazarro (USA, Ret.), interview by author, November 2001.

⊰ CHAPTER 15 ⊱

THE CRUCIBLE OF DUTY:
WEST POINT, WOMEN, AND SOCIAL CHANGE

Lance Janda

As the beneficiaries of more than 200 years of research and writing about the United States Military Academy, modern scholars could be forgiven for assuming they understand everything there is to know about the Long Gray Line. After all, the Library of Congress alone contains almost 2,300 entries on the Academy, while the number of journal articles, feature films, documentaries, internet sites, government studies, television shows, newspaper accounts, and magazine exposes is too large to estimate.[1] We have access to historical monographs, sociological models, psychological profiles, and insider accounts, to say nothing of statistical overviews, coffee table pictorials, novels, biographies, and the works of Academy graduates and dropouts alike. Each promises unique insight into the mystery, tradition, or history of West Point, and as the Academy begins a third century of service to America there appears to be no letup in the rapid pace of publication on the horizon.

Despite this avalanche of interest, however, most works concerning West Point or its graduates focus on cadet training, on the education and character development of its "great" leaders, or upon the Academy's long legacy of producing battlefield commanders. Few consider West Point or the other service academies as agents of social change, as evolving crucibles that help shape new social mores as well as leaders of character. Such a role is certainly not the raison d'étre of West Point, nor is there any evidence Congress originally intended the Academy to function as a sociological laboratory. Yet the ability to shatter cultural convention in the name of duty stands among the foremost contributions made by the armed forces and West Point to American life. The military demonstrated that ability in 1948 by desegregating long before mainstream society did so, and again in the 1970s by leading the way in institutionally advancing equity and even equality for American women. In neither case did the armed forces seek a leading role in promoting social change; indeed, in both cases they campaigned forcefully against it. Yet the government chose the Army, Navy, Air Force, Coast Guard, and Marines for the difficult challenge of setting new social standards anyway, because they represent the most traditional and respected institutions in the United States, and because whatever social norms are common in the military become an ideal for much of American society to emulate.[2]

This is especially true for the Army, which by virtue of its size has a larger impact on American society than any other branch of the armed forces, and perhaps truest for West Point. As the oldest and most prestigious military academy in the United States and one of the most influential in the world, West Point has an enormously powerful effect on what constitutes American military and social norms. It enjoys a lofty status at home and abroad because of the high caliber of its graduates, faculty, and staff, and this in turn means that changes at the Academy often represent watersheds in American and even global history. For when members of any social group graduate from West Point it is seen as a triumph for the group as a whole, as proof that it is fully included in the fabric of American life in principle if not yet in fact. Moreover, historians typically mark the first time members of any group graduate from West Point as a landmark event, one that forever changes perceptions of that group in the minds of the American people. This is true for African-Americans and Native Americans among others, and most importantly for American women. In fact, the admission and successful graduation of women cadets from the U.S. Military Academy make clear that

West Point is among the strongest and most resilient institutions in America, and one of the most important in leading social revolutions that fundamentally alter our society in the long run.

Those first women cadets, all 119 of them, arrived at West Point on 7 July 1976 because the U.S. House of Representatives passed Public Law 94-106 as an amendment to a military appropriations bill by a 303-96 vote on 20 May 1975. Senate passage quickly followed, and on 7 October President Gerald Ford's signature made the new law official.[3] It called upon each of America's federal military service academies to admit women the following summer, and in so doing ended the 174-year-old tradition of an all-male West Point.[4]

Many people were outraged by the law. During brief Congressional hearings in 1974, opponents of admitting women argued that each of the military academies existed primarily to train combat officers.[5] Women were barred from direct combat by either tradition or statute in the armed forces at the time, and a number of Americans concluded that no compelling rationale existed for placing women in training slots designed to produce front-line warriors. They also defended the unique all-male environment at West Point, arguing that women would destroy esprit de corps and introduce an element of sexual tension and competition that could damage training and morale among the Corps of Cadets. Most importantly, military opponents universally condemned the move as a threat to unit cohesiveness and combat effectiveness, a point made time and again by the services as they closed ranks before Congress to oppose the admission of women to any of the nation's service academies.[6] Retired Army Gen. Matthew Ridgway, a hero of both World War II and the Korean War, added his support to their cause with a letter to President Ford, which concluded that the admission of women to West Point would "prove to be an ill-considered action inimical to the best interests of the nation."[7]

Supporters of admitting women responded on many fronts. First, they attacked the proposition that West Point was designed exclusively to produce combat officers. They argued that the Academy mission statement had never specifically mentioned training officers for combat service, and cited a memo written by Brig. Gen.

L. Gordon Hill, Jr., for the Department of the Army, which read, "[T]here is . . . no prohibition to the admission of women in the mission of West Point. The commissioning of officers to lead in battle is only an implied and derived mission."[8] Additionally, supporters denied claims that all Academy graduates actually served in combat, a point buttressed by Paul D. Phillips, the Acting Assistant Secretary of the Army for Manpower and Reserve Affairs. In March of 1974 he collected data on active duty senior officers who were West Point graduates, finding that the combat arms "argument is a weak one since we seem to average less than 70 percent in CA (combat arms) over the years, less than 75 percent in the first five years, and about 80 percent. . . for the 1973 class [at West Point]."[9] A Government Accounting Office study that reviewed 102 randomly chosen service records of USMA graduates to determine the percentage serving in combat or combat related assignments in the same year confirmed Phillips's analysis. In results verified by the Army, the study found that only 50 percent of the officers in question served or had served in combat or combat-related assignments.[10]

The second major argument for admitting women concerned equality. Supporters pointed out that women were already commissioned as Army officers via Officer Candidate School (OCS) and through Reserve Officer Training Corps (ROTC) programs at civilian universities, and it made no sense to suggest that women were good enough for OCS and ROTC but somehow not good enough for West Point.[11] Moreover, proponents argued that educations at West Point as well as the Air Force and Naval Academies were critical first steps on the road to general officer which could not be duplicated anywhere else in the world. In that light, the question of admitting women had serious equal opportunity and equal protection implications.[12] This point arose in a number of court cases during the 1970s, most notably in a suit brought by California Representatives Jerome Waldie and Don Edwards on behalf of female constituents who wanted to attend the Air Force and Naval Academies. It began to appear likely that federal courts would eventually open the doors to women at West Point if Congress chose not to do so.[13] Finally, supporters argued passionately that the Army and the nation needed the services of the outstanding young women who would be attracted to West Point and the other service academies. Representative Pierre DuPont suggested it was "ridiculous, wasteful, and anachronistic to maintain that the best officer training our Nation has to offer should be limited to men only. . . . The only way we can take advantage of the most talented young women is to open the service academies to them."[14]

Ironically, the majority who supported the admission of women were largely unaware of the revolutionary changes they were setting in motion. To them, sending women cadets to America's service academies seemed simply a matter of equality. Women were already encouraged to become officers through ROTC or OCS in each service of the military, and it seemed natural to extend another outstanding educational opportunity to them by breaking down the gender barriers at West Point, Annapolis, and Colorado Springs.[15] Few saw the move as a step towards a greater sharing of power over the armed forces between men and women, and they failed to appreciate how in the long run the presence of women cadets at the leading officer training institutions in the world would be used as proof that women should serve in a greater variety of combat and combat support roles. What Congress debated in 1974 and 1975 was actually a very large issue indeed, involving as it did the question of what kind of military culture best suited the defense requirements of the nation, and how much opportunity should or should not be tied to a person's sex. These issues, however, were too controversial and abstract for most politicians, who focused instead on the issue of equity on a small scale, taking whatever political and social gain they could from supporting the admission of women and moving on. Most seem to have believed they could allow women to wear academy rings and undergo combat training while still somehow barring them from the front lines once fighting began. That is, they believed equality of opportunity did not ultimately mean equality of responsibility or risk.[16]

One person who did fear the connection between the legislation and the future role of American women in combat was Representative G.V. "Sonny" Montgomery, a Democrat from Mississippi. He echoed the military position that the admission of women was tied inextricably to the question of whether Americans were willing to commit their daughters to battle. "I am concerned that if we have the adoption of this amendment, this really is a foot in the door of putting women into combat," he said. Others echoed his concern, suggesting that it was nonsense to label all distinctions based on sex as discrimination, that opening the academies to women would pave the way for men incapable of combat duty to apply for admission, and that women would inevitably drag down physical performance standards.[17]

These arguments were echoed at West Point, where superintendent Sidney Berry called the admission of women the Academy's "most significant change since 1802," the year when Congress founded West Point on the banks of the Hudson River.[18] His assessment reflected the fact that no institution dedicated exclusively to training professional military officers anywhere in the world admitted women in 1975. A similar institution, the United States Merchant Marine Academy, had begun admitting women in 1974, but was considerably newer, far smaller, and committed to a very different mission than West Point. It fell under the auspices of the Department of Commerce rather than the Department of Defense, and trained officers for the U.S. Naval Reserve rather than for the active duty Navy. While useful as a point of departure in conceptual planning, the Merchant Marine Academy therefore provided little guidance to Berry on how he might admit women to the society of warriors and West Point and train them at a legendary school dedicated in principle if not in fact to preparing officers for the wholly unique universe of ground warfare. He and his staff faced the challenge of overcoming the male dominance of officer education that transcended national boundaries and extended backward to the beginning of recorded history. They had to find a way to make sexual integration work with no precedent to guide them, and in the aftermath of the American effort in Vietnam, a time when public confidence in the armed forces reached an alarming low. During the early 1970s Army recruitment became so challenging that even the Academy had difficulty finding qualified candidates, and in that era West Point sought only men. No one really knew how West Point could attract women cadets with no recruitment plan, no known pool of qualified applicants, and no previously established and culturally sanctioned role for cadet women already in place.[19]

Many of these problems were anticipated long before women actually arrived. As early as 1972, when the Equal Rights Amendment seemed likely to pass Congress and induce sweeping personnel changes within the armed forces, the Academy had quietly begun contingency planning for the admission of women. That planning accelerated, of course, following the passage of Congressional legislation in 1975 mandating the admission of women the following year, and continued unabated long after Berry and the rest of his staff had transferred to other assignments. Despite this lead time, however, the spirit of denial remained in full flower at West Point. No one at the Academy really thought women would ever arrive, and when Congress actually passed the requisite legislation most West Pointers were shocked. As Lieutenant General Berry wrote later: "Right down to the day in May 1975 that Congressman Stratton took the issue to the floor of the House of Representatives, the senior people in Washington seemed confident that Congress would maintain the service academies as male institutions."[20] Contingency plans existed, he admitted, "but nobody thought we would ever have to use them."[21]

West Point had only eight months between the time President Ford signed P.L. 94-106 and the day the first female cadets arrived at the Academy. It was in a rush, therefore, that the recruiting of women cadets began and new rules covering everything from cadet uniforms to social relations were developed. Academy planners adopted these rules in hopes of creating an environment in which women could quickly assimilate into the Corp of Cadets and find their specific group needs met, but no one really knew whether they would be successful or not.[22]

One of the most controversial decisions came in the realm of physical fitness. Army planners, fearful that women could not meet the minimum requirements established for male cadets, chose to adopt a different set of performance standards for women. This fueled persistent rumors that the presence of women at West Point was eroding physical fitness throughout the Army by lowering the standards for *all* cadets. This canard was reinforced by the fact that the Army at large has always had different physical fitness requirements for men and women, and it is ironic because the current two-track system at West Point—one for men, one for women—is manifestly not what Congress intended. Representative Stratton demanded equal treatment for men and women at the Academy in 1975, saying: "Mr. Chairman, I do not want any special concessions for women. I think they should be required to follow the same program, they should be required to meet the same standards."[23] Yet, West Point leaders, fearful of a high attrition rate among the first women cadets and consequent angry political repercussions, proposed that Congress insert language into P.L. 94-106 which read: "Academic and other relevant standards required for appointment, admission, training, graduation, and commissioning of female individuals shall be the same as those required for male individuals, except for those *minimum essential adjustments in such standards required because of physiological differences between male and female individuals*" (emphasis added).[24]

In the ensuing decades, the single greatest source of resentment toward women at West Point has been the differing physical fitness standards that evolved out of that language. Perhaps such language was necessary for West Point to avoid the public relations debacle that in all likelihood would have accompanied massive dropouts among the first women, or perhaps more women could have met the male standards than anyone predicted. Regardless, absent such concessions, either women would have met the single standard in sufficient numbers, or, in the event of widespread failure, Congressional and Army leaders would perhaps have followed with more meaningful discussions regarding the place of women in the armed forces and the merits of a single physical fitness standard. In hindsight, either of those possibilities seems preferable to the dual-track chosen by the Army, for it condemned women to second-class status at West Point from the very beginning and without giving them a chance.

In many other areas the Academy was far more successful, though it could not initially contain the angry response of some male cadets to the invasion by females of their historic home. Within a short time it became clear that some of the men were dedicated to simply running women out of the Academy. While the exact number of those men is impossible to know, it is important to remember that in the rigid hierarchy of West Point even a small number of men with rank could pose a real threat to women in the classes beneath them. If only one percent of the approximately 4,000 men at West Point chose to engage in some sort of vicious anti-female hazing or violence, for example, that would have meant that 40 men with rank in a closed environment still had the opportunity to harass individual women cadets on a daily basis. And that conclusion of course assumes a static number of harassers, when in reality the number fluctuated depending on mood, peer pressure, opportunity, and the ongoing battle in male cadet minds between what they were officially told to do (treat women fairly) and what many perceived as their real duty and/or what some upperclassmen and isolated members of the Academy staff and faculty were subtly suggesting that they do (run women out).[25]

The harassment and personal attacks that did occur stemmed from a cultural ambivalence regarding the role of women in American society as a whole, and blended with more specific Academy antagonisms toward female cadets to create an atmosphere in which few women could really relax or feel comfortable. Some male cadets liked having women around because they liked women in general or they thought their presence was a boon to the Army. Others were more conflicted. They might like women in theory, or be attracted to women cadets as individuals, but at the same time despise women cadets as a group because they threatened the exclusive hold men had on being warriors and seemed to threaten the traditions of the Academy. After all, if graduating from West Point had historically been a way to prove one's manhood, what would it mean if women were successful there? With a heavy dose of adolescence and youthful testosterone thrown into this volatile mix, the results were as dramatically good or bad as they were intense. Some male cadets immediately began pursuing or dating their female peers, some formed lifelong friendships with women and developed a greater respect for women over time, and a minority became truly abusive.

When it came, that abuse fell hardest on the very first women cadets, those who entered with the Class of 1980. Of the 119 admitted in 1976, 62 eventually graduated in 1980. Those who succeeded did so despite a few men who were willing to go to almost any lengths to persuade women to leave West Point. At a company inspection during the first eight weeks of cadet training (a period known as "Beast Barracks") one squad leader howled, "I'm gonna get everyone one of you fuckin bitches out of here!"[26] Another upperclassman made similar remarks privately. While discussing the prospect that female cadets might one day graduate from the Academy he leaned in and whispered to one woman, "Never. You are never going to graduate from West Point. I am going to make sure of it."[27] Another woman in the Class of 1980 found herself called into an upperclassman's room every day for a week so he could explain to her how much men respected West Point, how she was ruining it, and then ask her how in good conscience she could possibly stay.[28] In another case, a squad leader told the women in his squad that he would not recommend them for formal admission to the Corps at the end of their plebe (freshman) year because "God did not make women to be soldiers."[29] And in one regiment, a company commander held regular (and prohibited) formations of all the plebe women in his unit every morning before reveille for weeks so he could viciously haze them and remind each one of his personal intent to eliminate every woman from his command.[30]

On a more routine level, female cadets who called out "Good morning, Sir" when passing upperclassmen often heard "Good morning, Bitch" in return, and in one infamous exchange an upperclassman responded: "It's not going to be a good morning until you goddamn bitches get out of here."[31] Women saw sexual slurs on barracks walls, had condoms placed on their bunks, and received vibrators through the mail. Some were pawed during inspections while doing pull-ups or flexed-arm hangs, and a few had dress sabers thrust through their pillows and bed linens or even through the middle of their mattresses.[32] Others had water balloons, eggs, tomatoes, and condoms full of water thrown at them from barracks windows or into their rooms, or had salt thrown in their beds.[33] If they were considered too feminine men called them "fluffs," while those deemed too masculine were "dykes."

Some women tried to blend in by lowering their voices and avoiding makeup, and a few even had "command voice practice down in the locker room."[34] Others deliberately starved themselves and became anorexic, because losing their curves made them harder to identify at a distance.[35] Some men resented them anyway. They made fun of women for their typically inferior upper body strength and endurance, and their longer hair, and they especially resented the attention women received from tourists, who cadets dubbed the "Great American Public." Men particularly hated the fact that tourists stopped to take pictures of female cadets at every opportunity, fawning on them, as one cadet put it, like the "bears at Yellowstone."[36] Few seem to have considered the possibility that women hated the attention too.

With few exceptions, women endured whistling, name calling, and pats on the behind. Some struggled with upperclassmen entering their rooms and watching or groping them at night without permission, offenses made easy by the fact cadets did not have locks on their doors.[37] Rumors abounded about how each of the gender-integrated companies in the Corps actually functioned as brothels, and in one company a group of men organized a contest to reduce every woman in the unit to tears at least once.[38] Some upperclassmen regularly entered cadet rooms and used their sabers to scratch female shoes and belt buckles, only to return later to write up those same cadets for having damaged equipment.[39] Older graduates sometimes joined in the harassment by refusing to return female salutes at Hops or ceremonial occasions, and a few even accused female cadets of lowering the martial spirit of the Academy and contributing to the poor performance of the Army football team.[40] One approached a female cadet inside the West Point Officer's Club and bluntly asked, "What the hell are you doing at West Point?"[41] Even food became a weapon, much as it had been during the late 19th and early 20th centuries when Academy hazing was at its height. One male platoon commander flatly refused to allow women to eat at his table in the mess hall until told to do so by the chain of command,

and the use of food deprivation became so widespread in some companies that members of the Academy staff began routinely sneaking female plebes food.[42] Those who could eat suffered in a different way, particularly if they gained weight. Upperclassmen jeered women who added pounds consuming West Point's 4,000 calorie daily diet, accusing them of having caught the dreaded "Hudson Hip Disease." A running cadet joke began with the question, "What is the difference between a female cadet and a squad car?" The answer: "It takes two squad cars to make a roadblock."[43]

In the midst of this litany of harassment against women it should be noted and emphasized that *every* cadet faced hazing or abuse of some kind in the competitive, rigidly hierarchical world of West Point, and that many male cadets suffered as well. It is also true that the majority of male cadets never maliciously hazed or harassed women, that many befriended their female peers and tried to protect them, and that women received widely varying levels of abuse from one cadet company to another. The issue, therefore, is not whether women were the only cadets harassed, whether all women were harassed all the time, or whether all male cadets were guilty of persistently harassing women. None of those statements is true. Instead, the issue is how much women were targeted, what kind of harassment they faced, and why it occurred. Viewed that way, there is no question that female cadets as a group endured greater and more frequent harassment than their male peers, and that they often suffered solely because they were women, rather than because they were poor cadets or physically out of shape. The latter failings were a sure invitation for hazing for any cadet, regardless of sex, and it is fair to say a few women cadets drew abuse because they were, in the vernacular of the Academy, "tie-ups." Yet for women the hazing never came for that reason alone, and sooner or later every female cadet was told she did not belong at West Point simply because she was a woman and could never fit in. In contrast, no man was ever told that the mere fact of his being male precluded meaningful service to the nation at West Point or in the Army, and none were ever expected to justify the presence of their entire sex at the Academy or within the armed forces. Women faced such accusations on a regular basis.

That female cadets endured this sort of abuse in a society uncertain about military service and the "proper" role of women is hardly surprising. Nor is it a shock that molestations and assaults took place in a culture as preoccupied with sex as our own. What is significant, however, is that with quiet perseverance West Point overcame this entrenched resistance within roughly a decade, leading an unassuming role in revolutionizing the place of women in the Army and in American society. Women are now part and parcel of the fabric of Academy life, a part of the habit and custom of the institution. As the Roman poet Ovid wrote, "Nothing is stronger than custom," and with a strong commitment to duty and the success of sexual integration the staff and faculty at West Point made the customs of their institution change rather quickly.[44]

They did so because the professional ethic of the institution—duty—made the armed forces in general and West Point in particular the venue where political leaders could mandate change in the status of women and be assured that those changes would be made as quickly as possible. They were made immediately after Congress demanded action in 1975, and continually fine-tuned thereafter until the presence of women cadets was no longer worthy of special notice.

This does not mean that Academy efforts were without flaw, for it is certainly true that the experience of women cadets at West Point differs in varying degrees from that of their male peers. Moreover, a number of women cadets have been constrained to leave who might have made great contributions to the country and to the Army. Yet, for all these failings the Army and West Point are among the only institutions in the world where men and women holding identical ranks and are paid the same, and where it is unremarkable to see women leading and training men. Female cadets who endured and suffered year after year to make their presence "business as usual" at West Point deserve the most credit for changing the culture there, but the Academy also merits praise for making the matriculation of women largely successful in less than a generation. Studies showing women can succeed at the Academy are now "factual, provable, and empirical," and though we still debate on a national level the place of women in combat, few seem to question the place of women at West Point.[45]

That fact represents an accomplishment of deep significance, for West Point played a critical role in revolutionizing the place of women in the armed forces. It did not accomplish this feat in a vacuum, obviously. The removal of the two percent ceiling on the number of active duty military women by Congress in 1967, the admission of women to the Air Force (1969), Army (1972), and Navy (1972) ROTC programs, and the creation of the All-Volunteer Force following the end of the draft in 1973 were among the many important milestones in this process.[46] Still, the importance of what happened at the Academy should not be minimized. Like the final snowflake that fells the bough of a mighty oak tree, the arrival of women at the most elite officer training school in the world marked the point beyond which there could be no turning back. As women overcame the challenges of West Point and began to excel in the Army, it became progressively more difficult to talk of what women could *not* do. They had become part of the Long Gray Line that included such luminaries as Ulysses S. Grant, John J. Pershing, Dwight D. Eisenhower, Matthew B. Ridgway, and Norman Schwarzkopf, and there could be no stopping talk of what they *could* do.

Indeed, the high-profile success of women at West Point and the other service academies, and the attendant publicity that accompanied them, became so widely noticed that it had repercussions for civilian and military societies throughout the world. In the U.S. Army, it led directly to the abolition of the Women's Army Corps in 1977, and it accelerated the move toward gender-integrated commissioning and training programs in almost all of the armed forces.[47] Within American culture as a whole, photographs and news stories demonstrating the achievements of women at the academies made it increasingly difficult to argue that women should not move even farther into formerly all-male domains, and they proceeded to make many such moves. To be sure, other cultural forces were at work affecting this transformation, and it is impossible to trace the expansion of opportunities for women in the United States over the last 30 years to any single act of Congress or military decision. Still, the admission of women into West Point was a highly important symbolic event, covered in the national and international news media and thus impossible to ignore as a harbinger of serious social change. In the years that followed their admission, women found their way into military academies around the world; they rose steadily in numbers in the armed forces of dozens of nations; and today they find themselves flying military aircraft in more than 23 countries, assigned to combat ships in 16, and eligible for assignment to ground combat units in more than 14.[48]

Air Commodore Julie Hammer became Commandant of the Australian Defense Force Academy in 2002, and every member of the North Atlantic Treaty Organization now accepts women into its armed forces.[49] Again, these developments are not all traceable exclusively to the admission of women to West Point. But by 2003 women made up 15 percent of the active duty strength of the armed forces in the United States (and almost 15 percent of Army officers), as opposed to less than two percent in 1969. Certainly the ensuing explosion in the number of military women and the duties in which they can serve in America and overseas is attributable in at least some small way to the presence of women cadets at the Academy.[50] Even if their presence only accelerated an existing trend, it did so in a way that no other institution in the United States could have duplicated. After all, there is only one West Point.

The story of West Point's evolution as a coeducational institution is a reminder that the armed forces, despite their historical and understandable commitment to hierarchy, remain ideologically more equitable than most other institutions in the United States. Napoleon once said that every man in his army carried a marshal's baton in his knapsack, meaning that those with talent could earn promotions based on their ability rather than their race, ethnicity, family lineage, or political connections. So it is in the American Army, where Gen. Andrew J. Goodpaster, who succeeded Lieutenant General Berry as West Point Superintendent in 1977, began quelling resentment against women cadets with a very simple argument. He reasoned that if women were going to be in the Army there had to be female officers, and they had to have "preparation equal to that of the men." That meant admitting them to West Point rather than establishing a separate training regime, because, as he put it, "We know from past experience that separate but equal is not equal."[51] Everyone in the Army, he argued, needed the same chance to succeed.

Another legacy of the admission of women is the growing number of female graduates and civilian faculty on the Academy staff. In 1976 only three women taught at West Point; by 1997 there were 63.[52] Perhaps most importantly, women now represent the Regular Army by serving as tactical officers for the Corps of Cadets, and they are as responsible as any man for passing along the traditions of the Long Gray Line. That men now draw inspiration from military women less than 30 years after the first female cadets were almost hounded out of West Point is a testament to how much the Academy has changed since the 1970s. In other ways, however, the Academy has not changed at all. Faculty members and tactical officers still hope to instill in cadets the foundational virtues of Duty, Honor, and Country. As one female instructor from the Class of 1980 put it, "I want them [cadets] to be able to be courageous and make the right decisions," and to "protect the sons and daughters of America in the future."[53] She recalled her considerable amazement upon returning to West Point for the first time after graduation and seeing the progress made in gender relations. Today, she said, "There is absolutely an institutional norm that says, 'This is a co-ed institution.'"[54]

As a coeducational institution, West Point produced 2,235 female graduates between 1980 and 2001, many of whom have served with distinction.[55] Between 1993 and 2000, 10.1 percent were recognized as Distinguished Cadets for superior academic performance (compared to 9.5 percent of male cadets), while 25.5 percent (versus 22.1 percent for men) received the Superintendent's Award, which recognizes overall excellence in academic, military, and physical fitness programs. Since 1980, 14 women have earned postgraduate academic scholarships, including Rhodes Scholar Andrea Hollen, who graduated in 1980. Kristin Baker became the first female Cadet First Captain in 1989; Rebecca Marier became the first woman ranked at the top of her class in 1993; and Karen Short earned distinction as the first women to command cadet basic training in 1985. In fact, women have now served in every high-level cadet position West Point has to offer, and it remains only for female graduates to become commandant and superintendent for the litany of firsts to come to a close.

Women have generally left the Academy before graduation at a higher rate than men over the years, with female attrition at 34.2 percent and male attrition 27 percent since 1980. In light of a general lack of social incentives for women to join the armed services, however, it is perhaps amazing that the differences between the sexes is not any larger. Those women who do graduate are slightly more likely than their male peers to receive promotion and stay in the Army, and their example is paving the way for the admission of more women cadets than ever before. Between 1997 and 2000, the proportion of female cadets entering West Point averaged 16 percent, a healthy improvement over 1975-1976 when the Academy had to scramble to find the 119 women who paved the way so that others might follow.[56]

Perhaps the most astonishing legacy of the admission of women to the Academy is their ever increasing level of physical fitness. In 1980, graduating cadet women ran the two-mile run with a mean time of 17 minutes and 22 seconds (17:22). By 1995, graduating women had a mean time of 15:20, 34 seconds *less* than the minimum acceptable time for men. Women also improved from a mean of 43 sit-ups in the Class of 1980 to 92 for women in the Class of 1990, which is particularly compelling when compared to the mean of 59 sit-ups performed by the men of the USMA Class of 1959. Similarly, women in the Class of 1990 had a mean of 47 pushups during their third year, while men in the Class of 1962 were performing only 36.[57]

This is not to say that women cadets can compete on an even playing field with their male counterparts across the board, for male cadets have improved their level of physical fitness over the last two decades as well. But it does indicate that the gap in physical performance between men and women is narrowing, and that West Point women have dramatically improved their level of physical fitness since 1976. Cadet Jeannie Huh personified that improvement by graduating first among the Class of 2002 in physical performance, and examples of physical prowess like hers are a powerful factor in facilitating the further integration of women into the Corps of Cadets and the Army as a whole.[58] The idea that West Point should attract such quality people and serve as the place where the nation showcased its desire to promote equality and open the Army to the talents of all Americans is hardly new. In fact, it was summarized in a 1975 letter from Prof. Sidney Forman to Superintendent Berry, who at that time was struggling with how women were to be assimilated into the Corps of Cadets. Forman, who at one time directed the library at West Point, noted that the admission of women signified an occasion when the Academy could adapt itself to the changing needs of the nation. This sort of adaptation, he said, formed a vital part of West Point's role in American history. The admission of women, he continued, represented a positive development because continuing to keep women out meant denying the Army invaluable human resources. It would represent, he said, a decision to "disarm ourselves in the face of the enemy." Further, he noted that the admission of women offered a challenge well suited to the "tradition of flexibility and responsiveness to national needs" that characterized the Academy. "This change," he wrote, "which will bring all of our children into the officer corps, is in the best tradition of West Point and our democratic society."[59]

Today, Forman's words seem prophetic, and not because the Army or West Point needs to do women the "favor" of allowing them to join the Long Gray Line. Instead, it is the armed forces in general, and the Army and West Point in particular, which depend on the willingness of young people to direct their talents toward the service of their country. In an era of unprecedented abundance, the fact that thousands of Americans from every state and all walks of life compete for admission to West Point each year remains the surest sign the Academy has remolded itself from the conservative bastion that opposed the admission of women in 1976 into a leading model of diversity directed toward progress and constructive change. It has overcome the hurdles of the past, openly confronted its problems, and moved on with a characteristic sense of purpose and a willingness to confront any enemy and overcome any cultural hurdle if ordered to do so. In making that journey, West Point has proven once again that it can play a leading role in revamping American culture, that it can be a crucible in which we remold social mores and produce a stronger society in the long run.

Serving society by setting an example is one way West Point serves the nation, but the Academy's most important mission is producing leaders of character to lead the Army and the nation in times of crisis, especially on the battlefield. With that in mind, it is reasonable to ask whether the admission of women has served the national security interests of the nation, whether women officers offer more than a politically correct response to societal pressure, and whether West Point is the proper training environment for women in any event. Such questions are particularly important in light of the current war on terrorism and in light of the considerable controversy still generated by debates probing the degree to which American women should be thrust into combat units in the future.

Within those parameters, the Academy's own evaluation criteria suggest that the presence of women at West Point strongly benefits the Army and the United States. West Point uses a variety of indicators to measure the effectiveness of its program of study; they include cadet academic achievement, physical fitness, officer promotion rates, length of service in the armed forces, and performance in combat. As noted earlier, women cadets have excelled academically, generally outperforming men as a group, and have made enormous strides in physical performance. Women graduates are slightly more likely than their male counterparts to be promoted (with six women from the original 62 who graduated in 1980 making full colonel), and slightly more likely to stay in the Army until retirement. The test of combat duty is the most difficult to judge. Women from West Point have served in combat environments like Somalia and Iraq and with units like the 82nd Airborne Division, but regulations limit their opportunity to serve in most combat positions. The data, therefore, is incomplete in this regard, but that is solely because of policymakers and not the doing of the women themselves. In every other category the Academy's own research indicates that women have earned their place at West Point. Indeed, West Point has become a primary source for female leaders of character, just as it has been for men since 1802.

Yet one significant issue lingers. No one who encounters a male graduate of West Point who is lacking in character or physical fitness or who left the Army at the first available opportunity ever concludes that men do not belong at the Academy. In contrast, many are more than willing to extrapolate from an encounter with a female graduate who did not meet their expectations, thus drawing the conclusion that women have no place in the Long Gray Line. The subtle influence of sexism within our society is partly to blame, as is the persistence of cultural stereotypes about women in the face of decades of experience and research demonstrating that women can and do serve with distinction. So is the pervasive influence of sexual harassment, which often has a tendency to re-ignite debates over military women and induce some critics to suggest that the way to stop sexual attacks is to simply remove women from the threatening environment. That argument amounts to victim-blaming, of course, but like all the other controversies surrounding military women it promises to stay with us for the foreseeable future.

Still, there is no denying the progress that has been made. On a micro-level, one of the most revealing indicators of the change in attitude about women in the military, and of the effectiveness of the West Point crucible, is the fact that two male cadets currently at West Point chose to follow in the footsteps of their *mothers* to attend the Academy. In another case, the daughter of parents who are both members of the Class of 1980 recently joined the Long Gray Line as a member of the West Point Class of 2007.[60] In the midst of the statistics and the emotion and the history, those facts speak most eloquently to the great changes West Point has wrought in the Army and in the status of women in American life.

The importance of this contribution is difficult to quantify, especially at a remove of 28 years and in a time when the reality of military women serving in a wide variety of roles all over the world seems so unremarkable.[61] Yet American culture retained enough ambivalence regarding women at military academies to make the entrance of female cadets to the Virginia Military Institute and The Citadel national news in the mid 1990s, despite the fact that at West Point women cadets had become commonplace long before. That perhaps is a cogent reminder that Americans lack a sense of histori-cal memory, and that resistance to changes in the traditional role of women remains stronger than some Americans might like to admit. Yet it also demonstrates how far West Point and the Army have come since the 1970s, reminding us that the armed forces, more than any institution in our society, need and deserve the presence of the most gifted individuals our country can produce. No matter how we measure talent, some of those individuals are certain to be women, and it is in our collective national interest to marshal their abilities in as many ways as possible, regardless of stereotypes suggesting certain groups are restricted to particular roles in our society.

---

[1] An online "Guided Search" of the holdings of the Library of Congress utilizing the terms "West Point" or United States Military Academy" revealed 2,256 entries.

[2] Gallup polls have shown that Americans have respected the military more than any other societal institution for more than a decade. See www.gallup.com.

[3] Though not subject to the legislation, the U.S. Coast Guard Academy voluntarily announced in August of 1975 that it too would admit women in 1976. See John Lovell, *Neither Athens Nor Sparta? The American Service Academies in Transition* (Bloomington: Indiana University Press, 1979), 313.

[4] Judith Hicks Stiehm, *Bring Me Men and Women: Mandated Change at the U.S. Air Force Academy* (Berkeley: University of California Press, 1981), 36-37. Congressional action stemmed from pressure by ordinary citizens, members of the House of Representatives, and the federal courts. California representatives Jerome Waldie and Don Edwards sued Secretary of Defense James Schlesinger on behalf of female constituents who wanted to attend the Air Force and Naval Academies; after suffering defeat in U.S. District Court, they won a reversal in the U.S. Court of Appeals in 1974. The reversal called for a new and full trial of their case on its merits; given the tenor of the times and the questionable constitutionality of the ban on women cadets, it is possible the courts might have forced open academy doors by 1976 without Congressional action. When Congress opened them in 1975, the case became moot.

[5] The United States operates five federally funded service academies: the United States Military Academy, the United States Air Force Academy, the United States Naval Academy, the United States Coast Guard Academy, and the United States Merchant Marine Academy. The first three produce officers who serve in the regular armed forces; the Coast Guard Academy produces officers for the Coast Guard; and the Merchant Marine Academy trains officers for service on U.S.-flagged merchant ships who are usually members of the U.S. Naval Reserve.

[6] A short list of those who opposed the admission of women before Congress in 1974 includes the Secretaries of the Army, Air Force, and Navy; the superintendents of West Point, the Air Force Academy, and the Naval Academy; Department of Defense General Counsel Martin Hoffman, Lt. Gen. Leo Benade, Adm. Worth H. Bagley, Gen. George Brown, Gen. Fred Weyand, and Jacqueline Cochran, who directed the Women's Airforce Service Pilots (WASPs) during World War II. See Lance Janda, *Stronger Than Custom: West Point and the Admission of Women* (Westport, CT: Praeger, 2002), 18.

[7] M.B. Ridgway to President Gerald Ford, 9 June 1975, United States Military Academy (USMA) Official Historian files.

[8] Brig. Gen. L. Gordon Hill, Jr., Memorandum for Headquarters, Department of the Army (DAPE-ZA), "The Admission of Women to the United States Military Academy," undated, USMA files.

[9] Paul D. Phillips, Memorandum to Colonel Dyke, "USMA Graduates in Combat Arms Branches," 13 March 1974, USMA files.

[10] See Maj. Gen. Harold G. Moore, Jr., Memorandum for Deputy Chief of Staff for Personnel, "Attendance of Women at the United States Military Academy," 8 November 1974, 1-2, USMA files.

[11] See U.S. Congress, House, Committee on Armed Services, Subcommittee No. 2, *Hearings on H.R. 9832.* "Statement of Lt. Col. Grace M. King, U.S. Army Reserve," 226-37. King also argued that West Pointers had a distinct edge when it came to promotions, and that women could not compete fairly unless they were also admitted to the Academy.

[12] Janda, *Stronger Than Custom.*, 15-23.

[13] Stiehm, *Bring Me Men and Women*, 36-37.

[14] *Congressional Record*, 94th Congress., 1st session., House, 1975, 15450-51.

[15] Stiehm, *Bring Me Men and Women*, 2.

[16] Very few proponents in Congress took military views seriously. Representative Samuel Stratton of New York, for example, said the bulk of opposition to women in the service stemmed from "inertia and resistance to change," that "the services need qualified women today more than the women need the service academies," and that the oft-mentioned combat mission of the Academy was merely a smokescreen hiding "sophomoric, Neanderthal traditional practices that still apply at West Point. . . ." Ultimately, he said, the issue was "a simple matter of equality." See "Statement of Samuel S. Stratton, Representative from New York," 35-39, in U.S. Congress, House Committee on Armed Services, Subcommittee No. 2, *Hearings on H.R. 9832.* No doubt the low standing of the armed forces in the minds of the American public following Vietnam contributed to Stratton's dismissal of military opposition, and to the overwhelming majority which passed the legislation admitting women to U.S. service academies.

[17] *Congressional Record*, 1975, 15452-54.

[18] *Assembly*, December 1975, inside front cover.

[19] Ironically, West Point women were not the first to be recruited to a military school which stressed discipline and academics. Among the first in the United States were the women who attended Fairfield Seminary and Military College in the 1890s. Located in Fairfield, New York, the school modeled itself after West Point and served as a preparatory school for both sexes. See Susan Finlay Watkins, "It Is No Longer a Matter of Comment to See a Body of Young Ladies Under Military Training," *Assembly*, June 1980, 6-7.

[20] Letter from Lt. Gen. Sidney B. Berry to Col. E.H.B., 3 July 1975, 1, USMA files.

[21] "Address by Lt. Gen. Sidney B. Berry, Superintendent, United States Military Academy, Before the Defense Advisory Committee on Women in the Services," 16 November 1976, 6, USMA files.

[22] See Janda, *Stronger Than Custom*, 35-51.

[23] *Congressional Record*, 1975, 15449.

[24] Judith Hicks Stiehm, *Bring Me Men and Women*, 10; and a cadet interview (hereinafter referred to as CI) with Lance Janda, 24 June 1995, author's notes. I conducted interviews with over half the women of the Class of 1980. Each consented to an interview

with the promise their names would be kept in confidence. Some agreed to have their interviews tape recorded, and in those cases I have listed on which side of an audio tape their comments can be found. Others allowed me to prepare transcripts of their comments, and in those instances I have listed page numbers for their remarks. A handful preferred I take only handwritten notes, in which case I have used the phrase "author's notes".

[25] See Janda, *Stronger Than Custom*, 103.

[26] CI, 16 May 1997, author's notes; CI, 3 August 2000, author's notes; and a cadet exit interview (hereinafter referred to as EI), 8 May 1980, 5. Exit interviews with almost all of the women who graduated from West Point were conducted by West Point Historian Dr. Stephen Groves during the spring of 1980. The transcripts of those interviews are protected by privacy restrictions, but in many cases I was able to contact the female cadets in question and obtain their permission to review their remarks. Like the interviews I conducted, they are quoted anonymously.

[27] EI, no date, 5.

[28] EI, 17 April 1980, 12.

[29] EI, April-May 1980, 3.

[30] CI, 20 June 2000, side A.

[31] EI, May 1980, 8; and Rick Atkinson, *The Long Gray Line* (Boston, MA: Houghton Mifflin Company, 1989), 411.

[32] CI, 11 July 1996, side A.

[33] EI, 22 April 1980, 7, and CI, April-May 1980, 4.

[34] EI, 9 May 1980, 12.

[35] CI, 19 May 1996, side B.

[36] West Point is one of the nation's premier tourist attractions, drawing more than three million visitors a year. Prior to the terrorist attacks on New York City and the Pentagon on 11 September 2001, the Academy was also an open post, meaning cadets on parade, in formation near the barracks, or walking between classes were at the mercy of tourists and their cameras, and women cadets routinely drew a great deal of attention. Recent security changes have closed much of West Point to public access, but tour buses still crisscross the Academy grounds on a regular basis, and cadets still make jokes about the leering "Great American Public."

[37] EI, 9 May 1980, 18.

[38] Atkinson, *The Long Gray Line*, 411, 413.

[39] CI, 20 June 2000, side A.

[40] EI, no date, 10. It was a spurious claim. The Army football team did struggle during these years, but losing records were nothing new in the late 1970s. In 1973, for example, the "Black Knights" of West Point went 0-10, and were beaten 51-0 by the rival midshipmen of the United States Naval Academy.

[41] EI, May 1980, 18.

[42] EI, 17 April 1980, 6; and CI, 9 July 1996, side A.

[43] CI, 8 May 2000, author's notes.

[44] Graves Haydon Thompson, *Selections from the Ars Amatoria and Remedia Amoris of Ovid, with Introduction, Notes, and Vocabulary* (Hampden-Sydney, VA: Privately Published, 1953), 63. The original Latin phrase is "nil adsuetudine maius."

[45] CI, 16 May 1997, author's notes.

[46] The Naval Officer Candidate School (OCS) graduated its first co-ed class in 1973, while the Marine Corps followed suit in 1977. See Maj. Gen. Jeanne Holm, USAF (Ret.), *Women in the Military: An Unfinished Revolution*, Revised Edition (Novato, CA: Presidio Press, 1992), 192-203, 246-59, 270-71.

[47] Ibid., 270.

[48] These figures were current as of 2003. See Lory Manning and Vanessa R. Wright, *Women in the Military: Where They Stand*, 4th edition (Women's Research and Education Institute, 2003), 29.

[49] E-mail to the author from Kathryn Spurling, ADFA faculty member, 14 February 2002; and ibid., 28.

[50] Manning and Wright, *Women in the Military*, 10-11.

[51] Janda, *Stronger Than Custom*, 145.

[52] USMA Public Affairs Office Fact Sheet entitled "Women on USMA Faculty, 1976 to 1997," undated.

[53] CI, 11 July 1996, side A.

[54] Ibid.

[55] USMA Public Affairs Office Fact Sheet entitled "Women at USMA: Classes of 1980-2000." Between 1980 and 2000, 20,348 cadets graduated; between 1802 and 2000 the number of graduates was 57,518.

[56] Karen Fralen, "20th Anniversary of the First Women Graduates: Part II," *Gray Matter E-Mail Newsletter*, 16 June 2000, 4-5, and USMA, Public Affairs Office, telephone interview, 20 November 2000, author's notes.

[57] USMA Public Affairs Office Information Paper, received 12 October 2001, author's files.

[58] See http://www.us-irelandalliance.org/scholars/jeannie_huh_bio.phtml for a brief synopsis of Huh's West Point record.

[59] Letter from Sidney Forman to Lt. Gen. Sidney B. Berry, 22 July 1975, 2, USMA files.

[60] Robert Fix and Michael Linnington (both USMA Class of 2005) are the male cadets in question. Their mothers (Debbie Lopez Fix and Brenda Zachary Linnington) graduated from the Academy in 1981. Jennifer MacGibbon, the daughter of Kevin V. and Carol A. (Young) MacGibbon (both USMA Class of 1980) entered the Academy in the summer of 2003.

[61] The absolute number of women fighting in Afghanistan is small, but it should be remembered that 30 years ago there would have been no women in combat at all. In addition, the numbers will increase over time. Almost 14 thousand (13,935) women served in Bosnia during the late 1990s, while 5,660 saw duty in Kosovo. See Manning and Wright, *Women in the Military*, 3.

PART V:

EDUCATING FUTURE LEADERS

Introduction

In celebration of the West Point centennial in 1902, Academy leaders published a two-volume memorial containing, in part, histories of the ten academic departments: Chemistry; Drawing; Engineering; Law and History; Mathematics; Mineralogy and Geology; Modern Languages; Natural and Experimental Philosophy; Ordnance and Gunnery; Practical Military Engineering; and Tactics. The curriculums offered by these departments were much simpler than those of a century later. Their principal purpose was to "subject each Cadet . . . to a thorough course of mental as well as military discipline" necessary for success as an Army officer.[1] Hence, the cadets' entire curriculum was prescribed, with heavy doses of mathematics, science, and engineering. There was no allowance for discipline-specific majors, minors, or electives, and the only choice a cadet had was the language—French or Spanish—he opted to study.

The curriculum has changed dramatically over the past 100 years. Where there were ten departments then, there are now 13: Behavioral Science and Leadership; Chemistry and Life Sciences; Civil and Mechanical Engineering; Electrical Engineering and Computer Science; English; Foreign Languages; Geography and Environmental Engineering; History; Law; Mathematical Sciences; Physics; Social Sciences; and Systems Engineering.[2] A core curriculum still exists, but it now constitutes only about 75 percent, rather than the entirety, of the cadets' four-year academic program. Moreover, the core is now balanced between subjects in mathematics, science, and engineering on the one hand and humanities and social sciences on the other. The core curriculum, which comprises the "professional major" needed for a career as an Army officer, complements discipline-specific majors and the hundreds of elective courses offered by the departments.

The chapters that follow bring the academic history of the Military Academy up to date. Although not every department is represented, these nine chapters reflect the balanced curriculum that now defines the cadets' academic experience. They document the fundamental changes in the philosophy and structure of the academic program, as well as the organizational changes necessary for implementation. The evolutionary—in some cases revolutionary—advances in curriculum design and content, particularly over the last 50 years, challenge the notion that West Point is an irredeemably conservative institution.

Ironically, the changes documented in these chapters speak more of continuity than of change. Despite the tremendous growth in the number of majors and elective courses, the Academy's leadership is as committed now as ever to preparing graduates for a "lifetime of service" to the nation as commissioned officers. Leaders past and present may disagree on the best methods of doing this, but their goals are in consonance. The record of performance of West Point graduates during the 19th and 20th centuries is the surest evidence that the curriculum changes at West Point have kept pace with the changing security needs of the nation.

—Editor

---

[1] United States Military Academy, *The Centennial of the United States Military Academy at West Point, New York, 1802-1902*, vol. 1 (Washington, DC: Government Printing Office, 1904), 245.

[2] Between 1902 and 2002, the number, name, and organization of departments have changed frequently; the 13 departments listed here are the ones in existence at the time of this writing. A 14th department, Military Instruction, is organized under the Commandant of Cadets rather than the Dean of the Academic Board. Although not an "academic" department, it provides some of the instruction formerly offered by the departments of Ordnance and Gunnery, Practical Military Engineering, and Tactics.

CHAPTER 16

THE EVOLVING USMA ACADEMIC CURRICULUM, 1952–2002

George B. Forsythe and Bruce Keith

Introduction

The story of curriculum change, *any curriculum change*, is generally the story of an evolving consensus about what is valuable for students to learn. West Point's curricular history over the past half century is no exception. Curricular change normally involves several competing influences in a rational process informed by assessment data, changes in various fields of inquiry, and implicit or explicit judgments of professional requirements. At other times, the path selected is partially contingent upon the availability of resources. And certainly, such change is also political, manifested in decisions about competing values and dependent upon the strength of various actors in the pursuit of those values. Sometimes, curricular change is under the control of agents internal to the institution; often external forces are involved.

In this chapter, we summarize the evolution of the structure and content of the Military Academy's academic curriculum over the second half of the 20th century. We show how USMA has been responsive to a changing world and national security concerns that occurred between 1950 and 2002. Toward this end, we concentrate on two important issues. First, we document the evolving debate on the balance between curricular breadth and depth, focusing on prescriptive versus elective design. Second, we concentrate on the changes in broad subject areas in the core curriculum. Our focus is on curricular structure and not teaching practices. Moreover, we are oriented toward the history of organizational changes themselves rather than the actors involved in these changes. Throughout this chapter, we illustrate how the curriculum evolved toward a more balanced coverage of the arts and sciences, provided greater coherence within the core and concordance between the core and elective programs, offered increased opportunities for cadets to study fields in greater depth and choose courses consistent with their selected programs, and ensured that these changes reflected concerns over cadet time.

We attempt to capture this evolutionary process through an examination of six historical periods, to include 1962-1965, 1971-1978, 1982-1984, 1985-1990, 1993-2002, and 2005 and beyond. We selected these periods because they correspond with distinct shifts in the curriculum and involve unique configurations of political, rational, and external change agents. Furthermore, we selected 1952 as a reference point against which to document subsequent change. We chose this year, before the introduction of any elective courses in the curriculum, because it allows us to show how the curriculum evolved through the Cold War and into the post-Cold War era. From a historical perspective, the cross-sectional illustrations we present are likely to represent ideal typologies of curricular structures rather than the actual curriculum completed by any single graduating class covered during the period of our review. To illustrate, during this era, considerable curricular change occurred, particularly during the late 1960s and beyond; indeed, change occurred at such a rapid pace between 1967 and 1974 that the course structure presented in any particular catalogue may not adequately represent the actual curriculum taken by any of the four classes for which it was intended.[1] Thus, insofar as our challenge is to explain the historical patterns of curricular change at West Point, our presentation represents curricular trends and temporal themes and not necessarily the courses actually completed by any particular year group.

A Description of Curricular Change

The curriculum of 1952 was distinctly different from that of 2002; it was 32 percent larger, possessing 14 more core courses than did the curriculum of 2002. As we show in Table 16-1, of the 70 core courses for which instruction was offered between 1952 and 2002, only 16 (23 percent) were consistently maintained during the 50-year interval we reviewed. There were no electives in the 1952 curriculum; in 2002 cadets selected from one of over 25 majors or fields of study representing hundreds of elective courses. Despite these differences, there were important similarities between the two curriculums. The curriculums of 1952 and 2002 both possessed a set of common core courses to be completed by all cadets at the Military Academy. Although the balance between the two groups has shifted significantly, both curriculums combined a broad range of courses in the fields of mathematics, basic sciences, and engineering on the one hand, with courses in the humanities and social and behavioral sciences on the other. Indeed, Stephen Ambrose noticed these same similarities in comparing West Point's curriculum of 1965 with the underlying structure of its counterpart from 1820—a curriculum centered on a core program that offered instruction characterized by small sections, close supervision of cadets' work, frequent grading, cadet participation, and cadet assimilation of a large quantity of material.[2]

The academic curriculum of 1952 was characterized by its heavy emphasis on mathematics, science, and engineering. As shown in Table 16-1, of the 44 courses representing approximately 163 credit hours in 1952, 25 (112 credit hours) were in the mathematics, science, and engineering domain.[3] By 1963, the Military Academy required cadets to complete 48 courses, largely reflective of changes in the structure of several engineering courses. In particular, the 1952 versions of Electricity I and Electricity II were reorganized into four courses by 1963; moreover, courses on military topography and graphics evolved into two new courses in engineering fundamentals. This change produced an increase in engineering credit hours in 1963 relative to the 1952 curriculum. Certainly, the most momentous change during this era, as would become evident over time, was the introduction of electives into the curriculum.

Table 16-1. USMA Core Curriculum by Academic Year, 1952-2002.

Academic Program Core Courses	1952	1962	1972	1982	1992	2002
Academic Program Core Courses	44	48	40	30	31	30
Mathematics						
Algebra & Trigonometry	‖‖‖	‖‖‖				
Analytic Geometry	‖‖‖	‖‖‖				
Dynamical Systems					‖‖‖	‖‖‖
Calculus I	‖‖‖	‖‖‖	‖‖‖	‖‖‖	‖‖‖	‖‖‖
Calculus II	‖‖‖	‖‖‖	‖‖‖	‖‖‖	‖‖‖	‖‖‖
Differential Equations	‖‖‖	‖‖‖	‖‖‖	‖‖‖		
Probability & Statistics	‖‖‖	‖‖‖	‖‖‖	‖‖‖	‖‖‖	‖‖‖
Science						
Graphics I	‖‖‖					
Graphics II	‖‖‖					
Military Topography I	‖‖‖					
Military Topography II	‖‖‖					
Physical Geography		‖‖‖			‖‖‖	‖‖‖
World Geography		‖‖‖	‖‖‖			
Planetary Science			‖‖‖			
Introduction to Computing/IT I				‖‖‖	‖‖‖	‖‖‖
Information Technology II						‖‖‖
General Chemistry I	‖‖‖	‖‖‖	‖‖‖	‖‖‖	‖‖‖	‖‖‖
General Chemistry II	‖‖‖	‖‖‖	‖‖‖	‖‖‖	‖‖‖	‖‖‖
General Physics I	‖‖‖	‖‖‖	‖‖‖	‖‖‖	‖‖‖	‖‖‖
General Physics II	‖‖‖	‖‖‖	‖‖‖	‖‖‖	‖‖‖	‖‖‖
General Physics III			‖‖‖			
Engineering						
Electricity I	‖‖‖					
Electricity II	‖‖‖					
Direct & Alternating Circuits		‖‖‖	‖‖‖			
Power Circuit Machinery		‖‖‖				
Electronics		‖‖‖	‖‖‖			
Atomic & Nuclear Physics		‖‖‖				
Basic Electrical Engineering				‖‖‖		
Eng. Fundamentals I: Earth Measurements		‖‖‖	‖‖‖			
Eng. Fundamentals II: Engineering Graphics		‖‖‖	‖‖‖			
Thermodynamics	‖‖‖	‖‖‖	‖‖‖	‖‖‖		
Fluid Mechanics	‖‖‖	‖‖‖	‖‖‖			
Engineering Mechanics	‖‖‖	‖‖‖	‖‖‖	‖‖‖		
Mechanics and Materials	‖‖‖	‖‖‖				
Structural Analysis	‖‖‖	‖‖‖				
Structural Design	‖‖‖	‖‖‖				

	1952	1962	1972	1982	1992	2002
Academic Program Core Courses	44	48	40	30	31	30
Soils & Concrete	IIIIIIIII	IIIIIIIII				
Ordnance Engineering	IIIIIIIII	IIIIIIIII				
Ordnance Engineering	IIIIIIIII	IIIIIIIII				
Engineering Science I—Sequence			IIIIIIIII	IIIIIIIII	IIIIIIIII	IIIIIIIII
Engineering Science II—Sequence					IIIIIIIII	IIIIIIIII
Engineering Science III—Sequence					IIIIIIIII	
Engineering Design I—Sequence			IIIIIIIII	IIIIIIIII	IIIIIIIII	IIIIIIIII
Engineering Design II—Sequence					IIIIIIIII	
Humanities & Social Sciences						
English Composition	IIIIIIIII	IIIIIIIII	IIIIIIIII	IIIIIIIII	IIIIIIIII	IIIIIIIII
Literature	IIIIIIIII	IIIIIIIII	IIIIIIIII	IIIIIIIII	IIIIIIIII	IIIIIIIII
Advanced Composition	IIIIIIIII	IIIIIIIII	IIIIIIIII	IIIIIIIII	IIIIIIIII	IIIIIIIII
Advanced Literature	IIIIIIIII	IIIIIIIII				
History of the Military Art	IIIIIIIII	IIIIIIIII	IIIIIIIII	IIIIIIIII	IIIIIIIII	IIIIIIIII
History of the Military Art	IIIIIIIII	IIIIIIIII	IIIIIIIII		IIIIIIIII	IIIIIIIII
Constitutional and Criminal Law	IIIIIIIII	IIIIIIIII	IIIIIIIII			
Military Law	IIIIIIIII	IIIIIIIII	IIIIIIIII			
Constitutional and Military Law				IIIIIIIII	IIIIIIIII	IIIIIIIII
Foreign Language I	IIIIIIIII	IIIIIIIII	IIIIIIIII	IIIIIIIII	IIIIIIIII	IIIIIIIII
Foreign Language II	IIIIIIIII	IIIIIIIII	IIIIIIIII	IIIIIIIII	IIIIIIIII	IIIIIIIII
Foreign Language III	IIIIIIIII	IIIIIIIII	IIIIIIIII			
Foreign Language IV	IIIIIIIII	IIIIIIIII	IIIIIIIII			
General Psychology	IIIIIIIII	IIIIIIIII	IIIIIIIII	IIIIIIIII	IIIIIIIII	IIIIIIIII
Military Leadership	IIIIIIIII	IIIIIIIII	IIIIIIIII	IIIIIIIII	IIIIIIIII	IIIIIIIII
History, Government, & Geography I	IIIIIIIII					
History, Government, & Geography II	IIIIIIIII					
World or United States History I		IIIIIIIII	IIIIIIIII	IIIIIIIII	IIIIIIIII	IIIIIIIII
World or United States History II		IIIIIIIII	IIIIIIIII	IIIIIIIII	IIIIIIIII	IIIIIIIII
History of Modern Asia	IIIIIIIII	IIIIIIIII				
Comparative Government/Politics	IIIIIIIII	IIIIIIIII	IIIIIIIII			
Economics		IIIIIIIII	IIIIIIIII	IIIIIIIII	IIIIIIIII	IIIIIIIII
American Government/Politics		IIIIIIIII	IIIIIIIII	IIIIIIIII	IIIIIIIII	IIIIIIIII
International Relations	IIIIIIIII	IIIIIIIII	IIIIIIIII	IIIIIIIII	IIIIIIIII	IIIIIIIII
American Institutions				IIIIIIIII		
Philosophy			IIIIIIIII	IIIIIIIII	IIIIIIIII	IIIIIIIII

Curricular change persisted in the late 1960s and mid-1970s. The 1972 academic catalogue described a core curriculum consisting of 40 courses, with cadets required to select six electives.[4] Moreover, the number of engineering credit hours in the 1972 curriculum was, at 28.5, nearly half of what it had been 20 years earlier. The core courses in the curriculum continued to give way to an expanding electives program so that by 1982 there were only 30 core courses, constituting 104 credit hours.[5] In subsequent decades, the number of courses in the core curriculum remained essentially constant, with 31 in 1992 and 30 in 2002. However, during this period, the number of credit hours associated with the core gradually declined to 100 in 1992 and 97 in 2002.[6] Concurrently, the number of required elective courses shifted from ten in 1982 to nine in 1992 and ten by 2002.[7] Similarly, the credit hours associated with elective courses continued to rise, from five in 1962, to 15 in 1972, 24 in 1982, 27 in 1992, and at least 30 in 2002.[8]

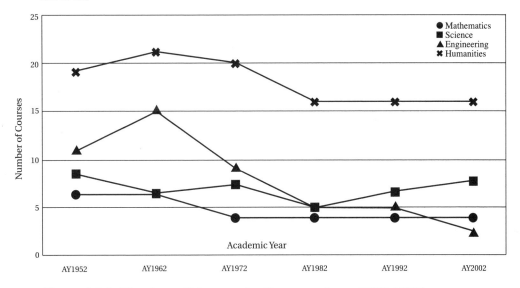

Figure 16-1. Number of Courses by Program Area, 1952–2002

Thus, as shown in Figure 16-1, the Military Academy has witnessed a gradual decline in the number of core courses while concurrently realizing an increase in the number of electives. Similarly, as illustrated in Figure 16-2, areas associated with engineering have seen the greatest decline in core credit hours between 1952 and 2002, from 64 credit hours in 1952 to nine credit hours in 2002 (a reduction of 86 percent). The areas associated with mathematics and the basic sciences also witnessed important but modest reductions during this same time interval, experiencing declines in credit hours of 33 and 40 percent, respectively. By contrast, the humanities and social and behavioral sciences have slightly increased their representation in the core curriculum during the past six decades, from 51 to 53 total credit hours (an increase of 4 percent). In sum, during the past 50 years, the academic curriculum at West Point has changed in two important ways: (1) a downward shift in the size of the common core curriculum, which was replaced by a much larger concentration of electives; and (2) a reduction of credit hours in the fields of mathematics, science, and engineering while largely holding

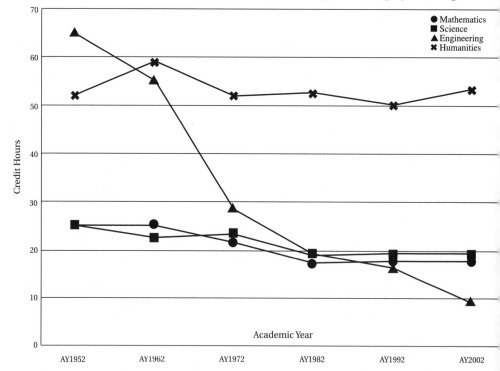

Figure 16-2. Number of Credit Hours by Program Area, 1952–2002

constant those in the humanities. Hence, by 2002, the courses in the humanities and social and behavioral sciences represented a much greater proportion of the core curriculum than they did in 1952 (55 versus 31 percent).

The curriculum of 1952 was prescribed in its entirety on the underlying assumption that the Military Academy, in preparing its graduates for a career as military officers, could identify a singularly "best" program of study.[9] Perhaps more important was the sense of tradition in the curriculum—it had always consisted of a prescribed common core, which was thought to establish a feeling of oneness and unity among the Corps of Cadets.[10] In 1960, shortly before his departure from West Point, Superintendent Lt. Gen. Garrison Davidson initiated the first curricular departure from this tradition by instituting elective courses to be taken during the First Class (senior) year.[11]

This initiative began with a report centered on the Army officer of the future. The report acknowledged concerns about choice, recommending that cadets be given opportunities to select electives during the First Class year.[12] This report, commonly referred to as the Ewell Report after the committee's chairman, Col. Julian Ewell from the USMA Department of Tactics, was followed by an internal review of the curriculum, which recommended, among other things, that "all departments provide at least one overload [i.e., additional to the prescribed core] elective course. . . ."[13] Not entirely satisfied with this recommendation, Superintendent Davidson convened an external curricular review group consisting of seven members and chaired by Frank Bowles, then President of the College Board. This team strongly recommended that the curriculum not include "overload" electives but instead institute a total of two elective courses with an additional two courses available to cadets who held advanced academic standing. In addition, this group recommended a balanced core curriculum that was slightly weighted in favor of mathematics, science, and engineering.[14]

Based on these recommendations, the Superintendent sought to provide electives for in-depth study, increase opportunities for acceleration within the curriculum, and expand the basic scientific content of the curriculum.[15] Ultimately, the Academic Board, swayed more by the tradition of a core, granted the inclusion of two electives and the opportunity for cadets to validate (i.e., receive credit based on equivalent study elsewhere) material in the core but did not permit substantive changes to the curriculum.[16] Nonetheless, this action set a precedent for adding flexibility to West Point's academic curriculum. By 1961, cadets were able to select two electives during their First Class year.

The next ten years witnessed major changes to the organizational structure of the academic departments and the curriculum. Several departments merged while others were renamed. For example, the department of Military Topography and Graphics became the Department of Earth, Space, and Graphic Sciences while the Department of Electricity was renamed the Department of Electrical Engineering. The Department of Chemistry and Physics was split into two separate departments. Moreover, Military Art was separated from Engineering, the latter being merged with the Department of Ordnance to become the Department of Engineering. Military Art merged with the Department of Social Sciences' history program to become the Department of History.

These organizational changes, along with the Superintendent's Curriculum Study of 1958-1959, resulted in several important curricular changes. By 1961, cadets were given an opportunity to select two electives from among 16 courses. This number was expanded to four electives by 1965. To offset the addition of two new electives to the curriculum, modifications were made to several engineering courses, particularly in terms of contact hours. For example, EL302—Power Circuits and Machinery, a two-credit course, was dropped from the core curriculum as was ME304—Engineering Mechanics II, a four-credit course.[17] During Academic Year 1970-1971, four areas of academic concentration were authorized, providing cadets with some measure of formal specialization in the selection of elective course work. Cadets were allowed to select a concentration in one of four areas: Basic Sciences, Applied Sciences and Engineering, National Security and Public Affairs, and the Humanities. To make room for these changes, the engineering curriculum was further reduced from 41 credits in 1966 to 33 credits in 1970. Specifically, the two courses in ordnance engineering and the two core courses in civil engineering were eliminated. Cadets, instead of completing these four courses, were given a choice of completing a two-course engineering sequence in either ordnance or civil engineering.[18] By 1973, cadets were allowed to select two additional electives, increasing to six the number of elective courses available. This addition was made possible by further reducing credit hours associated with core engineering courses; the number of courses remained the same (seven core plus a two-course engineering sequence) but the credit hours associated with these were reduced from a total of 33 to 28.5. Thus by 1973, because of significant reductions to the core engineering curriculum, cadets enjoyed far more choice in their course selection than their predecessors of 1960.

The Superintendent's Curriculum Review Study of 1972 sought to align the curriculum with nine USMA goals, in part by eliminating courses that did not clearly contribute to the Military Academy's mission.[19] During the next decade, the number of credit hours in core engineering courses was further reduced from 28.5 to 18.5. ME302—Fluid Mechanics served a dual purpose during Academic Year 1974-1975 in that it could be substituted as an elective for cadets pursuing an area in either the humanities or national security. By 1979, this course was completely eliminated from the core curriculum. The two-semester electrical engineering sequence was reduced to a single course on basic engineering in 1980, with a corresponding reduction from 8 to 4.5 credit hours. This change also resulted in the elimination of EE304—Electronics. Furthermore, the two engineering fundamentals courses, a mainstay in the curriculum dating back to the early 1950s, were removed from the core in 1982. This change eliminated the last remaining engineering courses of the Fourth Class (freshman) year. These adjustments created greater academic choice for cadets, more balance in the core curriculum, and enhanced opportunities for in-depth study.

Other important changes were made to the curriculum between 1973 and 1983. Calculus was reduced by five credit hours, from 14 to nine. A third semester of physics was removed from the curriculum (a loss of 3.5 credit hours), along with the two courses on environment (five credit hours); there was a one credit-hour reduction in the two chemistry courses (CH101 and CH102). Simultaneously, a course in computer programming (CS105) was added to the curriculum (3 credit hours), along with a 2.5 credit hour course on terrain analysis (EV203). The total impact on mathematics and science was a further reduction of nine credit hours from the core curriculum.

These changes were due, in part, to the cheating scandal of 1976. The Borman Report, an investigation of the incident by a special commission, concluded that cadets' time was overscheduled and recommended that the total number of courses and academic credit hours be further reduced.[20] The members of the commission concurred with a curricular study group's recommendation, released in 1977, that the number of courses in the curriculum be reduced further from 48 to 42 to more effectively balance cadet load. In this way, they were making a stand in favor of quality over quantity in course content and coverage.

In time, the spirit of this recommendation was implemented. By 1985, the core consisted of 31 courses with eight electives. Furthermore, the potpourri of engineering courses in the core curriculum was concentrated in a single engineering sequence with depth and coherence. The two-course engineering sequence was revised to include four engineering courses in a single field. By 1990, this sequence was expanded to five courses, providing cadets with a balance between engineering science and engineering design within the context of a single field. Cadets fulfilled their engineering requirement through the selection of one sequence from among six distinct engineering fields.[21]

After two decades of incrementally adding flexibility to the curriculum through elective courses, the Academic Board finally allowed for the creation of 16 optional majors beginning with the Class of 1985.[22] While the previous vehicle for specialization—the field of study—had provided cadets with an in-depth concentration of a selected field, the optional major allowed cadets to extend this depth component to a level more comparable to the disciplinary standards found at colleges and universities across the country.[23] The Superintendent's decision to create optional majors was due in part to the Military Academy's desire to seek accreditation of its engineering programs through the Accreditation Board for Engineering and Technology (ABET).[24]

While the majors and field of study concentrations provided cadets with opportunities to pursue study in a chosen field, the core curriculum retained a focus on preparing cadets for the multitude of challenges they were likely to encounter as Army officers. The Military Academy's internal self-study, completed in preparation for the 1989 reaccreditation by the Commission on Higher Education of the Middle States Association of Colleges and Schools (MSCHE), provided a venue in which to articulate the rationale and scope of the core curriculum. The Academic Program's stated purpose was to "enable its graduates to anticipate and to respond effectively to the uncertainties of a changing technological, social, political, and economic world."[25] Contributing to this overarching goal were a set of Academic Program goals intended to develop graduates who, as officers, could anticipate and respond effectively to change. Nine broad educational outcomes were established: creativity, moral awareness, skill in communication, commitment to continued intellectual development, engineering thought process, facility in mathematics and science, historical perspective, cultural perspective, and an understanding of human behavior.[26]

In noting the importance of intellectual preparation for future Army officers, USMA officials acknowledged in their institutional self-study report to MSCHE that demands on cadet time attendant to military and extracurricular activities made it difficult for cadets to achieve excellence in academics pursuits. The 1989 MSCHE accreditation team agreed with this perspective and encouraged USMA decision-makers to integrate the nine goals within the Military Academy's more comprehensive framework on leadership. Specifically, the MSCHE evaluation team recommended that greater attention be given to the integration of the academic, military, and physical education programs in the Military Academy's preparation of officer leaders.[27]

During the next several years (1994-2000), the Academic Program vigorously pursued the design, implementation, and assessment of cadet outcomes for each of the nine program goals. In 1994, the Dean and department heads adopted a system to assess the design, implementation, and outcomes of the Academic Program.[28] A multi-disciplinary faculty committee dedicated three years to the design of this assessment system. The resulting framework was cadet-centered and goal-based, responsive to educational decision-makers at all levels, methodologically sound, and focused on the improvement of cadet learning.[29] Faculty teams constructed learning models for each of the Academic Program's nine goals, which eventually were codified in a single document, *Educating Army Leaders for the 21st Century*.[30] These models became the basis for curriculum planning and assessment.[31] With the adoption of this system and its integration into educational planning, curricular change became primarily informed by the assessment of learning processes and educational outcomes.[32] These efforts marked a second major shift in the management of curricular change at West Point, a shift that was much more conceptual than structural. The addition of electives changed the structure of the curriculum. In linking the curriculum to educational goals relevant to the military profession, the Military Academy established a concept for managing curricular change that connects planning and assessment.

The most recent change to the curriculum occurred in 2000. Lt. Gen. Daniel Christman, then Superintendent, called for a review of the curriculum to ensure that the Military Academy was preparing cadets for the challenges of leading a diverse, globally engaged Army in an information-rich environment. His primary focus was on enhancing cadets' understanding of foreign cultures, but he encouraged a wider look at the curriculum with regard to the issue of cultural exposure. He challenged the Military Academy leaders to consider assessment results in light of changing Army needs, thus initiating a strategic review based on both internal and external assessments. This review resulted in the reduction of the engineering sequence from five to three courses while concurrently creating a required course in information technology (IT305) and an "integra-

> ## Table 16-2. USMA Academic Program Goals, 2002.
>
> **Graduates anticipate and respond effectively to the uncertainties of a changing technological, social, political, and economic world.**
>
> *Upon achieving this overarching academic program goal, graduates will be able to:*
> - Think and act creatively,
> - Recognize moral issues and apply ethical considerations in decision-making,
> - Listen, read, speak, and write effectively,
> - Demonstrate the capability and desire to pursue progressive and continued intellectual development,
>
> *and demonstrate proficiency in six domains of knowledge:*
> - Engineering and Technology
> - Math and Science
> - Information Technology
> - Historical Perspective
> - Cultural Perspective
> - Understanding Human Behavior

tive experience"—a culminating academic undertaking that would require cadets to consider the interplay of technological, social, political, and economic forces regarding issues relevant to their majors or fields of study. In addition, a tenth Academic Program goal was added, drawing attention to the importance of information technology. These goals, drawn from *Educating Future Army Officers for a Changing World*, are shown in Table 16-2.[33]

The Academic Program's overarching program goal was given a specific structure, within which the ten program goals were managed. Cadets' achievement of the overarching program goal was not represented simply by the accomplishment of the ten individual goals alone, but in addition by the integration of cadets' elective programs with the core curriculum. This amalgamation was achieved through the creation of an "integrative experience," a required component of each elective program that presents cadets with a complex but coherent problem or situation embedded in their selected program of study. The selected problem requires cadets to analyze uncertainties or potential change in each of four domains: social, technological, economic, and political. These domains constitute key components of the core curriculum. Cadets are expected to anticipate and respond to uncertainties in each domain as relates to the selected problem under investigation. Furthermore, the product of the integrative experience must be in the form of a concrete deliverable, such as a research paper, briefing, or project.

Discussion: Major Themes

Throughout the past five decades (1952-2002), the curriculum of the U.S. Military Academy has undergone a considerable metamorphosis. In 1952, it was heavily dominated by instruction in the fields of mathematics, science, and engineering, with 112 of the total 163 credits devoted to them. By 2002, 44 of the 97 total credit hours were located in the mathematics, science, and engineering fields. The percentage of mathematics, science, and engineering in the core curriculum has thus declined from 69 percent to 45 percent of the whole. What was once a predominantly engineering curriculum has gradually shifted toward a balance between the technical and social areas of study.

The impetus for curricular change at the Military Academy developed from a set of factors, perhaps best characterized as five distinct themes. First, the Military Academy's leaders came to recognize the need for greater depth—as opposed to breadth—in the cadets' educational experience. In the past five decades, the proportion of mathematics and science courses in the core curriculum has remained relatively constant. However, the engineering breadth of 1952 has given way to engineering depth through a narrow focus on one engineering sequence. Today, cadets select a major or field of study, which provides them with additional opportunities for the in-depth study of a field. Second, the Military Academy's leaders realized the need for better balance in the core curriculum between mathematics, science, and engineering fields and the humanities, social science, and behavioral science fields. In 1952, only 31 percent of the core curriculum was devoted to study in the humanities and behavioral and social sciences; in 2002, 55 percent of the core curriculum was devoted to these fields. Third, changes in the Army and throughout higher education made it desirable to offer cadets more discretion in fashioning their academic programs, thus leading to an evolution of the curriculum from one of complete prescription to one that offered choices, including the study of a particular academic discipline in greater depth. In 1952, cadets could express only a single course preference within the prescribed curriculum—which foreign language among German, French, Russian, Spanish, and Portuguese they would study (and even here their first choice could not always be granted). Today, in stark contrast, they can select from over 600 courses that span 24 majors. This change illustrates a commitment toward flexibility, allowing cadets opportunities for study in academic subjects that are of interest to them.

Fourth, persistent concerns over curricular depth, balance, and choice have gradually resulted in a curriculum that is much more coherent and integrated than its predecessor of 1952. The curriculum of 2002 is explicitly aligned with the Military Academy's published goals and the Army's perceived needs in a manner previously implicit at best. The current configuration of courses is carefully aligned with a set of ten Academic Program goals (Table 16-2), each being linked to several specific identifiable objectives. The curriculum of 2002 provides coherence, integration, and accountability to a much greater extent than was present in 1952. Fifth, the Military Academy's leaders have designed a curriculum that is sensitive to cadet load and the time demands imposed by the total USMA experience. The Borman Report brought to light the need to refine the curricular structure so that it enabled cadets to build the intellectual foundation necessary for success as commissioned Army officers and still have time and opportunity for military, ethical, physical, and social development.[34]

These five themes—study in-depth, balance, choice, coherence, and load—accurately represent the impetus behind curricular change at West Point. None of these factors was solely responsible for the evolution of the curriculum, but, taken together, they explain why West Point's curriculum changed in the manner depicted by our study. The 1958-1959 Superintendent's Study focused on flexibility and coverage. Over time, related concerns regarding curricular coherence and balance began to surface. Ultimately, with the advent of the 1976 cheating scandal, cadet load became a concern in its own right and concomitantly called for further attention to coherence and balance.

The early focus on breadth gave way to depth and cadet choice. The logic that culminated in the establishment of an electives program also led to a reexamination of institutional purpose and mission.[35] In time, Military Academy leaders adjusted the curriculum to align with specific educational and professional outcomes rather than prescribed disciplines associated with established departments. The first major paradigm shift occurred in 1961 when the Military Academy formally broke from a standard prescribed curriculum to include cadet choice in the selection of course work. The second occurred nearly 30 years later with a specific goal-based focus on the interplay of cadets' academic experiences. The second shift speaks to the power of goals and strategies for outcome assessment.[36]

Conclusion

West Point's process of curricular change was largely evolutionary, not revolutionary. Certainly, one can point to particular periods when greater change occurred in the curriculum relative to other eras. Nonetheless, the curriculum in 2002 is not so much the result of a single dramatic force as it is the gradual outcome of evolutionary growth. These curricular reforms were driven by both external and internal change agents. Superintendents' initiatives contributed to some of this change, as did concerns over the alignment of the curriculum around higher educational expectations and the changing needs of the Army. Throughout the past five decades, the Military Academy has retained a large core curriculum while increasingly providing opportunities for choice, depth, and integration. As with its forerunners, the present curriculum represents the rational and political consensus about how best to prepare cadets for service as

Army leaders. Nonetheless, the curriculum of 2002 will evolve further in the years ahead to remain responsive to the Army's evolving needs.

---

[1] This type of investigation would require an analysis of transcripts.

[2] Stephen E. Ambrose, *Duty, Honor, Country: A History of West Point*. (Baltimore, MD: Johns Hopkins University Press, 1966), 323.

[3] Credit hours were not calculated prior to the publication of the 1961 catalogue. Nonetheless, classroom contact hours were computed based on the number of classroom lessons and length of sessions. From this information, we were able to estimate credit hours in a manner that is comparable to those computed in the 1960s.

[4] United States Military Academy. *Academic Programs, 1972* (West Point, NY: Office of the Dean, United States Military Academy, 1972), 22-23.

[5] United States Military Academy, *Academic Program, AY 1982-1983* (West Point, NY: Office of the Dean, United States Military Academy, 1983), 39-41.

[6] United States Military Academy, *Academic Program, AY 1992-1993* (West Point, NY: Office of the Dean, United States Military Academy, 1993), 32-33; United States Military Academy, *2001-2002 Catalog* (West Point, NY: United States Military Academy, 2002a), 32-33.

[7] *Academic Program, AY 1982-1983*, 2-1; *Academic Program, AY 1992-1993*, 23; United States Military Academy, *Academic Program, AY 2001-2002* (West Point, NY: Office of the Dean, United States Military Academy, 2002b), 26.

[8] United States Military Academy *Academic Programs, 1963* (West Point, NY: Office of the Dean, United States Military Academy, 1963), 7-9; United States Military Academy, *Academic Program, AY 1972-1973* (West Point, NY: Office of the Dean, United States Military Academy, 1973), II-1, II-2; *Academic Program, AY 1982-1983*, 2-1; *Academic Program, AY 1992-1993*, 23; *Academic Program, AY 2001-2002*, 26.

[9] John P. Lovell, *Neither Athens Nor Sparta: The American Service Academies in Transition* (Bloomington: University of Indiana Press, 1979), 93.

[10] Lovell, 94.

[11] Ibid., 108-119.

[12] United States Military Academy, *Superintendent's Curriculum Study: Report of the Working Committee on the Present Curriculum and Future Trends* (West Point, NY: United States Military Academy, 1958).

[13] United States Military Academy, *Superintendent's Curriculum Study: Report of the Working Committee on the Present Curriculum and Future Trends*, VIII-15.

[14] United States Military Academy, *Report of the Curriculum Review Board* (West Point, NY: United States Military Academy, 1959), 2-3.

[15] United States Military Academy, *Annual Report of the Superintendent* (West Point, NY: United States Military Academy, 1959), 11.

[16] Lovell, 112-118.

[17] United States Military Academy, *Academic Programs, 1965* (West Point, NY: Office of the Dean, United States Military Academy, 1965).

[18] United States Military Academy, *Academic Program, AY 1969-1970* (West Point, NY: Office of the Dean, United States Military Academy, 1969), II-1, II-2, V-1-V29.

19 United States Military Academy, *A Study of the Programs of the United States Military Academy* (West Point, NY: United States Military Academy, 1972), 36-38.

20 The Secretary of the Army appointed a Special Commission on the United States Military Academy on 9 September 1976 to conduct an external assessment of the 1976 cheating incident that occurred in the EE304 course during the Spring term of 1976. Col. Frank Borman, USAF (Retired), was appointed as the chairperson of this special commission. The findings were published in *Report to the Secretary of the Army by the Special Commission of the United States Military Academy,* 15 December 1976.

21 United States Military Academy, *Academic Program, Volume II, Field Tables and Course Descriptions for AY 1989-1990* (West Point, NY: Office of the Dean, United States Military Academy, 1989), 23-26.

22 Letter from Lt. Gen. Willard W. Scott, Jr., USMA Superintendent, to Gen. Edward C. Meyer, CS Army, 26 October 1982.

23 Of the 16 optional majors made available to cadets, eight were in the Humanities and Public Affairs track while another eight were in the Mathematics, Science, and Engineering track. The former track included majors in Behavioral Sciences, Economics, Foreign Languages, Geography, History, Literature, Management, and Political Science; the latter track included majors in the fields of Chemistry, Civil Engineering, Computer Science, Electrical Engineering, Engineering Management, Engineering Physics, Mathematical Science, and Mechanical Engineering. For further information, see United States Military Academy, *Academic Program, AY 1983-1984* (West Point, NY: Office of the Dean, United States Military Academy, 1984), 4-2, 4-3.

24 United States Military Academy, *Institutional Self-Study: A Report to the Commission on Higher Education of the Middle States Association of Colleges and Schools in Preparation for the 1989 Decennial Reaccreditation* (West Point, NY: United States Military Academy, 1988), 34-35.

25 United States Military Academy, *Institutional Self-Study: A Report to the Commission on Higher Education of the Middle States Association of Colleges and Schools in Preparation for the 1989 Decennial Reaccreditation,* 28.

26 United States Military Academy, *Institutional Self-Study: A Report to the Commission on Higher Education of the Middle States Association of Colleges and Schools in Preparation for the 1989 Decennial Reaccreditation,* 28.

27 United States Military Academy, *Report to the Faculty, Administration, Superintendent, and Corps of Cadets of the United States Military Academy by an Evaluation Team Representing the Commission on Higher Education of the Middle States Association of Colleges and Schools* (West Point, NY: United States Military Academy, 1988), 39.

28 United States Military Academy, *Final Report of the Academic Assessment Committee* (West Point, NY: United States Military Academy, Office of the Dean, 1994).

29 United States Military Academy, *Educating Army Leaders for the 21st Century* (West Point, NY: United States Military Academy, Office of the Dean, 1998).

30 United States Military Academy, *Educating Army Leaders for the 21st Century.*

31 George B. Forsythe and Bruce Keith, "Assessing Program Effectiveness: Design and Implementation of a Comprehensive Assessment Plan," *Journal of Staff, Program, and Organization Development* (1999): 16, 19-34.

32 United States Military Academy, *A Decennial Assessment of the Academic Program: A Summary Report* (West Point, NY: United States Military Academy, Office of the Dean, 1999; Bruce Keith, Joseph LeBoeuf, Michael J. Meese, Jon C. Malinowski, Martha Gallagher, Scott Efflandt, John Hurley, and Charles Green, "Assessing Students' Understand-

ing of Human Behavior: A Multi-Disciplinary Outcomes-Based Approach Toward the Design and Assessment of an Academic Program Goal," *Teaching Sociology* (2002):30, 430-53.

[33] United States Military Academy, *Educating Future Army Officers for a Changing World* (West Point, NY: United States Military Academy, Office of the Dean, 2002), 6.

[34] *Report to the Secretary of the Army by the Special Commission of the United States Military Academy.*

[35] United States Military Academy, *Preparing for West Point's Third Century: A Summary of the Years of Affirmation and Change, 1986-1991* (West Point, NY: United States Military Academy, 1991).

[36] The evolutionary change described throughout this chapter has continued unabated at USMA. During 2003, the Academic Board eliminated the Field of Study as an option and adopted the major as a USMA graduation requirement, beginning with the Class of 2007. In addition, the established additional study-in-depth options, including the honors major and minor, remain. The USMA has a very well-defined core program of 30 courses that constitutes the professional major, plus a study-in-depth program that is standardized according to disciplinary best practices in American higher education.

CHAPTER 17

THE HISTORY OF HISTORY AT WEST POINT

Robert A. Doughty and Theodore J. Crackel

In 1801, when a military academy at West Point became a reality, and in 1802, when it received Congressional sanction, no thought was given to offering courses in any kind of history or, for that matter, in any of the humanities or social sciences. In its first years the Military Academy was little more than a small mathematics school, but it soon grew, and as it did its curriculum broadened. This is the story of the teaching of history—political, social, and military—at the U.S. Military Academy at West Point, and of the ultimate evolution of the Department of History there.

Political and Social History at West Point, 1808-1861

In its early years the Academy offered little more than mathematics and rudimentary military engineering, and, after 1803, drawing and French.[1] By 1808, however, Jonathan Williams, the first Superintendent, was considering an expansion of the curriculum—adding natural philosophy and engineering.[2] Joseph Gardner Swift, second in command of the Corps of Engineers and the Academy's first graduate, recommended that in addition cadets should receive instruction in ancient and modern history, geography, and morality.[3] It was the first suggestion that history should be taught at West Point, but Williams was not ready to go that far. He did, however, propose occasional instruction in architecture, chemistry, and mineralogy, but these subjects would be taught by visiting civilian professors.[4]

Williams also asked that the Academy be moved to Washington. Congress, however, ignored his requests and the Academy continued as it had for several more years.

Williams resigned in 1812, and Swift became Chief of Engineers and Superintendent of the Military Academy. That same year Congress finally authorized the curriculum changes Williams had recommended, and Swift immediately appointed professors of Natural Philosophy and Engineering.[5] In 1813 he secured approval to appoint a professor of geography, history, and ethics who would also serve as chaplain. His choice for the position was Adam Empie. Just how much history, geography, and ethics Empie taught is not clear, but given Swift's obvious interest, it is likely that some such instruction was presented. Alden Partridge, who supervised the Academy on a day-to-day basis during Swift's frequent absences, seems to confirm this—reporting that courses in geography, history, and ethics were then being taught as a regular part of the curriculum. The course, however, may have consisted wholly of lectures; no textbooks appear to have been purchased or assigned.[6]

In 1817, the arrival of Sylvanus Thayer marked the beginning of a new era in the academic life of the school. Chaplain Empie left that same year and was replaced by Thomas Picton. In 1818, Thayer and the academic staff drew up a plan for a four-year curriculum and implemented it the next year. That plan included "a course of Geography, History, Moral Philosophy and National law for the senior or First Class, to be pursued collaterally with" the engineering course which was given from early September through mid-March.[7] The chaplain's courses were taught sequentially—geography first, then history, then ethics, and finally, if there was time, law. Picton recommended as a history text Tytler's *Elements of General History, Ancient and Modern*, a Scottish work which had only recently come into print in the United States. The scope of the course was to reflect "the extent contemplated" by Tytler's text which covered ancient and modern history including the peace of Versailles in 1815.[8]

The course in geography was allotted the most time; it started in early September and continued into the first weeks of the second term. The balance of the second term was divided between history, ethics, and law. Picton's course in history, based on the Tytler text, likely began in mid-February and was finished by the end of March, consuming two hours each day except Sunday.[9] Ethics would have received about the same attention—early April to mid-May; law, a somewhat shorter term—from mid-May until the examinations in mid-June.[10] Picton taught these courses each year, from 1819 until he left West Point in 1825. His departure, unfortunately, marked the end of history instruction at West Point for more than a quarter-century.

Chap. Charles P. McIlvaine, who succeeded Picton, replaced history with a rhetoric course.[11] Over time, this component of the chaplain's course expanded to include grammar and belles lettres, as well as rhetoric. The reason for this change is not clear, but the lack of any record of a discussion concerning this change suggests some unanimity among the faculty. Possibly the incoming cadets' deficiencies in basic grammar—some could barely read or write—outweighed the perceived benefits of a course in history. Whatever the reason, for nearly 30 years the only history cadets received was the little bit they might glean from the courses in geography and constitutional law.[12]

In 1854, when the Academy introduced a five-year curriculum, the "English Studies" course was expanded and given to both the Fourth Class and the new Fifth Class. At that point Chap. William T. Sprole added instruction in history to his Fifth Class course. At first, the subject seems to have been limited to a brief view of the history of the United States, using Benjamin Lossing's *Pictorial History of the United States*.[13] The next year the chaplain expanded the history program, adding a course in general history for the Fourth Class—using Weber's *Outline of Universal History*.[14] Chaplain Sprole left West Point in 1856 and was replaced by John W. French. Shortly thereafter the Fourth and Fifth Class English courses (with the history component of the latter) were consolidated in the Fifth Class curriculum. It appears that the new course consisted of English in the first term and history in the second. In this reorganization the Lossing text was dropped, and the focus of the course became European history.[15] Cadet William H. Harris, who was taking the course in 1858, wrote twice of it to his father. In January he reported that he was studying the Persian Wars. By April the class was examining recent European history: "In History," he wrote, "we have been studying the French Revolution and Napoleon's campaigns and these have come hard to me as I have never read much about them, but I have 'maxed' it so far on them. We have a large room in the Academic Building, on the walls of which are painted very large maps of Napoleon's campaigns. It is called the 'Napoleon room' & cadets are taken in there to study his marches and battles. The officers are very particular about the study of all military campaigns and they are generally well 'posted' on them, so that the study is interesting."[16]

In the fall of 1858, French added a history segment to his First Class ethics course—again using Weber's *Outline of Universal History*. Although it is not certain, it is likely that this new (probably brief) component focused on the history of the United States, for the Weber text did include a section that would support such instruction.[17]

Despite the attraction of things Napoleonic or the utility of American history, both courses were discontinued in the early fall of 1861. With the coming of the Civil War, the War Department directed that the five-year course be abandoned. The Academic Board adopted a four-year curriculum which did not include history. It would be another two decades before modern history would again be presented to cadets at West Point.

The Science of War and Military History, 1802-1871

More often than not, instruction at West Point in what was called the "Science of War" was conducted as a part of the course in engineering. Military history—to whatever degree it was offered from year to year—was usually taught in conjunction with it. But even that was slow to develop. In 1802 only rudimentary engineering ("the elements of fortification") was offered, and it was more than a decade before any formal training in the science of war was offered.[18] Military history was an even later addition. Nonetheless, despite discussion of some of Napoleon's campaign in the chaplain's on-again, off-again course, the tradition of teaching both the science or art of war and military history as a part of the engineering curriculum was established by the end of the Civil War.

Alden Partridge, who stayed at West Point as an instructor after graduation in 1806 and did not leave until Thayer arrived in 1817, is reported to have had a special fondness for drilling the cadets. He is said to have demonstrated ancient battles to them in the process. Be that as it may, little else that resembled either military art or military history was presented at West Point in the Academy's first years. It was not until after Thayer's arrival in 1817 that any formal course in the military art was conducted.

Immediately upon assuming the superintendency at West Point, Sylvanus Thayer arranged for the translation of a text that he had seen being used at the Imperial Polytechnic School in France—Gay de Vernon's *Traité élémentaire d'art militaire et de fortification*.[19] The first volume was ready for use by that fall, and in December Thayer urged the translator, John M. O'Connor, to complete the last volume. "It is all important," he wrote, "that the studies of the class should not be interrupted."[20]

The Gay de Vernon text contained all that was envisioned by Thayer in the course in military engineering and the art of war, but O'Connor added an appendix on the principles and maxims of war. In this he drew on such military writers as Guibert, Lloyd, Templehoff, and Jomini.[21] Of these, said O'Connor, Jomini stood out: "[His] work is considered a masterpiece, and as the highest authority. Indeed no man should pretend to be capable of commanding any considerable body of troops, unless he have [sic] studied and meditated on the principles laid down by Jomini."[22]

In 1819, grand tactics—an element of the military art—was made an explicit part of the engineering course, but it was offered only to the first (most advanced) of the two sections of the First Class. The "Grand Tactics" element of the course was described as "Organization of armies, Marches, Orders of Battle, Battles, General Maxims deducted from the most important operations, [and] Castramentation"—the latter being the arrangement of encampments.[23] The second section, using only the first volume of Gay de Vernon's work, was restricted to the study of field engineering.[24] The Academy continued to use O'Connor's translation of Gay de Vernon into the mid-1830s, but it is doubtful that cadets in either section were ever assigned the appendix that would have exposed them to the teachings of Jomini. Neither Claude Crozet nor David B. Douglas, in turn, the professors of engineering from 1817 until 1830, seems to have had much interest in strategy or grand tactics. Crozet complained that the subject was left to him in 1819 when no other professor would take it.[25] Douglas, in turn, was absorbed in adding civil engineering to the course.[26] By the 1830s, the teaching of grand tactics had been almost wholly abandoned.

Even Dennis Hart Mahan, who took over the Department of Civil and Military Engineering in 1830, and who is thought to be the father of American military strategic thinking, seems to have had little affection for Jomini. He was particularly put off by O'Connor's presentation of that Swiss theorist in his appendix to the Guy de Vernon work; it was too abstract, too lengthy, and too pedantic, he thought.[27] Mahan moved as quickly as he could to replace Gay de Vernon's work with engineering texts of his own and simply ignored grand tactics. In 1833, the Board of Visitors noted in their report that "the Principles of Strategy or Grand Tactics" were not being presented and suggested that they "might be taught with advantage." At the same time the board recognized the practical difficulty in doing so. "It is true that there is no work treating of those subjects," they wrote, "which is sufficiently condensed and at the same time unexceptional in its principles and illustrations." Still, they suggested that "the same industry and talent which has furnished text books in other departments of military science might be employed for this purpose with great success, and furnish a series of lectures embracing a definition of the technical terms, and of such general principles as admit of the clearest and most exact illustrations."[28]

Mahan, however, did not immediately take up the challenge. At the time he had more immediate concerns with the engineering course itself, and over the next several years he produced a series of texts for the technical side of that subject.[29] It was not until 1847 that Mahan completed *Outposts*—his own attempt to present the subject of grand tactics at a level appropriate to the students who would soon be Army lieutenants.[30] Even in this work, however, Mahan did not feel it necessary to illustrate his points with historical examples.

Possibly he believed that because *Outposts* was designed to teach the conduct of operations of small independent bodies of troops, historical examples of larger battles and campaigns did not serve a useful purpose. His usual excuse, however, for not offering historical studies was that there was simply not time in the course for them.[31]

Although Mahan did not favor including military history as a discrete course in the Academy's curriculum, he did believe in its later study as an element of an officer's program of professional development. At West Point, he started the Napoleon Club where officers studied and discussed the battles and campaigns of that famous soldier. He also came, in time, to believe that military history could be useful to illustrate specific points—particularly in a lecture format. In 1854, when the academic program at the Military Academy was expanded from four to five years, he sketched out a series of lectures in military history for use in teaching the science of war. To support these lectures, however, he said that he needed large maps of campaigns which he hoped would be painted on the walls of the section rooms.[32] This project—lectures and classroom maps alike—seems somehow to have languished.

Nonetheless, Mahan's suggestion may have loosed the spirit of reform within the Academy's Department of Engineering. In June 1857, Mahan and his engineering course were attacked for being out of date, the attack coming from Lt. James St. Clair Morton, acting assistant professor of engineering under Mahan. Morton sent a paper to the Board of Visitors in which he argued for a complete restructuring of the engineering course. Regarding the sub-course on the Science of War his recommendations included: (1) broadening the Outposts course by adding "a foreign text book, possibly in French, on strategy and the art of war," (2) adding a new course in military history which would cover the campaigns of Frederick and Napoleon—a course that would be taught, not by Mahan, but by the chaplain's department in conjunction with its modern history offering, and (3) adding to the course on fortifications examples from the Crimean War which had ended just the year before.[33] That Morton went over Mahan's head to the board strongly suggests his belief that the professor would not make changes such as these without pressure from the outside.

The Board of Visitors applauded Morton's suggestions and appended them to their report. "We are fully persuaded that the best interest of this institution and of the army at large requires a careful and liberal consideration of the paper," they wrote, adding that "the spirit of reform which it exhibits cannot fail . . . to produce the most beneficial results." Much of what Morton had suggested, said the Board, was a "subject of discussion" often heard "in the engineering branch of the service."[34]

Mahan complained to Secretary of War John B. Floyd that the Board of Visitors had not consulted him at all on Morton's paper, and he objected to the implication "that a spirit of reform and improvement has not been exhibited in this department." He had been occupied for some time, he said, in identifying the changes necessary in his courses.[35]

Floyd, however, was unsympathetic. Two years later, after Mahan had made little or no progress in modifying either his courses or his texts, the Secretary decided that "important advantage probably would result by transferring from the Department of Engineering to that of Tactics . . . all that relates to Strategy, General Tactics, Army Organization, &c."[36] The matter was soon put before the Academic Board, with Floyd offering the board no choice. It complied, placing under the Commandant of Cadets that portion of the engineering course indicated by the Secretary and moving the instruction from the First Class to the Second Class year. The transition was made in Academic Year 1859-1860. That year Mahan gave the strategy course to the First Class, while the Commandant presented it to the Second Class.[37]

The Commandant, in teaching the strategy course to the Second Class in the spring of 1860, had been quick to make changes in the texts. He retained Mahan's *Outposts* but added Jomini's *Art of War*,[38] extracts from McClelland's *Military Commission to Europe*,[39] and Thomas Thackeray's *Military Organization and Administration of France*.[40] Mahan, for his part, also used the Jomini and McClelland books and his own *Outposts,* but not Thackeray.[41]

In June 1860, as the Commandant was preparing to assume full responsibility for the strategy course, Congress established a commission that was to examine the organization, discipline, and instruction at West Point.[42] The commission, informally called the Davis Commission because of Senator Jefferson Davis's key role in establishing and then chairing it, first met at West Point on 17 July 1860. They soon began to hear testimony on the broad range of subjects under their charge, including suggestions concerning the new strategy course.

Lt. Richard Dodge of the Tactical Department, who was teaching the new course, said that the new texts were good choices and suggested that the course would improve as it evolved. His immediate concerns were practical ones—the lack of maps and inadequate time devoted to the subject. There was, he said, "barely sufficient [time] to give the cadet a tolerable knowledge of the principles of the art; while a proper application of those principles, which should be the true object of study, is, and must of necessity be, almost entirely neglected." Dodge then described the conduct of the course: "The heads of the subject under discussion are written on the board, the subject itself explained and discussed in detail, elucidated by such examples from history as come within the knowledge either of the cadet or instructor."[43]

In his testimony Mahan told the commission that the frequent change of the Commandant "may render it difficult always to have in the position a person competent to teach the subject of strategy, military history, etc. If the Commandant has not been a reading man, nor prepared by precise study, the course would suffer. The officer who would make the best commandant might from having been on active service, without opportunities for study, be deficient in the proper requirements . . . to master the course."[44]

The Davis Commission applauded the changes that had been made at Floyd's direction, but its own recommendations were soon overcome by events.[45] The election of Abraham Lincoln in the fall of 1860 not only brought a new administration to Washington but also triggered the secession of the southern states and the creation of the Confederacy with Jefferson Davis at its helm. In Washington after that, everything with any connection to Davis became anathema, and the Davis Commission's recommendations were soon buried and forgotten.

Nonetheless, the changes that the Commandant made had seemingly breathed new life and vigor into the teaching of military art (and military history) at the Academy, but all of that quickly changed with the outbreak of war. In the spring of 1861 the Second Class curriculum (including the strategy course) was concluded a few weeks ahead of schedule, following which the Second Class was given a much abbreviated version of the First Class course and graduated a year ahead of schedule as the class of June 1861.

Events then conspired to return the strategy course to Mahan's Engineering Department. When the Civil War began, the Academy moved to a four-year curriculum that the Academic Board had designed in 1858.[46] This had the effect of restoring the course in strategy to Mahan. A new superintendent, Alexander Bowman, raised no objection, and the new Secretary of War, Simon Cameron, was much too occupied with the war to give the issue a second thought.

Mahan immediately dropped the new texts that had been adopted by the Commandant, including Jomini's work, retaining only his own *Outposts*. He did, however, begin to restructure the course to include more historical examples—though it could still hardly be called a military history course. By the spring of 1862, he had added a short series of lectures in which he introduced a few of Napoleon's campaigns, although here Mahan focused almost entirely upon the tactical positions involved.[47] At the same time, moreover, Mahan revised his *Outposts*, adding a new chapter titled "Principles of Strategy and Grand Tactics" which summarized some of Napoleon's most celebrated campaigns. The revised text was issued late in 1862.[48]

In 1865 Mahan again expanded the military history content of the course with the addition of a description of the sieges at Sebastopol, Vicksburg, and Fort Wagner.[49] In 1868, the Board of Visitors remarked positively on the results: "First in order was the examination of the first class in *Engineering and the Science of War*. The topics principally discussed were: the mechanics of engineering, fortifications, and a consideration of the great campaigns and actions in history, from the earliest times. Among those actually recited on were the battle of Zama, Leuthen, and other campaigns of Frederick, several of Napoleon, and, in the recent war, Antietam, Gettysburg, Nashville, the siege of Fort Wagner, the great campaign from the Rapidan to the surrender of Appomattox, and a general discussion of the defense of the Atlantic coast." The board underscored "the importance of discussing these great campaigns, especially those of Napoleon, because they establish principles which are of the greatest value to the military student, and draw how conformity to these principles leads to success, while a violation of them must end in disaster."[50] Mahan must have appreciated the board's positive view of the work he had accomplished. It contrasted sharply with the criticism he had received a decade earlier.

The Military Academy had offered very little in the way of military history in the years before the Civil War, and even in the early 1860s only threats and coercion seemed to have moved Mahan to incorporate it into his course. Still, by the time of his unfortunate death in 1871, Mahan had expanded the historical lectures given by his department to encompass 14 battles (from Leuctra in 371 B.C. to Wagram in 1809) and five campaigns—addressing events as recent as the campaign and battle at Nashville in 1864 and the Sadowa campaign of the Austro-Prussian War in 1866.[51] The strategy course had belatedly (and somewhat begrudgingly, it seems) become a course in military history—and such it would remain.

Political and Social History at West Point, 1861–1969

In the years before the Civil War the Academy had offered ancient or modern history for only two brief periods—from 1814 to 1825, and from 1856 to 1861. In the next century of the Academy's existence, history would fare better, although not so much in the early years of that era.

After modern history was dropped from the curriculum in 1861, there was no apparent effort to reestablish it until Chaplain William M. Postlethwaite arrived in December 1881. Postlethwaite immediately added lectures on universal history to those he gave on ethics to the Fourth Class. Then, in the fall of 1884, after three years of "patient and persistent endeavors" at the meetings of the Academic Board, he convinced his colleagues to reinstate formal courses in geography, history, and ethics for the First Class.[52] Postlethwaite's new course in world history met three times a week for two hours (some 50 lessons) during the fall term. In that course he used Swinton's *World History* as a text and also Labberton's *Historical Atlas.*[53]

At Postlethwaite's death in 1896, the responsibility for teaching history (other than military history) was transferred to the Department of Law, which then became the Department of Law and History. In September 1896, under the new auspices, the course was expanded, meeting twice a week in both semesters of the First Class year. The added lessons allowed the cadets to complete the study of ancient history in the first term and to take up medieval and modern history in the second. Over the next five years several texts were used,[54] but in 1900 the department settled on Duruy's *General History of the World.*[55]

In 1906 the department began to experiment with the course. The length was curtailed, and it was offered only in the fall term (54 lessons). In addition, attention was newly directed to sociology and political science. To accomplish these additions the text was supplemented by articles such as "The Origin of the Village Community," "The Oriental Empires," and "Tax-taking and Legislating Empires." In addition, lectures by Prof. James H. Canfield of Columbia University augmented the readings and the classroom work. Canfield's topics included: "The Advance Made by the Greeks," "What the Germans Have Accomplished," "The Influence of France," and "The Place and Value of the English."[56] The course continued on much this same line until 1908, when the Department of English and History was created.

John C. Adams, a Yale graduate, was hired in 1908 to head this new department. At the same time the course was moved from the First Class to the Fourth Class year. There is no record of which text Adams used during this first year, but the course purported to have "for its object a proper knowledge of social and political science and the development of present national and municipal governments; historical geography with special reference to military geography."[57] The next year (AY 1909-1910) the focus of the course was shifted further—eliminating all vestiges of ancient and medieval history. Now the course was to cover "political, social, and economic history from the end of the Middle Ages to the present day," and the forms and practices of modern government.[58] The texts then introduced were Schevill's *Political History of Modern Europe*, and Robinson and Beard's *Development of Modern Europe*.[59]

When Adams was replaced in 1910 by Lucius Holt, also of Yale, the course already established was continued, but with two additional texts: a book of readings in modern history by Robinson and Beard, and Gettell's *Introduction to Political Science*.[60] The next year Holt dropped Schevill's text and replaced it with Hazen's *Europe Since 1815*.[61] Holt fine-tuned the program in subsequent years, often substituting his own texts for outside readings. In 1915 he replaced the Gettell book with his own *Introduction to the Study of Government*, and in 1918 he dropped the Robinson and Beard reader, and added two texts of his own—first, *History of Europe, 1862-1914*, in 1918, and then *History of Europe, 1789-1815*, in 1919.[62]

In 1921, the Department of English and History was effectively split into the Department of English and the Department of Economics, Government, and History, although the new arrangement was not formalized until 1926. When the two new departments were first created, the history course was shifted from the Fourth Class to the Third Class year, but it followed the same general plan devised by Adams over the years since 1908. Although it was ostensibly a course on the history of Europe "from the outbreak of the French Revolution to the present day," it delivered a significant dose of political science as well.[63] That general outline was followed until 1925, when the top section was given a mini-course on United States history while the lower sections were being examined.[64] The mini-course proved popular and was retained.

In 1925, Holt chaired the First Class Committee of the Academic Board and conducted a study of how "better coordination in the History instruction at the Academy" might be achieved. The study proposed the revision of the courses in both political and military history. For Holt's course the committee recommended an 80-session "survey of general history from ancient times to the present."[65] In the process, the new course shed the political science elements that had been part of it since 1906. To accomplish this change, Holt abandoned the Hazen volume and his own text on the era of the French Revolution and Napoleon, substituting for them Meyers's *General History*[66] and Robinson's *History of Western Europe*;[67] two years later he added Webster's *History of the Modern World*.[68] Holt left the Academy in 1930 and was replaced by Herman Beukema, who would later become a distinguished presence in the Department of Social Sciences. Holt's influence lingered, however. The course he had crafted in 1925 was maintained with only incidental text changes until the start of World War II.[69]

In 1935, Beukema made a perceptive and interesting change in the mini-course that was first offered a decade earlier. The topic was changed from recent U.S. history to history of the Far East, using Vinacke's *History of the Far East*.[70] In 1942, the material developed in this mini-course on the history of the Far East was incorporated into the general program, using the Vinacke text. At the same time, a new mini-course in Latin American history was developed using Kirkpatrick's *Latin America, A Brief History*.[71]

In September 1942, the new term began under the four-year plan, but, barely two weeks into the course, the Academy moved to a three-year curriculum. The course in European history was reduced from 80 to 60 lessons and the special mini-course in Latin American history for the upper sections was replaced by two even briefer offerings—the "American Problem of Government" and the "Governments of the Major Foreign Powers." In 1943, these two courses were incorporated into the general curriculum. Four years later, the last year of the three-year curriculum, the history course was dropped for a year as part of a transition to a four-year curriculum in which the course would be offered to the Second Class rather than the Third Class.

The new four-year curriculum in 1948 provided for a history course in the Second Class year to be conducted by the Department of Social Sciences—as the old Department of Economics, Government, and History had been redesignated. This new two-semester course (roughly 65 lessons) once again abandoned ancient and medieval history in favor of a more detailed look at the history of modern Europe. The text chosen initially for the history course was

Schevill's *History of Europe.*[72] It was replaced in 1952 by R. R. Palmer's *History of the Modern World*, followed in 1953 by C.J.H. Hayes's *Modern Europe to 1870.*[73] Still, the focus of the course remained on the history of modern Europe.

In 1957, George A. Lincoln, now the head of the Department of Social Sciences, modified the course once again by inserting some American history. The intent was to provide "an integrated survey of the history of Europe and America since 1500 with emphasis on the interrelationship of European and American developments."[74] At the same time, a course in Modern History of the Far East was added to the curriculum and was also taught in the Second Class year. In 1960, the department began a complicated transition involving a shift of the survey course in European and American history from the Second Class to the Third Class year. At the same time the course in Asian history was moved to the First Class year and then dropped altogether shortly thereafter.

By the fall of 1962 (AY 1962-63), the transition was completed and the new two-semester survey course, now given to the Third Class, was in place. The fall semester of the new course covered the history of Europe to 1900; the spring semester was divided into two parts: a history of America to 1900, followed by instruction on Europe and America from 1900. This design persisted until 1969, when the Social Sciences Department surrendered its modern history program to the newly formed Department of History.[75]

For a few years, in the late 1950s and early 1960s, qualifying examinations were given in the history of modern Europe and America. Those who passed were allowed to take a more advanced program— History of Russia and History of the Middle East—in lieu of the usual survey courses. That program was dropped after 1962.[76]

In 1963, in place of the "advanced" courses, the department began to offer a seminar program which carved out of the survey course a few class meetings that would be devoted to study in depth of one period or subject selected from the historical time-frame of the course. In 1963, two seminar topics were offered, and the cadets were asked to choose which they preferred. By 1969, as many as eight different seminar topics were offered in each semester of the survey course. Typical of these were: Napoleon and the Americas; The Social and Political Impact of Industrialization, 1750-1848; The American Revolution; and The Role of Ideas in Shaping the Eighteenth Century Revolutions.[77] These seminars were popular with cadets and even more popular with the faculty.

Filling out the modern history offerings of the Department of Social Sciences were the electives. In 1959, the Academic Board allowed cadets to take two electives, and in 1965 two more were added. By 1969 the Social Sciences Department offered cadets three electives in history: History of Russia, History of U.S. Foreign Relations, and Seminar in History.[78]

This was the nature and scope of the modern history program—survey courses and electives—passed from the Social Sciences Department to the new Department of History in 1969.

Military Art and Military History at West Point, 1871–1969

Junius Wheeler, who became Professor of Engineering following Mahan's death in September 1871, inherited the engineering course, including its science of war component. The new academic year was already under way, and Wheeler made few, if any, immediate changes. The following year, however, told a different story. In the Science of War course, Wheeler dropped Mahan's *Outposts* and replaced it with Dufour's *Strategy and Tactics.* He retained Dufour's work until 1879, when he introduced his own book, *Elements of the Art & Strategy of War.*[79] Upon Wheeler's retirement in 1884, James Mercur took the helm of the department. Like Wheeler, Mercur did little innovating, and the science of war course remained very much the course Mahan had created. In 1879, Mercur introduced his own *Elements of the Art of War,*[80] but his text, like Wheeler's, was largely a revision of Mahan's *Outpost.* Neither work expanded the use of military history in any significant way.

It was not until Gustav Fiebeger took the reins of the engineering department from Wheeler in 1896 that military history came into its own at West Point. In 1899, Fiebeger replaced Mercur's text with Arthur Wagner's *Organization and Tactics and Service,* a work widely used in the active service.[81] In the years that followed, Fiebeger began to expand the science of war program. In 1906 he assigned pamphlets prepared by the department on strategy, campaigns, and battles. At the same time, he added his own text, *Battle of Gettysburg*,[82] and the Army's *Field Service Regulations*. By 1910, the course had come to embrace "the study of the organization of armies, employment of the different arms in combination, logistics, and strategy"—all taught largely through the medium of the history of some 20 battles and campaigns. The introduction of his *Elements of Strategy* (1911) continued to broaden the application of military history. This work is replete with examples drawn from a wide range of battles and campaigns that illustrate Fiebeger's points, and it demonstrates his extensive reading of military history and his remarkable grasp of the subject.[83]

In 1913, Fiebeger introduced the "staff ride" concept that had become popular in the Army itself and took the First Class cadets in the course on a visit to the battlefield at Gettysburg.[84] The course continued as he had laid it out until it was abridged in AY 1917-1918 as a result of U.S. entry into World War I. His "course in military art and history" had come to comprise the "study of the organization of armies, elements of strategy, and the development of the military art as shown in military history."[85] In AY 1921-1922 the Engineering Department taught the first complete military science and history course since 1917. In the years between, the course had been stitched together differently for each successive class—abbreviated in one form or another for each. Fiebeger retired in 1922, but the course that was his legacy had truly become during his tenure a course in military history.

Fiebeger's successor, William Augustus Mitchell, started down the same path. He did make some changes in the course—omitting "the detailed study of the campaigns of the Civil War and [substituting] therefor the campaigns of the World War." At the same time, Mitchell reorganized the department, dividing the instructors into two groups—one teaching military engineering and the other teaching military history.[86] This approach seemed promising, but it was aborted in 1923 when military history came under unexpected attack by the Army outside the Academy's walls.

That year, the Department of the Army dictated that the military science and history course go to the Tactical Department.[87] In the years after World War I, the Army reexamined the courses taught at its various schools. Military history had played an important part in the development of professionalism in the prewar Army, but in the years immediately after the war its role had diminished.[88] In 1922, the McGlachlin Board examined the Army school system and, among many other things, questioned the use of military history. The Board complained that West Point was not adequately preparing cadets to perform the duties of a second lieutenant. Academics should give way to tactical training, it said.[89]

When the War Department approved the McGlachlin Board's recommendations, Mitchell immediately sought permission to drop military history entirely.[90] In the end, the military art course was not given at all to the Class of 1924. The Commandant, who was once more to take over the military art course, offered to fill the gap in history as well. In October 1923, the Academic Board agreed, and on 1 January 1924, the transfer was completed.[91] The Department of Tactics first taught the course in AY 1924-1925.[92]

In 1925, after the first iteration of the course by the Commandant, the First Class Committee of the Academic Board, under the chairmanship of Lucius Holt, looked at the history being taught at the Academy and submitted "an outline of a proposed revision of the courses in Political and Military History, planned to assure better coordination in the History instruction at the Academy." The military history course the committee proposed would "trace the development of the principles, technique, and methods of tactics, and to a very minor extent, of strategy, during the entire historical period. To this end, campaigns and battles will be described in greater or less detail as may be necessary to give particular illustrations of the principles and developments enunciated." The course would consist of 13 periods and would be conducted largely as lectures, they suggested, until a satisfactory text could be identified.[93] The program was dramatically reduced from what Fiebeger had offered and was modest even in comparison with what Mahan had provided in the years just before his death. Still, it is likely that 13 periods was as much as the times would allow.

The Commandant divided his course into two parts. The first part, military art, was to prepare new graduates to exercise tactical command as platoon leaders and to understand their role as a part of the combined arms team. The course consisted of 35 periods devoted to lectures on the organization, tactics, and techniques of the separate branches, written reviews (examinations), and map problems. The second part of the course, military history, consisted of 13 periods—11 devoted to lectures and two to examinations. The lectures were on decisive battles from ancient to modern times, showing what took place on the field of battle and explaining the principles of war involved. Toward the end of the course, each cadet wrote a short paper on a military topic.[94] The course began about the first of September and continued until late October.[95] The text for the first part was *Command, Staff, and Tactics* until 1926, when it was replaced with *Tactics and Techniques of the Separate Branches*.[96] There was no text for the military history segment.

In 1928, the Academic Board decided to return the course in military art and history to the Department of Civil and Military Engineering, and Mitchell set the instructors of the department to writing a series of pamphlets covering different eras of military history. These were ultimately combined into his *Outlines of the World's Military History*.[97] Possibly Mitchell had enjoyed some epiphany relating to the subject, or more likely he began to realize that the engineering his department was teaching was becoming increasingly vulnerable to attack from without and within, and that military history might not be subjected to these same forces. The latter motive would certainly have been prescient in the light of later events, for in the next decade more and more of his engineering course was parceled out to other departments. As the years progressed, the Engineering Department taught less and less engineering and more and more military history. In recognition of this, in 1943 the Department of Civil and Military Engineering became the Department of Military Art and Engineering (MA&E). The military art course grew from 48 sessions in 1929 to 50 in 1930, then 69 in 1933, and finally to 92 in 1935. It remained at 92 class sessions until World War II. During the war the course again grew—finally reaching 101 sessions in September 1945.[98]

As the course added hours it broadened in scope, a development reflected in the choice of texts. By 1935, Mitchell added Dodge's *Napoleon,* and two texts on the Civil War—the first by Ropes and Livermore, and the second by Woods and Edmonds.[99] Mitchell also used pamphlets created within the department dealing with selected subjects from World War I.[100] As more and more hours became dedicated to military history, the course lost its earlier, more formal attention to army organization, equipment, and duties.

By 1938, when T. Dodson Stamps became Professor and Head of the department, the Art of War element of the engineering course had once again become a military history course. Stamps, in fact, now used the term "military history" to describe the course in the annual reports.[101] Stamps adjusted the course in only minor ways, but did select new texts in 1940,[102] picking Dodge's *Captains,* Jomini's *Life of Napoleon,* Steele's *American Campaigns,* and McEntee's *Military History of the World War.*[103] In 1942, the course entailed a study of "the great captains prior to Napoleon, Napoleon's Campaigns, the Civil War, the World War, and the present war."[104] In 1943, the department issued its own text on three of the world's great military thinkers, *Jomini, Clausewitz, and Schlieffen,*[105] and added it to the reading list.

During World War II, the department prepared a number of pamphlets on various American campaigns. These were used as texts in examining the ongoing war effort in the last lessons of the military art course. These pamphlets turned out to be popular throughout the Army; "almost every day requests are received for copies."[106] By 1944, the department was using in class ten of these pamphlets and the U.S. Army Signal Corps films of the same campaigns.[107]

In 1946, the department began a series of "great leader" lectures, and, the following year, introduced "a short reading subcourse . . . during which the cadets read two notable books on military history."[108] The course continued with only minor modifications until 1948, when a four-year curriculum was reinstated. At that time, Dodge's *Captains* was dropped along with the subcourse on great captains before Napoleon, and Jomini's work on Napoleon was replaced by Wartenburg's *Napoleon as a General.*[109] In 1950, Stamps and Vincent Esposito, the deputy head, introduced their own *Short*

History of World War I to replace McEntee's work on that war. In 1954, their *Short History of World War II* replaced the pamphlets the department's instructors had prepared during that conflict.[110]

Esposito took over the department upon Stamp's departure in 1956 and began to reshape the course in his own image. In 1957, he reintroduced two subcourses—the first on great captains before Napoleon, and the second on some of the world's most influential military thinkers and interpreters. He also included two texts written by members of the department: *Great Captains before Napoleon* and *Jomini, Clausewitz, and Schlieffen.*[111] Esposito then put the instructors to work once more, creating new texts and revising the older ones, while he himself undertook two new books, *The West Point Atlas of American Wars* (1959) and *A Military History and Atlas of the Napoleonic Wars*[112] (1964). New editions were issued of *Great Captains Before Napoleon* (1965) and *Jomini, Clausewitz, and Schlieffen* (1967), and, in 1968, the department published *Revolution in America, 1775-1783.*[113] Beginning in 1968, the department's own texts became the books prescribed for the military history course—now called "History of the Military Art." The sole use of department-prepared materials was justified by the explanation that, although there were "many excellent books on most phases of the course," they were not sufficiently condensed to be "managed by cadets during the time available for preparatory study."[114]

By 1968, the Department of Military Art and Engineering also offered three courses as electives: Revolutionary Warfare, Evolution of Modern Warfare, and Twentieth Century Warfare. These elective courses plus the flagship core course, History of the Military Art, comprised the package that the deputy head of the department, Thomas Griess, carried with him when he became the first Professor and Head of the new Department of History in 1969.

Creation of the Department of History, 1958–1969

In the late 1950s and early 1960s, the Military Academy completed several studies in which the role and contribution of history were studied carefully. This period of assessment began in November 1957 when the Superintendent, Lt. Gen. Garrison H. Davidson, initiated a broad effort to examine the curriculum of the Military Academy with a view toward instituting reform. Most appropriately, the effort began with a careful look at historical aspects of the curriculum for the period, 1802-1945.[115] It continued with the appointment of a board of officers to look toward the future and assess the "qualities and attributes which will probably be essential to an officer of the Regular Army during the period 1968-1970." As chair of this board, Col. Julian J. Ewell was directed to "make a comprehensive and critical self-evaluation to determine whether our curriculum as presently constituted provides the best means of meeting the probable requirements of the next couple of decades."[116] In its report of January 1958, the Ewell Board foresaw the Army's entry into an era of enormous change, observing, "[R]evolution rather than evolution will characterize future changes in the Army and in the art of war." In its consideration of the revolution in military art and science," the Ewell Board strongly supported the study of history, recommending that each officer be provided "a firm basic knowledge of fundamentals on which he can continue to build throughout his career." Two important parts of this goal were "knowledge of military art and science derived from the study of military history" and "better knowledge of history and geography—particularly of our allies."[117] In a separate report the Ewell Board also discussed the "advisability of electives" and supported offering "a few elective courses" during the cadets' First Class year.[118]

General Davidson next appointed a committee to study the curriculum. In November 1958 the Evaluation Committee, chaired by Col. Walter J. Renfroe, Jr., completed its work. The committee recommended creating a single engineering department by combining the Department of Ordnance with the engineering component of the Department of MA&E. Renfroe's committee also looked at combining the History of the Military Art (HMA) component of the Department of MA&E with the leadership component of the Office of Military Psychology and Leadership (MP&L), but concluded that leadership instruction should remain under the Commandant.[119] The issue of history in the curriculum also arose in a study General Davidson asked Col. Richard G. Stilwell and two other officers to conduct on the military and physical programs.[120] Colonel Stilwell, who later became Commandant of Cadets, strongly supported taking HMA from MA&E and merging it with MP&L's leadership program, but the narrow focus of his committee limited his suggesting any major changes in organization. In the end the committee's report said nothing about merging military history and leadership into a single department, but it did offer a ringing endorsement of the reading of military history and further strengthening of the military heritage course taught by the Department of Tactics with the assistance of the Department of MA&E.[121] Another committee looked more broadly at the Military Academy but also addressed curriculum issues and academic organization. This group, like Renfroe's Evaluation Committee, saw the wisdom of combining the engineering component of the Department of MA&E with the Department of Ordnance. Although the report said little about history other than military history itself, it did suggest that the cadet begin his "studies of the social sciences" in his Fourth Class year.[122] Like the other reports, the tone of the final report was very conservative and cautious, and those seeking dramatic changes in the Military Academy's curriculum were disappointed.

In late 1960 and early 1961, the Military Academy looked seriously at making significant changes in the organizations and responsibilities for teaching history. In January 1961 an ad hoc subcommittee of the Curriculum Committee considered various combinations of history of the military art, military fundamentals, military heritage, leadership, and history, which were being taught by several different departments at the time. The subcommittee also considered the creation of a new department with responsibilities for instruction in military art, leadership, and military heritage. Lt. Col. George A. Rebh, a member of the Department of Social Sciences, was chair of this subcommittee. His report observed:

> The regular HMA course is unique to the Military Academy. Neither of the other Service Academies nor any known civilian school teaches a course like it. This uniqueness stems primarily from the stated purpose of the course—to trace the evolution of the art of war . . . . The uniqueness of the

HMA course has gained for itself a wide and favorable recognition. This recognition together with the acceptance of
department-prepared texts and the proficiency of its personnel have resulted in a significant non-teaching workload.[123]

Though the report did not address the combining of all history
courses under a single history department, it did note that there was
greater similarity between the history taught by Social Sciences and
that taught by MA&E than between the leadership taught by MP&L
and the history taught by MA&E. The subcommittee also noted that
instruction on "military heritage" had a direct relationship with the
military art instruction and was in fact an "adjunct" of the HMA
course.[124] Despite these observations, the subcommittee offered
no recommendations for fundamental changes in organizations or
responsibilities.

The Dean of the Academic Board, Brig. Gen. William W. Bessell,
Jr., responded to the cautious report by forming another committee
and directing it to review the Rebh Subcommittee report and make
further recommendations. While the Rebh Subcommittee included
no department heads, the new subcommittee included three department heads (Lincoln from Social Sciences, Esposito from MA&E, and
Russell K. Alspach from English). This subcommittee also recommended against any major changes except for the creation of a separate Department of Military Art if the engineering component of the
Department of MA&E was combined with the Department of Ordnance.[125] Apparently impatient for change, the Superintendent, Maj.
Gen. William C. Westmoreland, directed the Commandant and Dean
in June 1961 to examine the matter of separating the Department
of MA&E into two departments. The Superintendent proposed that
"the Department of Military Art expand its coverage to a sequential
course involving all four classes [and] absorbing the course by the
Tactical Department on military heritage, the scope of the course to
include heritage, military history, and the historical study of leadership." He also proposed leaving the Office of MP&L under the Commandant, but shifting its focus to "the practice of military leadership
and management."[126]

Despite all these careful analyses of curriculum and organization, no real changes occurred in the late 1950s or early 1960s. The idea of combining "heritage, military history, and the historical study of leadership" remained under discussion for a short while, but the departure of General Westmoreland from West Point and the retirement of General Bessell as Dean drained momentum for the effort to merge the three subjects. In the late 1960s, however, an opportunity for changes in the responsibility for history appeared again with the retirement of the Head of the Department of Ordnance. Those desiring to form a separate Department of Engineering from the engineering courses in the Department of Ordnance and the Department of MA&E moved quickly, thereby reopening the question of the disposition of the "military art" component of MA&E.[127]

The opportunity to form a Department of History could have slipped away, but Colonel Griess, then the Deputy Head of MA&E, succeeded despite the ardent opposition of Colonel Lincoln, the Head of the Department of Social Sciences. The issue of creating a Department of History by combining military art with the history courses taught by the Department of Social Sciences came up first in deliberations of the National Security and Public Affairs Committee (consisting of the heads of the departments of Social Sciences, Law, MP&L, and MA&E). Despite the strong objections of Colonel Lincoln, the NSPA Committee recommended that "a Department of History be established concurrently with a Department of Engineering to consist initially of those courses in HMA and related electives."[128] The NSPA Committee recommended the new department be formed on 1 September 1969 and the "modern" history core courses and electives from the Department of Social Sciences be added a year later. At the NSPA Committee and the Academic Board meetings, Colonel Lincoln supported formation of a Department of Military Art but objected strongly to moving the modern history courses and faculty from his department.[129] In his minority report, Lincoln made several points, but the crux of his argument appeared in his assertion that "history is the core of the Social Sciences at USMA." He explained, "There may be some feeling that the Department is primarily a 'political science' department. More correctly, it is an integrated, interdisciplinary entity focused around a history course." He added, "[H]istory belongs with political science—to which it is intimately tied—rather than with Military Art, to which it is but distantly related."[130] Despite Lincoln's objections, the Academic Board approved by a vote of 13 to 3 on 6 November 1968 the formation of a Department of History.[131] On 15 June 1969, the Department of MA&E was formally "terminated" and the Department of History established.[132]

Department of History, 1969–1990

The first years of the Department of History's existence proved to be busy and challenging. Building a cohesive team from the officers who had come from two different academic departments required much of Col. Griess's time and effort. Friction came not only from their somewhat different approaches to history but also from age differences, the officers who came from MA&E generally being more experienced and older than those who came from Social Sciences. The Department gradually jelled, however, as the faculty worked together to offer strong history courses to cadets. Shaping healthy, stimulating elective programs also proved challenging. Cadets initially chose a broad area of concentration and then an elective field within that concentration. Those cadets who were interested in history chose National Security and Public Affairs as their area of concentration and then chose either the History Field or the Military Studies Field.[133] Cadets also could take history electives as part of other fields. The number of electives increased from six in AY 1970-1971 to seven in AY 1977-1978.[134] By the late 1970s the Department of History had strong core and elective programs.

As Colonel Griess worked to consolidate and improve the new department, he embarked on a massive rewrite of the instructional materials for the core military history course. In a memorandum written in 1974 to explain the philosophy and process involved in the rewrite, Griess summarized the revision that had been "worked out in 1965-1968." He wrote:

> My experience leads me to believe that it is very difficult to find any group of commercial texts which provide the coverage this unique course requires or which the cadet can afford

> or master in the time allowed. For this reason, we have
> begun to develop our own texts; I have no illusion, how-
> ever, about how these texts will continue to be refined by
> succeeding generations of instructors. At the same time,
> when suitable extracts or small texts are in print and can
> be folded into readings, I have no bias against leaning on
> such scholarship.

He also explained the decision to "abandon" the "text-atlases" on Napoleonic and American wars: "Their coverage is too narrowly oriented and the price of reprinting has become a problem. Moreover, the maps can be better designed to suit our purposes." The project involved not only writing new texts but also providing extensive "Notes for Instructors." Sensitive to possible criticisms of inflexibility, he wrote, "Conceived some years ago in recognition of the tremendously broad scope of the subject of military history, they [the notes] reflect an attempt to guide the instructor to more effective and stimulating teaching. They should assist him in being more discriminatory in his preparation, but they are not intended to restrict his academic freedom or to curb his initiative."[135] Slowly but surely, Griess's efforts to provide special materials for the core military history course yielded several volumes of what came to be known as the "Gray Books."

Under Colonel Griess's leadership, the Department soon began to play a leading role in reminding the Army of the importance of military history and in providing experienced, academically qualified officers to teach officers in other Army or military schools, and to lead and manage that academic effort. Evidence of this contribution is most apparent in Griess's chairing the Department of the Army's Committee on the Army Need for the Study of Military History in the early 1970s[136] and in the leading role departmental alumni played in the creation and founding of the Combat Studies Institute in June 1979 at the Command and General Staff College at Fort Leavenworth.[137] The flow of talented and dedicated departmental alumni into the Army's school system ensured a high level of excellence that otherwise would not have been attainable.

Despite the success of the Department, the Military Academy modified the history program substantially in the wake of the 1976 cheating scandal. Prompted by the West Point Study Group,[138] the Curriculum Committee and General Committee reviewed several alternatives for modifying the core curriculum. The existing curriculum included 48 courses, seven of which were electives, but the suggested alternatives had only 28 or 30 courses in the core curriculum.[139] During the period 12-16 December 1977, the General Committee met in three formal sessions and one informal to analyze and debate the curriculum alternatives. As noted in a memorandum from Col. Jack M. Pollin to the Superintendent, Lt. Gen. Andrew J. Goodpaster, "little general support" existed among the department heads for any of the three main alternatives considered. Pollin added, "[T]o adopt an institutional curriculum which does not have a reasonable measure of support from the faculty would be tragic."[140]

Pollin noted, however, that nine members of the General Committee would support a revised 31-course core curriculum. When all the discussions ended and the decisions were finally made, the Military Academy had only 31 semester-long courses in the core curriculum, three of which were history. The number of courses in the core curriculum had gone from 41 to 31. Cadets were required to take two semesters of "modern" history (with 40 lessons in each semester) in their Fourth Class year and one semester of military history (with 62 lessons) in their Second Class year. The Department of History also offered a two-semester military history course (HI387-302) which replaced the one-semester military history course (HI300 or 400) but required the use of one elective. About one quarter of the cadets chose the HI387-302 sequence, which strongly resembled the two-semester course of the past with 47 lessons in each semester.[141]

The reduction from two semesters to one in the core course on the History of the Military Art disrupted Griess's careful planning and preparation. Moreover, the challenge of providing cadets a solid foundation in military history in one semester proved formidable. In November 1979 a study of possible modifications to the one-semester core course (during the first semester in which the abbreviated course was taught) complained about having to reduce substantially the coverage of the period prior to World War II and emphasized the need to find new readings for the compressed lessons on the Napoleonic Wars and World War I if such a modification occurred.[142] Col. Roy K. Flint, who headed the teaching of military history concluded, "Experience with the new format has convinced the Department of History that it cannot inculcate cadets with what they need to know about their profession in one term—even a long one."[143]

The Military Academy's decision to reduce the core military history course from two to one semester brought outcries from all quadrants. One of the most articulate objections came from Gen. Garrison H. Davidson, the former Superintendent who had led the effort to reform the curriculum in the late 1950s. In a carefully crafted letter in July 1983, Davidson complained, "The paucity down through the years of such instruction [in the history of the military art], so basic to the very art the Academy was and is supposed to teach, never ceases to baffle me." He emphasized:

> Study of the use of the history of the military art to derive wisdom from the past is a fascinating experience and represents the only way by which the soldier can gain vicarious experience in his profession. The deeper one delves into the subject, the more impressed he becomes, not only with the benefits that can derived, but more importantly, with the uncertainties and the dangers of superficiality in the considerations.[144]

Other criticisms came from outside the military. Jeffrey Record, for example, chastised all the service academies for their inadequate emphasis on history, concluding starkly, "Ignorance of history is dangerous."[145]

At the end of the first year under the new curriculum, the Dean of the Academic Board, Brig. Gen. Frederick A. Smith, Jr., asked each department head to make an "interim evaluation" of the new curriculum. Other reviews occurred as the Military Academy approached the 1980 Decennial Accreditation by the Middle States Association of Colleges and Schools. Despite positive comments in the institutional report prepared for the 1980 Decennial Accreditation,[146] many of the department heads and faculty had strong reservations about aspects of the new curriculum. Those reservations soon resulted in an extensive evaluation of the academic program. During the same period the Military Academy considered seeking accreditation from the New York State Accreditation Board for Engineering and Technology (ABET) and establishing majors. In March 1981 the Curriculum Committee provided an assessment of areas for "potential reform," including improvements in the course in the HMA. The committee's report stated:

> The "History of the Military Art" is a preprofessional intellectual experience essential to the preparation of cadets for officership because it provides a vicarious involvement in war and the acts and decisions that officers must make. Reducing that course to 62 lessons and compressing it into one term severely limited coverage of the historical evolution of tactics, weapons, strategy, leadership, military institutions, and their dynamic relations with social, economic, political, and technological change. Consequently cadets can no longer develop historical-mindedness so essential to the analysis of developments that even now shape the future character of war and of their profession. With a limited grasp of the antecedents of modern warfare, cadets have difficulty understanding the reasons for its present character; with an even less adequate grasp of cause and effect in war's evolution, cadets cannot sense the impact of processes that have altered—and continue to alter—the nature of war over the long sweep of history.[147]

In October 1981 the Academic Board met to discuss the transition to a new curriculum. That transition included changing the one-semester core military history course to a "two-semester, 40-lesson per semester course in AY 83-84."[148] Although the transition affected almost every academic department, the Academic Board approved it unanimously.[149] The last rendition of the one-semester military art course occurred in AY 1983-1984.

A new emphasis on history, particularly military history, appeared at the Military Academy when Lt. Gen. Dave R. Palmer became the

Superintendent in July 1986. From 1966 to 1969 Palmer had taught military history in the Department of MA&E, and he obviously aimed to make the place of history more significant within the overall curriculum. Shortly after his arrival he authored a paper in which he outlined the concept of military history as the flagship academic area. This concept paper began with a definition:

> Military History occupies a preeminent position as the flagship of the cadet's academic and military development at the United States Military Academy. By virtue of the emphasis and resources it receives within the West Point experience, Military History is the discipline that charts, illuminates, and focuses the cadet's intellectual preparation to practice the art and science of war. Military History signals to the cadets, the Army, academia, and the American people the unique mission of the United States Military Academy— to prepare its students for professional service as officers of the Regular Army.[150]

As part of the "flagship" effort, the Superintendent convened a special committee to assess the teaching of history and the degree to which "historical mindedness" permeated activities at West Point. Composed of four distinguished historians who viewed the 1971 report of the Ad Hoc Committee on the Army Need for the Study of Military History as a model, the committee completed its report in December 1988, offering several suggestions. While the overall tone of the report was positive, the committee recommended moving the HMA course to Third Class year, providing an "overall conception" for military heritage, and hiring a few civilian faculty members with PhDs in history. The committee, however, recommended against creating a master's degree program in military history at West Point, one of the prime objectives of the Superintendent.[151] While Palmer's interest and emphasis produced hopes in the Department of History for additional resources and visibility,[152] very little changed except for the addition of "historical mindedness" to the academic program goals of the Military Academy.[153] The idea of military history being the "flagship" of the curriculum did not resurface after Palmer departed West Point.

As the Department of History focused on teaching history in the 1980s and 1990s, it responded to the changing international situation and the ending of the Cold War. One of the most important changes during this period involved the deletion of the core course in European history and its replacement by a world history course.[154] Colonel Flint, who succeeded Griess as the Department Head, initiated the change. The Department had introduced a world history survey course in AY 1977-1978,[155] and for a number of years cadets took either American, European, or world history as their core two-semester history course in their Fourth Class year. The last offering of the European history course occurred in AY 1985-1986. As the world history course evolved, the faculty debated issues pertaining to teaching such a broad course: area or regional coverage (Europe, Latin America, Middle East, Africa, or East Asia); themes (political, economic, social, diplomatic, or cultural); chronological starting and ending points; and reading materials. Other changes occurred in the core HMA course. One of the main achievements proved to be the preparation of another military history text, a task begun reluctantly because of the huge effort expended in the writing of the Gray Books in the 1960s. After a ten-year effort, the new textbook was finally finished in 1995.[156] In addition to providing more flexibility in the course and more opportunity for outside readings, this two-volume anthology titled *Warfare in the Western World* facilitated the Department's efforts to place greater emphasis on the post-Vietnam period and to include more coverage of "small wars" and "wars of intervention."

Other changes in the Department affected the electives program. These included such adjustments as compressing the courses on the History of Russia and History of the Soviet Union into a single-semester course on the History of Russia and modifying the elective on the History of Revolutionary Warfare by taking a broader perspective than the 1960s focus on "communist insurrections."[157] All in all, these changes illustrated the Department's continuing commitment to adjusting the curriculum to help prepare cadets for the challenges they could face in the evolving international environment.

The Department also remained attentive to providing outreach to the Army. An example of such efforts appeared in 1984 when Lt. Col.

Kenneth E. Hamburger and a group of officers from the Department of History completed a study for the Officer Personnel Management System Study Group.[158] The study focused on leadership in combat, and a shortened version eventually was assigned for use by the U.S. Army Cadet Command for instructing ROTC cadets in leadership. The Department also continued offering the Summer ROTC Fellowship. Beginning in the 1960s the Department had offered a summer program in military history for officers assigned to teach history in Army ROTC programs. In the early 1980s, however, after the Army decided to have civilian professors from the universities at which ROTC was offered teach the required military history course, the summer program was offered only to civilians and quickly became widely acclaimed. The committee that reviewed "historical mindedness" in 1988 had described the Fellowship as a "national treasure," observing that "no program radiates within and outside our Army with greater influence in the military history field than the ROTC workshop."[159] Although funding remained problematic, the Department continued having approximately 30 university professors spend a month at West Point during the summer to study the teaching of military history. Other contributions included sending officers on temporary duty to various military operations: two officers joined combat units in the Persian Gulf War, one officer served as a historian with Allied forces entering northern Iraq after the war, and another as a historian with Operation Uphold Democracy in Haiti.[160]

Amidst this success serious questions about the place of "modern" (or non-military) history in the core curriculum appeared with the appointment of Brig. Gen. Gerald E. Galloway, Jr., as Dean of the Academic Board. In his first visit to the Department in August 1990, he received a briefing about its organization and program and asked, "Why do you need two semesters to teach plebe history?"[161] That question proved to be the opening shot in a campaign to address "culture" more explicitly in the core curriculum. In August 1991, after Lieutenant General Palmer departed, Brig. Gen. Galloway directed the Curriculum Committee to assess "what is needed and whether we now have . . . enough [culture]" and consider "whether it would be advisable to add a formal course to solve the problem (real or perceived) of inadequacy of cultural education in the baseline curriculum."[162] Much of the discussion in various committees formed to address different aspects of culture focused initially on defining the term culture, a task that proved daunting because of the different methodologies of the social sciences, behavioral sciences, and humanities. In other discussions the Department was required to explain its coverage of culture in the history courses taken by Fourth Class cadets as part of the core curriculum. Moreover, the Department was put in the position of having to defend not only offering two semesters of American or world history but also offering American history at all. In the end the Academic Board agreed that the plebe history courses provided excellent coverage of culture, and the Department refined its system and criteria for deciding whether Fourth Class cadets would take HI103-104—History of the United States, or HI107-108—History of the World.

As the second century of the Military Academy's existence drew to a close, the Department of History continued to educate and inspire cadets. Upon his retirement in 1981, Colonel Griess observed, "History will judge whether USMA made the correct move in creating a Department of History. I remain convinced more than ever that it did."[163] Evidence of the Department's success in educating cadets appeared in the distinction that history majors achieved in the national essay contest sponsored by Phi Alpha Theta (the national honor society for history). A national committee accepted papers each year from students who were members of Phi Alpha Theta and selected the best ones. Between 1997 and 2002, individuals who had majored in history at the Military Academy won 22 of the 30 national awards, including six first-place winners, an achievement unmatched by any other institution in the nation. A more important indication of success, however, came in the number of graduates who had majored or concentrated in history and who remained in the military service. As of January 2002, 64.6 percent of the West Point graduates from 1985 to 2000 who majored or concentrated in history had remained on active duty past their mandatory service, compared to 55.3 percent of all graduates from those years who did so. The Department of History had provided an outstanding educational experience for cadets in its history courses but had also inspired them toward pursuit of a military career and provided them the skills necessary for success.[164] Clearly, the Military Academy had made the "correct move" in creating a Department of History.

---

[1] Jonathan Williams to Henry Dearborn, 14 October 1802, Letterbook, Williams Papers, Lilly Library; Henry Dearborn to Jonathan Williams, 10 March 1802, Williams Papers, Lilly Library.

[2] Jonathan Williams to Thomas Jefferson, 5 March 1808, Williams Papers, Lilly Library.

[3] Joseph Gardner Swift, "Sketch of a Plan for the Conducting of a Military Academy," January 1808, Swift Manuscripts, USMA Library.

[4] Jonathan Williams, "Military Affairs" [A report on the progress and present state of the Military Academy], 14 March 1808, U.S. Congress, *American State Papers: Military Affairs*, 7 vols.(in *American State Papers: Documents, Legislative and Executive, of the Congress of the United States*, 38 vols. [Washington, DC: GPO, 1904]), 1:229-230.

[5] Theodore J. Crackel, *West Point: A Bicentennial History* (Lawrence: University Press of Kansas, 2002), 73. Hereafter cited as Crackel, *West Point*.

[6] "Course of Study and Instruction pursued by the cadets at the Military Academy at West Point, New York," [ca. 1815], Alden Partridge Papers, USMA Library. There is no record of any requests for texts in either history, geography, or ethics, and no mention of earlier texts in 1819 when texts were discussed and adopted. Staff Records, Records of the Academic Board, USMA Library, 1:57. Hereafter cited as Staff Records. By 1818 the corporate body of professors was known as the Staff or the Academic Staff. The term Academic Board came into use a few years later.

[7] Staff Records, 1:57. The fact that the committee discussed the organization and scope of these classes in geography, history and ethics without reference to any earlier course designs, suggests that earlier courses in these subjects were not organized in any regular manner but instead were merely periodic lectures.

[8] Staff Records, 1:57. Alexander Fraser Tytler [Lord Woodhouselee, 1747-1813] was Professor of History at the University of Edinburgh. Tytler first published his *Elements of General History* in Edinburgh in 1801. An edition was printed in the United States in 1809 by Francis Nichols in Philadelphia based on the 4th British edition. Nichols issued a new edition in 1812, based on the 5th British edition, and reissued that text in 1813, 1817, and 1818, the latter two published in New York. In 1818 a new American edition (based on the 7th British edition) was printed by Samuel Goodrich of Hartford, CT (Alexander Fraser Tytler, *Elements of General History, Ancient and Modern: to which are added a comparative view of ancient and modern geography, and a table of chronology; the history continued from the close of the seventeenth century to the general peace of Europe in 1815, by Thomas Robbins*, 2 vols. [Hartford: Samuel G. Goodrich, 1818]). That edition was reprinted in 1819 in New York by E. Duyckinck, D.D. Smith, and George Long. It is not clear which of these editions was chosen for use at the Military Academy, but Goodrich's works were the most current. The work was revised again in 1823 (Concord, NH: Isaac Hill), adding a brief history of the United States, but there is no evidence yet found that any copies of this edition were purchased for use at West Point.

[9] "Report of the Working Committee on the Historical Aspects of the Curriculum for the Period 1802-1945," for the Superintendent's Curriculum Study, West Point: United States Military Academy, 31 June 1958, 11. (Hereafter cited as 1958 Curriculum Study.) The Working Committee reported that "Geography and History as known today were completely ignored after 1820." The committee was wrong. It is clear from the records of the Academic Board (Staff Records) that both geography and history continued until 1825; examinations in both subjects were held each year until then. Moreover, Geography continued to be taught for a number of years. A note in a report on the curriculum of 1839-1840 indicates that "in teaching Geography much use is made of the black board, a considerable part of every recitation being taken up in exercising the cadets in the drawing of maps . . . of all principal countries of the world." Staff Records, 2:243.

[10] The course in Geography, History, Ethics, and Law was offered to First Classmen for two hours a day from early September until the middle of June, a period of just over nine months. Two weeks of that time—one in January and one in June—were devoted to examinations. The division of time among the courses was estimated, based on a perusal of the subjects addressed in the winter and spring examinations. Geography was the only topic in the chaplain's course that was tested in the January exams, and it was touched on again in the June examinations—suggesting that this course consumed all of the first term and extended into the second. History, ethics, and law were covered only in the June examinations. Staff Records, 1:136, 152, 157, 276, and 289.

[11] Although it is clear from the Staff Records that history was replaced by rhetoric, the records are silent as to the reason for this change.

[12] The first law text appears to be Vattel's *Law of Nations,* which was adopted in 1819. (Staff Records, I:58.) By 1840 the Academy was using Kent's *Commentaries.* (*Official Register of the Officers and Cadets of the U.S. Military Academy* [West Point, NY: United States Military Academy, June 1841.]) This annual publication is hereafter cited as the *Official Register,* (date).

[13] *Official Register,* June 1855. Benson J. Lossing, *Pictorial History of the United States* (New York: F. J. Huntington, Mason Brothers, 1854).

[14] *Official Register,* June 1856. George Weber, *Outlines of Universal History: from the Creation of the World to the Present Time,* tr. M. Behr (Boston: Hicking, Swan and Brown, 1856).

[15] *Official Register,* June 1857. Although Weber's text did include a section on the history of the United States, it appears that the focus of the course after 1856 was on European history.

[16] William H. Harris to Ira Harris, 24 January and 4 April 1858, William H. Harris Papers, New York Public Library. The "Napoleon room" that Harris refers to was the home of the Napoleon Club which was presided over by Professor Dennis Hart Mahan. This club, in its time, was the focal point of the officers' intellectual life at West Point. The club was given a room in the Academic Building by Robert E. Lee while he was superintendent (1852-1855), and Mahan had supervised the painting of large maps of the theater of Napoleon's campaigns in Spain, Italy, and Germany. Although the club's membership was limited to the officers, cadets were sometimes brought into the room to see the maps and hear lectures on the campaigns. Crackel, *West Point,* 118.

[17] *Official Registers,* June 1859 to June 1860.

[18] Memorandum, Jonathan Williams to Henry Dearborn, 14 October 1802, Williams Papers, Lilly Library.

[19] The work was translated by John M. O'Connor, the son-in-law of Jared Mansfield, the professor of Natural Philosophy. (Gay de Vernon, Simon Francois, baron, *Traité élé-*

mentaire d'art militaire et de fortification: A treatise on the science of war and fortifica-tion: composed for the use of the Imperial Polytechnick School . . . and translated . . . for the use of the Military Academy in the United States. To which is added A summary of the principles and maxims of grand tactics and operations by John Michael O'Connor [New York: J. Seymour, 1817]). Hereafter cited as Gay de Vernon, *Treatise.*

20 Sylvanus Thayer to John M. O'Connor, 11 December 1817, Thayer Papers, USMA Library.

21 Jacques Antoine Hippolyte, Comte de Guibert; Henry Lloyd; Georg Friedrich von Templehoff; and Antoine-Henri Jomini.

22 Gay de Vernon, *Treatise,* v. O'Connor was among the very first American military writ-ers to introduce Jomini's works to an American audience. Only William Duane, in his *American Military Library* (Philadelphia, 1809), preceded him. On Duane, see Theo-dore J. Crackel, *Mr. Jefferson's Army, Political and Social Reform of the Military Estab-lishment, 1801-1809* (New York: New York University Press, 1987), 84.

23 Staff Records, 29 January 1820, I:105.

24 Staff Records, 19 April 1819, I:57. Instruction in tactics and drill, as opposed to grand tactics, was presented by the Tactical Department under the Commandant of Cadets.

25 Robert F. Hunter and Edwin L. Dooley, Jr., *Claudius Crozet, French Engineer in Ameri-ca, 1790-1864* (Charlottesville: University Press of Virginia, 1989), 22.

26 Crackel, *West Point,* 97-98.

27 Russell F. Weigley has insisted that Jomini's influence on Mahan was so pervasive that the latter's writings were based on the precepts of the former (*The American Way of War: A History of United States Military Strategy and Policy* [New York: Macmillan Publishing Co., Inc, 1973], 81-87). John I. Alger, however, has argued persuasively to the contrary. Although Mahan did admire Jomini, argued Alger, he rejected much of the foundation of Jomini's argument—his principles of war (*The Quest for Victory, The History of the Principles of War* [Westport, CT: Greenwood Press, 1982]). On Mahan's aversion to O'Connor's summary of Jomini, see Thomas Everett Griess, "Dennis Hart Mahan: West Point Professor and Advocate of Military Professionalism, 1830-1871" (Ph.D. diss, Duke University, 1969), 219. Hereafter cited as Griess, "Dennis Hart Mahan."

28 "Report of the Board of Visitors," June 1833, USMA Library.

29 These included works on field fortifications and civil engineering such as *A Complete Treatise on Field Fortifications, with the General Outlines of the Principles Regulating the Arrangement, the Attack, and the Defense of Permanent Works* (New York: Wiley & Long, 1836); and *An Elementary Course of Civil Engineering, For the use of the Cadets of the United States Military Academy* (New York: Wiley and Putnam, 1837).

30 D.H. Mahan, *An Elementary Treatise on Advanced-guard, Out-post, and Detachment Service of Troops: and the manner of posting and handling them in presence of an enemy. With a historical sketch of the rise and progress of tactics, &c., &c. intended as a supplement to the system of tactics adopted for the Military Service of the United States, and especially for the use of officers and volunteers* (New York: Wiley and Putnam, 1847). Mahan regularly updated his work, but stayed with the same title and same publisher. The various editions are hereafter cited as Mahan, *Outposts* (year).

31 Griess, "Dennis Hart Mahan," 235.

32 Griess, "Dennis Hart Mahan," 233-36. It is possible that Mahan's suggested lectures were merely a ploy to justify the painting of campaign maps—not on the classroom walls, but in the room (in the academic building) that the Napoleon Club had only recently been given. The Napoleon Club's maps were painted at about this time.

[33] James St. C. Morton, "Paper submitted to the Board of Visitors," in the *Report of the Secretary of War, 1857* (Washington, DC: GPO, 1857), 210, 216-17. Cited hereafter as Morton Paper. In the first recommendation Morton is probably referring to Jomini's *Art of War.* Cadet William Harris's letters to his father (see n. 16 above) show that the Chaplain's course was already offering some discussion of Napoleon. Possibly Morton simply wanted to formalize that coverage.

[34] Report of the Board of Visitors, 1857, in the *Report of the Secretary of War, 1857* (Washington, DC: GPO, June 1857), 200.

[35] Dennis Hart Mahan to John B. Floyd, 6 July 1857, Mahan Papers, USMA Library.

[36] John B. Floyd to Lt. Col. R.E. DeRussy, 26 August 1859, in Staff Reports, 7: 25-26, USMA Library.

[37] Staff Reports, 2 September 1859, 7:25-27; Official Register, June 1860.

[38] *Official Register,* June 1860; Antoine-Henri Jomini, *Summary of the Art of War,* trs. O.F. Winship and E.E. McLean (New York: Putnam, 1854). The only USMA classes of this era to be assigned the Jomini text were the Classes of 1860, May 1861, and possibly June 1861, although the strategy course for the latter class was substantially compressed.

[39] *Official Register,* June 1861; George B. McClelland, *Extracts from the report of Captain Geo. B. McClellan, for the use of the cadets at the U.S. Military Academy* (Washington, DC: 1860).

[40] *Official Register,* June 1861. Thomas James Thackeray, *The Military Organization and Administration of France* (London: T.C. Newby, 1856).

[41] *Official Register,* June 1860; Mahan, in AY 1859-60, taught the class which graduated in 1860.

[42] Report of the Commission appointed under the eighth section of the act of Congress of 21 June 1860, to examine into the organization of the United States Military Academy at West Point, Senate Misc. Doc. No. 3, 2d Sess., 36th Cong. (Washington: GPO, 1860), 1. Report hereafter cited as Davis Commission Report.

[43] Davis Commission Report, 183-84.

[44] D.H. Mahan testimony, 17 August 1860, Davis Commission Report, 137.

[45] Davis Commission Report, 23. The recommendation that "memoirs" be prepared was obviously intended to improve the cadets' ability to express themselves in writing; the recommendation asked that "special attention to the style of composition to be given."

[46] In 1858, the Academic Board had proposed a new four-year curriculum, and it was approved by the Secretary of War in October of that year and instituted immediately. In April 1859, however, Floyd reversed himself and the five-year program was reinstated. Edward C. Boynton, *History of West Point and its Military Importance during the American Revolution* (New York: D. Van Nostrand, 1863), 250. For a cadet perspective on these changes see William H. Harris to Ira Harris, 10 October 1858, and 10 April 1859, William H. Harris Papers, New York Public Library.

[47] Robert Johnston Taylor Wilson, [Cadet Notebook], Robert Johnston Taylor Wilson Papers, USMA Library. Wilson's notebook includes notes and drawings that reflect a series of four or five lectures, beginning on 21 May 1862. Mahan mentioned Jomini in at least one of his lectures, but if Wilson's notes are any measure—and they do seem rather thorough—the professor did not deal with the Swiss writer's interpretation of Napoleon at all. See also, "Brief historical sketch of the department [of engineering], giving dates of establishment, its scope in the beginning, and important steps in its development." *Annual Report of the Superintendent of the United States Military Academy,* 1896 (Washington, DC: GPO, 1896), 161. Hereafter cited as *Annual Report,* (year).

48 Mahan notes that this new material on Napoleon was drawn from the writings of Adolphe Thiers and August-Henri Dufour. He does not mention the works of Jomini. Mahan, *Outposts* (1862).

49 The new material is found in the most recent edition of *Outposts*. Mahan, *Outposts* (1864).

50 "Report of the Board of Visitors," 1868, USMA Library.

51 Lectures of Lieutenant Garrett J. Lydecker, 1869-1872, Papers of Garrett J. Lydecker (file 2020), USMA Library.

52 *Official Registers*, June 1882-June 1885; *The Centennial of the United States Military Academy at West Point, New York. 1802-1902...*, 2 vols. (Washington, DC: GPO, 1904), 1:373. Hereafter cited as *Centennial History*.

53 *Centennial History*, 1:373; *Official Register*, June 1885; William Swinton, *Outline of the World History: Ancient, Mediaeval, and Modern, with special relation to the history of civilization and the progress of mankind* (New York: Ivison, Blakeman, Taylor, and Co., 1880); Robert Henlopen Labberton, *An Historical Atlas; a Chronological Series of one hundred and twelve Maps at successive periods, from the Dawn of History to the Present Day* (New York: T. MacCoun, 1884). Postlethwaite used these texts until his death in 1896.

54 *Official Registers*, June 1897-June 1899. The texts used during the period 1897-1899 include: Philip Van Ness Myers, *A General History for Colleges and High Schools* (Boston: Ginn & Company, 1896); George Park Fisher, *Outline of Universal History* (New York: Ivison, Blakeman, Taylor & Co., 1886); George Park Fisher, *A Brief History of the Nations and of their Progress in Civilization* (New York: Cincinnati American Book Co., 1896).

55 *Official Register*, 1901; Victor Duruy, *A General History of the World* (New York: T. Y. Crowell & Co., 1898).

56 *Official Register*, 1906, 63.

57 *Official Register*, 1909, 64.

58 *Official Register*, 1910, 64.

59 *Official Register*, 1910; Ferdinand Schwill [Schevill], *A Political History of Modern Europe from the Reformation to the Present Day* (New York: Scribner's Sons, 1908); J. H. Robinson and C. A. Beard, *Development of Modern Europe* (Boston: Ginn & Co., 1907).

60 *Official Register*, 1912; J. H. Robinson and C. A. Beard, *Europe since the Congress of Vienna*, Vol. 2 of *Readings in Modern History*, 2 vols. (Boston: Ginn & Co., 1908-09); Raymond G. Gettell, *Introduction to Political Science* (Boston: Ginn & Co., 1910).

61 *Official Register*, 1912; Charles Downer Hazen, *Europe Since 1815* (New York: H. Holt, 1910).

62 *Official Registers*, 1916, 1919, and 1920; Lucius H. Holt, *Introduction to the Study of Government* (New York: The Macmillan Co., 1915); Holt and Alexander Wheeler Chilton, *History of Europe, 1862-1914* (New York: The Macmillan Co., 1917); Holt and Chilton, *History of Europe, 1789 to 1815* (New York: The Macmillan Co., 1919).

63 *War Department Information Relative to the Appointment and Admission of Cadets to the United States Military Academy*, 1924. This annual publication is hereafter cited as *Information on Admission*, (year).

64 *Information on Admission*, 1925. The text chosen for the mini-course on U.S. history was John Spencer Bassett, *A Short History of the United States* (New York: Macmillan, 1913). Cadets, since the time of Thayer, had been divided in each course into sections based on their standing in that course. The first section—and later, as the size of the

corps grew, the top several sections—was sometimes excused from the semi-annual examinations. This was the case in History at this time.

65 "Revision of the Courses in Political History, 3rd Class, and Military History, 1st Class," 10 April 1925, Staff Records, 54-55.

66 Philip Van Ness Myers, *A General History for Colleges and High Schools* (Boston: Ginn & Company, 1923). An earlier edition of this text was used briefly at the Academy in the late 1890s. See n. 54 above.

67 James H. Robinson, *An Introduction to the History of Western Europe* (Boston: Ginn & Co., c1924-26).

68 Hutton Webster, *History of the Modern World* (Boston: D. C. Heath & Co., c1925).

69 In 1934, Beukema make a number of textbook changes, but retained the focus of the course that Holt had created. He replaced all the older texts with just three new ones: George C. Sellery and A.C. Krey, *Medieval Foundations of Western Civilization* (New York: Haskell House, 1929; Volume 1 of Carlton J.H. Hays, *A Political and Cultural History of Modern Europe*, 2 vols. (New York: Macmillan, 1932); and Volume 2 of Hays, *A Political and Social History of Modern Europe*, 2 vols. (New York: Macmillan, 1930). In 1937, the second volume of Hays's *Political and Social History* was replaced by the second volume his *Political and Cultural History*.

70 Harold Monk Vinacke, *A History of the Far East in Modern Times* (New York: A.A. Knopf, 1928).

71 Frederick A. Kirkpatrick, *Latin America: A Brief History* (New York: The Macmillan Co., 1939).

72 Ferdinand Schevill, *A History of Europe from the Renaissance to the Present Day* (New York: Harcourt, Brace, 1949). An older text of Schevill's was used decades earlier at West Point. See n. 59.

73 R.R. Palmer, *History of the Modern World* (New York: Knopf, 1950); Carlton J.H. Hayes, *Modern Europe to 1870* (New York: Macmillan, 1953).

74 *Catalogue of the United States Military Academy, [AY] 1960-1961,* 67. This annual publication is hereafter cited as *Catalogue,* (years).

75 New texts were selected in 1968 for the survey course: Louis L. Snyder, *The Making of Modern Man: From the Renaissance to the Present* (Princeton, NJ: Van Nostrand, 1967); and David L. Dowd, *The Age of Revolution, 1770-1870,* Vol. 5 of *Critical Issues in History,* ed. Richard E. Sullivan (Boston: D. C Heath & Co., 1967).

76 *Catalogues,* AY 1958-59 to AY 1961-62.

77 Course End Reports, SS 301-302, AY 1963-64 to AY 1968-69, Records of the Department of Social Sciences, USMA Library.

78 *Catalogue,* AY 1968-69.

79 Guillaume Henri Dufour, *Strategy and Tactics,* tr. Wm. P. Craighill (New York: D. Van Nostrand, 1864); J.B. Wheeler, *A Course of Instruction in the Elements of the Art & Strategy of War* (New York: D. Van Nostrand, 1879).

80 James Mercur, *Elements of the Art of War* (West Point: USMA Press, 1889).

81 Arthur L. Wagner, *Organization and Tactics,* 2d ed. (Kansas City, MO: Hudson-Kimberly Publishing Co., 1897).

82 G.J. Fiebeger, *The Campaign and Battle of Gettysburg* (West Point: USMA Press, 1915).

83 G.J. Fiebeger, *Elements of Strategy* (West Point: USMA Press, 1917).

84 *Official Registers,* 1911 and 1913.

85 *Information on Admission,* 1923.

[86] *Annual Report*, 1922, 13.

[87] *Annual Report*, 1923, 5.

[88] On the Army's use of history, see Carol Reardon, *Soldiers and Scholars, The U.S. Army and the Uses of Military History, 1865-1920* (Lawrence: University Press of Kansas, 1990).

[89] U.S. War Department, Board of Officers Appointed to Study the Army School System, *Report of Proceedings* (Washington: 1922). The board was headed by Maj. Gen. Edward F. McGlachlin, then commandant of the U.S. Army War College.

[90] William Augustus Mitchell, [proposal to consider omission of some history], 13 July 1922, Staff Records, Committee on Physical and Technical Science, card file (heading: schedules). Mitchell's motive in this is not at all clear, but it is hard not to conclude that he was pleased at this turn of events.

[91] Commandant's course in Military Art, 27 August 1923, Staff Records, Curriculum file.

[92] The Commandant proposed his own courses in Military Art to the Academic Board on 27 August 1923 and again on 13 July 1924. The board appears to have agreed to his proposal in October 1923. It may have been judged too late to initiate the new course in AY 1923-24. The 1924 proposal appears to have been a mere revision of his earlier submission which would be put into effect in the fall of that year. Staff Records, 35 (1923):186, and card file (heading: curriculum).

[93] "Revision of the Courses in Political History, 3rd Class, and Military History, 1st Class," 10 April 1925, Staff Records, 37: 54-55.

[94] "A Study of the Curriculum of the United States Military Academy by the Academic Board," 1927, Staff Records, File: 351.051 "Curriculum 1926-1927," 17, USMA Library.

[95] *Official Register*, 1925, 20.

[96] *Command, Staff and Tactics* (Fort Leavenworth, KS: Army Service Schools Press, 1923); and *Tactics and Techniques of the Separate Branches*, 3d ed. (Fort Leavenworth, KS: Army Service Schools Press, 1925).

[97] William A. Mitchell, ed., *Outlines of the World's Military History* (Washington, DC: National Service Publishing Company, 1929); "Committee review of the first nine chapters of *Outline of the World's Military History*," 28 December 1928, Staff Records, card file (heading: textbooks).

[98] *Official Registers*, 1929 and 1930; *Information on Admission*, 1933 and 1935; *Annual Report*, 1945.

[99] Theodore Ayrault Dodge, *Napoleon, A History of the Art of War* (Boston: Houghton, Mifflin Co., 1904-07); John C. Ropes and William R. Livermore, *The Story of the Civil War* (New York: G. P. Putnam, 1933); and W. Birkbeck Woods and J. E. Edmonds, *A History of the Civil War, 1861-1865* (New York: G. P Putnam, 1905).

[100] *Information on Admission*, 1935.

[101] *Information on Admission*, 1940.

[102] *Ibid.*

[103] Theodore Ayrault Dodge, *Great Captains: A Course of Six Lectures Showing the Influence on the Art of War of the Campaigns of Alexander, Hannibal, Caesar, Gustavus Adolphus, Frederick, and Napoleon* (Boston: Houghton, Mifflin and Co., 1889). [Although all indications are that the Dodge text was used from 1940 to 1948, one should note that the Department of Military Art and Engineering had published its own text on this subject as early as 1941: *Great Captains before Napoleon* (West Point: USMA, 1941). This text was issued again in 1944, 1949, and 1965. The book was finally adopted as a course text in 1957.] Antoine-Henri Jomini, *Life of Napoleon* (West Point:

United States Military Academy, 1940). [Jomini's work was first published in 1827. This is a republication of the H.W. Halleck translation done in 1864. Included in the volume is an atlas prepared by the Department of Civil and Military Engineering, USMA.] Matthew Forney Steele, *American Campaigns* (Washington, DC: United States Infantry Association, 1935). Girard Lindsley McEntee, *Military History of the World War* (New York: C. Scribner's Sons, 1937).

104 *Information on Admissions*, 1942.

105 *Jomini, Clausewitz, and Schlieffen* (West Point: USMA, 1943). This text was republished at West Point in 1945, 1948, 1951, 1964, and 1967.

106 *Annual Report*, 1943, 8.

107 *Annual Report*, 1944, 9.

108 *Annual Report*, 1946, 14; *Annual Report*, 1947, 9.

109 Maximilian Yorck, Graf von Wartenburg, *Napoleon as a General* (London: K. Paul, Trench, Trubner & Co., 1902).

110 *Annual Report*, 1954. T. Dodson Stamps and Vincent J. Esposito, *A Short History of World War I* (West Point: United States Military Academy, 1950); and Stamps and Esposito, *A Short History of World War II* (West Point: United States Military Academy, 1953).

111 Department of Military Art and Engineering, *Great Captains before Napoleon* (West Point: USMA, 1949); and Department of Military Art and Engineering, *Jomini, Clausewitz, and Schlieffen* (West Point: USMA, 1951).

112 Vincent J. Esposito, *The West Point Atlas of American Wars* (New York: Praeger, 1959); Vincent J. Esposito and John Robert Elting, *A Military History and Atlas of the Napoleonic War* (New York: Praeger, 1964).

113 Dave R. Palmer, *Revolution in America* (West Point: USMA, 1968).

114 HM401 Course Notebook, 1968, 6-7, Records of the Department of Military Art and Engineering, USMA Library.

115 USMA, Superintendent's Curriculum Study, Report of the Working Committee on the Historical Aspects of the Curriculum for the Period 1802-1945, 31 July 1958, USMA Library.

116 MAGC, Memorandum, Lt. Gen. Garrison H. Davidson to Col. J.J. Ewell, Subject: Board of Officers, 12 November 1957, USMA Library.

117 Report, MAGC, Col. J.J. Ewell to the Superintendent, USMA, Subject: Report of a Board of Officers Appointed to Estimate Qualities and Attributes Essential to the Future Officer, 31 January 1958, 4, 41, 42, USMA Library.

118 Memorandum, Col. J.J. Ewell to the Superintendent, Subject: Supplement to a Report, The Army Officer of the Future, An Estimate of His Qualities and Attributes by a Board of Officers appointed by the Superintendent, USMA, 31 January 1958, 5-6, USMA Library.

119 USMA, Superintendent's Curriculum Study, Report of the Evaluation Committee, 18 November 1958, 29, 41, USMA Library.

120 Letter Orders Number 53, MACS, CWO Mark M. Kriebel to Col. Richard G. Stilwell, Subject: Curriculum Review, 30 September 1959, USMA Library.

121 Report, Col. Richard G. Stilwell to the Superintendent, Subject: Transmittal of Report, Superintendent's Curriculum Study, Report on Military and Physical Education Components, 26 January 1960, 4, USMA Library.

[122] USMA, Superintendent's Curriculum Study, Report of the Working Committee on the Present Curriculum and Future Trends, 31 August 1958, VIII-3, VIII-5, XI-4, VIII-4, USMA Library.

[123] Ad Hoc Subcommittee, A Study Regarding Reorganization Based upon Certain Courses Taught by Academic Departments and the Department of Tactics, 31 January 1961, Annex C, 4, USMA Library.

[124] Ibid., Annex I, Appendix 1, 2, 3.

[125] Memorandum, Col. G.A. Lincoln to Curriculum Committee, Subject: Academic Reorganization, 6 April 1961, 10, USMA Library.

[126] Memorandum, MASP, Maj. Gen. William C. Westmoreland, 20 June 1961, 1, USMA Library.

[127] Col. Thomas E. Griess, Memorandum for Record, Subject: Creation of the Department of History at the U.S. Military Academy, 13 August 1981, 2-3, 4, Author's Files. These papers will become a part of the Robert Doughty papers at the USMA Library.

[128] National Security and Public Affairs Committee, Subject: Investigation of a Department of History, 3 October 1968, 17. (Enclosure to Proceedings of the Academic Board, 6 November 1968).

[129] Letter, Col. G.A. Lincoln to Superintendent, Subject: Minority Report Presented under Provisions of Par. 2.06 *Rules of the Academic Board*, 7 November 1968 (Enclosure to Proceedings of the Academic Board, 6 November 1968).

[130] Enclosure to Minority Report on Department of History, 2 October 1968, 1, 9 (Enclosure to Proceedings of the Academic Board, 6 November 1968).

[131] United States Military Academy, Proceedings of the Academic Board, 6 November 1968.

[132] Headquarters, United States Military Academy, General Orders Number 129, Reorganization, 23 May 1969, USMA Library.

[133] USMA, Office of the Dean, Academic Program, 1970-1971 (Redbook), 17 February 1970, V-1-V-3, V-27, V-29.

[134] Ibid., p. V-1; USMA, Office of the Dean, Academic Program, 1977-1978 (Redbook), Change 1, 4 April 1977, 3.

[135] Letter, MADN-K, Col. Thomas E. Griess to Associate Professor, Military History, Subject: Revision of Course in the History of the Military Art (HI 401-402), 17 January 1974, 1, 2, 5. Author's Files.

[136] Report, Department of the Army Ad Hoc Committee on the Army Need for the Study of Military History, West Point, NY, 15 May 1971, 4 vols.

[137] ATZL-SWI, Colonel Stofft, Fact Sheet, Subject: Combat Studies Institute (CSI), 18 June 1981, Author's Files.

[138] Department of the Army, Final Report of the West Point Study Group, 27 July 1977, 74, USMA Library. The "Model Standard Curriculum" included one semester of modern history in the cadet's Third Class year and two semesters of military history in the Second Class year.

[139] MADN-I, Memorandum, Brig. Gen. Frederick A. Smith, Jr., to the Superintendent, Subject: Curriculum Proposal, 8 December 1977 (Enclosure to Proceedings of the Academic Board, 20 December 1977).

[140] Memorandum, MADN-A, Col. Jack M. Pollin to the Superintendent, Subject: Curriculum Proposal, 19 December 1977, 1 (Enclosure to Proceedings of the Academic Board, 20 December 1977).

[141] USMA, Office of the Dean, Academic Program, AY 1978-1979 (Redbook), 9-7—9-9.

[142] Memorandum, MADN-K, Maj. John W. Mountcastle to Col. Thomas E. Griess, Subject: Possible Modification to Course Structure, HI 300/400, 21 November 1979, Author's Files.

[143] Draft Memorandum, Col. Roy K. Flint to Col. Thomas E. Griess, n.d., 1, Author's Files.

[144] Letter, Lt. Gen. Garrison H. Davidson, 1 July 1983, 3, USMA Library.

[145] Jeffrey Record, "The Fortune of War," Harper's 260 (April 1980): 23.

[146] Col. William F. Carroll, et al., The United States Military Academy in Perspective, 1969-1970, An Institutional Report Prepared for the 1980 Decennial Accreditation, December 1979, 54, USMA Library.

[147] Memorandum, MADN-J, Lt. Col. James R. Golden to the Dean of the Academic Board, Subject: The Core Curriculum, 27 March 1981, 5-6 (Enclosure to Proceedings of the Academic Board, 17 April 1981).

[148] Memorandum, MADN-A, Brig. Gen. Frederick A. Smith, Jr., Subject: Curricular Transition, 16 July 1981, 3 (Enclosure to Proceedings of the Academic Board, 14 October 1981).

[149] USMA, Proceedings of the Academic Board, 14 October 1981.

[150] Paper, "The Concept of Military History as the Flagship Academic Area," n.d., 1, Author's Files.

[151] Memorandum, DAMH-ZA, Brig. Gen. William A. Stofft et al. to the Superintendent, Subject: Report of the Committee on Historical Mindedness at West Point, 10 December 1988, passim, Author's Files.

[152] Memorandum, MADN-K, Col. Robert A. Doughty to the Superintendent, Subject: Enhancing the Study of Military History, 2 February 1988, passim, Author's Files.

[153] USMA, Office of the Dean, Change 2 to Academic Program, AY 1990-1991 (Redbook), 10 January 1992, 11. The "flagship" concept did not appear in the Superintendent's strategic guidance. See: USMA, Office of the Superintendent, 2002 and Beyond: A Roadmap to our Third Century, Strategic Guidance for the United States Military Academy, 1990, USMA Library.

[154] Report, MADN-K, Col. Stephen J. Wager to Col. Roy K. Flint, Subject: Final Report on Creation of New Two-Semester Fourth Class History Course, 2 January 1985, Author's Files.

[155] USMA, Office of the Dean, Academic Program, AY 1977-1978 (Redbook), 121.

[156] Robert A. Doughty and Ira Gruber, eds., Warfare in the Western World, 2 vols. (Lexington, MA: D. C. Heath and Company, 1996).

[157] Memorandum, MADN-K, Col. Robert A. Doughty to Brig. Gen. Gerald E. Galloway, Subject: Curriculum Changes in Response to the Ending of the Cold War, 23 February 1994, Author's Files.

[158] Department of History, Lt. Col. K. E. Hamburger, Leadership in Combat: An Historical Appraisal, A Study for the Officer Personnel Management System Study Group, Department of the Army, U.S. Military Academy, 1984, Author's Files.

[159] Memorandum, Colonel Stofft et al. to the Superintendent, Subject: Report of the Committee on Historical Mindedness, 7.

[160] Gordon W. Rudd, "One More Tile on the Mosaic, 6 April-15 July 1991," Typescript, 1991, Author's Files; Memorandum, MADN-K, Capt. Thomas G. Ziek, Jr., to Professor and Head, Department of History, Subject: After Action Review of History Augmentation to Operation Uphold Democracy, 11 November 1994, Author's Files.

[161] Colonel Doughty, Notes, Book IX, 16 August 1990, Author's Files.

[162] Memorandum, MADN-3, Brig. Gen. Gerald E. Galloway, Jr., to Colonel Lamkin, Chairman, Curriculum Committee, 8 August 1991, Author's Files.

[163] Memorandum, MADN-K, Col. Thomas E. Griess, Subject: Creation of the Department of History, 6.

[164] For information about the methods of the Department, see Robert A. Doughty, "History is Alive and Well at West Point," *Assembly* 41 (December 1982): 16-17, 40; Cole C. Kingseed, "Inspiring Warrior Leaders," *Assembly* 57 (November-December 1998): 30-31, 76-77.

CHAPTER 18

EVOLUTION OF THE DEPARTMENT OF GEOGRAPHY AND ENVIRONMENTAL ENGINEERING

Peter Anderson and James B. Dalton, Jr.

Introduction

The world's burgeoning population has made the study of geographic and environmental sciences essential to national security. West Point graduates, as leaders of an Army that operates in virtually every corner of the globe, must understand the manifold ways that humans interact with their environment. The Department of Geography and Environmental Engineering (G&EnE) of the U.S. Military Academy is devoted to helping cadets understand these relationships; in this process, they heighten their awareness of foreign cultures and become better Army officers.

G&EnE's history goes back to the founding of the Military Academy in 1802. Over the course of 200 years, the department evolved through five distinct periods to its present configuration: Landscape Drawing (1803-1876), Technical Drawing (1876-1942), Mapping and Topography (1942-1960), Consolidation and Expansion (1960-1991), and Contemporary Integration (1992-2003). The curricular and organizational changes that surfaced in each period reflected the important work of a series of academic leaders who endeavored to shape the department to the needs of the nation. Throughout the history of the Academy, external events helped define what was needed within the curriculum, while internal discussion shaped the way in which G&EnE responded to those events. The present department configuration is the result of this long history of adaptation and change.

Landscape Drawing, 1803–1876

In the Academy's early years, the drawing teacher's responsibility was to teach the basic principles of drawing so as to produce officers and gentlemen who had a grasp of the fine arts. Drawings of the time were predominately human figures and natural landscapes completed in ink and watercolors. The drawing of human figures and landscapes was a traditional component of officer training in European military schools. The tradition was passed down to the U.S. Military Academy by the European professors who were hired to teach drawing and by the American officers who studied in Europe and later returned to teach at West Point.

Drawing instruction in the early years of West Point was characterized by faculty turbulence and imprecise academic standards. Although Congress authorized a Teacher of Drawing to be hired in 1802, the position went unfilled for a year; between 1803 and 1833, the incumbent changed five times.[1] The first Teacher of Drawing was François Désiré Masson, a Frenchman, who was succeeded in 1808 by Christian E. Zoeller, a Swiss citizen. Two years later, Zoeller gave up the office and Masson was again appointed to the position of Teacher of Drawing. In 1812 Masson was once more replaced with Zoeller, who remained in the position until 1819. Replacing Zoeller was another Frenchman, Thomas Gimbrede. When Gimbrede died, he was succeeded by Charles Albert Leslie, an established artist, but an individual not suited for the remote situation of the Academy in the 1830s.[2] After Leslie's short tenure, he was replaced by Robert Weir, whom we shall have more to say about shortly. Not surprisingly, these frequent faculty changes undermined the effort to design a coherent, rigorous, and well-balanced academic program.

Making matters worse was the drawing teacher's added responsibility of teaching French (see Chapter 21). Most of the engineering texts were written in French, necessitating that cadets acquire a reading competency in the language to conduct their studies. For the first few years of the Academy's existence, Congress expected the drawing teacher to be able to handle both subjects. The teachers did their best to balance their responsibilities, but in the end both subjects suffered.

Despite these problems, the drawing instruction program did experience some modest improvement. The principal drawing method used through the mid-1820s was literal copying of great works of art. Cadets practiced by tracing the original (or a copy) on a primitive light table topped with a piece of glass illuminated by a candle, and tracing the artwork. Despite tracing's technical benefits—accuracy and perspective, in particular—it gradually lost favor as a pedagogical technique. It was too prescriptive, too suppressive of the cadets' creative impulses. Some faculty members even believed it was demoralizing to the cadets.[3] The deemphasis on copying great works of art led to greater stress on observation and analysis by cadets, particularly when attempting to draw a human figure or natural landscape. This improvement helped cadets become better observers of the natural landscape.

Robert Weir's tenure as Teacher of Drawing (1833–1876) brought a period of stability and prominence to the Drawing Department at the Academy. Unlike his predecessors, save for Leslie, he came to West Point as an established artist, and his solid reputation helped to put the drawing program on a rigorous academic footing; additionally, he was not burdened by the requirement to teach French. Weir added both substance and breadth in to the drawing program. As a teacher, he established high academic standards and demanded that his cadets achieve them. An 1836 Board of Visitor's Report records the efforts and results of his efforts: "We were much gratified in perceiving that the commodious room, 75 x 22 feet, is now fitting up for the exhibition of drawings and paintings of those cadets that have distinguished themselves. . . . [This was] the result of the laudable industry of the present professor executed during his leisure hours."[4]

Throughout his distinguished teaching career, Weir continued the traditional emphasis on drawing human figures and natural landscapes. He and his students completed several important works, for example, "Hudson River with a Distant View of West

Point" by Cadet Seth Eastman (1834) and "Embarkation of the Pilgrims" by Professor Weir (1844). The works of his students clearly reflect the emphasis on natural settings and the human form. Weir's watercolor titled "Study of Entwined Trees" reflects his interest in using the surrounding natural landscape to focus the viewer's attention on the main object of the work.[5]

Weir designed his drawing curriculum to develop the cadets' appreciation of the landscape. He demanded that cadets learn techniques for depicting the natural terrain employing particularly "blended tints, shading mountains, rocks, trees, and other objects appertaining to wild and uncultivated countries."[6] These techniques were the standard at the time for topographic maps; [they] required the cartographer to use survey data along with artistic interpretation to depict elevation contours. Field survey training, which had begun in the summer of 1802, was the source of elevation data for many of the local properties, providing valuable land data for the early maps. Additionally, surveying was an essential skill for many of the future engineers. Surveying instruction was taught by several separate departments, but for the majority of the last 200 years it has been taught by the Drawing Department or its descendants, as it is today[7].

By establishing high standards of excellence in his field, Weir garnered considerable prestige for the institution. Most important, he endowed cadets with many of the technical skills they would need as officers in the Army. Ulysses S. Grant was one of the beneficiaries of Weir's excellent instruction. His "Watercolor of Indians and Trader," on display in the Academy Museum today, is a testament to the high standards that cadets achieved under Weir's tutelage.[8] His pedagogical innovations, in addition to his considerable talents as an artist, brought national recognition for him and the Academy.

Technical Drawing, 1876–1942

During the last years of Weir's tenure as Professor of Drawing, technical drawing assumed greater prominence within the Drawing Department. Technical drawing used geometric principles in the construction of the drawing. Cadets turned greater attention to detailed graphical portrayals of machinery, buildings, fortifications, and topography. Surveying had become an instrumental part of the departmental offerings, using mathematics to guide cadets in the depiction of the topography. The subject was taught during summer training as practical survey.[9] This technical evolution occurred over time; Weir's students, later officers, would be the ones to continue providing the support and impetus for the ever increasing mathematical orientation of the Army and nation.

Charles W. Larned (USMA 1870) arrived at West Point in August 1874. As a first lieutenant assistant instructor in the Department of Drawing, his qualifications included his experience as an assistant instructor under Weir during his cadet days. Using talented cadets as assistant instructors was not uncommon in the 19th century, when the permanent faculty was not always large enough to manage the teaching load. Cadets selected for teaching duty had shown unusual aptitude in the given discipline; hence it is likely that Larned was reasonably well prepared to join the permanent faculty. Larned's other major qualification was his experience with the 3rd and 7th Cavalry, which instilled in him a sense of the field officer's educational needs. When Weir retired in 1876, Larned was appointed Professor and Department Head. The academic board does not appear to have looked for or considered a civilian artist for the position of Professor of Drawing, as was the case when Weir was hired.[10]

Professor Larned departed from the previous methods of instruction in an effort to improve the drawing curriculum. Specifically, he moved away from copying existing works of art to the instructional model used in the Mathematics Department that focused on training the future officers' mental facilities.[11] Larned introduced methods designed to train the "eye to see properly and the hand to execute accurately."[12] The drawing course under Larned's guidance changed substantially from Weir's course, especially when compared to Weir's pre-Civil War drawing instruction when technical drawing had not yet begun to assert itself in the curriculum. Professor Larned moved immediately to increase the mathematical and topographic nature of the drawing program.[13]

Cadets were quick to discern the changes. In 1877, only one year after Larned had become the head of the department, Cadet Charles Noyes noted,

> Professor Larned has instituted a new feature in his Department of Drawing. He is going to give practical instruction in making military surveys. Work started with cadets following the road from the South Gate to Fort Putnam, making notes as they progressed. [14]

A month later, Noyes reported that Larned was "getting very much interested in my drawing. We are now engaged in making the topographical sketch of the survey which was made last month."[15]

Table 18-1. Comparison of Courses Taught in the Department of Drawing, 1876 and 1900.[17]	
Courses, 1876	**Courses, 1900**
Topography	Plane and Descriptive Geometry*
Landscape	Shades and Shadows*
Pencils and Colors	Linear Perspective and Isometrical Projections*
	Topography and Plotting Surveys
	Field Reconnaissance, Contouring, and Sketching
	History of Cartography and Topography
	Triangulation and Large Surveys
	Free Hand Drawing and Landscape
	Mechanical and Architectural Drawing
	Military Landscape, Sketching in the Field
	Memory Drawing
	Free Hand Mechanical Drawing without Instruments
	Building Construction, Working Drawings, and Isometric Sections

Noyes's comments suggest an appreciation among cadets of the usefulness of the new drawing curriculum.

Larned oversaw the development and implementation of a new program concentrating on surveying, topography, cartography, and construction engineering.[16] A comparison of course work in 1876 to that of 1900 illustrates the extent of Larned's changes (Table 18-1). One sees that in 1876, though instruction was more technical compared to pre-Civil War instruction, it still focused on landscape appreciation, with topography being the only departmental course using mathematical methods.

By 1900, however, the department had assumed responsibility from the Mathematics Department for its three courses directly related to the topographic and cartographic sciences, thus increasing the number of courses within the Department of Drawing to 13. Six of those courses applied mathematics directly to technical drawing.

Larned's vision of a revised curriculum involved deliberations that went beyond the department to the Academy as a whole. His seniority on the Academic Board and leadership of the curriculum revision committee were instrumental in his work to turn the vision into reality. In a memorandum to the superintendent, dated 17 May 1910, Larned reported the results of the work completed between 1905 and 1906 in curriculum review. He also described the committee's recommended revisions and how the implementation of the changes was progressing. The three topics addressed were: (1) methods of instruction; (2) number and nature of the courses; and (3) amount of material to be assimilated by cadets. The committee believed that the revisions had been helpful, but reserved final judgment until they had been in effect for a longer time.[18] This memo suggests that Larned was successful in assisting the Academy in changing.

The revised curriculum reflected Larned's appreciation of the changing needs of the Army and the nation. As the new century began, Larned realized that the Army needed officers who were well trained in topographical skills and could apply these skills regardless of where they were deployed. Following America's conversion to colonial-power status after the Spanish-American War, officer deployments could now reach to various places around the world.

All of America's previous major wars had been fought on the continent, without the impediments of long lines of communications and underdeveloped infrastructure requiring technically innovative solutions. The Academy's instruction in technical drawing was thus well conceived to help prepare graduates for the far-flung challenges that would now inevitably begin to emerge.

Upon Larned's death in 1910, Lt. Col. Edwin R. Stuart (USMA 1896) was appointed Professor of Drawing and Department Head. Stuart continued implementation of the reforms started by Larned's committee at the turn of the century. Additionally, he wrote two texts that embodied the emergent emphasis on technical drawing.[19] The texts brought together three of the four areas of Larned's new program, marking the full evolution of technical drawing's orientation toward mapping and topography and away from graphic depictions of machinery and structures. Though Stuart suffered a premature death in 1920, he can be credited with the continued evolution of the curriculum away from landscape drawing and toward technical and topographic drawing.

When Stuart died, Superintendent Brig. Gen. Douglas MacArthur appointed Maj. Roger G. Alexander (USMA 1907) as Professor and Head of the Department of Drawing.[20] Alexander would remain in this position until September 1945. Alexander came to the Department of Drawing soon after returning from Europe, where he gained invaluable practical experience during World War I while serving in the American Expeditionary Force.[21] His bucolic roots in rural Missouri—with its "earth, horses, seeds, harvests, storms, mud, heat, cold, and country schools"—also influenced his military career, since any good topographer has to appreciate the elements of nature. [22] He had spent two years at the University of Missouri, where he was involved with student teaching in rural schools.[23] His subsequent decision to pursue a career in the military brought him to West Point, where he graduated number two in his class.

Five years after graduation, he returned as an assistant professor of surveying and topography in the Department of Practical Military Engineering, serving in this capacity from August 1912 to September 1916. During this early assignment, he displayed a particular affinity for "the world of maps, photos, graphics, and their application to the military."[24] While in Europe, from May 1917 to July 1919, Alexander was in charge of topographical work and even established a printing plant for the production of maps to be supplied to allied forces.[25]

Back at West Point as department head, he made numerous curricular changes aiming to modernize the material presented. His wartime experiences were particularly useful in suggesting the practical changes that needed to be made. At MacArthur's urging, Alexander began to place increased emphasis on "battle map preparation." Then, in short order, "surveying and descriptive geometry were added to the courses taught by the department."[26] Characterization of terrain and representation of landscape features via topographic mapping became important components of the curriculum. Owing to Alexander's leadership and continuous drive to modernize instruction and course material during his 20 years as department head, the numerous graduates who would see combat duty during World War II were far more effective officers in the field.

Mapping & Topography, 1942–1960

On 2 January 1942, the Department of Drawing was renamed the Department of Military Topography and Graphics (MT&G) so as to reflect the changes in the department's academic focus. The areas of predominant concern were military sketching and mapping, map and air photo interpretation, surveying, and graphics and mechanical drawing.[27] Despite the many curricular changes over the years, much continuity remained. Drawing and surveying, for example, had been taught for 150 years.[28]

During the 20th century, technological advances required the Army, the Academy, and the Department of Drawing to continue to adapt and change. Although the diminution and then elimination of landscape drawing meant a potential loss of cadet landscape analysis, characterization, and appreciation, other skills and knowledge were acquired. These new skills enabled cadets to function in an increasingly technological milieu. Through lecture and practical exercises, cadets were expected to be able to read, understand, and use maps and technical drawings.

During the Technical Drawing period, cadets received two hours of drawing instruction and practical exercise on alternate afternoons. With an increased number of courses in MT&G, Fourth Class cadets received instruction in graphics, surveying, and military topography, while Third Class cadets concentrated on military topography and graphics.[29] During World War II, course schedules and criteria for graduation were modified to enable cadets to graduate earlier. The country needed officers—lots of them—faster. Shortened and compressed academic programs facilitated earlier graduations. As department head, Alexander, now a colonel, was instrumental in adjusting the curriculum of his department to meet the needs of the Academy and the Army during these difficult wartime years.

Early September 1945 brought another change to MT&G. Alexander was elevated to the position of Acting Dean, an action formalized by act of Congress on 20 June 1946. In that year, Col. Lawrence E. Schick (USMA 1920) took over as department head, having just returned from Korea where he had been the Provost Marshal General. This would be Schick's third tour of duty at West Point, the previous two also having been with the Department of Drawing under Alexander's tutelage.[30] His first tour of duty at the Military Academy lasted five years, beginning in 1925. He returned as assistant professor from 1934 to 1938, during which time he developed expertise in engineering graphics, descriptive geometry, and surveying.[31]

Schick had served for almost five years in the Far East—Alaska, Okinawa, Korea—before returning to West Point to become Professor and Head of MT&G. He brought with him the experience of two world wars and the Korean War, at a time when the curriculum would receive extensive review in light of the experience gleaned from those conflicts.[32]

Throughout the 1950s, military lessons learned during World War II and Korea as well as academic advances and technological developments were incorporated into courses at the Military Academy. MT&G was in the thick of these changes.[33] Schick sought to reduce vocational style training and instill in the cadets more theory and fundamental principles.[34] Lessons in astronomy and geology were added to the topography course. Courses in geology, established in 1837, but eliminated from the Academy curriculum during MacArthur's superintendency, would soon return to the curriculum.[35]

Also contributing to departmental modernization was Col. Charles R. Broshous (USMA 1933), who assumed the duties of professor and deputy head of the department in 1948. Broshous's first tour of duty at the Academy was in 1937 as an instructor in the Department of Civil Engineering. During World War II, then Captain Broshous was one of the first American staff officers sent to England to prepare the way for the millions of American soldiers who would follow. His specific task was to establish the Southern Base Section installation, from which many of the D-day invasion forces would depart.[36] He helped supervise the construction of roads, campsites, hospitals, and marshaling areas that soon were teeming with soldiers and airmen.[37] These and other wartime engineering experiences gave Broshous a clear vision of the types of geographical and mapping skills that cadets would need as officers.

Colonel Broshous had a clear vision of the nexus between an army's map and terrain analysis skills, on one hand, and its success in war, on the other:

> Modern warfare emphasizes the utter dependence of all ranks on maps. Experiences during World War II and in Korea have further substantiated the need for the mastery of map and terrain analysis. As a consequence, additional emphasis has recently been placed on certain phases of the course in Topography.[38]

In accordance with this concept, the department increased its emphasis on map and air photo interpretation, military sketching, and terrain analysis, with the latter showing greater attention to geology and physical geography. During periods of "acceptable weather" (a term always broadly construed), cadets spent time outside learning the fundamentals of military sketching and practicing map reading. These fundamentals were considered particularly important in light of the frequent complaints by returning Korean War veterans that in the theater they had experienced "great difficulty in matching terrain with the map, and vice versa, as the terrain is practically devoid of man-made features which assist in orientation."[39] Addressing this problem, while incorporating new land navigation technologies in the existing courses, provided stiff challenges for the department.

Consolidation and Expansion, 1960–1991

During the late 1950s, Colonel Schick chaired a review committee on the mathematics, science, and engineering curriculum which led to the introduction of curriculum changes during the 1960-1961 academic year.[40] Some of the changes directly affected his department, which, on 10 October 1960, received a new name—Earth, Space, and Graphic Sciences (ES&GS)—and a new academic focus.[41] Henceforth, ES&GS would have a twofold mission: teaching human and physical environmental studies as well as engineering fundamentals.[42] To undertake the new mission, Schick added courses in astronomy-astronautics, geology, physical geography, the digital computer, and engineering fundamentals; additionally, he revamped existing courses in graphical calculations, techniques, and representations.[43] The world geography course was transferred from the the Department of Social Sciences to ES&GS.

In parallel with the new mission, the department reorganized courses into two instructional groups: the Engineering Fundamentals Group (EFG) and the Environment Group (EG).[44] The former presented a course in earth measurements, which, as a cornerstone of science and engineering, was a subject with obvious military relevancy. Also presented by the EFG were courses in graphic science that had migrated from the old Department of Military Topography and Graphics; they included surveying, descriptive geometry, topographical drawing, engineering drawing, and graphical mathematics. These courses provide a medium through which technological developments could be more easily understood and applied. Schick was adamant in his view that illiteracy in these areas was "unthinkable for officers of the armed forces."[45]

The EG courses were physical geography, astronomy-astronautics, and world geography. The purpose of these courses was to increase cadets' awareness of the natural environment, its history, and its effects on human activities. Additionally, the courses required cadets to apply their knowledge in practical settings and evaluate the results. The curricular changes in ES&GS had a significant impact on the faculty selected to teach the new courses. In the Environment Group, former military topography instructors had to be retrained as geography and astronomy-astronautics instructors.[46] All instructors would teach the new physical geography course, while half would teach world geography and half would teach astronomy-astronautics.[47]

Training for these changes had begun during 1959. Some instructors monitored the economic geography course in the Department of Social Sciences and consulted with outside geographers such as Dr. Preston James of Syracuse University, whose text was adopted.[48] The physical geographers also received instruction from noted authorities in the field, such as Dr. Arthur Strahler of Columbia University, whose book, like Preston's, became a course text for the cadets.[49] Besides mastering the new course material and developing their syllabuses, the instructors also had to procure the maps, globes, readings, and other teaching aids that the new courses required; meanwhile, classrooms were adapted to accommodate new courses.[50] Schick and Broshous carefully supervised these developments to avoid damage to the distinguished heritage of MT&G as it transformed into ES&GS. This old department with a new name and focus would remain a leader at the Military Academy in geographic and environmental sciences.

When Schick retired in 1961, Broshous became the department head.[51] He continued to refine the courses, improve and modernize the department, and demand excellence from his instructors.[52] One of his most important legacies was to encourage development of instruction in computers and automated technology.[53] Broshous often commented that the cadets were increasingly better prepared for academic, military, and social life at the Academy than their predecessors. "As an instructor in the Department of Engineering in 1937," he recalled, "I taught vector analysis to First Classmen. In Earth, Space, and Graphic Sciences, we now teach it to Plebes. We are pushing forward in knowledge."[54]

Broshous retired as head of ES&GS on 29 February 1972, and Col. Gilbert W. Kirby (USMA 1949) was appointed as the new department head. Kirby's first assignment at the Military Academy had been in 1956 as a member of MT&G. Upon his return to West Point in 1967, he accepted an appointment as a permanent professor in ES&GS.[55]

From 1975 to 1978, Kirby devoted a great deal of attention to implementing changes recommended by USMA curriculum review groups.[56] His goal was to strengthen the curriculum in consonance with advances in technology and to better prepare future officers to meet the challenges that awaited them as commissioned officers. Accordingly, he added electives in physical geography, astronomy, regional geography, automated cartography, and geographic information systems, while shifting the world regional geography course from the core to the elective program.[57] He established an environmental studies program that focused on "matters of national environmental concern, emphasizing scientific research and encouraging thoughtful alternatives and solutions through sound engineering."[58] In the engineering field, Kirby gave increased emphasis to the core course in computer science, computer operations, and particularly computer applications in the military.[59]

Kirby and his staff also addressed means for improving map and landscape interpretation and integration skills by Academy graduates. In 1977, the department introduced a new core course for the Third Class, EV203—Terrain Analysis.[60] The course, which brought together elements of the old military topography course and instruction in physical geography, included cartography, advanced map interpretation, and remote sensing integrated with meteorology, climatology, and geomorphology. The intent of this course was to increase cadets' "understanding and appreciation of the environment over which they will operate as soldiers and in which they will live as members of society."[61] The current version of this course, EV203—Physical Geography, continues with this goal.

In 1989, the department's evolving mission led to yet another name change: ES&GS became Geography and Computer Science (G&CS). Although on the surface there appeared to be a new face, the broad nature of the department remained very similar to the old

Department of Drawing, still encompassing analysis, interpretation, understanding, and presentation of Planet Earth as the home of mankind. The department also continued its adaptation to an increasingly technological society. Courses were offered providing cadets with the knowledge and tools that would enable them to use computers to perform modern engineering design and data manipulation.[62] The use of computers was closely allied with the department's historical role in the teaching of engineering fundamentals. As Colonel Kirby wrote in 1980:

> The cartographic component of Geography carries on the tradition of earlier days and provides the cadets opportunities to pursue interests in the descriptive aspects of engineering and topography. Cartography and Surveying courses are key to understanding map development and engineering planning, while the Graphics course provides the fundamental skills in engineering drawing.[63]

General MacArthur's earlier-expressed desire that battle maps be improved and the concern of World War II and Korean War veterans for improved map interpretation and terrain analysis skills continued to be addressed during Kirby's tenure. During Cadet Field Training at Camp Buckner, Third Class cadets received instruction in land navigation that helped them interpret terrain using maps. G&CS faculty continued to provide leadership as instructors during this training. With regard to EV203, lessons in meteorology, climatology, soil and vegetation analysis, geomorphology, and map and air photo interpretation furthered the cadets' knowledge of landscape analysis. EV203 culminated in a capstone terrain analysis exercise. Upon successful completion of the course, the cadet was judged "competent to pick up a map and develop in his or her mind a visualization of the terrain depicted on the map and the limits that this terrain will place on military and civilian activity."[64]

Kirby continued his predecessor's practice of incorporating new technology, particularly computers, into the curriculum. As expressed in *Assembly* magazine on the occasion of Colonel Kirby's retirement,

> through his foresight and initiative, his department embraced computing at its genesis and guided the Military Academy into the computer age. . . . Kirby argued the academic merits of computer science and built the discipline into a substantial field of study and academic major including 26 electives and one core course.[65]

Introduction to computers and computer programming were presented in a one-term core course taken by Fourth Classmen (see Chapter 23 for a fuller exposition of the history of computing at West Point). Kirby continued to keep the department, its courses, and the staff and faculty current with changes occurring in the computer field.[66] During the period in which Kirby was head of G&CS, fields of study were established in geography and computer science, resulting in the creation of many new courses in these disciplines. Geography courses continued to focus on the physical aspects of Planet Earth and its interactions with humanity. Complementing these courses were faculty-authored publications that Kirby initiated and guided to publication: *The Atlas of Landforms, The Landscape Atlas of the USSR,* and *A Bibliography of Military Geography.*[67] These and later G&CS publications found widespread use in military and academic communities outside West Point. Colonel Kirby had clearly met his goal of designing a geography curriculum that would give cadets "a better understanding of the environment in which the soldier and civilian operate."[68]

Contemporary Integration, 1991–2003

Col. Gerald E. Galloway, Jr., (USMA 1957) became the head of G&CS upon Colonel Kirby's retirement on 27 January 1989. Galloway had been the deputy head of G&CS and a member of the department since 1977, his principal academic interests being military geography, water resources management, and microcomputer use on the battlefield.[69] During Academic Year 1987-1988, he served as USMA Chief of Staff and Deputy Post Commander, an experience that no doubt helped groom him for the appointment as Dean of the Academic Board that would occur on 1 July 1990.[70]

During his brief tenure as department head, the department experienced still another name change. In July 1989, computer science and electrical engineering were consolidated under the newly created Department of Electrical Engineering and Computer Science, with what remained of G&CS becoming the Department of Geography. Later that year, the Department of Geography was redesignated the Department of Geography and Environmental Engineering (G&EnE). The new name reaffirmed the departmental focus that had evolved from the 1960s—an appreciation of physical landscapes and their modification by human activity, with the goal of mitigating or preventing the harmful aspects of human activity.

To lead this newly reorganized department, the Academy turned to Col. John H. Grubbs (USMA 1964). His long and varied engineering experience was ideally suited for the challenges of bringing the department's new environmental engineering component up to the high standards of the Academy. Grubbs would serve as the department head from 1991 until his retirement in 1998. Succeeding him was Col. Wendell C. King, the current head. Grubbs and King moved the department toward an integrated curriculum that combines geographical studies with environmental engineering. They oversaw the development of five sub-programs—human-regional geography, environmental geography, environmental science, environmental engineering, and geospatial information science—that continue today.

Conclusion

One of the first courses offered at West Point was surveying, taught by the Superintendent Maj. Jonathan Williams in 1802. The cadets' integrative project in that course was to create a map of West Point and its environs. Throughout the Academy's history, topographical mapping and interpretive skills have been an enduring focus. These skills have been taught successively in the Department of Drawing, MT&G, ES&GS, G&CS, and G&EnE, as well as in the former Department of Practical Military Engineering. The surveying course has survived by following a similar pathway, maintaining its relevance throughout the last two centuries. Mapping and surveying courses continue to reside in G&EnE today.

It is true that courses in drawing and geography at West Point never enjoyed the status of those in mathematics, civil engineering, and French, particularly during the 19th century when the Academy's focus was on producing engineers. However, drawing and geography courses have been among the most enduring of the Academy's curriculum, outlasting other courses that were more fashionable at the time but less relevant in the long term. Knowledge imparted to cadets through these subjects directly furthered accomplishment of the Academy's mission—producing leaders of character.

In a profession that demands a mastery of land, whether for fighting on it or for living on it, the Department of Geography and Environmental Engineering continues to play a vital role in West Point's academic agenda.

---

[1] Michael Moss, "Robert W. Weir as Teacher," in *Robert W. Weir of West Point: Illustrator, Teacher and Poet* (West Point, NY: United States Military Academy, 1976), 35.

[2] Ibid., 36.

[3] Charles Larned, *The Centennial of the United States Military Academy at West Point, New York, 1802-1902*, vol. 1 (Washington: Government Printing Press, 1904), 291, 293.

[4] Moss, 39.

[5] Ibid., 38.

[6] Larned, *The Centennial*, 294.

[7] Charles Broshous, "The Department of Military Topography and Graphics, U.S.M.A.," *Assembly*, no. 4 (1953): 2.

[8] Moss, 42.

[9] Larned, *The Centennial*, 295.

[10] George Pappas, *To the Point: The United States Military Academy, 1802-1902* (Westport, CT: Praeger, 1993), 378.

[11] Francis Greene, *Annual Report, Forty-third Annual Reunion of the Association of the Graduates of the United States Military Academy at West Point, NY* (West Point, NY: United States Military Academy, 1912), 33.

[12] Ibid., 33.

[13] Sidney Forman, *West Point: A History of the United States Military Academy* (New York: Columbia University Press, 1950), 159-160; Larned, *The Centennial*, 295-296.

[14] Pappas, 393.

[15] Ibid., 393.

[16] Greene, 34-35.

[17] Ibid. The three courses, Plane and Descriptive Geometry, Shades and Shadows, and Linear Perspective and Isometric Projections, were transferred to the Department of Drawing from the Department of Mathematics.

[18] Charles Larned, Memorandum for the Superintendent on Revision of the Course of Instruction. West Point, NY, U.S. Military Academy, 17 May 1910.

[19] *Topographical Drawing* (1917) and *Map Reading and Topographical Sketching* (1918) were written by Colonel Stuart and published while he was the department head.

[20] Ibid., 3.

[21] Theodore Crackel, *The Illustrated History of West Point* (New York: Harry N. Adams, 1991), 214.

[22] Lawrence E. Schick, "General Alexander Rretires," *Assembly*, no. 3 (1947): 2.

[23] Ibid., 2.

[24] Lawrence E. Schick, "The Department of Earth, Space, and Graphic Sciences," *Assembly*, no. 2 (1961): 29-31.

[25] Schick, "General Alexander," 3.

[26] Gilbert W. Kirby, Jr., "The Department of Geography and Computer Science: A New Name for an Old Department," *Assembly*, no. 4 (1980): 12.

[27] Stanley Tozeski, *Preliminary Inventory of the Records of the United States Military Academy* (Washington, DC: National Archives and Records Service, 1976), 16.

[28] Broshous, 2.

[29] Francis Wilby, *The Annual Report of the Superintendent of the United States Military Academy* (West Point, NY: United States Military Academy, 1945), 3.

[30] "General Schick Rretires," *Assembly*, no. 3 (1961): 8.

[31] Ibid., 8.

[32] Ibid., 7.

[33] Ibid., 6.

[34] Ibid.

[35] Tozeski, *Primary Inventory*, 13.

[36] "Colonel Russ Broshous," *Assembly*, no. 3 (1969): 25.

[37] Ibid., 25.

[38] Broshous, 4.

[39] Ibid.

[40] "General Schick retires," 7.

[41] Schick, "The Department of Earth, Space, and Graphic Sciences," 29.

[42] Tozeski, 16.

[43] William W. Bessell, Jr., "Lawrence Edward Schick," *Assembly*, no. 1 (1968): 117.

[44] Schick, "The Department of Earth, Space, and Graphic Sciences," 29.

[45] Ibid.

[46] Ibid., 30.

[47] Ibid., 31.

[48] Ibid.

[49] Ibid.

[50] Ibid.

[51] "Colonel Russ Broshous Retires," *Assembly*, no. 4 (1972): 22.

[52] Ibid.

53 Lawrence J. Lincoln, "Charles Russell Broshous," *Assembly,* no. 3 (1985): 140.

54 "Colonel Russ Broshous," 46.

55 Jeffrey LaMoe, "Brigadier General Gilbert W. Kirby, Jr., Retires," *Assembly,* no. 1 (1989): 7.

56 Kirby, 13.

57 Ibid.

58 LaMoe, 7.

59 Kirby, 13.

60 LaMoe, 7.

61 Kirby, 33.

62 Ibid., 12.

63 Ibid., 34.

64 Ibid., 33.

65 LaMoe, 7.

66 Ibid.

67 Ibid. Complete citations for these three works are as follows: H. Allen Curran, Phillip S. Justus, Drew M. Young II, and John B. Garver, Jr., *Atlas of Landforms* (New York: John Wiley and Sons, 1965); Thomas F. Plummer, Jr., William G. Honne, Edward F. Brunner, and Christian C. Thudium, Jr., *The Landscape Atlas of the USSR* (West Point, NY: U.S. Military Academy, 1971); Eugene J. Palka and Dawn M. Lake, *A Bibliography of Military Geography,* 4 vols. (West Point, NY: U.S. Military Academy, 1988).

68 Kirby, 34.

69 Ibid., 8.

70 Ibid.

CHAPTER 19

EVOLUTION OF SOCIOLOGY AT WEST POINT, 1963–2001[1]

Morten G. Ender and Thomas A. Kolditz

Introduction: Origins of Sociology

The origins of the discipline of sociology are not easy to pin down precisely. Edward Byron Reuter notes that sociology has always been around—that it is "as old as associated life and as universal as human thought."[2] In other words, human history is replete with human organization where people have attempted to make sense of their relations in groups. Thus, "sociology begins when [people] reflect and generalize about social reality and human relationships."[3] James Henslin takes a narrower view—he argues that sociology began in the wake of the American and French revolutions when people were encouraged to rethink social life.[4] The traditional ideas of monarchies gave way to the conviction that individuals had rights and that they are inalienable. Henslin further argues that western imperialism around the world fostered increased contact with divergent cultures thus surfacing a need to understand those cultures. Finally, he concludes that sociology would not have developed without the success of the natural sciences and the use of the scientific method.

Despite these divergent views, it seems clear that modern sociology started in Western Europe sometime in the mid-19th century. Social thinkers such as Auguste Comte, Herbert Spencer, Karl Marx, Emile Durkheim, and Max Weber reflected on the social milieus of industrialization and urbanization. All were deeply concerned over the sweeping social changes occurring during their lifetimes and impacting every aspect of human life. Work, family, religion, the economy, migration, and interpersonal relationships were greatly affected by the Industrial Revolution and the demographic shift from rural to urban living.

The early centers of American sociology were at the University of Chicago and the University of Kansas. The sociology programs set up by such schools had several distinguishing characteristics. First, many of the early sociologists were ministers and reformers. They had experienced the social world prior to theorizing about it. Second, women and blacks were welcomed early on—social reformers Jane Addams and W.E.B. DuBois, for example, had backgrounds in sociology. Third, the early sociology programs emphasized practical application of theoretical knowledge; consequently the focus was on the belief that the human condition could be improved through human intervention, reform, the study of human subcultures, the use of science to understand the human condition, and local issues.

These characteristics seem to possess relevancy in the unique educational environment at West Point. Sociologists have noted that the narrow focus of professional schools such as the Military Academy, as opposed to the broader scope of traditional liberal arts institutions, make them ideal places to establish sociology programs.[5] They argue that professional schools could benefit from a discipline devoted to understanding the nature of organizations in general and professions in particular. In fact, the Academy sociology program addresses these topics; additionally, it has assumed the tradition of pragmatism characteristic of early American sociology, with its application to problems at the Academy, to other academies around the world, and within the Army at large.

This chapter begins by describing the origins of sociology at West Point relative to the role of educating future officers. Next, we focus on the slow and steady growth of the sociology program and sociology curricular change to include a focus on courses and pedagogy. Next, we discuss the social history and demography of cadets by drawing relevant comparisons with civilian students and within the Corps of Cadets itself. We also remark upon the post-graduation experience of our graduates. Here too we discuss structural changes in the most recent sociology program at West Point, including strategies for evaluating program results. The USMA sociology faculty and their academic backgrounds are covered as well. The chapter is concluded with a brief comparison of 21st century-Academy sociology with American sociology as it existed in the late 19th and early 20th centuries.

The principal method of analysis will be a social autopsy of sorts. Data sources include Academy archives, documents, reports, assessment data, interviews with key figures, and Department of Behavioral Sciences and Leadership (BS&L) records. We shall find that sociology at the Academy has followed the trends of sociology in the larger society, educational institutions, and the Army. West Point and the Army, like the greater society and higher education in general, are experiencing a moderate renaissance in student/cadet interest as people come to recognize the utility of sociology in institution-building.

Origins of the USMA Sociology Program

No sociology program existed at West Point prior to World War II. An in-house memorandum suggests that prior to 1946, the Academic Board resisted the establishment of formal courses in psychology and leadership "on the grounds of time [instructional hours] and relevance, arguing that the subjects of psychology and leadership were irrelevant or not possible to teach, respectively."[6] Gen. Dwight Eisenhower disagreed. After the war when be became Chief of Staff of the Army, Eisenhower wrote a letter to the West Point Superintendent Maj. Gen. Maxwell Taylor expressing his concern with future leaders' ability to handle the human dimensions of leadership and personnel issues. The letter, dated 2 January 1946, is here quoted at length:[7]

> A feature that I should like very much to see included in the curriculum is a course in practical or applied psychology. I realize that tremendous advances have been made in the matter of leadership and personnel management since I was a Cadet. Nevertheless I am sure that it is a subject that should receive the constant and anxious care of the

Superintendent and his assistants on the Academic Board
and these should frequently call in for consultation experts
both from other schools and from among persons who have
made an outstanding success in industrial and economic
life. Too frequently we find young officers trying to use
empirical and ritualistic methods in the handling of individuals—I think that both theoretical and practical instruction
along this line could, at the very least, awaken the majority
of Cadets to the necessity for handling human problems on
a human basis and do much to improve leadership and personnel handling in the Army at large.

Eisenhower's appreciation of the social and psychological sciences probably emerged from his experience in commissioning
researchers to study the morale of soldiers during World War II. The
researchers were civilian scholars who had considerable experience
in conducting human affairs research. Led by Harvard sociologist
Samuel A. Stouffer, the researchers published their findings in 1949
under the title *The American Soldier*.[8] The study broke new ground
as an interdisciplinary effort to address difficult human attitudinal,
situational, motivational, and leadership issues associated with military service. Eisenhower probably did not know that the researchers
were principally sociologists, but he was certainly impressed by the
quality and usefulness of their work, which has never been replicated.[9]

In the latter part of 1946, pursuant to the Chief's wishes, the Academic Board established the Department of Military Psychology and
Leadership (MP&L), placing it in the Department of Tactics under the
Commandant of Cadets.[10] Cadets were to be "trained" in psychology
and leadership rather than "schooled" under the aegis of a bona fide
academic discipline. Again, prior to 1946, both the Superintendent
and the Academic Board had refused to officially include a leadership and psychology course in the academic curriculum.[11] However,
the subject of military leadership was treated through occasional lectures, incidental integration in the regular academic classes of other
disciplines, and sundry other expedients—all under the Dean with

support by the Commandant. Though lacking the form, stature, and coherence of an actual curricular course, the subject was nominally addressed. The gradual crystallization of the Department of Behavioral Sciences and Leadership (BS&L) as we know it today occurred over a 35-year period, from 1946 to 1977. The issue was extraordinarily controversial and polarizing, with slow, halting movement toward resolution marked by numerous sharp turns, false starts, and see-saw motions as deans, commandants, and superintendents came and went, each seemingly with views somehow at odds with those of their predecessors or of the other principals. For example, as early as 1950, the Department of the Army recommended that a Department of Management, Psychology, and Leadership be established as an academic department under the Dean. The Dean, Brig. Gen. Harris Jones, opposed the idea and no further movement was made until his departure in 1956.[12]

During the 1950s, most of the argument centered on two related issues: Should responsibility for psychology and leadership instruction be assigned to the Dean or to the Commandant? And should instruction take the form of a baccalaureate course entailing the teaching of disciplinary history, theory, and practice by appropriately credentialed academics, or should it be approached as field-oriented, "how-to" military training taught by officers and NCOs using the Army's time-proven rote-and-drill instructional methods? Regardless of where they stood on these issues, however, everyone did appear to agree that both psychology and leadership courses were necessary.

As early as 1962, the Commandant, Brig. Gen. Richard G. Stilwell, favored the establishment of a new Department of Behavioral Sciences to include courses in both sociology and psychology.[13] In 1970 there was considerable movement toward reorganizing the Department of MP&L in that direction. However, the senior leadership charged with making changes—both the Commandant of Cadets and the Director of Military Psychology and Leadership—changed again with the incoming Commandant and Director both opposing such changes. The new Commandant recognized, however, the utility of both sociology and psychology to buttress the study of leadership.

By the early 1970s, the utility and fruitfulness of leadership development and training, psychology, and other behavioral sciences were fast being recognized. A curriculum review committee in 1972 found "increasing emphasis at Department of Army on the application of the behavioral sciences to the solution of current Army problems."[14] Moreover, the committee proposed the transfer of such academic courses to the academic side of the house. The committee's report, known as the Kappel Report, resulted in the brief establishment in 1973 of the Office of Military Leadership (OML), which split formal organizational responsibilities for leadership instruction between the Dean and the Commandant. A few years later, the Borman Commission, citing earlier studies to include the Kappel Report, recommended that a Department of Behavioral Sciences and Leadership be established as an academic department under the Dean.[15] The Department of Behavioral Sciences and Leadership (BS&L) was established on 1 September 1977. Courses in sociology were included in the curriculum as recommended.

Sociology Curricular Evolution

Prior to the establishment of BS&L, sociology in the curriculum was represented almost entirely by psychology and leadership. The few sociology elective courses offered were slanted toward applied and practical aspects of military organization. An introductory sociology elective course called Sociology: Society and Culture was first offered at West Point during the 1963-1964 academic year. Another elective course in military sociology titled American Military Institutions and Manpower was first offered in 1965-1966 as part of a new military studies program. Social Psychology and Organizational Theory were first offered in 1969 and 1971, respectively. These courses were based largely on research as reported in *The American Soldier* series published immediately after World War II by Stouffer and his associates. Sociology of Minorities was added to the curriculum during the 1970-1971 academic year, reflecting the marked racial turbulence not only in American society but in the military as well. These courses were no longer offered in 1974, when the Department of Military Psychology changed to the Office of Military Leadership

(OML). However, by the 1975-1976 academic year, Introductory Sociology and Sociology of Minorities, and later (1976-1977) Military Sociology, were again offered under the title Topics in Sociology on a rotational basis.

Prior to 1985, West Point did not offer a traditional academic major based on a disciplinary specialty as found at almost all colleges.[16] The establishment of the major at West Point has been an incremental process. Prior to 1960, cadets had no choice of electives. After 1960, upperclassmen could choose electives including one of two sociology electives. In 1970, an "Area of Study Concentration" gave cadets a choice of six to seven electives in their academic program. Moving toward a major, the "Field of Study" (FOS) was developed in 1979, allowing cadets heavier concentration in a specific academic discipline, with nine courses. In anticipation of the FOS, an optional sociology/psychology FOS was added to the curriculum during the 1977-1978 academic year. Marriage and the Family, a popular staple course of any sociology program in the country, was offered for the first time in 1977-1978 after some resistance on the part of the administration.[17] Introductory Sociology had also been available to cadets and offered as an elective in two of the areas of concentration offered at West Point in 1977—Humanities and Public Affairs. Finally, in 1985, the traditional academic major was introduced, permitting study in-depth of an academic discipline on the basis of 13 required courses. Fourteen cadets graduated with a major in sociology the following year—three being women. The FOS continued to be offered for those cadets who wanted a concentration in the discipline but short of a major.

The period from 1980 to 1994 saw rapid growth in the sociology program at West Point. New courses, including Research Methods; Class, Status, and Power; and Group Dynamics, were added, while Organizational Theory was restored to the curriculum in 1980-1981. A year later, the department began rounding out sociology offerings with Mass Media and Society and Theoretical Perspectives in Sociology. Moreover, the sociology program saw its first movement toward a traditional civilian sociology major in terms of structure. Two capstone courses, Colloquium in Sociology and Independent Study were added in the mid-1980s to complete the course of study in the field of sociology. The fortuity of having a criminologist on the faculty, along with growing interest in the topic itself, resulted in the introduction of the course Criminology and Criminal Justice Studies in Academic Year 1990-1991, thus further broadening the program. By the early 1990s, BS&L featured 17 elective courses that had a sociological focus, offering cadets a breadth and depth of specialization comparable to that of highly regarded liberal arts colleges around the country.[18]

The enrollments of cadets in sociology courses has fluctuated within fairly narrow bounds for the past 17 years. There are several reasons for the popularity of sociology courses, including schedule flexibility, increased awareness of social issues in the military, and changes in the composition of the Corp of Cadets such as the integration of women. The data in Table 19-1, from a study conducted by BS&L visiting professors David and Mady Segal and BS&L Department Head Col. John Wattendorf,[19] show the mean enrollments in nine sociology courses at West Point for the selected Academic Years 1985-1986 through 1988-1989, 1996-1997 through 1997-1998, and 2000-2001 through 2001-2002. During the late 1980s, the courses Introductory Sociology and Marriage and the Family[20] were the most frequently offered and enjoyed the highest enrollments. Group Dynamics, Social Psychology, and Research Methods were also in high demand. By the mid to late 1990s, Introductory Sociology and Criminology and Criminal Justice Studies had the highest enrollments, with some drop in the number taking Marriage and the Family. Armed Forces and Society as well as Social Inequality have emerged as staple course offerings for sociology, popular among students both in and outside of BS&L majors. For example, a number of students from outside BS&L enroll in Social Inequality, seeking a course that satisfies their inquisitiveness, addresses diversity at both the individual and societal levels, and offers some systematic and in-depth study of this broad issue. Summing up, the early 21st century shows modest decreases in enrollment from previous years but stable numbers for all courses with the exception of Marriage and the Family, which has fluctuated.

Table 19-1. Frequency of Selected West Point Sociology Courses (one semester each) and Average Course Enrollments Per Semester—for Three Representative Periods.*

Courses	Frequency of Presentation			Average Course Enrollments Per Semester**		
	Sep '85- May '86	Sep '96- May '98	Sep '00- May '02	Sep '85- May '86	Sep '96- May '98	Sep '00- May '02
Introductory Sociology	6	8	4	58	131	64
Marriage and the Family	6	2	2	55	31	27
Research Methods	8	***	4	45	***	69
Group Dynamics	4	***	2	45	***	32
Mass Media and Society	4	***	***	21	***	***
Social Psychology	8	***	5	20	***	73
Armed Forces and Society	2	3	3	19	50	44
Social Inequality	4	4	2	12	55	34
Criminology	***	12	7	***	199	112

*Averages are rounded to the nearest whole number.

**Maximum size for sociology classes at West Point is small (18) because of the emphasis on Socratic dialogue in the classroom. Enrollments larger than 18 indicate the course was presented in multiple sections.

***Courses not offered or data was not available at the time of writing.

All the sociology courses have relied on traditional and standard sociology content but deviate somewhat in the application of that knowledge. While instructors used standardized pedagogical resources, the cases and examples used in the classroom were intended to illustrate and to enliven the applicability of sociological theories, concepts, and research findings to the profession of arms.[21]

Thus, as the Segal research team reported 13 years ago, the sociology curriculum at West Point diverges from more conventional sociology curriculums at civilian universities in three major ways: (1) the professional application component of each course; (2) emphasis on military leadership and social structure of the military; and (3) inflexibility in scheduling introductory sociology courses. On the last point, the USMA core curriculum precludes BS&L cadets from taking Introductory Sociology until the second half of the Third Class (i.e., sophomore) year, and often later. The late start creates a timing problem for cadets wishing to take sociology as a major (entailing 13 elective courses) or as a field of study (ten elective courses).[22] Non-sociology cadets encounter sociology late in their academic experience—thus their schedule usually precludes their taking advanced electives in sociology. Similarly, sociology cadets must take a heavy dose of sociology courses in their final two years; in the end, however, they complete the back-loaded program as a rich complement to their other professionally focused studies.

Cadets in Sociology: Future Leaders

The percentage of cadets majoring in sociology at West Point has conformed to national trends fairly closely over the years, following a sine-wave pattern.[23] Nationally, bachelor's degrees in sociology peaked at nearly 36,000 in 1973, declining to just over 12,000 in 1986. In subsequent years, the number has risen steadily to just over 24,000 in 1996, the last year for which reliable figures are currently available.[24] With regard to trends in the number of sociology degrees awarded in the United States as compared to trends at West Point, the data show a consistent rise in civilian degrees over the decade from 1986 to 1996, but a fluctuating number of bachelor's degrees for USMA over the identical period and up to the present as well. The highest yields at USMA were in 1986 and 2003, with 14 cadet sociology majors graduating in each of those years. The lowest yield was only three graduates in 2001. A decline following 1997 resulted from significant changes in the program, including substantial loss of faculty and courses, but a strong rebound occurred in 2001.

The rise in sociology majors in the United States has resulted from several factors, including greater proportions of women and other nontraditional students entering higher education (e.g., first-generation college students), a new generational civic consciousness orientated toward social problems, especially criminal justice, and the flexibility of the sociology major in preparing students for graduate education in areas such as teaching, social work, law, private sector management, and not-for-profit and government administration. Similar considerations account for cadets coming into sociology at

West Point. In addition, our anecdotal evidence suggests cadets are genuinely concerned about and focused on studying social issues for their own sake.

The marked upturn of cadet sociology majors following 2001 reflects a rigorous restructuring of the sociology program. A number of changes were implemented, the four main ones being: (1) creation of greater curriculum flexibility by offering more electives both in BS&L and the other departments that enrich the sociology core and its electives; (2) establishment of a more stable and cohesive program by hiring two civilian professors working in conjunction with permanent and rotating military faculty; in addition, both vertical and horizontal cohesion within the program were enhanced by increasing faculty, promoting greater cadet interaction among the three upper classes, and emphasizing team projects within classes and study groups; (3) fostering a subculture of sociological excellence through such activities as establishing a local chapter of an international honor society, attending professional conferences, applied learning, and participating in student paper competitions; and (4) improving extra-institutional outreach during the Fourth Class and Third Class years.[25] Overall, the 18-year trend of the sociology program at USMA is duplicative of the 35-year trend nationally, with both ending on an upswing.[26]

A closer examination of West Point sociology graduates reveals interesting similarities and dissimilarities to a cross section of the Corp of Cadets. Data is based on 159 cadets who completed or are expected to complete the sociology program during the period 1986-2004 as compared with the 15,601 cadets who graduated from West Point between 1986 and 2001. (Data is unavailable for the Corp of Cadets from 2002 to 2004; data for the sociology program cadets is extended to 2004 instead of 2001 to provide a more valid sample size. The number 159 represents about one percent of the total number of graduates.) The data in Table 19-2 provides selected socio-demographic characteristics of the two groups.

Cadets from the sociology program compared to a cross section of the Corp of Cadets reflect a disproportionate percentage of women (41 percent vs. 12 percent, respectively), African-Americans (17 vs.

Table 19-2. Selected Socio-Demographic Characteristics of West Point Sociology Majors and Field of Study Graduates from 1996 to 2004 and All Cadet Graduates from 1986 to 2001.

Characteristics	Sociology Cadets, 1986-2004 (N=159)*		All Cadets, 1986-2001 (N=15,601)*	
Gender				
Female	65	40.9%	1,786	11.5%
Race				
African-American	27	17.0%	1,008	6.5%
American Indian	**	**	82	.5
Asian	8	5.0	703	4.7
Caucasian	115	72.3	13,057	83.7
Hispanic	8	5.0	642	4.1
Other	1	.6	82	.5
USMAPS	41	25.8%	2,034	13.0%
Recruited Athlete	50	31.4%	3,079	19.7%
Father West Point Grad	7	4.4%	616	4.0%
Status				
Major	47	29.6%	9,994	64.1%
Field of Study (FOS)	112	70.4	5,607	35.9

*Totals for both are less than N due to numerous factors (e.g., separation after graduation).
**Native Americans included in "Other" category.

7), U.S. Military Academy Preparatory School (USMAPS) graduates (26 vs. 13), and recruited athletes (31 vs. 20). Additionally, cadets studying sociology as a field of study outnumber those who major in sociology (70 percent vs. 30 percent)—nearly the reverse of the situation in the Corp of Cadets overall (36 percent of cadets opt for their field of study vs. 64 percent who major). Sociology cadet graduates are similar to their peers in terms of whether their fathers graduated from West Point and religious affiliation (not shown in Table 19-2).

The data in Table 19-3 reveals some modest percentage underrepresentation of male sociology graduates in such ground combat branches as Armor, Infantry, and Engineers. The reason for this difference is unclear and could benefit from more study in depth. There is over-representation of sociology graduates in such support branches as Quartermaster, Ordnance, Transportation, and Military Police. The over-representation of sociology graduates in these four branches is accounted for by an imbalance in favor of female graduates. Since women are systematically excluded from assignment to the ground combat arms, they must be assigned to the support branches. When women graduates also happen to be over-represented in sociology or any other discipline, they may cause that discipline to be over-represented in particular support branches even while male sociology graduates are not necessarily over-represented in the same support branches.

An explanation for the high concentration of women in sociology comes from outside of West Point. The discipline of sociology has consistently drawn women in great numbers at all levels of education, but especially at the undergraduate level.[27] There is indirect evidence that similar nationwide trends are occurring for African-Americans.[28] Finally, we suspect, based on anecdotal evidence through informal interaction with cadets, that over-representation of USMAPS and recruited athletes in the sociology program results from such factors as slightly older cadets, prior service, more varied life experiences, and familiarity with sociology through the USMAPS curriculum.[29] It should be noted that the Superintendent of the USMAPS at the time of this writing, Col. Michael A. Anderson, held a Ph.D. in sociology from the University of Chicago, taught sociology courses in BS&L for a number of years, and provided some exposure to the "prepsters" through sociological readings in the USMAPS English courses.[30]

Moreover, with respect to athletes, we would argue that they are looking for disciplines that provide sufficient flexibility for them to become more well-rounded at USMA, to include excelling in leadership positions and academics as well as sports. Some have argued that sociology is perceived by college athletes and others as an academically easy major, but recent studies have debunked the myth that sociology courses are a free ride, which certainly has no validity at West Point in any case.[31] The Academy sociology program is as rigorous as that of any other discipline; the unfair perception that it

Table 19-3. Branch Selections of West Point Sociology Majors and Field of Study Graduates.*

Branch of Service	Sociology Cadets, 1986-2004 (N=159)		All Cadets, 1986-2001 (N=15,601)	
	frequency	%	frequency	%
Air Defense	11	9.2%	938	6.1%
Adjutant General	3	2.5	238	1.6
Armor	9	7.6	1,909	12.0
Aviation	8	6.7	1,790	11.6
Chemical Corp	0	0	77	.5
Engineer	3	2.5	1,808	11.7
Field Artillery	21	17.6	2,478	16.1
Finance	3	2.5	104	.7
Infantry	17	14.3	3,009	19.6
Military Intelligence	6	5.0	853	5.5
Military Police	6	5.0	320	2.1
Medical Service Corp	3	2.5	176	1.1
Ordnance	6	5.0	375	2.4
Quartermaster	12	10.1	415	2.7
Signal Corp	2	1.7	596	3.9
Transportation Corp	9	7.6	309	2.0
Totals **	119	100.0	15,395	100.0

*Excludes cadets not commissioned, interservice transfers, foreign nationals, and medical school.
**Totals for both groups are less than N due to numerous factors (e.g., separation after graduation).

is easy is probably the result of the flexibility that BS&L designs into the program to overcome the scheduling difficulties already noted. For example, sociology courses provide for more out-of-class writing and community-related assignments compared to in-class drills, problem-solving, and standardized examinations. In addition, the department is philosophically oriented toward alternative assignments, student-centered pedagogical approaches to knowledge acquisition and application, and self-paced assignments. Cadet athletes and senior leaders appreciate these flexible techniques which allow them to reconcile their academic commitments with the time-consuming responsibilities associated with their sports, clubs, and leadership activities.

Perhaps the best indicator of the sociology program's (or any academic program's) effectiveness is how well USMA graduates perform as commissioned officers. Army field data tends to confirm the strength of the sociology program at West Point.[32] In general, commanders' ratings of West Point graduates as well as graduates' self-assessment of their field performance indicate that West Point's academic program goals are being met. In particular, cadets who studied sociology as a field of study or major earn slightly higher ratings. If West Pointers are doing well overall, those who study sociology seem to be doing even better.

The Sociology Curriculum: Rebounding from Reversal

The 1994-1995 academic year marked a downturn in the sociology program. Sociology lost three electives, viz., Sociological Theory, Mass Media and Society, and Class, Status, and Power. Although loss of the theory course seriously undermined the program, loss of the other two courses could have been compensated for easily within the department with other electives had the option been available. The program faltered for a few years. The reason for the decline was related to the competitive nature of the system, that is, the growth of other programs in the interdisciplinary BS&L. BS&L encompasses four programs (psychology, leadership and management, engineering psychology, and sociology) under one department and a single Department Head. The structure of the West Point curriculum is such that any gains in the number of new courses require corresponding losses elsewhere in order to maintain a rough balance among faculty, cadets, and resources. In the case of BS&L, the rapid and significant growth of enrollments in the management program during the 1994-1995 time frame impacted negatively on sociology enrollments.

The hiring of a second full-time and civilian sociologist with a Ph.D. in 1998 marked a new milestone, providing a further opportunity to stabilize the core sociology courses and the program. Likewise, new rotating faculty members with terminal M.A. degrees in sociology from premier graduate programs specializing in military sociology such as the University of Maryland, Northwestern University, and Texas A&M University helped to strengthen the sociology curriculum and stimulate increased enrollments.

Today, the sociology program at West Point has been refocused and revitalized. Sociological Theory returned to the curriculum as a foundational course required for cadets in sociology. Other required sociology program core courses are Research Methods, Introductory Sociology,[33] Social Inequality: Race, Gender, & Ethnicity, Armed Forces and Society, and Advanced Study in the Behavioral Sciences. These required courses are supplemented with electives from BS&L departmental programs; the electives include Marriage and the Family, Social Psychology, Personality and Adjustment, Criminology and the Criminal Justice System, Leadership Theory and Development, and a new course, Cinematic Images of War and the Military.[34] In addition to these core and elective courses, cadets enrich their education in sociology with complementary electives in other disciplines. Such courses include Cultural Studies (Department of English); Korea, Vietnam, and the American Military Experience (History); Comparative Military Systems (Military Instruction); German Civilization (Foreign Language); and Political and Cultural Anthropology (Social Sciences). In sum, sociology has been revitalized through several measures: the stabilization of the core sociology program; the abandonment of the "lockstep" curriculum that limited course selections; the opening of the sociology major/field of study with a student-centered curriculum through electives; and, finally, the resourcing of sociology with experienced, committed, and enthusiastic faculty.

West Point Sociology Faculty: Applying Knowledge

A 1990 study of the West Point sociology program concluded that the curriculum "is quite conventional by the standards of a civilian liberal arts college, but the faculty is not."[35] Thirteen years later, that conclusion is less valid. The curriculum remains, but faculty have changed somewhat. Continuing an earlier tradition, the West Point faculty remains composed primarily of active-duty Army officers to provide cadets role models as soldier-scholars. Senior military officers with Ph.D.s make up about 15 percent of the faculty; rotating military faculty officers with master's degrees represent 62 percent. What is new are civilian professors with Ph.D.s, who in recent years have assumed a larger role in cadet education; today they comprise 23 percent of the West Point faculty.

The recent structure of the BS&L faculty parallels that of the USMA faculty overall. For example, during Academic Year 2000-2001, BS&L had 38 faculty members. Of these, seven (18 percent) were senior military officers with Ph.D.s, while 24 (63 percent) were rotating military officers with master's degrees from highly ranked civilian graduate programs. Civilian professors number seven, or 18 percent.

As mentioned earlier, the West Point sociology faculty earned their degrees primarily from universities with strong military sociology programs. Table 19-4 lists the universities employed. The four faculty members from the University of Chicago earned their degrees under the tutelage of the world's preeminent military sociologist, Morris Janowitz, prior to his death in 1988. Since then, USMA faculty members have been taught by Janowitz's students at the University of Maryland, Texas A&M, and Northwestern University. Additionally, other fine schools—Vanderbilt, University of Michigan, and Stanford University have well established sociology programs that have attracted people bound for the USMA faculty.

Civilians began joining the sociology faculty at West Point in 1987. In that year, BS&L sponsored Dr. Robert M. Carter as a visiting professor.[36] Two other prominent military sociologists, Drs. David R. Segal and Mady Wechsler Segal, were Visiting Professors in BS&L during the 1988-1989 academic year. Carter left after one year, but was re-hired as a visiting professor from 1989 to 1992. In 1996 he was hired yet again—this time as a Title 10 faculty member with the rank of associate professor.[37] That same year, the Dean hired sociologist Dr. Bruce Keith as the Associate Dean for Academic Assessment. In 2000, Keith was promoted to Associate Dean for Academic Affairs. With promotion to full professor in 2001, Dr. Keith became the first

Table 19-4. Graduate Departments Attended by USMA Sociology Faculty through June 2002.	
University	**Number of Graduates**
University of Maryland at College Park	8
Northwestern University	4
Stanford University	4
University of Chicago	4
University of Texas at Austin	3
Texas A&M University	2
College of William and Mary	1
Harvard University	1
Tulane University	1
University of Alabama	1
University of Michigan	1
University of Nebraska	1
University of New Hampshire	1
University of North Carolina at Chapel Hill	1
University of Oklahoma	1
Vanderbilt University	1

Professor of Sociology at West Point.[38] In 1998, BS&L hired a second full-time sociologist, Morten G. Ender, who was promoted to associate professor in 2000.

The scholarly output of the USMA sociology faculty has been notable. Seventeen articles were published in refereed journals between 1990 and 2001, for an average of 1.5 articles per year. This impressive rate of scholarly productivity is comparatively greater than during the pre-1990 years, when few articles were being published by the sociology faculty at West Point. The themes of the articles have related principally to military sociology (12), undergraduate education (3), and other areas (2). The articles have been published mostly in such journals as *Armed Forces & Society* and *Teaching Sociology.*

Conclusion

To recall briefly the introduction of this chapter, early sociology was primarily pragmatic in orientation with a focus on meliorism, reform, ethnography, empiricism, and locality. This approach represented turn-of-the-century American pragmatism and the earliest traditions of American sociology.[39] Meliorism refers to the improvement of the social conditions of specific groups at the turn of the century such as women, immigrants, and other disenfranchised peoples. Reform deals with civic action and a view of longer-term structural changes through social and political action and policy changes. Ethnography, as practiced at that time, was based primarily on descriptions of the social world inhabited by the peoples under study, though quantification and analysis were not absent. Empiricism—reflecting an orientation toward systematic analysis of direct experience in the empirical world—preceded the advance of abstraction and theorizing. Finally, the early Chicago scholars used locality—that is, the local populations—to advance the study of sociology and make local community life situations better through the scientific method. For example, Albion Small, a prominent early figure in American sociology, viewed the study of the surrounding city of Chicago as offering opportunities for the community under study, for the discipline of sociology itself, and for his students—an obvious "win-win-win" situation.

Sociology at West Point has maintained a variant of this broad pragmatic tradition. The early teaching in the Department of BS&L involved the Socratic method and problem-focused teaching. In recent years, both an active and service-learning approach has been integrated into sociology courses. Active learning involves engaging students in the application of knowledge gleaned to personal, professional, or social situations and contexts. Service-learning involves bridging between theory and real world situations outside the classroom. For example, sociology cadets have been conducting evaluative research of a boarding school for at-risk youth over the past two years. The sociology program stresses the scientific method, encouraging cadets to examine quantitative as well as qualitative data sources. Notably, cadets appear to be more interested in reading and carrying out ethnographic research than statistically-oriented studies. The locality examined by cadets is often the local community of the Corps of Cadets, considered specifically as a subculture, followed more generally by the larger Army of which the Corps is part. Instances can be observed in such senior thesis titles as: "Tattoos and the West Point Cadet" (Cadet Mary Tobin); "Masculine Sex Role Strain at the United States Military Academy" (Cadet Sara Ewing); "Dual Career Couples in the Army" (Cadet Katie Powell); and "A Qualitative Analysis of Military Academy Cadets and their Perceptions of Alcohol Use" (Cadet Mike Izzo).

The sociology faculty recognize and build upon this pragmatic orientation by employing examples from both cadet military experiences in the Corp of Cadets and anticipated experiences to come in the Army. The orientation toward reform is tempered, developing through an understanding that as leaders they will be positioned to make social changes that will improve the lives of their soldiers and their families, their military units, the Army, and potentially the nation and the international community.

The overarching academic program goal expects West Point "graduates to anticipate and to respond effectively to the uncertainties of a changing technological, social, political, and economic world."[40] James Henslin tells us that "sociology is the scientific study of society and human behavior [to include] the impact that various forms of government have on people's lives, the social consequences of production and distribution, culture, [and] the consequences of material goods, group structure, and belief systems."[41] Thus there is clearly a strong relationship between sociology and educating army leaders. The relationship is not as mature as it could be, but it is already rich, committed, valued, and vital—and becoming more so with each passing year.[42]

---

[1] Previous versions of this chapter were presented at the International Sociological Association Meetings, Brisbane, Australia, 7-13 July 2002; and the "Making History: West Point at 200 Years" Conference, West Point, New York, 7-9 March 2002. The authors wish to thank Deb Butler, Bruce Keith, Remi Hajjar, Scott Hampton, Anita Howington, John Hurley, Lloyd Matthews, Shirley Sabel, and David Segal for their assistance with the preparation of this chapter. The views of the authors are their own and do not purport to reflect the position of the United States Military Academy, the Department of the Army, or the Department of Defense. For correspondence, contact Morten G. Ender, Associate Professor of Sociology, Department of Behav-

ioral Sciences and Leadership, United States Military Academy, West Point, New York 10996-1784, U.S.A. or email: morten-ender@usma.edu or visit the website at http://www.dean.usma.edu/bsl/default.htm.

[2] Edward Byron Reuter, *Handbook of Sociology* (New York: Dryden Press, 1946), 4.

[3] Ibid.

[4] James M. Henslin, *Sociology: A Down-to-Earth Approach* (Boston, MA: Allyn & Bacon, 2003).

[5] See Mady Wechsler Segal, David R. Segal, and John M. Wattendorf, "The Sociology Program in a Professional School Setting: The United States Military Academy," *Teaching Sociology* 18 (1990): 156-163.

[6] Department of Behavioral Sciences and Leadership, "The History of the Department of Behavioral Sciences and Leadership: Issues, Events, and Current Events," unpublished memorandum, West Point, NY: United States Military Academy, no date.

[7] Dwight D. Eisenhower, "Letter to Major General Maxwell D. Taylor." unpublished document, Department of Behavioral Sciences and Leadership, West Point, NY, 2 January 1946.

[8] See Samuel A. Stouffer, Edward A. Suchman, Leland C. DeVinney, Shirley A. Star, and Robin M. Williams, *The American* Soldier, vols. 1 and 2 (Princeton, NJ: Princeton University Press, 1949). See also William H. Sewell, "Some Reflections on the Golden Age of Interdisciplinary Social Psychology," *Social Psychology Quarterly* 52 (1989):88-97.

[9] Also on Eisenhower's staff was Morris Janowitz, who would become one of the world's foremost military sociologists after the war. Janowitz worked as a propaganda analyst on Eisenhower's staff prior to the invasion of Normandy. See also Segal et al., "The Sociology Program," 157; and Sewell, "Some Reflections," 89.

[10] Department of Behavioral Sciences and Leadership, *The History of the Department of Behavioral Sciences*, 1.

[11] Ibid., 1.

[12] Ibid., 2.

[13] Ibid., 3.

[14] Ibid., 4.

[15] The Borman Commission, chaired by Col. Frank Borman, was appointed by the Secretary of the Army in 1976 to investigate the 1976 West Point honor scandal. See John P. Lovell, *Neither Athens nor Sparta? The American Service Academies in Transition* (Bloomington and London: Indiana University Press, 1979).

[16] For a discussion of the academic curriculum and its evolution, see chap. 16 of the present volume.

[17] Lt. Col. James R. Swinney, USA Ret., devised, co-developed, and co-taught the first Marriage and the Family courses in BS&L. In a written communication on 18 March 2003, he informed us that the administration of the Academy felt the Marriage and the Family course was "outside the purview of cadet needs and not a scientific field of study." However, with the arrival of the Class of 1980 women in 1976, there were very clear signals to many at the Academy that the military family, dual careers, and issues of sexuality were very much on the minds of the cadets. With the assistance and encouragement of then Department Head, Col. Harry S. Buckley, the Academic Board obstacle was overcome. Lieutenant Colonel Swinney, a trained sociologist, and Lt. Col. Woodie Caine, Ph.D. in social psychology, recognized the importance of family issues at both the interpersonal and institutional level as new research was beginning to emerge about the significance of military families. The courses were overwhelm-

ingly popular, with multiple sections presented in the first couple of years (see table 19-1 in this chapter) employing both Swinney and Caine as fulltime Marriage and the Family instructors.

[18] See Eric P. Godrey, ed., *Teaching Sociology at Small Institutions* (Washington, DC: American Sociological Association, 1998).

[19] Segal et al., "The Sociology Program," 158.

[20] Empirical evidence showed that cadets gained substantial new knowledge from the Marriage and the Family course, both personally and professionally. See Edna J. Hunter and John M. Wattendorf, "De-mystifying Marriage for West Point Cadets: Effects of a Marriage and Family Course," paper presented at the 10th Psychology in the Department of Defense Symposium, U.S. Air Force Academy, Department of Behavioral Sciences and Leadership, Colorado Springs, CO., 16-18 April 1986.

[21] Segal et al., "The Sociology Program," 159.

[22] The field of study will be phased out at West Point by 2005. Since the mid-1980s it has provided cadets the discretion to study a discipline in depth (although not as deeply as in a major) while allowing room for electives in other areas. In place of the field of study, cadets will have the option of taking a minor to supplement their studies in a major. Those who qualify will be able to opt for an honors major.

[23] See the American Sociological Association, "After the Fall: Growth Trends Continue." Available on-line as of March 2003 at: http://www.asanet.org/research/bagrowth2/figure1.html; and the American Sociological Association, "Frequently Asked Questions." Available on-line as of March 2003 at: http://www.asanet.org/research/faqintro.html.

[24] Ibid.

[25] A chapter of Alpha Kappa Delta (AKD): The International Sociological Honor Society was established in the sociology program at West Point in 2001. The official name of the USMA Sociology Program Chapter is *Alpha Phi of New York*. It is a democratic and international society of scholars dedicated to the ideal of Antropon Katamanthanein Diakonesein ("to investigate humanity for the purpose of service"). The purpose of AKD according to its constitution is "to promote excellence in scholarship in the study of sociology, research of social problems, and such other social and intellectual activities as will lead to improvement of the human condition." Membership requirements for AKD include official declaration of sociology major status or demonstration of a serious interest in sociology, at least a junior standing, an accumulated equivalent of an overall grade point average (GPA) of 3.0 (four-point scale), and maintenance of the equivalent of a 3.0 GPA in sociology courses taken at USMA prior to initiation. Other information is available at our website: http://www.dean.usma.edu/bsl/default.htm.

[26] American Sociology Association, "Frequently Asked Questions."

[27] Ibid.

[28] Ibid.

[29] For admission, West Point requires that candidates be at least 17 years of age and not yet 23 years of age on 1 July of their year of admission.

[30] Of special note, USMAPS alumni have a higher graduation rate compared to the entire population of West Point graduates. Over-represented by prior enlisted, African-Americans, and recruited athletes, the "Prep School," as it is known, is essentially a fifth year of high school. For discussion, see Charles C. Moskos and John Sibley Butler, *All That We Can Be: Black Leadership and Racial Integration the Army War* (New York: Basic Books, 1996).

[31] A recent newspaper article by Bryan Strickland examines this myth in some detail. See Bryan Strickland, "ESPN Report: Is Duke Making the Grade?" Available on-line at: http://www.heraldsun.com/sports/18-199696.htm (26 February 2002).

[32] Office of the Dean, *Feedback from the Field Army: Officer Performance of USMA Graduates from the Class of 1996* (West Point, NY: Office of the Dean, United States Military Academy, 2000).

[33] The *Introductory Sociology* course guide used for this course is published among 20 top-rated sociology courses in the United States and published as a model for other courses. See Morten G. Ender, "Introductory Sociology (PL371): Course Guide," in James Sikora and Teodora O. Amoloza, eds., *Introductory Sociology Resource Manual*, 5th ed. (Washington, DC: American Sociological Association Teaching Resources, 2000), 55-66, 156-161.

[34] The course guides for two courses—Armed Forces and Society and Cinematic Images of War and the Military—will be published in John MacDougall and Morten G. Ender, eds., *Teaching the Sociology of Peace and War: A Curriculum Guide,* 3rd ed. (Washington, DC: American Sociological Association Teaching Resources, in press).

[35] Segal et al., "The Sociology Program," 159.

[36] Dr. Robert Carter earned a co-degree in both Sociology and Criminology at the University of California, Berkeley.

[37] Civilian faculty have three possible designations at West Point: (1) Endowed Chairs, (2) Distinguished Visiting Professors, and (3) Title 10 faculty. The latter comprise the vast majority of the civilian faculty. Title 10s are authorized by the Secretary of the Army through Public Law 102-484, Section 523, Title 10, Section 4331, U.S.C. USMA is authorized over 100 civilian faculty to serve in academic departments, in the Department of Physical Education, and on the Dean's staff.

[38] Dr. Keith is an adjunct faculty member for the sociology program and teaches Social Inequality: Race, Gender, and Ethnicity in addition to serving as a faculty advisor for senior sociology cadet projects.

[39] See Morten G. Ender and Shihlung Huang, "Revisiting Regional Traditions: An Emerging Sociology of the Great Plains," *The American Sociologist* 30 (Spring 1999):37-54, for an application of these ideas to another region of the country.

[40] Office of the Dean, *Educating Army Leaders for the 21st Century* (West Point, NY: Office of the Dean, United States Military Academy, 1998); and *Educating Future Army Officers for a Changing World: Operational Concept for the Academic Program of the United States Military Academy* (West Point, NY: Office of the Dean, United States Military Academy, 2002).

[41] Henslin, *Sociology: A Down-to-Earth Approach*, 4.

[42] For a compelling argument in behalf of the utility of sociology in educating future Army officers, see Scott Efflandt and Brian Reed, "Developing the Warrior-Scholar," *Military Review* 4 (August 2001):82-89.

⇥ CHAPTER 20 ⇤

THE HISTORY OF LAW INSTRUCTION AT WEST POINT

Patrick Finnegan

I never discussed the Constitution very much, and I
never made many speeches upon it, but I have
done a good deal of fighting for it.

—Lt. Gen. Philip Sheridan[1]

The study of law at the U.S. Military Academy is almost as old as the Academy itself. Fourteen years after Congress established the school at West Point in 1802, Academy regulations prescribed that "a course in Ethics shall include Natural and Political Law."[2] Two years later, Congress passed a statute providing for "one Chaplain stationed at the Military Academy at West Point who shall be Professor of Geography, History and Ethics, with the pay and emoluments allowed a Professor of Mathematics."[3] The resulting Department of Geography, History, and Ethics, headed by the Chaplain, the Reverend Doctor Thomas Picton, became the fourth established academic department, following the Departments of Philosophy, Mathematics, and Engineering.[4] Since those early days when the Chaplain was charged with teaching natural and political law, the Academy has maintained required courses in the study of law as an essential part of the preparation and education of future officers.

Early Subjects and Texts

Although the newly established department began teaching geography, history, and ethics in 1818, there is no record that any law instruction was actually given before 1821, when Monsieur De Vattel's *The Law of Nations*,[5] a treatise on international law, was adopted as a textbook.[6] An 1823 Military Academy Regulation prescribed that First Class cadets (seniors) would attend four hours of this instruction every week.[7] The Chaplain and the other officers who assisted him, although not lawyers, also taught moral philosophy, the origin of civil society, principles of civil liberty, modes of civil government, and constitutional law, in addition to the law of nations.[8] The study of natural and political law was intended to foster the intellectual and cultural growth of the cadets, as well as to develop their reasoning ability and instill in them the basic principles of a society based on the rule of law.[9]

As the study of law evolved in West Point's early years, cadets studied a variety of topics and read from multiple sources. From 1821 to 1842, the various chaplains and professors adopted the Reports of the United States Supreme Court as addenda to the textbooks.[10] The study of American constitutional law replaced natural law (which emphasized international law) in 1827, but by 1838 the course of study in law provided for instruction in both constitutional and international law.[11] During this period, William Rawle's *A View of the Constitution of the United States of America*[12] may have been studied by some cadets in the late 1820s, but it was never officially adopted as a textbook.[13] Rawle's treatise concluded that a state has a legal right to secede from the Union, and this was most likely the basis for the post-Civil War argument that West Point had taught "secession" for decades and thus was responsible for many West Point graduates fighting for the Confederacy.[14] Although it is impossible to know the precise extent of Rawle's influence, his ideas had a profound effect on at least some cadets. Gen. Robert E. Lee, Class of 1829, confided in Bishop Joseph Wilmer of Virginia that, if he had not read Rawle's work as a cadet, he would never have left the Union.[15]

Rawle's book was in use for less than two years before James Kent's well-known *Commentaries on American Law* replaced it in 1828.[16]

The latter volume, covering both international and constitutional law, remained in use as a textbook at the Academy for over 30 years.[17] Rather than arguing that the states had a right to secede, Kent concluded that the distinguishing feature of the U.S. Constitution was to bind the states in union with each other. In this regard America's constitutional system differed markedly from the political system that prevailed under the Articles of Confederation, which allowed states to effectively veto proposals or ignore policies of the central government.[18] Ever since constitutional law was introduced into the curriculum in 1827, it has been a required course and an essential part of the professional education of cadets who upon commissioning swear to support and defend the Constitution. Hence, except for a brief period during which a secessionist viewpoint appeared in a book available to cadets, the Academy's law curriculum was unequivocal in emphasizing the legitimacy of the Constitution and the inviolability of the Union.

The Antebellum Period and the Civil War

Although the Academy emphasized law instruction during its first 50 years, unfortunately none of the teachers were lawyers. Had lawyers been available, the instruction certainly would have been better, but there were simply not enough lawyers in the Army to justify assigning them to the faculty. Tellingly, the same Act of 16 March 1802 that established the U.S. Military Academy abolished the position of Judge Advocate of the Army.[19] When the Army needed judge advocates, Congress would periodically pass statutes providing for their inclusion in the force structure, but from 1821 until 1849, there were no statutory enactments related to judge advocates and no full-time lawyers in the Army.[20] When judge advocates were needed for courts-martial, the Army typically would appoint line officers to fill the duty temporarily.[21] Congress finally reestablished the position of Judge Advocate of the Army in 1849; 13 years later, as the Army expanded to fight the Civil War, Congress enacted legislation creating the Judge Advocate General's Corps. [22]

The Military Academy worked hard to refine the law curriculum despite the unavailability of Army lawyers as instructors. With so few judge advocates in the Army, the need for line officers to understand and apply the principles of law became even more apparent. In 1858, the Academy instituted the study of military law, which included the Rules and Articles of War, criminal law, and evidentiary procedures for courts-martial.[23]

Nine years later, the Academic Board discontinued instruction in the subjects of geography, history, and ethics and directed the Chaplain to focus solely on the teaching of international, constitutional, and military law.[24] During this period, the instruction emphasized the relation of law to moral values, as well as philosophical aspects of international and constitutional law.[25] Military law, a subject of great professional interest to future Army officers, included study of War Department General Order 100 of 1863, in which Francis Lieber codified, for the first time in history, a compilation of the Laws of War.[26]

As the American military became more professional in the mid-19th century, the benefits of understanding military law were clear. There were never enough qualified Army lawyers in the field, and line officers therefore assumed greater responsibility in meeting legal requirements and in courts-martial. To help address the legal needs of the Army, the Board of Visitors of the Military Academy recommended in 1849, and again in 1858, that a separate Department of Law be established.[27] Congress finally acted on those recommendations in 1874, over 50 years after the start of law instruction at West Point.

The Department of Law, 1874–1908

The establishment of the Department of Law reflected the Army's priority on improving the officer corps's legal skills. The 1874 statute authorized the Secretary of War to "assign one of the senior Judge Advocates of the Army to be Professor of Law."[28] This was a significant step, considering that the Congress had passed another law that year which reduced the Judge Advocate General's Corps from a total of eight officers to four.[29] The latter law was part of a major compilation of U.S. statutory law that included a reorganization of the Army Staff, revision of the Articles of War of 1806, and reduction in the size of the Army to 25,000 men.[30] Additionally, the law authorized a new type of wartime court-martial, known as the field officer's court and run by commissioned officers.[31] These statutory innovations underscored the importance of continued and improved instruction in law at West Point, and they may have significantly influenced the decision to assign 25 percent of the Judge Advocate General's Corps to the Academy.[32]

The *Army and Navy Journal*, a leading service publication, called the law "a step in the right direction" and summed up the rationale for its unanimous passage:

> The study of the general principles of law . . . and the study of the Constitution of the United States and of the administration of justice in the Army . . . have, since the Rebellion, become matters of primary importance [for] every individual holding a military commission.[33]

The Civil War and Reconstruction highlighted the need for commissioned officers to be savvy practitioners of military law. They had to be able to enforce court processes while protecting civil liberties, as well as to understand rules of evidence, courts-martial procedures, and military criminal justice. In light of these requirements, the *Journal* concluded, "The necessity for such a department seems to have been long felt."[34]

The professors who headed the new Department of Law were distinguished scholars and soldiers who made significant contributions to the Academy and the nation. The first Professor of Law (and the first lawyer ever to teach law at the Military Academy) was Maj. Asa Bird Gardiner, appointed to the position on 29 July 1874.[35] An 1860 graduate of New York University Law School, he gave up his legal practice to fight for the Union in the Civil War.[36] He was wounded in an engagement at Carlisle, Pennsylvania, in 1863 and was awarded the Medal of Honor for action during the Battle of Gettysburg.[37] President Ulysses S. Grant appointed Gardiner as a major in the Judge Advocate General's Corps in 1873; one year later, the Secretary of War named him Professor of Law.[38]

Gardiner initiated numerous curricular changes. He sharpened the focus on military law and the law of war, including systematic study of the Lieber Code as a supplement to the course on international law.[39] His text on court-martial forms and procedures became the basis for teaching cadets the rudiments of the military court-martial system.[40] Gardiner discontinued the use of Kent's *Commentaries*, which cadets had been using for 30 years, substituting a new work on constitutional law[41] by respected scholar Professor John Norton Pomeroy.[42]

Although his tenure lasted only four years, Gardiner's contributions were significant. He had organized the new department, mentored instructors, taught cadets, designed courses, and wrote textbooks. He earned more enduring fame, however, for his work after he left the Department of Law. In 1881, he served as prosecutor in the memorable case of Cadet Johnson C. Whittaker, who claimed that he had been attacked and mutilated by masked assailants. [43] Academy leaders believed that Whittaker had faked the attack in an effort to avoid taking final examinations.[44] Gardiner's skill as a prosecutor helped convince the court-martial to convict Whittaker, despite relatively ambiguous evidence.[45] Perhaps in recognition of that skill, Gardiner was selected in 1884 to prosecute charges brought against the Judge Advocate General of the Army, Brigadier General David Swaim, for fraud and conduct unbecoming an officer.[46] That prosecution also resulted in a conviction.[47]

Maj. Guido Norman Lieber, son of Dr. Lieber, author of the Lieber Code, succeeded Gardiner in 1878.[48] Lieber graduated from Harvard Law School in 1858 and served with distinction during the Civil War. Besides serving as aide-de-camp to the General-in-Chief, Gen. Henry Halleck, he received two brevet promotions for gallantry.[49] Following the war, he served tours as Judge Advocate for Army Departments and Divisions ranging from the Atlantic to the Dakotas.[50] As Professor of Law, Lieber introduced Rollin A. Ives's *A Treatise on Military Law*[51] and replaced Pomeroy's text on constitutional law with a textbook by Judge Thomas M. Cooley[52] that remained in use for almost 20 years.[53] After four years, Lieber left West Point to become the Assistant to the Judge Advocate General, Brig. Gen. Swaim.[54] Following the latter's 1884 court-martial conviction, Lieber was appointed Acting Judge Advocate General in the rank of brigadier general and early the next year named Judge Advocate General.[55] He retired from the Army in 1901, after serving 16 years as the Judge Advocate General, the longest tenure of any of the 36 officers who have held that position.[56]

Following the relatively uneventful tenure of Lt. Col. Herbert Curtis from 1882 to 1886, the Judge Advocate General appointed Lt. Col. William Winthrop as Professor of Law. Winthrop, an 1853 Yale Law School graduate, had served with distinction during the Civil War. Commissioned in the infantry, he was wounded several times and promoted to captain for gallantry before becoming a judge advocate.[57] Prior to his assignment as Professor of Law, he completed the revision of the 1806 Articles of War, which Congress approved in 1874. Additionally, he published *Military Law*,[58] the first major scholarly compilation of military law cases and principles of the United States.[59] When he served as Professor of Law from 1886 to 1890, *Military Law* was introduced as the cadet textbook on military law.[60] Winthrop returned to Washington after his tenure at West Point, where he served as deputy to Acting Judge Advocate General Lieber and ultimately as Assistant Judge Advocate General.[61] Upon retirement in 1895, after almost 34 years service, Winthrop updated his treatise and renamed it *Military Law and Precedents*.[62] That text became the most influential book ever written on military law, as it preserved and codified more than a century's worth of military jurisprudence and established a tradition of careful legal scholarship for military attorneys.[63] His text in still quoted in military law cases and has been cited many times in opinions of the United States Supreme Court. It was so authoritative that the War Department issued reprint editions in 1920 and 1942, despite the lapse in time since its first publication in 1886.[64]

For more than a decade straddling the turn of the century, the Department of Law reunited with the discipline of history. In 1896, after the death of Professor (Chaplain) Postlethwaite, the Department of Geography, History, and Ethics was discontinued and the Chaplain no longer had academic duties.[65] The study of history moved to the newly named Department of Law and History until 1908, when it migrated anew to the Department of English and History.[66]

Col. George B. Davis, West Point's most renowned Professor of Law, became department head in 1896. As an enlisted soldier and junior officer in the Civil War, Davis had distinguished himself in the Army of the Potomac, participating in more than 25 battles and engagements.[67] After the war, barely 18 years old, he entered West Point from the ranks, graduating in 1871 as the First Captain of the Corps of Cadets.[68] He fought the Apache Indians on the frontier before returning to West Point in 1883 for the first of three tours there that would total 16 years.[69] As a faculty member, his primary responsibility was to instruct on law, but he also taught Spanish, French, mineralogy, geology, history, ethics, and geography.[70]

Colonel Davis greatly influenced law instruction at West Point. While Professor of Law, he wrote texts on military law and courts-martial, the basic elements of law, and the elements of international law. [71] The latter two texts remained in use in the department for over 20 years.[72] Cadets respected Davis for his ability to combine his vast knowledge of law with ample doses of practical experience as a soldier. His intellect, patience, and good humor could make any subject interesting.[73]

Davis firmly established the core curriculum in law during his tenure. In their First Class year, cadets would take two courses of one semester each: Elementary and Constitutional Law in the first semester, and International and Military Law in the second.[74] Cadets attended those law classes for two hours each Monday, Wednesday, and Friday afternoon. [75] Davis's law curriculum, with occasional minor adjustments, remained in place for almost a century, until a reorganization of the curriculum in 1989.

In 1901, Colonel Davis left West Point with a promotion to brigadier general and an appointment as the Judge Advocate General of the Army, a position he held for nearly ten years.[76] During that time, he represented the United States as Delegate Plenipotentiary to the Geneva Conferences of 1903 and 1906, and the Hague Conference of 1907, all of which were landmarks in international agreements and codification of rules and laws for warfare.[77]

The refinement of the law curriculum since the formal establishment of the Department of Law was showcased during the Spanish-

American War and its aftermath. West Point graduates, relying in large part on the law instruction they received as cadets, successfully administered martial law, organized and conducted civil affairs, and facilitated the establishment of civil governments in Cuba, Puerto Rico, and the Philippines.[78] The Department of Law had proved its worth in helping West Pointers combine intellectual understanding of the principles of law with practical guidance that proved useful in confronting military legal issues.

Shifts in Emphasis, 1908–1946

Gradual change characterized the law curriculum in the first quarter of the 20th century. Although course content varied little, instructor emphasis shifted gradually from the theoretical toward the more practical application of the law.[79] Additionally, whereas constitutional law continued to be a core course, the department dropped the subject of international law from required instruction, since it had less practical utility.[80] In place of the latter offering, the Department of Law in 1921 added instruction in criminal law and evidence, which provided cadets greater concentration of study in topics relevant to their military careers.[81] Under the court-martial system, line officers had significant responsibilities as court members, prosecutors, and defense counsel, and their West Point law education helped to prepare them for those responsibilities.[82]

The Department of Law coupled education with training. Beginning around 1915, it conducted military moot courts to enhance cadets' understanding of the roles they would have as officers in courts-martial.[83] The new officers had plenty of opportunities to use what they learned. Following World War II when occupied countries were under martial law, recent West Point graduates wrote to cadets advising them to save every book and pamphlet from the Department of Law and to memorize everything they were learning.[84] West Pointers typically were the "only officers with legal training to be found in a unit — especially in the occupied territories."[85] Lt. Gen. Frank S. Besson, Jr., a 1932 USMA graduate who served in both the European and Pacific Theaters during World War II, recalled the importance of his instruction in law:

> A knowledge of the basic principles of law has been invaluable to me in my military service. I believe that in my day-to-day administrative problems, no single subject taught to me at the Military Academy with the exception of English has been more directly applicable.[86]

Gen. Andrew J. Goodpaster, a member of the Class of 1939 who later served as Supreme Allied Commander, Europe, and as Superintendent of the Military Academy, had a similar perspective:

> I have found over the years that my law course was of very great value to me. . . . [A]n understanding of the principal structure of law is essential equipment for an Army officer if he is to be effective within a unit, on higher staff, or as a military representative in the highest circles of government.[87]

The reputation of the department among cadets and in the legal profession during this period continued to be excellent. Cadets noted that studying law developed the capacity to think logically, stimulated intellectual curiosity, imparted a sense of values, and taught the application of knowledge to practical problems.[88] The 1935 edition of the *Howitzer*, the cadet yearbook, noted:

> The Law Department in setting its precedent did something at once radical and unique, something which causes the First Classman to wonder, to marvel, and then to rejoice. It allowed the cadet freedom of speech and freedom of thought such as no other department has ever done. The cadet became an individual not only in point of grading but also in point of mental action and self-expression. Response was spontaneous and profitable both to department and to cadet alike.[89]

Reflective of the fine reputation of the Department of Law was the decision of the American Bar Association (ABA) in 1941 to recognize high-achieving cadets. The ABA award, presented annually to the graduating cadet with the highest standing in law, continues to this day.[90]

Although all Professors of Law and some of the assistant professors were lawyers, a large part of the department's faculty still consisted of line officers. In an effort to ensure high standards of teaching, the Law Department began sending its officers who were not lawyers to receive training at law schools.[91] Between 1915 and 1953, members of the department attended courses at Columbia, Georgetown, Virginia, Yale, and The Judge Advocate General's School in Charlottesville, Virginia.[92] Many of these non-lawyer officers, benefiting from their experience teaching law, went on to serve the Army in significant leadership positions. Among them is Capt. Frederick Irving, a member of the West Point Class of April 1917, an infantry officer who taught in the department from 1922 to 1924.[93] From 1941 to 1942, Brigadier General Irving returned to West Point as the commandant of cadets, and, after serving as the 24th Infantry Division Commander in World War II and in other important leadership positions in the Army, he returned yet again to West Point as Major General Irving to serve as Superintendent of the Military Academy from 1951 to 1954.[94] Major General Irving is the only person in the history of West Point who has served as an instructor in an academic department, commandant, and superintendent.[95]

Two former Professors of Law served with great distinction during World War I. In 1917, when General Pershing was chosen to command the American Expeditionary Force in France, he selected Col. Walter Bethel, Professor of Law from 1909 to 1914, to be his judge advocate.[96] Colonel Bethel held that position throughout the war, participating in the Meuse-Argonne offensive and receiving the Distinguished Service Medal; subsequently he served as The Judge Advocate General of the Army from 1923 to 1924.[97] Col. Edward Kreger, who had been awarded the Distinguished Service Cross for heroism in battle in the Philippines, followed Colonel Bethel as the Professor of Law, a position he held from 1914 to 1917, when he was assigned as the Judge Advocate General's representative to the American Expeditionary Force and received the Distinguished Service Medal for his outstanding service.[98] Following the war, Colonel Kreger supervised the writing of the 1921 *Manual for Courts-Martial* and was appointed The Judge Advocate General of the Army in 1928.[99]

Continuation and Expansion, 1946–1989

From the time the Department of Law was established in 1874, the Professor and Department Head was an officer of the Judge Advocate General's Corps detailed to the Academy for a regular tour of duty.[100] As was the case for all Army lawyers, his assignment and tour length were determined by the Judge Advocate General of the Army.[101] A change came in 1946 when Congress authorized a permanent Professor of Law at West Point; henceforth the Head of the Law Department would be a tenured professor equivalent in academic rank to the heads of the other academic departments.[102] Moreover, selection of Professors of Law would follow the same statutory and regulatory procedures as those for other department heads. Once the Senate confirmed the selection, the Professor of Law would leave the Judge Advocate General's Corps and become part of the Corps of Professors.[103] Like other tenured professors, Professors of Law may remain on active duty until their 64th birthday and, at the discretion of the President, may retire in the grade of brigadier general in recognition of "long and distinguished" service.[104]

Col. Charles W. West, who had served as Professor of Law since 1943, was selected as the first permanent Professor in 1946 and served in that position until his retirement in 1962.[105] His 19 years as Professor of Law is the longest tenure of any officer who has held that position. Colonel West enhanced the professional competence of the faculty by mandating, with the concurrence of the Judge Advocate General, that all officers serving in the Law Department be fully qualified lawyers and members of the Judge Advocate General's Corps.[106] In 1953, 79 years after Congress authorized the Secretary of War to appoint an Army lawyer to head the Department of Law, all instructors were members of the bar for the first time in the history of the department.[107]

The Department of Law adjusted its curriculum in the early 1950s to keep pace with Congressionally mandated changes in the military judicial system. The 1951 Manual for Courts-Martial, promulgated after Congress passed the Uniform Code of Military Justice, included significant military justice roles for line officers. Because they would be involved in investigating, processing, prosecuting, and defending cases at courts-martial, law instruction placed heavy emphasis on familiarizing cadets with the framework of the military justice system.[108] By 1953, the law faculty (now consisting of the Professor of Law, an associate professor, an assistant professor, and nine instructors[109]) taught First Class cadets a two-semester course centered on the subjects of constitutional law, criminal law and evidence, and military law.[110]

A decade later, as the Academy looked for ways to revise the curriculum, in part to find room for elective courses, the Academic Board considered reducing the instruction in law.[111] In 1963, the Superintendent, Maj. Gen. William C. Westmoreland, ordered a review of the law curriculum. He formed an ad hoc committee and directed its members to analyze three options: maintain the curriculum as currently structured; increase the emphasis on legal training while reducing the emphasis on legal education; or provide minimal law instruction during the academic year under the supervision of the USMA Staff Judge Advocate with supplemental training during summer training periods.[112] Although the orders appointing the committee directed that they make no specific recommendations,[113] the committee report stated, "It would not be in the best interest of the United States Military Academy to reduce the current coverage of law."[114]

During their study, committee members had sought the advice of prominent military officers familiar with the program of law instruction. Maj. Gen. Charles Decker, a 1931 USMA graduate serving as The Judge Advocate General of the Army, was unequivocal in his support for a strong law curriculum:

> I am convinced that the study of law at West Point *does* contribute to the graduate's overall education and cultural background and *does* materially assist him in solving the military and administrative problems he encounters throughout his military service. If a poll were taken of any group of West Point graduates I believe there would be few dissenting voices. . . . While I believe the [law] course at West Point is essential for other reasons, its inclusion in the curriculum can be justified for its scholarly and intellectual values alone.[115]

Decker noted other benefits of studying law in an increasingly complex and dangerous world. Army officers, he observed, are increasingly drawn "into the legislative and administrative fields of government, international relations, procurement involving . . . billions . . . of dollars, and the direction of large numbers of men and women both in and out of the service."[116] In virtually every field of professional endeavor, a solid grounding in legal education and training would assist Army officers in meeting their responsibilities.

While Major General Decker could be expected to speak in favor of the law curriculum by virtue of his position, other prominent officers who were not lawyers did likewise. For example, General Goodpaster[117] observed,

> I am constantly interested to see that in important areas of
> the military profession, the fine points turn out to be the key
> points, and precision of thought is essential. Law certainly
> conditions and disciplines the mind in that direction. At
> the same time, an understanding of law in its relation to the
> Constitution, and hence to the process of self-government
> in its basic sense, is indispensable in the military profession
> within a democracy.[118]

In the end, no substantial changes were made in the law program. When Colonel West retired in 1962, he was succeeded by Col. Frederick C. Lough, West Point Class of 1938, who served in North Africa and Italy during World War II.[119] That year the Department of Law consolidated its operations with those of the USMA Office of the Staff Judge Advocate and assumed the responsibility for providing all legal services to the West Point community.[120] Under Lough's tenure, the Law Department began to offer a small number of elective courses to complement the core course in Constitutional and Military Law. By 1974, the department offered electives in Public International Law as well as Business and Procurement Law. Also, for cadets of the First Class, a seminar in Military Aspects of International Law was presented.[121]

During the late 1960s and early 1970s, the Department of Law joined the other academic departments in recognizing the need for permanent military faculty beside the department head. In 1969, the Judge Advocate General established the first of two such positions in the Department to assist with continuity, long term projects, and Academy governance.[122] Judge Advocate General's Corps officers filled these positions, with the intent that they would remain on the faculty until their mandatory retirement. In 1983, for a variety of reasons, a successor Judge Advocate General withdrew support for the permanent positions, with the apparent acquiescence of Col. Robert W. Berry,[123] who had succeeded Colonel Lough as Professor of Law in 1978.[124] The officers filling those jobs were reassigned, and the department head again became the sole permanent faculty member.

Around this time the law faculty, which had been exclusively white male Army officers, became more diverse with the gradual addition of women, minorities, and civilians. In 1979, Capt. Christine Czarnowsky became the first female officer to teach law at West Point, and in 1982 Maj. Nolan Goudeaux was the Law Department's first African-American officer. To assist and mentor military faculty members, to help evaluate the law program, and to reach out to other academic institutions involved in teaching law, the Department began to participate in the Academy's Visiting Professor program in 1979, hosting a visiting professor from a prominent law school or undergraduate institution for a year or semester.[125] The list of visiting professors includes such distinguished names as Prof. Daniel J. Meador of the University of Virginia, Prof. John F.T. Murray of the University of St. Louis, Professor and former Judge Advocate General of the Air Force Walter Reed of the University of South Dakota, Prof. Joseph Conboy of Texas Tech University, Prof. Donald Zillman of the University of Maine, Prof. Stephen Dycus of the University of Vermont, and Prof. Jonathan Lurie of Rutgers University.[126]

The cadet cheating scandal erupting in the spring of 1976 had a significant impact on the Department of Law. Because the department had been consolidated with the Office of the Staff Judge Advocate, many law instructors had to serve as either prosecutors or defense counsel in cases involving cadet cheating.[127] The situation caused potential conflicts of interest, as some law instructors found themselves simultaneously serving the interests of two competing parties—the Academy and the cadets accused of honor violations. After resolution of the cases, the Secretary of the Army appointed a Special Commission on the United States Military Academy (known as the Borman Commission, named after the Commission's Chairman, Frank Borman, former astronaut and member of the Class of 1950).[128] The commission's mission was to study the problems that led to the cheating scandal and recommend ways to correct them. In the course of its deliberations, the commissioners noted the ill effects of using law instructors as military defense counsel: "The system of having the same officer teach law and act as defense counsel places him in the difficult position of appearing to attack the basic policies of the institution to which he owes allegiance is his role as a faculty member."[129] Accordingly, the Commission recommended that "judge advocates who defend cadets should have no teaching duties."[130] In 1977, coincident with the retirement of Colonel Lough and the selection of Colonel Berry as Professor of Law, the Law Department and the Staff Judge Advocate once again separated their functions and offices after 15 years of consolidated activities. The separation remains in effect today.[131]

The law curriculum at West Point has kept pace with changes in the military justice system. Reflecting legal reforms in the civilian sector, the Military Justice Act of 1968 and the subsequent Manual for Courts-Martial revision in 1969 included more legal safeguards for the accused. Henceforth military lawyers—not line officers—would act as prosecutors and defense counsel in virtually all courts-martial, and military judges would preside over the courts.[132] Consequently, cadets no longer needed the heavy emphasis on criminal procedure and evidence that had been previously required to help prepare them to conduct courts-martial. Moreover, the moot courts that had been a part of law instruction since the early 1900s were discontinued by the mid 1970s.[133]

Despite these changes, officers still played key roles in the military justice system. They needed to understand legal principles and procedures that would be essential for duty as a company grade officer and commander.[134] The law curriculum adapted to this requirement by focusing on practical legal issues such as the rules for lawful searches and safeguards against self-incrimination. The department complemented this instruction with continued emphasis on constitutional law, an understanding of which is essential to officers in a democracy.

Although the instruction continued to emphasize military justice and constitutional law, the total number of lessons was reduced as the Academic Board revised the overall curriculum to create room for additional elective courses. In Academic Year 1978-79, the Academy reduced the core course in law from 80 lessons taught over two semesters to 62 lessons in one semester.[135] In 1985, the course once again became a two semester course, but only two lessons were added, for a total of 64.[136] In the early 1980s, electives in Environmental Law and in Constitutional Law were added to the existing electives in International Law and Business and Government Contracting Law, but the department discouraged cadets from taking more than two law electives.[137] In part, this was because the leadership of the department at that time believed that law courses and electives should supplement other academic areas and concentrations rather than comprise an independent field of study.[138]

New Directions and Challenges, 1989–Present

In the early 1980s, the Academic Board initiated a major review and revision of the curriculum. Significant changes included a reduction in the number of courses required for graduation and the opportunity for in-depth study in academic areas of interest. For the first time, cadets could major in an academic discipline; those who preferred less work in a specific area than a major entailed still could concentrate in a "field of study."

These changes directly affected the Department of Law. In 1989 the core course in law was reduced to 40 lessons in a single semester to allow cadets the opportunity to take an additional elective course.[139] Despite its curtailment, the core course retained a value of 3.5 credit hours instead of the normal 3.0 by virtue of 70-minute class periods (versus the normal 55 minutes). That is how the core course in Constitutional and Military Law is structured today, with essentially two-thirds of the course related to Constitutional Law, including how constitutional rights and authorities may be different in the military context. The remaining third of the course is devoted to criminal law and military justice, with a continuing emphasis on the role of the officer and commander in a constitutional system based on the rule of law.

The Academic Board's decision to establish a component of the curriculum devoted to disciplinary concentration significantly influenced the law program at West Point. At the same time the core course was shortened to one semester, the Department of Law shifted gears and decided to begin offering the electives necessary to support a 10-course field of study in the American Legal System. Col. Dennis R. Hunt,[140] who succeeded Colonel Berry as Professor and Department Head in 1987, oversaw creation of the new approach, including a cohesive elective program. In addition to electives in Business Law, Environmental Law, Constitutional Law, and International Law that had previously been offered, new or revised courses included a National Security Law Seminar, Jurisprudence, Introduction to the Legal Method, Special Topics in the Law, and Development of Military Law.

Just prior to Colonel Hunt's retirement in 1998, the Law Department took the next logical step by developing a 12-course academic major in the American Legal System. Up to then, Law had been the only department not to offer a major; upon receiving the Academic Board's approval in 1999, Law joined every other department in offering both a field of study and a major.[141] The principle difference between the American Legal System field of study and the major, besides the two extra electives, is the requirement for majors to write a 30-page thesis on a narrow legal topic as part of a one-semester project. Cadets must conduct in-depth research and study to complete the thesis, and they must orally defend their work upon completion. Beginning with the Class of 2005, the thesis project will extend over both semesters of the First Class year.

For a number of years, part of what was dropped from the core course to fit it into one semester was made up as part of military science instruction during the two week period in January known as the Military Intersession. In conjunction with the Department of Military Instruction, the Department of Law taught First Class cadets some of the practical aspects of military law essential for company grade officers to know. The topics included such areas as nonjudicial punishment, administrative separations, reports of survey and other administrative actions, and law of war and rules of engagement.[142] Because the requirement to teach approximately 1,000 cadets in a two week period was beyond the capability of the assigned law faculty, the department relied on Army Reserve attorneys to assist in teaching Intersession subjects.

In 2002 the Superintendent, Lt. Gen. William J. Lennox, decided to eliminate the intersession and return all military science instruction to the academic year. The department therefore reincorporated some of the legal topics covered during the intersession, particularly those related to military justice and administrative actions, into the last third of the core course. Additionally, it assisted the Department of Military Science in designing lesson plans and teaching subjects related to the law of war and rules of engagement as part of the military science instruction for First and Second Classmen.

Even so, reductions in the core course in law and periodic decreases in the amount of time allocated to the Department of Law during the intersession created a significant gap. Cadets were not receiving adequate instruction in the Law of War (particularly the basic rules of the Geneva and Hague Conventions), or any appreciation for Operational Law, increasingly important because of frequent Army deployments. The department coordinated with the Department of Military Instruction and the Commandant to incorporate law-of-war instruction and law-related scenarios into the summer field training exercises for Third Classmen at Camp Buckner. The revised training program took effect for Operation Highland Warrior, the cadets' culminating field training exercise, in the summer of 2000.

Responding to Congressional direction, in the early 1990s the Military Academy began supplementing the military faculty with limited numbers of civilian professors. In 1992, Prof. Edward Hume became the first civilian faculty member to join the Department of

Law.[143] When the department gained another position four years later, Prof. Gary Solis, a retired U.S. Marine Corps lieutenant colonel who had earned a Ph.D. in the Law of War at the London School of Economics, came aboard.[144] Professor Solis completely revamped the course in Development of Military Law to create a new elective, Law of War for Commanders, that became an essential part of the American Legal System program.

The Academic Board's approval of the American Legal System major in 1999 enabled cadets in the program to be eligible for recognition at the Superintendent's Award Convocation, held during graduation week. Through the generosity of Col. Ron Salvatore, U.S. Army ret., a former Law faculty member and current Academy Counsel, the Maj. Gen. John D. Altenburg, Jr., Award was initiated with the Class of 2001 to recognize the graduating cadet who had the best academic record while majoring in the American Legal System.[145]

As an adjunct to the classroom component of the American Legal System major, the Law Department developed an extensive intern program. The internships take place in the summer for up to three weeks; the fact that cadets often forgo their leave to take part in them suggests the quality and value of these experiences. In recent years cadets interns have served at the United States Supreme Court, the Department of Justice, the Office of the Army General Counsel, Staff Judge Advocate Offices throughout the Army, and the Office of The Judge Advocate General.[146] In the summer of 2002, additional internships became available at district attorney offices around the country, as well as at the American Embassy in Rome. An internship at the International Criminal Tribunal for the Former Yugoslavia was added in the summer of 2003.[147]

The department has also embarked on several long-term initiatives designed to enrich the academic major in law. It has expanded its relations with other military academies, particularly in areas related to International Law and the Law of War. At the instigation of Professor Solis, the Law of War for Commanders elective conducted Law of Armed Combat written exercises, initially with cadets from the Air Force Academy. The exercises quickly expanded to include the Naval Academy, the Coast Guard Academy, and the Royal Military

College (RMC) of Canada. These exercises were the impetus for the first-ever service academy competition in the Law of Armed Conflict, conducted in March 2002 at the International Institute for Humanitarian Law in San Remo, Italy.[148] Six West Point cadets, all majoring in the American Legal System, participated, along with representatives of all other U.S. service academies, RMC, and cadets from military academies in Russia, China, Ireland, Greece, and Belgium.[149]

Members of the department were also instrumental in establishing the Consortium for Undergraduate Law and Justice Programs. In 2002 at Amherst College, representatives of the Department of Law met with faculty members from other schools having undergraduate legal programs. The group decided to create a formal non-profit consortium, which was founded in 2003. Moreover, they agreed that membership would be open to academic institutions instead of individuals, and that consortium meetings would occur annually. In April 2004, the Department of Law hosted the first consortium conference, with the theme of Law and Terrorism.

The composition of the law faculty has continued to change in ways that only help strengthen the department. The current authorized strength of the law faculty is 16, including four civilian professors, one of whom is a visiting professor.[150] Five members of the faculty are rotating JAG Corps officers who typically serve a three-year tour primarily teaching the core law course. Another quarter of the faculty consists of rotating JAG Corps officers who report to the department after earning a Master of Laws (LL.M.) degree (this in addition to the earlier basic law degree qualifying them for commissioning in the JAG Corps) in one of four disciplines: Constitutional Law, Government Contract Law, International Law, or Environmental Law.[151] These faculty members use their expertise in these areas to manage the associated elective courses offered by the Department of Law. Additionally, they and the other rotating military faculty bring to the classroom their expertise from the practice of law in the field.

Prior to 2001 (except for the period 1969-1983), the Law Department was the only academic department with no permanent military faculty members other than the Department Head. In contrast, no other department had fewer than five permanent military professors. Without additional permanent faculty, the Department of Law would lack continuity in important areas—in particular, curriculum development, course design, resource allocation, and Academy governance. The Judge Advocate General of the Army, Maj. Gen. Walter B. Huffman, recognizing this state of affairs as a disadvantageous aberration, therefore approved the conversion of two JAG Corps positions in the department to Academy Professor positions, beginning in the summer of 2001.[152] After a hiatus of 18 years, the Department once again had the undeniable benefit of permanent military faculty. Academy Professors in the Law Department continue to be members of the JAG Corps, but they will remain permanently assigned to the law faculty until retirement.

Although the Department of Law is unique in several ways, it has evolved in parallel with the development of the academic program at West Point. Despite the many organizational and curricular changes, however, the purpose for law instruction has remained constant. When the department was created more than 125 years ago, the *Army and Navy Journal* noted that the study of law and the Constitution was of primary importance for any commissioned officer.[153] The Department of Law exists to educate future officers about their Constitutional rights and duties, including protection of the rights of all citizens, and to familiarize cadets with the military justice system and the criminal law process. The Constitution requires commissioned officers to swear an oath to support and defend its principles. Those officers must understand the meaning of that oath, their essential role in protecting the liberty of all citizens, and their duty to uphold and enforce the law in a society and country based on the rule of law. For more than 200 years the Military Academy has accomplished this mission, and the Department of Law has played a major role in that success.

---

[1] General Sheridan's response to the Toast to the Army made at the Constitution Centennial Celebration in Philadelphia, PA, in September 1887. At the time, General Sheridan, USMA Class of 1853, was Commander in Chief of the Army.

[2] Regulations of the United States Military Academy, 10 July 1816.

[3] Act of April 1, 1818, ch. 61, 3 Stat. 426.

[4] Keith L. Sellen, "The United States Military Academy Law Department—Yesterday and Today: Purpose—Challenge—Reward," *Federal Bar News and Journal* 37 (May 1990): 231. See also George B. Davis, "The Department of Law," in *The Centennial of the United States Military Academy at West Point, New York, 1802-1902*, Volume I (New York: Greenwood Publishers, 1902), 367.

[5] Monsieur de Vattel, *The Law of Nations; or Principles of the Law of Nature applied to the Conduct and Affairs of Nations and Sovereigns*, 4th American Edition (Philadelphia: Nicklind and Johnson, 1823), reprinted from London edition of 1797.

[6] Charles W. West, "Department of Law, U.S.M.A," *Assembly* XII (April 1953): 3.

[7] Department of Law Information Pamphlet (1987), 1.

[8] Sellen, "Law Department," 231.

[9] Ibid.

[10] Information Pamphlet, 1.

[11] Preliminary Inventory of the Records of the U.S. Military Academy, prepared by the Academy Archives in 1976, 21. See also Frederick C. Lough, "The Centennial of the USMA Department of Law," *Assembly* XXXII (March 1974): 8.

[12] William Rawle, *A View of the Constitution of the United States of America* (Philadelphia: Carey and Lea, 1825).

[13] *The Howitzer*, Class of 1928, 46.

[14] Ibid.

[15] Richard O'Connor, *Thomas, Rock of Chickamauga* (New York: Prentice-Hall, Inc, 1948), 66; Wilbur Thomas, *General George H. Thomas* (New York: Exposition Press, 1964), 63. See also Douglas S. Freeman, *R.E. Lee: A Biography* (New York: Scribner's Sons, 1943), I, 78-79. Although Jefferson Davis graduated from West Point a year before Lee, he stated that he did not use the Rawle text but was taught using Kent's *Commentaries*. Freeman, *R.E. Lee*, 78-79. For a further discussion of this issue, see John W. Brinsfield, "The Military Ethics of General William T. Sherman: A Reassessment." *Parameters: Journal of the U.S. Army War College* XII, no. 2 (June, 1982): 38. In contrast to Lee and others, Gen.William Tecumseh Sherman, an 1840 USMA graduate, whose favorite textbook in the Chaplain's course was Kent's *Commentaries*, left his position as Superintendent of the Louisiana State Seminary and Military Academy to return to the Union Army when the Civil War started. Sherman stated that he would fight for the Union "as long as a fragment" of the "Old Constitution" remained. Ibid., 39-40.

[16] James Kent, *Commentaries on American Law* (New York: G. Halstead, 1826).

[17] Davis, "Department of Law," 367-68.

[18] Kent, *Commentaries*, 353-54.

[19] *The Army Lawyer: A History of The Judge Advocate General's Corps, 1775-1975* (Washington, DC: U.S. Government Printing Office, [1976], 27.

[20] Ibid., 35.

[21] Ibid.

[22] By Act of 4 July 1862, Congress created the foundation for the Judge Advocate General's Corps. Ibid. at 49-50. By Act of 2 March 1829, Congress re-authorized appointment of a Judge Advocate of the Army. Ibid. at 42.

[23] Lough, "Centennial," 8; Information Pamphlet, 1-2.

[24] Davis, "Department of Law," 368-69. The main objection to geography, history, and ethics was that they competed with the supposedly more important courses in mathematics, science, and engineering. Law instruction remained in the curriculum

because of its relevancy to the missions that cadets would perform upon graduation. The experiences of graduates during the Civil War and during Reconstruction dramatized the need for a thorough grounding in constitutional law and the military justice system. Much of the information in this note was provided by Dr. Stephen Grove, USMA Historian.

[25] Lough, "Centennial," 8.

[26] Ibid. Known as the Lieber Code, this first codification of the rules and laws of war served as the basis for much of the developing law of war. Variations of the Lieber Code were adopted in several European countries and many of its provisions were later incorporated into the Geneva and Hague Conventions.

[27] *The Howitzer* (1928), 46. General Sherman, who had enjoyed his courses on law and ethics at West Point, believed in the utility of knowing the law as an Army officer. In fact, he studied the law intermittently from 1839 to 1859 and eventually became a practicing attorney. Brinsfield, "Ethics of General Sherman," 37-38. Many Southerners might doubt Sherman's adherence to legal principles based on his Civil War campaigns in the South. Chaplain Brinsfield's article explains how Sherman attempted to reconcile his belief in the law with the death and destruction of war. Sherman's interest in the law continued after the Civil War. The curriculum at Fort Leavenworth's School of Application included law at his personal direction. Robert W. Berry, "The Department of Law, USMA," *Assembly* XLIII (December 1984), 17.

[28] Act of June 6, 1074, ch. 217, 18 Stat. 60.

[29] *The Army Lawyer*, 72.

[30] Act of June 23, 1874, ch. 458, 18 Stat. 244. See also *The Army Lawyer*, 71-72; Sellen, "Law Department," 232.

[31] *The Army Lawyer*, 72.

[32] Sellen, "Law Department," 232.

[33] *Army and Navy Journal*, 4 July 1874, 745.

[34] Ibid.

[35] Sellen, "Law Department," 233; Preliminary Inventory of USMA Records, 21.

[36] Sellen, "Law Department," 233; Lough, "Centennial," 8.

[37] *The Army Lawyer*, 83.

[38] Ibid.

[39] Davis, "Department of Law," 369.

[40] Sellen, "Law Department," 233.

[41] John Norton Pomeroy, *Introduction to the Constitutional Law of the United States* (Boston: Houghton, Mifflin, 1886).

[42] Davis, "Department of Law," 369.

[43] *The Army Lawyer*, 77. See chap. 8 of the present volume for a more detailed discussion of the Whittaker case.

[44] Ibid., 77-78.

[45] Sellen, "Law Department," 233.

[46] *The Army Lawyer*, 79.

[47] Sellen, "Law Department," 233.

[48] *The Army Lawyer*, 85.

[49] Ibid.; Lough, "Centennial," 8.

[50] Sellen, "Law Department," 233.

[51] Rollin A. Ives, *A Treatise on Military Law* (New York: D. Van Nostrand, 1879).

[52] Thomas M. Cooley, *The General Principles of Constitutional Law in the United States of America* (Boston: Little, Brown, 1880).

[53] Davis, "Department of Law," 369.

[54] *The Army Lawyer*, 86.

[55] Ibid.

[56] Ibid.

[57] Ibid., 96-97.

[58] William Winthrop, *Military Law* (Washington, DC: W. H. Morrison, 1886).

[59] Ibid., 98.

[60] Davis, "Department of Law," 370.

[61] *The Army Lawyer*, 99.

[62] Ibid. William Winthrop, *Military Law and Precedents* (Boston: Little, Brown, 1896).

[63] Ibid., 99-100.

[64] Ibid., 99; Lough, "Centennial," 9.

[65] *The Howitzer* (1928) , 46; Preliminary Inventory of USMA Records, 21.

[66] Ibid.

[67] Sellen, "Law Department," 233; *The Army Lawyer*, 101.

[68] Lough, "Centennial," 9.

[69] Ibid.; Sellen, "Law Department," 233.

[70] Lough, "Centennial," 9.

[71] George B. Davis, *A Treatise on the Military Law of the United States: Together with the Practice and Procedure of Courts-Martial and other Military Tribunals* (New York: J. Wiley & Sons, 1898); George B. Davis, The Elements of Law: *An Introduction to the Study of the Constitutional and Military Law of the United States* (New York: J. Wiley, 1904); George B. Davis, *The Elements of International Law: With an Account of its Origin, Sources, and Historical Development* (New York and London: Harper & Brothers, 1900). See also Sellen, "Law Department," 233; Davis, "Department of Law," 370.

[72] Sellen, "Law Department," 233. Colonel Davis wrote the International Law text the same year he graduated from law school. It was used as a text at West Point even before he was Professor of Law. Ibid., 238, n. 64.

[73] Ibid., 233-34.

[74] Lough, "Centennial," 9.

[75] Ibid. On Tuesdays and Thursdays, the cadets received two hours of history instruction from their law professors.

[76] *The Army Lawyer*, 102.

[77] Ibid.

[78] Sellen, "Law Department," 231.

[79] Lough, "Centennial," 9.

[80] Information Pamphlet, 3.

[81] Lough, "Centennial," 9.

[82] Sellen, "Law Department," 236.

[83] Ibid.

[84] Ibid., 236, 239, n.13.

[85] Ibid., 231 (quoting from the 1947 edition of *The Howitzer*).

86 United States Military Academy Report of the Superintendent's Ad Hoc Committee on the Coverage of Law at the Military Academy (1963), Letter to the Committee from Lt. Gen. F. S. Besson, Jr., 67. At the time he wrote the letter, Besson commanded the Army Materiel Command.

87 Report of Ad Hoc Committee, Letter from Maj. Gen. Andrew J. Goodpaster, 80. When he wrote the letter, Goodpaster was serving as Assistant to the Chairman of the Joint Chiefs of Staff. After retiring from the Army following his assignment as SACEUR, Gen. Goodpaster was recalled to active duty as Superintendent of the Military Academy in 1977.

88 *The Howitzer*, Class of 1941, 53. "The Academic Board has come to realize that the study of Law has special training values particularly useful to military men—the development of powers of analysis and a sense of relative values. These developed faculties furnish an officer a sound basis for his 'Estimate of the situation,' so important in a successful military career."

89 *The Howitzer*, Class of 1935, 43.

90 West, "Department of Law," 5.

91 Sellen, "Law Department," 232.

92 Ibid.

93 Information Pamphlet, 3.

04 Berry, "The Department of Law," 18.

95 Ibid. Another distinguished alumnus of the Department of Law is Lt. Gen. Paul Caraway, an infantry officer who taught law at USMA from 1938 to1942. Caraway, a 1929 USMA graduate, earned a law degree from Georgetown Law School while stationed in Washington, DC, but never served in The Judge Advocate General's Corps. He worked for Gen. George C. Marshall during World War II and participated in almost every significant postwar conference, including Yalta and Bretton Woods. Caraway later served as a special Vice Presidential aide to Richard Nixon and culminated his military career as Commanding General and High Commissioner of the Ryukyu Islands.

96 Lough, "Centennial," 9.

97 *The Army Lawyer*, 139.

98 Lough, "Centennial," 9.

99 *The Army Lawyer*, 149.

100 West, "Department of Law," 4.

101 Ibid.

102 Ibid.; Information Pamphlet, 4.

103 Congress enacted legislation establishing permanent professors of the Military Academy. *U.S. Code*, Vol. 10, section 4336 (1956). Once selected and approved, the officer becomes a Professor, United States Military Academy, (PUSMA) which is its own military branch, the smallest in the Army. This statutory position is a separate category from Academy Professors, who remain in their basic branch but are assigned to the faculty until they retire.

104 As an exception to other statutes governing retirement based on age or years of service, *U.S. Code*, Vol. 10 section 1251 (1980) permits a permanent professor of the Military Academy to retire "on the first day of the month following the month in which he becomes 64 years of age." *U.S. Code*, Vol. 10, section 3962 (1956) permits retirement as a brigadier general, at the discretion of the President. The Secretary of the Army may, at his discretion, retire any permanent professor who has more than 30 years commissioned service. *U.S. Code*, Vol. 10, section 3920 (1956).

[105] Information Pamphlet, 4.

[106] Ibid.

[107] Sellen, "Law Department," 232.

[108] Information Pamphlet, 3-4.

[109] West, "Department of Law," 4.

[110] Ibid., 3.

[111] Report of Ad Hoc Committee, 1-3.

[112] Report of Ad Hoc Committee, 39-40.

[113] Ibid., 40.

[114] Ibid., 34.

[115] Ibid., 71 (Letter from Maj. Gen. Charles L. Decker).

[116] Ibid., 73.

[117] See note 87 above and accompanying text.

[118] Report of Ad Hoc Committee, 80 (Letter from Major General Goodpaster). Goodpaster's West Point classmate, Col. Julian J. Ewell, serving as Executive to the Chairman, Joint Chiefs of Staff, wrote "A well educated man, particularly in public service, must understand the part that the law plays in both civil and military pursuits. There is also an aspect of the law which is even more intangible. This is the philosophical, historical, and cultural understanding which the regular officer, the professional soldier, and the temporary citizen soldier should bring to their role as a citizen in our democracy. I have in mind here the duties of each citizen as a voter, a taxpayer, a soldier." Ibid., 58 (Letter from Col. Julian J. Ewell). Ewell later commanded the 9th Infantry Division in Viet Nam, served as Military Representative to the Viet Nam Peace Talks Delegation in France, and retired from the Army as a lieutenant general.

[119] Lough, "Centennial," 8.

[120] Ibid., 9.

[121] Ibid.

[122] Department of Law Historical Files and Personnel Records. The first officer selected was [then] Lt. Col. Thomas Oldham, who served from 1969 to 1975. The second Permanent Associate Professor, as they were then designated, was [then] Maj. Daniel Shimek, who began in that position in 1974. When Col. Oldham retired in 1975, he was replaced by [then] Lt. Col. Hugh Henson.

[123] Colonel Berry, a Harvard Law School graduate, served as an enlisted soldier during World War II and as an officer in the Korean War, prior to completing law school. Although he did not serve on active duty in the JAG Corps before selection as Professor of Law, he had a long prior association with the Military Academy and served as the General Counsel of the Army from 1971 to 1974.

[124] Memorandum of Maj. Gen. Hugh J. Clausen, The Judge Advocate General, for the Deputy Chief of Staff for Personnel, US Army (10 February 1982), Subject: Permanent Associate Professors of Law at USMA. Although the precise reasons for eliminating these positions is not clear from the historical record, Colonel Berry did not believe (and still does not) that permanent military faculty positions were good for the Department of Law. In addition, he and Colonel Henson had differing views of how the department should operate. That conflict was almost certainly exacerbated by the fact that Colonel Henson, the senior Permanent Associate Professor who served as Acting Head of the Department for the year preceding Colonel Berry's arrival, also contended for the Professor of Law position for which Berry was selected. The Judge

Advocate General, Major General Clausen, did not approve of some actions that the other Permanent Associate Professor, Lieutenant Colonel Shimek, had taken while serving as the Staff Judge Advocate for USMA during a period when the Department of Law was responsible for both teaching and rendering legal advice to the USMA leadership. Exercising his statutory authority over assignments of all officers in the JAG Corps, Clausen reassigned Henson and Shimek.

[125] Sellen, "Department of Law," 232.

[126] Ibid.; Law Records.

[127] Information Pamphlet, 5.

[128] The cheating scandal, the most widespread in Academy history, resulted in a comprehensive review of many of the policies and procedures at West Point. The Secretary of the Army asked Col. (retired) Frank Borman to head the review commission because of his reputation for integrity, clear thinking, and common sense.

[129] Information Pamphlet, 5.

[130] Ibid.

[131] Berry, "The Department of Law," 17.

[132] The Military Justice Act of 1968 and the 1969 *Manual for Courts-Martial* essentially removed line officers from court-martial roles other than as court members or witnesses. Henceforth the prosecution and defense functions were assigned to members of the har; moreover only qualified attorneys could be military judges. This revision was part of a continuing effort to make courts-martial fairer for accused soldiers and to more closely align the military justice system with the federal criminal court system.

[133] Sellen, "Department of Law," 236.

[134] Berry, "The Department of Law," 17.

[135] Memorandum of Colonel Dennis R. Hunt to Curriculum Reduction Study Committee (1 May 1989), 1.

[136] Ibid.

[137] Berry, "The Department of Law," 17.

[138] Col. (ret) Daniel Shimek, interview by author, 5 February 2004.

[139] Colonel Hunt memorandum, 1-2; Law Records.

[140] Colonel Hunt, a Harvard Law School graduate, had served as the Chair of the Criminal Law Department, The Judge Advocate General's School, and as Staff Judge Advocate, 24th Infantry Division, Fort Stewart, GA, prior to his selection as Professor of Law. He retired as a brigadier general in 1998 and currently teaches law at the University of Southern Mississippi.

[141] Because she was able to adjust her schedule to meet the additional requirements for a major, Cadet Erin Scheu, Class of 2000, became the first graduate to major in the American Legal System.

[142] *Tools of the Profession: The Leader's Legal Role*, Department of Law Reference Book (New York: McGraw-Hill [2001]).

[143] Department of Law Records.

[144] Professor Solis brought favorable notice to the department throughout his five years at West Point and was a frequent national commentator on law of war and military law issues. He devised a new elective on Law of War for Commanders that has become an essential part of the American Legal System program. He received his law degree from The University of California-Davis and served two tours in Viet Nam as a Marine platoon leader and company commander. His book *Son Thang: An American*

War Crime, is an excellent study of the application of the law of war and the operation of the military justice system during wartime. It is now a required supplemental text for cadets who major in the American Legal System. When Solis departed in 2001, Lt. Col. (ret.) Mark Welton, who had just completed his second teaching assignment in the department, was hired as a civilian to replace him. In addition to a law degree from Georgetown University and two master's degrees, Professor Welton has earned both an LLM and a Doctor of Juridical Science (S.J.D.) degree from the University of Virginia School of Law. While on active duty, in addition to teaching assignments at West Point and the International Law Department of the Judge Advocate General's School, he served as Chief of International Law for US Army, Europe, and as Deputy Staff Judge Advocate, US European Command. Professor Welton not only has a wealth of experience in International Law, he is also one of the United States' leading experts on Islamic law. Two additional civilian faculty members, hired in the summer of 2000 (Prof. Tim Bakken) and the summer of 2001 (Prof. Margaret Stock) also brought specialized expertise, particularly important as the department increased the depth and breadth of law instruction for an expanding number of cadets who major in the American Legal System.

[145] Major General Altenburg culminated a distinguished military career that included service in Viet Nam and the Gulf War with a four-year assignment as The Assistant Judge Advocate General, from 1997 to 2001. Throughout his career, he was a strong supporter of teaching law and of the Department of Law. He has a son and daughter who are both members of the West Point Class of 1995.

[146] Department of Law Pamphlet, "American Legal System Academic Individual Advanced Development Program, Summer 2002."

[147] Ibid.

[148] The San Remo Institute is a world renowned organization that teaches law of war, international law, and humanitarian law courses to military officers and other interested individuals from around the world.

[149] Patrick Murphy, "West Point Cadets Receive Top Honors," *Pointer View* 59 (12 April 2002): 1. The competition has continued annually, with the Department of Law providing cadet teams and instructors each year.

[150] The number of faculty is the smallest of any academic department by an order of magnitude—the next smallest department is twice the size. All military members of the Law Department are in the same branch of the Army—the Judge Advocate General's Corps—while cross sections of all other branches are represented in the other departments.

[151] The Academic Board approved significant changes to the curriculum beginning with the Class of 2005. As a result, the Department of Law will offer a new elective in Comparative Law, particularly useful as the Army deploys to many areas of the world. To assist in devising and teaching that course, one of the LL.M.s for faculty positions was shifted from Environmental Law to Comparative Law, effective the summer of 2003. The first faculty member to specialize in that subject will complete his LL.M. at the London campus of the University of Notre Dame Law School in the summer of 2004.

[152] Memorandum of Maj. Gen. Walter B. Huffman to Professor and Head, Department of Law, Subject: Academy Professors, Department of Law, USMA, dated 24 October 2000. After the application and selection process, the Academic Board approved the nominations of Lt. Col. Maritza Ryan (USMA Class of 1982) and Lt. Col. David Wallace as the first Academy Professors in the Department of Law.

[153] See notes 33-34 above and accompanying text.

⫷ CHAPTER 21 ⫸

TEACHING FOREIGN LANGUAGES AT WEST POINT[1]

Patricia B. Genung

Introduction

Foreign language instruction at West Point began in 1803, just one year after the founding of the Military Academy. At that time, most educated men had a classical background. Drilled from childhood in the declensions, conjugations, and vocabulary of Latin and Greek, the more proficient among them were able to read the works of Virgil, Cicero, Plato, and Aristotle. This prepared them well for politics or for a life of leisurely contemplation of art and literature, but such an education had little value in training Army officers for an increasingly technical army. To educate artillerymen and engineers, the U.S. Military Academy needed to educate cadets in modern mathematics and science, for which purposes the classical languages were of little use.

In the early 19th century, leading scientists, mathematicians, and engineers often wrote in French. Accordingly, the early textbooks at West Point included Vauban's *Traités de fortifications,* Hackett's *Traité des machines,* and Sganzin's *Programme d'un cours de construction.*[2] Even into the 1830s the renowned West Point mathematician, Charles Davies, before he had written his own influential texts, used as teaching texts Bourdon's *Élements d'algèbre* and Legendre's *Élements de géométrie* (which in 1794 had replaced Euclid's classical work).[3] Clearly, the cadets needed to read French.

Whether they taught Greek, Latin, or French, 19th century language instructors used the same methodology: grammar and translation. This methodology remained in vogue well into the 20th century. Through extensive oral and written drills, students memorized noun declensions, verb conjugations, and long lists of vocabulary words along with their English meanings. Eventually the students progressed to translating sentences, paragraphs, and entire documents. Students acquired pronunciation through the oral recitation of grammar exercises and by reading aloud from original texts; however, they did not acquire the ability to communicate orally in the language since oral communication was not necessary for the comprehension of written text.

The "First Teacher of French"

In view of the necessary use of foreign language texts and the concomitant need for foreign language instruction at the Military Academy, Congress established the position, First Teacher of French, in February 1803. The French teacher was also the drawing teacher, and Congress (perhaps to emphasize the primacy of military officers on the faculty and the predominant disciplines of science and engineering) stipulated that his pay could not exceed that of a captain.[4] The first man to hold the position, beginning in July 1803, was a civilian native speaker, François Désiré Masson. Masson had lost his plantation in the West Indies during a slave revolt and immigrated to the United States, ultimately finding employment at West Point.[5] Masson wrote his own textbooks, including *French Grammar* and *French Reader*. Upon his departure from West Point in 1810, Masson went to the Military College at Sandhurst as an instructor and was succeeded by his brother, Florimond Masson.[6]

In 1815, another French-speaking civilian, Claudius Berard, arrived at the Academy to take the position First Teacher of French from Florimond Masson. Berard, wishing to avoid service in Napoleon's armies, purchased a substitute to serve in his place. When the substitute was killed in Spain, Berard fled to the United States. He taught first on the faculty of Dickinson College in Carlisle, Pennsylvania, before arriving at West Point.[7] Like François Masson, Berard developed his own grammar. He also assigned as reading exercises the first volume of *Histoire de Gil Blas*, a work also used at Harvard by Superintendent Sylvanus Thayer's friend, George Ticknor.[8] Ticknor, like Thayer, was interested in moving education out of the classical mode.

Berard's tenure as First Teacher of French extended through 8 August 1846 when Congress granted him the title Professor of French.[9] He and his successors carried that title for many years. Berard died in 1848, and the Second Teacher of French, Hyacinthe Agnel, succeeded him as Professor of French. Congress had authorized a Second Teacher in 1818 as cadet enrollments increased, and Agnel was the third person to hold the position following Joseph Du Commun (1818-1831) and Julian Molinard (1831-1839).[10] After he rose to the position of Professor of French, his successors in the position of Second Teacher received the title Assistant Professor.[11] Agnel was Professor of French until his death in February 1871.

Language Instruction, 1803–1854

During West Point's early years, the amount of French instruction cadets received was inconsistent. Until 1812, there were no annual graduating classes, so the length of cadets' academic programs varied according to their pre-admission educational level. There is some indication that in 1805 there were French recitations, probably one hour in duration, held between 11 a.m. and 1 p.m., alternating daily with the drawing lessons.[12]

With the establishment of a more structured curriculum after 1812, Academy officials organized cadets into annual graduating classes, and instructors administered yearly examinations to determine whether cadets could advance to the next class. In 1816 it was announced that a "course of French shall consist in pronouncing the language tolerably, and translating from French into English, and from English into French with accuracy."[13] Nevertheless, with regard to the examination in 1817, it was noted that "but few cadets could translate with tolerable facility the easiest French author."[14] Three years later, the Academy explicitly added an ability to read French to the stated aim for French instruction.[15]

The earliest official mention of a specific allotment of time to French instruction appears in a report of the Academic Board in July 1816. It recommends the study of French with 310 hourly recitations during Fourth Class (freshman) year in connection with English, noting that this study should be completed by the Third Class (sophomore) year. There is no record as to whether this proposal was accepted.[16]

Throughout the next decade, the amount of French instruction continued to fluctuate. In 1820, the Academic Board recommended daily French instruction five days a week for the first two years at the Academy, thus increasing the number of recitations to 360. Four years later, the number of recitations increased to 400; however, by 1826, while daily one-hour recitations in French continued for the Fourth Class, during the Third Class year the recitations alternated with English. This decreased the number of recitations in French to 290.[17]

Another curriculum change in 1845 resulted in one hour of French on alternate days for the Fourth Class, January to June, with either English or history taken on the off day. French recitations were stepped up to daily during the Third Class year. This system brought the number of French recitations to 272.[18] Notably, during the entire period from 1803 to 1854, cadets were also exposed to the language on a daily basis during their last two years at the Academy through the use of the aforementioned French language texts for their study of mathematics, fortifications, and construction.

Spanish Enters the Curriculum

Over time, Army leaders added other languages to the curriculum, the first of these being Spanish. The Board of Visitors recommended adding Spanish in 1825; however, Thayer, already in the throes of an argument against the Board's suggestion that civil engineering be added to the Academy's curriculum, was not inclined to entertain any other changes. Thayer stated, "Those who are not satisfied with the existing studies . . . have not reflected upon the nature and object of the Institution and have not considered that this is a special school designed solely for the purpose of a *military* education."[19]

It was not until an 1854 expansion of the Academy course of study from four years to five that Spanish found room in the cadet course of study. Actual instruction under the new curriculum began in 1856, the Third Class year for the cadets under the new curriculum.[20] From 1855 to 1857, Professor Agnel held the title Professor of French and Spanish. Congress established a separate position, Professor of Spanish, in February 1857, and the Academy hired Patrice de Janon to fill it.[21] Thereafter, from 1856 until 1940 (with a brief break in 1919), all cadets took both French and Spanish.

In addition to Thayer's opposition to curriculum change, another likely explanation for the Academy's failure to add Spanish in 1825 was that (without an expansion of the core curriculum) it would have required a significant decrease in some other area, probably French. In fact, even with the expanded curriculum, the number of French recitations was cut from 272 to 238 to accommodate Spanish. Spanish recitations alternated with French from September to January in the Third Class year, resulting in 170 Spanish recitations.[22] Given the importance of French as a vehicle for understanding the curriculum's foreign texts, and the documented difficulties cadets experienced in learning the language, an initial resistance to the addition of Spanish with a concomitant decrease in French instruction is perhaps understandable.

In 1858, the Secretary of War expressed his desire that the Academy return to the four-year course of studies. The Academic Board suggested that French should return to 272 hours of instruction rather than the 238 that had been necessary to accommodate Spanish. This change could be made only at the expense of some other course of study. The Secretary preferred that French be dropped from the Fourth Class program entirely, thus reducing the number of French recitations to 218. The Academic Board, which had the final say, declined the Secretary's recommendation, which would have reduced the total amount of time devoted to the study of foreign languages, French in particular. They embraced this position because of the importance of the language [French] and also on account of it being one of the best exercises for precision in the use of language, because of the remarkable care of its structure, and the exact signification of its words received from some of the most acute minds and lucid writers.[23] French instruction thus remained at 238 hours for the time being.

With the outbreak of the Civil War in 1861, the course of study at the Academy was finally reduced from five years to four years. At that point, the Academic Board got its wish, and the number of French recitations returned to 272. In the same year, Spanish instruction was cut from 170 to 110 recitations, these being presented in the Fourth Class year.[24] The Academic Board clearly saw more value in the study of French than Spanish.

Over the years, the cadet language program underwent a number of adjustments. In 1867, Spanish was moved to the Third Class year, and back again to the Fourth Class year in 1877, with the number of recitations remaining at 110.[25] In 1867, Congress established English grammar, geography, and history as requirements for admission to the Academy. English was accordingly deleted as an academic subject, and French instruction was increased from 272 to 290 recitations.[26]

While the possibility of adding Spanish to the curriculum came in 1854 with the expansion from four years to five, the underlying impetus for the study of Spanish at West Point was the experience of graduates during the Mexican War (1846-48). Through them, the Army discovered the difficulties associated with the conduct of military operations where commanders are unable to communicate with the local populace. In retrospect, it is clear that with the addition of Spanish instruction at West Point, two important themes emerged: the importance of foreign languages to an army ordered to project power outside the borders of its own country, and the need for officers in that army to be able to communicate orally as well as read and write in languages other than English. Unfortunately, those themes were not clear to the language professors at the time.

Language Teaching Goals and Methodology, 1803–1900

Throughout the 19th century, the language teaching methodology at the Academy remained unchanged from the grammar and translation methods in use in 1803. In 1840, French instruction included pronunciation drills, reading with correct pronunciation, recitation of grammar rules, and translation from French to English and English to French. Only with the upper sections (the best students) could instructors ask cadets to attempt to speak French.[27] In 1853, the French teaching goals were the same, except that there was no longer any mention of speaking. By 1882, cadets studying either Spanish or French learned grammar and reading and writing. They translated from texts and also orally from English to the foreign language and from the foreign language to English.[28] They received no instruction in conversation, nor did they have the opportunity to use either Spanish or French in a social context. The result was that cadets did not learn to speak either language.

As a case in point, Capt. Edward O.C. Ord of the 3rd Artillery Regiment, testifying before the Davis Commission in 1860, noted that while at West Point he "was never called on to *speak* French or listen to it spoken, though I recited upon grammar, Leçons Françaises, and Gil Blas; and have since learned more Spanish from Mexican senioritas in two months than I did French at the Point in two years."[29]

In a similar vein, Cadet Adelbert Ames, a First Classman at West Point, also testifying before the Davis Commission, noted that although he completed the French course, "I cannot read French with entire facility, and in my present knowledge, would select the translation in preference to the original."[30] Ames was even more disparaging of his facility in Spanish: "Have finished also the Spanish course. I cannot speak Spanish at all."[31] Ames was not a bad cadet. He finished 17 out of 50 in Spanish and 13 out of 52 in French.[32]

The Foreign Languages Teaching Faculty

Between 1854 and 1941, the year the next language, German, entered the West Point curriculum, the foreign language faculty underwent a fundamental change. In the early 19th century, the belief was prevalent that native speakers should give language instruction, and at West Point during that period all of the native-speaking professors and instructors of French and Spanish were civilians. However, in the mid-19th century, an Army officer, Théophile d'Orémieulx, a native of France, arrived as a second lieutenant and served continuously teaching French until he resigned as a captain in 1856.[33]

In 1860, Professor Agnel, then the Professor of French, advanced arguments in favor of officers rather than civilian native speakers as instructors based on theory and his own experience.[34] The growing sentiment in favor of military instructors also applied to professors. In 1871, Col. George L. Andrews became Professor of French. He was the first Army officer and the first non-native speaker of French to hold that post. Known to the cadets as "Pop," he graduated first in the Class of 1851.[35] On 23 June 1879, Congress declared that

> when a vacancy occurs in the office of professor of the French language or in the office of the professor of the Spanish language at the Military Academy, both of these offices shall cease, and the remaining one of the two professors shall be professor of modern languages. [36]

Thus, upon Patrice de Janon's retirement in 1882, Colonel Andrews became Professor and Head of the Department of Modern Languages until he retired in 1892.

Beginning in 1877, the Department of Modern Languages acquired responsibility for teaching English as well as French and Spanish.[37] The teaching methodology for all three languages was grammar and translation. The study of English literature or any other literature at the Academy lay far in the future.

During his tenure as Department Head, Andrews changed many of the texts and made classroom methods of instruction in all three languages even more uniform. He also revised the testing methodology. Prior to 1873, oral examinations in all aspects of French instruction were the rule. After that time, grammar exams were in writing, but cadets did oral reading exams.[38] Nevertheless, the emphasis on learning grammar rules and producing accurate and natural translation, as opposed to oral conversation, continued.

Col. Edward E. Wood, who graduated sixth in the Class of 1870, succeeded Andrews as Department Head. Wood's service at the Academy, beginning as instructor of French in 1872, was frequently interrupted by field assignments. He served as aide de camp to Lt.

Gen. John Schofield from 1879 until 1882, when he rejoined the Eighth Cavalry Regiment. He returned to West Point in 1883 only to leave again in 1886 to participate in the campaign against Geronimo. He returned as assistant professor of Spanish in 1887 and served as Professor and Head of the Department of Modern Languages from 1892 until his mandatory retirement in 1910. In his obituary, Wood is described as being of a scholarly disposition, widely read in French history, especially the era of Louis XIV and the French Revolution.[39]

Like his predecessors, Wood concentrated cadet learning on grammar. As former cadet Williston Fish recalled: "He delighted in asking us for a rule in grammar—not so much for the pleasure of seeing us fail on it—though that was a great satisfaction—as for the scholarly delight of showing what a noble and hard rule it was."[40] Wood's claim to fame seems to have been his addiction to chewing tobacco. Fish reported that Wood "was always chewing tobacco. . . . When he got a [class] about lost in the rules of grammar he would take a fresh chew, and presently lose him[self] entirely, and seem to be in a rapture—or perhaps I should say ecstasy." Wood's nickname among the cadets was "Monkey Wood." [41]

Like the cadets who testified before the Davis Commission nearly two decades earlier, Fish, in response to the question, "What do you think of the French course at West Point?" responded: "The French course had its defects. The instructors were Army officers who, with some exceptions, had learned their French at West Point."[42] Fish also noted that he could not comprehend spoken French.[43]

In 1894, the elements of French instruction were grammar, reading, writing, the study and use of idioms, military terms, written and oral translation of English to French and vice versa, and the study of English synonyms. The requirements for Spanish were the same except that there were no provisions for the study and use of Spanish idioms or military terms.[44]

Under Wood, as under his predecessors, no attempt was made to teach cadets to speak either French or Spanish. The 1896 Superintendent's Annual Report notes, "The power to speak with even moderate fluency a foreign language cannot be and never has been acquired in a classroom."[45] The fact that fluency was not acquired in the classrooms of the time can be directly attributed to the fact that cadets, like language students in many other comparable institutions, were given no opportunity to acquire it. The grammar and translation methodology simply did not require, nor did it allow, students the opportunity to converse or otherwise communicate their own ideas in the foreign language. Furthermore, students of the time were given no opportunity to hear the language used in conversational settings.

The next Professor of Modern Languages was Col. Cornelis De Witt Willcox.[46] He was the first of the military professors to have solid academic qualifications for the position. Born in Geneva, Switzerland, he lived as a child with his family in Annaberg, Germany, and Brussels, Belgium. He graduated fourth out of 39 in the West Point Class of 1885; prior to that, he graduated with honors and was a member of Phi Beta Kappa at the University of Georgia where his father was Professor of Modern Languages. Prior to coming to West Point to take up his position, he studied the two languages abroad in Spain and France. He also served as instructor and assistant professor in the Department of Natural and Experimental Philosophy.

Willcox's military career included service in both the Spanish-American War and World War I. He was called to service in France in October 1917, serving first at the American General Headquarters and then at the French General Headquarters as the head of the American Mission. For his service he was named an Officer of the Legion of Honor and was awarded the Croix de Guerre with Palms. He wrote a French-English military dictionary and a handbook of War French which "proved of considerable value to our government and its allies during the Great War." [47] Willcox returned to West Point from his wartime service in France in June 1918. During his absence, he was indicated as being on "detached service" in the minutes of the Academic Board. Willcox died in Naples, Italy, in 1938 and was buried at West Point.

Language Teaching Goals and Methodology, 1900–1941

By 1902, there was a significant change in the number of hours devoted to Spanish and French. Though it is not clear how "recitations" (the term used in earlier documents to describe units of language instruction) were translated into "class hours," in 1877 cadets took 622 class hours of French and only 232 class hours of Spanish. A quarter of a century later, however, the figures had equalized somewhat, with 422 class hours of French and 318 class hours of Spanish. The increase in hours devoted to Spanish was partially compensated for by reducing mathematics instruction by 40 periods of instruction.[48] The Army's experience in the Spanish-American War and the increased availability of English language texts in math and engineering undoubtedly contributed to the increase in emphasis accorded to Spanish.

Of course, some were still dissatisfied with the relatively low priority given to the study of foreign languages in the West Point curriculum and to the failure to teach the spoken language. The Academy drew some pointed criticism from President Theodore Roosevelt. On 11 January 1908 in a letter to the Secretary of War, Roosevelt remarked:

> It seems to me a very great misfortune to lay so much stress upon mathematics in the curriculum at West Point and fail to have languages taught in accordance with the best modern conversational methods. I should like to have this matter taken up seriously. I have several times called attention to it, but nothing has been done. Mathematical training is a necessary thing for an engineer or an artilleryman, doubtless; but I esteem it of literally no importance for the cavalryman or infantryman. If tomorrow I had to choose officers from the regular army for important positions in the event of war, I should care no more for their mathematical training than for their knowledge of whist or chess. A man who learns a language by studying a book, but cannot speak it, loses at least half the benefit obtainable. I would like a full report on this matter.[49]

As reasonable as Roosevelt's request seemed to be, the Superintendent, Col. Hugh Scott, was unmoved. He sent the president the following unreceptive response in which he tried to defend the Academy's focus on mathematics as a tool for honing mental discipline:

> It is believed that mathematical training at the Military Academy has been the main factor in all the accomplishments of graduates; that it, more than any other factor, has generated the power of the graduate for profound logical thinking; it has been the means for the installation of proper self-confidence, for undertaking unhesitatingly the unfamiliar, and for going unerringly and indomitably after results whenever demanded by duty of any nature.[50]

Scott's letter notwithstanding, Willcox apparently agreed with President Roosevelt regarding the importance of learning to speak a language. By 1916, two superintendents later, he had developed a mission statement that reflected the new focus. Henceforth, the objective of the Department of Modern Languages would be "the acquisition of the ability to converse in French and Spanish and to have a working knowledge of the printed languages."[51] This aim stood in sharp contrast to the grammar and translation goals that had dominated language teaching at West Point since its beginning in 1803. As if to underscore the wisdom of the new language instruction aims, Superintendent Samuel Tillman in 1918 brought professors from Harvard University to summer camp to instruct cadets in spoken French, the language most important to Army officers fighting in Europe.[52]

To accelerate the output of officers for the war, the West Point curriculum was temporarily condensed and shortened beginning in 1917. The Class of 1917 graduated in April 1917; the next month, the following class, which had arrived in 1914, started a shortened version of their senior year studies. They graduated as the class of August 1917. A second three-year class graduated in June 1918. In July, Tillman received War Department approval for a three-year curriculum for all cadets.[53] This curriculum change resulted in a temporary deletion of Spanish instruction until 1920. At the end of 1920, the four-year curriculum, including instruction in both French and Spanish, resumed for all cadets.[54]

Throughout the first 150 years of language instruction at the Academy, the West Point faculty developed most of their textbooks and other teaching materials. Not only are these textbooks useful in describing the teaching methodologies employed during the various phases of the Academy's existence, they also provide revealing glimpses of cadet life. Included in one of the French texts published in 1918 are descriptions of "R" Day (Reception Day), selection of roommates, the cadet barracks, guard duty, and other aspects unique to cadet life. Additionally, the text takes readers on a tour of West Point to Trophy Point, lunch in the Mess Hall, summer camp, the hospital, concerts, marching, the gymnasium, 100th Night, June Week, dinner at an officer's quarters, a journey to New York City, and a trip to the nation's capital, among other topics.[55] This text was still in use in the 1930s, as indicated by the daily schedule of Cadet T.W. Morris inserted inside the front cover of the copy currently in the author's possession. He was Section Marcher (the cadet responsible for reporting attendance), and the names of the other 13 cadets in his section are also listed.

Faculty, Curriculum, and Teaching Methodologies, 1941–2000

Col. William E. Morrison became Department Head in 1925, when Willcox retired. For the first 15 years of his professorship, language teaching at the Academy remained static. Upon the outbreak of World War II, however, Morrison secured the addition of two other languages to the curriculum and significantly changed the teaching methodology for all foreign languages at the Academy.

German instruction began in 1941, followed swiftly by Portuguese the following year. Morrison developed a plan to determine which languages the cadets would learn and when.

> All cadets will study Spanish the first year; some will study French, some German, and the remainder Spanish the second year; and in the third year the French group will continue its work in that language, the German group will continue in German, and the Spanish group, having already had two years of that language, will take one year of Portuguese.[56]

Although cadets still did not choose the languages they would learn, this was the first time any cadet would graduate from the Academy without having studied exactly the same core courses as all of his classmates. It is interesting to note that a number of instructors were trying to learn German while teaching French and Spanish, and no instructor was yet qualified to teach Portuguese.[57] Fortunately, Morrison's plan gave the faculty an additional year to learn German, and two years to learn Portuguese.

Morrison's Annual Report to the Superintendent states the teaching objectives for 1941 as follows:

> The main objective was the customary one, to impart a thorough knowledge of the rules of pronunciation and grammar to be used later by the cadet in his career as an officer as a foundation upon which to build a working knowledge when occasion may arise. A secondary but very important objective was to develop facility at reading, writing, understanding, and speaking the language taught.[58]

Notably, although speaking the language was an acknowledged goal, it was secondary to learning grammar, and was listed after reading, writing, and understanding the language taught. Clearly Willcox's emphasis on spoken language did not survive beyond his retirement.

Once again, because of the exigency of war, Academy leaders shortened the curriculum (from four years to three) beginning in 1942. Under the revised curriculum, cadets took just two years of one language. Cadets were discouraged from continuing a language they had already studied before coming to the Academy. The department believed that developing a basic knowledge of a second foreign language was more beneficial than gaining a thorough familiarity with only one.[59] The wartime shortage of officers made it difficult to provide the needed instruction. To solve the problem, Morrison selected four upperclassmen to teach Spanish. One of those cadets, William Knowlton, returned 27 years later as the Superintendent.[60] Russian was the next language to be taught at the Academy. In Academic Year 1944-1945, selected faculty members began learning Russian in anticipation of adding that language to the curriculum in the fall of 1945.[61]

During the 1940s, the Academy established quotas for the number of cadets studying a particular language. With minor exceptions, the quotas remained quite constant for over 20 years: Spanish, 33.33 percent; French, 25 percent; German, 16.67 percent; Russian 16.67 percent; Portuguese, 8.33 percent. With the Cold War heating up, the Department of the Army in 1948 mandated a reversal of the French and Russian percentages, but after three years the percentages were reversed again. The reason for this change back to 25 percent for French was that some cadets assigned to study Russian struggled with the language, finding it more difficult to learn than French.[62]

The decade of the 1940s saw further change in the composition of the department faculty. The first foreign exchange officer, from the Mexican Army, arrived in the department in 1942.[63] Later, other officers would arrive to make up a contingent of allied officers representing Brazil, France, and Germany, in addition to Mexico. In 1946, the first civilian instructor since 1871 arrived for duty. Mr. Nicholas Maltzoff, who taught Russian and was known to the cadets as *Gospodin* Maltzoff, was the first of a number of civilian instructors hired in an effort to bring back the native-speaker flavor to language instruction at the Academy.[64] The growing emphasis on cadets learning to *speak* the languages they studied necessitated a pool of native speakers to assist both cadets and military faculty in the correct pronunciation and usage of the languages presented. Over time, other civilian native speakers joined Maltzoff on the faculty. Pepi Martinez was the native Spanish speaker. Others included Fred Garcia, Portuguese; Fritz Tiller, German; and Claude Violet, French. Samuel Saldivar, Arthur Reetz, and Mike Solo would eventually replace Martinez, Tiller, and Maltzoff, respectively, as civilian faculty members. These civilian instructors were housed in government quarters at the Academy and wore Army green uniforms with field grade hats and U.S. Military Academy collar insignia, but no rank insignia. One of their primary duties was to rotate among the language classrooms drilling the cadets on their oral pronunciation. They also held seminars for the rotating military faculty and eventually taught elective courses on the literature and culture of their native lands.[65]

The pressing need for language proficiency during World War II and in the postwar occupations significantly influenced how the Army approached the teaching of foreign languages. Responding to military wartime needs in the area of language acquisition, civilian universities developed the "Army Method" of instruction; the hallmarks of the program were an emphasis on oral work and the near total immersion of students in the target language. [66] The Army Method could not be ignored at West Point, and in 1947 the Military Academy formally declared the primacy of speaking in the acquisition of a foreign language. Henceforth, language instruction would be characterized by "greatly increased importance attached to oral work and the acquiring of oral fluency, with a corresponding deemphasizing of the conventional written work based on the study of rules."[67]

The "new" audio-lingual methodology that grew out of the Army Method eventually found its way into the West Point foreign language classrooms and remained in place into the mid-1990s. Characterized by the memorization and recitation of dialogues in the target language, and hours of listening to language tapes in language laboratories, the audio-lingual methodology also used written dictations and both oral and written grammar exercises to teach learners to speak, read, write, and comprehend both spoken and written language.

On 17 January 1948, an article in the post newspaper, *The Pointer View*, described the foreign language instruction that thousands of graduates remember well. Cadets studied one language for two years. Language choice was based primarily on the quota system and the cadet's own language background.

> The cadet follows a course in his selected language throughout the first two years. His program starts with a thorough study of pronunciation and then proceeds to practice in speaking. Reading and writing practice and study of the grammar are limited at first but thorough in the end. In the first year the cadet completes the grammar and acquires considerable familiarity with the spoken language. In the second year he proceeds to composition, reading (partly military), comprehension of lectures in the foreign tongue on the civilization of the countries where it is spoken and further constant practice in speaking.[68]

In July 1947, Col. Charles J. Barrett, Jr., became Professor of Modern Languages. Now, two military officers held this title, and the second of these would take over the department chairmanship upon the death, retirement, or disability of the first. When Colonel Morrison retired the following year, Barrett succeeded him as Head of the Department of Modern Languages. Language-related extra-curricular activities began during this time, the first of these being language clubs. Cadets could join one of the clubs and as members participate in various field trips broadly designed to enhance cultural understanding.[69]

In January 1949, Lt. Col. Walter J. Renfroe, Jr., became Professor of Modern Languages, filling Colonel Barrett's now vacant position as the second professor. Renfroe had come to the department during World War II as a French instructor, but he took up German during the war and was in charge of all German instruction when he was appointed professor. The same year the department name was changed to the Department of Foreign Languages. During Colonel Barrett's tenure, the course objectives in the Department remained constant, i.e., "a practical proficiency in one language and a basic acquaintance with the culture of its speakers."[70]

In the summer of 1955, 25 plebes (freshmen) were given the opportunity to take an advanced course in French. Based on the success of that endeavor, a similar course in German was added in 1956, followed by an advanced Spanish course in 1957.[71]

In 1958, West Point installed its first language laboratory, consisting of 21 booths and a reel-to-reel tape console that allowed the instructor to monitor individual cadets as they practiced the language. Cadets were encouraged to listen to tapes and to record their own voices as part of their normal class preparation.[72]

With the introduction of electives at West Point in 1961, the Department of Foreign Languages began offering one-semester courses in readings in literary masterpieces by French, German, Brazilian, Russian and Spanish-American writers. There were also follow-on advanced seminars in the literature of the five languages.[73] By 1966, the number of electives offered in the Department had mushroomed to 30 courses. These included third and fourth-year classes in all five languages in both civilization and literature as well as specialized courses in military and scientific readings in French, German, and Russian.[74]

Colonel Barrett died after a short illness in June 1963, and Colonel Renfroe became Department Head. Col. Sumner Willard, who held a bachelor's degree, master's, and Ph.D. in Romance Languages from Harvard University, replaced Colonel Renfroe as the second Professor of Foreign Languages. In 1966 Colonel Renfroe proposed adding Mandarin Chinese to the curriculum. Fortunately, the department already had a qualified instructor. Lt. Col. James Ross was serving in the department as a Russian instructor. Born in China, Ross had learned the language as a child. He then studied Chinese in the Army Specialized Training Program in 1943-1944 and served as an interpreter with the Chinese 38th Division in Burma. He attended a refresher course at Middlebury College before teaching at West Point[75]

To accommodate those cadets taking Chinese, Renfroe proposed new quotas for cadets enrolled in each language: Chinese 1.0-1.5 percent; Portuguese 8.5-9.0 percent; Russian 18 percent; and French, German, and Spanish, 24 percent each. Colonel Renfroe explained that he selected Chinese rather than Arabic, Italian, Japanese, or Korean, which were also considered, because "at present and for the foreseeable future Chinese appears to have the principal strategic and cultural importance among those languages named above."[76] Chinese instruction began during the fall semester of 1966.

The issue of a seventh language arose in November 1973, when Deputy Secretary of Defense W.P. Clements presciently suggested that the Academy consider teaching Arabic. The reasons were clear: the growing strategic importance of the Middle East owing to its oil reserves and the continuing Arab-Israeli conflict. Nothing happened immediately, and in January 1976 Clements became more insistent. In a memo to the service secretaries he noted: "The need for qualified Arabic linguists will continue indefinitely." Going further, he directed the superintendents of the three service academies to "examine the feasibility of adding the Arabic language to their respective curricula."[77] The Department of Foreign Languages began teaching Arabic in September 1976.

Upon Colonel Renfroe's retirement in August 1977, Colonel Willard became the new department head. He retired in 1980 after only three years as head, having reached the mandatory retirement age of 64. During his chairmanship, the foreign language elective program was expanded though the Academic Board reduced the core foreign language requirement from four semesters to three semesters for all cadets. The reason for the change was an event that shook the Military Academy to its very foundations.

In the spring of 1976, the Academy separated more than 100 cadets in the Class of 1977 for violating the Cadet Honor Code by cheating on an electrical engineering exam. It was the largest honor scandal in the Academy's history, leading to a bottom-up review of every aspect of the cadet experience. Astronaut Frank Borman, Class of 1950, headed the principal investigating commission. The comprehensive findings of the Borman Commission identified a number of issues, and the Superintendent referred them for action to a special committee—the West Point Study Group. The most pertinent result for purposes of the present chapter was the Study Group's recommendations regarding the core curriculum. Prior to 1977, the West Point core curriculum included 41 courses. According to the West Point Study Group, this large allocation of core courses "limited the depth of the cadets' educational experience by restricting the number of electives they could take in a specific field."[78]

In 1977, the Superintendent established the Military Academy Curriculum Committee to review curriculum issues and provide recommendations. After reviewing the work of the Borman Commission and the West Point Study Group, the committee recommended revisions to the academic program intended to "reduce fragmentation, sustain a substantial core curriculum and provide for a broad general education, and expand opportunities for more elective study in depth."[79] The new curriculum reduced the core requirement to only 30 courses, allowing cadets to choose ten electives from the 240 electives available. The aforementioned reduction of the core language requirement from four semesters to three was one of the side effects of the 30-course core curriculum. Foreign language instruction would be administered during the entire Fourth Class year and the first semester of the Third Class year.[80]

In addition to such curriculum revisions, the face of the department faculty began to change during this period. Early in the 1970s, the first African-American in the department was a young Spanish instructor named Fred Gorden; just over a decade later, he returned to the Academy as the Commandant of Cadets. Upon joining the department, Maj. Jack Child became the first non-West Point graduate since Colonel Willard and the first of the non-permanent faculty members to be a "non-grad." With the first female cadets entering the Academy in 1976, women joined the department faculty. The first woman to teach foreign languages was a reserve officer, Capt. Linda Bird, called to active duty in July 1975 as a French instructor. [81] Dr. Sheila Ackerlind was the first civilian female faculty member. She served initially as a visiting professor in 1985-1987 and then joined the permanent faculty in 1989.[82]

Colonel Willard's successor in 1977 as the second professor in the department was Col. John J. Costa, who later, in 1980, succeeded him as department head. Costa had many years of field experience to include command of an infantry brigade. He was the first professor in the department whose language teaching specialty was not French. As a cadet in 1945, Costa had been in the first group to study Russian, and he first returned to the Academy as a Russian instructor from 1957 to 1961.

Another important curriculum change in April 1981 led to a decrease in the amount of foreign language instruction given to some cadets. In order to facilitate the implementation of the majors program at the Academy, and in order to allow the engineering departments to offer the courses required for professional accreditation of the engineering programs, the Academic Board voted to reduce the core foreign language requirement from three semesters to two semesters for cadets concentrating in math, science, and engineering. The vote was far from unanimous—13 for, 7 against. Moreover, the study of foreign languages would not begin until the Third Class year for all cadets except those who expressed an interest in majoring in foreign languages during New Cadet Training. They could begin language instruction during Fourth Class year.[83] Cadets majoring in the humanities and social sciences would continue to take three semesters of foreign languages. Even that standard was shortly discarded when, in September 1984, the Academic Board extended the two-semester minimum to all cadets, a policy that prevails to the present day.[84]

In May 1982, the Academic Board approved the nomination of Col. Edward Thomas as the second professor in the department with the title Permanent Professor and Deputy Head, Department of Foreign Languages.[85] Colonel Thomas succeeded Colonel Costa as department head when the latter retired in 1989, and the deputy position was left unfilled. When Thomas retired unexpectedly five years later, the senior officer, Col. William G. Held, became Acting Department Head while a search committee was formed to locate a new department head. In May 1995, the Academic Board recommended the appointment of Held as the Department Head and Lt. Col. Patricia B. Genung as the Deputy Department Head. Upon confirmation by the Senate a year later, Genung became the first woman in the Academy's history named as Permanent Professor.

Teaching Foreign Languages Today

In the fall of 2000, the Academic Board again undertook a revision of the core curriculum, effective a year later for the Class of 2005. The result was a reduction of the core engineering sequence from five semesters to three for cadets not majoring in engineering. One of the deleted engineering courses was replaced by a mandated information technology course; the other provided room for a free elective intended to increase cadet exposure to foreign cultures. Although there are many options available for meeting the cultural requirement, one of the most popular has been to take a third semester of foreign language.

Today, despite the long-term decline of foreign languages in the core curriculum, the department's electives program remains strong. The number of cadet concentrators in foreign languages and in the department's foreign area studies programs exceeds 220, approximately 7 percent of the upper three classes. Under the tutelage of the Department of Foreign Languages faculty, cadets visit more than

36 countries every year through an extensive program of exchanges with other military academies. The principal vehicles for these visits are the Foreign Academy Exchange Program, operative during the academic year, and a summer academic enrichment program. Cadets participating in the latter program travel to many countries to experience foreign cultures and military training, and to study the politics, industry, and society of other nations.

Since the mid-1990s, the teaching methodology in the department has changed from the "memorize and repeat" techniques of audio-lingual methodology to a learner-centered communicative classroom teaching style in which cadets are encouraged to create language and express their original thoughts in the target language from the first day of class. Reading, writing, and grammar, while still included in the course of study, take a backseat to learning to speak and comprehend spoken language. Department language laboratories currently include facilities for a variety of computer-assisted language learning techniques. Research in voice recognition technology and its application to language learning takes place within the department in the Computer Technology Enhanced Language Learning division.

Over the 200 years since its founding, language instruction has played a central role at the Academy. In 1803 the French language provided the key to studying the only extant math, science, and engineering texts. By the mid-19th and early 20th centuries, the Army began to recognize the importance of foreign languages to a nation and to an army intent upon projecting power onto the global stage. World War II and the Cold War continued this trend, with foreign language instruction at the Academy expanding to include the strategically important languages of the mid to late 20th century.

The teaching methodologies and teaching faculty, along with the language curriculum and classroom technology, have changed at West Point over the last 200 years as they did at civilian institutions. Sometimes the Academy lagged behind, and sometimes it found itself at the forefront, in presenting the discipline of foreign languages. In the year 2003, the Department of Foreign Languages proudly enters its third century at the U.S. Military Academy, still very much a vital part of cadet learning and development.

[1] I am indebted to a former Department of Foreign Languages colleague, Lt. Col. Robert L. Doherty, for the general outline of this paper. Much of my initial knowledge of the topic came from reading his dissertation, "Foreign Language Studies at the United States Service Academies: Evolution and Current Issues" (Ph.D. diss., Teachers College, Columbia University, 1983).

[2] Roswell Park, *A Sketch of the History and Topography of West Point and the United States Military Academy* (Philadelphia: C. Sherman, 1840), 91.

[3] Sidney Forman, *West Point: A History of the United States Military Academy* (New York: Columbia University Press, 1950), 52.

[4] Robert H. Hall, compiler, *Laws of Congress Relative to West Point and the United States Military Academy from 1786-1877* (West Point, NY: United States Military Academy Press, n.d.), 6, 40, 46. Although it is not clear how much salary the first First Teacher of French received in 1803, in 1850 the Professor of French received $1,500 per annum. Notably, professors of engineering, philosophy, mathematics, ethics, and chemistry received $2,000 each. The Professor of French did not receive the same pay as his counterparts until 1855.

[5] Stephen E. Ambrose, *Duty, Honor, Country: A History of West Point* (New York: Johns Hopkins University Press, 1999), 27.

[6] Park, 54; United States Military Academy, *Annual Report of the Superintendent of the United States Military Academy 1896* (Washington, DC: Government Printing Office, 1896.), 132.

[7] Forman, 52-54.

[8] Forman, 52.

[9] Hall, 37-38.

[10] Park, 83.

[11] *Annual Report of the Superintendent of the United States Military Academy 1896*, 132.

[12] Ibid.,133.

[13] Ibid.

[14] Ibid.

[15] Ibid, 136.

[16] Ibid., 134.

[17] Ibid.

[18] Ibid.; James Morrison, Jr., *"The Best School in the World": West Point, 1833-1866* (Kent, OH: The Kent State University Press, 1998), 92, 160.

[19] Quoted in Theodore J. Crackel, *West Point: A Bicentennial History* (Lawrence, KS: University Press of Kansas, 2002), 97. Italics in original.

[20] Ibid., 139.

[21] Ibid., 139-40.

[22] Ibid., 134.

[23] Ibid.

[24] Ibid., 140.

[25] Ibid.

[26] Ibid., 135.

[27] Ibid., 137.

[28] Ibid., 141.

[29] Congress, Senate, *Report of the Commission*, 36th Cong., 2nd sess., 1860, S. Doc. 3, 334. Emphasis in original.

[30] Ibid., 109.

[31] Ibid.

[32] Ambrose, 143

[33] *Annual Report of the Superintendent of the United States Military Academy 1896*, 132.

[34] Ibid. There is no elaboration as to what theory he cited or what experience led him to this conclusion.

[35] Ambrose, 204.

[36] Hall, 104.

[37] Sixty recitations were taken from French to accommodate English. This lowered the number of French recitations to 260. In 1878, English appears to have been combined with French to some degree. The number of French recitations increased to 280 and remained there until 1882. *Annual Report of the Superintendent of the United States Military Academy 1896*, 135.

[38] Ibid., 138. Details of the course of instruction for 1878-79 may be found in Appendix B of the reference.

[39] United States Military Academy, *The Association of Graduates Fifty-sixth Annual Report* (Saginaw, MI: Seeman and Peters Printers, 1925), 145-46.

[40] Williston Fish, *Memories of West Point, 1877-1881*, edited and reproduced from the unpublished typescript by Gertrude Fish Rumsey and Josephine Fish Peabody (Batavia, NY, c1957), 3:869.

[41] Ibid. Emphasis in original.

[42] Ibid., 3:870.

[43] Ibid.

[44] *Annual Report of the Superintendent of the United States Military Academy 1896*, 145, 147. Details about classes, class reports, and examinations during this period may be found in pp. 150-56 of reference.

[45] Ibid., 152.

[46] As is not infrequently the case, the spelling of names in the 19th century shows considerable elasticity. In the 2002 edition of *Register of Graduates and Former Cadets* published by the Military Academy, the name appears as "Cornelis deWitt Wilcox" in the Class of 1885 roster (p. 4-69). However, in the Alphabetical Locator (p. 2-139), the name appears as "Cornelius deW Willcox." The Library of Congress uses "Cornelis De Witt Willcox" with the acute accent (´) over the e in Cornelis. Documents preserved in Willcox's hand confirm the double l according to Ms. Susan Lintelmann, Manuscripts Curator, USMA Library. The usage adopted in the present chapter is that of the Library of Congress, without the acute accent.

[47] United States Military Academy, *The Association of Graduates Sixty-ninth Annual Report* (Newburgh, NY: The Moore Printing Company, 1938), 133-36.

[48] United States Military Academy, *Superintendent's Curriculum Study: Report of the Working Committee on the Historical Aspects of the Curriculum of the Period 1802-1945* (West Point, NY, 1958), 49, 67.

[49] President Theodore Roosevelt to Superintendent Hugh L. Scott, 11 January 1908, as quoted in United States Military Academy, *Superintendent's Curriculum Study: Report of the Working Committee on the Historical Aspects of the Curriculum of the Period 1802-1945* (West Point, NY, 1958), 81.

[50] United States Military Academy, *Superintendent's Curriculum Study: Report of the Working Committee on the Historical Aspects of the Curriculum of the Period 1802-1945* (West Point, NY, 1958), 82.

[51] John R. McCormick, "History of Foreign Language Teaching at the United States Military Academy," *Modern Language Journal* 54 (1970): 321.

[52] Ambrose, 253.

[53] Crackel, 185.

[54] Forman, 196.

[55] Charles F. Martin and George M. Russell, *At West Point: A Practical Course in Speaking and Writing French* (New York: D.C. Heath, 1918).

[56] Colonel Morrison to the Superintendent, United States Military Academy, Subject: Program of Language Instruction, 18 December 1941, in United States Military Academy, *Proceedings of the Academic Board 1941*.

[57] Doherty, 27.

[58] United States Military Academy, *Department of Modern Languages Annual Report* (West Point, NY, 10 July 1941), 3; quoted in Doherty, 27.

[59] United States Military Academy, *Department of Modern Languages Annual Report* (West Point, NY, 9 August 1945), 1; quoted in Doherty, 28.

[60] United States Military Academy, *Department of Modern Languages Annual Report* (West Point, NY, 30 June 1943), 1; quoted in Doherty, 28.

[61] Brig. Gen. (ret.) John J. Costa. Interview by the author, March 2002.

[62] Colonel Renfroe to the Academic Board, Subject: Introduction of Teaching of the Chinese Language in the USMA Curriculum, 11 April 1966, in United States Military Academy, *Proceedings of the Academic Board 1966*.

[63] Dr. Samuel Saldivar. Interview by the author, February 2002. Saldivar has been on the faculty at the Academy longer than any other current faculty member.

[64] Costa.

[65] Saldivar.

[66] Doherty, 30.

[67] United States Military Academy, Public Relations Office "Change in United States Military Academy Method of Language Instruction," Release No. G-40 (West Point, NY: Public Relations Office, 26 March 1947), as cited in Doherty, 30.

[68] "The Department of Modern Languages," *The Pointer View*, 17 January 1948; quoted in Doherty, 31.

[69] Costa.

[70] United States Military Academy, *Department of Foreign Languages Annual Report* (West Point, NY, 1 August 1951), 1; quoted in Doherty, 32.

[71] United States Military Academy, *Department of Foreign Languages Annual Report* (West Point, NY, July 1956), 1; quoted in Doherty, 32.

[72] United States Military Academy, *Department of Foreign Languages Annual Report* (West Point, NY, 1959), 1; quoted in Doherty, 33.

[73] *United States Military Academy Catalogue 1961-62* (West Point, NY: USMA Admissions Office, 1961), 59.

[74] *United States Military Academy Catalogue 1966-67* (West Point, NY: USMA Admissions Office, 1966), 89-93.

[75] United States Military Academy, *Proceedings of the Academic Board 1966*, 162.

[76] Colonel Renfroe to the Academic Board, Subject: Introduction of Teaching of the Chinese Language in the USMA Curriculum, 11 April 1966, in United States Military Academy, *Proceedings of the Academic Board 1966*, 158.

[77] United States Department of Defense, Office of the Deputy Secretary of Defense, "Teaching of Arabic Language at the Service Academies, " Memo to the Secretaries of the Army, Navy, and Air Force (Washington, DC: Office of the Deputy Secretary of Defense, 29 January 1976); quoted in Doherty, 36.

[78] *The United States Military Academy in Perspective 1969-1979: An Institutional Report Prepared for the 1980 Dicennial Accreditation*, 38.

[79] Ibid., 39.

[80] Ibid.

[81] Dr. Stephen B. Grove, United States Military Academy Historian. Interview by author, 9 June 2003.

[82] Dr. Sheila Ackerlind. Interview by the author, March 2002.

[83] United States Military Academy, *Proceedings of the Academic Board 1981*, 25 April 1981.

[84] United States Military Academy, *Proceedings of the Academic Board 1984*, 11 September 1984.

[85] United States Military Academy, *Proceedings of the Academic Board 1982*, 12 May 1982. Another title, "Professor, United States Military Academy" (PUSMA), has been used since the mid-1960s to denote the small group of military faculty members (primarily Department Heads and Deputy Department Heads, Vice Deans) who are appointed by authority of Title X, U.S. Code, and who provide institutional continuity and senior leadership at the Academy; PUSMAs may serve on active duty until their 64th birthday. The PUSMAs are different from the "Academy Professors" (formerly called "Permanent Associate Professors") in that the latter group must retire in accordance with Army regulations—for most upon reaching 30 years of commissioned service. The terms PUSMA and Academy Professor refer only to the job or position title. The academic rank—assistant professor, associate professor, or professor—of a military faculty member is a separate matter.

⊰ CHAPTER 22 ⊱

NATIONAL SECURITY STUDIES AT WEST POINT

Jay M. Parker

Introduction[1]

Maj. Michael George was halfway through the morning's lesson in the National Security Studies Seminar when a cadet came running in the classroom. "Turn on the television!" It was a scene being repeated at that moment on 11 September 2001 in classrooms all over West Point. Cadets watched as the World Trade Center collapsed and the Pentagon burned. For most Americans, it was something they could never have envisioned. But for Major George and the cadets in his National Security Studies Seminar, the lesson already on the syllabus for that day was terrorism and non-state actors.

In the months following the terrorist attacks, the staff and faculty of West Point assessed how the curriculum would need to change to adjust to this tragedy. The answer for the National Security Studies program was, "Very little." One should expect nothing less. For more than 200 years, the purpose of the U.S. Military Academy has been to provide leaders who will take responsibility for the nation's security. The education and professional development of the next generation of Army officers must focus on the demands of the future as well as the lessons of the past. Clearly, the Academy's approach to national security education was meeting this difficult challenge.

However, such foresight had not always been the hallmark of West Point's approach to the teaching of national security. Graduates such as Grant, MacArthur, and Eisenhower—through self-directed study, brilliance, experience, and attentive mentors—developed these skills post-West Point. They were decades past their graduation when called on to exhibit their talents as grand strategists. It was more than 150 years into the Academy's history when, to reflect changes in the nation's place in the world following the Second World War, formal classes in national security studies entered the curriculum.

Until then, America's concept of national security did not include an Army needing junior officers with a clear sense of grand strategy and their role in its execution. As it has throughout history, West Point adapted its curriculum to meet the specific needs of the evolving roles of the nation and its Army. However, this relatively recent addition of formal instruction on grand strategy and national defense policy making does not mean that West Point ignored national security education for the first century and a half of its history.

Long before the events of 11 September 2001, soldiers and their civilian counterparts had struggled not just with the demands of national security, but with the very definition of the term.[2] As West Point continues to prepare young men and women to assume the responsibilities of commissioned service, the institution must determine how best to adapt the curriculum to new national security imperatives while addressing those traditional aspects of national security that remain unchallenged. To understand how West Point will meet this critical challenge in the years ahead, one must first examine the Academy's past. How did national security studies become a formal part of West Point's curriculum? Was it through a refinement of previous instruction, the complete replacement of outdated or misguided concepts, or the introduction of entirely new and unique courses?

The history of national security education at West Point is the history of the entire curriculum. That curriculum is not composed of discrete course blocks. It is a comprehensive, integrated educational experience designed to prepare officers for the national security challenges of tomorrow. This chapter outlines how West Point's teaching of national security has adjusted to America's changing views of national security over the course of the nation's history, and then discusses what it does today to prepare future Army leaders for the years ahead. In concluding, it advances the position that West Point today provides a timely, relevant, and comprehensive education in national security studies, one that is unique both in West Point's history and in American higher education.

West Point and The Changing Nature of American National Security

Thomas Jefferson was not a fan of standing armies. Like many Americans who shared his views, he was particularly suspicious of a professional military—led by an elite officer corps—that might endanger the nation's fragile new experiment in democracy. In his view, the best defense was a national militia of well armed, loosely organized citizen soldiers. When others—particularly his archrival Alexander Hamilton—proposed a national academy whose purpose would be to train such a professional officer corps, Jefferson was solidly opposed. His fears were not entirely unwarranted. Revolutionary War officers already had threatened to take control of the reins of government.[3] Among Jefferson's first acts as president was to reduce the nation's already minuscule Army by almost half.

In 1802, however, the U.S. Military Academy at West Point opened its doors with the president's blessing. Jefferson's change of heart can be ascribed mainly to three sobering strategic and educational realities of the time. First, any hope of continued American isolation was wishful thinking. The wide Atlantic to the east was little protection from dangerous neighbors to the north and on the frontiers of the west and south. In fact, the oceans themselves provided the greatest dangers. The ink on the 1783 Treaty of Paris was barely dry before America found its ships attacked by pirates and "legally" boarded and seized on the high seas by the navies of other nations.

Second, the nature of 19th century warfare demanded officers educated and skilled in sciences and engineering. It is no accident that West Point was first seen as a school of artillery and military engineering. The tasks of leading massed infantrymen armed with muskets or charging cavalrymen with sabers were ones that could be learned through rote battle drills. America's limited military experience to this point fueled the Minuteman mythology of hastily assembled local militias led by courageous and intelligent amateurs. However, the mathematics of cannon artillery and the complex intricacies of constructing and defending (or, for that matter, attacking and destroying) siege fortifications were not skills learned on the parade ground. Furthermore, when the young American Army required these skills, it had to rely largely on European expatriates to serve as instructors.

Third, American higher education in the early 1800s reflected the primacy of humanities and the liberal arts taught in the classic European tradition. Those very few colleges and universities already established could not be relied on to provide young men educated in the sciences and mathematics and motivated to take up the profession of arms. Engineering as an academic discipline was virtually unheard of in the United States.[4]

There was also a compelling political reason for Jefferson to support such an academy. In the years following the American Revolution, many officers who remained in military service were Federalists and allies of one of Jefferson's fiercest rivals, Alexander Hamilton. In Jefferson's view, the new school could help "Republicanize" the nation's Army or—at a minimum—balance competing ideological views within the officer corps.[5]

Soon after the first cadets reported, Jefferson acquired another, more acceptable reason for establishing the Academy, but it had little to do with warfighting. With the Louisiana Purchase, an Army would be needed to secure and develop this massive expanse of new territory. For the first West Point cadets, "national security" had a broader definition than just the use of military forces to deter aggression and defend the state. "We must get up early," one 19th century cadet explained, "for we have a large territory; we have to cut down the forests, dig canals, and make railroads all over the country."[6] The teaching of national security issues in the modern sense was at best limited. In the pre-Clausewitzian era, this new American nation had not yet fully come to terms with the education of a professional military, and the role of that military in a modern democratic state. For the first generation of Academy graduates, "the common defense" was best served by building a sound national infrastructure. America's demand for professional soldiers was tied to needs of the growing national economy. Engineering took precedence over tactics. [7]

Under the leadership of Sylvanus Thayer, the superintendent from 1817 to 1833, West Point became the nation's premier institution for civil engineering, modeled principally after France's École Polytechnique. But in addition to laying a firm academic foundation for the Academy, Thayer also instilled a strong sense of the military.[8] He did not entirely neglect the art of war for the science of engineering. His protégé Dennis Hart Mahan was one of several West Point faculty members who studied and taught the lessons emerging from the European campaigns of Napoleon [9] Those lessons were not limited to tactics. Napoleon waged war at the operational and strategic levels. By learning the lessons of the European wars and the context of those struggles, cadets added a strategic military dimension to an education focused primarily on domestic nation-building.

However, this instruction was minimal at best. A review of the early Academy curriculum reveals that even the most generous count of the hours devoted to topics remotely related to "national security" was little more than half the hours devoted to French instruction and less than the time dedicated to instruction in drawing.[10] Classifying Mahan's courses as "national security" instruction or even tactics must be heavily qualified. His principal focus is reflected in the course title, "Military Art and Engineering."

American ambivalence about the composition and organization of the military made Thayer's tasks all the more difficult. Americans were still suspicious of an army subject to the whim of a single ruler rather than to the institutions of democratic governance. When Thayer resigned the superintendency after a political battle with President Andrew Jackson over the latter's attempts to use the "spoils system" to fill the Army and West Point with political allies, West Point graduates had still not convincingly faced the ordeal of war, the ultimate test of the Academy's utility.[11]

In the War of 1812 and the Seminole Indian Wars beginning in 1818, West Point graduates were called on to lead American troops in battle. They acquitted themselves well, displaying courage and intelligence, but they were still only a small portion of the officer corps. In the War with Mexico (1846-1848), however, an Army increasingly dominated by West Point graduates first began to fill the classic role of those charged with the nation's security. A generation of officers schooled primarily to harness rivers rather than defend against foreign enemies clearly established themselves as leaders in a major war with strategic implications.

The Civil War was a far sterner struggle, testing West Point graduates at the tactical, operational, and strategic levels of war. Many who proved themselves in Mexico now served with distinction on both sides of the conflict. In virtually every significant engagement of the war, West Point graduates faced off across the battlefield. Specifically, of the 60 major battles of the Civil War, West Pointers commanded both sides in 55 of them. In the remaining five, Academy graduates commanded on of the two sides.[12]

But while many graduates are remembered for their success in battle, the war highlighted what some felt were flaws in the Academy product. After the war, this criticism surfaced. For example, though some West Point graduates, now remembered as Civil War heroes, were quickly promoted from junior officer rank to senior leadership roles, some older graduates were found wanting in battle. Gifted civilian amateurs such as Joshua Lawrence Chamberlain had proven to be the battlefield equal of their West Point peers. Most damning was the charge that a West Point education had not instilled a sense of duty and national loyalty in all its alumni. The President of the Confederacy, Jefferson Davis, was a West Point graduate, while distinguished graduate and former Superintendent Robert E. Lee led the forces of the rebellion. Some 313 officers resigned their commissions in the Union Army to join that of the Confederacy.[13]

The Civil War era coincided with changes in West Point's status in American higher education. While the Academy's curriculum remained largely the same, it now began to win praise for its emphasis on science and mathematics at a time when colleges and universities still stressed a classic education grounded in the humanities. But West Point was no longer the sole engineering school nor was it the only institution offering a military education. Virginia Military Institute was established in 1839, and the Citadel began instruction in 1842. The Morrill Act of 1862 marked the beginning of the modern state universities, with many schools choosing a West Point style curriculum balancing science and liberal arts, rather than the more traditional degree programs stressing the classics.[14] These Land Grant institutions would eventually evolve into the modern American public universities with curriculums like West Point's, shifting from the classical model in order to better meet the particular economic, political, and social demands of the nation.

With the end of the Civil War, the Regular Army was once again a constabulary force. Many contemporary commentators forget that most of the Army's missions involved what are today referred to as "military operations other than war." The building of the nation's infrastructure continued while the Army sometimes fought, sometimes negotiated with, sometimes guarded and policed, and sometimes coexisted with the tribes of Native Americans. The battles in the west were motivated and framed by the same broad political, economic, technological, and social issues that defined all war, but the immediate focus of West Point graduates was narrow. These were brutal, isolated clashes fought by units so small and concentrated that a regimental commander could still physically observe and control his troops on the battlefield. With no demand from the field for junior officers with a strategic perspective, little changed in the formal structure of national security studies at West Point. An officer's education in the nuances of America's security challenges in the late 1800s reflected professional responsibilities as engineers and builders rather than as warrior-diplomats.

At the turn of the century, propelled mainly by the Spanish-American War, America moved dramatically from relative isolation toward significant involvement in the world's leadership. West Point graduates, by the nature of their traditional service mission and the limits of force projection capabilities, were not in the immediate forefront of those changes. It was Dennis Mahan's son Alfred and his patron Theodore Roosevelt who redefined the nation's strategic outlook by expanding the role of the U.S. Navy.[15] But while the Navy's "Great White Fleet" may have ensured the emergence of America's new role in the world, it was soldiers on the ground who sustained it. They fought in Cuba and the Philippines among other places. These battles highlighted the need for new weapons and new tactics applied under a new strategic vision. Likewise, the new American colonial role in Asia and the Caribbean put West Point engineers and logisticians in situations foreshadowing those faced by graduates throughout the 20th century. Around the globe, young officers found themselves in far-flung locations they never imagined in their days as cadets.

As the world and the Army's role in it changed, so did the curriculum at West Point. The 1902 curriculum incorporated more detailed instruction in tactics. History was taught as a separate discipline. However, hours assigned to course work in the art and science of war were even fewer than those allocated in 1823.[16] The curriculum would change again in 1912, with an end to required courses in fencing, but there was still nothing that could clearly be considered formal course work in national security. Courses related to the profession of arms remained at the tactical level, with instruction in drill, riding, and gunnery.[17]

Of course, national security courses were not likely to be found in civilian institutions either. The discipline of political science was relatively new, and formal course work in international relations still lay in the future.[18] This was also a time when the military and its entire professional education system were undergoing dramatic change under the impetus of visionary leaders such as Secretary of War Elihu Root. A West Point education now provided the foundation for a career-long series of military schools and training programs. The introduction of service war colleges (Naval in 1885, Army in 1901) meant that national security education would now be provided to officers, but only after long years of service and education in tactics and operational art.

With the end of the First World War, America was forced to reconsider its role on the international stage. Added to this motive for change, the Army of the Great War had found some West Point officers wanting as small unit leaders. Furthermore, those few junior officers of exceptional skill and talent were rapidly promoted to staff and command positions, where they required a broader perspective on the strategic dimensions of warfare. Douglas MacArthur—witness to the performance of Academy graduates on the battlefield and conscious of the Army's new roles—returned to the Academy to serve as Superintendent. This development precipitated the most significant changes to West Point in 50 years. Advances over the next two decades included the practice of sending West Point instructor designees to civilian graduate schools, accreditation from the Association of American Universities, and authorization to grant Bachelor of Science degrees.[19] Curricular attention to new technologies began to surpass that of classic fortifications. Electricity—totally absent from the Class of 1912's transcripts—consumed 154 hours of instruction for the Class of 1923.[20]

By 1923, military history had become a separate course with 47 hours of instruction. Twelve years later, military history instruction expanded to 120 hours.[21] Officers also had to be conversant with international affairs and the economic and political demands of national mobilization. Meeting this requirement was the responsibility of the Department of Government, History, and Economics (later renamed the Department of Social Sciences when History became a separate department) headed by Dwight Eisenhower's classmate, Col. Herman Beukema.[22] The nation's mobilization effort for the First World War and the significant depression era civilian role in federal agencies like the Civilian Conservation Corps put West Pointers in direct interaction with and sometimes in direct control of large sectors of the domestic economy.[23] The changes in West Point's curriculum reflected those demands.

With the coming of another world war, those demands sharply increased. Cadets entering a wartime West Point in 1942 spent more hours on courses in the Department of Social Sciences than in physics, chemistry, or ordnance. Despite such significant curriculum changes, it was not until after World War II that the specific topic of national security entered West Point's academic curriculum.

Creation of a National Security Curriculum at West Point

After World War II, the challenges confronting young officers multiplied enormously. Their first task was to assist in the occupation and rebuilding of Europe and Asia. Without precedent in peacetime, the nation's defense now depended on a large, forward-deployed military rather than on the small home defense force that had always seemed to reappear after previous overseas conflicts[24] During the Cold War, the new threat of nuclear annihilation was too close and complex and the consequent risks too great to allow for the traditional American process of deliberate national mobilization as a prelude to hostilities. Meanwhile the old colonial order collapsed as age-old forms of guerrilla warfare reemerged. Cold War Army officers now led a large conscript force, reflecting both the strengths and weaknesses of the American society from which it sprang.

Meanwhile, the technological transformation of the Army, begun in World War I, had continued unabated. In the Class of 1928, graduates entered the horse cavalry and aviation in almost equal numbers. Less than 25 years later, the old riding hall had been converted to an academic building, the Army Air Corps was a separate force soon to have its own Academy, and nuclear weapons and space age technology—both pioneered by West Point graduates—defined the modern battlefield. The math, science, and engineering portions of the core curriculum were still salient in the nuclear age, and little changed in that portion of instruction.

But the social, political, and economic dimensions of war were enlarging dramatically. In a world where American security depended on strong, institutionalized political alliances, the line between diplomat and soldier blurred. New links between the economy and the military had also materialized. America's economic recovery from the Great Depression was nearing completion, but the defense spending that helped fuel that recovery was still at unprecedented levels for peacetime. New conflicts were not confined to external enemies. Whereas the Army and Navy had clearly divided their responsibilities at the water's edge in centuries past, the postwar era saw intense interservice rivalry, manifested in bureaucratic and political battles over roles and missions and the defense budget that underwrote them.

Taken together, these developments illustrate perfectly the Clausewitzian conception of national strategy. War, in Clausewitz's oft-quoted view, is an extension of policy. A nation's defense policy, and the grand strategy it spawns, rests upon military might joined with social, political, and economic power. In America's democracy, civilian leaders must be the ones to set policy. As always, officers must execute that policy on the battlefield. In this new era, officers—not just senior officers but junior officers as well—had to understand fully the bigger strategic implications of their tactical and operational actions. Developing such officers required new elements in the West Point education.

Responding to this challenge was George "Abe" Lincoln. A Rhodes Scholar from the Class of 1929, Lincoln was—like many of his class-mates—the beneficiary of rapid promotions. He quickly became the youngest general in the Army. Lincoln witnessed the grand strategic level of modern warfare at close hand while serving on the staff of Gen. George C. Marshall. As a war planner, he played a significant role throughout World War II and in the early phases of postwar reconstruction. He was a key player at virtually every significant alliance conference and treaty negotiation. Few officers understood the new dimensions of international security better than Lincoln. Turning down choice postwar assignments, he took a reduction in rank from major general to colonel to join Herman Beukema in West Point's newly renamed Department of Social Sciences. Arriving at West Point in 1947, Lincoln soon introduced a new elective course titled The Economics of National Security.[25]

Lincoln also initiated an annual lecture presented to the entire Second Class (juniors) on the general topic of national security. The lecture was part of core instruction in international relations, newly introduced to the Academy curriculum.[26] Assuming the leadership of Social Sciences upon Beukema's retirement in 1954, Lincoln continued to press the Academic Board for an expansion of elective offerings and the introduction of academic majors.[27] At the same time, he began to develop the Academy's first elective national security seminar. This course would serve as the founda-tion for a wide range of related elective courses that would eventually become the Department's first field of concentration and, later, an academic major.

As Lincoln developed new courses and fought the inevitable battles within the academic bureaucracy, global events served to reinforce the wisdom of his initiatives. The American military's clear-cut triumph in World War II was followed by its ambiguous advisory role in the Greek Civil War, the bloody stalemate of Korea, and the growing insurgency threats to American allies throughout the world. In the mid-1950s, plans for a space satellite were shelved when a political battle with the Air Force delayed a launch that would have put America in space before the Soviet's Sputnik.[28] In 1956, a fierce interservice battle over budget resources became a public feud. The nation's press reported that the Army Staff was in open revolt over cuts in forces and spending.[29] This bureaucratic battle stemmed from the Eisenhower Administration's determination to cut the defense budget by relying on nuclear deterrence at the high end of the spectrum of conflict and covert CIA intervention at the low end. While Eisenhower argued that the threat of "massive retaliation" would ensure "more bang for the buck," the Army's role in the resulting continuum of conflict was not yet clearly defined.

The Military Academy faculty could, and did, contribute to the debates over national strategy, Army doctrine, and interservice budget battles. Lincoln's personal papers reveal considerable correspondence on these matters with members of the Army Staff. Memos from Eisenhower would often find their way to the desk of White House aide Gen. Andrew Goodpaster with the handwritten notation, "See what Abe thinks. DDE." Such involvement in the day-to-day policy arena—while valuable to both the Academy and the policymakers—was not West Point's primary mission. The faculty's primary focus would be the long-range task of preparing graduates for military careers in an increasingly complex world, not resolving ephemeral issues treated in the daily headlines.

In 1956, the Academy leadership initiated a major historical review of the curriculum as a first step toward revising the instruction to better meet the demands of the future. The task of preparing a comprehensive history of the Academy curriculum was assigned to a faculty group which reviewed the changing course mix since1802, with special attention to the broader strategic, political, and educational context.[30] Graduates were surveyed, particularly those who served in the Second World War and were still serving in positions of significant responsibility. Even President Eisenhower was consulted.

The President's input, dictated to Goodpaster, reinforced Lincoln's views. In response to the request to indicate courses needing to be expanded, the institution's highest-ranking graduate replied, "Economics and International Relations; History, Government and Geography." The President added that additional instruction was also needed "on the broad subject of the Army in American Society."[31] Responding to a report on the progress of the curriculum review and revision, Eisenhower in 1959 reiterated his earlier views, highlighting the importance of a new voluntary elective titled, "National Security Problems." [32]

Eisenhower's note officially acknowledged the new seminar, developed by Lincoln, that represented the first Academy course devoted entirely to the subject. Lincoln had spent several years reviewing courses in the newly emerging field of national security studies and corresponding with the faculties at other schools. West Point was not the only school in the nation to offer such a course, but it was certainly among the first.[33] The study of national security extended from nuclear deterrence to guerrilla warfare. Out of interest as well as necessity, Einstein and Mao were studied side by side at West Point. By 1961, as a limited number of electives were added to what had previously been a prescribed curriculum, the two-year-old National Security Problems course had the highest enrollment of any Academy elective.[34]

As the Cold War domestic consensus turned sour over Vietnam, West Point was reminded of the importance of domestic politics in the definition and execution of its mission. It was not enough for officers to understand what went on in Moscow or Hanoi if they did not understand the political realities in American society itself. The Army confronted the open hostility of the civilian population, many of whom saw the military as the prime agent of the nation's unpopular foreign and defense policies. The graduates of Jefferson's school for engineers now faced security challenges far greater in breadth than those ever imagined by Thayer and Dennis Hart Mahan.

In the 1970s, junior officers were key to the rebuilding of an Army torn and demoralized by the Vietnam War. The draftee Army was gone, but the new volunteer force bore little resemblance to the small Regular Army of decades past. Leadership challenges increased rather than diminished. With ad slogans like "Today's Army Wants To Join You!" the American military struggled to maintain a sufficient Cold War force without conscripts in a society where the military was openly despised in ways that even Jefferson might not have understood. Furthermore, weapon systems and doctrine neglected in a time of jungle and guerrilla warfare desperately needed modernizing as the continuing Cold War returned the Army's focus to Europe.[35]

To help meet all these political and economic challenges and to expand on the domestic politics addressed in the National Security Studies Seminar, a separate course titled The Politics of Defense Policy-Making was added to the curriculum. In the early 1970s, the Department of Social Sciences further expanded elective course offerings in response to the Academy's introduction of an academic concentration titled National Security and Public Affairs. This "concentration" was upgraded to a formal academic major by the decade's end.

In the late 1980s, West Point's entire curriculum underwent significant revision. The numerous piecemeal course adjustments and additions since the end of World War II had added considerable volume as well as depth to course content. The gradual result was an academic course load which, combined with military training and other requirements, had come to demand more hours of the day than nature provided. Moreover, the institution itself was struggling to meet both academic accreditation standards and the needs of an Army strapped for more fully educated officers. The world was not going to reduce the pressures and demands placed on 20th century Army officers. How could West Point come to terms with such apparently contradictory demands?

The answer lay in a series of adjustments that succeeded in preserving the extensive core curriculum while reducing the overall course load. Engineering academic major programs were better able to meet their accreditation requirements. Those students not majoring in engineering nonetheless obtained the scientific and technical foundations for the Bachelor of Science degree by taking a concentrated five-course sequence in an engineering field of their choice. While still an exhausting regimen by civilian university standards, this academic program represented a more realistic approach. There would continue to be only a modest amount of discretionary time in a cadet's day. The time available, however, would be adequate to meet the study requirements of the course load.

Over the course of more than 35 years, the gradual addition of three key social science electives—Economics of National Security, Politics of the Defense Policy-making Process, and the National Security Seminar[36]—served to reinforce the basic lessons on national security taught in the two core courses, American Politics and International Relations. Two additional elective courses were subsequently introduced to further expand national security education at West Point.

The first reflected a challenge to old subject matter frameworks for national security studies. Scholars had now begun to argue over how broadly or how narrowly to define the term "national security." Critics argued that security studies were narrowly focused on the use of force to secure, defend, and advance national interests.[37] Others broadened the term to incorporate a range of threats to national survival, stability, and sovereignty to include environmental hazards, domestic crime, economic growth, and questions of social justice. Some even questioned the ultimate utility of force. Concepts such as "soft power" and "comprehensive security" began to emerge in international relations literature previously dominated by traditional realism and power politics. Some even went so far as to question why security studies warranted separate attention within the broader field of international relations.[38] A new course, International Security Studies Seminar, served as West Point's response to this debate. The course examined the new interpretations of security studies while providing a comparative perspective, looking at the concept of security from the perspective of developing or transitioning nations.

The second course addition reflected important academic concerns about the realities of budgetary politics. The demand for a post-Cold War "peace dividend" resulted in the sharp drawdown of military forces following the collapse of the Soviet Union. The end of the 40-year national Cold War consensus on security spending highlighted the domestic political struggle that traditionally determines the nation's defense budgets. With the endowment of the Bernard Rogers Chair of Defense Economics, the department added an elective course, Defense Economics, to provide a domestic economics complement to The Politics of Defense Policy-Making.

The Army that witnessed the end of the Cold War and then turned from Europe to the Mideast to challenge Saddam Hussein bore little resemblance the Army of 1973.[39] As the former Soviet adversary crumbled and the facade of its power was stripped away, many on both sides of the former Iron Curtain came to recognize the superior quality of America's Army and the prominent role West Point graduates played in winning the Cold War. "Our problem," said one former Soviet official, "was our generals were not trained by West Point economists."[40]

Consistent with the Academy's comprehensive curriculum concept, the Department of Social Sciences had several partners in building the national security curriculum at West Point. The Department of History offered elective courses in such topics as Revolutionary Warfare and Diplomatic History. The Department of Law expanded its course roster to include an elective in National Security Law. Courses in the Departments of Behavioral Sciences and Leadership, Geography and Environmental Sciences, and Foreign Languages enhanced the national security curriculum and ensured that cadet study of this critical topic would not be limited to academic majors associated with a single department.

In civilian institutions, the post-Cold War academic debate raged over alternative approaches to national security. Meanwhile, West Point's national security curriculum continued to evolve. Within the Department of Social Sciences, the International Relations core course required of all cadets now reflected a broader range of perspectives on international politics. This broadening is best exemplified by publication of a new course text, designed and compiled by department faculty to reflect the breadth of intellectual tools available to analyze international politics. Now in its fourth edition and in use at several other universities, *Understanding International Relations: The Value of Alternative Lenses* exposes cadets to the debates within the discipline, challenging them to draw on the full range of their broad undergraduate education to address the challenges of international politics.[41]

There would be one more significant academic program revision initiated at the beginning of the 21st century. Keenly aware of the new demands placed on young officers assigned to post-Cold War missions and fully aware of the challenges that would arrive after 11 September 2001, the Academic Board, with encouragement from the Secretary of the Army, implemented narrow but important curriculum changes. Through the reduction of the engineering sequence for non-engineering majors from five to three, the engineering departments were given greater resources to concentrate on the demands of maintaining the accreditation of their nationally ranked programs. All cadets also took an additional course in information technology and would now have the option of at least one additional course in the language, history, politics, or culture of a nation or region of the world.

Finally, a new national security elective course, The Policy, Strategy, and Tactics of Information Warfare, was added to the curriculum in 2001. Jointly developed by the Department of Social Sciences and the Department of Electrical Engineering and Computer Science, this course recognizes the critical role of information technology in security. It soon received national recognition for both its content and its pedagogy. The final stages of implementing this new curriculum were underway on 11 September 2001.

National Security at West Point Today: Three "Classes" Each Year

In the wake of 11 September, West Point was inundated with visiting journalists. It seemed that almost every news media query began by asking what West Point would now teach, given that these horrible events were beyond the scope of anything previously taught and anything the Army had ever dealt with.[42] The most obvious error underlying these questions was the assumptions. In the latter half of the previous century, the Academy's academic program evolved in a timely manner to deal with emerging security challenges, often anticipating them well in advance. Prior to the 9/11 terrorist attacks, the Department of Social Sciences had regularly offered such elective courses as Terrorism, Middle East Politics, International Security Studies, and Ethnic Conflict. Comparably relevant course offerings could be found in the Departments of Foreign Languages, Geography and Environmental Engineering, History, Law, and other departments.

Moreover, when it comes to understanding the current state of national security education at West Point, the broad nature of the de facto "alumni" is every bit as important as any specific course syllabus. The students of national security at West Point comprise more than the generic graduating class. In the words of Brig. Gen. Daniel Kaufman, Dean of the Academic Board, the Academy graduates three "classes" of national security students each year. The first "class" is the obvious one, seen each spring parading into Michie Stadium to receive their diplomas and commissions. The second class is a large subset of the first. These graduates chose an academic major focused on some aspect of national security. The third and often overlooked class is those officers assigned to the West Point faculty following graduate study who complete their assignments as instructors and then return to the field Army.

Every Cadet A National Security Studies Student

All West Point cadets experience a curriculum that embraces a broad conception of national security without rejecting or subordinating the traditional elements of the term. In particular, they study the use of force to secure and defend vital national interests. By creating, developing, and integrating a curriculum consistent with the Academy's mission, West Point aims is to provide a baccalaureate experience that first and foremost prepares its graduates for the unique demands of their chosen profession. Further, the curriculum prepares them not just for their early years as junior officers, but for the long haul of a military career. [43]

The foundation of the West Point educational experience is the core curriculum. Currently consisting of 30 courses in a wide range of disciplines, it is far broader than those normally found at other colleges and universities. All cadets take the same core courses in mathematics, philosophy, literature, composition, physics, chemistry, physical geography, computer sciences, history, psychology, leadership, law, and military art, as well as a foreign language and a three-course sequence in an engineering field. In addition to the academic core, there are required courses in military science and eight semesters of physical education.

This design of the core curriculum reflects a belief in the importance of a truly common educational experience. There are no watered-down sections of physics for history majors. Chemists take the same literature class as English majors. There is no "math for poets" at West Point. In a reconciliation of Hamilton's professional model and Jefferson's scientific ideal, West Point cadets must master a range of common disciplines.[44]

Among those common courses are several with direct bearing on the subject of national security. Three are taught by the Department of Social Sciences. These include:

> **American Politics.** Drawing on earlier required courses in history and philosophy, this course covers the philosophical roots of modern democracy, the Constitution, American political institutions, and the politics of making and implementing policy. This second-year course also examines the legal and professional obligations of American military officers, preparing them for later courses in military and constitutional law. Finally the course teaches the dynamics of the policy-making process with a special emphasis on defense policy. Cadets address the fundamentals of conventional studies of national security, reviewing political and policy elements of a nation's decisions to use force to secure and defend its national interests.

> **Principles of Economics**. This is a one-semester course in the basic principles of economic analysis and their appli-

cation to contemporary economic problems. Taken the second year, the course covers microeconomics, macroeconomics, and international economics. It prepares students for further applications of economics in the required course in international relations. Cadets consider the implications of economics for national security and defense and the use of economic analysis in decision-making as Army officers.

International Relations. This third-year, one-semester course poses two key questions: "Why do states do what they do?" and "Does the international environment reflect conflict or cooperation?" Building on a foundation of classic readings in international relations, cadets review these questions through classic realism and international systems explanations, theories of international political economy, and internal nation-state dynamics. Cadets use multiple "lenses" to view international events and are taught to value intellectual pluralism. Through the use of case studies, individual research, and course exercises, cadets focus on questions of power, wealth, security, and stability. This course also serves as the Academy's capstone course in cultural understanding.

These three courses cannot stand alone. They are integrated with classes in other disciplines such as history, behavioral science, military instruction, philosophy, law, and geography. Moreover, they complement courses in science and engineering. As in Jefferson's time, perhaps even more so, an understanding of all the dimensions of national security requires an understanding of technology. Studies in science, math, and engineering are theoretical as well as applied.

Cadets have the opportunity to apply what they have learned to real-world defense issues both in the classroom and in outside research opportunities. Classroom learning in all fields is supplemented with summertime Academic Individual Advanced Development (AIAD), offering opportunities that enhance classroom work and complement summer military training and orientation assignments to military units. AIAD experiences include venues ranging from a weapons research laboratory, to a nongovernmental organization in Africa, to a government agency in Washington, DC.

National Security Studies and Academic Majors

Many cadets choose to go beyond the core curriculum in their study of national security. The creation of a majors program in the late 1970s was a significant addition to the West Point academic program. With 19 majors and an additional nine fields of study (normally interdisciplinary programs), West Point provides an opportunity for in-depth study in a wide range of fields. Among the majors are four—American Politics, Comparative Politics, Economics, and International Relations—offered by the Department of Social Sciences. These four majors serve as examples of how cadets major in specific aspects of national security studies.[45]

Majors in Economics and the three political science stems are structured much as one would expect to find in any college or university. Required courses in basic methodologies are followed by a wide range of electives. The Department of Social Sciences offers more than 50 political science and economics electives. These include such standard courses as Legislative Politics, Government and Politics of East Asia, Econometrics, Finance, and International Political Economy. But while the curriculum mirrors those of many other nationally recognized programs, there are two elements that distinguish it from the others.

First, all course work includes at least some consideration of national security issues as they relate to the specific course topic. This does not come at the expense of the essential core material of the class. It does, however, provide a focus for case studies and course research. Second, every cadet is required to take at least one capstone course integrating elements from all other courses. Four of these capstone courses—Defense Politics, National Security Studies, International Security Studies, and Economics of National Security—explicitly deal with national security as the course theme. Economics majors are required to take courses in defense sector economics, and many also opt for classes in international political economy and comparative economic systems. With economics and political science both taught in the same department, some cadets develop programs of study that allow them to take full advantage of both.

Department of Social Sciences AIAD experiences also provide unique opportunities for cadets to apply what they learn. Cadets from the course in East Asian Politics witnessed the return of Hong Kong to the sovereignty of the People's Republic of China. International Political Economy students studying in Maastricht experienced the continuing development of the European Economic Community. American Politics majors worked in Congressional offices and the Pentagon. Upon their return to West Point, they bring their on-site knowledge back to the classroom. In the spring, some will do senior theses on specific research questions that emerged from their experiences and their course work.

At the end of four years at West Point, cadets regardless of major have completed a fully integrated degree program with the broad skills needed to allow them to meet the Academy's Concept for Intellectual Development: "To enable its graduates to anticipate and to respond effectively to the uncertainties of a changing technological, social, political, and economic world." West Point thus provides a comprehensive "national security" education.

The "Graduating" Faculty

A third and often overlooked group to benefit from the national security curriculum consists of the West Point rotating faculty who return to the field at the end of their three-year Academy assignments. Supervised by a small group of permanent senior faculty, reinforced by distinguished scholars in endowed chairs, and complemented by a civilian faculty, the largest component of each department's faculty is the rotating junior military faculty. As with other departments, officers for the Department of Social Sciences are selected in a highly competitive process after successful company, troop, or battery command in their basic branch of service, usually during their seventh year of service. Military performance and potential for future service are weighed in addition to academic potential. Along with an outstanding academic record, a young officer must also present an outstanding military file.

Officers are then sent to outstanding graduate schools for two years to earn a master's degree. Some of these complete all requirements for the Ph.D. but the dissertation, continuing dissertation research and writing on their own while assigned at West Point.[46] The average instructor will teach four sections per semester, with normal section size being 15 cadets. There are no graduate student assistants at West Point. The instructors are responsible for individual course development, instruction, grading, and related counseling and additional instruction. As role models and mentors, they also take part in a wide range of other activities, to include Cadet Honor Code instruction, sponsorship and supervision of cadet activities, and summer military training. It is a demanding assignment, but there are specific rewards that benefit both the individual officer and the Army as well.

For example, these young officers have an opportunity to obtain a first-class graduate education. This opportunity contributes to their intellectual development by putting them in touch with their civilian counterparts, many of whom have had little or no contact with the military, but who will serve later in policy-making roles in the defense and foreign policy communities. Officers further develop their intellectual skills while teaching and conducting research. They provide valuable assistance to Army agencies on everything from weapons modernization to regional culture. The Department of Social Sciences is not unique in this regard. Officers in every department at West Point provide their relevant expertise to the Army.

Their services do not end when the officers "graduate" from teaching after three years and leave the Academy. The combination of education and experience ensures continued utility for the Army. Many of the Army's senior leadership—to include several Army Chiefs of Staff—served a tour on the West Point faculty. In key Army and Joint Staff positions, in high-level commands, and as part of important research and development programs, former West Point faculty members continue to develop and apply their national security expertise. Moreover, the rotating faculty serve as the seedbed from which future permanent uniformed faculty are selected.

Meeting the Changing Needs of the Army and the Nation

West Point graduates will always confront a mix of human and technological challenges. As the changing security environment alters requirements for Army officers, the West Point curriculum will adjust. As the course changes are developed, debated, and implemented, which courses truly need to remain and which should be moved aside? How will the Academy meet the broad needs of the future Army while developing pockets of functional expertise? The program that emerges must conform to the scientific education vision of Jefferson and the professional development objectives of Hamilton. Breadth must be continuously balanced with depth.[47]

The early national security components of the West Point curriculum were limited at best. But as the role of the Army changed, so did the demands on young lieutenants. West Point's curriculum reflected first the demands for engineers, then for platoon leaders and company commanders skilled in small-unit leadership and basic tactics. With World War II, America needed an Army capable of thinking and operating at the strategic level. Furthermore, those officers often had to assume these duties at an early stage in their careers, well before the opportunity to attend the War College. West Point's response to that demand was modest at first, but the program that evolved in the latter half of the 20th century is robust and forward-looking.

The current West Point catalogue includes SS483—National Security Seminar. Each year, approximately 60 cadets enroll in this course. These cadets represent little more than 10 percent of their graduating class. It is a mistake, however, to assume that these are the only individuals studying national security at West Point. When asked what West Point does that relates to the study of national security, it is not much of an overstatement to answer, "Everything." Throughout a four-year integrated curriculum—constantly under review to ensure academic quality and professional relevance—cadets study all the dimensions of national security while talented junior faculty better prepare themselves for positions of senior leadership. Upon graduation, both groups are uniquely qualified to serve as national security professionals and, if West Point has succeeded, they will continue to learn and develop while assigned to positions of increasing responsibility in their service to the nation.

---

[1] Some portions of this chapter are revisions of Daniel J. Kaufman and Jay M. Parker, "Teaching National Security at West Point," *National Security Studies Quarterly* 3, no. 4 (Autumn 1997).

[2] David A. Baldwin, "Security Studies and the End of the Cold War," *World Politics*, no. 48 (October 1995); Lawrence Freedman, "War," *Foreign Policy* (July/August 2003); Keith Krause and Michael Williams, "Broadening the Agenda of Security Studies: Politics and Methods," *Mershon International Studies Review*, no. 40 (1996); Jessica Tuchman Mathews "Redefining Security," *Foreign Affairs* 67, no. 4 (Spring 1989).

[3] This abortive coup, commonly referred to as the Newburgh Conspiracy, has been chronicled in many historical accounts of the American Revolution and its aftermath. See for example Richard H. Kohn, "The Inside History of the Newburgh Conspiracy: America and the Coup d'Etat," *William and Mary Quarterly* (Third Series), 27 (April 1970): 187-220. For a look at the conspiracy in broader context, see Kohn's later work, *Eagle and the Sword: The Federalists and the Creation of the Military Establishment of America, 1783-1802* (New York: Free Press, 1975).

[4] C.E. Covell, et al., *Superintendent's Curriculum Study, United States Military Academy: Report of the Working Committee on the Historical Aspects of the Curriculum for the Period 1802-1945* (West Point, NY: U.S. Military Academy, 1958), 3-4. This document is sometimes referred to as the Forman Report.

[5] Theodore J. Crackel, *West Point: A Bicentennial History* (Lawrence: University Press of Kansas, 2002), 46.

[6] Pamela Lowry, "Projects to Develop U.S. Infrastructure—From the Revolution to the Civil War: Capt. Basil Hall Visits The Infant City of Rochester, New York (1827)," reprinted in *Executive Intelligence Review* (January 1992), <http://members.tripod.com/~american_almanac/earlyinf.htm>.

[7] See Samuel Huntington, *The Soldier and The State* (Cambridge, MA: Belknap Press of Harvard University Press, 1957), 198-200. Huntington notes the Jefferson-Hamilton clash on the nature of the American military and the need for an academy. He argues that the eventual product of this debate was an institution more compatible with Jefferson's view of a scientific and technical institution focused on domestic infrastructure development rather than a professional military with a focus on war and international affairs. Russell Weigley also cites Huntington's "technicism" argument in *The American Way of War* (Bloomington: Indiana University Press, 1977), 491, but stresses the development of West Point as a center for the study of war under legendary Superintendent Sylvanus Thayer and his protégé Dennis H. Mahan. Huntington thoroughly reviews the long history of attacks on West Point. Some range from those demanding more direct benefit to civil society to those demanding more of an exclusive focus on military professionalism. Other criticisms came from those who saw the creation of an aristocratic military elite foreign to our political culture while others feared a military too reflective of society's diversity. See also John Masland and Laurence Radway, *Soldiers and Scholars: Military Education and National Policy* (Princeton, NJ: Princeton University Press, 1957), 76-79. Note that all these works also extensively document the transformation of the Army's role throughout American history.

[8] Huntington, 198-199; Masland and Radway, 76-79; Weigley, 81-82. For an amusing and well-researched discussion of these early West Point years—particularly the pre-Thayer Academy—see James B. Agnew, *Eggnog Riot: The Christmas Mutiny at West Point* (San Rafael, CA: Presidio Press, 1979).

[9] Weigley, 82-84, 87. It is commonly said that Mahan, father of naval strategist Alfred Thayer Mahan, taught all the winning generals of the Civil War. It is usually quickly noted that he also taught most of the losers.

[10] Covell et al., *Superintendent's Curriculum Study*, appendix 11.

[11] Huntington, 208-209, outlines the attacks by both Congress and Jackson on the elitism of West Point. Masland and Radway, 77, argue that Thayer's views of discipline conflicted with Jackson's views of democracy and elitism. See Chapter 7 of the present volume.

[12] John W. Chambers, ed., *The Oxford Companion To American Military History* (New York: Oxford University Press, 1999), 4.

[13] James M. McPherson, *The Battle Cry of Freedom: The Civil War Era* (New York: Ballantine Books, 1988), 281, 328.

[14] Huntington, 20-22. Many of these institutions incorporated military training into their required curriculum, a practice that continued until Vietnam era protests led to the end of required Reserve Officer Training Corps (ROTC) at public universities.

[15] Alfred Thayer Mahan, *The Influence of Seapower on History* (New York: Hill and Wang, 1957). See also Philip A. Crowl, "Alfred Thayer Mahan: The Naval Historian," in *Makers of Modern Strategy: From Machiavelli to the Nuclear Age*, ed. Peter Paret (Princeton, NJ: Princeton University Press, 1986), 444-77. For a broader discussion of the role of the American military through the early part of the 20th century, see Weigley's "American Strategy from its Beginnings through the First World War," in Paret, 404-43.

[16] Covell et al., appendix 15.

[17] Ibid., appendix 16.

[18] The American Political Science Association did not hold its first conference until just after the turn of the century.

[19] Stephen E. Ambrose, *Duty, Honor, Country: A History of West Point* (Baltimore, MD: Johns Hopkins University Press, 1966) 228-91.

[20] Covell et al., appendix 17.

[21] Ibid., appendices 17 and 18.

[22] Morris Janowitz notes the role of Beukema in transforming the study of national security at West Point and further states that Beukema "anticipated post-World War II intellectual trends." See *The Professional Soldier: A Social and Political Portrait* (New York: The Free Press, 1971) 132, 441.

[23] The graduates who served in key leadership roles during World War II and the postwar years, to include Dwight Eisenhower and Omar Bradley, spent the bulk of their careers in the undefended, under-trained, and (for one month) unpaid Army of 1919 to 1940. Their service also included participation in such non-traditional missions as leadership of units in the Civilian Conservation Corps. Ironically, the CCC's role was close to that envisioned for the Army at West Point's founding. For a summary of this period, see T.A. Heppenheimer, "Build Down," *American Heritage* 44 (December 1993): 34-46.

[24] For a discussion of the end of the so-called "expandable Army" concept, see Charles R. Miller, "Serving Two Masters: Doctrinal Evolution in the 20th Century U.S. Army" (Ph.D. diss., Columbia University, 2002), 58-62.

[25] Roger H. Nye, "George A. Lincoln—Architect of National Security," *Issues of National Security in the 1970s: Essays Presented to Colonel George A. Lincoln on his Sixtieth Birthday*, ed. Amos A. Jordon (New York: Frederick A. Praeger, 1967), 3-20.

[26] United States Military Academy Special Collections—George A. Lincoln Collection (USMASC-GAL), Box 38, File 2: Lincoln Lectures; "Department of Social Sciences, United States Military Academy, "Selected Readings In International Relations," 1956.

[27] Nye, 3-20; Memorandum: Committee on the Major-Minor Issue, 10 September 1953, USMASC-GAL, Box 98, File 12: Curriculum-The Major/Minor Issue.

[28] James M. Gavin, Oral History, Army Military History Institute Archives, Carlisle Barracks, PA. See also Gavin's *War and Peace in the Space Age* (New York: Harper and Brothers, 1958), 14-19.

[29] Jay M. Parker, *The Colonels' Revolt* (Cambridge, MA: Harvard University Press), forthcoming. See also David Halberstam, *The Best and The Brightest* (Greenwich, CT: Fawcett, 1975), 575-78. See also Michael Meese, "Defense Decision Making Under Budget Stringency: Examining Downsizing in the United States Army" (Ph.D. diss., Princeton University, 2000); David T. Fautua, "The 'Long Pull' Army: NSC 68, the Korean War, and the Creation of the Cold War U.S. Army," *Journal of Military History* 61 (January 1997): 93-120.

[30] Covell et al.

[31] "Answers to questions in Comment Booklet for USMA Graduate Questionnaire," 10 June 1957, Dwight D. Eisenhower Library, White House Office Files (DDE-WHOF), Office of the Staff Secretary, Box 25, File: West Point 7/53-7/61 (2).

[32] Memorandum for General Goodpaster, 13 August 1959, DDE-WHOF, Office of the Staff Secretary, Box 25, File: West Point 7/53-7/60 (4); Interview, MG (ret.) John Stoner, 7 June 2003.

[33] See USMASC-GAL, Box 186, File: 1956-1961 Study of NSS Courses. Among those schools offering this instruction were Harvard and Ohio State.

[34] "Memorandum for: Head of Each Academic Department, Subject: Enrollment of First Classmen in Elective Courses, Second Semester, 1960-61," 13 January 1961, USMASC-GAL, Curriculum Files, Box 98, Proposed Curricula Changes.

[35] See James Kitfield, *Prodigal Soldiers* (New York: Simon and Schuster, 1995).

[36] Note that there are several courses listed in this chapter with similar titles. In some instances, differences in course titles represent minor administrative wordsmithing over time, while other title changes represented significant course revisions designed to better reflect broader Academy curriculum changes.

[37] John Mearsheimer "A Realist Reply," *International Security* 20, (1995); Richard Schultz, Roy Godson, and Ted Greenwood, eds., *Security Studies for the 1990s* (New York: Brasseys, 1993).

[38] Baldwin, "Security Studies"; Mathews, "Redefining." This academic battle foreshadowed a policy debate over the Army's role that would follow in the decade after the Cold War. New missions (often only older, traditional Army missions thinly disguised with new titles and acronyms like OOTW and PKO) challenge young lieutenants with new responsibilities tied to new concepts of national security.

[39] Ibid.

[40] "Lebed Plan Attacks Crime, Corruption," *Moscow Times* (20 May 1996).

[41] Asa A. Clark IV, Thomas F. Lynch III, and Rick Waddell, eds., *Understanding International Relations: The Value of Alternative Lenses*, 1st edition (New York: McGraw-Hill, 1993). Subsequent editions have kept pace with the dynamics of

international politics while adding timely, relevant case studies in a supplemental text. See Daniel J. Kaufman, Jay M. Parker, and Kimberly C. Field, eds., *Understanding International Relations: The Value of Alternative Lenses*, 4th edition (New York: McGraw-Hill, 1999); and Daniel J. Kaufman, Jay M. Parker, and Suzanne C. Nielsen, eds., *Through Alternative Lenses: Current Debates in International Relations*, 2nd edition (New York: McGraw-Hill, 2000).

[42] A representative array of these interviews by journalists from around the world can be found at http://www.usma.edu/PublicAffairs/inthenews.htm.

[43] Often lost in the debate over West Point's strengths or weaknesses is the need to evaluate results over time, accounting for changes in curriculum, military training, and post-West Point professional experiences. The success or failure of senior Army leaders in 2003 is not an accurate measure of the quality of the USMA Class of 2004.

[44] While USMA provides the Army with less than 25 percent of its officer accessions each year, it provides almost 60 percent of the new officers with scientific and technical educations.

[45] This is not to say that other departments do not provide the same opportunities to focus on national security as a major. Many cadets who major in history or who choose to emphasize national security and international law as part of the American Legal System major are clearly focusing on important dimensions of national security. Cadets in the Military Art and Science program study tactical and operational level aspects of national security. A key assumption of the majors program is that once in the force, the combined skills of officers from a wide range of majors will provide the Army with a breadth of expertise essential to contend with a broad range of national security challenges.

[46] As a result of the assignment of officers to top graduate schools, academic departments are continually revitalized with the latest developments in their fields. This process also insures a broader perspective on these academic disciplines. For example, the international relations curriculum is thus better able to integrate the full range of approaches to national security studies.

[47] The current framework for achieving this balance is outlined in the United States Military Academy Academic Program Goals. See *Academic Programs: Field Tables and Course Descriptions AY 1995-1996 ("The Redbook")*, Office of the Dean, United States Military Academy.

⫸ CHAPTER 23 ⫷

COMPUTING AT WEST POINT: REVOLUTION TO PURPOSEFUL EVOLUTION

Kenneth L. Alford, Gregory J. Conti, David B. Cushen,
Eugene K. Ressler, Jr., William Turmel, Jr., and Donald J. Welch

Introduction

In many ways, the U.S. Military Academy led the Army and the civilian undergraduate educational community in the vast changes sparked by the rise of computers as a facet of life in the late 20th century. While business, government, the military, and, eventually, the whole of U.S. society struggled with similar change, West Point has been conspicuous in the effectiveness with which it embraced new technology and made it work. Early on, the Military Academy adopted computer technology as a tool both for the education of cadets and for operations of the Academy and all its programs. In tracing the evolution of computer technology at West Point, a common, repeated cycle emerges. Each cycle invariably began with a person or agency taking up the role of champion of a new, technology-related vision and winning institutional support for it. Implementation followed, usually with the dedication of significant Academy and Army resources. Finally, there was a period of assessing results and forming the corporate opinion that set the stage for the next vision, and the rise of the next champion.

Change is seldom simple, and the cycles that characterized the adoption of new information technology were no exception. Some innovations were easily implemented and broadly accepted. Others were technically or organizationally difficult and widely resisted. There were amazing successes and notable setbacks. Nevertheless, there were common threads through all such initiatives. The first is that the cycles were almost invariably driven by the emergence of new technologies in the marketplace, where the landscape of the early 1980s was an ever-accelerating tumult of new developments and rapidly obsolescing older ones. Second, individuals and small groups of technological visionaries at West Point repeatedly emerged to exploit this chaos. Characteristically, an individual or small group of faculty or staff members would envision how a particular emerging technology could be applied in the USMA mission context and then garnered the help of colleagues to work out the idea. They were consistently able to convince senior decision-makers to adopt their thinking and to provide resources for implementation, often with no sure prospect of success. Overall, the Academy's senior leaders were courageous in accepting the risks associated with the new technology; their conduct in this regard was in sharp contrast to the fabled reluctance of their predecessors to rapidly embrace change.[1]

Implementation of fledgling technologies was seldom a problem; the military penchant for planning and energetic execution saw to this. Most projects successfully achieved their goals and saw a new technology integrated into USMA's organization and daily life. On the other hand, there were unintended consequences in nearly all the cycles, thus forming the third common thread. For better or worse, the breadth, depth, and type of change wrought by a new technology were frequently different than anticipated, sometimes vastly so.

The fourth and last thread through USMA's technology adoption cycles is gradual institutional change in response to the consequences of technological change. Organizational structures, leadership, policies, and physical infrastructure evolved to make sense of the never-ending stream of new technology impacts and to make preparations for the next arrival.

The Mainframe

American attitudes toward technology in the late 1950s were shaped by the Cold War and the sense of urgency it inspired for improving national prowess in science and engineering. The nascent computer technology of the time promised rapid advances in these areas. The U.S. military had successfully used the primitive ENIAC (Electronic Numerical Integrator and Computer) to compute weapon trajectory tables during World War II, and visionaries had extrapolated from this application to see the possibilities for war gaming, simulation, and other employments of computers far in advance of their practical implementation.[2] Nowhere was the investment in computer technology greater than in the military, and computer-related developments at West Point were part of this larger trend. The emerging commercial availability of relatively economical computing resources for academic research and educational use starting in 1955 was another spur to its adoption at the Academy.[3]

The earliest attitudes toward computers at the Academy mirrored the Army's. People knew that computers harbored untapped potential, but realizing this potential was a nascent art. Not surprisingly, the initially modest efforts at the Academy centered on incremental speedups and improvements of existing processes of administration, finance, and logistics. Finally, in Academic Year 1961-1962, the sense that something must be done regarding computers in cadet education jelled in the form of several hours of computer instruction in courses taught by the Electricity and Ordnance Departments.[4]

The head of the Department of Military Engineering, Col. Charles H. Schilling, and the head of the Department of Electricity, Col. Elliott C. Cutler, Jr., assumed the champions' role for computers in the Academy curriculum. In their quest for the proper educational place for computers, they had a staunch ally in the Dean of the Academic Board, Brig. Gen. William W. Bessell, Jr., former head of the Mathematics Department. In contrast with the Academy's administrative structure today, Bessell had little staff and only limited centralized control over the resources needed to effect change. He therefore combined forces with Colonel Schilling and enlisted Lt. Col. William Luebbert, a faculty member in Colonel Cutler's Department and an avid computer proponent, to exploit the only power at hand—persuasion and the modest bully pulpit of his position.[5]

General Bessell established the ad hoc Academic Computer Committee, with Schilling as the chairman and Luebbert as secretary. Says one witness close to the scene, these latter two officers "dredged out every paper, pamphlet, booklet, or book they could and fed them" to the committee members and the senior faculty.[6] Their enthusiasm was contagious, and by 1961 they had established a set of ambitious goals that, in retrospect, proved to be prescient. They believed that every cadet should have practical exposure to computers, including the writing, running, and testing of computer programs to solve real problems. In addition, the cadets should work with computers during the plebe (freshman) year so that the new skills might be exercised periodically in all four years of a cadet's education. To guide the use of computers at West Point, each academic department would examine and report on the usefulness of computers within its own disciplinary sphere.

Finally, the committee placed a high priority on making computer power ubiquitously available in every academic department, every cadet company, and, eventually, every classroom of the Academy.[7] It is clear that the committee also recognized, long before it was feasible, the importance of making computers available where people do their work. The committee members were at least dimly aware of the potential for computers to serve the communication needs of cadets, staff, and faculty as well as the computational. In short, they anticipated the power and utility of modern enterprise computer networks.

The committee also concluded, by a simple economic argument, that a central Academic Computing Center, with a radiating array of communication lines, was the most rational way to provide the requisite computing power to cadets. This essentially academic service, with incidental technical support and instructional training staff, naturally fell to the Dean to administer. Colonel Cutler eventually agreed to the reassignment of Luebbert as the Dean's staff director for computing, with the Academic Computing Center as his primary responsibility. In this manner, the Computing Center became an important part of an increasing array of centralized educational and administrative services that today is known as the Office of the Dean. Luebbert, who was appointed one of the Military Academy's first four Permanent Associate Professors, became the prototype for the Dean's staff officers that followed.[8] He established the model for these positions—an officer who had both teaching and operational skills as well as the administrative savvy necessary to run a computer automation program.

Luebbert acted with energy and intelligence, acquiring three computer-smart officers for his budding organization and establishing an informal agreement with Army personnel managers to receive a stream of college-educated, computer-oriented enlisted soldiers immediately after their basic training. The team Luebbert assembled provided a core of expertise that, in a few years, propelled the Academy and its curriculum far into the lead among comparable programs in the use of computers for educational purposes. The Academic Computer Center opened its doors in December 1962, offering the use of a newly procured General Electric 225 digital mainframe to all faculty members and cadets. Nine months later, the Academy sponsored a data processing seminar for Army general officers to educate them on the power of computer technology and to enlist their support in keeping West Point at the forefront of computer research and application. To mark the extremely qualified young enlisted technicians who operated the Center as worthy of special respect by cadets, they wore pale yellow lab coats over their uniforms.[9] As West Point graduates spread word of these soldiers' expertise, the Academy "Goldcoats" became widely known as the Army's elite computer technology experts.

While technology implementation proceeded apace, curricular change proved more difficult. The academic departments of the Academy then, as today, prided themselves on providing programs—curricula, courses, and classes—that operated as well-oiled machines, steadily tuned and refined over time. Changing a machine while it runs is difficult and risky, especially when the consequences of the change are unclear. This realization acted against the ambitious goals of Schilling's Computer Committee. It would take another visionary to provide the necessary impetus. That visionary would have to be a department head. West Point had built the technical foundation for computing, but lacked a pedagogical one. Only a department head would be in a position to both see the general educational benefits of computers and possess the curricular and resource control to do something about it.

The Academic Computer Committee's vision of computer exposure starting in the plebe year narrowed the field to two candidate departments. The Department of Mathematics, headed by Col. Charles P. Nicholas, and the newly reorganized Department of Earth, Space, and Graphic Sciences (ES&GS), under Col. Charles R. Broshous, had responsibility for the Fourth Class core courses where numerical computation was required. The Department of Foreign Languages expressed interest in treating the newly emergent programming languages FORTRAN and COBOL (both, incidentally, products of military-sponsored research) as new domains for its own language program, though, in retrospect, this proffer could not have been a serious proposal.[10]

Nicholas decided against adding computer instruction because he considered the plebe mathematics curriculum to be too crowded as it was; moreover, he had doubts that this new technology was a viable topic of study in the long term. It remained for Colonel Broshous, amid personal qualms over further burdening a new and still-reorganizing department, to reluctantly agree to incorporate computer instruction into the plebe core courses in Engineering Fundamentals. The first block of instruction was four hours, an important first step. The Department of Electricity chimed in with an elective in 1963. EL483—Digital Computers was the first full course on computing offered at the Academy, and one of the first in-depth courses on the subject offered anywhere.[11] The computer revolution had begun at West Point.

Instruction in computer technology expanded quickly, and West Point began to experience the first stress owing to rapid technological advance. Maj. Herbert Hollander, Deputy Director of the Academic Computing Center, professed, "You have to start off at a dead run just to keep up with this field."[12] By 1965, the Mathematics Department had come around. The GE225 mainframe processed about 3,500 cadet programs that year. Cadets were assigned five math problems to solve using computer programs, and the goal for cadets to "use the computer for assistance in problem solving during all four years at West Point" had received broad support.[13] Fifteen courses spanning six departments included computer work.

The institution began to showcase its leading-edge, high-tech outlook. The National Intercollegiate Debate held at West Point in 1964 sported an experimental system for scoring debates based on a complex set of criteria processed through computer software. The Army-Citadel football game half-time program of September 1964 included a narrative on computer education for cadets.[14]

Computer use and infrastructure grew quickly. Within a few years, the Computer Center found itself taking on the unanticipated mission of cadet administrative information processing, which, though considered secondary at the time, would soon assume a role of over-riding importance to the institution. The dual role of computers as both a subject of education and a tool for educational support thus appeared for the first time. By 1968, the Computer Center was processing over 100,000 programs per year, and a new "time-sharing" network of 15 teletype machines provided access in areas remote from the glass-enclosed mainframe on the ground floor of Thayer Hall.[15] ES&GS instructors had implemented the FORTRAN language for the West Point faculty and a simplified version, CADETRAN, for cadets, who coded programs for processing using the new technology of penciled "mark sense" forms.[16] By 1971 there were 71 teletypes scattered around the campus, which made the Military Academy the "largest time-share user of Honeywell-developed computer software in the nation."[17]

The unexpectedly large task of administrative computing, initially assumed as a secondary mission of the Academic Computer Center, was formalized in 1972 in the creation of a separate Academic Management Information Center under the Dean.[18] Its mission included maintaining archival information on cadets in an electronic format allowing rapid retrieval. This innovation realized a vision of the Office of Institutional Research, allowing the staff to better record and analyze the cadet experience.

The establishment of the Academic Management Information Center represented a bold step forward in applying computer technology to managing enormous quantities of information quickly and efficiently. It brought West Point national recognition as a leader in management information systems.[19] Among many other activities, the center processed grades on a weekly basis. With 120 remote-access terminals by 1974, cadets could now view on-line their current grade and class standing in each course and overall.[20] Ironically, in the wake of the 1976 Special Commission Report following the EE304 cheating scandal of that year, the Academy concluded that frequent access to continuously updated grades played a part in the unhealthy competitive environment that led to the scandal. Because of this unanticipated side effect, grades were thereafter processed only four times per semester.

Explosive growth continued in computer use at West Point. By 1974, the Academic Computer Center was processing over 450,000 programs annually using three mainframe computers. The faculty had coined the term "Computer Center riots" to describe the flocking of hundreds of cadets to the Center on the bottom floor of Thayer Hall and to terminal clusters throughout the academic area in the hours preceding project due dates.[21] The number of electives in the new discipline of computer science had grown to 15, and in light of the growth of the computer curriculum, the Secretary of the Army approved the renaming of the Department of ES&GS to the Department of Geography and Computer Science (G&CS) in December 1979.[22]

At the institutional level, Superintendent Lt. Gen. Andrew Goodpaster, after studying the growing decentralized array of computing capabilities, in 1978 combined organizations to form the Directorate of Automation and Audiovisual Systems. Within the Directorate, the computer systems division combined the roles of the Academic Computer Center, Academic Management Information Center, and the Adjutant General Data Processing Branch, the latter of which had assumed the mission of data processing for everyone assigned to West Point except cadets. Computing had found an integral role in all phases of Academy operations and cadet education.[23]

The formal promotion of computer science to a full-fledged discipline of academic study at West Point and the consolidation of computing facilities were important milestones. Nonetheless, Academy leaders were increasingly aware that centralized "mainframe computing was not the answer to meeting the long-range computing needs of the academic program."[24] Capitalizing on recommendations of the West Point Study, another response to the 1976 EE304 cheating scandal, the Academy formed the Automation Planning Committee to set out a five-year strategy. As in the case of Brigadier General Bessell's Academic Computer Committee nearly a score of years earlier, visionaries rose to the fore. The next major cycle of technology adoption was about to begin.

The Personal Computer

The strategy for academic computing that gradually emerged from the Automation Planning Committee—"to be a leader of colleges and universities in the use of computers in education"—was based on an immature technology that many serious automation professionals of the time considered a toy—the personal computer or PC.[25] The Apple computer of the late 1970s had, at most, a few ten-thousands of characters of chip memory, displayed a few lines of 40 characters on a converted television, used an audio cassette for data storage, and sported a tiny assortment of software of questionable usefulness. Still, in certain quarters, the concept of personal computing evoked the same visceral sense of freedom as would, in other populations, a fine sports car. Such sentiments aside, the members of the Automation Planning Committee realized that if the problems of mainframe computing flowed from the bottleneck of a single shared computing facility, then a new kind of computing based on at least one computer processor per person was a way forward. If the personal computers of the day were too limited, then time was sure to fix the problem.

Indeed, time was short, as requirements for computers were expanding rapidly. In 1980, the Academic Board approved a "computer thread" proposal of the Committee requiring computer usage in 11 core courses.[26] It formally approved FORTRAN, long a de facto standard, as the programming language of record for the core curriculum.[27] Computer science electives required increasing resources as computer science itself matured as an academic discipline. Computing facilities had become far more common in graduate programs throughout the nation, so that newly arriving officers of the junior faculty created a fresh demand for computing power. To them, its usefulness was obvious. The Academy's centralized computing facilities strained under the combined cadet and faculty loads.

An interim solution for increasing core course computing resources was the installation of approximately 100 Terak "microcomputers" in 1983 to replace the obsolete mainframe time-sharing terminals. The microcomputers supported FORTRAN and also the Pascal language that the Academic Board adopted as the new standard in 1985. They also supported a homegrown word processor called FMT, created by G&CS faculty member Capt. Francis Monaco, who later commanded the Academy's Information Management Directorate as a colonel from 1994 to his retirement in 1998. A small but technologically advanced network, also based on locally written software, allowed Terak users to send documents to shared printers in the nearby "microcomputer laboratory" rooms. Despite its flexibility, however, the Terak was expensive and slow. A Terak, as configured for the Academy, with 56,000 characters of storage and an eight-inch floppy disk drive (with floppy disks capable of storing only one-fourth of one megabyte) cost $8,935. Preparing a small computer program to run on a Terak, a process repeated many times by cadets in the completion of a single assignment, could require several minutes each time. Only two years later, however, each such iteration would be nearly instantaneous for any cadet working in his or her barracks room with a personal computer.

The concept of practical and reasonably priced PCs for the Corps of Cadets was moving toward fruition by 1984, when the Cadet Personal Computer Planning Subcommittee convened to work on the idea of an individual cadet computer in earnest. The IBM PC, introduced in 1981, had advanced the state of the art immensely. The air was also thick with announcements of the brash new Apple Macintosh, and research universities were connecting offices and computer centers in increasing numbers to the newfangled ARPA-NET, progenitor of the Internet. The PC's usefulness for education generally equaled that of the Academy's centralized facilities, and its speed and cost easily bested the Teraks. Therefore, it is not surprising that in May 1985, the "Dean and Superintendent approved the committee recommendation that each cadet and faculty member should have a networked personal computer."[28] The newborn Cadet Personal Computer Project adopted three ambitious goals: [29]

- Provide a tool to enhance learning by the cadet and teaching by the faculty.
- Increase the quality of cadet work while saving them time in preparation.
- Assist in graduating lieutenants who are prepared for our technology-dependent Army.[30]

Accomplishment of these goals would reflect the evolution of the computer at West Point through the latter 1980s. Whereas the Academic Computer Committee's 1961 goals had focused on the academic uses of the technology, the new goals went on to acknowledge the role of computers as an essential professional tool for Academy graduates.

The first computers purchased by cadets in the fall of 1986 were the sturdy and reliable Zenith 248 IBM-PC "clones." Class of 1990 cadets paid about $1,700 for their computers. In another of the prescient strokes that pervade the Academy's computing history, their software included the rarely used and little-appreciated graphical user interface Microsoft Windows Version 1.0 and the word processor called Word, also Version 1.0. Successor versions of these software packages were to be the basis of Microsoft's overwhelming success in the software industry. Members of the Class of 1990 eventually became the most junior officers present in the Desert Shield and Desert Storm campaigns in Iraq. Some of these officers executed their wartime missions with their cadet computers or identical ones, since Zenith 248s were widely employed due to the large annual purchase contracts let at the time for service-wide acquisition.[31]

At West Point, each faculty member also received a Zenith 248, through the same government contract. The coincidence was serendipitous for the Department of Geography and Computer Science, which had the highest concentration of computer science advanced degrees of any organization in the Army at that time. The Head of the Department, Col. Gilbert Kirby, saw opportunity. The small, research-oriented Computer Graphics Laboratory organization he had cobbled together within the department through external funding support from the Defense Mapping Agency and others had, by this time, developed considerable expertise in the writing of microcomputer software for mapping and satellite imagery analysis. Kirby directed a focused effort to export Computer Graphics Laboratory software products to field units in a form that would work on the Zenith 248.[32] The Department mailed hundreds of floppy disk copies to users throughout the Army, many of whom used the software during the Gulf War. Portions of the software are still in use, 15 years after its creation.[33]

The Cadet PC Project has also continued uninterrupted to the present. Each August during Reorganization Week, the new class of plebes, fresh from their field training at Lake Frederick, file through carefully organized issue lines to receive new PCs and software. Back in their rooms, with the help of the still extant Goldcoats and other support personnel, they make themselves computer-ready for the academic year. In a coincidence that appears to involve the friendly intercession of the Norse god Odin, it has never rained on a PC issue day.[34] To the knowledge of current Academy technology leaders, no organization—academic, civilian, or military—has exceeded the record set annually by plebes since 1986—1,200 new computers set up for operation in one day. Thus, the PC has become a Military Academy tradition. But the PC itself is not the whole story.

The Network

The Cadet Barracks Local Area Network (CBLAN) project, completed in September 1987,[35] was the longstanding vision of Lt. Col. Lanse Leach, who took over as Director of the Dean's Academic Computing Division in 1983. The CBLAN, along with similar networks at the Naval and Air Force Academies, was among the very first computer networks ever extended to all the living spaces of a collegiate institution.[36] Why did the Academy, with Leach taking the lead, undertake this massive project?

Forces strongly rooted in the Academy's computing history were at work. Cadets and faculty had always associated the usefulness of computers with having their capabilities close at hand, where work was done. Academic Computer Center planners and operators steadily pushed ever-larger numbers of terminals to remote areas of the post until the Academy system was one of the world's biggest. Still, computing demand exceeded capacity during peak usage periods, causing such problems as the "Computer Center riots" alluded to earlier. In response, Academy planners resorted to personal computers so that users could enjoy, in their individual workstations, computing power that previously had to be shared on the Academy's cumbersome mainframe. Processing bottlenecks and dependence were no longer a problem.

On the other hand, the thousands of new personal computers at West Point were separate computing islands. Printing and sharing electronic information required copying information to a removable diskette (a "floppy") and physically carrying it to another computer. The small networks that afforded Terak users access to shared printers hinted at a better way. Leach saw clearly how the personal computer could serve the Academy mission more directly by exploiting its communication capabilities in addition to its computational ones. In the Academy's computer-rich environment, only communication network infrastructure was lacking.

The network that emerged was remarkable for its time. As early as 1982, officers arriving from graduate school had experienced the embryonic ARPANET, with its somewhat clumsy electronic mail, bulletin boards, chat facilities, network storage and printing, and remote access to computing power. Under the technical leadership of a brilliant software engineer, Chief Goldcoat Master Sergeant John Junod of the Dean's Academic Computing Division, Cadet Barracks Local Area Network (CBLAN) technicians adapted the capabilities of the ARPANET to the West Point environment.[37] Centered on a bank of minicomputers to provide the centralized services named above, the new network radiated a web of communications lines throughout the academic and cadet barracks areas, carrying data at the modest rate of 9,600 raw bits (about 1,000 characters) per second. [38]

Both the promise and the unintended consequences of computer-based communication were finally realized. Electronic mail and other electronically delivered information seemed to force themselves, unbidden, into the daily personal working lives of each faculty and staff member and each cadet. Starting in 1988, network traffic experienced steady, exponential growth extending roughly through 1998, when it finally leveled off with each person receiving an average of over 50 e-mail messages per day.[39] Initially a text-only messaging service, late-1980s electronic mail was generally viewed by the faculty as a novelty and a research experiment. It was the plebes who arrived in 1988, the Class of 1992, who sensed the possibilities.

The CBLAN had been coolly received by the upper classes. The cadets in the Classes of 1988 and 1989, who had not purchased personal computers, could access the network only through the scattered microcomputer labs, where new PCs had replaced the Teraks. In 1988, only one in six First Classmen did this on a typical day, and less than one in five of the Second Class. The Third Classmen, even with their own computers, were slow to revise their habits. Only about one-fourth touched the network on a given day. [40]

The plebe class, however, used e-mail extensively, probably because the Fourth Class system of discipline made it expedient. Through the skillful use of this device, plebes could exchange required knowledge, organize team operations, and plan Navy Week pranks safe from the watchful eyes of the upperclassmen. Nearly half of all plebes logged in to the CBLAN each day in the first year.[41] As no entertainment aspect of computer networks had yet arisen, usage declined precipitously on weekends.

Cadets were ingenious in developing new uses for early e-mail technology. The longstanding practice of passing the word when the Officer-in-Charge entered the barracks was one example. Officers noted how their arrival in a company area was marked by the squeal of "e-mail arriving" beeps down the hallways and stairwells as cadets spread news of the impending inspection.[42] Accordingly, the cadet mantra of "cooperate and graduate" gained new meaning in the context of a networked environment.

Day-to-day operations of the faculty underwent a similar transformation. The faculty logged in with about the same frequency as the plebes during this period, but a few organizations were more aggressive. By 1988, Geography and Computer Science faculty members were required to check e-mail daily because frequent department meetings were replaced by e-mail broadcasts of important information. Word processing had transformed procedures for lesson assignment and exam preparation, not always for the better. Drafts were edited and corrected on the screen instead of on hard copy, thus leaving no visible audit trail. People found that the loss of such visual cues as to the trail of revision had a deleterious effect on proofreading, but no one went back to the old methods.

The retirement of the Department Head, Gilbert Kirby—after 46 years of active duty—was accompanied by a major realignment of academic disciplines among the academic departments at West Point. The computer science program moved from Washington Hall to Thayer Hall at this time, forming, along with Electrical Engineering, the new Department of Electrical Engineering and Computer Science (EE&CS). Members of the EE&CS Department today find it fitting that their offices and classrooms occupy the same space as Colonel Luebbert's original Academic Computer Center.

By 1992, instructions, assignments, and question-answer exchanges were routinely communicated between cadets and faculty members by electronic mail. When technical problems sometimes caused loss of mail or delays in routing of a few hours, system operators were under the gun. Usage was ramping up. Expectations were rising, and the limits of CBLAN capacity were in sight.

Beginning in 1993, the Military Academy initiated an uninterrupted process of network capacity and service upgrades that continues to the present day. The technology selected to replace the original CBLAN promised a thousandfold speedup in data flow to cadet desks—up to one million characters (ten megabits) per second—but the transition was not to be easy. Three thousand upper class cadet computers were opened for the installation of entirely new hardware. All network switching and routing hardware and software were new technology never employed in such a large installation. Miles of wiring in barracks and academic buildings designed for the lower capacity of the old network were pressed into service for the new one, with unpredictable results. A new, exotic "backbone" for moving ten million characters (100 megabits) of data per second from building to building was installed, employing fiber optic cable for the first time at West Point.

Any new technology entails a significant period of unreliability and trial-and-error learning by support personnel. Academy network planners had taken a large, perhaps excessively large, risk in adopting so much new technology at once. As the school year began in August 1993, only about two-thirds of the cadets were able to access the upgraded CBLAN due to technical problems. Fixing those problems involved painstaking troubleshooting of each cadet computer, a process not completed until the following December. The Academy chain of command noted the importance of the service loss and placed emphasis on repairs. Although network operators and the Goldcoats were exhausted by the ordeal, it was now clear that the requirement for their services and support had moved from the periphery of the Academy's operations to their very core.

Brig. Gen. Fletcher Lamkin, Dean of the Academic Board starting in 1996, launched the project that finally brought to full realization the vision of the 1960s Academic Computer Committee—he would extend the CBLAN to all of the Academy's more than 300 classrooms. It was not network or computer technology that drove this change, but rather the arrival of comparatively cheap and reliable large-format projectors for computer images. The new equipment enabled instructors to enhance learning to a previously unattainable extent. Through digital imagery projected on a large screen, cadets could better visualize three-dimensional mathematics, unit movements on Civil War battlefields, stresses on cantilever beams, and many other abstract or dynamic depictions. The project required three years of work, with completion in 1998. The faculty continues to discover new and illuminating applications of this capability to the present day.

Though he presided over the largest expansion of technical means to support cadet education since the CBLAN, Lamkin's vision for technology in the academic program focused outside the classroom. He reasoned that the learning activities of cadets in the barracks area provided the greatest fresh opportunities for technology to enhance cadet education. Computer and network support could, for instance, make reading a richer experience through multimedia, provide "virtual" learning experiences through simulation (chemistry and physics experiments were a favorite example), guide cadets toward productive use of time, and provide more out-of-class interaction with instructors. He urged the faculty in these directions.[43]

However, he saw the 55 minutes of classroom meeting time with cadets for each lesson as particularly precious. He viewed the computer as a third party, a potentially disruptive addition to the fragile, essentially two-way human communication between instructor and student. The least experienced junior military faculty members, having no previous experience with college-level teaching, would be particularly prone to misusing classroom technology. He cautioned the faculty to be careful in this regard, to inject technology in the classroom only in a well-considered and graduated manner.[44]

The World

The CBLAN was expanded in another important way in 1966 when, on the basis of Lamkin's recommendation, Superintendent Lt. Gen. Daniel Christman became convinced that it was high time to connect cadets through their PCs to the Internet. The Academic Board had long been familiar with this issue. Board members debated whether the benefits of Internet access outweighed those of a Spartan lifestyle and insulation from pop culture in the development of cadet self-discipline. Some held that the Internet would provide an untoward distraction. Generals Lamkin and Christman took a different position: since Army leaders in the field were increasingly confronted with a bewildering sea of information delivered by electronic data networks, cadets would be better served by an Academy experience that trained them to deal with it. They reasoned that the best training for such an environment was immersion in a similar environment at West Point, and that the Internet was a good start.

The Internet had come to the Academy through the Department of Geography and Computer Science as the MILNET in 1987, another of Colonel Kirby's innovations.[45] Initially available only to members of the Department through its own minicomputers, access expanded by 1989 to include the whole faculty. Initial capacity was tiny by modern standards—a single line with a capacity of about 5,000 characters (56 kilobits) per second expanded to about 120,000 characters (1.5 megabits) a few years later. In most departments, the early Internet remained the narrow province of computer specialists and automation professionals until the next technological breakthrough allowed an explosion in its use.

The World Wide Web crept into the collective consciousness of the Academy from the grassroots. In 1993, just as members of the computer science faculty were reading about the skeletal beginnings of the web in academic publications, a junior civilian computer technician in the Department of Mathematical Sciences, Erich Markert, acting under the guidance of Lt. Col. John Robertson, erected the first web server and web page at the Academy. The faculty was quick to see the educational possibilities.

In the fall of 1994, while serving as Vice Dean, Col. Fletcher Lamkin delivered luncheon remarks to the Army Executives for Software (ARES), a general officers' conference at West Point, capturing the thoughts of the day regarding the web:

> The question is this. What are the effects of providing this capability directly to each cadet's desk in the barracks? Will Internet etiquette need to be part of Regulations USMA? Will we restrict what one can "download" from the net? What about documentation standards for things gathered from the net? We have discovered "essay services" on the net. For a fee, these will provide a paper on most any subject tailored to the buyer's specifications. What are the honor implications of this? Here it is too early even to propose how we will study the problem, but experience dic-

tates the general course: we will try it out for a small number of cadets and watch carefully. We will extrapolate that
experience to the Corps in a comprehensive staff action,
and we will make a decision.

Although West Point was not one of the first organizations worldwide to embrace the web, it was an early adopter within the Army.
By 1995, EE&CS faculty members were advising the Chief of Staff of
the Army on the implications of the web and multimedia for staffing
and publishing Army doctrine and technical publications. The next
summer, two computer science majors, Cadets Christa Chewar and
Anthony Iasso, worked in the Chief's office, making a series of recommendations in this area. The web address www.usma.edu appeared
on the Internet in 1995, providing the rest of the world a virtual
window into West Point. Just as important, the USMA Web Presence
Policy, staffed and approved concurrently, established the groundwork for a separate internal web, which could publish documents
and provide services meant for exclusive use by Academy personnel. The Academy had thus anticipated academic intranets, which
became common at many institutions over the next few years. The
wheel continues to turn. In 2004, now Capt. Christa Chewar, Ph.D.,
is scheduled to return to the Department of EE&CS as a computer
science faculty member.

If total immersion in a digital environment was Dean Lamkin's goal
for cadets, then West Point still had work to do. In 1997, the scarcity of
pay phones prompted increasing numbers of cadets to purchase cell
phones, with the additional benefits of saving time and enhancing privacy. There was a single television set for each company of 120 cadets.
Rapidly expanding internet traffic overloaded the barracks network.
The old CBLAN wiring, installed in 1989, was growing increasingly
saturated and unreliable. Replacement had been planned to occur
during an ongoing series of barracks renovations, but these would not
be complete for at least seven years, unacceptably late.

The Academy exploited a public-private partnership to solve
these problems much more quickly and at less cost to the government. A concept later known as the Barracks Information Technol-

ogy (BIT) project, which had been discussed for a number of years in Academy automation circles, was approved by the Superintendent on Brigadier General Lamkin's recommendation. Under the plan, the Academy invited commercial telephone contractors to bid on a single project that included installing and providing a new telephone service for cadets. In addition to wiring for telephones, the contractor was required to replace the old CBLAN wiring and to install a new closed circuit television network that extended to each cadet desk.[46] The new infrastructure was in full operation by the fall of 1998.[47] The cadet desk was now the nexus among Internet, CBLAN, television, and telephone, and the ability of cadets to communicate with the world outside of West Point was unprecedented.[48]

The BIT project was an important component of a larger campaign to make computing at West Point dependable and secure. Network administrators began focusing on security and dependability issues in 1993, as the major network upgrade of that year temporarily hindered access to e-mail and other services. Additionally, there was growing concern over the proliferation of computer viruses that periodically caused major disruptions to computer use and the loss of digital files.

By 1996, the revitalization of the CBLAN allowed the Academy to adopt what are today called "information assurance" measures for its student body. No similar practice was documented by other educational institutions of the time.[49] Cadet computers of that year incorporated operating system software that was normally reserved for business and scientific use and was thus more robust than home-oriented software.[50] Security measures were applied automatically by the Goldcoats to cadet computers as they logged in to CBLAN. The Goldcoats' central monitoring facility identified misconfigurations and vulnerabilities. The teetering legacy of Master Sgt. John Junod's 1989 mail system and two experimental alternatives was finally jettisoned in 1996 to be replaced by a single integrated and reliable multimedia messaging and calendar facility. The Goldcoats of 1999 were commonly able to verify that 99.3 percent or more of cadet computers were operating on the CBLAN each day.

The Academy was also an early leader in the vital area of information assurance education. This topic, deemed increasingly important to national defense as the new millennium arrived, became a fixture in the curriculum with the establishment of the Information Technology and Operations Center (ITOC), whose focus was information assurance. It was founded in the Department of EE&CS in 1999, a descendent of Gilbert Kirby's Computer Graphics Laboratory. ITOC personnel made the case for information assurance in the computer science curriculum, with the result that the first course in this topic, CS482, was offered in 1999. Supporting the course was a one-of-a-kind laboratory where cadets could practice cyber attacks and defenses in an electronic network environment isolated from the CBLAN. By the end of 2000, information assurance topics were treated in the courses of nine of the Academy's 13 academic departments. For innovations in the field of information assurance education, the Academy became the first undergraduate institution certified by the National Security Agency as an Information Assurance Center of Excellence.[51]

Lessons for Today

What does the foregoing discussion of the cycles of technology adoption at West Point suggest about the future? One clear lesson is that the emergence of new technology will continue to drive change and improvements in Academic mission accomplishment. This chapter has traced five major technology change cycles over some 30 years: mainframe computing (1962), time-sharing remote access (1968), microcomputers (1982), networks (1987), and the Internet (1994). If we examine the agenda of the current information technology staff at West Point, we find technology changes of comparable scope and significance that will be completely implemented in the next five or six years: portable computers, handheld devices, wireless networks, video teleconferencing, course management software, and educational simulations, among others. Thus, an ever-accelerating stream of new technologies will continue to enhance accomplishment of the Academy mission.

That a succession of technological visionaries has appeared in the past bodes well for the Academy's future. The presence of active, even aggressive, attitudes toward technology within the West Point faculty and staff shows no evidence of decline. On the contrary, it is no longer necessary to convince most young officers arriving at West Point, many of whom have had early experience with digitized brigades and divisions, that computer and network technology are in the Army to stay. The West Pointers among recent crops of instructors and tactical officers are members of the first classes who received personal computers and who first "organized for battle" against the upper classes and the officer-in-charge using e-mail. For them, solving problems with technology is already a known essential part of leadership. Hence, there is much room for optimism that people of the right technological vision will continue to appear and that they will find the necessary institutional support, even at the inevitably accelerating pace with which it will be needed.

There have been many unintended consequences—some positive, others not—of the Academy's embrace of information technology. Is it possible that technology-induced change could be counterproductive because of the dizzying array of unpredictable side effects? In fact, there is evidence that the most potentially harmful side effects are in the past. The transition from manual to electronic document management, for instance, cannot recur. The broad paradigm of asynchronous electronic messaging (e-mail, in particular) has been absorbed into the collective psyche, a transition in human habits that need never happen again. Rather, looking at the current slate of planned innovations, we see only incremental expansions in the quality, convenience, and level of accessibility of technology in human experiences, not the wholesale upheaval of the past. The evolutionary framework within which the expansion will occur already exists.

Moreover, the organizational and individual trauma of technological assimilation appears to have inured cadets and faculty alike to change in this form. When new technologies are today introduced in the West Point environment, they are matter-of-factly tried and either adopted or discarded on their merits. Unanticipated side effects are apparently fewer, smaller, and less disruptive than in the past. Few cadets or faculty and staff members are dogmatic, either for or against technology. It is merely a fact of life. Although technical malfunctions and computer system quirks have grown scarcer and less severe over time, when they do occur, people "work around" and "make do" with the same stoical acceptance long reserved for automobile breakdowns and power failures. The revolution in computer technology seems to be over for the time being; purposeful evolution has replaced it.

Of course, unintended consequences are by definition unforeseeable. Still, there is cause for confidence in the resilience of West Point's organization. The Academic Computer Center of 1962 was itself a technological innovation. It served to illustrate the scope and speed of change that technology entails. The incorporation of such change into the fabric of West Point itself continued with the Academic Computing Division of the late 1980s, which was deliberately flexible in both capability and composition. The modern Dean's and Superintendent's technology staffs have fully incorporated technological innovation and change into each step of mission accomplishment and the planning therefor. In a similar manner, curricular change has been facilitated by the adoption of routine programmatic assessment of the connections between the outcomes of cadet studies and the needs of the Army. Not surprisingly, assessment has consistently pointed to the need for even more technology in the core curriculum and to continuing investment in the Academy's technology infrastructure. An acutely technology-aware form of adaptivity has become a mature aspect of the organization that is West Point, equipping it to learn and grow in its third century of existence.

---

[1] The complacency of the Academic Boards of the late 19th and early 20th centuries is well documented, but perhaps most clearly by Stephen E. Ambrose, *Duty, Honor, Country: A History of West Point* (Baltimore, MD: Johns Hopkins Press, 1966).

[2] William T. Moye, "ENIAC: The Army-Sponsored Revolution," *Army Research Library* (1996); par.1 [journal online]; available from http://ftp.arl.army.mil/~mike/comphist/96summary/.

[3] I. Bernard Cohen, "The Computer: A Case Study of Support by Government, Especially the Military, of a New Science and Technology," *Science, Technology, and the Military* 12 (1998): 143.

[4] Gilbert W. Kirby, Jr., interview by Capt. David B. Cushen, 5 October 2001.

[5] William F. Luebbert, interview by Capt. David B. Cushen, 29 November 2001.

[6] Op. cit. Gilbert W. Kirby, 5 October 2001.

[7] Ibid.

[8] Ibid.

[9] United States Military Academy, *Annual Report of the Superintendent*, 1963, 18.

[10] William F. Luebbert, interview by Capt. David B. Cushen, 29 November 2001. Today it is broadly understood that computer languages are so specialized as to be fundamentally different from human languages. Housing both in the same academic department is a quaint notion.

[11] United States Military Academy, *Catalogue of the United States Military Academy*, 1961.

[12] "Computers Quicken the Pace in the Cadet Race Against Time," *Army-Citadel Football Program* (September 1964): 41.

[13] United States Military Academy, *Catalogue of the United States Military Academy*, 1965, 10.

[14] "Computers Quicken the Pace," 41.

[15] United States Military Academy, *Annual Report of the Superintendent*, 1968.

[16] *Communications of the ACM*, 7 (December 1964): 722-23.

[17] United States Military Academy, *Annual Report of the Superintendent*, 1971, 15.

[18] United States Military Academy, *Annual Report of the Superintendent*, 1972, 11 and 1973, 14.

[19] United States Military Academy, *Annual Report of the Superintendent*, 1971, 67.

[20] United States Military Academy, *Annual Report of the Superintendent*, 1973, 15.

[21] Gilbert W. Kirby, Jr., interview. General Kirby highlights the time of the "riots" that occurred when the computer center was in the basement of Thayer Hall.

[22] United States Military Academy, *Annual Report of the Superintendent*, 1980.

[23] United States Military Academy, *Annual Report of the Superintendent*, 1977, 70.

[24] Col. Lanse M. Leach, "Academic Computing: Past Present, and Future," *Assembly* (May 1990): 6.

[25] United States Military Academy, *Annual Report of the Superintendent*, 1980.

[26] Leach, *Academic Computing*.

[27] Ibid.

[28] Ibid.

[29] Ibid.

[30] Ibid.

[31] Whether any of the Class of 1990 carried their cadet computers to the Persian Gulf region is uncertain, but the Army was still using many thousands of Zeniths of the same model at the time.

[32] TerraBase Military Terrain Information System, User's Documentation, Computer Graphics Laboratory, Department of Geography and Computer Science, U.S. Military Academy, West Point, NY, May 1988.

[33] The Laboratory's model for external support of research performed by USMA faculty members continues to the present day in the 12 Centers of Excellence within the Dean's sphere.

[34] The Norse god Odin is invoked in chants by cadets hoping for a quick, parade-canceling rainstorm.

[35] Academic Computing Division, Office of the Dean, USMA, CBLAN Test Plan and Schedule, Issue 8, 17 July 1989.

36 Northwest Missouri State University claims to be the first publicly-supported university to install a networked computer in every dormitory room in 1987. This claim is made on their web page which can be found at http://www.nwmissouri.edu/compserv/ecnorthwest.htm and was last assessed 21 January 2003. If it was the first, then West Point's network, which was also available in 1987, could not have been far behind.

37 As of this writing, John Junod is the Chief Technology Officer of IpSwitch, a network software firm, which he co-founded after retirement from the Army.

38 Academic Computing Division, Office of the Dean, USMA, CBLAN Test Plan and Schedule, Issue 8, 17 July 1989. For comparison, today's barracks network is 10,000 times faster.

39 Based on the number of e-mail messages processed per day and the number of users of the current USMA e-mail system.

40 Academic Computing Division, Office of the Dean, USMA, Unique Logins by Class, 1 September 1988 to 31 December 1988, undated.

41 Ibid.

42 Gregory J. Conti, USMA Class of 1989, personal experience.

43 Lt. Col. Eugene K. Ressler, Associate Dean for Information and Educational Technology under General Lamkin from 1996 to 2000.

44 Ibid.

45 Maj. Daniel R. Judy did the staff and technical work. Today, as a colonel, he commands the Joint Battle Center and is an Advisory Board member for the Department of Electrical Engineering and Computer Science.

46 A notable sidebar is that between initial BIT planning and award of the contract, average long distance service rates fell by nearly 50 percent. This completely changed the financial basis for the project. Bids were much higher than estimates. USMA found the money, and BIT went forward.

47 Lee barracks was, at this time, gutted for renovation. The building's BIT installation was completed the following year.

48 The cadet computers issued starting in 1997 were equipped to view television through the computer monitor.

49 Lt. Col. Eugene K. Ressler, Associate Dean for Information and Educational Technology, was responsible for cadet computers from 1995 to 2000. Personal literature survey, 1996.

50 This was Microsoft Windows NT Version 3.51, rather than the far more popular, but less secure and reliable Windows for Workgroups.

51 "Introduction to the Centers of Academic Excellence in Information Assurance Education Program," http://www.nsa.gov/isso/programs/coeiae/index.htm, 1 August 2003. USMA achieved Center of Excellence certification in March 2001. The other 22 institutions certified through 2001 all had graduate programs.

⫷ CHAPTER 24 ⫸

201 YEARS OF MATHEMATICS AT WEST POINT

V. Frederick Rickey and Amy Shell-Gellasch

Mathematics is the study which forms the
foundation of the [United States Military Academy
curriculum]. This is necessary, both to impart to
the mind that combined strength and versatility,
that peculiar vigor and rapidity of comparison
necessary for military action, and to pave the way
for progress in the higher military sciences. All
experience shows that the mind, in order that it may
act with efficiency, must be accustomed to exertion.
It should be taught gradually to develop its own
powers, and as it slowly learns their capacity and
the manner of employing them, the increasing lights
which are thrown upon its course will enable it to go
on for an unlimited extent in the path
of improvement.

**—Committee on Military Affairs
United States Military Academy, 17 May 1834**[1]

The Department of Mathematical Sciences at the U.S. Military
Academy celebrated its bicentennial on 21 September 2001, for it
was on that date in 1801 that the first mathematics class was taught
at West Point. Though the Academy would not be signed into law

and officially founded by Thomas Jefferson until 16 March 1802, his Secretary of War, Henry Dearborn, hired George Baron as Teacher of the Arts and Sciences to the Artillerists and Engineers in July 1801.[2]

Dearborn ordered Baron to purchase 15 to 20 copies of *A Course in Mathematics*, a two-volume text by English mathematician Charles Hutton, so that cadets could study algebra, geometry, plane and spherical trigonometry, conic sections, and surveying.[3] Joseph G. Swift, the first USMA graduate and second individual to serve as Superintendent, described his first lecture as a cadet thus: "Professor Baron furnished me with a copy of Dr. Hutton's Mathematics, and gave me a specimen of his mode of teaching at the blackboard in the academy."[4] Soon afterwards, Swift and Baron got in a shouting match, and Baron was court-martialed and resigned before the Academy was even officially established.[5] Counting Baron as the "zeroeth" head of the Mathematics Department at West Point, in the following two centuries, there have been 20 more department heads, ten in each century. For ease of reference during the course of this chapter, we detail them in Table 24-1.

After Jared Mansfield graduated from Yale, he taught school in New Haven and Philadelphia. In 1802, he published *Essays, Mathematical and Physical*, the first mathematics book published in the United States that contained original work. President Thomas Jefferson was so impressed with the book that he appointed Mansfield captain in the Corps of Engineers so that he could teach mathematics at West Point. He was noted as a kindly teacher and the cadets liked him. Mansfield left the Academy in 1803 when he was appointed Surveyor General of Ohio and the Northwestern Territory, replacing Rufus Putnam, the namesake of Fort Putnam, the best-known of the satellite defense works protecting fortress West Point during the Revolutionary War. He returned to West Point in 1812 as Professor of Natural and Experimental Philosophy and stayed until he retired in 1828.[6]

William A. Barron (the "two r" Barron), who had an impressive flair for teaching, had been a tutor at Harvard before he accepted a captaincy in the Corps of Artillerists and Engineers. After two years, he was assigned to West Point. A year later, in 1803, he purchased 14 copies of *Geometrical and Geographical Essays* by George Adams for

	Professor	Born-Died	Education	Tenure of Mathematics Department Heads
0	George Baron	1769-1812		6 Jan 1801-11 Feb 1802
1	Jared A. Mansfield	1759-1830	Yale 1777	3 May 1802-14 Nov 1803
2	William A. Barron	1769-1825	Harvard 1787	6 Jul 1802-14 Feb 1807
3	Ferdinand R. Hassler	1770-1843		14 Feb 1807-31 Dec 1809
4	Alden Partridge	1785-1845	USMA 1806	13 Apr 1813-1 Sep 1813
5	Andrew Ellicott	1754-1820		1 Sep 1813-29 Aug 1820 †
6	David B. Douglass	1790-1849	Yale 1813	29 Aug 1820-1 May 1823
7	Charles Davies	1798-1876	USMA 1815	1 May 1823-31 May 1837
8	Albert E. Church	1807-1878	USMA 1828	1 Jun 1837-30 Mar 1878 †
9	Edgar W. Bass	1843-1918	USMA 1868	17 Apr 1878-7 Oct 1898
10	Wright P. Edgerton	1852-1904	USMA 1874	7 Oct 1898-25 Jun 1904 †
11	Charles P. Echols	1867-1940	USMA 1891	29 Jun 1904-30 Sep 1931
12	Harris Jones	1892-1977	USMA 1917	1 Oct 1931-1 Sep 1947
13	William W. Bessell, Jr.	1901-1977	USMA 1920	1 Sep 1947-Sep 1959
14	Charles P. Nicholas	1903-1985	USMA 1925	Sep 1959-Sep 1967
15	John S. B. Dick	1913-2004	USMA 1935	Sep 1967-Jan 1974
16	Jack M. Pollin	1922-	USMA 1944	Jan 1974-Jun 1985
17	David H. Cameron	1927-	USMA 1950	Jun 1985-Jun 1988
18	Frank R. Giordano	1942-	USMA 1964	Jun 1988-1995
19	David C. Arney	1949-	USMA 1971	1995-25 Dec 2000
20	Gary W. Krahn	1955-	USMA 1977	25 Dec 2000-

† Died while serving as Department Head

Table 24-1. USMA Mathematics Department Heads.

teaching practical applications of mathematics.[7] During these early days instruction was from 8 a.m. until noon, with Mansfield teaching algebra and Barron doing "geometrical demonstration."[8] Superintendent Jonathan Williams taught surveying in the afternoons.

One of the early students at the Academy was Alden Partridge. Williams and Barron examined the cadets on 17 October 1806 and declared Partridge "the best mathematician in the academy."[9] Unfortunately, this is a hard claim to judge, but there is an undated manuscript at Norwich University, a school that Partridge founded in 1819, showing that Partridge knew enough about "fluxions" (the Newtonian version of calculus) to calculate the inflection points of a conchoid. Following graduation in 1806, Partridge was promoted to first lieutenant, one of only two graduates to receive this rank upon graduation.[10] He stayed at West Point after graduation to teach mathematics under Barron and later under Ferdinand Hassler, who taught at West Point from 1807 to 1809. On 13 April 1813, Partridge became the first official "Professor of Mathematics" at West Point (the position was not established by Congress until 29 April 1812), but held the office for only a few months. On 1 September 1813, he accepted the position of Professor of Civil and Military Engineering, becoming the first person in the country to hold a professorship in engineering.

Without doubt, Ferdinand Hassler was the most colorful professor the department has ever had. Born in Switzerland, he studied in France and Germany and assisted in a survey of his native canton of Bern. He was an avid collector of books but sold half of his collection before immigrating to the United States. His plan was to set up a utopian farming community in South Carolina. On the voyage across the Atlantic, the captain of the ship had a stroke, and Hassler took over the navigation to Philadelphia.

Upon arrival he learned that one of his business partners in the farming venture no longer had the funds to buy land, so he turned to other pursuits. Hassler quickly impressed the intellectuals of Philadelphia with his versatility and scientific knowledge, his set of surveying instruments (including a copy of the standard meter and kilogram), and his library of 3,000 scientific books. Reports soon reached President Jefferson about Hassler's talents. He was appointed Professor of Mathematics at West Point with a salary of $700 per year in 1807. Reports on his teaching are mixed—he was good for the good students and bad for the bad ones. While teaching at the Academy, Hassler wrote *Elements of Trigonometry*, the first work on analytic trigonometry in English (not published until 1826). He thus became the first mathematics professor to write a book while at West Point. Despite these distinctions, his stay at West Point was short-lived because Secretary of War William Eustice, who wanted to abolish the Academy, interpreted the law to mean that civilians could not teach at West Point.

Andrew Ellicott had a considerable reputation as a surveyor when he came to West Point in 1813 to replace Partridge. His most memorable achievement was the surveying of the "ten-mile square" that became the District of Columbia. Interestingly, in that historic task he was aided by the mathematical practitioner Benjamin Banneker, a free Black. Ellicott had a reputation as a good teacher, and it appears that under his leadership the teaching of mathematics was much less tied to the text, although he continued to use the Hutton book noted at the beginning of this chapter. In a letter to Swift dated 10 February 1815, Ellicott writes that the students "have made great progress—these classes are in Conic sections, one of which will be in fluxions before the end of next month."[11] We also know that seven cadets were examined by Ellicott in calculus in 1815. Curiously, one member of that class, future Department Head Charles Davies, was not examined at this time. He must have learned his calculus through private study and under the tutelage of Partridge and Ellicott. While 1815 is the earliest documentation of a class in calculus at West Point, we conjecture Davies was tutored because earlier Partridge tutored the sons of Jonathan Williams in the subject in 1810.

Ellicott was a kindly and friendly man, well liked by the cadets for his interesting stories. They nicknamed him "Old Infinite Series," revealing that the topic was indeed taught to the Corps. He was famous for the perfect geometrical constructions he made at the blackboard with cord and straight-edge. He even had a small slate and sponge attached to his buttonhole so that he could do mathematics on the spur of the moment. He died in 1820 at West Point and is buried there.

One of the most useful advances in military engineering of the late 18th century, the mathematical discipline of descriptive geometry, was the creation of the French mathematician Gaspard Monge. The idea was to produce a two-dimensional representation of a three-dimensional object; today, the subject has evolved into computer-aided design. In Monge's day it allowed moderately quick geometrical solutions of problems that had been done by laborious arithmetic, such as in calculating specifications for construction of fortifications and optimum emplacement of guns. Descriptive geometry was brought to the Academy by Claudius Crozet, a student of Monge at the École Polytechnique in Paris, who immigrated to the United States in 1816 and immediately took up the position of Assistant Professor of Engineering at USMA.

Crozet undertook to teach descriptive geometry, but the cadets were not prepared to comprehend the material. Since the level of descriptive geometry texts available, all in French, was above the capacity of cadets, Crozet wrote *A Treatise on Descriptive Geometry* in 1821 explicitly for the use of the cadets at the Academy, but it was not published until 1826. Crozet relied heavily on the blackboard for the teaching of descriptive geometry, and since his time the blackboard has been in almost daily use at the Academy.[12] The subject of descriptive geometry was taught in the Mathematics Department from Crozet's arrival in 1816 until 1929 when it was transferred to the Department of Drawing.

To augment the teaching of descriptive geometry, a set of 26 string models was procured from the firm of Pixii in Paris in 1857 for about $500.[13] Designed by another student of Monge, Theodore Olivier, these models depict the intersection of various three-dimensional ruled surfaces, such as cones and hyperboloids. They were used by cadets as models for their two-dimensional drawings. Drawing, both artistic and technical, was an important part of the curriculum (see Chapter 18). As officers in the Corp of Engineers, graduates would be called on to make detailed and accurate drawings of landscapes as well as road and bridge designs as part of the exploration and development of the nation that took place during the 19th century.

The Olivier models are on display today in the Department of Mathematical Sciences. Also, examples of the precise and beautiful drawings done by cadets during this period can be seen both at the USMA museum and in the Special Collections of the USMA Library. Two favorites are signed by Class of 1843 member U.H. Grant, who was later to adopt the name Ulysses S. Grant. After graduation, Grant wrote Professor Church several times requesting to be an instructor in the Mathematics Department.[14] Church turned him down and so today the wags claim that "it is harder to become an instructor in mathematics at West Point than President of the United States."

After the difficult experience of the War of 1812, national leaders became more concerned with the quality of instruction at West Point. Secretary of State James Madison accepted Swift's recommendation to send Lt. Col. William McRee and Capt. Sylvanus Thayer to Europe "to gain a knowledge of the European military establishment, their fortifications, Military Schools and Military workshops, and also to collect Books, Maps, Plans and Instruments for the Military Academy."[15] They arrived in Europe in May 1815 shortly after the Battle of Waterloo and returned in May 1817. In particular they visited the École Polytechnique in Paris and brought back almost 1,000 French mathematical, scientific, and military texts from the best authors of the period.[16] The École was founded in 1794, and within a few years had become Europe's premier military and scientific institution. Prominent scientists and mathematicians such as Laplace, Lagrange, and Fourier developed a program there that produced some of the best minds of the century. Thayer rebuilt the U.S. Military Academy both militarily and academically using the École as his model. Some of the reforms were already under discussion by the faculty and Superintendent Alden Partridge, but few changes had actually been made. By the end of the second decade of the 19th century, under the superintendency of Sylvanus Thayer, the Academy would take the shape that we are familiar with today.

David Douglass graduated from Yale in 1813, was commissioned a second lieutenant in the Corps of Engineers and ordered to West Point, but was called away by the War of 1812. He was breveted captain for his "distinguished and meritorious service" in the defense of Fort Erie. Returning to West Point, he married Ann Eliza Ellicott, daughter of Prof. Ellicott, in 1815. For the next five years he served as the Principal Assistant Professor of Natural and Experimental Philosophy. Upon his father-in-law's death in 1820, Douglass succeeded him as Professor of Mathematics, serving until 1823 when he became Professor of Engineering, remaining in that position until his resignation in 1831. He later became president of Kenyon College in Ohio.

Charles Davies, under the auspices of the Chief of Engineers, Joseph G. Swift, came to West Point in December 1813 and graduated in December 1815.[17] There were no openings in the Corps of Engineers so he took a less desirable position in artillery, serving a year in garrison duty before being transferred to the Corps of Engineers in August 1816. He resigned from the Army on 1 December 1816 to accept a position at West Point teaching mathematics. He served under Department Heads Andrew Ellicott and David Douglass, and then taught natural and experimental philosophy for two years. He subsequently became Professor of Mathematics in May of 1823 when Douglass became Professor in Philosophy. The use of Hutton's text, which had served yeoman duty since the inception of the Academy, was discontinued at this time.

As professor, Davies began a long and lucrative career as the author of textbooks, initially for use at the Academy but then for use throughout the country. The books he published while at West Point covered the entire Academy mathematics curriculum:

> *Elements of Descriptive Geometry* (1826)
> *Elements of Geometry and Trigonometry* (1828)
> *Elements of Surveying* (1830)
> *A Treatise on Shades and Shadows, and Linear Perspective* (1832)
> *The Common School Arithmetic* (1833)
> *Elements of Algebra: Translated from the French of M. Bourdon* (1835)
> *Elements of the Differential and Integral Calculus* (1836)
> *Elements of Analytical Geometry* (1837)[18]

Not surprisingly, the effort of producing eight books in 11 years left Davies exhausted. He resigned in May of 1837 to tour Europe, restore his health, and then "continue to write and revise wildly successful mathematics textbooks."[19] All of these works except the arithmetic were used as textbooks at West Point, most for long periods of time. Several of them began as translations and then were revised and improved for the Academy and the American market. Owing to the large number of graduates who taught mathematics after leaving the Army and to the wide recognition of the value of these texts, the books of Davies were extensively used in both colleges and schools.[20] The 1828 text, *Elements of Geometry and Trigonometry,* was his most popular book. During the period from 1828 to 1895, it appeared in 33 editions/printings and some 300,000 copies.[21] In his lifetime Davies published 49 different titles appearing in at least 492 editions/printings. They covered the ground from elementary arithmetic through college mathematics (though none was higher than calculus). By 1875, Davies was selling about 350,000 books every year and reached a total of seven million sold by that year.[22] He completely dominated mathematics textbook writing in the 19th century.

Davies was succeeded by Albert Church, who, as we have seen, would one day refuse a future U.S. president the opportunity to teach mathematics at West Point. When Church arrived at West Point in June of 1824 at age 16, the entrance requirements were simply arithmetic, reading, and writing. During the summer the cadets "received daily and very thorough instruction" in arithmetic by Cadet Dallas Bache, and recited daily to him. Bache had served as Acting Assistant Professor of Mathematics the previous year, and was about to enter his First Class (senior) year. It was then the practice to have a few outstanding cadets serve as instructors, and Bache was outstanding (he eventually became Superintendent of the U.S. Coast Survey).[23] Bache's examination of the "fully qualified" was "hurried and slight," with not more than one or two questions asked, but the proficiency of the weaker cadets was "fully tested." Moreover, every cadet was "required to read and write in the presence of the Academic Board."[24]

During his first year Church and his classmates studied algebra. "The best textbook that could be obtained in the English language was a poor translation of Lacroix," so it had to serve.[25] Also, they used Legendre's *Geometry,*[26] Lacroix's *Trigonometry,*[27] both in translation, and Crozet's book on descriptive geometry.[28] These were all useful books, providing an excellent basis for learning. During the second year, Church and his classmates in the higher sections used the analytic geometry text of Biot and the calculus text of Lacroix, both in

French. [29] Thus the French the cadets studied every afternoon of their plebe (freshman) year was necessary for their study of mathematics during their yearling (sophomore) year. It is noteworthy that in 1825 all cadets were learning some calculus.

Albert Church graduated first in the Class of 1828 and, like Davies, was commissioned in the artillery, there being no vacancies in the Corps of Engineers. Thayer requested that Church stay at West Point to teach mathematics, and there he remained except for two years from 1832 to 1834 when he joined his artillery unit. In 1837 he became Professor of Mathematics when Davies resigned. Church served as professor until his death in 1878, a total of 50 years of service, 48 of them at West Point.

The reports on Church as a teacher are not good. Morris Schaff, who graduated in 1862, called him "an old mathematical cinder, bereft of all natural feeling."[30] Arthur Hardy, an 1869 graduate who taught mathematics at Dartmouth in the 1890s and was also a novelist with a national reputation, observed, "The mathematical recitation was a drill room. In my opinion the result was a soldier who knew the maneuvers, but it did not give an independent, self-reliant grasp of the methods of research."[31]

But Church was influential, both through his guidance of the department and through his own textbook writing. His four texts were used extensively at the Academy and saw moderate success across the country as well.

> *Elements of Differential and Integral Calculus* (1842)
> *Elements of Analytical Geometry* (1851)
> *Elements of Descriptive Geometry* (1865)
> *Plane and Spherical Trigonometry* (1869)

These texts were noteworthy in that they were meant merely as improvements on what was already being taught. There was no broadening or deepening of the curriculum. Church himself admitted that once the mathematics curriculum was set in place, it did not change substantially for the rest of the 19th century, although the annotations in many textbooks in the library show that there was constant tinkering with the presentation of the mathematics.

When Professor Church died in 1878 at the age of 70, Edgar Bass, who had never previously taught mathematics, replaced him. From 1869 to his appointment in mathematics in 1878 he had been Assistant Professor of Natural and Experimental Philosophy, except for 16 months during the period 1874-1875 when he served as assistant astronomer of the U.S. expedition to New Zealand to observe a transit of Venus. Bass was not satisfied with the foundations and clarity of the calculus book of Church, so he worked hard over many years writing his own. As portions were finished, he published them as pamphlets and issued them to the cadets. In 1889 he finally published the completed work under the title *Differential Calculus*. A decade later he retired because of poor eyesight.

If we look at the Academy curriculum from the earliest years, it is clearly "the product of an evolutionary development which, over the years, has reflected the changing requirements of the military profession and advances in the field of higher education."[32] A good example occurred in 1879, when Department Head Bass introduced into the curriculum a course in least squares, a method of statistical analysis for finding the best trend line for a set of empirical observations. This method was invented by Carl Friedrich Gauss and used by him in his spectacular 1801 rediscovery of the first observed asteroid, Ceres. The technique became a standard method for the astronomer and surveyor to correct observational and measurement errors. It was a tool that every military engineer should have in his tool-kit. In 1879 the Board of Visitors recommended the use of *Treatise on the Method of Least Squares*, written by William Chauvenet, one of the founders of the U.S. Naval Academy. The book was used until 1889 when it was replaced by *The Theory of Errors and Least Squares* by W. W. Johnson, which itself was used until 1932.

There is a copy of the latter in the USMA library that reveals a good deal about teaching at West Point. Notes in the book, once in Bass's personal library, indicate which sections of the book were to be covered on which days, and which sections were to be assigned solely to the advanced sections. In 1942, when Col. Harris Jones was Department Head, a portion of the least squares course was replaced by a course in statistics. When William W. Bessell, Jr., was head, all sections studied the same material, which by this time had developed more broadly into statistics. Electronic computing machines were introduced into the statistics course in 1947 to do the tedious computations that the method of least squares requires. With the development of modern computers the method has been reduced to an exercise in multivariable calculus and a black box on the computer. However, the study of statistics has remained a central part of the curriculum, and the discipline is expected to play an even more important role in the curriculum of the 21st century because familiarity with the applications of statistical analysis has become a vital tool for the educated citizen.

Another noteworthy contribution of Professor Bass was the adoption of special lectures in the history of mathematics in 1896.[33] During the first year, cadets attended a special lecture on the history and early development of geometry and algebra. In the Third Class year, cadets attended one or more lectures on the history of descriptive geometry, which included a comparison of algebraic and geometric methods and a short introduction to projective geometry. Another special lecture during the Third Class year was on the development of calculus, to include the Newton-Leibniz controversy over who first discovered the calculus.

Wright Edgerton was appointed Department Head in 1898. He had much more military experience than his predecessors, having served in the line Army for eight years at ten locations in six states. In 1882 he returned to West Point to be the Principal Assistant Professor of Mathematics, second in the department to Professor Bass. In 1893 he became Associate Professor of Mathematics, the first in the department to hold that title. He made two important changes in the curriculum. Since Thayer's time, algebra and geometry had been taught in that order, but Edgerton decided to teach them simultaneously, with recitations on alternate days. The other change still echoes today. He started giving written tests for the general reviews, thereby allowing students who did well on them to be exempt from the final exams. It had been customary throughout the century to have three kinds of classes, "advance" where new material was covered, "partial reviews" where a portion of the material was revisited, and then a "general review" before the examination. Beginning with Edgerton, cadets took written partial reviews (or WPRs, to use familiar Academy lingo), which were actually tests. In 1902, to create more time for Spanish instruction, the mathematics curriculum was reduced and surveying was transferred to the Department of Practical Engineering.[34] Professor Edgerton died in 1904, at age 51, from the lingering effects of disease contracted in the summer of 1898 while he was serving as a volunteer aide-de-camp during the U.S. seizure of Puerto Rico from Spain.

Charles P. Echols became head of the Mathematics Department in June of 1904. At the end of the fall term he declared 40 percent of the yearlings deficient in mathematics. This incensed Superintendent Albert Mills, who ordered Echols on a study tour of eastern colleges to observe instruction in mathematics. Then he ordered him to Europe for the following academic year to study military instruction there. In his absence the department experimented with eliminating daily marking in Fourth Class mathematics, and a committee studying the curriculum reduced the mathematics curriculum for the second time in two years.[35]

In 1908, President Roosevelt wrote that it was "a very great misfortune to lay so much stress upon mathematics in the curriculum at West Point and fail to have languages taught in accordance with the best modern conversational standards."[36] The Academic Board dismissed the idea, reiterating the long-held view that a technical curriculum instilled mental discipline. Indeed, it went on to claim, "Mathematical training at the Military Academy has been the main factor in all the accomplishments of graduates."[37]

The workload for the professors was particularly heavy and got even worse during World War I. For example, during Academic Year 1918-1919, there were 18 instructors in mathematics operating under an emergency schedule. Each instructor was in the section room from 8:00 a.m. to 12:35 p.m. daily—three periods of 85 minutes each. According to the Annual Report of the Superintendent, this "is at a rate of twenty-five and a half hours per week of actual section room instruction, which, it is safe to say, is not undertaken ordinarily at any college in the country by an instructor in such subjects."[38]

Brig. Gen. Douglas MacArthur assumed the superintendency at West Point on 12 June 1919, the youngest superintendent since Thayer. When appointing him, Gen. Peyton March, Chief of Staff, told him, "West Point is forty years behind the times."[39] Thus MacArthur's task was to revitalize the Academy. This required reinstatement of the four-year curriculum (although March wanted three) after the abridged terms during World War I. The Academic Board was assigned the task of revising the curriculum, with the work lasting for an entire year. MacArthur approved the Board's report on 20 July 1920, with the result here described by Academy historian Roger Nye:

> The system of recitations was reaffirmed; the practice of assigning review lessons after a few advanced lessons was continued; frequent grading and merit sectioning were retained. Finally, the report reaffirmed the essentiality of a faculty of Academy graduates, suggesting only that a year's assignment to a civilian school would improve their instruction, and that a four-year tour was highly desirable.[40]

Among curricular changes, the mathematics program was cut by a third. Professor Echols, who had 21 years of experience in higher education as opposed to MacArthur's just-completed first year, was incensed, so he issued a minority report. Echols was particularly disturbed by the dropping of descriptive geometry from the curriculum, a subject that had been taught at West Point for a century, and "a subject taught with painstaking elaboration at all the important military schools in the world."[41] Although the new curriculum was approved in Washington, Echols waged a guerrilla campaign. At the end of the fall term, Echols reported that 95 of 572 plebes were deficient in mathematics. The Academic Board saved 11 by reducing the passing mark from 37.5 to 35.3.[42]

MacArthur appointed an ad hoc committee of three lieutenant colonels, each with only their two-year cadet experience in mathematics, to investigate the high failure rate. In historical terms, Echols's 16.6 percent failure rate was not particularly high, for the 1924 *Superintendent's Annual Report* reveals that 24 percent of each plebe class was academically deficient after their first semester at

West Point. This fact notwithstanding, the committee issued, in the words of Roger Nye, "the most careful denunciation of the Professor of Mathematics officially recorded at the Academy."[43] Through actions such as this, MacArthur lost the support of the Academic Board, and soon after he left in 1924 his revisions of the mathematics curriculum were rescinded.

In the penultimate year of Professor Echols's incumbency, the mathematics curriculum was described as follows in the *Howitzer*:

> In the fourth class year algebra is completed in alternation first with plane and solid geometry, then with plane and spherical trigonometry. Plane analytical geometry is begun. The third class year embraces plane and solid analytical geometry and descriptive geometry, both being concluded in alternation. The calculus, differential and integral, and the theory of least squares complete the course.[44]

Harris Jones, who served as Department Head from 1931 to 1947, attended Harvard for two years before entering West Point. As a cadet he earned the nickname "Prof" for his ability in mathematics and willingness to help his fellow cadets. He graduated first in the Class of 1917 and was commissioned as a first lieutenant. A month later he was promoted to captain and led an engineer company into World War I. He earned the Distinguished Service Cross and was back at West Point the next fall. The following year he attended the Massachusetts Institute of Technology for a year of advanced study and then rejoined the field Army for eight years. He returned to West Point in 1931 as a colonel to become the Department Head.

Along with academics, the Academy has always been strong in athletics. The football program, in particular, was a strong competitor in the early decades of the 20th century. The athletic prowess of Army teams and the military nature of the institution, however, led to skepticism among some civilian educators about the quality of West Point's educational methods. In 1932 West Point was called upon to defend its academic honor after Army had won the Army-Harvard football game that year by a score of 46-0. President Abbott Lowell of Harvard commented to Superintendent William Connor at a post-game gathering at the home of Mrs. William Putnam that even though Army could beat Harvard in football, Harvard would surely win at an academic contest. Superintendent Connor could not ignore the challenge, so they agreed on a mathematical competition to be held at West Point on 19 and 20 May 1933. Ten sophomores from each school would be tested in plane and solid analytic geometry and the differential and integral calculus; the contest was restricted to the first two years of collegiate mathematics because that was all that was taught at West Point. The cadets trained as if for an athletic contest and received all the special treatment normally given to the athletic teams; one of their three coaches was future department head Lt. Charles Nicholas. Newspaper articles anticipating the event appeared in the *Pointer* and even the sports section of the *New York Times*. The cadets' hard work paid off as they beat the Crimson handily. "Army 'Mathletes' Defeat Harvard 98-112," reported a headline in the *New York Times*. Each contestant received a gold medal and a book.[45]

With support from the Putnam family, the contest was expanded in 1938 to a national event, and the Putnam Competition continues to this day as the most prestigious contest in the nation for mathematics undergraduates. Alas, West Point has not won since the zeroeth competition in 1933, primarily because the exam covers the whole range of undergraduate mathematics. Until majors were introduced in 1982, cadets could not have acquired the requisite knowledge. In recent years, cadet teams have participated in the International Mathematical Contest in Modeling and done very well, ranking in the highest category, "Outstanding," in each of the past four years.

A milestone occurred on Prof. Harris Jones's watch in 1943, when the Mathematics Department took over instruction in the slide-rule from the Department of Physics. Glancing ahead, we may note that the Class of 1978 was the last class to be issued this venerable instrument, by means of which thousands of cadets learned to quickly make any mathematical calculation amenable to logarithmic solution—with surprising accuracy.[46]

Also during Professor Jones's period of office was the assignment of the first mathematics instructor at West Point with a Ph.D. (in mathematics). He was Capt. Robert C. Yates, Corps of Engineers, who arrived for duty on 15 June 1942 as a member of the Army Reserve. In contrast, other engineering colleges and universities had been hiring instructors with Ph.D.s for half a century. Yates received his undergraduate degree at the Virginia Military Institute in 1924 and his doctorate at Johns Hopkins in 1930. One of his duties at West Point was to design and teach a course for new instructors on techniques for teaching mathematics to cadets: "In performing this duty he was considered a superior instructor and also an excellent teacher of teachers."[47] The author of five books and over 60 papers, his text on differential equations was in use at the Academy from 1950 to 1963. The next individual in the department to have a Ph.D. (in systems engineering) was the 16th department head, Col. Jack Pollin. Col. David Arney, who received his Ph.D. in 1985, was the first department head to have a Ph.D. in mathematics.

The 1942 *Howitzer* noted:

> As war becomes more and more mechanized, the
> study of mathematics assumes a greater importance
> in the education of a soldier. Without a background in
> mathematics it is impossible for one to study properly
> those sciences with whose principles one must be familiar
> in order to understand the functioning and operation of
> modern weapons.[48]

Even though the cadets recognized the military applicability of mathematics, and this is doubtless more true today, in the same paragraph as that above they cite the older rationale for studying mathematics—a view championed by the Academic Board throughout the 19th century—as "one of the best methods of training a mind." It was this narrow viewpoint that retarded the development of the mathematics curriculum. The cadets had noted this stagnation two years earlier when they remarked that "in 1835 the course was fundamentally the same as it is today."[49] They were only partially right, for a statistics course had been newly added. This was during World War II, and it is noteworthy that the department once again had to resort to cadets as instructors in some classes, a practice not previously seen since the Civil War.

The *Howitzer* of 1947, the final year of Professor Jones's tenure, gives the cadet view of the department. We quote it in full:

> From the day he first responds to the immortal battlecry of "Take boards!" to the day he graduates, a cadet at West Point makes constant use of the principles he learns at the capable hands of the Mathematics Department. To the cadet, no portion of his academic instruction is more important. During his Fourth Class year he wades through algebra, solid geometry, analytical geometry, and trigonometry. Barely able to distinguish an ellipse from a hyperbola, he is plunged into his Third Class course of differential and integral calculus and statistics. Emerging from this battle with sines, cosines, derivatives, integrals, and their assorted brethren, he possesses a sound mathematical foundation on which to base his scientific education. Although formal instruction in Mathematics finishes with his Third Class year, he continues to use his prowess throughout his courses in physics, chemistry, mechanics, and ordnance; for if he forgets his math in any of them, he's lost![50]

This unmistakable cadet style betrays both the callowness of youth and an emerging maturity. It provides a good basic summary of the curriculum, an acknowledgment that the department is doing a capable job, and an understanding that what they are learning is useful.

Col. William Bessell replaced Jones as Head of the Department in 1947. The Academic Board selected him for Professor from a pool of 31 nominees: 19 Army officers and 12 civilians, several of whom went on to become world-class mathematicians. To join the Corps of Professors, Bessell was required to give up the star that was pinned on him in 1944 during World War II. Bessell's 12-year tenure as Department Head was filled with important accomplishments. One of his first decisions was to offer the probability and statistics course to all cadets, rather than just to the upper sections. Desirous of improving the Academy's teaching facilities, he conceived the idea of converting the 1911 Riding Hall—it served for little more than a parking lot after equitation was discontinued in the 1940s—into a modern academic building. The renovated structure "of structural steel framing with reinforced concrete, completely air conditioned and practically windowless," became Thayer Hall and the home of the department.[51] To complement the new academic building, Bessell modernized the mathematics classrooms by adding overhead projectors and mechanical computers. Additionally, he was one of the early visionaries in the establishment of a computer center, which found its first home in Thayer Hall (see Chapter 23). Finally, he was instrumental in the Academic Board's decision to require incoming military faculty members to earn advanced degrees prior to their arrival at West Point.

In 1959, Col. Charles Nicholas became the Department Head upon Bessell's elevation to the deanship. During World War II he was a pioneer in the new field of scientific intelligence, serving on the organizing committee for the Central Intelligence Agency of which he was Deputy Assistant Director during the period 1947-1948. Undoubtedly his most important contribution in mathematics was a series of Special Topics Memoranda (STMs). As he revised them, they were repeatedly typed by Ms. Frida Clogston, who served as departmental secretary for over 40 years. The STMs were assembled into a 1,200-page text, *Differential and Integral Calculus*, especially designed for the method of instruction used at the Academy. This was a rigorous book, explaining every detail. The STMs earned their nickname—"The Green Death"—from the color of their covers (and, truth be told, their content).

In 1960, the Academy instituted elective courses to be taken during First Class year. The following year the department offered its first elective courses: abstract algebra with military applications, matrix algebra, and advanced calculus. By 1971 there were tracks of study in the department—one standard and three advanced—each concordant with the particular area of engineering the cadet was interested in, as well as their mathematical ability and interest.[52] The first concentrations or fields of study, the predecessor to majors, became effective with Academic Year 1975-1976. In 1980 the operations research field of study was added to the mathematics offerings, which would grow into the predominant mathematics degree in the department when majors were finally introduced for the Class of 1985 (cadets no longer had to take an engineering degree, and within a few years more than half the corps would pursue degrees in fields outside of engineering).

John S.B. Dick, after serving seven years as Deputy Department Head, became the 15th head of the department with the retirement of Colonel Nicholas in 1967. Having previously earned a master's degree in civil engineering from the Massachusetts Institute of Technology and a master's in mathematics from the Rensselaer Polytechnic Institute, as deputy head he oversaw a successful advanced placement program that allowed qualified cadets to validate (i.e., receive credit for) some mathematics courses. He was an excellent instructor and faculty mentor who focused on cadet character development. He stressed the importance of assisting cadets in the mastery of logical reasoning and enlightening them concerning the applications of mathematics. He retired in 1974 after serving for a few months as Acting Dean.

Col. Jack M. Pollin graduated from the Academy in 1944 and had a distinguished military career, commanding in Germany, Korea, and Vietnam. He earned a master's degree in electrical engineering from the University of Pennsylvania in 1949, another in mathematics from the Rensselaer Polytechnic Institute in 1957, and a Ph.D. from the University of Arizona in 1969. He became Department Head in 1974. It was under Pollin that a mathematical modeling course was introduced. He was also head of the department during the exciting years when women were first admitted to the Corps of Cadets.

The typical cadet entering in 1976 would take a 12-credit hour calculus course as a plebe; and then multivariable calculus (4.5 hours) plus differential equations, probability theory, and statistical inference (4.5 hours) as a sophomore. The content of these courses was similar to what was being taught across the country at the time. The cadet with advanced preparation would replace the plebe calculus course with multivariable calculus and introduction to linear algebra, the standard probability course, and an elective. The electives available included linear programming, abstract algebra, complex analysis, numerical analysis, and real variable theory—standard courses that mathematics majors could take at most schools.[53]

The first civilian in the department in the 20th century was Prof. Iso Schoenberg, who joined the faculty as a Visiting Professor in Academic Year 1977-1978. He was a vigorous 72-year-old with a distinguished career in mathematics—he had single-handedly created the field of splines, which are used to approximate a complicated curve by a sequence of shorter, simpler ones. While at West Point, he wrote a popular book, *Mathematical Time Exposures*, which is still in print by the Mathematical Association of America. Moreover, he provided a reminder of the benefits of physical fitness to the junior members of the faculty. One winter night there had been a major snowstorm, bad enough to keep the young officers on the faculty from getting to the office on time the next morning. When they finally arrived they were surprised to find Professor Schoenberg already there, working quietly at his desk. Asked how he got there, he nonchalantly replied that he had skied from his quarters in the Lee housing area. Schoenberg got the visiting professor program off to a good start, and it has continued almost every year since.

In addition to the visiting professor, the Department of Mathematics benefited from the addition of a second visiting civilian faculty position starting in 1994.[54] The Army Research Laboratory, eager to exploit the talents of the mathematics faculty, agreed to provide one of its scientists to the department each year. Dr. Peter Plostins was the first ARL scientist so designated. The Math-ARL relationship led to cooperative and productive research on a variety of important research topics, which are showcased by annual joint conferences.

Col. David Cameron was the Head of the Department from 1985 to 1988. He earned master's and Ph.D. degrees from Princeton in civil engineering as well as a master's in mathematics from Rensselaer Polytechnic Institute. An excellent teacher, Cameron taught the first course in advanced mathematics offered by the department and directed the redesign of the mathematics curriculum to take advantage of computers in the classroom. Under his guidance, a mathematics-consulting element was established that allowed faculty members and students to support the research needs of the Army.

It was under Colonel Cameron's period of office that the first female Academy graduates returned to teach mathematics.

Capt. Kathleen Snook and Capt. Bobbi Fiedler-Prinslow, both from the Class of 1980, joined the mathematics faculty in 1987. They were the first women graduates to teach in mathematics.[55] Snook's career was similar to that of many of the rotating faculty members who have served in the department. After five years as an officer in the line Army, she spent two years in graduate school earning a master's degree in applied mathematics. She then reported to West Point and taught mathematics for four years (one year longer than usual). Upon completion of their teaching duties most officers return to the active Army; many use their mathematical skills to contribute to the Army in operations research and related fields. Capt. Snook followed a different path. Selected to return to graduate school for a Ph.D., she returned a few years later on a permanent basis as an Academy Professor. She retired In 2002.

Col. Frank Giordano was the Head of the Department from 1988 to 1995. After graduating from the Academy in 1964 he served two tours in Vietnam. During the period 1971-1974 he was an Olmstead Scholar at the University of Madrid and the University of Arkansas. Earning a Ph.D. in 1974, he then reported to West Point. He was the first department head since Davies to have a substantial publication record (including both books and journal articles) and a presence in the national mathematical community. Giordano modernized the mathematics classrooms with mobile classroom computers, overhead display devices, and advanced computational software. In recognition of the faculty's expanding interest in applied mathematics, operations research, and computation, he proposed that the department be redesignated the Department of Mathematical Sciences. The suggestion was approved in 1990.

Giordano's most important legacy was the revision of the four mathematics core courses taught to cadets in their first two years. Particularly significant was the introduction of discrete dynamical systems, which blended the old and the new mathematics. The old was the theory of finite differences, a discrete form of the calculus which goes back to Leonhard Euler (1707-1783) and earlier; the new was the theory of dynamical systems, which analyzes the long-term behavior of mathematical systems. The other three courses were also changed substantially. The combined changes became known by the catch phrase "seven into four," where seven mathematical subjects—differential calculus, integral calculus, multivariable calculus, differential equations, linear algebra, probability and statistics, and discrete mathematics—were condensed into four semesters. This seemingly impossible task was neatly accomplished by omitting material that could be treated more easily using a computer algebra system, a technology introduced into the curriculum at the time, and by carefully coordinating topics. In addition there were five mathematical thread objectives which were revisited in each course: mathematical reasoning, mathematical modeling, scientific computing, communicating mathematics, and history of mathematics.

By this time, teaching in the Mathematics Department had evolved. Cadets no longer had daily recitations in front of the instructor and they were not graded every day, but remnants of these traditions remain. Today cadets work problems at the board on a daily basis and brief their classmates on their solutions. This style of instruction is unique to West Point and places the Academy at the forefront of progressive, interactive learning.

Another significant change during Giordano's tenure was the addition to the faculty of full-time civilian professors (in addition to the visiting professors). In the fall of 1991, Prof. Donald Small, who is still a member of the faculty, joined the faculty in this capacity. He came from the University of Maine, where he had written the calculus textbook, *Calculus: An Integrated Approach* (1990). Today he has a deep interest in helping historically black colleges and universities to improve their teaching of algebra and frequently travels under National Science Foundation support to help them. Over the next decade four others joined the department as senior civilians. All are still on the faculty, with the exception of Prof. Lida Barrett, onetime president of the Mathematical Association of America, who retired in 1998 at the age of 72 after three years at the Academy. Younger civilians joined the faculty in 1992, some as Title X faculty who teach full time and some as Davies Fellows, a position created in 1996. The Davies Fellows, named in honor of the seventh Department Head Charles Davies, teach one semester and do research in conjunction with a senior researcher at the Army Research Lab during the next semester and summer. The department made the decision to hire these young Ph.D.s on three-year tours to assure a constant pool of vibrant young Ph.D.s in the department.

Giordano passed the baton to Col. David Christopher Arney in 1995. Graduating from the Academy in 1971, Arney earned two master's degrees from the Rensselaer Polytechnic Institute, one in mathematics in 1980, another in computer science in 1982. In 1985, again from RPI, he received his Ph.D. in mathematics. He too has a very substantial publication record. Under his leadership, the department continued to modernize the classrooms. Personal computers found their way into each classroom in addition to use of the internet as a tool for mathematics. His goal was to help the cadets become competent, confident problem-solvers; his motto for the Department, "To Infinity and Beyond," was meant to inspire them in this regard.

The core mathematics program for the bicentennial Class of 2002 started with discrete dynamical systems, turning to differential calculus about two-thirds of the way through. The second semester picked up with integral calculus as supplemented by work on linear algebra and differential equations. The yearling year began with multivariable calculus and concluded with a semester of probability and statistics.

The 20th and current department head is Col. Gary Krahn, whose Ph.D. was awarded by the Naval Postgraduate School in 1994 for work in applied mathematics. Under his leadership the department is focusing the core program on problem-solving through modeling and inquiry, as supported by mathematical concepts and techniques. The purpose of this real-world, problem-based mathematics program is to emphasize the breadth and variety of mathematics; to develop graduates equipped to find answers to vexing practical problems having their roots in the social, information, and physical sciences as well as in operations research, engineering, and technology; and to promote the process of life-long learning.

The U.S. Military Academy has held an honored place in American history. It has been a world leader in the education of scientifically trained military officers. As the oldest and largest department at West Point, the Department of Mathematical Sciences has played a significant role in the shaping of the Academy. Mathematics, which comprises the largest component of the core academic program, provides cadets with a sound foundation for the rest of their quantitative course work. This has been achieved through the unique influence of the departmental staff, through the curriculum and teaching methods, and through departmentally-prepared texts such as *Discrete Dynamical Systems*, by Colonels Arney, Giordano, and John S. Robertson. This influence has spread outward to the rest of the nation for the whole of the Academy's history. Members of the department have influenced education across the nation, both directly by taking the West Point methods to other institutions, and indirectly through textbooks written at West Point. West Point exists to build leaders for the nation, but in accomplishing that goal West Point has also been an institution that built education for the nation.[56]

---

[1] U.S. Military Academy, *Annual Report of the Superintendent of the United States Military Academy* (Washington, DC, 1896), 47. Available on the web at http://www.library.usma.edu/search/. Hereafter cited as *Annual Report of the Superintendent.*

[2] Dearborn-Baron correspondence, 11 April, 11 May, 6 June 1801. Available at http://www.dean.usma.edu/math/people/rickey/dms/DeptHeads/Baron-George.htm.

[3] *Annual Report of the Superintendent*, 1896, 42.

[4] *The Memoirs of Gen. Joseph Gardner Swift*, ed. Harrison Ellery (1890), 27. Available on the web at http://www.library.usma.edu/archives/special.asp. The original spelling, both here and in all subsequent 19th-century documents quoted from, will be preserved intact.

[5] Baron moved to New York City where he founded the first mathematical journal in the United States, *The Mathematical Correspondent*. See Edward R. Hogan, "George Baron and the Mathematical Correspondent, the First Mathematical Journal Published in this Country," *Historia Mathematica* 3 (1976): 403-15.

[6] For additional information about Mansfield and his work, see Joe Albree, "Jared Mansfield (1759-1830): Janus Figure in American Mathematics," in *History of Undergraduate Mathematics in America: Proceedings of a Conference Held at the United States Military Academy, West Point, New York, 21-24 June 2001*, ed. Amy Shell-Gellasch (West Point, NY, 2001), 73-94. Copies of this volume are available through the authors. Hereafter cited as *HUMA Proceedings*.

[7] Edgar Denton III, "The Formative Years of the United States Military Academy" (Ph.D. diss., Syracuse University, 1964), 41. University Microform 6501551.

[8] *The Centennial of the United States Military Academy at West Point* (1904), 221, 224.

[9] For a transcription of the report on this examination, see http://www.dean.usma.edu/math/people/rickey/dms/doc/1806-exam.htm.

[10] The other was Oliver G. Burton, Cullum #37, Class of 1808. He served as storekeeper at West Point from 1815 to 1820.

[11] Sylvanus Thayer, *The West Point Thayer Papers, 1808-1872*, ed. Cindy Adams (West Point, NY: Association of Graduates, 1965), USMA Library. Unpaginated. Letters arranged chronologically. Available on the web at http://www.library.usma.edu/search/. Hereafter cited as *Thayer Papers*.

[12] For some history of the blackboard, see Charles Anderson, *Technology in American Education* (Washington: U.S. Dept. of Health, Education and Welfare, 1962), 16-19.

[13] Amy Shell-Gellasch, "The Olivier models at West Point," *Rittenhouse Journal of the American Scientific Instrument Enterprise* 17 (December 2003): 71-84. Photographs of the string models may be viewed on-line at http://www.dean.usma.edu/math/people/rickey/dms/OlivierModels.html .

[14] U.H. Grant stands for Ulysses Hiram Grant. Grant reports in his autobiography, *Personal Memoirs of U.S. Grant* (New York: C.L. Webster & Co., 1885-1886), 40, that the reason he came to West Point was to gain the knowledge to become a professor of mathematics.

[15] Quoted without attribution in Robert F. Hunter and Edwin L. Dooley, Jr., *Claudius Crozet: French Engineer in America, 1790-1864* (Charlottesville: University Press of Virginia, 1989), 19.

[16] There is no catalogue of "Thayer books," but USMA librarian Alan Aimone is preparing one.

[17] Henry Eugene Davies, *Davies Memoir. A Genealogical and Biographical Monograph on the Family and Descendants of John Davies of Litchfield, Connecticut* (privately printed, 1895).

[18] The titles of these works have been shortened (both here and below). For details about the pre-1917 mathematics books in the USMA library, see Joe Albree, David C. Arney, and V. Frederick Rickey, *A Station Favorable to the Pursuits of Science: Primary Materials in the History of Mathematics at the United States Military Academy* (Providence, RI: American Mathematical Society, 2000).

[19] Amy K. Ackerberg-Hastings, "Mathematics Is a Gentleman's Art: Analysis and Synthesis in American College Geometry Teaching" (Ph.D. diss., Iowa State University, 2000). University Microform 9977308.

[20] A list of USMA graduates who taught mathematics at other schools, including which schools, is being compiled. See http://www.dean.usma.edu/math/people/rickey/dms/OldestSchools.html.

[21] Amy K. Ackerberg-Hastings, "Charles Davies, Mathematical Businessman," in *HUMA Proceedings*, 119-132. Almost all of the books of Davies appear in multiple "editions," but many are so alike they should be called "printings."

[22] *First Century of National Existence; the United States as They Were and Are ... by an Eminent Corps of Scientific and Literary Men. Illustrated with Over Two Hundred and Twenty-Five Engravings* (San Francisco: L. Stebbins, 1875), 268. Available on the web through the Humanities Text Initiative: http://www.hti.umich.edu.

[23] *Annual Report of the Superintendent*, 1821, as quoted in the 1896 *Annual Report*, 44, states, "The superintendent was authorized to detail cadets to act as assistant professors, each to receive $10 per month for extra services." However, Lester A. Webb, *Captain Alden Partridge and the United States Military Academy, 1806-1833* (Northport, AL: American Southern, 1965), 172, indicates that cadets were already being used as instructors in 1816. There is no evidence that either Davies or Church was a cadet instructor.

[24] Albert E. Church, *Personal Reminiscences of the Military Academy, from 1824 to 1879* (West Point, NY, 1879), 39-41. Available on the United States Military Academy Library web: http://usmalibrary.usma.edu/.

[25] Silvestre François Lacroix, *Elements of Algebra* (1st edition 1818). In 1821, neither mathematics Prof. David Douglass nor Superintendent Thayer was aware that John Farrar had published this English translation of Lacroix (Norton to Thayer, 13 August 1821, in *Thayer Papers*). The 1823 Board of Visitors report indicates that an English translation was used, so that this confirms Church's recollection. The 1825 Board of Visitor's report lists Lacroix's *Algebra*, but whether it was in French or English is unclear. The "Tentative List of Text-Books" in the first *Centennial* volume indicates that a French edition of the work was used; moreover, an 1825 French copy in the library bears the stamp "Textbook West Point 1823 to ____ ," but we have come to distrust these stamps, which were probably inserted when Edward Holden was preparing the *Centennial* volumes. Professor Davies must have been very unhappy with the Farrar translation to have the cadets instead use the French original.

[26] Adrien-Marie Legendre, *Elements of Geometry* (first edition 1818) is the edition that Church used. This is a translation of *Éléments de géométrie avec des notes* (first edition 1794). The West Point library has the tenth (1813) edition in French in a Thayer binding, indicating that it was purchased by Thayer while in France. For information on which editions are in the West Point library, see Albree et al., cited in note 18.

[27] Silvestre François Lacroix, *An Elementary Treatise on Plane and Spherical Trigonometry* (first edition 1820) by John Farrar.

[28] Church confirmed his use of these books. See *Personal Reminiscences*, 46-47.

[29] Jean Baptiste Biot, *Essai de géométrie analytique, appliquée aux courbes et aux surfaces du second ordre* (second edition 1805); Silvestre François Lacroix, *Traité élémentaire de calcul différentiel et de calcul integral* (first edition 1802); Jean-Louis Boucharlat, *Elémens de calcul différentiel et de calcul integral* (first edition 1812). Thus use of textbooks in the original French, and especially which editions, is difficult to document due to the paucity of records. There is a copy of Silvestre François Lacroix's *Traité élémentaire de trigonométrie rectiligne et sphérique* (1813 edition) in the West Point library that was owned by Lt. Samuel Stanhope Smith. He graduated in 1818, but the fact that he included his rank may indicate that he procured this book later while teaching mathematics at West Point from 1818 to 1823. After that he taught Natural and Experimental Philosophy until his death in 1828.

[30] Morris Schaff, *The Spirit of Old West Point* (Boston: Houghton, Mifflin, 1907), 68, as quoted by James L. Morrison, Jr., *"The Best School in the World": West Point, the Pre-Civil War Years, 1833-1866* (Kent, OH: Kent State University Press, c1986), 52.

[31] Cited by Florian Cajori, *The Teaching and History of Mathematics in the United States* (Washington, DC: Government Printing Office, 1890), 124.

[32] *Catalogue of the United States Military Academy*, 1970/1971, 17. These are available on the web at http://www.library.usma.edu/archives/archives.asp.

[33] *Annual Report of the Superintendent*, 1896, 74.

[34] Roger H. Nye, "The United States Military Academy in an Era of Educational Reform, 1900-1925" (Ph.D. diss., Columbia University, 1968), 199-200. University Microform 6812943.

[35] Ibid., 205, 211.

[36] Ibid., 231, 253.

[37] Ibid., 233.

[38] *Annual Report of the Superintendent*, 1919, 27.

[39] Douglas MacArthur, *Reminiscences* (New York: McGraw-Hill, 1964), 77, as quoted by Nye, 302.

[40] Nye, 310-11; Nye cites *Annual Report of the Superintendent*, 1920, 37.

[41] Nye, 321, who quotes from Echols's minority endorsement to the Board's curriculum revision report.

[42] Ibid., 321.

[43] Ibid., 322.

[44] U.S. Military Academy, *Howitzer* (1930), 30.

[45] David C. Arney, "Army Beats Harvard in Football and Mathematics!" *Math Horizons*, September 1994, 14-17; Arney and George Rosenstein, "USMA-Harvard Math Competition" at http://www.dean.usma.edu/math/about/history/mathcomp.htm. See also U.S. Military Academy, *Annual Report of the Superintendent*, 1933, 3.

[46] *Annual Report of the Superintendent*, 1933, 3.

[47] Quoted in "Note About the Author" (p. viii) in Robert C. Yates, *Curves and Their Properties* (reprint; National Council of Teachers of Mathematics, 1974). Yates's original appeared in 1952.

[48] U.S. Military Academy, *Howitzer* (1942), 46.

[49] U.S. Military Academy, *Howitzer* (1940), 58.

[50] U.S. Military Academy, *Howitzer* (1947), 44.

[51] *Catalogue of the United States Military Academy*, 1959-1960, 107.

[52] *Catalogue of the United States Military Academy*, 1971-1972, 74.

[53] *Catalogue of the United States Military Academy*, 1975-1976, 75-76.

[54] Earlier there were visitors from the National Security Agency, Nathan Thiesse in 1992-1993 and Roman Tarnawski in 1993-1994.

[55] The first women faculty members in the department (and their years of service in the department) were Captains J. L. Taylor (1980-1983), Karen L. Perkins (1981-1985), and Joan L. Black (1983-1986), who were not Academy graduates. The first civilian woman in the department was the late Edith Luchins, who was the Visiting Professor in 1991-1992.

[56] We would like to thank Joe Albree and Col. Joseph Myers for their helpful comments on an earlier draft of this paper.

About the Contributors

Kenneth L. Alford is a colonel in the U.S. Army and is the Information Systems Engineering Program Director at the U.S. Military Academy. He is a 1979 graduate of Brigham Young University, holds master's degrees from the University of Southern California and the University of Illinois at Urbana-Champaign, and earned a Ph.D. in computer science from George Mason University. His research interests and most recent publications involve computer science education, software engineering, handheld computing, and information assurance. Colonel Alford has served as a personnel, acquisition, and automation officer in a wide variety of assignments in the United States and Europe, including service on the Department of Army staff at the Pentagon and two teaching assignments in the Department of Electrical Engineering and Computer Science at the U.S. Military Academy.

Peter Anderson is Assistant Professor of Geography at the U.S. Military Academy where he teaches courses on physical geography and environmental geography. He holds a B.A. and M.A. from the State University of New York at Albany and a Ph.D. from the University of Utah. His research interests focus on forest ecology and dynamics, mountain geography, and land use and conservation. His most recent publication is "Biogeography" in Eugene Palka and Frank Galgano, eds., *North Korea: Geographic Perspectives* (McGraw Hill, 2003).

Lance Betros is a colonel in the U.S. Army and Professor and Deputy Head of the Department of History at the U.S. Military Academy. He is a 1977 graduate of the Academy and holds a master's degree in national security strategy from the National Defense University and an M.A. and Ph.D. in history from the University of North Carolina at Chapel Hill. Colonel Betros was commissioned in the infantry branch and has served in command and staff assignments in the United States and Europe. His current research interests and recent publications are in the fields of civil-military relations and the U.S. Army officer corps.

Thomas M. Carhart III is a 1966 graduate of the U.S. Military Academy and holds two Purple Hearts from his service with the 101st Airborne Division in Vietnam. He earned a J.D. from the University of Michigan Law School and a Ph.D. in American and military history from Princeton University, and has been an Adjunct Professor of American History at Mary Washington College in Fredericksburg, VA. Dr. Carhart is the author of five military history books, including *West Point Warriors* (Warner Books, 2002) and *Lost Triumph* (G.P. Putnam's Sons, 2004).

Gregory J. Conti is a major in the U.S. Army and an Assistant Professor of Computer Science at the U.S. Military Academy. He holds a master's degree in computer science from Johns Hopkins University and a Bachelor of Science in computer science from the U.S. Military Academy. His areas of expertise include network security, interface design, and information warfare. Major Conti has worked at a variety of military intelligence assignments specializing in signals intelligence. Currently he is on a Department of Defense Fellowship and is working on his Ph.D. in computer science at Georgia Tech. He is conducting research into denial of information attacks.

Donald B. Connelly is a historian at the U.S. Special Operations Command and is currently working on studies of special operations forces in the war on terrorism. He is a retired U.S. Army military intelligence officer and former military history instructor with the Combat Studies Institute, U.S. Army Command and General Staff College. He holds a master's degree in national security studies from Georgetown University and a Ph.D. in U.S. history from the University of Houston. His dissertation, "Political Soldier: John M. Schofield and the Politics of Generalship," is undergoing revision for the University of North Carolina Press.

Theodore J. Crackel is Director and Editor of *Papers of the War Department 1784-1800* at East Stroudsburg University of Pennsylvania. He was Visiting Professor of History at the U.S. Military Academy in 2001-2002. He did his undergraduate work at the University of Illinois (1962) and earned an M.A. and Ph.D. in history at Rutgers University. Dr. Crackel was a career Army officer, serving in Germany and twice in Vietnam before teaching assignments in history and strategy formulation at West Point, the Command and General Staff College, and the Army War College. His books include *Mr. Jefferson's Army: Political and Social Reform of the Military Establishment, 1801-1809* (New York University Press, 1987), and *West Point: A Bicentennial History* (University Press of Kansas, 2002).

David B. Cushen is a captain in the U.S. Army and is currently assigned as a tactical officer for Company D-1, U.S. Corps of Cadets, at West Point. He is a 1994 graduate of West Point and holds master's degrees from the University of Long Island and the University of Missouri at Rolla. Captain Cushen has served as a platoon leader, company commander, and personnel manager in the U.S. Army Corps of Engineers. His assignments include postings in the United States and Europe. His current research interests are leader development at the small-unit level and personal crisis management.

James B. Dalton, Jr., is a lieutenant colonel in the U.S. Army and Assistant Dean for Plans, Analysis, and Personnel at the U.S. Military Academy. He is a 1979 graduate of Providence College and holds a master's degree in national security and strategic studies from the Naval War College and a Ph.D. in geography from the University of Minnesota at the Twin Cities. Lieutenant Colonel Dalton has served in command and staff positions in the United States, Korea, and Europe. His current research interests are historical geographies and impacts on current events. His most recent publication is "Historical Geography" in Eugene J. Palka, ed., *Afghanistan: Geographic Perspectives* (McGraw-Hill/Dushkin, 2003).

Dik Alan Daso, (B.S., U.S. Air Force Academy; M.A., Ph.D., University of South Carolina) is curator of modern military aircraft at the Smithsonian Institution, National Air and Space Museum, Washington, DC. A retired Air Force lieutenant colonel, he has served as an RF-4C *Phantom* instructor pilot, F-15 *Eagle* pilot, twice as a T-38 *Talon* instructor pilot, instructor of history at the U.S. Air Force Academy, and chief of Air Force doctrine at Headquarters Air Force, Pentagon. During his career, Daso accumulated over 2,700 total flying hours. He contributed a chapter to *The Air Force*, an illustrated history of that service. Daso has also written three books: *Architects of American Air Supremacy: Gen. Hap Arnold and Dr. Theodore von Kármán* (Maxwell AFB, AL.: Air University Press, 1997); *Hap Arnold and the Evolution of American Airpower* (Washington, DC: Smithsonian Institution Press, 2000), winner of the 2001 American Institute of Aeronautics and Astronautics History Manuscript Award; and *Doolittle: Aerospace Visionary* (Washington, DC: Brassey's, 2003).

Carlo D'Este graduated Magna Cum Laude from Norwich University and was commissioned in the U.S. Army in 1958. After serving in command and staff assignments in Europe, the United States, and Vietnam, he retired as a lieutenant colonel in 1978 and has since been a military historian and biographer. He holds a master's degree from the University of Richmond (1974) and an honorary doctorate of humane letters from Norwich (1992). He is the author of six books, including *Decision in Normandy* (New York: Dutton, 1983); *Patton: A Genius For War* (New York: HarperCollins, 1995); and, most recently, *Eisenhower: A Soldier's Life* (New York: Henry Holt, 2002). He currently is writing a biography of Winston Churchill.

Robert A. Doughty is a colonel in the U.S. Army and has been the Professor and Head of the Department of History at the U.S. Military Academy since August 1985. His awards and decorations include the Silver Star and Bronze Star as well as the Combat Infantryman's Badge. His publications include: *The Seeds of Disaster: The Development of French Army Doctrine 1919-1939* (Archon Books,

1985) and *Breaking Point: Sedan and the Fall of France 1940* (Archon Books, 1990). His book *Seeds of Disaster* won the Birdsall Prize from the American Historical Association in 1986. He currently is working on a book-length manuscript tentatively titled "Pyrrhic Victory: French Strategy and Operations in the Great War."

Morten G. Ender earned his Ph.D. in sociology from the University of Maryland. He is currently Associate Professor and Sociology Director in the Department of Behavioral Sciences and Leadership at the U.S. Military Academy at West Point, where he teaches Marriage and the Family, Sociological Theory, Cinematic Images of War and the Military, and Armed Forces and Society. He has been a research fellow at the Defense Equal Opportunity Management Institute and the Walter Reed Army Institute of Research. His research areas include military sociology, social psychology, and teaching sociology. His more recent scholarly publications appear in *Armed Forces & Society, Teaching Sociology, The American Sociologist,* and *Death Studies.* He is the editor of *Military Brats and Other Global Nomads: Growing Up in Organization Families* (Westport, CT: Praeger, 2002). His current research examines civil-military relations and representations of the military in social texts such as films and books.

Patrick Finnegan is a colonel in the U.S. Army and the Professor and Head of the Department of Law at the U.S. Military Academy. He is a 1971 graduate of the Academy and holds an M.P.A. from the Kennedy School of Government at Harvard University and a J.D. from the University of Virginia School of Law. Colonel Finnegan has served in a variety of assignments in the United States and Europe, including duty as legal advisor to the Joint Special Operations Command, the U.S. Special Operations Command, and the U.S. European Command. His current research interests include the law of armed combat and military and legal responses to terrorism. He has published articles in the *University of Virginia Law Review, Military Review,* the *Military Law Review,* and *The Army Lawyer.*

George B. Forsythe is a colonel in the U.S. Army and Professor and Vice Dean for Education at the U.S. Military Academy. A 1970 graduate of the Academy, he holds an M.A.C.T. (social psychology) and a Ph.D. (higher education) from the University of North Carolina at Chapel Hill. Colonel Forsythe has served in command and staff positions in Europe and Korea, and recently returned from Afghanistan and Iraq where he assisted with the establishment of national military academies in both countries. His current research interests are in leader development, officer education, and program assessment; he has published numerous books, book chapters, and journal articles on these topics.

Patricia B. Genung is a colonel in the U.S. Army and Professor and Deputy Head of the Department of Foreign Languages at the U.S. Military Academy. She is a graduate of Duquesne University and holds a master's degree in history from Indiana University and a Ph.D. in linguistics from Cornell University. Colonel Genung has served as a military intelligence officer in numerous command and staff assignments in the United States and in Europe. Her current research interests include second language acquisition and the language of women in command. Her most recent publication, with James P. Lantolf, is titled "I'd rather switch than fight: An activity theoretic study of power, success, and failure in a foreign language classroom," in Claire Kramsch, ed., *Language Acquisition and Language Socialization: Ecological Perspectives* (New York: Continuum, 2002).

Lance Janda is an Assistant Professor of History at Cameron University and the author of *Stronger than Custom: West Point and the Admission of Women* (Westport, CT: Praeger, 2002). His research interests include the U.S. Military Academy and the changing role of women in the armed forces. He serves as book review editor for both H-Minerva and the journal *Minerva: Women and War*. He teaches military and modern U.S. history at Cameron, and is currently researching a history of American military women since 1945.

Tanya Kabel-Ballard is a major in the U.S. Army and is currently assigned as a tactical officer for the U.S. Corps of Cadets at West Point. Major Kabel-Ballard is a 1993 graduate of Western Maryland College where she earned her baccalaureate degree in history and American studies. She was commissioned in the air defense artillery branch and has held command and staff positions in Louisiana, Texas, and Saudi Arabia. Her most recent tactical assignment was as the commander of E Battery, 2-43 ADA, Ft. Bliss, TX. Major Kabel-Ballard holds a master's degree in education from Long Island University.

Bruce Keith is Professor of Sociology and Associate Dean for Academic Affairs at the U.S. Military Academy. His research examines the influence of higher educational contexts on the production and dissemination of knowledge, with a focus on the competing structures of institutional status and quality. His most recent book is *Contexts for Learning: Institutional Strategies for Managing Curricular Change Through Assessment* (New Forums Press, 2003). Other publications have appeared in *Social Forces* (1991, 1998, 2002); *Teaching Sociology* (1995, 2002, 2003); *The American Sociologist* (1992, 1994, 2000, 2001); *Research in Higher Education* (2001); *American Educational Research Journal* (1999); and the *American Journal of Education* (1996).

Thomas A. Kolditz is a colonel in the U.S. Army and currently Professor and Head of the Department of Behavioral Sciences and Leadership at the U.S. Military Academy. He holds a B.A. degree with double major in psychology and sociology from Vanderbilt University; M.A. and Ph.D. degrees in social psychology from the University of Missouri; M.M.A.S from the School of Advanced Military Studies; and M.A. in strategic studies from the U.S. Army War College. Colonel Kolditz's research and teaching activities span applied social psychology and leadership development, to include ethnographic field research examining cohesion during the recent hostilities in Iraq. His most recent publication, with L. Wong, R. Miller, and T. Potter, is titled *Why They Fight: Combat Motivation in the Iraq War* (Strategic Studies Institute Monograph, 2003).

Charles D. Krumwiede is a major in the U.S. Army and is currently attending the Command and General Staff College at Fort Leavenworth, KS. A 1991 graduate of the U.S. Military Academy, Major Krumwiede was commissioned in the infantry. He has served in leadership and command positions in infantry units at Schofield Barracks, HI, and Ft. Drum, NY, with operational deployments to Somalia and Haiti. Recently, he served as a tactical officer for the U.S. Corps of Cadets and as the aide-de-camp to the Superintendent of West Point. Major Krumwiede holds a master's degree from Long Island University in leader development and counseling.

Brian McAllister Linn was born in Honolulu and is a graduate of the University of Hawaii. He received his master's and doctoral degrees from The Ohio State University where he specialized in American military history under the direction of Prof. Allan R. Millett. He is now Professor of History at Texas A&M University. He is the author of three books, including *Guardians of Empire* (Chapel Hill: University of North Carolina Press, 1997) and *The Philippine War, 1899-1902* (Lawrence: University of Kansas Press, 2000), both of which received the Society for Military History's Distinguished Book Award, as well as over a dozen articles and book chapters. He has been an Olin Fellow at Yale University, the Susan Dyer Peace Fellow at the Hoover Institute, the Harold K. Johnson Visiting Professor of History at the Army War College, and a John Simon Guggenheim Memorial Foundation Fellow. He is currently writing a book on American military thought.

Gerardo V. Meneses is a major in the U.S. Army and is currently assigned as the executive officer, 184th Ordnance Battalion (Explosive Ordnance Disposal), Ft. Gillem, GA. A 1992 graduate of the U.S. Military Academy, he served first as an armor officer for four years and then in the Ordnance Corps. Major Meneses has held command and staff positions in a variety of tactical units. As commander of the 18th Ordnance Company (EOD), Ft. Bragg, NC, he deployed in support of Operation Bright Star 1999 and supported North Carolina's Weapons of Mass

Destruction Domestic Preparedness Program. Following command he returned to West Point as a tactical officer for Company E-1, U.S. Corps of Cadets. Major Meneses holds a master's degree in counseling and leader development from Long Island University.

Robert S. Norris is a Senior Research Associate with the Natural Resources Defense Council in Washington, DC. His principal areas of expertise include writing and research on all aspects of the nuclear weapons programs of the United States, Soviet Union/Russia, Britain, France, and China, as well as India, Pakistan, and Israel. He received his Ph.D. in political science from New York University in 1976, and has taught at Miami University in Oxford, OH, Miami University's European campus in Luxembourg, and American University in Washington, DC. His most recent book, *Racing for the Bomb: General Leslie R. Groves, the Manhattan Project's Indispensable Man* (Steerforth Press, 2002), won the Distinguished Writing Award for Best Biography of 2002 from the Army Historical Foundation.

Jay M. Parker is a colonel in the U.S. Army and Professor of Political and International Affairs in the Department of Social Sciences at the U.S. Military Academy, where he serves as Director of International Relations and National Security Studies. A graduate of the University of Arizona, he holds master's degrees from Arizona State University, University of Southern California, and the Naval War College, and a Ph.D. from Columbia University. Commissioned in the infantry, he served in command and staff positions in Europe and the United States. His teaching and research areas include American foreign policy, East Asian politics, civil-military relations, and mass media. Colonel Parker is currently completing a manuscript titled "The Colonels' Revolt" for Harvard University Press. He served on advisory committees for the Museum of Television and Radio Satellite Seminar Series and appeared in "Reporting America at War," an Insignia Films production for PBS.

Eugene K. Ressler is a colonel in the U.S. Army and Deputy Head of the Department of Electrical Engineering and Computer Science at the U.S. Military Academy. He served formerly as Associate Dean for Information and Educational Technology at West Point. He is a 1978 graduate of the Academy and holds a Ph.D. in computer science from Cornell University. His military assignments include command in Europe and engineering staff work in Korea. Colonel Ressler's research interests include neural signal processing and computer science education. He is currently developing a patent for electronic devices inspired by the human auditory system that provide for very high speed, high quality digital processing of analog phenomena.

V. Frederick Rickey is a Professor of Mathematics at the U.S Military Academy and a well-known authority on the history of mathematics. He earned a B.S., M.S., and Ph.D., all in mathematics, from the University of Notre Dame. His research focuses on the history of calculus, the use of history in teaching mathematics, and the history of the Department of Mathematical Sciences at West Point. He is coauthor of *A Station Favorable to the Pursuits of Science: Primary Materials in the History of Mathematics at the United States Military Academy* (American Mathematical Society, 1999). He has numerous other publications in mathematical logic and in the history of mathematics. His first historical paper, "An Application of Geography to Mathematics: History of the Integral of the Secant," was recently republished in the collection titled *Sherlock Holmes in Babylon & Other Mathematical Tales* (Mathematical Association of America, 2003). Professor Rickey is currently finishing a volume titled *Historical Notes for Calculus Teachers*, to be published by the Mathematical Association of America in 2005, and is also writing a volume on the history of the Department of Mathematical Sciences at West Point.

Amy Shell-Gellasch is currently a freelance historian of mathematics living in Grafenwoehr, Germany, where her husband is a major in the U.S. Army on a three-year tour of duty. She received a bachelor's degree from the University of Michigan in 1989, a master's from Oakland University in Rochester, MI, in 1995, and a doctorate from the University of Illinois at Chicago in 2000, all in mathematics. Her dissertation was published as "Mina Rees and the Funding of the Mathematical Sciences," *American Mathematical Monthly* (December 2002). She edited a volume titled *History of Undergraduate Mathematics in America: Proceedings of a Conference Held at USMA, June 21-24, 2001*. Most recently, she conducted research with V. Frederick Rickey on the history of the Department of Mathematical Sciences at the U.S. Military Academy, where she was an Assistant Professor. She is widely involved with the community of historians of mathematics through her work in the Mathematical Association of America's Special Interest Group on the History of Mathematics and the Canadian Society for the History and Philosophy of Mathematics.

William B. Skelton is Emeritus Professor of History at the University of Wisconsin-Stevens Point. His research centers on the military profession, civil-military relations, and the social history of the U.S. Army in the 18th and 19th centuries. He is the author of *An American Profession of Arms: The Army Officer Corps, 1784-1861* (University Press of Kansas, 1992), as well as articles in *Journal of Military History, Armed Forces & Society, William and Mary Quarterly*, and other scholarly journals. He is currently working on a book tentatively titled "The Commanding Generals and the Problem of Command and Civil Control in the U.S. Army, 1815-1903."

Lewis Sorley is a biographer and historian concentrating on the Vietnam War. He is a third-generation graduate of the U.S. Military Academy and holds a Ph.D. from Johns Hopkins University. As an armor officer he served in tank and armored cavalry units in Germany, Vietnam, and the United States, in staff positions in the offices of the Secretary of Defense and the Army Chief of Staff, and on the faculties of West Point and the Army War College. Subsequently he was a civilian official of the Central Intelligence Agency. His most recent book is *A Better War: The Unexamined Victories and Final Tragedy of America's Last Years in Vietnam* (Harcourt Brace, 1999). His edited two-volume work *Vietnam Chronicles: The Abrams Tapes, 1968-1972*, is scheduled for publication by Texas Tech University Press in 2004. Dr. Sorley is Secretary of the Board of Directors of the Army Historical Foundation and Executive Director of the Association of Military Colleges and Schools.

William Turmel, Jr., is a major in the U.S. Army and is currently attending the Command and General Staff College, Ft. Leavenworth, KS. He holds a bachelor's degree in economics from the University of Hawaii and a master's degree in computer science from Northwestern University. Major Turmel has served in light and airborne infantry units, in Special Forces, and as an automation officer at the U.S. Military Academy. His current research interests include information assurance, network security, and incident handling.

Frank J. Walton is a major in the U.S. Army and is currently assigned as a tactical officer for Company H-2, U.S. Corps of Cadets, at West Point. A 1993 graduate of the U.S. Military Academy, Captain Walton was commissioned in the infantry and has served in a variety of command and staff positions, including that of rifle platoon leader during operations in Haiti. His most recent operational assignment was with the 173d Separate Infantry Brigade in Alaska. Captain Walton holds a master's degree from Long Island University.

Donald J. Welch is a colonel in the U.S. Army and the Associate Dean for Information and Educational Technology at the U.S. Military Academy and an associate professor in the computer science program. He is an active researcher in information assurance and software engineering with over 25 publications in those disciplines. He is a recipient of the Apgar award for innovation and excellence in teaching. He has served as the chief of software engineering in a special operations unit, and he has also been the human resources manager for the Army's professional information technology workforce. He has managed information technology support for the Department of Electrical Engineering and Computer Science at West Point and for a branch of the Army Personnel Command. He has also commanded various light infantry units. He has a B.S.

from the U.S. Military Academy, an M.S. in computer science from California Polytechnic State University, and a Ph.D. in computer science from the University of Maryland at College Park.

Robert P. Wettemann, Jr., is an Assistant Professor of History at McMurry University in Abilene, TX, where he teaches courses in U.S., military, and public history. A 1993 graduate of Oklahoma State University, he holds both a master's degree and Ph.D. from Texas A&M University, where he studied U.S. and military history. His contribution to this volume was taken from his dissertation, "'To the Public Prosperity': The U.S. Army and the Market Revolution, 1815-1844," which he completed in 2001. His current research interest is the development of field expedient solutions by U.S. servicemen during World War II.